THE SEVENTH STREAM

D0189339

The Seventh Stream

THE EMERGENCE OF

Rocknroll

IN AMERICAN

POPULAR MUSIC

PHILIP H. ENNIS

Wesleyan University Press
Published by University Press of New England
Hanover and London

ML
3534
·E55
1992

WESLEYAN UNIVERSITY PRESS
Published by University Press of New England, Hanover, NH 03755
© 1992 by Philip H. Ennis
All rights reserved
Printed in the United States of America 5 4 3 2 1
CIP data appear at the end of the book

SEP 6 1994
102751 p

To the Memory of ARTHUR ENNIS

Contents

Figures and Tables

FIGURES

TABLES

Acknowledgments

This work has been long in the making. My debts, new and old, are great, reaching back to "The Bureau" at Columbia University in the early 1950s. Thus to William N. McPhee my primary thanks for starting me into the major and minor tactics of the trout stream called social research. To the late Russell Sanjek, I owe a debt of friendship and scholarly exchange that lasted for almost twenty years and lives today in his magisterial volumes on American popular music. To my departed friends Vernon K. Dibble and Hanan C. Selvin, a salute for their luminous presence in my life.

A number of scholarly colleagues, some of whom have participated as full actors in the history of rocknroll, have given me both their critical reading and their personal assessment of parts of this work. They are not responsible for the outcome. I thank Robert Farris Thompson for those valuable letters and articles of many years ago, trying to get me to appreciate the richness and depth of black vernacular dance. Priscilla Meyer, Stewart Gillmor, and Oliver W. Holmes, my colleagues at Wesleyan, and Howard S. Becker have given me continuing encouragement over the years of joint venturing. I am grateful to Leonard B. Meyer, Nat Hentoff, Paul DiMaggio, Walter Wallace, Stephen Milner, H. Stith Bennett, Reebee Garofalo, Robert Kotlowitz, and Tim Riley for their readings, questions, and kind words.

I am appreciative of the steadiness and creative help that I received from Ben Lyons, and grateful for the research assistance from Bruce MacLeod, Vince Brownell, and Rob Lancefield, for the unstinting help and presence of Sam Gilmore, and for the encouragement and stimulation from Corinne A. Kratz.

There are too many Wesleyan students to name individually those who worked with me over the years and who suffered my early formulations and overstatements about a subject they themselves were experiencing directly. I thank them all as well as, for their specific contributions, Joel Schwartz, Ann Duncan, Doug Berman, Mady Kraus, Peggy Kobacker, Walter Rassbach, and Marty McDonough.

For the endless typing so cheerfully done, I thank Loredona Chapman, Debbie Sierpinski, and Christine Cordone. My thanks to Irene Spinnler for years of assistance in times rough and smooth.

I cannot thank enough the librarians at Wesleyan's Olin Library for their always cheerful and accommodating assistance in searching for the endless documentation required.

I am indebted to the many within the music industry who have rendered with courtesy the information I asked for. To Broadcast Music, Inc., the Academy of Recording Arts and Sciences, *Billboard*, *Cash Box*, and the American Music Conference, I am most thankful.

To Bill Randle who told it like it was in the winter of 1952 and who confirmed it in 1982, my deep thanks. And to all those disk jockeys of the 1950s who started this work and rocknroll itself, my thanks.

I am more than grateful for the help and support from Mary Beth Harhen whose understanding of rock is from the inside out. Mindy Keskinen has participated in almost every part of this book's making; my deepest thanks for her dedication, skills, and steadiness. I thank Harrison White and John Morthland for their strong words recommending the first draft of this book. To Terry Cochran my thanks for his light but valuable hand on the editorial rudder, and to the staff of the University Press of New England goes my appreciation.

To Reita Collins Ennis whose patience and sustenance are wondrous. To Michael M. Ennis and to Sarah Ennis-Ruff, my unfailing appreciation for how they made their own separate collections of life and music a shared one for us all.

Middletown, Connecticut   P.H.E.
March 1991

THE SEVENTH STREAM

Introduction

In the children's game, "paper-scissors-rock," each of the two players presents the other with either "paper," indicated by an open hand, or "rock," shown by a closed fist, or "scissors," made with two fingers held up in the "V" for victory sign. The winner of the round is determined according to these rules: paper covers rock, rock breaks scissors, scissors cut paper. The relations among art, commerce, and politics are something like that game; each has some strong power over one other but, at the same time, is vulnerable to the third. In the kids' game, that power is absolute and one directional. In real life, the power of each of the three realms varies considerably and can go either way. But within wide ranges, it can still be said that, in American society, art validates money, money regulates politics, and politics defines art.

The opposite of these rules, however, can also be quite plausibly asserted. Money validating art is more than just outrageous auction prices for a dead painter's neglected works. Money lends legitimacy, a state as much sought after as it is feared by artists. Politics tries to regulate money and, within some limits, does the job. From the Securities and Exchange Commission to copyright law, commerce is guided by rules set through the hurly burly of politics. And art defines politics in ways both subtle and blunt. From the campaign poster and its rhetoric to the cut of the politician's cloth and turn of phrase, artists, as the masters of the senses, clothe political actions and shape political goals. Even during their most normal operations, then, all three of these realms are thoroughly entangled in making up the arts of any society.

This study is about the stormy meeting of art, commerce, and politics when, after the end of World War II, a change occurred within the several American popular musics. That change was the appearance of a new kind of music, different from the others not just artistically but in the way it engaged politics and commerce. Rocknroll,[1] for such was its name, provoked trouble right from the start in all three of these areas, and it still does.

Commitment and Release

The story of rocknroll, told many times before, illuminates deeper social issues not generally addressed. These include the nature of social and artistic boundaries, their creation and maintenance, their violation and repair. The making of boundaries is essential to all human societies, and the alternation between commitment to and release from those boundaries is one of the deepest rhythms of all social life.[2] Unrelieved commitment, like unrelenting reality, is insupportable. The established alternations, from the coffee break to the annual vacation, recognize this fact. Leisure, the name for this institutionalized envelope, invites individual versions of release under its protective banner of "free" time.[3]

Other institutions recognize the imperative for the momentary escape from time, gravity, and lies. One of the most powerful of such institutions is the brief experience known from time immemorial as ecstasy.[4] The search for ecstatic release in religion, the arts, nature, the lover's couch, the bottle, even madness are well known. As long as they are individual and random choices, they are harmless steam valves, adding personal piquance to life. If, however, they become entangled in some social movement, trouble lies ahead. History is littered with the wreckage of such joinders; yet the attempts to achieve the ecstatic cessation of time and merge it with the flow of everyday life returns again and again.

Along with the conflict of social groups for power, most familiarly stated in Marxian terms as the struggle for control of the means of production there is another, equally pervasive, but perhaps less visible struggle. It is the ceaseless battle of organized powers of society for control and monopoly over the means of ecstatic expression.[5]

That battle is fought mainly in symbolic terms these days, but symbolic representations of social boundaries are as necessary to their preservation as are the blood and bodies of their makers. The symbolic resources of a people, those symbols that give fantasy its shape and substance, provide not only release but the means and motivation to continue with everyday life. It is arguable that fantasy is, in fact, the deepest guide to the reality of everyday life as well as being its only cure.

Music is one of fantasy's best helpers. It is a strange language understood by all without instruction, although its creation is foreign to most (in the United States, at least). Music is a way of holding off time, making the present fill all space. It joins us with others yet defends our privacy.

It lifts the spirit, assuages grief, and sometimes teaches as well. Above all, music creates values, along with a social structure that nurtures, defends, and celebrates those values. Music does all this vividly, and does it twice; once in the first hearing, when the music-maker has you as joint voyager, then again and infinitely more times as the rehearing merges the music with the remembered experience of that first and subsequent hearing. Is it any wonder that the history of music is so quarrelsome given this inevitable confusion of nostalgia with taste?

Further, music has its own internal boundaries to regulate. Its division of labor, stratification of styles, and competition for audiences make the different musics of a society engage in political and economic actions similar to those of any other political economy. Symbolic politics are real politics. The economics of symbol creation and exchange is consequential economics. Each musical tradition wants its own name and distinct presence, yet all join together, legitimately or otherwise, at their boundaries, realigning, blurring, sometimes disappearing into each other. These encounters are like those of a wave coming through a jetty to the beach. Where they touch there is disturbance and change, yet wave, jetty, and beach preserve themselves for their own expirations. In just such a way did rocknroll emerge from the other musics of the day.

Who Controls the Music

Most of the several American popular musics were developed within a money framework politically crafted by narrow legislative and judicial regulation of intellectual property, embodied in the Copyright Act of 1909. The story of rocknroll is anchored, therefore, in the commercial struggles that defined and allocated property rights in music at the turn of the twentieth century. It was at that moment, not coincidentally, that the popular music of the day consolidated itself into the standard three-minute song still being sung today.

The dominant influence in music at that time was the group of music publishers located mainly in New York. It was their job to bring the songwriters and composers together with the performers to give audiences a continuing supply of song and dance. The publishers' catalogue—their accumulated songs protected by copyright law—was the key entity in assembling, retrieving, and shaping the main reservoir of American popular music.

Those catalogues, the concretization of cultural capital, were the basis for music production's economic viability. Any music outside the catalogues was in the public domain, either in the form of composed music that had exceeded the period of legal protection (twenty-eight years, with renewal for twenty-eight more)[6] or in the great anonymous pool of folk music. Music in the catalogues and in the public domain provided all the raw material used in the primary artistic act, that is, the making of new ones out of old ones.

When communication technology took a giant step forward in 1920 with commercial radio and the mass sale of phonograph records, the music publishers faced an entirely new situation. Not only was the making and selling of music done differently, but its costs fell on different shoulders. Radio and the phonograph record gradually shifted popular music from a reliance on the home piano and its sheet music to broadcast and recorded performance as the primary experience. A struggle soon began between the young radio broadcasting industry and the music publishers, with the record companies an active third party. The battle, on the surface, was about who was to pay how much for the use of copyrighted music on the air.

A much deeper issue was at stake, however: control over the nation's musical culture. The old braggart's cry that to write a song for the people's heart brings more power than is held by their king rings true, for America's popular musics defined the contours of everyday life. While the nation's employers set working hours and rates of pay, the New York music publishers laid out more important matters: the pleasures and pains of being an American (immigrants poured in through Ellis Island until 1924), how one's ease was to be taken, how the display of pride was to be manifested, what it was like to be in love and out of love. This musical framing of experience marked the range of its listeners' aspirations, telling them what to expect as they journeyed from poor to rich, from country to city, from downtown to uptown.

Radio and phonograph increasingly accompanied that journey, and there soon ensued a thirty-years' war over the control of American popular musical culture. The publishers, represented by the American Society of Composers, Authors and Publishers (ASCAP), were not willing to hand over to a bunch of engineers and financiers either the control or the money involved in steering American musical life. By the early 1950s, the situation had reached a standoff. The broadcasters had their own licensing organization, Broadcast Music Incorporated (BMI), and their catalogue strongly leaned toward hillbilly and black pop material. They also had significant control over much of the phonograph industry. The publishers, watching the rise of competitive musics controlled by other interests, angrily asked how the heirs to the great songwriting traditions of Jerome Kern, George and Ira Gershwin, Cole Porter, Irving Berlin, could have been displaced by upstarts and unknowns.

What had happened? The entertainment press offered diagnoses and dirges from prominent and/or knowledgeable "tradesters," who collectively agreed on only one thing: that radio broadcasting and its creatures were somehow responsible. That diagnosis led some members of the New York music establishment to declare a series of political-legal battles.

The Disk Jockey Study

In 1953 Arthur Schwartz, a popular composer of first rank during the 1920s and 1930s, a lawyer himself, and a senior presence in ASCAP, spearheaded a civil suit on antitrust grounds against BMI, its top executives, the major networks, and their chiefs. The plaintiffs joining Arthur Schwartz were a pantheon of American music ranging from Ira Gershwin to Virgil Thomson.[7] Schwartz argued that the broadcasters, by virtue of their ownership of BMI, could and did unduly influence their station personnel—disk jockeys especially—to favor music licensed by BMI rather than ASCAP. The additional air play received by BMI songs resulted not only in an actual diminished income to ASCAP members but, in their eyes, a diminished quality of popular music for the nation. The power of the radio disk jockey was being used to deprive young Americans of great musical riches from the golden era of American song.

Sidney Kaye, the founding and leading figure of BMI, respected his adversaries. ASCAP's legal staff and political allies had already revealed their wiliness and strength during the past three decades of negotiation. He went uptown to Columbia University's Bureau of Applied Social Research for help. Paul Lazarsfeld, director of "The Bureau," as it was called, had previously served BMI in a technical capacity and was an innovative scholar of the mass media. The research team he assembled, of which I was a part, applied the Bureau's familiar research approach: map out the specific institutional contexts of decision making in the radio exposure of popular music and estimate the relative strengths of the various influences on the nested series of decisions leading to the final choice of songs to be played on the air.

The study concluded that the disk jockeys on AM radio were the key figures in making the hits of the day, and BMI, the creature of the broadcasters, was essentially irrelevant in the hit-making game.[8] BMI, for its part, was satisfied with this conclusion but wanted more evidence that it had little influence over the direction pop music was heading. So Kaye returned to Lazarsfeld for further advice, while the Schwartz case ground on. The result of this second study, which focused on the recent success of rhythm and blues records and was based on a close examination of *Billboard*'s music popularity charts, showed that disk jockeys tended to follow rather than lead popular taste. They "do not appear to have exerted a determining influence on the 'popularity' of particular rhythm and blues disks," the study concluded.[9] BMI was thus doubly exonerated. First, it was cleared of the charge of controlling the agents who played the records, and second, these agents were shown to have no commanding influence on the current popularity of this new rhythm and blues fad.

The Bureau was now finished with the matter, although the Schwartz case would continue to move glacially forward over the following years. A full Dickens novel's worth, the case finally fell exhausted, dismissed with prejudice in June of 1971, eighteen years after its inception and long after ASCAP and BMI had reconciled their differences.[10]

What Was There to Understand about Rocknroll?

I was not content, however. In the first report we had established what everyone in the industry already knew—that the disk jockey was "king," that collectively disk jockeys made the hits. The second report announced what everybody also knew as a fact—that the "fad" was bigger than the "king." This unresolved paradox between the two reports went completely unnoticed; but it rankled me, and through the following years, I suffered the worst case of the Zeigarnik effect known to Western medicine.[11] I knew the disk jockey report was not really done. Only gradually did I come to see that the disk jockey's role was pivotal in the formation of rocknroll, which was not a fad after all.

It is now obvious why I didn't understand better, at the time of the Bureau studies, for nowhere in either the disk jockey report or in the rhythm and blues fad study was the word "rocknroll" mentioned. Rocknroll was simply not a word in the vocabulary of the people in the music business I dealt with in the years 1952 through 1955. If I had listened to the radio, however, I would have found the beginnings of an answer. Rocknroll was indeed not a hula hoop. It was here to stay. As the tumult of the 1960s linked its music to the youth movements of those times, I surrendered to the fact that, if I was to make peace with my long unresolved disk jockey questions, I would need a full review of the facts of rocknroll's birth and growth, on the one hand, and some kind of a theoretical framework on the other. Both the study that follows and the theory guiding it, reported elsewhere,[12] are premised on a pair of observations and their implications.

One observation is that the cohort of Americans born just at the end of World War II was not just especially large, a demographic burst, but was also a spawn with a specific cultural heritage. The set of beliefs held by its progenitors, its parents and teachers, was founded on the optimistic promise of peace and plenty won by the military victory over the Axis powers. The children were to be guided in achieving the fruits of that victory. By the time they got to high school in the late fifties, however, it was clear that the promise had been broken, or at least was not coming out the way the kids thought it should. Their response was to question, raise hell, do anything to avoid doing what the adults wanted.

The paths they took, while indeed personal and individual, were also collective. They were rewriting the code on what constituted commitment and what was release. When they proclaimed peace and love, were they not critiquing the regnant learning theories that used punishment and reward as equivalent tools?[13] When they demanded freedom, were they not challenging an economy of scarcity and repudiating the conventional definitions of work and play? In this process, the music, their own rocknroll, brought these young people together and opened wide the perspectives for seeking alternative answers.

The second observation is that the explosion of all the arts after the end of World War II was an efflorescence of great breadth, bringing the old arts and some new ones to millions of Americans. Although there was no vast extension of the so-called elite arts after the war, there was, through the GI Bill and mass marketing (the economic mechanism of democratization), a greater penetration of all the arts into the American population than ever before. More importantly, young artists formed a new set of cohorts who quite self-consciously adventured considerably past the boundaries set by their teachers.

It is in their work that the term "efflorescence" has its locus. In the literary arts, the paperback revolution of the early 1950s brought the reprinted literary storehouse of the past to a new postwar audience. On top of that, a huge cascade of fresh novels and poetry poured out of a bursting literary fountain. A comparable energy, richness, and diversity characterized the visual arts, with abstract expressionism transforming New York City into a world avant garde center of painting.[14] Dance also experienced a rebirth, yielding the bewildering world of "postmodern" dance that eventually erased the boundaries separating theater, ballet, and opera.[15] Music shared in this rapid creative growth. From the musical theater's *Oklahoma!* by Richard Rodgers and Oscar Hammerstein II and Benjamin Britten's *Peter Grimes* to John Cage and Harry Partch, popular and "serious" music refashioned their boundaries, simultaneously unleashing the other popular musics from their wartime restrictions and dislocations. The design of postwar architecture, household products, and clothing flourished with a genuine and creative freshness.[16]

In feast or in famine, each of these arts is carried within a basic social molecule consisting of four parts: (1) its artists, who make the pieces, (2) the distributors, who select among them for presentation to (3) the audience, whose presence and approval (or disapproval) is essential, and (4) the critics, upon whom the public responsibility of evaluation rests. This "diamond," as I call it, is as necessary to creative life as the family is to reproductive life, and just as varied. Every culture has its unique configuration of the arts, and all its separate diamonds constitute the "Parade of the Muses." No one had ever seen that Parade, of course, because it just won't assemble. The reason is that the arts are too busy quarreling over their individual claims about who should be first in line for that grand attempt to give the assembled people a helluva show. Moreover, the arts are so intermingled in personnel and artistic resources that it is difficult to draw the boundaries between them. Worse, what is to be done when a new art form emerges with a mixed parentage? Where should it be placed in the Parade, or should it be kicked out of the Parade entirely? It should be noted here that the entire Parade of the Muses is always on trial for its morals. This scrutiny occurs not only because the Parade marches in the realm of release—an acknowledged dangerous realm— but it also occurs because the arts are generally on the wrong side of town, placed among the taverns, the cheap hotels, the whorehouses, and the gaming parlors.

The appearance of rocknroll as a new member of music's ranks brought the question of positioning onto the table. An art primarily for kids traditionally goes to the back of the Parade, but an art that pays its own way moves to the front. Where, then, would rocknroll go, especially since it was oppositional if not criminal? And this question raised the recalcitrant issue about how the *internal* criteria for judging an art's place in the parade are perpetually invaded by *external* concerns. The two most important of these externalities are the state and the corporation. If the Czar likes ballet dancers, ballet moves forward; if the President is a movie actor, film moves closer to the head of the Parade. The contemporary face of commerce is more than a small group of Dutch burghers sustaining their portrait painters; it is filled with enterprises whose wealth and power are greater than that of most sovereign countries and who are now dictating to artists a bottom-line dollar story. A specific study of rocknroll, I thought, would illuminate how the encroaching power of both the state and the swelling corporate affect the arts generally.

The struggles over money and leadership of New York's musical culture that began years before with ASCAP and the broadcasters thus generated not just a new kind of music but a whole youth-led politics that challenged the institutions of the entire society. The irony of those struggles is that the music young people championed and indeed made for themselves has turned into economic enterprises of gigantic proportions, and the politics they fought for has dissipated. But what an instructive story of one moment's meeting of art, commerce, and politics.

A Musical Odyssey

I was not chosen for the disk jockey project accidentally, nor did I relish that assignment without cause. I had been well cooked in American musical culture before I started work on the project. In my parents' home in Baltimore, we listened to the music on the radio, but we had no phonograph. My mother's move was to put a grand piano (not an upright) in the living room of the first house we owned. Neither she nor my father could play it, and neither could sing. Nevertheless, from the bathroom often came my father's rendition of "Ah Sweet Mystery of Life." I measured his performance against Nelson Eddy's version, and though I found my father's a lesser achievement, I enjoyed it more. It was like wallpaper to me, familiar and comforting. The song might have been sung for himself, but it was given to me. My affection and respect for all American popular musics comes, I think, from that gift. It has brought me to recognize that someone else's words and music will allow you to say your heart in ways you couldn't do yourself. The collaboration of artist and audience is like that between the flagmaker and the wind.

Listener only I was not to be, but the sacrificial morsel to the god of the piano and I was, of course, burnt in the offering. I bear no bitterness toward the teacher; but when I knew I was not going to teach myself or enjoy the doing, I gave it up. The much misunderstood term "frustrated artist," a mischievous notion if there ever was one, nevertheless carries a germ of truth explainable by any number of psychohydraulic theories about all that creative fluid bottled up and looking for an outlet.

My mother accepted defeat at the piano but inflicted much more interesting inducements to land me on the path of "culture": live concerts, live theater, and, finally, live opera. That supreme musical form was permanently destroyed for me by a traveling company doing the standard double bill *Pagliacci* and *Cavalleria Rusticana*. Pagliacci, in the passionate midst of his betrayal, sang just as I had heard him on the radio, with Milton Cross purring the story sung by the Metropolitan Opera Company on its New York stage. But, being the tacky company it was, the knife held aloft in desperation, rehearsing the steely blow to be delivered, waggled like the rubber knife it was. The strictures of realism imposed by regular Saturday afternoons at the movies were completely violated. So much for the opera for a twelve-year-old kid. But every art is in danger at any moment of being stabbed by Pagliacci's rubber knife.

Music in Baltimore's Forest Park High School was completely uncomfortable and incomprehensible—dressing up for dances I couldn't do and listening to music that made no sense and gave no pleasure. Glenn Miller's 1941 "Moonlight Cocktail" will always signify that distasteful puzzlement. It was only much later, after I had heard records of the Basie band of those years, that I could reconstruct what most of the white swing bands were trying to do and feel some relief that I wasn't entirely at fault.

Black popular music simply didn't exist for me in high school and never would have except for the accident of having a particular fraternity brother. Irvin Feld and his brother owned a drugstore in Washington, D.C., and invited me to work there on Saturdays. It was a new world,

Seventh Street, one of the main drags in black Washington. At the drugstore's doorway was stationed a dried up little man with a "pet" gila
monster selling "Nature Tonic." Into the street blared the latest race records. Enough street traffic was lured into the store to fill half its interior
with cartons of those records, all 78s and simply wonderful. The record
"Jelly Jelly," surely Earl "Fatha" Hines' own composition, went round in
my head for months. The Feld brothers must have known that the entertainment on Seventh Street was the main road, not Nature Tonic or the
rest of the drugstore. Their move to radio and talent management in the
1950s and then to ownership of the greatest circus in the world attests to
that instinct.

If music really could be as powerful as it was in Washington's black
ghetto, why wasn't I getting any? Where was my music? Hearing what
was being sung in the synagogue was short-circuited because my family
didn't belong. Again, years later in a Brooklyn Jewish neighborhood during High Holy Day Services, I was struck down by the cantor, discovering
that power for the first time, but too late.

Politics and music made an easier but not very intense connection for
me; I was taken to the traveling company of *Pins and Needles* and saw
an exciting Broadway show with political commentary and fun, but
nothing to set me afire. Also uninspiring were the skits and "folk" topical
musical shows done in the Washington Book Shop (the same place that
attracted many Baltimore-Washington left-liberal cultural types, including one of the young Ertegun brothers).[17] Music was still too distant from
me, from the Saturday morning kiddie concerts by the Baltimore Symphony Orchestra (was Walter Damrosch really there on occasion?) to
burlesque at the Gayety Theater where the crackerjack, the comedians,
and the luminous Valerie Parks gave a definite piquance to my arts education. I absorbed everything but found nothing that really spoke to my
condition.

In 1943, like millions of others in the armed forces, I heard white
Southern music for the first time. Roy Acuff's "Great Speckled Bird,"
though recorded in 1937, was still strong in the jukebox, as was Bob
Wills' "San Antonio Rose." In the barracks, his "Ah Haa San Antone"
was the cry that signaled preparations for a two-day pass. The distance
from home and the solitude of KP late at night made popular music, for
the first time in my life, a companion. The Mills Brothers' "Paper Doll"
and "It's Only a Paper Moon" stayed with me for years.

Nevertheless, pop music of every land retreated from my awareness
when I returned to college after the war. The early years of exposure to
classical music finally got to me, and I worked through the record stores
indiscriminately. I wore out an album of Beethoven's *Emperor* Concerto
in a month of daily playing and did the same for Lizst's *Les Preludes*, not

knowing or caring about the differences in their value. At the same time, I listened to the folk music that was appearing on my campus. I bought and relished the obligatory *Six Songs for Democracy* (the Spanish Civil War songs), the Almanac Singers' (Pete Seeger's pre-Weavers group) rendition of *The Talking Union*, and Josef Marais' *Songs of the South African Veld*.

The same pattern of immersion in classical music and casual listening to the folk scene continued in graduate school. Harvard and Boston in the late 1940s were drenched with live music. I heard the Budapest Quartet do the full cycle of Bartok quartets live in Sanders Theater, heard Paul Hindemith conduct an evening of his music there, dwelled in an overwhelming Berlioz Requiem, and on occasion went to the Sunday morning organ recitals that E. Power Biggs broadcast from the Germanic (now the Busch-Riesinger) Museum. The newly developed "long playing" record made that repertoire immediately accessible, providing me with an intense personal discovery of "pure" music. I must have bent my body out of shape a hundred times getting through the unending finale of the third movement of Beethoven's C-sharp Minor Quartet and making an equal number of trips through Bach's *Actus Tragicus* (Cantata no. 106).

About this time (1948–1950), pop music reentered my life, accompanying my household chores and studying. An AM station in Boston unobtrusively presented the "hit" game—"Here's number six jumping up two notches; Here's the number one song." It was familiar but varying wallpaper. This easy coexistence of "serious" and popular music continued when I moved to New York in 1950 and added to my fare the musical theater, jazz at Birdland, and the young City Center Ballet Company, then headquartered in the old mosque-like theater on Fifty-sixth Street. There was no incongruity or invidious comparison among these different musics. They all coexisted quite easily. "My" music had become, without any grasping, practically everything in town.

On the Road Again

The invitation to join the research team Paul Lazarsfeld assembled for the BMI project in 1952 brought me to the heart of New York's music business in midtown. That realm was nicely poised, I thought, between two other cultural marketplaces, Seventh Avenue South (the garment trade) and Seventh Avenue North (publishing and the art galleries). The intensive preparation the BMI staff gave us included a tour through the rehearsal rooms of a major music publisher, a compulsory visit to Guy Lombardo (then regally ensconced at the Roosevelt Grill), a brief chat with Mitch Miller, and considerable stories of show biz ways delivered mainly by George Marlo at Al and Dick's.

I have the clearest memory of the tone and belief that permeated all our discussions. New York was considered, as a matter of course, the music capital of the nation, and that belief was not in any sense embattled. It was believed, though, that the city was isolated from the main action. "You can't make a hit in New York any more" was the insistently repeated statement. I didn't know then why this was the case, but I quickly learned that the industry was willing to go wherever the hits were made. Every Sunday evening the flights from La Guardia to the Midwest and to the West Coast were filled with song pluggers and record company men flying to visit disk jockeys from Pittsburgh to Seattle, from Detroit to Phoenix. The disk jockeys in New York City, though star-studded with such luminaries as Martin Block, Ted Husing, Art Ford, and Rayburn and Finch, were not the types to break the hits. We were to discover in the cities outside New York who did make the hits and how they did it. The disk jockey study called for intensive interviews with a mix of "average" and the top fifty disk jockeys in the nation.

In Cleveland, my main interview was with Bill Randle, then presiding over WERE's popular music efforts. In the two days I spent with him, I learned what the whole hit-making game was about and how it was conducted. Paradoxically, Alan Freed, just down the street in a competing radio station, was neither on our list of "important" disk jockeys nor on the list of "average" disk jockeys, nor was he mentioned to me by Bill Randle. There I was in the city of rocknroll's founding, and I didn't find the founder.

In New Orleans I left the radio station ambiance for the French Quarter. There I stumbled onto a small record store selling Bill Russell's American Music recordings of Bunk Johnson, George Lewis, and Billie and Dee Dee Pierce. At the store I met Richard Allen (later curator of the William Ransom Hogan Archive of New Orleans Jazz at Tulane University), who invited me to join him and friends for an evening of music. The evening ended up lasting three days. For the first time, I was hearing New Orleans jazz live, in its natural habitat. I spent time at Luthjens ("The Old Folks Home," as it was called) where Dee Dee and Billie Pierce played, in the Paddock Lounge, at Manny's, at the Three Deuces, and even at the Famous Door where the young Asunto brothers were doing a more commercial version of the music (and where Pete Fountain was on the verge of his departure for a solo act wherein jazz would meet pop).

My sometime companion during those nights and days was Ken Colyer, whom I met en route. We listened into the morning to Paul Barbarin and to Papa Celestin's band, and we talked with them and with Bill Mathews and Alphonse Picou. We talked with Lizzie Miles and listened to her singing, but mostly we were at the club where George Lewis played. It was a wonder of nature to hear and see Slow Drag Pavigeaux, Jim

Robinson, Larry Marrero, and Baby Dodds, who played along with George Lewis (there was no trumpet in the group at that time). The fact that Colyer was British puzzled me, knowing nothing of the power that American jazz records had exercised on young British musicians since the end of World War II. Colyer had worked himself to New Orleans on a merchant ship after several years of mixed emotions over whether it was the sea or music he really wanted. He apparently found the answer in New Orleans, where he often sat in with George Lewis' band and spent a little time in jail due to immigration problems. He had the talent to match his passion, as did several young white musicians from the British Isles in subsequent years. Colyer was a model of that successful cultural transplant of traditional jazz from New Orleans to London. In a movement that was to be repeated again and again, reworked old American popular musical forms were filled with fresh material in London and shipped back to the States.[18]

I also brought back from New Orleans (and still play on occasion) a 78 rpm recording of Sister Lottie Peavey's "When I Move to the Sky" and "Nobody's Fault But Mine." These religious songs, accompanied by Bunk Johnson's Yerba Buena Jazz Band,[19] were a revelation to me. I had only known the refined grandeur of Mahalia Jackson's spirituals and Dorothy Maynor's concert versions of the sacred music of Handel and Bach, particularly her lofty "Let Every Tongue Adore Thee." The rough and urgent quality of Peavey's gospel rendition opened up another door to American music. I sensed then that both jazz and gospel had enormous capacities to realize themselves in the most diverse musical settings and even to merge successfully, in spite of the injunctions that sinful secular jazz and sacred gospel music should not mix.

Finally, upon my return from the South, I bought Hank Williams' "You Win Again," Webb Pierce's "Back Street Affair," Kitty Wells' "I Heard the Juke Box Playing," and the Louvin Brothers' "I Don't Believe You've Met My Baby," all current hits that I had been listening to on the radio from Fort Worth to Atlanta. These artists represented, and still do, that clean, direct honky-tonk style that dominated country music at the time. The Louvin Brothers' record, though I didn't know it then, was representative of the embattled but persistent mountain strain that was turning into the bluegrass movement.

By the time, then, that I realized rocknroll was not a fad but a definite and perhaps permanent part of American popular music, I had become a fairly knowledgeable and, on occasion, a fervent member of the audience for serious concert music, for pop (from Broadway to top 40), for country music, for rhythm and blues, and for jazz, folk, and gospel. I knew and liked them all, could generally tell the differences in style and quality among them, and enjoyed the intermingling at their boundaries. Leaving concert music aside as a distinctly different music, I could visualize the six streams of American *popular* music as having somehow produced rocknroll, the seventh stream.

The notion of *stream* had gradually worked itself into my thought; each of these seven popular musics was thus an entire world, in the sense that Howard S. Becker uses the term.[20] Being a Columbia trained sociologist, I sought to analyze those worlds to discover their component structural parts. I had already begun to work out elements of the "diamond" and "Parade" notions, and, as my study of rocknroll progressed, it became clear that the interconnections between the economy of rocknroll and various social movements required that it all be put together into one concept. The stream concept seemed to be at the right level of generality, with enough specificity to see how the whole thing worked. Hopefully, the story to follow, in all its historical detail and geographical meanderings, will illuminate the general notions offered here.

Just as rocknroll grew out of the other six streams and became a natural member of that family, it grew on me personally and must have done so for millions of young Americans who got there without knowing very much more than how to turn on the radio. But I must confess, I didn't like it very much in the late fifties. I even wrote these fatuous lines in a letter to Robert Farris Thompson, whose gifted descriptions of vernacular dance, particularly mambo, helped correct my unwarranted snootyness. "The problem of quality cannot be blinked; rock and roll is at the bottom of American music, the commercial sludge which lubricates the system enough to allow some musicians to play and record better stuff. Mambo is high octane, and some of its vapors infuse the highest jazz forms. . . ."[21]

My only excuse is that it was 1958, and I wasn't listening carefully enough. The popularity of this new stream in American popular music is, at least in personal, subjective terms, easy to understand and totally unproblematical. Young people all over the world take to it without instruction. It is only in the external, objective story of its formation and development that its complexity and wider contexts are revealed.

PART ONE

SIX STREAMS
ASSEMBLE:
1900-1940

1. The Organization of Popular Musics

A new music appeared in the United States around 1950. It received its name, rocknroll,[1] soon afterward, and by 1965 it had fully matured as the seventh stream of American popular music. It survives today, well and strong, among the six other streams that gave it life. Those other streams are called pop, black pop, country pop, jazz, folk, and gospel. Each of these musics, from their central cores and from their boundary zones with the others, successively touched and mixed, producing rocknroll. It was a boisterous and infectious music, directed to, and embraced almost exclusively by, young people. Rocknroll began with teenagers and was adopted later by college students and those of college age. Together they forged a musical ambiance in which they could sing and dance and that would accompany them on a journey of confrontation with the adults who ruled their homes, their schools, and their nation.

Once it was publicly named by the mainstream press, its defining social characteristic was instantly understood. Rocknroll was the music and the dance of the young. Its cultural meaning was also quickly and accurately identified; it was a stance against adult authority. This was unprecedented, for at no time in the nation's history had such a unifying cultural identity spread so widely and so deeply among the young of every social class, region, and race.

The way rocknroll originated is by now a familiar story:

The origins of rock'n'roll have been repeated so often it sounds like a litany. Black blues and white country music were the basis of rock 'n' roll. Both were products of the deep South, and the roots of rock really go back to one person with a guitar singing about hard times or letting it all hang out. This out-in-the-woods type music began to change as many of the musicians living in small towns in the country fell upon hard times and started to move to the bigger cities to find work and a better way of life. In the cities their life styles changed and their music changed with them.[2]

This simple genealogy, although not entirely the wrong "begat," omits the teenagers, the interior workings of the music business, and the other musical streams that joined to produce rocknroll. A more fruitful origin story tells how rocknroll got its name. The disk jockey Alan Freed is generally, and I believe correctly, credited with naming rocknroll in 1952. Here is one version of how that came about.

Billy Ward and his Dominoes were on a record promotion tour set up by their label, Federal Records. In Cleveland it was essential to visit two disk jockeys. One was Bill Randle, among the nation's highest paid and most successful hit-making record spinners whose long afternoon show on station WERE could put new records on the charts with unfailing ease. The other was Alan Freed, a classically trained musician who was scrambling for an audience on the nighttime slot of station WJW. The record store owner, Leo Mintz, had suggested to Freed that he build his show around "race" music because that was where the action was at the moment in record sales. So, with a mixture of black gospel, secular quartets, and jump bands, Freed enthusiastically became the white champion of black pop, not only on the air but as a promoter of live shows.

After appearing at one of these events, which packed some twenty-five thousand (a mammoth crowd for those days) young people, both black and white, into the Cleveland Arena, Billy Ward, lead singer of the Dominoes, paid his respects to Freed at the radio station.

Next day Freed and I were sitting in his studio still staggered by the unexpected success of the night before. We talked while "Sixty Minute Man" was playing. [The then recently number one hit on both black and white music popularity charts.] "You know, Billy," he said, rubbing his chin thoughtfully, "you've turned the music business upside down with this new music of yours. It's *not* authentic rhythm and blues, or jazz or pop. It has no classification, really. We've got to find a name for it. . . ." At this juncture our record boomed, "I rock 'em roll 'em all night long, I'm a Sixty Minute Man!" Freed leaped to his feet. "That's it!" he cried hoarsely. "Rock and Roll! That's what it is." Immediately he broadcast his name for our sound. And all the trade publications fell in line with his thinking. To my knowledge—and *Billboard* confirmed it—this was the first time this music that spread-eagled the rhythm and blues, jazz and pop fields became labeled "Rock and Roll."[3]

Like any mythic icon, this story compresses some of the main elements involved in bringing about rocknroll. The expression "rockin' and rollin'" had been in the American vernacular for a considerable time. It's many meanings, sexual and otherwise, coalesced in that moment and in such a way to enable Freed to communicate the simple but dangerous fact that he was bringing a black popular "party" music (risqué lyrics with a strong dance beat) to a mixed audience of black and white teenagers. The term did double duty. While signaling the musical crossing of sensitive racial and moral boundaries, it also masked that announcement. It was a truly artful naming, doing what a symbolic code always does—hiding while it reveals, revealing while it hides. But who is Billy Ward? The Dominoes? Why wasn't "Sixty Minute Man" real rhythm and blues? What was Federal Records? And why does Cleveland, Ohio, become so important? Within the answers to these questions lies the story of rocknroll.

The thesis of this book is that rocknroll appeared during the convergence of two changes that affected all of American society and each of its arts. One change affected the nation's several popular musics from the inside out, the other, from the outside in. The "outside in" part was the transformation of American society precipitated by World War II and its aftermath. That conflict and its echoes generated worldwide changes in politics, economics, and family life. In the United States, the Depression-era lines of social division, those of economic class, labor versus capital, though still operative of course, gave way to other concerns. Obscuring the deeper divisions of race and gender for the moment, the fears of communism abroad and at home unleashed the Cold War and the McCarthy witch hunts, both of which divided and numbed the American people for most of the fifties. Afterward, the civil rights movement and then the feminist movement, along with other comparable movements, started assembling their grievances into phalanxes of social action.

Most unexpectedly at that time, young people began to feel a great weight on their shoulders. As the postwar promise of peace and plenty energized the nation, redeeming the wartime pledge that this era was to be the Century of the Common Man,[4] the kids were told to get into their classrooms, pay attention to the work, obey parents and teachers, speak when spoken to, be nice, get a job, and shut up. While most dutifully did, some wouldn't and didn't. The screw had been turned too tight too fast. Among the several ways of saying no to adults (and there were more than one), was the new music of the day, which provided a strategic alternative. To listen to that music, to dance to that music, and to make that music was a political act without being political.

The "inside out" of rocknroll's origin came from the postwar changes within all the arts, changes that relocated their geography and redefined their uses, their meanings, and their forms of expression. The American music industry, among those arts, was already in the midst of decisive reorganization due to forces that dated back to the beginning of the twentieth century. Music publishing and its practices had earlier established a relatively simple music business. It offered song and dance in theaters and taverns, in concert halls and churches, bringing music into the American home via the piano and its sheet music. The mechanical technology of the player piano, then the electronic technologies of radio and phonographic recording began a series of changes that reworked the entire popular music system. The ensuing struggles over the property rights in all popular musics was a central factor in the creation of rocknroll.

The events leading to this new musical stream were rooted in the increasing antagonism between the music publishers and the radio broadcasters. The fight was over who would bear the costs of music production and who would receive its profits. This financially consequential battle took place just as the pop stream's musical resources were being exhausted, a decade-long process that went hand in hand with the self-destruction of its production and distribution apparatus. The battle came to a head just as World War II erupted, disturbing every aspect of life as well as the entire music business.

There is simply no way to understand rocknroll without taking these two aspects into account: the young audience with all its adventures and misadventures on the one side and, on the other, the convoluted story of the music industry's internal plumbing. Inside out and outside in met in the person of the radio disk jockey, an unlikely midwife attending the birth of a new musical stream born from the meeting of the other six. How did that occupation, "disk jockey," halfway between the staid radio announcer and the impish trickster impresario, appear in the first place? How did the job become so important? A larger picture is necessary to answer those questions, one that encompasses the surprising diversity of American popular music. It was within that diversity, indeed, that rocknroll incubated.

What Is a Musical Stream?

The premise that rocknroll is a full member in the company of the other six musical streams requires some elaboration. It is a mysterious thing when a new music appears. Since something does not come out of nothing, the new must come either from within one existing type of music or from the boundary of two or more different musics. The latter is the way rocknroll began. Further, a new music is either the work of one or a small number of inspired artists or it comes from the pervasive and powerful presence of an anonymous cohort.[5] In the case of rocknroll, it was both.

Rocknroll is not a fad, although for some time the music pundits in New York were convinced it was. Rocknroll is not a form; a sonata, a symphony, an opera, or a popular song are forms. Rocknroll is not a style; the Classical and the Romantic are styles. Rocknroll has its fads, forms, and styles, but it is more than all of them. These classifications—fads, forms, styles—cannot capture music's protean ways and its fecundity. Rocknroll is a stream, the seventh, that grew out of the meeting of the other six streams.

What, then, is a musical stream? It is more than a metaphor. A musical stream is a palpable part of social reality, made up of several elements: an artistic system, an economic framework, and a social movement. The first of these, its artistic system, is a four-part social molecule as durable and as ubiquitous as the family, and just as diverse. This basic "diamond" structure is made up of the artists, the distributors, the audiences, and the critics. Collectively they create, circulate, use, and evaluate the individual pieces, plays, poems, and pictures that taken together constitute the art forms called music, theater, poetry, painting, and so on. A musical stream, therefore, includes the people who invent and perform the music itself, whether notated and/or remembered, the instrumentation and vocal traditions, the media and performance sites, the distributors who organize the musical events, the audiences who, in exchange for some mixture of love and money, accept the music as their own, and the critics who set the standards of evaluation for each piece of music as well as for the whole canon and then apply those standards day by day, song by song.

Second, a musical stream is an economic entity of some complexity. That economy includes different kinds of exchange systems, each with its own legal skein of property rights. One kind of exchange is the conventional market structure in which consumers select the music they want (the diet) from fare offered by the producers and their distributors (the menu). The dynamic driving that system is thus the continuous matching and mismatching of menu to diet. Another economic arrangement guiding a musical stream is what can be called "third party choice," wherein someone like a librarian or a museum curator is given the money and the right to select the books or paintings for a number of consumers. The disk jockey works in that way, choosing the music for the radio station's listeners. Finally, and most enigmatic, is the system of gift exchange, by which music circulates through the system. Much more than "free" concerts, dedicated creations, or the exchanges of "friendship," the gift economy intertwines with the other exchange systems to produce a dense and opaque set of transactions. As a whole, music's economic institutions are an interconnected set of mixed enterprises, each offering a particular set of services. They range from one-man operations to giant corporations. They operate in a manner somewhere between full, open competition and oligopolistic dominance.

A third and vital component of a musical stream is its participation in some social movement. That movement may be concerned with the defense and enhancement of a specific race, class, caste, age group, gender, or of some geographical-cultural entity such as the South, the City, or the

Nation. It may be a social formation actively dedicated to a single idea: a search for social change, for sacred celebration, or just for a good time (the "party" party whose members are legion). It may be simply a symbolic accoutrement to a specific style of life, as the Viennese waltz, the cowboy song, or the Cajun two step. The movement may be a total and durable design for living (the Way of the Samurai). It may be as evanescent as the "Committee to Free Bobby Seale and All Other Political Prisoners." A musical stream, in short, is the sound of ordinary life generating its tribal cries as it seeks its tribal ties.

In any case, the leadership of most social movements considers music (and the other arts) a means to an end, or as a symbolic marker for its beliefs. The fate of such movements determines, therefore, the fate of their arts. When a movement dies of failure or of success, its music also dies except as a museum or shrine. At that point, most of the players, singers, dancers, and listeners go elsewhere, reassembling their resources for the longer haul on a different road.

These three parts of the stream—the artistic system, the economic arrangements, and the social movement—are but different aspects of one concrete reality. A song in any of the streams is at the same moment a "piece" in the artistic system, a "product" in its economy, and a unit of "propaganda" in its social movement. In the same way, the creative person is simultaneously the "artist," an economic "property," and a symbolic "leader" to its movement's followers. Those followers are, in turn, also "audiences" and "consumers." The distributor is at the same time an impresario, an entrepreneur, and a movement's "Minister of Propaganda."

The stream as a whole is a "loose structure," a term best understood in opposition to a "tight" structure.[6] It is the grapevine versus the chain of command. A loose structure connects all the nodes of a stream's formal organization and their penumbra of informal associations through networks of ties, weak and strong. As such it is fluid, restless, and hard to track. Statistical aggregates can turn into organized publics, just as "a newspaper is an association of its most constant readers," as de Tocqueville observed. The story of youth and their alternative culture is the story of an assembling loose structure.

Finally, there is the ethos of the streams. Each has an ineffable presence that is more than the sum of its parts. That presence is manifest in each stream's distinctive symbols and ways of behaving. Hair and clothing styles, language, gestures, and posture, as well as ceremonies of the ordinary and the consecrated, embody the values and beliefs of its people. This ethos is not a single, cohesive, or specific code but a set of cultural preferences, some quite remote from the immediate musical elements. Jazz, folk, and gospel, for example, have resisted an indiscriminate widening of their audiences. In contrast, pop leads an eager country pop and black pop into the search for audiences of unlimited size, irrespective of race, class, or nationality. Another instance—jazz's highest concerns are with the mastery, power, and originality of an individual's (or a band's) musical improvisation in the service of its community. The folk stream also dedicates its highest achievements to its cultural heritage, but it has never put such a high value on mastery of the musical craft or improvisational skill as has jazz.

This very difference between jazz and folk is the occasion for an unyielding quarrel. Jazz evaluates its performances in terms of standards set by its giants, from King Oliver to Charlie Parker. The folk stream asserts that every performance of a song is acceptable if it is honest and carries the story and passion of the people it celebrates. This unbridgeable gap is sharply expressed by Charles Rosen in his *Classical Style*:

> The history of an artistic "language" . . . cannot be understood in the same way as the history of a language used for everyday communication. In the history of English, for example, one man's speech is as good as another's. It is the picture as a whole that counts, and not the interest, grace, or profundity of the individual example. In the history of literary style or of music on the other hand, evaluation becomes a necessary preliminary. . . . This stands the history of a language on its head: it is now the mass of speakers that are judged by their relation to the single one, and the individual statement that provides the norm and takes precedence over general usage.[7]

All six streams participated in this argument over evaluation standards, and the discourse continued as rocknroll developed. The pop stream's variant of the issue complicated the situation; it had created an evaluative system that mysteriously transmuted commercial success into musical value. The star pop performer was a popular hero as much as a genius. Rocknroll would suffer through that confusion all through its development.

All the players in these musical dramas do their various jobs in ways that are rarely harmonious, rendering the entire world contradictory and confusing. That turbulence was exacerbated for rocknroll because it was born not only from six streams whose artistic heritages were different from one another, but also because its birth took place in the postwar untidiness. In other words, the usual and ancient conflicts among art, commerce, and politics were particularly smoky at the birth of rocknroll.

The Six Streams of American Popular Music

The several musical streams have been carried in the American experience since the nation's beginning as a fragile string of colonies along the Atlantic seaboard and in the Spanish Caribbean settlements.[8] Music in its various streams also accompanied the expansion across the North American continent, reflecting both grand adventures and everyday life. Its diverse traditions gradually crystalized around 1900 into six streams, each of which maintained its own boundaries by allowing only minimal and controlled exchange with the others. Two kinds of evidence support the 1900 date as the time of crystalization. One is a stylistic analysis of the music. Alec Wilder and James Maher offer a persuasive epic catalogue of the diverse American musics of that time:

Probably just before the turn of the century—the American popular song took on and consolidated, certain native characteristics—verbal, melodic, harmonic, and rhythmic—that distinguished it from the popular songs of other countries. It became a discrete musical entity. To be sure, it used the aural grammar of Western mensural, diatonic music, and it assumed many forms. In fact, it revelled in its variety. But the sum of its distinctions was unique.[9]

The other evidence is the growth in the music industry that occurred at this time. Between the years 1890 and 1909, the sale of sheet music tripled, and the manufacture of records and cylinders vaulted to more than 27 million units.[10] A powerful aggregation of capital and specialized personnel had suddenly assembled and were now serving the music needs of an expanding middle class and a flood of immigrants. These musical interests became six distinct streams:

   1. "Pop," the "commercial" music of the nation. The ranks of pop's great composers and lyricists included Jerome Kern, Lorenz Hart, Oscar Hammerstein II, Richard Rodgers, Irving Berlin, George Gershwin, Harold Arlen, and Cole Porter, to mention only the most familiar from its Golden Age. Pop led all the other American popular musics. It was able to reach the largest audience, outside and inside the home. Outside the home, it was ubiquitous in vaudeville and the Broadway theater, in hotels, restaurants, dance halls, night clubs, high school and college dances, juke boxes, movie houses, gambling casinos, ocean and air liners, trains and buses, offices and factories, and now, with the Walkman and the boom box, it virtually moves about with everyone. Inside the home, pop music enters through radio, television, recorded sound, the old-fashioned piano and sheet music, and the newer forms, the home computer and synthesizer. Pop enjoys a full diversity of musical forms. At one pole it emulates the symphony orchestra, with dance bands that carry choirs of brass, woodwinds, and strings; at the other, it is carried by the single instrumentalist or vocalist.

   Pop's three great departments span all the other musical art forms: theater music, movie music, and popular songs reach all across the nation and into every part of the cities. By the 1930s, the focus of the popular song industry and gradually drifted further uptown from its early West Twenty-eighth Street base in Manhattan. That move brought the new Tin

Pan Alley, exemplified by the Brill Building at 1619 Broadway, into close physical proximity to theater music's home base, "Broadway," radiating west out of Times Square. These neighborhoods were close to the old Metropolitan Opera House at Thirty-ninth and Broadway and to Carnegie Hall north on Fifty-seventh Street, connecting the pop stream directly to the concert, conservatory, and lyric theater music scene in the nation's cultural capital.

After 1928, when sound came to the motion pictures, most of the movie music branch of pop shifted to Hollywood and became a front seat partner to the film arts, a fact that influenced all popular music. The popular song wing, that is the Tin Pan Alley part of the pop stream, was thus anchored on both coasts. In subsequent years, its personnel would move to wherever its audiences, especially its dance audiences, summoned it.

2. "Black Pop" is the popular music of black Americans. In ways similar to other "folk" musics, black popular music became a commercially domesticated music around the turn of the century. It included versions of all popular Afro-American forms, blues, dance tunes, work songs, hymns, and psalms, as well as parodies and copies of white popular tunes. As with pop, black pop's musical instrumentation included everything from the huge dance orchestra to the lone singer with a guitar. It had its own musical vehicles, including vaudeville theaters, night clubs, dance halls, and organized tours that brought black entertainers to almost every town, from the deep South to the industrial cities of the North and West. From 1920 to 1948, it was known as "race music" or "race records," since its predominant form was phonographically recorded. The trade press used this label for its charts alternatively with such designations as "Folk and Blues," "What's Hot in Harlem," or "Sepia Hits," until 1948 when Paul Ackerman of *Billboard*, a major trade publication of the music industry, persuaded the industry to call this stream, "Rhythm and Blues" (R&B). It is still called "R&B" even though in 1969 it was officially renamed "Soul" by *Billboard*. Now in the 1990s, its name is once more under review. In alliance with its close neighbors black gospel and black jazz, it has been called "The American Music" and, more recently, "African-American" music, though *Billboard* has used the euphemism "Urban Contemporary" and currently uses "Black" as its designation.

3. "Country Pop" is the popular music of the American white South and Southwest. It includes the indigenous folk music of the South—tidewater, mountain, delta, and port city—and the music of the Western expansion, railroad and cowboy. Until the late 1950s, it was sung and played almost exclusively by whites to white audiences, though it did draw from black, Cajun, Spanish, and German sources and built upon

English-Scottish-Irish secular ballads and church hymns. Its musical forms were almost exclusively carried by stringed instruments. After World War II, prohibitions against drums and horns disappeared gradually as the boundary between white and black musics eroded.[11] Country pop appeared on radio and in movies, in dance halls, and in a myriad of outdoor forms, from country fairs to jamboree tours from the Gulf of Mexico to northern Michigan, from southern California to Connecticut. Until the war, this music was called "Hillbilly," but soon afterward the trade press designated it "Country and Western." In the 1960s, the term "Country Music" was more common, and now it, too, has been championed as "The American Music."

The three smaller streams are: (4) jazz, (5) folk, and (6) gospel. Each of these musics is a product of many earlier musical convergences, and each has within it several different strands. They are "smaller" only in that their annual dollar gross is less than that of the three larger streams. Jazz, folk, and gospel have been guided by powerful restrictions that keep them from establishing too close a relationship with the three "pop" streams. The "purity" parties within jazz, folk, and gospel stressed the strongly held values that pulled them away from the "commercial" music industries, even as they negotiated for a place in them. Although the three smaller streams share musical roots and continuing contact at their boundaries, they are unlike and antithetical to each other in important respects.

The jazz stream was, in its early days, a nighttime, city music associated with everything that walks on the wild side. It became a coherent entity in New Orleans at the end of the nineteenth century. It was almost entirely created and initially played by black musicians, but white players appeared early on the scene and have remained. Jazz had two sides. One played to white audiences in and around Storyville, New Orleans' sporting house district. The other played to black audiences at funerals, parades, dances, and other events in the black community. After 1917, when Storyville was closed by the U.S. Navy at the behest of the embarrassed forces of official morality, jazz dispersed. It left enough of its original performers and its musical traditions to survive a dormant twenty years, until the New Orleans jazz revival of the early 1940s.

Jazz migrated west to Texas, to the Territories, to the California coast, and up the Mississippi to Chicago before moving on to New York. It evolved slowly from a small improvisational orchestra of three or four main intertwining voices (trombone, cornet or trumpet, and clarinet) backed with the rhythms of drums, piano, banjo, string bass or tuba, into multiple choirs of these brass and reed instruments, guided increasingly by written arrangements. This development was rather paradoxical since jazz is predominantly a performer's medium, with the power and freshness of improvisation its most prized attribute. In the years following its release into national currents, jazz has produced at least two revolutions in its own style and has several times infused the other streams with powerful refreshments to their failing musical resources.

The folk stream is everybody's ancestor. All ethnic and regional cultures contribute to its enormous, untidy, and anonymous reservoir. It, too, is a paradox. How can the anonymous song and dance of peoples who do not make a commodity of music become a conventionalized part of the modern entertainment scene? The answer is that as folk performers entered contemporary music markets via recordings and tours to county fairs, the Continent, London, or concert halls in the great cities of the United States, they or their manager/discoverers simply appropriated the music in their own names. They then collected their copyright monies and gave interviews defending and elaborating their indigenous cultures. As every folk music tradition imaginable has become the raw material either for a performer's career or an impresario's steady living, the "folk" template has been enlarged to encompass the world's music. With world-pop-folk-rock as the generic designation, endless variations have evolved in the packaging of the folk stream's expanded reservoir.

The folk stream absorbs the music of the poor and oppressed—urban or rural, contemporary or ancient—and from developing and developed nations—providing, thereby, material for all kinds of entertainment and/ or protest. While some of this music is piped immediately into political channels, others parts are transformed by some performers into "art" songs or concert pieces without political urgency. Folk materials, moreover, have provided a major link to the serious or classical musics of several national traditions: the works of Brahms, Bartok, and Villa-Lobos, not to mention the American composers from Stephen Foster and George Gershwin to Aaron Copland and Charles Ives.

Gospel's primordial home is the church. In its popular forms, it is the religious music of Americans of every kind and condition. Its primary institutional locus is the individual house of worship, connected to a loose national mosaic of churches linked by radio, television, and the live performances of resident and touring "artists." Made up of soloists or groups of singers, gospel is almost entirely a vocal music. It has reached beyond the church circuit in recent years through phonograph records and the apparatus of the music industry to touch larger audiences. More importantly, it has provided personnel and musical materials for other streams. Black pop in particular has tapped black gospel resources to an extent that has engendered, on occasion, a troubled discourse on the separation of sacred and secular interests. In recent years the popularity given performers such as Ray Charles and Aretha Franklin have muted that quarrel, though the separation is still actively respected.

There are, of course, other popular musics. Every ethnic group in the United States has its own music industry, including the vigorous Polish,

Greek, Irish, Portugese, Puerto Rican, and Mexican-American musics that serve their communities through radio, records, and live performances. There are, in addition, thousands of choral and instrumental groups of every size and every degree of musical interest. These occasionally feed all the other popular musics; it is with no sense of disrespect that they are not treated here.

But what about the blues? In what stream, if any, does that important music flow? The complexities around the blues touch racial and political matters that will repeatedly arise in the story of rocknroll. The topic is of such emotional weight and cognitive imprecision that some clarification is essential.

Given the full range of usages of the term, there appear to be two clearly different meanings to "blues" music. One is a musical form whose origin lies obscure in American black history. Richard Wright defines them in the foreword to Paul Oliver's *The Meaning of the Blues* as "the blues, those starkly brutal, haunting folk songs created by millions of nameless and illiterate American Negroes in their confused wanderings over the American Southland and in their intrusion into the Northern American industrial cities." [12] As Oliver demonstrates fully, given this meaning, the blues are manifold in their range of subject matter, emotional range, sophistication, instrumentation, and adaptability to practically all the American popular streams, especially jazz and black pop.

The blues developed from field hollers and cries, spirituals and ballads that merged with European musical forms. Lyrically, its iambic pentameter meter is imposed upon a twelve-bar (or eight-, ten-, 16-bar) melodic phrase freely improvised around the "blue note" and a blue tonality. The blues were capable of endless emotion-drenched commentary on the travails of love and living poor and black. Their vocal and instrumental variations are the musical counterparts of those existential cries. The blues as musical form are neither pessimistic nor optimistic. They express how it is, and they express it to everyone. As Richard Wright noted, "In every large city of the earth where lonely disinherited men congregate for pleasure or amusement, the orgiastic wail of the blues, and their strident offspring, jazz, can be heard." [13]

The second meaning of the blues is simply the name of the black pop stream during the years beginning with the appearance of commercial phonographic recording and ending just after World War II. Black pop received that designation because the "blues" were the dominant music in that stream. The term took hold with the surprising and instantaneous success of Mamie Smith's "Crazy Blues" for Okeh in 1920. This first commercial hit by a black artist unleashed a blues recording craze that involved most record companies. Practically every kind of black music was subsumed under the "blues" name, and it came to mean the entire black pop stream. Dixon and Godrich, chroniclers of the early days of black recording, for example, state, "Blues and pop moved closer to-gether during the forties and fifties; today it is often difficult to distin-guish them." [14]

The two definitions of the blues are related, in fact, if you think of the blues as having been transformed from "a simple folk music to a form of sophisticated entertainment." [15] The previously established forms of vaudeville and the commitment to musical notation brought the blues into commercial usage. Further, the blues have always been a secular form, that is, strongly, if implicitly, nonreligious. They have been called, in fact, the devil's tunes; Peetie Wheatstraw, one of the steadiest bluesmen recording in the 1930s, was nicknamed to honor that notion—the Devil's Son-in-Law.

The blues, in both meanings, have been closely tied to black dance traditions. There has been a continuous exchange between highly skilled, professional dance performances and the enthusiastic amateur participa-tion in the dance, an exchange dating back to the days of post–Civil War minstrelsy. More than any other stream, black pop with its blues and its dance rhythms, has been the main carrier of American vernacular dance. The black pop stream's post–World War II designation as "Rhythm and Blues" was, I suggest, a succinct encapsulation of the intertwining of the blues and dance styles, whose polyrhythmic roots lay in West Africa. For example, in 1942 Jay McShann led one of the large prewar, Kansas City-based black dance bands, advertising itself as "the band that jumps the blues"; one of his best-selling Decca records was called "Jumpin' Blues." [16]

Practically every kind of American popular music has, on occasion, used the blues. If young Americans now regard the "blues" as sacred, it is in part because that holiness was the way in which the serious early rock musicians, especially the British, validated their use of black pop in appealing to their audiences of the early 1960s. At that time, young people were beginning to demand an authenticity to their music beyond that, say, provided by the Crests' "Sixteen Candles." In exactly the same way, a decade earlier an even younger American audience demanded more than Patti Page's "That Doggie in the Window."

The confusion between a form and a stream, which the term "blues" engenders and exemplifies, is understandable. Nevertheless, it is impor-tant to distinguish between the blues as a musical form and rocknroll as a musical stream.

Was Rocknroll a Conspiracy?

Among the oversimplified origin stories of rocknroll's beginnings are three conspiratorial tales. The first is that the popular music industry as a whole is more than a highly developed profit machine. It is a deliberately and secretly organized exploiter of young people's hopes and energies. Its major mission, in addition to making millions of dollars, is to keep the visibility of the social structure low, to divert people with the musical equivalent of bread and circuses. The music industry, this story claims, force-feeds its audience mindless commercial junk that must be endlessly replaced. When the melodic lodes it had been mining were exhausted in the early 1950s, the industry turned to rhythm and blues, a growing and successful version of white popular music for blacks, and this "pretested" style was forced into the gullible ears of young white American teenagers.

The second conspiracy theory is that the popular music industry generally, but especially during the early 1950s, stole black music in wholesale fashion and packaged it for whites, then kept all the money.

The third and most specific conspiracy tale is that Broadcast Music, Inc. (BMI), one of the two major American performance-rights licensing agencies, conspired with the radio broadcasting industry (its creator in 1940) to give BMI-licensed songs more air play than those licensed by the rival agency, the American Society of Composers, Authors and Publishers (ASCAP). Since BMI licensed more songs of a certain type— hillbilly and rhythm and blues—these were said to have received undue exposure, blotting out the "genuine" popular music guarded by ASCAP, thus preparing the ground for rocknroll. This conspiracy was formally charged to the broadcasters and BMI in 1953 by some members of ASCAP in the famous but now dead and forgotten Schwartz case.

Arthur Schwartz, erstwhile lawyer, distinguished composer ("Dancing in the Dark"), and senior presence in ASCAP, had mobilized a large group of prominent music figures associated with the New York music publishers to challenge BMI and the broadcasters. The radio stations were charged, under the antitrust laws, with unfairly excluding ASCAP-licensed music from air play in favor of BMI songs for the purpose of weakening ASCAP and diminishing the income of its members.

Popular music disk jockeys on AM radio stations throughout the country were thought to play strategic roles in all three of these conspiracies. They were either innocent dupes trying to "reflect" popular taste but falling into the clutches of an industry bent on pushing their product by any means, or they were venal hucksters playing certain records for a consideration, as was revealed in the so-called "payola" scandal. The rise and fall of the disk jockey is a central part of the story.

What is the verdict on these three conspiracy theories? As for the first, there is hardly any doubt that the music industry in its early days wanted little part in delivering "social" messages. Music publishers only wanted to sell songs, though topicality was not entirely out of place: There were songs about the First World War, the foibles of immigrants, the wonder of every new invention from the subway to the radio.[17] There were also songs about love, including sexual love, but by the late 1940s either the passion had weakened or its expression had exhausted itself. When any art form forgets how to sing persuasively of love and sex, to anticipate a part of the story to come, the young people have already left the room. More generally, the answer to the charges of diversionary irrelevance is that the popular music streams were doing their job of providing release from the cares of the day's commitment to job, family, country.

Did the music industry force-feed teenagers into the acceptance of rocknroll? To the contrary, it was almost the reverse. The "music industry" is no monolithic structure. Its various components—publishers, record companies, performers, talent agencies, radio stations, movie companies, night club and dance hall owners, and others—have their own perspectives and strategies. Most of those forces in popular music were at that point either blind, indifferent, or hostile to the rocknroll "craze" or "fad," as it was called. No one in particular wanted it, and most fought it for years before they belatedly sought to get a piece of the action. Indeed, some got rich, and a whole generation of performers and middlemen found their life's work. But beyond the ordinary levels of venality and chicanery, which even industry observers said exceeded that in most American business,[18] it is difficult to demonstrate any concerted and hidden planning that could make the *general* charge of conspiracy stick.

Can the same be said of the white theft of black music? From the earliest times, black contributions in composition and performance have had an influence on American music out of all proportion to the size of the black population. It can be argued that music was one of black people's most powerful weapons of individual strength and collective survival. Paradoxically, those varied musics were the languages of release for whites as well as for blacks in both sacred and secular forms. It is no surprise, therefore, that black music reached beyond its own boundaries to be used in the white parts of all the streams. This use included the borrowing, hiring, buying, and stealing (mainly "legal" theft) of the music and the musicians. It is beyond the scope of this work and my knowledge to fill and balance the scales of those historic exchanges. For every success story—from Ben Harney, Scott Joplin, and W. C. Handy to Johnny Mathis, Aretha Franklin, Gordy Berry, Jr., Quincy Jones, and Michael Jackson—each of which must have had its own unhappy subplots, how many crimes and disasters were there? And what could serve to recompense?

As for the third conspiracy, the Schwartz case took fourteen years to get out of pretrial hearings. As a speculative investment, its attractiveness waned as the factual and legal basis for sustaining its charges faded and as ASCAP and BMI settled their differences, but not before the still operative disagreements between publishers and broadcasters fueled the growth of rocknroll.

So much for conspiracy theories. The real trouble with such theories is not so much the facts of the case, but a matter of temperament, the way prayer for quick relief is answered by the myths of quick diagnosis. The music world is untidy and recalcitrant. It is too complex for neat conspiracies. Patient inquiry, at the risk of paralyzing affection and will, is the course to be taken.

Basic Processes: From the Inside Out

If it wasn't a conspiracy, then what did bring rocknroll into being? The factors from the inside out were informed by the most basic process shaping all the arts: the making of new pieces out of old pieces. That is, every new piece, a song or a dance, comes, somehow, from the reservoir of old pieces. Every new piece is some mix of current life and previous art.

Each of the popular music streams organizes its personnel and resources to generate a more or less orderly succession of pieces, its own hit parade. That flow of individual units is packaged into shows, or programs, that carry a mixture of old, current, and new pieces within recognizable formats and at a determinable speed. A certain number of old ones are needed to provide the audience with enough familiarity to accept or reject the new ones.

Old ones are also necessary for a stream's creators. They mine their stream's reservoirs by stripping parts of old songs—their melodies, harmonies, lyrics, instrumental or vocal styling—then recombine them to make new ones. Sometimes an overheard melody lies hidden in a composer's brain for years before its emergence as a "new" song. Sometimes last year's or last week's songs are literally taped together to make this week's newest rap record.[19] And on occasion, new pieces are drawn from distant sources: from nature's breathing, from foreign cultures' cornucopia. The recombinations can be within the boundaries of previous works or might breach those boundaries to open new styles, even new streams. But what exactly is transferred to new pieces from old pieces? In music, the transferred part is not, of course, the most elementary unit—the individual notes or chords—but rather a pattern of notes that become named and have a conventionalized range of variation. A melodic phrase, a rhythmic figure, a cadenza, the three-minute popular song, the call and response voicings, "taking a solo," all of these patterns are *schema*[20] that have several important properties. One is that they hold their name and form yet retain an infinite capacity for variation. Another is that they can be readily detached from one piece and put into another piece quite different in length, instrumentation, or performance context. The employment of various schema is not a denial of genuine creativity; it is its description.

When new pieces are no longer made, as in Egyptian funerary art, the stream is destined for the museum, useful and important no doubt as historical source and marker but creatively dead. Living arts all play their own "hit game." Whatever its rate of flow, each of the streams has procedures for teaching an audience to participate in choosing the succession of new songs and performers that climb up and down the ladder of popularity, from first introduction to final play.

Though there is no central authority setting the speed limit on how fast new hits replace old ones, the struggles between the music publishers and radio broadcasters over the financing of music inadvertently but decisively changed that speed. In the course of their moves and counter-moves, they set a new premium on new rather than old songs. In so doing, they shifted the rules guiding the pop stream's "hit game." Those rules evolved out of the inescapable fact of satiation (all music wears out sooner or later) and from the sad fact of the audience's fickleness, as well as from the chilling uncertainty about what makes a hit. No one knows really what makes one song successful, another a flop. In the face of that unpredictability, these two rules of the road emerged:

Rule 1. Whatever was a hit last week, find a song for this week as similar to it as possible, even up to the fencelines of a possible plagarism suit.

Rule 2. Whatever was a hit last week, get as far away from it as possible this week, preferably a song from another style, another country, or another stream, anywhere else.

These rules have an encrusted lore attached to them in music and related fashion-driven fields. The counterpart expression to Rule 1 in the garment trade is "knocking off" an item. In Hollywood circles, to paraphrase Rob Faulkner, when searching for a composer for a new film's music, the producer will say "Get me Harry Whatsisname" (currently the hottest composer in town). If that composer is unavailable, "Get me Harry Junior," and only when all the juniors can't be hired will you hear, "Get me the *new* Harry Whatsisname."

Rule 2 invokes the search for the next hit in left field, on the Left Bank, whatever had been previously left out. The category "novelty song" is the pop stream's grab bag for such material. The players in the music game had for years used these two rules in some alternating mixture, swearing by or at each as it produced or failed to produce a winner. As the postwar years unfolded, the usual balanced use of the rules tipped in favor of Rule 2. The search was on for new material, and rocknroll was born, in good measure, because of that search.

A second basic process in all the arts is the selection of a series of schema that form and wrap the pieces in their journey from artist to audience. It is the richness of these schema and their simultaneous presence in all the American popular musics that facilitated rocknroll's emergence.

Since the turn of the century, the basic medium that carried the individual song was the physical form of sheet music. In fact, sheet music constituted the largest source of income for American popular music publishers, until it was gradually replaced by the phonograph record. After the war, when the vinyl 45 rpm single and the 33 rpm long playing record replaced the shellac 78 rpm record, young people and grownups listened to different musics mainly because each group was using different music technologies, thus widening the gap between the generations, a consideration that also made and marked the road toward rocknroll.

Those technologies, radio and the phonograph, also reshaped the making of new songs. The dominance of the traditional guilds and loose networks (largely in New York) that organized songwriters, lyricists, publishers, performers, record producers, record company owners, and other technical personnel ended. A new crop of writer-performer-producer-owners appeared, many in places far across the Hudson River. These new centers provided the basis for rocknroll's own infrastructure. In a short time, the advances in studio sound recording and in live performance sites (soon to grow into huge rock concerts and festivals) rearranged both the artistic and management organization of all seven streams.[21]

Basic Processes: From the Outside In

Within larger social contexts, the six popular music streams, indeed, all the arts and entertainments that had defined the American way of life since colonial times, began changing after 1945. They started doing their job in new ways. They decorated and announced the social rankings that arrayed wealth and power, education and occupation, race and gender in their distinct and invidious orderings. The materials for this drapery came from all over the world, but it was shaped into a distinctly American style. Nevertheless, English aristocratic trappings of higher rank have been the single most important source for the symbolic expression of the American pecking order.[22]

At the same time, the arts hid these unpleasant social differences in an attempt to unite all peoples in shared cultural activities. This unifying effort was not always successful, given the ease with which the arts had become the instrument for rebellion against those invidious rankings. From the earliest times, theatrical or musical gatherings had been the assembling place and the flashpoint for unrest.[23]

The highly salient conflicts of workers against management in the 1930s, abated by the war mobilization, allowed other social divisions to command the political stage. These were largely concerned with matters of race, region, and nationality. Once more it was the South versus the rest of the nation. While the Cold War and Korean conflict dominated the front pages in the early 1950s, race relations gradually became a national preoccupation that spread steadily into every facet of political and cultural life. The civil rights struggles, as they accelerated, underscored the fact that each music has a white part and a black part, no matter how disguised or suppressed. Though there is still vigorous debate as to the specifics of this or that contribution, there is a fairly clear understanding that white and black musical traditions mingled at this time within each of the six streams, even though each has a predominant white or black senior progenitor.

The origins of each stream are entwined in the white and black cultural roots brought to the continent during that five hundred-year pulse of demographic journey and pause called North American civilization.[24] The significance of this mixed racial heritage is that no individual stream has been able to become the sole focus, the single true banner, of white or black social movements. Such movements, musical and political, are always searching for the purest black or for the purest white. This search, therefore, infuses all the streams with an unsettling and unresolving political presence.

Black pop and its religious partner gospel were almost entirely segregated within the black communities of the nation, just as white gospel and white country were tightly harnessed together. Jazz, a city music, spanned race and regional boundaries quite deliberately, though racial segregation and prejudice within the jazz world and its audiences were facts of life. The folk stream, depending upon the moment, was both white and black, rural and urban. Country music and its close gospel cousin were both overwhelmingly white and largely southern, but they spread from the South across the Midwest, from the Plains states to California's great agricultural belt. Pop, of course, reached everywhere, no matter where its production was centered. It had a national reach, and by its sheer size crossed regional and racial boundaries with magisterial generosity, inviting everyone down the road to stardom. However, pop's behind-the-scenes policies, especially in movies and broadcasting, were, paradoxically, implacably racist.

Gender politics, the renewal of earlier feminist movements, awakened in the 1950s, accompanied by a quiet but determined movement to free lesbians and gays of their social stigma and discrimination. Other minorities were soon testing their position and asserting their identities and rights.

Peculiarly, and most consequentially for the story to come, age was an insignificant social category, hardly worthy of political or cultural commentary before World War II. There had been incipient age-graded distinctions during the 1920s,[25] but these were thought to be mere flashes of cultural discontinuity. They were short-lived anyway, being arrested during the Great Depression and war years. The speed and extent with which age categories became important after the war was without parallel. Not only in the United States but in most of the developed nations in the West, most social institutions reoriented their perspectives along age lines. In Great Britain, for example, the Labor Party was swept to victory in 1945 on the promise that its welfare state would deliver care "from cradle to the grave" via programs for each specific age group, for example, infant care, youth services, all the way to specialized old-age facilities.

In the United States, the situation was not very different. The fruits of long-delayed peace and plenty were to be secured by concentrating on family needs for housing and schools. Life in the new suburbs and in the old cities made the schools a more or less self-contained, age-graded society. The high school, both in its standard architecture and its spirit, resembled something between the prison and the factory, batch processing its involuntary clientele through its prescribed four-year term. It was the focal point of dissatisfaction with the pressures to conform and to achieve. These pressures were spelled out in the approved programs of the high school authorities and in the age-targeted commodities provided by consumer industries eager to make lifelong customers. The road to the bright future was laid out as clearly as the schools and their advertising allies could make it. Just follow the directions.

But not every kid did. They were, in fact, spilling out in all directions, in such number and visibility so as to embarrass school officialdom and alarm parents. Reasons and excuses for what had gone wrong flowed freely, and after a decade or so of inquiry, social scientists concluded that most American youngsters either marched to conventional drummers or enacted domesticated versions of deviant tendencies. They also comforted the public with the observation that there really was not much increase in the rate of juvenile departure from the straight and narrow. Youthful rebelliousness, individually and in gangs, was in fact as American as apple pie, observable back beyond the turn of the century. The sources of that deviance, paradoxically, were to be found in the very values the adults put forward as models for youth to adopt. For whatever reasons, a minority of youngsters were not persuaded that schoolwork was worth the effort. Perhaps more threatening was their rejection of the "proper" behavior and attitude associated with such dedicated work.

There were several alternatives to the path of a dutiful student, each drawing upon a strong cultural tradition; David Matza named them De-

linquent, Bohemian, and Radical.[26] Criminal or near-criminal delinquency was the most familiar, fitting readily into the rubrics of scare
headlines and handwringing sermons. The high school's rough crowd, its
"hoodlums," "greasers," and so on, were the current embodiment. The
Bohemian direction of the early 1950s updated the yearnings of an earlier
generation for the Parisian "artists and models" life, still another Ameri-
canization of foreign escapes. This yearning was manifested in the "beatnik," translating the "beat" movement of their older brothers into high
school terms. The Radical direction, only thinly anchored in the high
schools, found its strongest constituency among college youth. A bagful
of diverse movements appeared, reviving and updating the repudiation of
the status quo, generally within a Marxian framework. Both Bohemian
and Radical students constituted smaller and less potent groupings at
least until the 1960s. There were other failures of conformity as well,
either dropouts into a retreatist drug culture or escapees into the world
of drifting and casual labor.

The key point is that, while most adults were poised for takeoff into a
future of steady work that promised steady rewards, a significant segment
of the young were looking elsewhere, and almost all of them felt that the
heat on the pressure cooker of an achievement-driven and consumer-
rewarded economy had been turned up too high and too fast. Rocknroll
can be understood as youth's response to a situation that was too intense
and too pervasive to cope with on the terms the adults had proffered. The
culture of teenagers and later of college-aged youth created a musical
language that went beyond the reach of adult authority. Young people
were using their culture for their own purposes; they were not going to
be batch processed. Their more durable message was that, if youth was
to be squeezed through a machine to fit the needs of parents, the government, and industry, youth was going to insist upon its own solutions to
some very important questions. What is work and what is play, and who
decides? These were refreshing openings to deeper matters than electoral
politics. Young people's agenda now included that more fundamental
question about the institutions of commitment and release and how ad-
herence to each would be negotiated. That youthful search for alternatives was the major engine from outside the music world that met the
changes within the industry to produce rocknroll. The alternative banners that were first raised with the appearance of rocknroll still fly as the
nation continues to argue about the nature and terms of those institutions
of commitment and release.[27]

The Geography of Rocknroll

Culture, including music, is not spread evenly over the landscape; it is
densely coagulated in some places, sparsely found in others. The familiar

Law of Raspberry Jam—the wider you spread it, the thinner it gets—is a recognition that cultural density in geographical terms is complexly related to cultural innovation and quality. Nor does culture stay in one place. It is almost always on the move, going from one center to another along routes that spread the news to places innocent of the arts. One of the most remarkable aspects of rocknroll's development was its participation in the nation's rearrangement of its cultural geography.

The most elementary geographical distinction is that music is connected to an audience in two ways; one, an out-of-home experience, the other offered within the home. As the postwar suburban explosion rearranged American patterns, all the arts scrambled to hold their audiences. During that hurly-burly, movies and television fought out their "either-or" battle (stay home and watch vaudeville retreads on the small screen or go out, for the "movies are better than ever"). Theater, à la Broadway, leaked out of the city to dinner theater and its cousins on Long Island, Bergen, and Westchester counties. Modern dance dug in resolutely at the city's center, as did painting and the other gallery-dominated visual arts.

The popular musics of every kind tried, as usual, to have it all ways. Though they sought a place in the new television programming, radio was where they found their main connection to the home audience. The FCC opened the door to radio by releasing broadcast licences held in abeyance during the war. With radio disk jockeys' use of the phonograph record, the in-home audiences for popular music were secured. What was its out-of-house locale? The solution to that question was different for young and old. The high school gymnasium, the alcohol-free teen centers, and other less savory dance halls were reconnecting the pop stream with vernacular dance, this time strictly for the youth. There was far less out-of-house music for the adults, a geographical fact of considerable portent for the future of rocknroll.

Next is the distinction between "uptown" and "downtown." This is close enough to the mischievous continuum, "high brow" to "low brow," to finesse that interminable confusion between the ranking of the arts according to internal considerations and the ranking that results from penetration of external forces. The most important of these external influences is the hierarchical ordering of American social classes. The "big house" on the hill in the fancy neighborhoods, the slums on the wrong side of town, and all the graduated statuses in between are geographical realities that place all the arts within a specific, class-ranked landscape.

Such realities defy the myth of a classless America propagated in its music. The pop stream, particularly, could simultaneously ignore and acknowledge social class, as Edward Marks, one of the prominent publishers at the turn of the century, recalls: "The best songs came from the gutter in those days. Indeed, when I began publishing in 1894, there was no surer way of starting a song off to popularity than to get it sung as loudly as possible in the city's lowest dives."[28]

Overall there was, and still is, a persistent distinction between "uptown" and "downtown" in all six streams. This is in part a sensitivity to the refinement and elegance of some of its audience at the top of the nation's social ladder and to the crudity and roughness of those at the bottom. Fastidiousness of manners, accuracy of diction, elegance of musical ideas, bluntness or explicitness of sexual allusions, degree of emotional restraint or excess have become geographically crystallized. Bessie Smith's torrid "Empty Bed Blues," for instance, reached "uptown" audiences at Carnegie Hall, but it was still quite a "downtown" statement. The record was almost certainly never played on the radio during Smith's lifetime due to the song's barely disguised anguish over sexual loss.[29]

A more extended geographical consideration is the location of music on the national scene, the changing patterns of concentration and dispersion. New York City long ago announced itself the capital of American culture. It held all the financial and organizational cards to back that claim and dealt them selectively across the country, which was pejoratively and in fact called "the road." New York nurtured and preened the most sophisticated audiences in the nation. As far back as the First World War, the New York audience was the standard to match. *Variety*, the senior trade publication of American entertainment, summed it up tartly for that period: "From the coast came Ken Murray's glorified vauderevue, *Blackouts*, which ran seven years in Hollywood and lasted seven weeks in New York."[30] The pop stream, ensconced in Manhattan's entertainment district, intertwined itself with the dance bands and the radio network scene, which dominated broadcasting after its 1920 commercial debut. New York was also the terminus of the London-New York loop, which circulated the fragile produce of the music trade as well as book publishing and the Broadway theater.

World War II ended New York's unchallenged hegemony in some cultural matters, including its centralized control of popular music. Los Angeles had entirely taken over the "creative" side of movies by the early 1930s, as well as significant sectors of writing, theater, and music, but the money was still in New York. The other major cities of the nation slowly inherited the collapse of New York's dominance as they became intersections where radio stations, stage show and dance hall circuits, night clubs, and record distribution and musical instrument outlets met. The regional musics of whites and blacks in the South were the primary beneficiaries of that dispersal. In the years after 1945, it became increasingly clear that the ability to make new hits out of old ones had crossed the Hudson River.

Those "regional musics," black pop and country pop, were growing into national musics as the interconnections among the cities elaborated into a loose national loop made up of individual "short loops" in each city. A short loop is the efficient arrangement by which a pool of performers is presented to a more or less homogeneous audience. That audience, doing what audiences have always done (that is, saying yea or nay to each performer's work), selects what it likes and rejects what it doesn't. That apparently simple system requires several more complex things. One is a continuous supply of fresh talent. Another is a forum that exposes that talent to the audience. Still another is a mechanism that organizes and promotes the performers the audience has initially favored. This task is the impresarial job, necessary in every art form. These components were put together in a dozen or so cities in every part of the United States, and they were done locally, by local entrepreneurs. Gradually these local efforts reached out, drawing fresh talent from distant cities into their own short loops. At a certain point, they formed a loose but efficient national network of audiences and performers held together by local radio stations, independent record companies, and small performance sites. Neither the major record labels nor the broadcasting networks could effectively reach those structures.

One other geographical notion is essential. Places are not just physical entities; they are moral enclaves, sometimes with deeply coiled symbolic powers. Just the names of cities such as Jerusalem, Rome, or Mecca invoke a certain attitude, as do the names Sodom and Gomorrah. The workings of a moral geography identifies, for instance, Cincinnati, Ohio, as a respectable town largely because its traffic over the Ohio River leads to the (once) wide open sin city of Covington, Kentucky. Similarly, there is an identification of specific cities or regions with certain musical streams. New Orleans is jazz's historical shrine of origin, the South as a whole serves as the heartland for country music, and New York and Hollywood have been the spatial focii of the pop stream. The seat of folk and gospel are, not surprisingly, less clearly located. They are, to be sure, American, and they seem geographically to be flourishing in small towns and rural areas. Black pop shares the double placement of the rural South and the northern city. Where, though, is the seventh stream's home?

The answer to that question is that rocknroll is located in the hearts, minds, and feet of young people all over the world; that its homeland is more a pilgrimage than a place, for instance in the memory of Woodstock. The shrines along that spiritual way include several genuinely historic locales but include others created with more mundane interests in mind than the celebration of rocknroll. Graceland in Memphis, Tennessee, is one such place that has overwhelmed its managers by the depth of the passions poured out to Elvis. The selection of Cleveland as the home of the Rock 'n Roll Hall of Fame was a political choice celebrating not only that city's historical significance in rocknroll's birth, as the scene of both Alan Freed and Bill Randle's pioneering disk jockey work, but something else as well. Cleveland is one of the leading port cities of the midwest. Boundary-crossing points have been especially fecund in their musical life. The cities and regions discussed in this story, New Orleans, Memphis, Kansas City, Chicago, New York, San Francisco, west Texas and the other border states ringing the deep South, all have strong "roots" musical traditions that have to be understood if their connections to rocknroll's origin and growth is to be appreciated. Above all, rocknroll was born in the United States, is at home everywhere coast to coast, border to border, and invites the popular (youth) musics of the world into its company.

Getting Ready for the Moment

The slow and steady organization of the hit game in all the American popular musics up to 1940 accelerated after the war. Most important was the gradual equalization of the rate of song replacement on each respective hit parade. In fact, it can be said that rocknroll could not have come into being had not the three commercial streams aligned themselves and begun moving at the same speed.

As the streams converged, the nature of musical literacy changed. New York publishers could no longer impose the standard of competency in reading and writing music on composers or performers as a prerequisite to participation. Songwriting and performing were opened to everyone. By the early 1960s, standards of performance had also shifted to where the whole question of technical musical competence was embroiled in an evaluation of the artist's credibility. And that issue of "credibility" was so interwoven with nonmusical concerns that it was impossible to make a clear judgment about the music itself. It is thus no surprise that Alec Wilder ended his analysis of American popular song in the year 1950, for that was a watershed year. Rocknroll was about to appear and an entirely different aesthetic would be required. Not quite as Götterdämmerung, James Maher's introduction to Wilder's book summarizes the reasons for Wilder's cut-off date in terms similar to my own:

By 1950 the professional tradition in song writing was nearing its end, for reasons too complex to summarize other than very roughly. Consumption patterns in popular music had changed rapidly in the post World War II years. Singers and singing groups enjoyed a new primacy in the ordering of economic priorities in the pop market. The big dance bands had priced themselves into oblivion. Further, most of them, as a result of their ceaseless replication of one another's styles, had lost all claim to the attention of the pop audience, a predominantly young consumer group that is notorious for its short attention span, and its insatiable hunger for the *new* (a word that has since given way to the word *now*, with its dreary implication of manipulated hysteria).
The rock era was about to begin.[31]

2. The Basic Struggle:
Publisher against Broadcaster

The music publishers, mainly in New York City, were a small-shop, labor intensive, undercapitalized industry whose most complex technology was a metronome. Radio broadcasting, on the other hand, was technologically advanced, at the leading edge where physics and engineering met high-flying corporate finance. The meeting of publisher and broadcaster would change the way music was to be brought into the American home.

Around the turn of the century, the publishers were mainly responsible for the crystallization of the new popular song into its short, three-minute form. Those publishers were a new breed that built upon the accumulated knowledge and lore, the physical plant and inventories, the network of personal and business relationships of the music trade that had been growing for a century and a half. All these had been carried forward by a small, monopolistically inclined group of publishers who just about controlled the whole industry.[1]

This new group of ambitious young men had little or no experience in music publishing. They grafted onto its slower pace the high-flying, high-pressure sales techniques that were pervading the rest of American economic life at the time. Sheet music as a "product" was to be sold just like corsets, patent medicines, and real estate. The new Tin Pan Alley publishers, exemplified by the firms of Leo Feist, Edward Marks, Jerome Remick, Isidore Witmark, and Shapiro-Bernstein, were quick to learn how to sell sheet music, their only source of income.

The Three-Legged Money Stool

In 1900 the music publishing business was simple. Selling sheet music was the sole activity of the one hundred or so music publishing firms, less than twenty of which were major players.[2] The Copyright Act of 1909 opened the way for two more sources of profit. One was the property right in the "mechanical" reproduction of a song; the other was a property right in its public performance. It took considerable time and ingenuity for the publishers to harvest these routes to profit. The system they devised, with only slight modifications, operates to this day.

New tunes had to fight their way into the ongoing musical vocabulary as old tunes waned. Repeated exposure was essential, however the publishers did not earn anything from exposing new music. In fact, they expended considerable treasure on securing live performances of their songs. The only way to recover those expenditures and earn something beyond was to get their sheet music onto the music rack of the living room piano. Sheet music was the first leg of the stool. Without the piano, there was virtually no at-home audience for the publishers' product, the sheet music. These times were, fortunately, the years of the piano's greatest expansion, with piano production more than doubling between 1900 and 1909.[3]

The trick for the publishers was to find a connection between the out-of-home listener and the in-home purchaser. Vaudeville was one of the entertainment forms that did that job. The congeries of minstrelsy, variety, burlesque, tent shows, museums, and melodramas that came together near the end of the nineteenth century and organized into large city theater chains became the major presenters of the emerging popular song to the remote reaches of the nation.[4]

Singers and orchestras, then as now, required a continuous flow of new songs. The whole process, from selection to exhaustion of the song, took about three years at the turn of the century. Performers, choosing songs for their repertory, balanced personal preference with the wisdom that their audience likes what it knows rather than vice versa. The publishers had to convince performers, therefore, that a new song was a "plug" tune, one that would produce both freshness and the requisite sense of familiarity. Such convincing required major resources, including salaries to song pluggers ("contact representatives," as they were formally called), payments for advertising in the trade press, and the costs of printing copies of the song and freely distributing orchestral arrangements to bands and singers.

In addition, somewhat more mysterious expenditures could ensure the tune's exposure to an audience. The publishers' smiling and persistent contact men cajoled singers and band leaders with every and any inducement to play their songs and play them repeatedly. They offered exclusive identification with a hit song (with the artist's picture on the sheet music cover) if the performer would sing it repeatedly. Cash subsidies to compliant vaudeville acts and cash payments to orchestra leaders were common. "Payola," as this practice is now called, went back at least to the Civil War.[5] Variations of this operating procedure continued during the growth of vaudeville. E. B. Marks describes the extent of such practices at the time as "a system of direct subsidy" by the music business. "At the height of the bidding the industry paid tribute of a million dollars per year."[6] The pay-for-play habit became so noisome during the first twenty years of the twentieth century that the publishers attempted self-regulation in concert with leading vaudeville figures. In 1917 the Music Publishers Protective Association, founded by the new Tin Pan Alley publishers, put the brakes on the worst excesses.

The second leg of the money stool, provided by the Copyright Act of 1909, was income from "mechanicals." This was a statutory fee payable to the copyright holder (the publisher) of not more than two cents for every song "mechanically" reproduced for an audience. The legislation was aimed at the player piano, with its perforated piano rolls, and at the phonograph record.[7] The player piano was invented in the late 1880s and marketed by several firms under a variety of trade names. At the turn of the century, the device was attached to less than 1 percent of all pianos, by 1909 15 percent were so equipped, and by 1919 over half (56 percent) of the pianos manufactured included the mechanical player.[8]

A marketable version of the phonograph and its wax cylinder was perfected in 1877 by Thomas Edison. After the usual struggles, the two major firms in the industry, Victor and Columbia, pooled their patents in 1902 to avoid a costly competitive fight, and both thrived. Sales of the earliest musical recordings on wax cylinders were mostly to owners of coin-operated music machines, the proto-jukebox. Only later did the sale of individual records for home use become dominant. All parties soon realized the musical imperatives of the popular song and accordingly extended the playing time of the two-minute wax cylinder to the three-to-four-minute shellac disk.[9]

Soon after the phonograph industry's highly visible "take-off" period, the music publishers sought their share of this lucrative market in the form of a mechanicals fee. The phonograph record companies opposed the secret arrangements between leading members of the Music Publishers Association and the Aeolian Company (the largest of the piano roll manufacturers) for a long-term exclusive link of their catalogues. These disputes were part of the general crisis about intellectual property that resulted in the 1909 Copyright Law. Part of that law provided that no such exclusive contract could be made; that, once a song was published, a "mechanical" license had to be issued to anyone who wished to reproduce it. The statute did not, however, offer any arrangement by which the publishers could collect their "mechanicals" income. Makeshift procedures gave way in 1917 to the organized efforts of the Music Publishers

Protective Association. In 1927 the Harry Fox Office was founded to bring modern auditing and collecting methods to the publishers' mechanicals income, which by that time was derived largely from phonograph records.

The 1909 Copyright Act also provided the third leg of the publishers' money stool, a separate and distinct property right to the copyright holder for the song's "public performance for profit." This right not only opened another source of income to the music publishers but initiated a chain of events that led to the formation of a powerful and centralizing pop stream organization.

ASCAP Leads the Pop Stream

Based on the European model of a performance rights society, the American Society of Composers, Authors, and Publishers (ASCAP) was formed in 1914. Its origin and early growth took place within the New York popular music world at a moment of rapid growth in the American economy. By 1900 New York City was the world's largest "repple depple" (a World War II term for "replacement depot"). Through the Port of New York passed millions of immigrants. The musical cultures they brought with them met and mixed with the commercial music already established in that city.

New York, by the early twentieth century, had also become the nation's financial capital and a major manufacturing center. Several monied elites contested for dominion over the city's culture. Diverse styles of entertainment clashed and blended with each other. The immigrant poor and monied elites met in a variety of ways that influenced the development of popular music, dramatically so in the cases of Irving Berlin and Benny Goodman. Both these poor Jewish musicians, on the basis of talent and energy, rose to fame and fortune, both marrying into leading families of the eastern establishment.

In New York there were meeting places for the full range of social classes, mainly in settings that combined food and drink with entertainment. The appearance of the cabaret, a new entertainment form, gave music publishers a strategic new venue for plugging their songs. The opening of the Folies Bergères at Broadway and Forty-eighth Street in 1911 brought together the traditions of uptown's elegant dining with downtown's more unbuttoned entertainment. Along with dining at table, the Folies presented what subsequently became the "floor show," which included ballets, singers, and large orchestras with professional dancing, plus the opportunity for dining patrons to dance as well. The cabarets were respectable; a man could take his wife there. There was good food and lively musical fare. This innovation was soon recognized in typical show business terms. On 3 December 1912, *Variety* headed an article, "Cabarets Mean Big Money." One year later, the *New York World* carried a story entitled, "The Cabaret Is No Longer a Fad—It's a Business" (13 April 1913).[10]

The cabaret was not just a new market; it also held an important specific advantage. It gave the music publishers an opportunity to collect fees for the performance of their music, a right that had been assured since 1909 but not exercised. The introduction of married couples into the cabaret's evening musical entertainment ensured a greater overlap between the out-of-home and in-home audiences. Sheet music sales for the home piano were now more closely linked to the song-plugging efforts of the publishers, whose tunes were heard in the cabarets. The expansion of the new cabaret business thus made it well worth the effort and cost to collect performance fees. Consequently, a group of new and standard publishers, together with theatrical producers, some influential composers and lyricists (notably Victor Herbert), and of course the lawyers, met over a period of several months. On 13 February 1914, ASCAP formally came into existence with a membership of 170 composers and lyricists and twenty-two publishers.[11]

The "Society," as ASCAP was called, received a cold welcome from the hotel and restaurant trades. Its first struggles to collect performance rights fees climaxed in the famous Shanley case, in which Justice Oliver Wendell Holmes, speaking for a unanimous Supreme Court, held that, indeed, Victor Herbert's music, played at Shanley's cabaret, had to be paid for. "If the music did not pay, it would be given up. It if pays, it pays out of the public's pocket. Whether it pays or not, the purpose of employing it is profit, and that is enough."[12] The highest court in the land thus affirmed the right of composers and authors to receive payment for the public performance of their works. ASCAP was, by default, the inheritor of the tasks of defining the amounts of those payments and of collecting them.

ASCAP was also soon charged with the additional duty of regulating piracy, the perennial scourge of popular music even to this day. It was hoped, too, that the Society could stop the other endemic drain on publishers' profits, the pay-for-play "payola." *Variety*, however, suggested a more dangerous purpose for the proposed Society: the collective establishment and holding of the price of sheet music at ten cents a copy.[13] By far the most important task the Society would undertake was in monitoring the changing technologies and uses of music and ensuring that its members got recompense for all of them. After bringing the Hotel Association, the restaurants, and the cabarets under license, the Society turned to its next target: the movies.

Thomas Edison invented what he called the "kinetoscope" in 1889.

Its first form was a peep show, one viewer, one screen, but it quickly progressed to a large screen with enhanced entertainment values and a story line. Next came the successful swallowing of vaudeville's theaters and its performers and the fateful move of the industry to the West Coast. Almost from the beginning, the "nickelodeons" (so named because of their five-cent admission charge) and the screen-projected movie parlors provided for a musical background to silent films, either in the form of piano, organ, or, increasingly, a small orchestra. The silent era of motion pictures was hardly ever silent. By 1926 there were twenty-two thousand musicians [14] employed in more than twenty-three thousand movie houses across the nation.[15]

The music publishers soon realized the potential exposure value of the movie houses and began to push their songs there. Their song pluggers fought a losing battle as the film producers began to insist upon total control over the viewer's experience.[16] The battle for access to the silent movies soon gave way to the battle for performance rights fees. ASCAP brought forth the same arguments successfully used against the hotels and restaurants. E. Claude Mills, the wily chairman of the Music Publishers Protective Association (MPPA), speaking for the Society, recounted that movie exhibitors

were earning large revenues, tremendous sums of money, through the works of the American composers, and the gentlemen who operated these theaters conceded that the value of the music to the program was forty per cent. In other words, the exhibition value of the picture as part of the evening's entertainment was *sixty* per cent and that of the music *forty* per cent [emphasis added], but there was no compensation for the service rendered by the men who contributed this forty per cent of entertaining value.[17]

Mills' "sixty per cent" and "forty per cent," a prophetic note, is supported by no evidence whatsoever to contradict the notion that he made up those numbers entirely. That same tactic, pulling numbers out of the air, was used repeatedly in battles with radio station owners over the next twenty years.

Dance Calls the Tune

Popular music is inescapably linked to dance. Though this linkage seems quite natural, it caused difficulty for the publishers, who had to juggle the relative importance of lyrics and "danceability" in their songs. The music sustaining a lyric is different from one pulsing a dance. Lyrics tell somebody's story, and dance brings a definite intimacy between different somebodys. On the one hand, the publishers believed that clearly sung lyrics helped sell sheet music. The early music popularity charts in the trade press reflected this belief by identifying the number of vocal

SAN JOAQUIN DELTA COLLEGE LIBRARY

versus instrumental renditions a plug song received each week. On the other hand, when dance rises in popularity, as it does from time to time, questions of the audiences' ethnicity, race, class, gender, and age also usually surface. This link has occurred in practically all the streams of American popular music, especially when dance directly involved matters of racial boundaries. Remarkably, these boundary crossings in music and dance have appeared frequently, unexpectedly, and practically independently of the state of race relations.

From the earliest days of the nation, music and dance have been secular entertainments appealing to all social classes and ages equally. The dances of the poorest and the most despised were shortly transformed into dance forms of the privileged, and vice versa. At the turn of the century, for example, "ragtime," the piano-based musical core of the emerging popular song, accompanied a new dance, the cakewalk. This black dance form was originally one of many satirical, mocking commentaries on the elegant European dances of the whites.[18]

After the cakewalk, a number of dance crazes continued to influence the course of popular music. Some were led by dramatically compelling performers such as Vernon and Irene Castle, who, around the time of World War I, made ballroom dancing a national titillation. Their musical director was James Reese Europe, whose collaboration with the Castles led to popularization of such black-originated dances as the turkey trot, the one-step, and the fox trot, which was the longest lasting ("invented," according to Irene Castle, by Jim Europe).[19] These dances were taught in the Castles' proliferating dance studios. For the dance schools to flourish, however, people had to have a place to dance. As noted above, the new midtown cabarets in Manhattan were ideal places to satisfy the dancing urge. The dance craze that radiated out of the cabarets widened the audiences for popular music, destroying the distinction between a dance to watch and a dance to perform.[20]

The explosion of these new audiences affected the manner of song plugging. The attention given popular singers of the day was extended to the dance world by the more aggressive and thoughtful publishers. Marks' memoir reports on his

regular hours of wriggly-wriggling, for the music business had gone on a dance basis. It ws the only way of checking on rival publishers' new tunes and getting the dancers' reaction to your own new numbers. Cup contests took place almost every night. We snapped up the winning couples, if they were young and prepossessing, and signed them up for vaudeville appearances. . . . They then would use our music exclusively.[21]

The leading couple "snapped up" by this energetic firm was the Castles themselves, who went on to international fame and epitomized the dance mania of the day.

This high point in vernacular dance came to its usual end in the usual

SAN JOAQUIN DELTA COLLEGE LIBRARY

way, which is in itself an instructive story. The tango, one of the most popular dances of the moment, produced its own demise not only because of the glut of tangoes with which most of the publishers had flooded the dance halls but because of the dance itself. Marks shrewdly observed:

It was the tango which broke the legs of the dance craze. The tango was a graceful and a highly developed dance at the time of its importation from South America, via Paris. The expert tangoists vied in the introduction of refinements. Soon few amateurs could dance it creditably. The cycle was complete. The new dances had achieved their tremendous vogue because they were easy to perform. Now the social dance had evolved from difficult through easy to difficult again, and the dancers quit." [22]

A later incident would lead to another resurgence of Latin music however. In 1940, while the newly formed Broadcast Music, Inc. (BMI) was engaged in a competitive battle against ASCAP, the first break for the broadcasters came when E. B. Marks' publishing firm signed with BMI. Their tremendous South American catalogue, tangoes and all, became a major source, in addition to tunes in the public domain, for radio broadcast music. The flood of Latin hits in 1940–1941 (e.g. "Amapola," "Frenesi") stemmed from that specific fact rather than from some "natural" turning of the American public to a Latin pulse. Before that event, however, dance lost its hold; music returned to song. This complex alternation can be seen again and again in strikingly parallel circumstances during the development of rocknroll.

To summarize the publishers' place in the evolution of the pop stream, it is clear that by the end of World War I they guided a more complex system than they had at the turn of the century. They were able to reach all social classes and encompass all styles, all across the nation, in the home and out. The hit-making engine was fine-tuned. By 1921, ASCAP was able for the first time to distribute to its members the fruits of its efforts. Performance rights income became a reality; it generated over $81,000, which was distributed to the members, half to the publishers, half to the writer-lyricists. [23] This amount was minuscule compared to the approximately fourteen million dollars earned from sheet music in that same year. [24] It was also trivial compared to "mechanical" earnings, the exact amount of which is difficult to estimate but was certainly in the millions of dollars at that time. But this situation was to change dramatically. The very next year, 1922, ASCAP requested the brand new commercial radio industry to pay for the use of its music.

The Rise of Radio Broadcasting

The theories of the electromagnetic spectrum that came out of the laboratories of Europe and the United States near the end of the nineteenth century produced two great industries. One used electricity for power; the other for communication. In the United States, the General Electric Company (GE), founded in 1892 as successor to Thomas Edison's original company, and the American Bell Telephone Company, founded in 1885 by the inventor of the telephone, Alexander Graham Bell, shared a number of patents but nevertheless struggled over property rights and for dominion in their overlapping markets. These legal and economic battles shaped the practices and strategies of the emerging phonograph, radio, and motion picture industries. The opposing views of these corporations and their offspring about what constituted proper musical fare for the nation, how that music was to be organized, presented, and paid for, set the trajectory for the development of popular music in the succeeding half century.

Guglielmo Marconi's discovery of "wireless telegraphy" in 1896 was speedily transformed into "radio" when he brought the invention from his native Italy to England, where he patented the device and formed a corporation to exploit it. The need of world navies for high-speed communication soon brought radio into the militias of all the major nations of the world. Though under the control of the U.S. Navy from 1914 to 1918, American radio technology made great advances. The government's ability to pool patents and concentrate research and production using the military imperative gave radio a strong industrial base. The federal government's ban on all amateur transmission from 1917 through 1919 restricted radio resources to a few large corporations, which angered and frustrated the tens of thousands of amateur radio operators. They were a feisty lot and would be heard from repeatedly during radio's stormy development.

After the war, the Navy, not surprisingly, was reluctant to turn the vast potential of radio over to civilians. They sought legislation that would "secure for all time to the Navy Department the control of radio in the United States, and will enable the Navy to continue the splendid work it has carried on during the war." [25] The Navy's arguments, couched in the political rhetoric of the day, claimed that the government was the "natural monopoly" best fitted to do this job, including the prevention of overlapping broadcast channels and the tendency of more powerful stations to override the signal of weaker ones.

The Admirals lost. Private enterprise, *American* private enterprise, was to be given the opportunity to develop radio. The air waves were defined, however, as a public resource to be federally regulated. In 1919, the highest levels of the federal government requested General Electric *not* to sign a pending contract with the British Marconi Company. [26] The contract, the Navy claimed, "would have almost certainly . . . fix[ed] in British hands a substantial monopoly of world communications." [27] After extended negotiations, GE accepted the government's proposal to form a new company devoted to using the capitalized resources developed for the war effort to maintain a strong American presence in peacetime international communications.

That new company was the Radio Corporation of America (RCA), chartered in October 1919 as a corporation in the state of Delaware.[28] General Electric was joined to Westinghouse, its chief competitor, to AT&T, and to the other participating companies with a series of cross-licensing patent agreements.[29] One of the main reasons for the consortium was that the patents requisite for a modern radio system, from transmission of powerful signals to their reception by individual radio sets, had fallen across the boundaries of corporate organization in such a way that no single firm could do it alone. Given the agreement, each party had the potential to construct and bring to the market a complete radio system. There was, however, a division of tasks among the corporate partners. RCA would market receiving sets, GE and Westinghouse would manufacture them, and AT&T would manufacture the transmitting equipment. These arrangements soon broke down, and corporate warfare over control of radio broadcasting continued for years. The source of this struggle was, of course, the very agreement that formed the merger. Once the patents were pooled, each of the corporate partners looked for an opportunity to use them all. This maneuvering began the moment the agreements were executed but took several years to manifest itself.

At the deepest level was the struggle between the House of Morgan, whose fortune was behind AT&T, and the Rockefeller interests that dominated GE. These two giants of American banking had different and distinct visions of the nation and different styles of expressing those visions. The difference in style between the House of Morgan and the Rockefellers was pervasive, manifesting itself even in the kind of architecture each chose to represent itself.[30] In the initial deal that formed RCA, to illustrate, some important Manhattan properties were transferred to GE. Since real estate values were the coin of contemporary corporate ambition, it was clear that the Rockefellers were triumphant. That victory was embodied in Rockefeller Center, begun in 1921 and completed in 1939. The eight-square-block monument consisted of fifteen midtown skyscrapers and other related structures, including the Time-Life Building, the RKO Building, Radio City Music Hall, and the centerpiece, the seventy-story shaft named for the RCA Corporation.

This enormous monument to a forward-looking and democratic alliance of science and industry, a brash statement of the optimistic Rockefeller philosophy, was in stark contrast to the more secretive, aristocratic, and European-linked world view of the House of Morgan. This is exemplified by the quiet sumptuousness of the Morgan family town house on 36th Street near Fifth Avenue, now serving as an elegant scholarly library, museum, and gift shop. RCA, on the other hand, housed in Rockefeller Center,[31] stamped radio with a quality of excellence that merged technological progress, cultural elegance, and moral uplift, all in the service of delivering the broadest program spectrum to the American home and family.

Sarnoff's Vision

The one person who, it might be said, embodied that cultural vision and who had the power to enact it was the young David Sarnoff. Among the personnel transferred from the American Marconi Company to the newly formed RCA, he was appointed commercial manager, and he came with a plan. Sarnoff had been an employee of American Marconi since the age of sixteen. His rise from office boy at $5.50 a week to president of a giant corporation was an American success story right out of Horatio Alger. As a rising young wireless telegrapher, he had had the fateful experience at age twenty-one of manning the only American wireless key to receive the signals from the sinking Titanic in 1912. He earned instant fame by continuously monitoring for seventy-two hours the messages to and from the dying ship. That experience apparently gave the young Sarnoff a sense of radio's enormous power and a belief that such power should be used in the service of the public. He was a company man though, and as early as 1916 he was thinking about the possibilities of radio from that peculiarly American perspective that seamlessly joins public good with private profit, a mode of thought later given aphoristic illumination in "Engine Charlie" Wilson's assertion that what's good for General Motors is good for the country.

In a letter to his superior in that year, Sarnoff outlined his idea for a "Radio Music Box." It was a bold yet practical notion, with a crisp battle plan: "I have in mind a plan of development which would make radio a household utility in the same sense as the piano or phonograph. The idea is to bring music into the house by wireless."[32] He then described the technical components of the radio set that would soon dominate millions of American living rooms, its economics guaranteeing RCA a profit. He presented a vista of its diverse programming under the grand headings of entertainment, information, and education, the entire plan yielding "tremendous" advertising for the company.

In the very first sentence of his memorandum, Sarnoff acknowledged the centrality of the three-way competition for the home entertainment market, or at least for its musical side. That competition continued throughout the 1930s and 40s with the piano, phonograph, and radio (and their successors) vying for the dollars and the commitment of the nation's families. From the start the major corporations in these markets attempted in every possible way to control all three forms, as well as their out-of-home counterparts.

By the time Sarnoff had become general manager of RCA in 1922, his premise that it would take specialists to do radio's job of entertaining, informing, and educating the public had crystallized into two questions:

   1. Who is to pay for broadcasting?
   2. Who is to do the broadcasting job?[33]

The answers, Sarnoff further suggested, had to be national in scope, and some new structure other than RCA had to be created to house the enterprise. Sarnoff's commitment to national broadcasting never wavered, but his strategies for achieving that goal changed as technology developed. When long-distance telephone lines were the only way to connect radio stations in distant cities, Sarnoff proposed to utilize those lines. When "super-power" (that is, wattage high enough to send a signal through the air across the entire continent) appeared, Sarnoff saw it as the new answer. He even considered the possibility of short wave as a useful resource when necessary. Conversely, any technological advance that threatened the national concept was not to be supported—FM radio and television being the main examples.[34]

Sarnoff's general aspirations pointed radio to the high road of American culture, with public service as its touchstone. Therefore, rather than having the set manufacturers control the programming, those trained in the arts and sciences should make the programs. At the same time, radio should adhere to the highest engineering standards possible. Radio would be bedeviled for decades by the confusion and blurring of these two sets of standards. Programming and engineering personnel would war with each other over the priority and content of programming versus engineering standards. More importantly, the federal regulatory presence would weave these two sets of standards in and around its shifting policies.

The fullest expression of Sarnoff's commitment to the public service nature of radio was his belief that the medium should not become a marketplace. To prevent this, he laid out a corporate strategy that made the radio set manufacturers responsible for the costs of broadcasting. Two percent of their gross receipts would be used to operate a specialized broadcasting entity. The estimated price of a radio set was seventy-five dollars. In 1920, this amount was a month's wage for the average manufacturing employee. A low-priced piano cost about two hundred dollars (with player attachment, $250); a popular phonograph cost half that amount.[35] Radio was thus attractively priced as well as offering much broader entertainment fare than either piano or phonograph. This price advantage was sufficient, Sarnoff thought, to spare radio from both the evils of advertising and the unreliability of public subscription. His estimates of radio sales were detailed and, as it turns out, accurate.[36] But he hedged his bet on the manufacturers' ability to support broadcasting with an explicit invitation to a public benefactor to do for radio what Andrew Carnegie had done for libraries. No such benefactor appeared.

The final question Sarnoff raised in 1922—Who is to do the broadcasting job?—has reappeared at every crucial point in radio's technological and organizational development. At that moment, Sarnoff's answer reflected his conclusions to the other problems he was facing. Broadcasting was to be national and noncommercial, run by a specialized and centralized organization, staffed by experts in entertainment, information, and education, and powered by a technology of continental reach. What would be needed to create and disseminate the programming of such an entity? The answer was the National Broadcasting Company (NBC), which took Sarnoff four years to create.

Radio's Other Voices

By the early 1920s, radio programming was growing like kudzu, largely without the scruples or large-scale planning that preoccupied Sarnoff. There were two major alternatives to the high-toned public service vision of NBC's national programming. Both, predictably, came from the participants in the original consortium that had created RCA back in 1919. One was the Westinghouse pioneer station KDKA in Pittsburgh; the other was the telephone company's station WEAF in New York City.

Westinghouse turned its high-level mastery of the vacuum tube wireless receiver and large electrical power apparatus technologies to the consumer radio market. It found its way there almost accidentally. An engineer at the company's Pittsburgh headquarters, Frank Conrad, an avid prewar radio amateur, began broadcasting from his garage with a U.S. Signal Corps transmitter Westinghouse had built for the Army. Like thousands of other amateurs all across the nation who began experimenting again after government restrictions were lifted in 1919, Conrad was more interested in the engineering than the programming side of radio. He broadcast phonograph records and played the piano, his son did a saxophone solo, he announced football and baseball scores, and he presented any other entertainment he could come up with. Such an approach was the opposite of Sarnoff's notion of what a radio broadcasting station should do. The station was inescapably and contentedly lowbrow and local.

It was, however, dramatically successful in increasing sales of phonograph records. Conrad had borrowed the records from a local music store and complied with the store owner's request to have the store mentioned as their source.[37] Local sales of radio parts and complete sets also spurted. Westinghouse executives soon saw that commercial broadcasting could spur the sale of its receivers. Thus in the fall of 1920, the former amateur station 8XK became the first Department of Commerce licensed commercial broadcasting station, KDKA.[38]

It made its mark immediately by broadcasting the 1920 presidential election returns, telephoned from the *Pittsburgh Post* to the "studio" hastily built on top of the tallest building in Westinghouse's facilities. After this coup, the company's management reasoned that, since radio's appeal lay in its ability to be present at a live event, expensive radio sets were wasted on phonograph records whose quality was far below that of live music. Conrad, still in charge, arranged for a series of live concerts by the Westinghouse band. Two aspects of this simple action had long-term consequences. First, it was entirely a company project; no outside fees for music or musicians were required. Second, valuable experience was gained in the creation and mastery of remote broadcasting. This experience was soon to be used in the extension of KDKA's programming to church services, sports, and public affairs events, all broadcast from their natural settings. The technique was to use the "wire," a radio pickup, at the site, then relay the signal to the broadcasting station via telephone lines, where it was rebroadcast over the air. Free music remotely picked up and rebroadcast would become the device by which the music publishers found their accommodation to the new radio medium, a new way to bring music into the home.

The other alternative to Sarnoff's version of radio broadcasting came from AT&T, full partner in RCA and the dominant force in telephonic communications in the United States. Bell Telephone executives sought some way to enter the promising radio broadcasting field and, after considerable thought, found a solution using the strengths of the telephone system. The idea was to create a radio broadcasting station whose service was modeled on the extant telephone system that is, individuals renting the phone company's equipment to make a call, point to point, for a fee. The radio version shared the broadcast signal on a "toll" basis, individuals and companies offering programs to the public for a fee. Anyone wanting to "talk" to the public over the radio would pay a fee to the broadcasting station for the privilege. The rental or licensing of telephone wires for long-distance transmission to more than one station, the network concept, was implicitly included in the Bell System's plan by their turning over the responsibility for the incipient broadcasting enterprise to its Long Lines Division.

After an initial period of experimentation, the telephone company created station WEAF in New York City. It broadcast its first commercial programs in August 1922, the first in the nation.[39] The sponsors included a Queens real estate corporation announcing its tenant-owned apartment houses, an oil company, and the American Express Company. Although some years would pass before commercial sponsorhip of broadcasting achieved public acceptance and financial success, WEAF persevered with subsidies from the parent company.

The programming notions of the telephone company fell somewhere between the elevated fare envisaged by Sarnoff's NBC and the melange of materials used by Westinghouse's KDKA. In the beginning, almost all WEAF's programming personnel were drawn from the ranks of the telephone company. With the exception of some slight use of phonograph records and piano roll music, the personnel were all amateur employees of the phone company, and the performances were live. These polite broadcast standards adopted by the phone company's radio station are nicely illustrated by the first hour and a half of the first evening program offered by WBAY, the phone company's experimental station predating WEAF.[40]

EVENING PROGRAM

Station WBAY—24 Walker Street, New York
August 3, 1922

7:30–8:00 Victor records and player piano music
8:00–8:07 Announcement of opening of station
           George W. Peck, Long Lines Commercial Department
8:08–8:22 Vocal selections, Miss Helen Graves, Long Lines Plant
           Department:
           (a) "Just a Song at Twilight"
           (b) Selected
           (c) Selected
           Mrs. M. W. Swayze, accompanist, Long Lines Commercial
           Department
8:23–8:33 Talk: The value of effective speech in talking by wire and
           radio, followed by recitation of James Whitcomb Riley's
           "An Old Sweetheart of Mine"
           Miss Edna Cunningham, Long Lines Traffic Dept.
8:34–8:44 Violin selections, Mr. Joseph Koznick, AT&T Drafting
           Department
           (a) Traumerei
           (b) Melody in F. Rubinstein
           Mr. William Schmidt, accompanist, New York Tel. Co.
8:45–8:59 Baseball Talk, Mr. Frank Graham, *New York Sun*

This schedule reveals the source of the conflict in the relations between broadcasters and the music world that lasted well into the late 1950s. The conflict was actually a three-sided struggle over programming's schema. Radio's preferences were for a technically based, precisely timed series of short segments. Advertisers' interests were in attaching commercial messages as proximately and as often as possible to the most appealing parts of the program. On the other hand, the separate music interests of publisher and record company demanded extended periods of time to fully expose each musical selection. Thus, three different versions of the schedule were vying for dominion in radio music. The battle would go through several different transformations as all of the streams came into radio during the subsequent decades and as the social and mechanical technologies of radio led to the disk jockey era.

In addition, there was the controversy over the payments for the broadcasting of music. Though the performers bypassed the musicians and other performers' unions by virtue of their amateur status, many of the songs were owned by publisher members of ASCAP. The Society granted the station permission to broadcast these performances without fee, conditional upon an announcement of ASCAP's proprietorship. The Society's early generosity in this regard soon gave way to demands for a fee structure.

Further, the WBAY evening schedule was to become a continuing model of evening programming. While the segments periodically lengthened and shortened over the years, the practice of building a program schedule from the concatenation of very brief temporal units became standard broadcasting practice. It provided the template for at least two ways of threading radio fare that operate to this day. One is the succession of musical units, a slow tempo piece followed by a faster one, a vocal followed by an instrumental, in endless permutations. The other is the alternation of music with speech. The latter would turn into the sandwiching of commercial messages between musical selections. Every variation in format would evolve from these basic patternings.

In the 1920s, radio broadcasting was one of the fastest growing sectors of the expanding American economy. All across the country, small stations started up either without any external support whatsoever or only with the capital and organizational support of local business, usually department stores or newspapers. Their programming ideas were most like those of KDKA, that is, local, informal, and certainly not aimed at the higher levels of the auditory brow. In the South, the ancient traditions of live music and wandering performers were easily assimilated into the practices of the new small stations, which spread like a rash across the southern states from the Carolinas to West Texas. In 1922, Atlanta station WSB first broadcast country, folk, and gospel singers live from their 500-watt studio. Within a year, the first square dance program, lasting an hour and a half, was broadcast from WBAP in Fort Worth, Texas.[41] The folk, country, and gospel streams were establishing their own conventions as to what constituted radio fare, taking into account their performers' repertoire, instrumentation, and vocal style.

Southern radio adopted some other practices, one of the most consequential of which was the unspoken rule that no black performers should be on the air. This pattern was followed quite rigorously for two decades, notwithstanding some notable exceptions.[42] Another Southern radio policy allowed the mixing of secular and sacred music, validating the belief among white musicians that those two realms were not incompatible. In the course of bringing unsophisticated folk and gosepl performers to their microphones, radio gradually transformed their style and their music into the emerging commercial country pop stream.[43]

Black music also was broadcast during the initial years of radio, but mainly from northeastern stations in popular musical programming rather than from a specifically black identification. Ethel Waters, Earl Hines' band, Duke Ellington's orchestra, the Southernaires, and the Mills Brothers were all on the radio in 1922. Each of the six streams, in its own stage of development, grew with radio broadcasting as it evolved.

The question of music was increasingly on radio's agenda. Where was it to come from; how was it to be organized and presented; who was to pay for it? The convergence of all these issues around the music problem is illustrated in the controversy in the 1920s between RCA's WJZ, the most powerful station in New York, and the smaller stations in the metropolitan area. The smaller stations had banded together as a group, using the courts and governmental regulatory agencies in an attempt to stop WJZ from blanketing the air waves and overriding and blocking their own broadcast signals. This maneuvering was Sarnoff's strategy at work. A trade press editorial succinctly showed the tension between the high and low musical roads open to radio and the linkage between programming and engineering standards.

It would be sheer nonsense to stop the operation of WJZ for one minute so that some dry goods store might send out a scratchy foxtrot phonograph record which is mixed up with a loud commutator hum and "blocking" of overmodulated tubes. The time has gone by when the public should have to listen to such stuff, because there are stations which have been properly designed and to which it is a pleasure to listen. . . . The only criterion which must serve to guide in the allocation of hours is excellence of program excellently produced.[44]

The outcome of this specific fight was, in essence, a draw. Every kind of station was to be allowed to compete, using any musical fare and any power it could muster in the scramble for a share of the erupting broadcasting industry. The growth in the sale of radio sets, to illustrate, was seen in RCA's income: an eightfold increase, from $1.47 million in 1921 to $11.29 million in 1922. There was an even faster rate of growth—thirtyfold—in the number of radio broadcasting stations, from less than twenty in 1921 to almost six hundred in 1922.[45]

The Network Era Begins

The early formative period of radio broadcasting ended in 1926 with AT&T's withdrawal from broadcasting and radio set manufacturing.

The original agreement that formed RCA required the phone company's complete break from radio set manufacturing, General Electric's bailiwick. The Bell System ceased direct broadcasting, and WEAF was sold to RCA. The long lines technology required to operate a network was sold to RCA/GE and became the basis of the National Broadcasting Corporation (NBC), RCA's broadcasting arm. The issue of who was to pay for broadcasting moved substantially in the direction of commercial sponsorship of radio programming.

NBC was strongly launched. By 1928 it had three networks. The Red Network consisted of twenty-three stations, with WEAF[46] in New York City as its flagship and the rest spread mostly throughout the Northeast. The Blue Network, with eighteen stations, was headed by WJZ, also in New York City. The Pacific Network, without a leading station, consisted of seven stations scattered from Nevada to Washington. A grand advisory board to guide the NBC networks' public service commitments was created. Walter Damrosch, the distinguished and popular conductor of the New York Symphony Orchestra, was appointed musical counsel, but the crowning mark of NBC's dedication to musical excellence was the creation and support of an orchestra for the world's premiere conductor, Arturo Toscanini. The high road was to be the main direction of the network's musical programming, even though "light orchestral" fare would drift down towards the music of B. A. Rolfe's Dance Orchestra, broadcasting the equivalent of Muzak dance tunes.

Even during the earliest days of NBC, music was the largest category of programming. How it was to be paid for was a nagging problem. Possible solutions were proposed by broadcasters and the various music interests all through the rapidly expanding radio industry. A considerable body of radio managers still believed that the free publicity a performer or a tune received far outweighed any fee for performance that might be paid and that the pool of amateur talent was deep enough to go on forever. This attitude fueled the fire between broadcasters and music publishers. The important distinction that had emerged with the victory of commercial sponsorship of programming, that between *sponsored* (advertiser-driven) and *sustaining* (publisher-controlled) programs, gave the publishers a foothold in radio's new and expanding national networks. Song plugging, a resource the music men were reluctant to give up, would be adapted to these different program types.

Actors' Equity, the American Federation of Musicians, and the organizations of the music publishers (the MPPA and ASCAP) had received from the broadcasters some recognition and schedules of compensation, including regular salaries. More importantly, the musicians' union had won an agreement that radio stations, graded by size, had to employ specified numbers of staff musicians. Nevertheless, the victory of these performers' organizations was neither total nor uniform. Some stations refused to pay the high fees prominent performers were getting. Some refused to pay for live music at all, substituting phonograph records instead. The choice of live versus recorded musical performance would be a flash point for a considerable period of time.

From the beginning, Sarnoff was against paying either the performers or the publishers. But he and the other broadcasters would need both and therefore had to deal with both. In 1926, Arthur Judson and George Coats presented Sarnoff with a proposition that appeared to solve these problems. Arthur Judson, concert booker and manager of the Philadelphia Orchestra, had extensive connections with the world of classical music. He saw that radio was both a threat to and an opportunity for the concert business and proposed to Sarnoff a venture of mutual benefit. Judson would supply, for a fee, musical talent for NBC, thus solving one part of its programming problem and at the same time securing work and public exposure for the artists he managed. Sarnoff refused to commit himself at that time.

A year later, still smarting from Sarnoff's rejection of their offer, Judson and Coats announced that they were forming their own network. The United Independent Broadcasting Network (UIBN) was incorporated, and within a few months, twelve stations had signed contracts with the stipulation that the new network provide each of them ten hours of programming and five hundred dollars a week. In addition to an initial lack of funds, the most formidable barrier to Judson and Coats' network plans was the unwillingness of the Bell System to lease their long lines. Coats went to Washington, threaded his way through the tangle of congressional committees and executive powers interested in radio, and turned on his considerable charm. AT&T revised its position in light of this political pressure, deciding to lease their long lines to Coats and Judson, after all.

The young network survived long enough to offer itself to the Columbia Phonograph Company at a time when the phonograph industry was experiencing a dry spell due to the introduction of radio. A sharp reduction in record and phonograph sales had taken place in 1923–1925, driving the industry into a two-party configuration (Victor and Columbia) with a large number of small companies tailing behind. Simultaneously, there came a radical advance in phonograph technology. In 1925, acoustic recording and reproduction gave way to electrification of both ends of the process.[47] Sarnoff wanted control of the Victor Record Company not so much for its recorded music but because the phonograph case was such a handsome piece of furniture within which to place his Home Music Box. RCA thus successfully absorbed the Victor Phonograph Company.

Columbia Records saw the Judson and Coats venture as a way to counter its competitor's alliance with radio. They bought into the sinking network, changing its name to the Columbia Phonograph Broadcasting System, but the capital that was injected was insufficient. Collapse of the network was averted when it was purchased by the owners of radio station WCAU, one of the first to sign with Judson and Coats. After pouring close to a million dollars into the network's apparently bottomless pit, however, WCAU wanted out. The twenty-six-year-old William Paley was invited to become investor and chief operating officer. He and his family bought controlling interest in the network. Paley had been managing the family cigar business in Philadelphia and had successfully advertised its products over WCAU's airwaves. He was prepared to oversee the new investment in New York and, by the end of 1928, was in charge of the seventeen-station network, now renamed the Columbia Broadcasting System (CBS). Within a few years, CBS and NBC dominated the evening prime listening hours. Each network ransacked vaudeville, Hollywood, the legitimate and musical stage, as well as the higher echelons of American and European concert halls to fill those hours and to compete for the largest audience.

In addition to CBS and NBC, with its three networks, still another network appeared around this time. This organization was called the Mutual Network, constructed in 1934 and organized on quite different principles. It served more as a device for pooling advertising contracts than as a system of centralized program initiation. WOR in Newark, New Jersey, and WGN in Chicago had initiated the cooperative pooling of resources, and by 1938 Mutual had made arrangements with 110 independent stations and with several smaller regional networks throughout the West and Southwest.

Radio stations soon spread throughout the entire nation, gradually saturating urban America; by 1940, about 90 percent of cities with populations over fifty thousand had at least one station, and most had anywhere from two to seven stations. Rural areas and small towns were less well served, yet gradually radio reached almost everyone, achieving a near total saturation of 96 percent of the population in 1950.[48]

The radio industry had become a diverse mix, held loosely together by fragile associational ties and common enemies. Almost all network programs originated from New York, though a few were transmitted from Chicago and Los Angeles. In all the major cities, the highest rated segments in the evening hours were network programs, a considerable amount of which contained musical fare. The independent stations found that music, recorded and live, was their best and most frequently used programmatic strategy against the networks.

ASCAP and the Broadcasters Face Off

Both independent and network affiliated radio stations soon found that ASCAP was a major and permanent irritation. Radio's dependence on music clearly meant that performance rights money from the stations was going to be the fattest leg of the Society's three-legged money stool. Realizing that it had near total command of the musical fare used in radio broadcasting, ASCAP initiated the first round of the battle in September of 1922, calling a meeting of the leading firms in the newly emerging network radio configuration. The main spokesmen for the music publishers were Nathan Burkan, general counsel of ASCAP, and E. Claude Mills, chairman of the MPPA. On the other side were leading executives from AT&T, RCA, GE, and Westinghouse. Representatives from the Department of Commerce also attended.

Mills laid out the music publishers' position: 1.5 million radios were in use, a number likely to grow to ten million in a few years. There were also six or seven million phonographs, selling at a price four times that of radio. There were five or six million pianos and six or seven hundred thousand player pianos. Denying that radio could ever replace the phonograph and piano, Mills nevertheless argued that to the extent that radio did so, the publishers' income from sheet music sales and "mechanicals" income would be diminished. The publishers, he continued, wanted their fair share of radio's $100 million sales and $2.5 million profit. Since they controlled 90 percent of radio's popular music, he argued, radio could not exist without an ASCAP agreement. Finally, according to the law, a public performance of a copyrighted piece of music had to be paid for.[49]

The industry representatives pondered ASCAP's position on a variety of questions. These included the legal basis by which the radio broadcast of phonograph records or piano rolls could be considered "a performance"; the basis upon which a fee structure established for theaters, dance halls, cabarets, and restaurants could fit radio broadcasting; the extent to which ASCAP really represented the nation's music publishers and writers; the extent to which music in the public domain was a feasible source of radio programming as an alternative to ASCAP-licensed music; what constituted broadcasting, that is, were the twenty thousand licensed amateurs to be considered radio transmitting stations; and, finally, the familiar question, Who is to pay?

ASCAP replied simply that *commercially licensed* radio stations should pay, since they are the immediate users of the music. Mills, for the Society, having first floated in the trade press the sum of one million dollars (a year) as the amount due ASCAP from the loss of sheet music sales, modestly suggested the sum of five dollars a day as a minimum for small stations, with an increasing scale for larger ones.[50] That money, he further offered, should come from radio's trade associations. These bodies should insure and regulate their payments to ASCAP, just as ASCAP regulated matters in its trade. The broadcasters were assured that neither the standard publishers (who were mainly re-releasing old favorites) nor the public domain could satisfy the public's demand for current tunes. Only ASCAP could do the job. Mills reviewed the Society's history of successful litigation with others and then invited the radio people to participate in a friendly suit to clarify the legal questions.

The second meeting of the group a month later was a much simpler business. The broadcasters flatly stated that they would not pay for using the music in ASCAP's catalogues. Mills again recommended that the Society file a friendly suit to test the situation. The invitation was declined. ASCAP then revoked all the temporary licenses it had issued to broadcasters. It established a fee structure ranging from $250–5000 a year depending upon the station's location, population served, and its profits, then invited radio stations to take out a license with the warning that further performances of ASCAP music without a license would be prosecuted as a copyright infringement.[51]

The response of the broadcasters was to dig in, organize, and fight. In April 1923, a group of broadcasters, mainly midwestern, met in Chicago and formed the National Association of Broadcasters (NAB). The group persuaded Paul B. Klugh to come out of retirement and accept the salaried position of managing director.[52] Klugh had been a piano roll manufacturer and was a veteran of ASCAP's wars with the piano roll industry. One of the NAB's first acts was to establish a music bureau, the first of many attempts to create a broadcaster-controlled pool of new popular music. The other resolution made at this meeting was to seek federal legislative relief from ASCAP's pressures, which included creating a national regulatory body that would guide radio's growth along "proper" business principles.

None of the NAB's strategies worked. The weight of accumulated court decisions gradually shifted against the broadcasters. As advertising became the dominant way of financing radio, the broadcasters' argument that there was no "performance for profit" collapsed. They did no better in Congress or in the state legislatures. The standard publishers joined ASCAP in 1924, thus closing off another pool of music that had been available in 1922. Soon after, the large radio stations agreed to pay ASCAP for a blanket license, which made available the entire ASCAP catalogue to those stations. ASCAP also offered a per program license for those stations whose policy precluded use of the full ASCAP catalogue. This license allowed the stations or sponsors to pay for specific popular music programs. The availability of this option allowed Sarnoff's wholly-owned NBC stations to accept, and they signed a full agreement in 1930. (CBS' owned stations had all signed in 1928.)

Then, in 1931, the broadcasters lost a crucial court case. The court held that each station in a radio network had to have its own ASCAP license rather than just the network itself.[53] The loss of this case, combined with diminishing audiences and falling sales due to the Depression, finally led the NAB to acknowledge ASCAP's legitimacy. In 1932, after strenuous legislative maneuvering in the U.S. Congress and attempts on both sides to divide and confuse the issues, the first comprehensive contract was signed between ASCAP and the broadcasters. This contract, it should be emphasized, was between ASCAP and each individual station. For a three-year duration, it stated, every radio station was to be granted a blanket license contingent on payment to ASCAP of a sustaining fee based on the station's size. In addition, for the first year of the contract, ASCAP was to receive 3 percent of the stations' gross revenues, 4 percent for the second year, and 5 pecent for the third year. Finally, for network broadcasts, the network's key stations were to bear the appropriate costs.

The music publishers and the broadcasters were now irrevocably linked to each other, despite continuing attempts to go it alone.[54] It was neither a friendly embrace nor a simple one. Moreover, each side had its own internal quarrels. Within the broadcasters' camp, network-affiliated stations and independents were suspicious of each other, and ASCAP continually played one against the other. Within ASCAP's own ranks, the younger and smaller publishers began increasingly to complain about the division of the Society's steadily rising income. Those complaints surfaced sporadically, reaching a peak as the 1930s ended. Further, the major publishing firms owned by the movies were dissatisfied. Warner Brothers Publishing actually resigned from the Society in 1935 during the fight with the broadcasters over copyright license fees. Also, the author/composer members frequently quarreled with the publisher members over the distribution of royalties, ownership, rights, and the voting procedures of the society.

Negotiations for a 1936 renewal of the contract between ASCAP and the broadcasters were even more tangled, acrimonious, and divisive than the original ones in 1932. They led to such a stalemate that the final solution was simply a continuation of the (by then) 5 percent assessment on every station's gross revenues for an ASCAP blanket license.

The 1930s decade, which began with the stock market crash of October 1929, ended with the start of the Second World War and the expiration of ASCAP's contract with the broadcasters on 31 December 1940. Those ten years were a more orderly period than the popular music industry had long experienced, in spite of the turmoil of the Depression and the New Deal and the continual low-level warfare between ASCAP and the radio broadcasters over money and procedure. All six streams developed their vehicles and their artistic resources in a regularized musical environment; all the participants enjoyed stable technologies and procedures, without any significant changes in the rules.

The New York publishers were firmly in charge of the pop stream, even though (or perhaps because) a third of its personnel and two-thirds of its income came from Hollywood. Although the Depression almost wiped out the record industry overnight and the piano industry was dealt a heavy blow by radio and the phonograph, the music publishers had defined a clear path. Their three sources of income—sheet music, "mechanicals" fees, and performance rights money—were legally secure, and their methods of making hit songs had successfully adapted to radio.

How the Publishers Made Hits on Radio

The publishers, with no great effort of mind but with their usual tenacity, transferred to radio the whole bag of tricks they had used in vaudeville to expose and exploit their new tunes. But radio, much more so than vaudeville, resisted and resented the soiling of their "cultural" medium by the sweaty process of hit-making.

Network programming of popular music had steadily increased over the decade, from about 60 percent of all music programming in 1933 to 75 percent in 1940.[55] Almost all the music on the network stations was from the pop stream, with each type of program having its characteristic mix of old favorites, current hits, and brand new songs. The two main program types were the expensive prime time evening show, fully sponsored by a single firm (for example, the "Chesterfield Hour" or "The Fitch Bandwagon"), and the remote broadcasting of a live band, generally from a hotel ballroom later at night.

The late night dance band "sustaining" programs rarely found a sponsor and were delivered by the "wire," an open telephone line connecting the dance floor to the station's transmitter. This arrangement was especially valuable for broadcasters since many of the larger stations were required by federal regulation to stay on the air longer than sponsors at that time would pay for. Those time slots were more or less turned over to the pop stream. The networks themselves were able to reap the general entertainment value of having some of the national adulation of name dance bands rub off onto their stations. In addition, these late night shows served a specific purpose for all stations, network and independent alike: It allowed them to end their broadcasting day with the strongest programming possible so that, when the listener turned off the radio for the night, the set was tuned to that same station the next morning. "Don't touch that dial" was the ruling commandment in radio even then.

At the time, there were almost three hundred regularly working and nationally known dance bands in that fiercely competitive field.[56] Securing a late night remote network broadcast was important for a dance band, not just for the prestige but for its audience-building effect. This boost was especially important for remotes emanating out of New York City, since the Midwest and West received the broadcasts one to three hours earlier, during evening prime time hours. Throughout the 1930s, most dance bands toured regularly, although some found more or less permanent venues. Touring bands were necessary for dance halls, hotels, and clubs, which thrived on a succession of changing acts rather than on a single "house band." The remote broadcast was deemed valuable in advancing the band's chances of getting those live bookings, record contracts, and, ultimately, a part in the movies. The hotels and clubs, in turn, received free publicity from broadcasting on the premises, not only to the local market but to a national constituency as well.

For music publishers, late night remotes became the most important exposure and exploitation points in their two- to four-month campaign for each "plug" tune. These programs provided national exposure, thereby augmenting sales of sheet music and records. They identified the tune with a prominent band or singer, and, most important of all, they provided an opportunity for their tunes to make the "sheet." This most important chart—the "Most Plugged Radio Songs," known in the trade as the "sheet"—appeared in Variety, Billboard, the Accurate Report, and the Sunday edition of the New York Enquirer.[57] Music popularity charts were evidence not merely of a song's popularity but of the publisher's commitment to the tune. The Variety "Breakdown of Network Plugs" chart reproduced here is typical of the late thirties (fig. 2-1).

There are several features of this chart that reveal how the pop stream operated at that time. First, only the main network stations are reviewed, not the independent stations. Next, the publisher of the song is identified rather than the performers. The key unit is the song, not the performer. The "source" column refers to the three great departments—motion pictures, musical theater, or the "money song"—in which the song originated. The "grand total" of plugs is the key unit of measurement. The chart makes two other distinctions of importance. One distinguishes a plug appearing on a commercial from a plug played on a sustaining show. The former was more desirable but, as the figures show, far less frequent. The other revealing figure was the number of plugs wherein the song's lyrics were sung. A vocal rendition in contrast to an instrumental one was thought to sell more copies of sheet music. The song pluggers' march-

Figure 2-1. (opposite) "The Sheet," Variety, Wednesday, December 22, 1937. © 1937. Reprinted with permission of Variety.

Breakdown of Network Plugs

Following is an analysis of the combined plugs of current tunes on WEAF, WJZ and WABC computed for the week, from Monday through Sunday (Dec. 13-19). Grand total represents accumulated performances on the two NBC links and CBS. 'Commercials' refers to all types plugs on sponsored programs. In 'Source' column, * denotes film songs, † legit tunes, and 'pop' speaks for itself.

Title	Publisher	Source	Grand Total	Commercials	Vocals
Rosalie	Chappell	*Rosalie	39	8	14
True Confession	Famous	*True Confession	30	6	22
You're a Sweetheart	Robbins	*You're a Sweetheart	30	4	22
Once in a While	Miller	Pop	29	13	24
Sweet Someone	Feist	*Love and Hisses	25	5	11
Nice Work If You Can Get It	Chappell	*Damsel in Distress	24	8	19
I Double Dare You	Shapiro	Pop	24	6	13
Bob White	Remick	Pop	22	6	16
You Too! Words Out of My Heart	Paramount	*Big Broadcast	21	3	18
There's a Gold Mine in the Sky	Berlin	Pop	21	9	14
Farewell My Love	Harms	Pop	20	2	12
In the Still of Night	Chappell	*Rosalie	20	3	10
Ebb Tide	Paramount	*Ebb Tide	20	5	9
You Can't Stop Me from Dreaming	Remick	Pop	18	7	15
Dipsy Doodle	Lincoln	Pop	18	3	12
Roses in December	Berlin	*Life of Party	18	4	6
When Organ Played O Promise Me	Morris	Pop	17	6	14
I Wanna Be in Winchell's Column	Feist	*Love and Hisses	17	3	14
I Still Love to Kiss You Good Night	Feist	*32d Street	17	5	9
Blossoms on Broadway	Famous	*Blossoms on Broadway	17	3	9
Josephine	Feist	Pop	16	5	4
I Want for Christmas	Harms	Pop	14	6	12
I See Your Face Before Me	Crawford	*Between the Devil	14	0	8
Sweet Stranger	Ager-Yellen	Pop	14	1	5
Mama, That Man Is Here Again	Paramount	*Big Broadcast	13	1	9
Everything You Said Came True	Remick	Pop	13	3	8
I've Hitched My Wagon to a Star	Harms	*Hollywood Hotel	13	1	7
Mission by the Sea	Shapiro	Pop	13	1	7
You Started Something	Marks	Pop	13	0	6
Thrill of a Lifetime	Marlo	*Thrill of a Lifetime	12	1	9
If It's the Last Thing I Do	Crawford	Pop	12	5	7
Vieni, Vieni	Witmark	Pop	12	4	6
Sail Along Silv' Moon	Select	Pop	12	1	6
Am I in Another World?	Witmark	*Start Cheering	12	1	6
Let's Give Love Another Chance	Robbins	*Hitting a New High	11	0	7
One Rose Left in My Heart	Shapiro	Pop	11	1	6
Cachita	Southern	Pop	11	0	3
Foggy Day	Chappell	*Damsel in Distress	10	3	6
Somebody's Thinking of You Tonight	Schuster-Miller	Pop	10	0	6
I Want a New Romance	Famous	*Love on Toast	10	1	5
Broadway's Gone Hawaii	Feist	*Love and Hisses	10	3	4
Mama, I Wanna Make Rhythm	Santly-Joy	*Manhattan Merry-Go-Round	10	0	4
She's Tall, Tan, Terrific	Mills	†Cotton Club Parade	10	2	2
I Hit a New High	Robbins	*Hitting a New High	9	3	8
Gettin' Some Fun Out of Life	Donaldson	Pop	9	3	6
My Heaven on Earth	Witmark	*Start Cheering	9	2	6
Every Day's a Holiday	Famous	*Every Day's a Holiday	9	2	5
I Told Santa Claus to Bring Me You	Santly-Joy	Pop	9	1	5
A Strange Loneliness	Donaldson	Pop	8	0	6
I've Got My Heart Set on You	Robbins	*Ali Baba	8	2	5
Have You Ever Been in Heaven?	Santly-Joy	*Manhattan Merry-Go-Round	8	0	5
This Never Happened Before	Robbins	*Hitting a New High	8	0	1
My Day	Mills	Pop	8	1	1
How Many Rhymes?	Remick	Pop	7	1	6
I'll Take Romance	Berlin	*I'll Take Romance	7	4	5
An Old Flame Never Dies	Robbins	†Virginia	7	2	5
You and I Know	Robbins	†Virginia	7	2	4
That Old Feeling	Feist	*Vogues of 1938	7	1	4
Greatest Mistake of My Life	Mills	Pop	7	1	4
Rollin' Plains	Schuster-Miller	*Rollin' Plains	7	1	4
Tune in on My Heart	Gilbert	Pop	7	1	4
Have You Met Miss Jones?	Chappell	†I'd Rather Be Right	7	1	3
Ten Pretty Girls	Crawford	Pop	7	1	3
Sailing Home	Words & Music	Pop	7	1	2
Remember Me?	Witmark	*Mr. Dodd Takes the Air	7	0	1
Rockin' the Town	Witmark	*Start Cheering	6	3	5
Jubilee	Famous	*Every Day's a Holiday	6	2	4
I Live the Life I Love	Words & Music	†Princeton Mask and Wig	6	0	3
Let's Waltz for Old Times Sake	Witmark	Pop	6	2	1
Toy Trumpet	Circle	Pop	6	1	0
Snake Charmer	Marks	Pop	6	1	0
Caravan	Exclusive	Pop	6	0	0
Goodby, Jonah	Robbins	†Virginia	5	2	4
I've Never Had a Sweetheart Like You	Ager-Yellen	Pop	5	1	4
Miles Apart	Davis	Pop	5	0	4
Silhouetted in the Moonlight	Harms	*Hollywood Hotel	5	1	3
Let's Make It a Lifetime	Jacob	Pop	5	0	3
Now They Call It Swing	Handman-Hirsch	Pop	5	0	3
So Many Memories	Shapiro	Pop	5	0	3
When You Dream About Hawaii	Kalmar-Ruby	Pop	5	1	2
Who Knows?	Chappell	*Rosalie	5	1	2
More Power to You	Miller	*Merry-Go-Round 1938	5	0	2
In an Old English Village	Exclusive	Pop	5	0	2
Let That Be a Lesson to You	Harms	*Hollywood Hotel	5	1	1
I'd Love to Play a Love Scene	Famous	*Love on Toast	5	0	1

ing orders are clearly indicated: Get as many plugs as possible; get as many commercial plugs as possible; get as many vocals as possible.

Advertising executives in charge of commercially sponsored network musical programming, musical directors of independent stations, performers and their managers, phonograph record executives, the whole pop stream, in fact, relied heavily on such charts. The late night remote network shows were a more controllable forum for the necessary repetition of a song than any other type of radio program. They were particularly accessible because most of them originated in New York (Chicago and Los Angeles to a lesser extent) where the publishers' song pluggers could reach the band leaders (or their arrangers). The band leader selected the tunes, keeping in mind the pressures and persuasions from the flock of song pluggers who surrounded him. A band leader's decision to play a new tune once or to add it to his repertoire was made given some mixture of the following encouragements from the plugger: that the tune was going to be the publisher's number one plug, that the band was going to be given an exclusive play period for the tune, that the leader or the entire band was going to be pictured on copies of the sheet music, that the leader was to be "cut in" to authorship of the tune, or that there might be other "tangible" evidence of the song plugger's friendship.

The crucial interchanges were between the music publishers' song pluggers and the bands' representatives. Radio personnel had almost nothing to say about the selection of music and the manner of its presentation. The network staff announcers who handled these live remote shows, for example, played almost no part in the plugging process.[58]

The prime time, commercially sponsored, network music show was organized in quite a different manner. Many of these programs were built around specific and resident musical performers, such as Kate Smith or Bing Crosby; others were headed by respectable dance orchestras such as Guy Lombardo, Horace Heidt, or Fred Waring. Other formats invited performers or dance bands for shorter periods of time.

Perhaps the most important of these prime time shows was the Lucky Strike Hit Parade on WABC (CBS). From 1939 to the mid-40s, this program was the most heavily listened to music show in the nation. It died in 1959, it is said, at the hands of rocknroll.[59] Just as important to the publishers as each appearance of a particular plug tune was the lesson taught to the nationwide audience about the rules of the hit game—this song is number one, this one is coming up, this one is on the way out. The participation of the audience in this game and their commitment to it (in terms of regular radio listening and regular sheet music and phonograph record purchases) were the jointly held aims of every part of the entertainment complex.

For commercially sponsored network programs, the selection of popular music was almost entirely in the hands of the advertising agency, and the "sheet" was therefore crucial. "As for the commercial programs overseen by ad agency men the repertoires still depend on how they stand on the most played list. If it isn't among the first 10 or 15, the agency producer no want."[60] Unlike the remote announcers, the announcers on *these* programs were free to "hype" the particular tunes being played live to a studio audience and were encouraged to build enthusiasm for the particular tunes being played.

The publishers' reliance upon network radio's late night dance band remote was a crucial factor in the transformation of the pop stream at the end of the thirties. The gradually accelerating abuses and conflicts among the parties were to render the entire system too fragile to withstand the changes that reached a breaking point by 1940.

The successor to that system was already developing in *independent* radio, which, during the 1930s, had maintained a different perspective. The independents by and large did not have the commitment to live music that the networks had so powerfully institutionalized. The American Federation of Musicians had successfully targeted the main network stations with demands for live musicians on staff. Among southern radio stations, independent and network affiliated live music was standard practice. Country pop had, quite early in radio's history, been threaded into the circuit of shows, from county fairs to the jamboree tours.

An important measure of the musical differences between network and independent programming is seen in the musical fare. In 1942, a moment of full maturity in the two types of broadcasting, four network and three independent stations were compared for musical programming. On the network stations, the average number of songs played three times or more during the two-week period under study was about fifteen. For the three independent stations, only about four tunes were played three or more times.[61] What accounted for this nearly fourfold difference in repeating songs (for the network stations, almost all of which were new plug tunes)? Why were the independent stations not the target of the song plugging efforts of the publishers? A major factor was that independent stations (including those in New York City) had developed a much closer association with the phonograph record industry than the networks had. This legacy had resulted from early radio's history, including the Westinghouse KDKA model.

By the mid-1930s, the pop stream of the record industry had begun a recovery from its near extinction in 1932. Radio stations, mainly the independent ones but some network stations as well, found that programs consisting of a sequence of popular phonograph records were an attractive alternative to live performances. By the late 1930s, network and independent use of the phonograph record began to diverge. The independents began to use the phonograph record as their main evening fare. The format combined the top dance records with a personality who both chose the records for the show and announced them. One of the first disk jockeys, Martin Block, made his "Make Believe Ballroom" the prototype, and it was soon imitated, varied, and elaborated by stations all across the nation.[62]

The publishers did not, prior to World War II, pay much heed to programs and their announcer-hosts. Their recording efforts were directed more toward getting the dance bands to record their top plug tunes. This strategy yielded not only a direct source of income from mechanical license fees but also, through record air play, was thought to stimulate the other two income sources—performance fees collected by ASCAP and the direct sale of sheet music.

The electrical means of disseminating music was creating industries far greater in size, wealth, and complexity than that run by the music publishers, who still steered new songs though the augmented tangle of presentational forms. A small group of writers, composers, and publishers in New York and Hollywood had created a nationalized hit-making process that connected them to dance bands, network radio, national advertisers, and the motion pictures. At the outer reaches of that machinery, following its directives a little more slowly perhaps, were country pop and black pop. At an even greater distance, insulated by special considerations, were the jazz, folk, and gospel streams.

3. Gospel, Jazz, Folk:
Their Paths in Development

The transformation of jazz, folk, and gospel into full-fledged streams was a long and untidy process. These initially "noncommercial" musics were only partially domesticated by the music publishers and their allies. All three had a special connection to their communities that resisted the commercial exploitation of the music. That connection was their participation in their people's ceremonial life.

Gospel sculpts and scaffolds the potent moments of a congregation's religious extravagance; jazz sparks the fleeting joinder of those voyaging through late nights on the town; folk music recreates for the assembled people fragments of their history and aspirations. In each case, the music is a concentrated ingredient binding a company together. A community, in other words, is more than an audience. The unresolvable problem of these three streams is how the music of genuine companies of conscience can hold onto its values and practices in the face of its dilution by, or incorporation into, commercially constructed audiences.

Although every part of the nation has influenced these streams, the South has been a particularly fateful setting for their character formation. That region, with all its diversity, still bears the marks of a rebellious slave plantation society defeated in a murderous civil war by a young and expansionist industrial power. The culture of the South, including its music, reveals the continuing presence of Appomattox a century and a quarter later. Though the following discussion of gospel, jazz, and folk emphasizes their southern traditions, it should be clear that these three streams are part of American life as a whole, in all fifty states.[1]

To see that rocknroll was not just the delivery of rhythm and blues and country music to a pop audience of white teenagers but rather was a music that, step by step, amalgamated all six streams, it is essential to review the separate paths by which the three smaller streams acquired their nature.

The Gospel Root

Music has accompanied worship since time before history, but the self-conscious composition of *new* religious songs is of relatively recent origin. In Protestant churches, it was the *Hymns* and *Psalms* of Doctor Isaac Watts, first published in England in 1715, that initiated the modern movement of making fresh religious music. The appeal and persistence of those songs was thought by some observers to be due to the fact that Watts "deliberately wrote down to the level of vulgar capacities, and furnished hymns to the *meanest of Christians*."[2] And the doctor was not above using secular tunes to entice believer and nonbeliever alike into the house of Methodism.

Those traditions, transplanted to the new American nation and intertwined with African religious culture, helped southerners, both black and white, slave and free, rich and poor, meet the crises and celebrations of their lives. These musical resources, fueled by the religious revival of the late nineteenth century, were fused with earlier American song styles to become the gospel stream, which, given the reach of racial segregation beyond the church door, was divided into a white part and a black part.[3]

Gospel is a performer's medium. It is also preeminently a vocal music; the human voice, solo and in choir, carries the heart, the heat, and the message. The skills of the vocal craft are the core of gospel; the piano, organ, guitar, and occasionally other instruments are but augmentation. Further, given that the singer and not the song is primary, then the audience is creatively implicated. Both the African and the European roots of American religious life made vocal music a joint venture of congregation and singers. Audience fervor in voice and movement magnified the performance's power.

Black Gospel

The history of black gospel music begins with the diverse African heritages that survived the Middle Passage and drenched the Christian hymns and psalms with its vast presence. Over and above the inventiveness of black instrumental music, its vocal reservoir was essential. Words, most often coded for protection, voiced the great questions of life and its daily travails in song that did not acknowledge the boundary between sacred and secular forms. The spiritual, reaching its completed form by 1870, had the capacity to express both the painful emotions of everyday life and the highest flights of religious joy. "Many unquestioned spirituals have no 'religious' phraseology; many so-called secular slave songs have deep 're-ligious' import."[4]

Late in the nineteenth century, the spiritual branched into two directions. One transformed into what is now the modern "gospel" movement. The other was directed at the secular concert hall. The religious branch originated in the black churches of the South and in northern cities. Its forms included not only the congregation itself as choir, but the singing preacher, the soloist, and the male quartet. All these configurations had white counterparts, many of which, particularly the male quartet, had first appeared and flourished in the most popular mass entertainment form of the day, the minstel show.[5]

The path to black participation in the nation's secular conservatory music began in 1871 with the formation of the Fisk Jubilee Singers. The transformation of spirituals into concert performance material was given validation and international currency through this choir's widely acclaimed European tour. Other artists continued the process. College jubilee choirs and their quartet offshoots considerably widened the base of trained black musicians, including a crop of composers. One notable was Henry Thacker Burleigh, composer and organist who, beginning in 1917, published arrangements for concert performance of such spirituals as *Swing Low Sweet Chariot*, *Deep River*, *Go Down Moses*, and hundreds of others.[6]

The concert performance of spirituals to white audiences was thus an acceptable and attractive path, one subsequently taken by many black gospel singers, Marian Anderson and Dorothy Maynor being the most prominent in the 1930s through the 1950s. Black composers, most notably William Grant Still, and concert singers such as Paul Robeson and Roland Hayes also widened their repertoire of spirituals with black secular materials and other "art" songs.[7] This tendency accelerated with the impressive number of gospel-trained singers joining the ranks of grand opera. This movement included the formation of black opera companies in the United States and appearances in European houses and, finally, in New York at the Metropolitan Opera Company, where in 1955 Marian Anderson was the first of her race to make an appearance.[8]

A clear separation between sacred and secular music had gradually emerged, reflecting the division of black cultural life into a set of passionate secular musics and a religious musical canon just as fierce. Between them was a high wall that was, on occasion, surmountable. Many gospel singers left the church circuit for secular settings; many secular musicians moved from the night club world into the church, either as gospel singers, preachers, or both. But there was still a definite division between sacred and secular, although many performers alternated between the two realms during their careers.

The Gospel Highway

How did the thousands of separate and scattered churches, each with its own traditions and musical repertoire, become organized into the gospel stream? Put another way, how did new religious music become organized as a more or less self-sufficient *national* entity, maintaining its separation from the other streams? The answer lies in the fact that the route was different for black and white gospel. For black Americans, racial segregation throughout the entire United States was the unifying experience underlying their culture, pervading all its institutions. It is little wonder, therefore, that the different black musics were all more closely related to each other than to their white counterparts. That is, black gospel is closer to black pop than it is to white gospel. At least, since the 1950s this close relationship has held true, for the black church has provided the personnel and the performance styles to much of black pop.

The black Protestant churches were among the most racially segregated institutions; they were also one of the most formative elements in the American black experience. As LeRoi Jones put it: "Any historical (or emotional) line of ascent in Black music leads us inevitably to religion, i.e. spirit worship. This phenomenon is always at the root in Black art, the worship of spirit." [9]

The segregation of the black church, though strengthening the solidarity of its members, also isolated each congregation.[10] The "gospel highway," a term coined by Anthony Heilbut,[11] was the instrument that soon linked these churches into what was to become the gospel stream. That highway consisted in part of a relatively small cadre of gospel performers who borrowed from the older practices of traveling musicians, perhaps even adopting their actual routes. The circuit, which reached coast to coast and South to North, trained a pool of performers as well as a set of audiences to the "canon," the full reservoir of old and new gospel music. Like any such loose structure sustaining a geographically dispersed audience, the gospel highway had not only its routes but its centers. Among these cities radiating gospel music was Memphis, Tennessee. This city sheltered on Beale Street not only the liveliest secular music but cast its rich gospel resources, especially its male quartets, all through the deep South, the border states, the Midwest, and even along the string of cities from Houston to Los Angeles.[12]

The gospel stream was soon embedded within the larger organizational entities of the black Protestant denominations at the local, state, regional, and national levels, suffering thereby the usual political machinations. It was, however, protected from the music publishers' hit-making machinery by the black church's segregation from whites. Not that religious music publishing didn't exist; it flourished within national or regional church entities. Hundreds of thousands of Bibles, hymnals, and collections of gospel songs were sold through these church organizations by publishing houses that had special and privileged connections to the various denominations.

These stable and comfortable arrangements were decisively, if gradually, upset after World War I with the massive migrations of southern blacks to northern cities—New York, Chicago, Detroit, and Cleveland, for example. The Depression generated a large number of small, independent, storefront Sanctified, Holiness, and Full Gospel churches that partially eclipsed the reach of the more established black churches. In these churches, given the desperate conditions of their parishioners and the emotionality of their services, the more sedate "spirituals" simply wouldn't do the job. A new gospel song form thus emerged. It was written and performed by a new group of men and women, some of whom were preachers as well. Many had previously been successful secular performers and writers who had entered (or more likely *re*entered) the church with fresh religious music rhythmically and melodically derived from the country blues, jazz, and the then-emerging commercial black pop streams.

One of the most important figures in this movement was the Reverend Thomas A. Dorsey (known in his earlier days as Georgia Tom). As a youngster, he had met and listened to Bessie Smith. Later on he was Ma Rainey's band leader and was a prolific composer of witty and strongly erotic blues. Yet, as the son of a preacher, he eventually found his way back to religious music.[13]

In 1931, in accordance with the prevailing practices of the national conventions of the Baptist and Holiness Churches, Dorsey published and distributed his first jazz- and blues-based "gospel songs," a term he claims to have coined in the 1920s. Throughout the thirties, Dorsey and the leading members of his musical entourage, Sally Martin and their later discovery, Roberta Martin, set an example by touring the national church circuit and writing, singing, publishing, recording, and broadcasting their own gospel music. This vertical integration became a model for other artists, and by the early 1940s, the gospel stream boasted "a good half dozen" highly successful publishing houses (most owned by the performers themselves) and hundreds of smaller firms as well.[14]

The black gospel stream, preeminently a performer's medium, extended its pantheon of stars to include a tide of male and female soloists and several outstanding male quartets. Most of these were known only along the gospel highway, but a few, such as Mahalia Jackson, Rosetta Tharpe, James Cleveland, the Dixie Hummingbirds, and the Soul Stirrers, were recognized by national audiences. Black youngsters listening to the Mills Brothers and the Inkspots would find in the gospel stream models for careers that would soon bridge the road to rocknroll.

Gospel Recording and Radio

The first known recorded black gospel music, in 1902, was by one of the important college quartet and jubilee groups that had been raising money for black schools, the Dinwiddie Colored Quartet.[15] It was only in 1920, when commercial recording had begun in earnest, that black recorded music, both pop and gospel, began to flourish. From 1920–1942, over one hundred record companies recorded over eighteen thousand record sides using approximately two thousand black artists, comprising about 10 percent of the total output of the phonographic industry over that period.[16]

Most labels recorded a mixture of black artists, typically a blues singer accompanied by a piano, guitar, or small studio band. Gospel singers, either a soloist, a vocal quartet, or occasionally a larger choir, were also recorded. In the rural South and Southwest, in the towns and cities of the border states, and in northern cities, music and record shops, drug stores, department stores, furniture stores, and general stores carried these "race" records. Pop and gospel mingled together and were often blared into the streets via loudspeakers. If the performers wouldn't mix the two, the distributors and the audiences did, and the musics themselves, gospel and blues, were the closest of cousins.[17]

From its start, also in 1920, radio did not offer much of a black musical presence. A decade later, the limited repertoire of black gospel radio music included such gospel trained groups as the Jordanaires, the Golden Gate Quartet, and the Southernaires. The programs mixed spirituals performed in secular concert style with elevated semiclassical and even popular songs. During the early 1940s, there were regular network performances by other gospel groups, including the Deep River Boys and Wings Over Jordan. After World War II, as black radio opened up, an expanding audience was formed not only for secular rhythm and blues but for gospel.

The "highway" had found the airwaves. In the same way that some black disk jockeys programmed the secularized gospel black pop of Ray Charles and the new postwar black pop vocal groups, others developed a black audience for the real thing. These programs were produced by many of the same independent labels that were to sweep the rhythm and blues field (for example, Savoy, Chess, Peacock), but they used black gospel performers whose reputations had been made in the cities and towns along the gospel highway. Some performers carried the gospel apparatus and intensity into black pop. The extraordinary energy that James Brown, Nina Simone, and Marvin Gaye, for example, released on stage gave every rock performer from Elvis onward a standard to emulate. Others followed a less-traveled road, exemplified by Little Richard's several dramatic pilgrimages back and forth across the sacred-secular boundary line. The tension at that border is also seen in Duke Ellington's later religious works, with "serious" concert settings providing the shochorn to force the secular foot into the sacred boot.

White Gospel

From the early 1800s onward in the South, especially in its non-plantation areas, the "shape note" music schools, with their pictured notation system, allowed the musically untrained to participate. Sacred Harp choirs and camp meetings further developed this entirely vocal music. The songs often were new words put to traditional hymns or to the popular ballads of the day. Everyone sang "in the plainest every-day language"; there was no audience apart from the singers. These aggregations stoked an emotional ambiance that often brought the meeting into a "singing-ecstasy."[18] The higher ecclesiastical authorities of southern white Protestanism opposed such unruly enthusiasm, as well as the untutored level of the music. The publication of officially sanctioned hymn books by the major southern denominations was one manifestation of that disapproval. These efforts were augmented by several religious music publishing houses, which not only brought gospel music into the home but taught sight-reading of its tunes at its schools and pioneered the development of the male quartet as the medium to present that music to out-of-home audiences. These respectable firms and their singing representatives were important influences in guiding respectable southern family life.[19]

There thus developed a "high" and a "low" religious musical expression in southern white gospel. Because the "low" road, the upcountry, "hillbilly" part mixed secular and sacred music so readily, the white country music performers could subsequently do the same. This style did not move into the cities as the South urbanized at the beginning of the twentieth century, nor did it carry to any separate extent into radio and records. Instead, as *secular* white southern music was recorded and broadcast, it brought along its religious country cousin.

White gospel in the South also found its way into radio in much the same way as had its black counterpart. A white gospel music program, in fact, had appeared on the first commercial station, Pittsburgh's KDKA, in 1922, and by that year, there were at least eighteen religious, noncommercial radio stations licensed and broadcasting programs that contained some gospel songs of the day.[20] A few years later, the male quartets moving across the Depression landscape, mostly in the South, in fleets of cars from church to church, singing and selling their songbooks, got a tremendous boost when radio stations, large and small, offered regular airtime for their music. The Stamp Quartet, the Blackwood Brothers, and others often broadcast for no pay other than the right to advertise their wares and announce their schedule of appearances.

On the radio stations all across the South, even below the Mexican border, live gospel music fought for its voice and its purity. The pressures, mainly from station management, to include commercial country tunes of the day were resisted just as firmly as in the black gospel stream. James Blackwood, one of the leading figures in white gospel quartet music, stated during the 1930s, "We knew we were Gospel singers. God had called us to sing Gospel, not country music."[21]

That line of separation between the sacred and the secular did not exist for the wing of the southern folk tradition that became commercial country music. Roy Acuff, one of its pantheon giants, established the pattern in his instrumentation and singing style, which "suggested the mountain churches. . . . On gospel numbers no attempt was made to achieve close harmony, for Acuff wanted to keep the style similar to that heard in his boyhood church."[22] Others were cooked in that same pot. In the fifties, Kitty Wells, one of the first women country performers, began her career as a gospel singer.[23] Red Foley, one of the most durable country artists, put such gospel favorites as "Peace in the Valley" and "Steal Away" on the charts, and other performers (e.g., J. Standley with "It's in the Book") revived the spoken religious word. Wink Martindale placed the "Deck of Cards" high on the country charts. Beyond the explicit religious content, some performers brought into their secular country performance the manner and intensity of the gospel voicing. The Everly Brothers sometimes used their tight harmony and loud, almost strangled vocal style to emphasize that side of their musical tradition in a manner akin to the Louvin Brothers, who often covered a secular song with a religious side on their records. The gospel element, expressed indirectly in this fashion or explicitly in new or traditional songs, still lives side by side with the secular side of country music.

Finally and paradoxically, it is the national appeal and, at the same time, the regional source of the gospel stream, white and black, that must be understood. Besides the Mormon Tabernacle Choir, which has enjoyed a national radio audience since 1928, there have been few nonsouthern religious musical presences regularly performing to the whole of the American people. Moreover, there had been, until the 1960s, a definite isolation of all gospel music. Among the many reasons for this isolation was the fact that gospel never developed, at least during its formative years, a national organizational structure beyond the "gospel highway," nor did it form a print-based critical press. General newspapers and magazines, both white and black, had no gospel "beat"; no one was writing about gospel.[24] The same can be said for black religious newspapers and magazines, except for sporadic "notices" about the appearance of visiting singers. The entertainment trade press, *Billboard*, *Variety*, and *Cash Box*, paid almost no attention to gospel. Occasionally, toward the end of the 1930s, there would be included in the listings of new record releases the titles of some "spirituals." But there was no regular coverage, no charts driving the hit game, until well after World War II. Gospel developed, in short, on its own, insulated from any speedy exhaustion of its creative resources, even while playing its own hit game.

The Jazz Root

The music and ceremony of West Africa was distilled in the Caribbean, enriched in the Spanish life of South and Central America, spread throughout the black belt of the American South, and, when blended with the American commercial entertainment world, formed a stream of popular music that came to be called jazz.[25] It emerged at about the same time the pop stream was born and appeared mainly in the coastal cities of the South.

The spiritual and physical home of jazz was New Orleans, a cosmopolitan entrepot that brought together all the New World's cultures in a remarkable mixture of sophistication and savagery. It was the city of such strongly opposed social and cultural antagonisms that only its stylish manners could keep a decorous peace as this seaport to the world went about its business. A part of that business, just as important as dutiful commitment to family and religion, law and commerce, and the ruling demeanors of order, hierarchy, and probity, was the opposite of propriety, its overturn in the excesses of Carnival. Protestant whites might run the commitment side, but Catholic Creoles of color inspired its release so that everyone, princes and pirates, rich and poor, could all gather downtown in the Vieux Carré to culminate a season in orgiastic release.

In the few days of its explosive climax and in the months of its preparation, the New Orleans Mardi Gras nurtured its local music, dance, costume, parade, and the like. The high honor given to that celebration gave jazz a special place in the embroidery of release. It also afforded an honest living to many artists, whose day jobs on the docks or in the warehouses in no way affected their status as respected members of this or that musical-fraternal organization. Mardi Gras and its permanent musical enclaves were also a major stop on the various tours that carried the music of Caribbean and Latin cultures into the American heartland.[26]

Jazz Beginnings

From its earliest formative moments late in the nineteenth century, jazz, though largely black in its musical heritage, was played by people of all colors, including whites. The Creole of color occupied a special position musically. They were driven out of white society by the post-Reconstruction segregation laws, losing their high status and elegant culture. Many Creole musicians were skilled, conservatory-trained instrumentalists who, upon entry into the black musical community, could read the most complex written scores but were not able to play jazz. They learned only as the black community began to accommodate its light-skinned cousins.[27] Trumpeter Buddy Bolden and his "Bolden Ragtime Band," generally considered the first black jazz band, played from the 1890s until Bolden's mental collapse in 1907. Jack Laine's Ragtime Band, contemporaneous with Bolden's, was the first white jazz band, the progenitor of the "Dixieland tradition."[28]

The beginning of the *national* jazz age is attributable to the Original Dixieland Jazz Band, a group of young white musicians who appeared in New York City in 1917. A few years earlier, they had been "hanging around and listening open-mouthed to the music" of Joe "King" Oliver at the 101 Ranch Cabaret in Storyville.[29] From the start, black and white musicians and audiences shared in the making of the jazz stream, though the black priority is clear.

The New Orleans jazz bands, playing in nightclubs and whorehouses mostly for whites, were often small detachments of larger parade organizations, which in turn were part of a large network of secret societies.[30] These formations offered social protection, strengthened the personal and social identities of their members, and provided economic benefits as well, including the important ceremonial functions of burial societies. The familiar funeral parades—somber and religious to the burial ground, joyful on the return—integrated both sacred and secular modes of experience. Jazz's exceptional status vis-à-vis religious music allowed for the recording of some jazz gospel combinations, but these were rarities.

The small jazz band was for dancing and relaxed listening. It consisted in its "classical period" of the front line—one trumpet or cornet, one trombone, one clarinet—whose intertwining voices were sustained by a rhythm section of mixed percussion plus combinations of tuba or string bass, guitar or banjo, or sometimes a piano. Gradually, the saxophone family was added; initially a parade instrument, it became one of the band's leading voices. The virtuosity and eminence of individual players did not diminish the ensemble nature of jazz performance. The spur to excellence was provided by the practice of "cutting" contests in which one band competitively attempted to drive a rival band off the stage or off the street corners with the power, inventiveness, and stamina of its playing. This practice harks back to eighteenth- and nineteenth-century competitive dance ceremonies in both West and East Africa.[31] The rivalries were the predecessors of similar "cutting" competitions in the great ballrooms of the 1930s, wherein the big swing bands fought it out to the delight of the audience, which was responsible for declaring a winner. Black jazz, as the small band and as the full parade orchestra, was thus anchored deeply in New Orleans' black community at every level of respectability, including Storyville, the city's official red-light district.

In those early days, it was the paradoxical rootedness of jazz in both the upright black community (via fraternal societies and the parade tradition) and in the most exotic Tenderloin of the South that served to insulate jazz from the publisher-dominated music industry. Jazz and the pop stream during the years 1920–1940 kept their mutual distance for another reason as well. Like gospel and folk, jazz was a performance-dominated music; the players were the true composers. Improvisation being its touchstone, jazz was not written as sheet music to be sold. Performance first, then publishing was the rule adopted by those few black musicians who had a talent for business. King Oliver was quite explicit about this practice. In 1926, he wrote to a friend:

If you've got a real good blues, have someone to write it just as you play them and send them to me, we can make some jack on them. Now, have the blues wrote down just as you can play them, it's the originality that counts.[32]

The Jazz Diaspora

When New Orleans' Storyville was closed in 1917 by the United States Navy, the jazz band, its instrumentation, its performance settings, and its audiences began a series of migrations and modifications. Many of its best professionals went up the Mississippi, some moved west through Texas and the "Territories," others reached Chicago. The Windy City was a wide open town during the roaring twenties; prohibition, the speakeasy, gangster wars, and jazz were as large in life as they were in the Hollywood movies about them.

The first significant change in jazz was the growing importance of the piano, leading the move towards a reliance on written notes. In the twenties and thirties, it was a matter of belief and pride (among both whites and blacks) that black jazz was superior to white because the players could *not* read music. But it was only a matter of time before all, or almost all, jazzmen would be forced to read. The era of the arranger began in the early thirties as the small black dance bands tried to compete economically with the large white bands, or at least to emulate their appeal. Use of the piano, with a player that read music, was a step in this direction. Lil Hardin (Louis Armstrong's wife), for example, was one of the first piano players added to a New Orleans band and one of the first women instrumentalists.[33]

Chicago, like New Orleans, was rich in piano players who found work in the various white clubs and pleasure houses and who played in black clubs and rent parties on Chicago's segregated South Side. When Louis Armstrong joined Oliver's band, the cornets were doubled, as were the other horns, and the rhythm sections were consequently augmented. Whether in conscious imitation of the large white bands or from internal personnel or musical pressures, all popular bands became larger aggregations. They were, in fact, often given the name "orchestra" in hopeful imitation of the seriousness and prestige of the symphony orchestra and its lesser cousin, the "semiclassical orchestra." Thus violins and cellos were included in some dance orchestras.

Just as in New Orleans, there were some young white musicians in Chicago who found in black jazz what they could not find in the more polite white dance orchestras. Bix Beiderbecke, the best known of these, organized the Wolverines in 1923. At about the same time, the Austin High School gang formed its band. Over the course of the twenties, a distinctive Chicago jazz style emerged. White and black musicians individually or in small groups "sat in" with each other's bands, exchanging ideas and manners with their colleagues.[34] The distinctive mark of Chicago jazz was its driving force, its fast tempo, and its ardor, sometimes carried to the point of chaos.

During the same period as the flowering of Chicago jazz, the Southwest became another focus of jazz development. "Western Swing" emerged in Texas, an amalgam of several streams over the course of the 1930s. Bob Wills and his band (first called the Lightcrust Doughboys, then the Texas Playboys) shaped that southwestern tradition, which continued through World War II. It brought together black dance music, the emerging commercial country and western styles, and the surprisingly diverse pockets of Mexican, German, and other ethnic musics, all held together and explicitly derived from the emerging jazz-pop meeting-ground called swing.[35]

Kansas City was at the center of this western variation, and it produced a musical style and several generations of artists very different from those of New Orleans or Chicago.[36] Kansas City, straddling the western edge of Missouri, was isolated from both the New Orleans jazz traditions and from the eastern music industry. It was the commercial capital of the western plains, where wheat and barley, cattle and hogs, and all the other products of farm and ranch came to market from as far south as Houston, as far west as Albuquerque, and as far north as Cheyenne, Wyoming. The men who brought the produce came for money and pleasure, both of which they found in abundance. A vital part of that pleasure was musical and black. The men and women who provided the music toured the dance and vaudeville circuits that reached into the farthest towns of the Southwest. They absorbed a variety of local styles and left seeds of inspiration and skills leading to the formation of hundreds of unknown but sometimes outstanding "Territory" bands, as they were called. Some of these bands, along with gifted individual performers, found their way back to Kansas City and points east.

Kansas City was an inland seaport; and, like New Orleans and Chicago, the same mix of diverse, transient populations, heavy money transactions, political corruption, and wide open vice and gambling with its necessary gangster-politician alliances all led to the comparable efflorescence of a rich and torrid night life. Black musicians of every variety performed in those cabarets, show bars, music lounges, nightclubs, taverns, saloons, public dance halls, taxi dances, plain honky-tonks, and even some lowly barbeque restaurants serving music with their ribs and chili. It was a city with the highest concentration of night spots in the nation.[37]

Kansas City's strategic geographic location, its special economic functions, its relative isolation, and, perhaps most important, the density and diversity of its black musical forms were favorable conditions for the emergence of a distinctive jazz style that modified the classic New Orleans musical source materials and its instrumentation. One important addition to the music was the infusion of current black popular tunes, many of which were also from the white pop stream. They were widely played by touring tent shows and circuses with their small bands and (mainly female) vocalists.

During the early 1920s, several changes in the jazz instrumentation of the Kansas City bands lent them a new coloration. One was that members of the saxophone family (centering on tenor but ranging from soprano to baritone) replaced the clarinet in the front line. The saxophone filled more space with less manpower than could the clarinet in the large, noisy tents, theaters, and nightclubs. It also may be that Kansas City, as a center of local and traveling brass marching and circus bands, simply had a lot more sax players than clarinet players.

A second change was the gradual replacement of the banjo by the guitar. Musically, the guitar may have been favored for its enhanced voicing and harmonic possibilities. The preference for guitar over banjo may also have been an expression of the band leaders' desire to emphasize their bands' musical elegance and sophistication, as opposed to the banjo's rougher, rural heritage.

Perhaps the most decisive change was the accumulation in Kansas City (and elsewhere) of a large pool of piano players, the leading carriers of the popular ragtime dance craze. Ragtime led a considerable number of musically literate composer-performers to the publishers' piano–sheet music complex. These included Scott Joplin, Ferdinand "Jelly Roll" Morton, and Eubie Blake, to mention only the most familiar names.[38] These changes in repertoire and instrumentation brought the black jazz band closer in size, instrumentation, and style to the black pop bands and, in turn, brought both closer to white pop dance orchestras. The developing jazz stream was, quite naturally, using the pop and the black pop streams as its models.

This whole process accelerated as the ragtime fad ended in the late

1920s and many of the musically literate piano player—composers became leaders of the changing jazz bands. Their special gift was in providing a solution to an emerging crisis: How could jazz, the essence of which
is *spontaneous collective improvisation*, be played from a pre-written
score of an individual composer? The "Professor," as the piano playing
composer came to be called, was able to raise the level of most of the
nonreading players to that of bands such as that headed by Bennie Moten
and his brother Ira, those of Jesse Stone, Ben Smith, Alphonse Trent,
Jay McShann, and, somewhat later, "Count" Basie, all of whom were
pianists.[39]

The technical device these pianist-leaders used to bring their compositional gifts to the rest of the players was the "riff." The riff is

a melodic idea stated in forceful rhythmic terms and is usually contained in the
first two bars. The simpler the germ idea the better, just as long as it has rhythmic
force. After the first two bars (or after the first four if the riff happens to be
longer), the same idea is restated, probably with harmonic shadings and instrumental coloring, but without any alterations. Once established, the riff idea is
repeated in the second eight-bar section. The third eight bars of the typical Kansas
City riff tune contains a counter theme, corresponding to the trio section of the
rag and weaker in character, so as not to interfere with the main statements. The
riff then concludes with a return to the original idea (A-A-B-A2). It is simple
enough, but it is precisely simplicity that is wanted. Simple, practical, readily
understood by everyone, the riff became for early Kansas City bands a kind of
musical ground rule for the real business at hand, improvisation.[40]

This solution could not have appeared had not ragtime, the pianists'
specialty, been the constructive basis for the popular songs of the day.
The riff, as a schema requiring ensemble playing by all or parts of the
band, was a vital constituent of the improvisational "jamming" that
made jazz such an exciting live performance event. The developing rock
canon would embrace the riff and all its cousins as part of its maturation
process.

The written popular song, the publishers' basic unit, thus became the
bridge to jazz, whose improvisational essence until then had kept the two
streams apart. The next step followed readily, but, as with practically
every important change in any of the streams, a geographical journey was
required. The center of jazz moved from Chicago and Kansas City to
New York, though the traffic between those three cities continued to be
strong and steady at least until the early 1940s.

In the course of the move to New York, the jazz band grew larger,
ultimately reaching in the swing era a standard fourteen members (including vocalist), divided into a brass section (trumpet and trombone),
reeds (saxophones and clarinets), and rhythm (drums, bass, guitar).[41] The
increased size of a jazz band threatened the simple "riff" solution developed in Kansas City; if more than six or eight players were going at the

same time, they interfered with the pattern, and no one could carry it or enjoy it. A compromise used by some of the large "sweet" bands was to hire a few "hot" jazzmen to take a solo once in a while to spice up the show. This tactic may have been more than a compromise; it was an easy and durable way for bands with links to publishers and networks to enhance the excitement that jazz had produced in the dance halls and night spots of Chicago and Kansas City, indeed, around the country.

Paul Whiteman as early as 1924 had become one of the major dance band leaders to understand the potential of jazz. His famous 1924 Aeolian Hall concert, entitled "Experiment in Modern Music," presented jazz to the New York musical establishment in a concert setting. George Gershwin's "Rhapsody in Blue" was introduced to the public for the first time at that concert, as the orchestra weaved back and forth across the two worlds of popular song and conservatory writing. The concert was judged by some as the end of jazz, a disastrous musical miscegenation of jazz and the European orchestral tradition. Others saw that concert as opening the road to jazz's wide and general acceptance. Whatever the critical outcome, conservative dance orchestras in the major cities immediately plucked away from the smaller young white bands the future stars of the swing ear.[42]

There was another solution to the problem of jazz improvisation in a large band, beyond sprinkling a few hot peppers into a soggy stew. It was forged by eastern black bands based mainly in Harlem. The answer was "the arranger." He was a specialist, often a performer, able to take a simple melodic piece of material and write out the harmonically organized parts for each of the sections (brass, reed, rhythm). Call and response patterns between sections were interspersed with solos for specific individuals, scored in endless variety yet open to improvisation. European, "modern" harmonies and musical colorations were added according to the interests and skills of the arranger.

The Fletcher Henderson band of the twenties, one of New York's pioneering black dance bands of the era, was one of the first to perfect this solution with the arrangements of the gifted Don Redman. When the white bands turned toward jazz, initiating the "swing" band style, ironically Fletcher Henderson's arrangements helped crown Benny Goodman and his band as the King of Swing. Soon, however, every ambitious sideman was learning how to "write." To become an arranger was the road to jazz composition, to a steady living, perhaps even to fame and fortune as a band leader. This road was successfully traveled by Glenn Miller, Quincy Jones, and many others.[43]

Although jazz was moving inexorably closer to the (white) pop stream in its musical structures, it nevertheless retained its own (black) culture and ethos. It did so mainly because its own cultural patterns used the racial segregation of the times to its own advantage. In addition, several institutions developed about this time to give jazz its own separate identity and strength.

The "rent party" was one such social institution. Even before the Depression, this custom was a widespread but informal practice in the northern cities, to which hundreds of thousands of black families had moved after World War I. The great Chicago boogie woogie pianists Jimmy Yancey, "Pine Top" Smith, Meade "Lux" Lewis, Albert Ammons, and others developed their styles and their repertoire in such places, isolated from other musics but in close touch with each other and with local audiences. When New York became the "vanguard" center of jazz in the thirties, the Harlem rent party was an important meeting ground for the jazz audience. Free from commercial pressures but challenged by the presence of knowledgable fans and players, jazzmen developed their craft and wove their culture. They also practiced their art in after-hours jam sessions. As far back as the early New Orleans days, jazz musicians from the same or from different bands gathered together to play for themselves when their work for a night was finished. In each stage of jazz's development, that is, at each successive geographical center, the jam session had its own particular ambiance. In New Orleans, there was an air of courtesy among players; in Kansas City, the atmosphere was more heated and competitive; in Chicago, it was wild and chaotic.[44]

Over the years, the jam session tested musical ideas, set high standards for performance, stiffened players' confidence, and, more importantly, brought unknown talents to the attention of band leaders. Whatever the ambiance, the jam session in each city served to bind the players and their leading audience together. It insulated them from the larger public and from the commercial interests of the pop stream, which crowded in steadily as the scene moved from Chicago to Kansas City and then to New York. The spirit of the Kansas City jam session went to New York with Charlie Parker, Charlie Christian, Lester Young, and other jazzmen, wherein it incubated the bebop style, an even more fundamental distancing from the pop stream.

Another locus of the emerging jazz culture was the studio. In the quasi-public studio sessions of the 1940s and 1950s, such producers as John Hammond and George Avakian created an atmosphere in which "serious" recording and relaxed jamming could, on occasion, merge into genuinely peak moments. These sessions were essential in celebrating the essence of jazz as a way of life. The small jazz club carried this essence to a small public that collected in seedy night spots scattered in cities throughout the country, a nearly closed society of voyagers. The later the hour, the greater was the feeling of joint participation, binding performer and audience into a single entity.[45]

There was one more element that strengthened jazz's separation from the music-entertainment industry: the existence of its own critical press, both in magazine and in book form and directed toward the jazz audience. The musical *trade* press, *Variety*, *Billboard*, and later *Cash Box*, paid only the slightest attention to jazz in their news columns after the end of the swing era. In their regular monitoring of the music industry's production (in popularity charts, reviews, and listings of newly released tunes and phonograph records), jazz was given only the most superficial coverage. On a global basis, however, especially after World War I, there were hundreds of periodicals devoted to jazz ranging from small-circulation, mimeographed, fanzine-type items to widely distributed and commercially successful magazines. The two most popular publications in the United States were *Down Beat*, which began to serve the jazz public in 1934, and *Metronome* (founded in 1883), which introduced a jazz policy in the 1930s.

Both these organs filled their pages with the usual puffery and advertising but also accomplished several important critical functions, as did the smaller publications. First, through their critical pieces on live and recorded performances, they laid down a set of evaluative standards that, along with the lively "Letters to the Editor" department, trained a literate and active audience. That audience influenced the system individually and collectively by their purchases, attendances, and even career choices. The annual polls inviting the jazz audiences to vote for their favorite band, soloist, singer, and so on reinforced the importance of the audience as counterfoil to the internal urgencies of commercial music.

A second task accomplished by this jazz press was the introduction of the individual jazz performer to the audience by name. Every leader and a surprisingly large proportion of side men became known to the fans. The American star system, which isolates and rewards only a few performers in almost all the arts, was resisted by jazz fans who maintained a more egalitarian stance towards artistic excellence. As jazz expanded its boundaries, that posture was bent toward the normal mass adulation of the star performer; nevertheless, a critical perspective was inculcated in jazz audiences and anchored in the jazz *performer's* depth and freshness of improvisation. This training in critical appraisal was done in many ways, including the always lively blind fold tests begun by Leonard Feather. In those sessions, the editors of *Down Beat* invited well-known jazz figures to listen to and comment upon current recorded performances of their peers. For years, this public forum gave jazz audiences a critical vocabulary right from the artist's mouth.

By the 1930s in the United States, and especially in France, the scholarly community began to recognize jazz as America's unique and premiere contribution to the world's arts. Journals, monographs, biographies, discographies, and bibliographies were only a small weapon defending the art against the commercial machinery of show business; they were nevertheless an important part of the jazz armor. They helped that stream's independent development, even as jazz crossed its boundaries to reinvigorate the pop stream and to sustain the black pop stream.

The Folk Stream

The folk stream is not the same as folk music. Folk music is the ultimate source of all six streams and therefore beyond the category of a single stream. Its definitions have included many components: music that is collectively owned, of ancient and anonymous authorship and transmitted across generations by word of mouth; a canon celebrating life in the past and urging change for tomorrow, the performance being on simple instruments in natural settings; meditations on everyday work and play; recapitulations of extraordinary moments of danger or disaster; and the joyful performance by specially gifted but not "professional" artists. Folk music's self-appointed custodians have been asserting, denying, and qualifying its nature and fate for over a hundred years. While scholars inside and outside the academy, musicians of every kind, and politicians of all stripes argued these definitional questions, they were all also harvesting folk music in their own ways for their own purposes.

The folk stream gradually took charge of folk music and arrogated to itself the right to designate what was or was not the real stuff. Those in charge began to fence the territory, certifying the folk authenticity of performers and their music or announcing their contamination by commercial interests, by too much contemporaneousness, or by too much art. The folk stream's custodians also assumed the job of stopping, or at least of regulating, the ransacking of folk music's resources by the other streams. The questions of property rights and musical purity were, as always, fully entwined. The difficulty of assigning some musicians and musics to one and only one stream, especially the folk stream, stemmed from the fact that all of them drew from the great unboundaried reservoir. As time went on and each stream increased its own canon, the proportion of music and performers coming directly from folk music naturally diminished; yet the deliberate spicing of each stream by external music, including folk music, was a common and necessary practice. Folk origins, it is still believed, legitimated and honored every stream.

The folk stream fought for its hegemony over folk music against the other streams' claims to folk music's history and resources. The reality and contentiousness of that fight is quite transparent in the way the folk stream protects its boundaries in the perennial arguments over how the skills and styles of art versus folk music should be related.[46] It shares with jazz and gospel an embattled stance, offering the commercial streams some of its riches while trying, at the same time, to keep itself intact and true to its standards.

The Construction of the Folk Stream

The organizational structure of the folk stream came to look quite different from that of the other streams, although it is generically the same. Its artistic system, which illustrates the most important of these differences, is inherently paradoxical. Where is the artist, the creative force in the stream? For a considerable period, the founding scholars of folklore (folk music's academic main house) contended that there were no individual composers or lyricists. "Pronouncements by Johann Gottfried von Herder and the brothers Grimm . . . had led to a concept of folksong as a spontaneous, autochthonous expression of the 'collective soul' of the people."[47] This denial of individual authorship, even when modified by the acceptance of individual but anonymous composition, kept the study of folk music within the precincts of the museum and in the hands of the collectors.

Francis J. Child, the leading American presence in folk music, retreated from this basically European doctrine, instead holding this view: "Though they do not write themselves, as William Grimm has said, though a man and not a people has composed them, still the author counts for nothing, and it is not by mere accident, but with the best reason, that they have come down to us anonymous."[48] The full consequences of this modification on authorship took fifty years to find expression; that is, it finally came to be realized and reluctantly accepted that *new* folk songs can be composed and, God forbid, performed to a live audience. This acceptance would eventually open the folk stream to new and unruly participants. In the first half of this century, however, the main branch of folk music studies was dedicated entirely to the unearthing and preservation of musical fossils.[49]

As long as the music stayed in the museum, the previously discussed argument between Charles Rosen and his opponents was moot. To open the argument would take not only an individual performer and/or composer but that individual's live performance as well. Was the music to be judged against the giants or simply placed in the musical discourse of peers? The question was soon to become operative.

Nevertheless, the changing organization of scholarship and its technologies during this period threatened the professors' hold on the emerging folk stream. To begin with, the original claim by the American Folklore Society, founded in 1888, of dominion over all of folk culture was gradually eroded during the first two decades of the twentieth century by the incursion of anthropology, linguistics, and musicology. During this very period, these disciplines were establishing their own professional associations, their own university departments, and their own publishing vehicles (i.e., books, monograph series, journals).[50] Folklore, as a result, lost control over folk music at least until the 1920s. It could not elude the stigma of antiquarianism and "Merrie Olde England" pedantry. In the case of black music, it was, with a few notable exceptions, still nursing views about the origin and nature of American black music that were subsequently to be demolished.[51] The scholar-folk musicians were being squeezed between anthropology and musicology. It was recognized that, without the training and credentials of these two rising fields, folklorists were in trouble.[52]

A major part of the problem was the reliance of folk music scholars on printed materials. The act of wrenching an aural culture out of its natural context and then stuffing it into the medium of print (both words and musical notation) could well justify the definition of the academic folk song collectors as the "creator" of folk music. They were creators in this peculiar and limited sense: In retrieving the "raw" folk songs and winnowing out their "false" (that is composed, degenerate, or borrowed) musical elements, thus freeing, as it were, the statue hidden within the marble block, the folk music collector became the "artist." In this strange way, the collector-scholars individually became the creators of folk music; collectively they owned the stream.

The development of the phonograph and its use both by commercial interests and by cultural and social scientists decisively ended that notion and that era. Live performances and the living performer entered the folk music scene. They were realities to be understood and accepted as a legitimate part, the central part, of folk music. They were also to be domesticated not only into a new form of scholarly output but into commercial properties and the weapons of social movements.

As the social context of the folk stream was thus widened, new actors appeared on the scene. The arena became larger, more crowded, and more complicated, an entity moving, nevertheless, toward the regularized structure of the other streams. Prior to the phonograph-radio watershed of the 1920s, the scholar-collectors talked mostly among themselves, and the "folk" sang and danced among themselves, with no interaction between the two groups.

The first new personnel that appeared after 1920 was a group of *distributors*. They were actually three kinds of distributors, each with its own perspective on which audiences wanted what kind of folk music for what purposes. The folk stream was thus split into three parts. One was the augmented scholarly network where the new generation of academics, now rooted in university departments of folklore, anthropology, and musicology, simply applied the technologies of sound recording to traditional pursuits. The second was a small but active corps of recording and presentational organizations, some commercial, some "not-for-profit," whose mission was to connect the relatively isolated world of folk music performance to larger, even national audiences. The third part was the corps of specialists attached to the diverse political movements roiling the American landscape during the 1930s. This tidy tripartite division—scholarship, performance, politics—vanishes instantly upon actual ground inspection, however. There were so many mixed and shifting elements in the folk stream that it might be more accurately described as being a structure very much like the vast and amphorous folk music reservoir it was trying to supervise.

Out of that complex mix began the Library of Congress' *Archive of American Folk Song* in 1928. Under its Music Division chief, Carl Engel, was gathered a large checklist (450 pages) of the thousands of recordings made from 1933 to 1942. These wide-ranging field records (including "Negro Prisons")[53] of the nation's "living libraries" were made by John A. Lomax and his son Alan.

Folk Performance

The Lomax recording efforts, which continued the 1910 influential collection of *Cowboy Songs and Other Frontier Ballads*, stimulated the organization of many statewide associations devoted to folk music, especially in the South and Southwest.[54] These societies served not only scholarly interests but those of the folk musicians themselves. The organization of folk music performances on a regular and a paid basis generated a more or less separate component to the folk stream. Such performance structures grew in many places and involved such representative individuals as Bascom Lamar Lunsford, one of the first collector-performer-impresarios. He was not only an accomplished singer but also a managerial virtuoso. He organized one of the earliest annual folk festivals (Asheville, North Carolina) in 1928 and, a year later, commercially published some of the songs he had collected. There soon developed throughout the South (and elsewhere in the United States) an expanding network of such fiddlers' and pickers' conventions. These were at first local but then widened to the county level and beyond, often being attached to the county fair, a vehicle that itself was developing under quite different auspices.[55]

John Jacob Niles and Carl Sandburg were two other leading collectors, performers, and composers who not only used the commercial publishing network, limited as it was, but also gave concerts and radio broadcasts and recorded folk songs commercially through the late 1920s and 1930s. Still other performers were mainly entertainers whose materials were drawn solely from folk sources or eclectically taken from anywhere. Richard Dyer-Bennett and Burl Ives are two well-known examples, though hundreds of "singers of songs" filled a niche between the pop stream's radio-based repertoire and the concert halls' art-song performer.

During this same period beginning in 1920, the record industry started its restless search for new material. The familiar story of Ralph Peer's tour through the South in that year for Okeh delineates the start of the commercial side of the folk stream development. Malone's description of Peer as the "indefatigable commercialist-folklorist"[56] accurately catches the fact that the southern musicians and their repertoire were being fought over by the emerging "hillbilly" commercial recording interests and by the noncommercial collectors. Although in those days it was unclear whether the Carter family and Fiddlin' John Carson were country or folk or to which stream Jimmie Rodgers, the "Singin' Brakeman," belonged, there was no difficulty placing Vernon Dalhart.

Born in Texas, Marion Try Slaughter was drawn to New York, where his waning career as a popular and light opera tenor was revived by his decision to try a hillbilly singing style. His stage name, Vernon Dalhart, was taken from two North Texas towns about one hundred miles apart. His record success for Victor in 1924 with "The Wreck of the Old 97" and the "Prisoner's Song" ("Oh if I had the wings of an angel") revived Victor records and further spurred the exploitation of that great southern reservoir.[57] Even a most casual hearing of Dalhart's records reveals the spurious nature of his claim to a hillbilly voicing, and the extended litigation over the authorship and property rights of the "Wreck of the Old 97" perfectly illuminates what was at stake in the control over that enormous lode of folk music material lying in the public domain.

The folk stream, country pop, and the pop stream itself were all engaged in the plunder and division of spoils. With no disrespect intended, even the lofty Lomaxes engaged in that most normal of pop stream's practices, being "cut in" on the composers' rights of a newly published tune. Huddie Ledbetter's (Leadbelly) hit song "Goodnight Irene," allegedly composed while he was in prison, is listed as follows in Nat Shapiro's *Annotated Index of American Popular Songs* (vol. 1, page 10):

Goodnight Irene

Words and music by Huddie Ledbetter and John Lomax. Ludlow Music, Inc. First recorded for the Library of Congress archives by Leadbelly (Huddie Ledbetter) while he was a prisoner at the Angola, Louisiana State Prison. Included in *Negro Folk Songs As Sung by Lead Belly*, edited by John and Alan Lomax and published by The MacMillan Co. in 1936. Best-selling records by The Weavers with Gordon Jenkins and his Orchestra (Decca) and Ernest Tubb and Red Foley (Decca).

This listing surely illustrates the earlier question about who is the "creator" in the folk stream, collector or performer.

The Broadway theater was not oblivious to the folk stream's riches. In the 1920s, the folk presence came to Broadway, in part from the Community and Little Theater movements that had their roots, from the early 1920s, in American small cities and towns. Paul Green won the Pulitzer Prize in 1924 for his *In Abraham's Bosom*, a southern play in a Negro dialect. His folk-based work culminated in the 1927 historical pageant about the settlement of Roanoke Island. He was a strong presence in that part of the folk stream that carved a niche between the pop commercial and the art-song world.

In 1935, George Gershwin presented, under the Theater Guild auspices, the folk opera *Porgy and Bess*. The all-black cast (including the veteran vaudeville dancers John Bubbles as "Sportin Life" and his partner Ford L. Buck in a lesser role), black street cries, shouts, spirituals, jazz, and Gershwin's own serious compositional efforts were blended into one of the most durable contributions to the American musical theater.[58] In 1938, Douglas Moore wrote the "folk opera," *The Devil and Daniel Webster*. Soon after in 1940 there appeared *Cabin in the Sky*, based on the folklike play of Lynn Root. The music was by Vernon Duke, an esteemed mainstream pop composer, with John La Touche's lyrics and with choreography by George Balanchine. The play yielded a polished blend of folk, pop, and serious dance. It was a commercial success and was made into an even more successful movie in 1943 starring Ethel Waters, who recreated her stage role.

Rodgers and Hammerstein's *Oklahoma!* (1943), based on the "folk" play *Green Grow the Lilacs* by Lynn Riggs, continued the tradition, as did their *Carousel* (1945), based on Ferenc Molnar's *Liliom*. A more direct use of folk music was the Theater Guild's 1944 production, *Sing Out Sweet Land*, built entirely on folk songs. The convergence of modern dancers with serious composers reached beyond the theater to produce such collaborations as *Billy the Kid*, with music by Aaron Copland and choreography by Agnes De Mille for the Ballet Theater.

This relatively brief and luminous touch of the folk stream on commercial musical entertainment laid the groundwork for subsequent extensions. One direction was into the work of serious composers. Theoretically, the issue about whether *new* folk music could be composed at all had been forced upon the folk stream's academic consciousness by the inescapable phonographic evidence of live performances.[59] Many serious American composers of the 1930s sought to break from the European canon. They turned to the full range of American folk musical experience, not only for melodic or rhythmic materials but for a deeper grounding that was only in part musical. A naive nationalism in the face of threatening foreign ideologies was at work.

The use of folk music for art composition, paradoxically, legitimized composers' work, for there was a European precedent for this use. Beethoven had incorporated Scotch and Irish folk songs into his work, and even earlier, the Italian composers of the early seventeenth and eighteenth centuries had used their own folk songs in a similar fashion. Contemporaneously, Villa-Lobos and Bartok, modern composers, were engaged in the retrieval, preservation, and above all the *creative incorporation* of their national folk musics into their work. These were models for American composers such as Aaron Copland, Ferde Grofé, and Morton Gould.

Near the other end of this performance continuum, that is, in the arena of the single singer with a guitar, could be found direct collages of folk materials, an important early example of which was Charles Seeger's "Midnight Special," a prematurely advanced form of folk composition. This second part of the folk stream gradually accumulated a loose set of strong vehicles that brought its performers to live audiences and to records. Impresarios like Moses Asch and his Folkways records and Emory Cook and his ethnographic recordings were important contributors to the performance side of the folk stream.

The Political Part

The political side of the folk stream heated and cooled with the political fires in the nation. It is probably not far off the mark to say that every flare of civil strife from colonial days onward was set to music. Every organized protest had its songsters. Consequently, the life span of the political protest controlled the durability of its musical side. It was an on-again, off-again business, the music treated as irrelevant discards. It is thus not surprising that most academics chose to ignore that strand of American folk music. They also ignored the organizational structures that created and carried early political folk song as well as its contemporary expression. As the folk stream gathered strength after the market crash of 1929, however, so too did efforts to retrieve the political side of the music.[60] Indeed, there was, from the early 1900s, an unbroken tradition of folk music in the service of political action, mainly on the left. The Wobblies, the International Workers of the World (IWW), made a lasting contribution with their *Little Red Songbook* (published in 1909).[61]

The trade union movement's use of folk music materials dates at least from the Knights of Labor in the 1880s, continuing through the coal and steel workers' organizing drives after World War I, and to the formation of the CIO in the 1930s. Some of the amateurs singing and shouting out labor songs went on to careers in show business. Others ran meetings, rallies, cabarets, and picnics wherever the political scene allowed music. A thin margin of commercial record companies and an equally small group of book and music publishers supported the cultural side of the political struggles.

The most prominent of the politically active folk singers were Woody Guthrie and, to a lesser extent, Huddie Ledbetter. They were both "authentic" personalities, guided by the Lomaxes and recorded for the Library of Congress' *Archive of American Folk Song*. Towards the end of the period, they both reached a national audience via commercial recordings. They were to constitute a bridge to the rapidly expanding folk stream that in the forties and early fifties had found a new and equally volatile audience, one whose politics were distant cousins to that of an earlier time.

Another part of that bridge were the Almanac Singers, assembled in 1940. They included Pete Seeger, Lee Hays, and Millard Lampell, joined later by Woody Guthrie. They toured the trade union and left-wing folk music circuits, recording an album of union songs that had wide circulation. In 1949, Seeger and Hays along with Ronnie Gilbert and Fred Hellerman organized the Weavers. They first performed in New York's Village Vanguard to the emerging new urban folk audience. In 1950 they recorded, with Gordon Jenkins on the Decca label, Leadbelly's "Goodnight Irene." This song was a top hit on the pop charts and a significant link in the chain connecting the folk stream to rocknroll.

Behind these public performers were the political bodies and cultural gurus of the left (mainly in the Communist party), its allies in the trade unions, and its organizations of intellectuals and their literary organs, largely in New York City. Their direct financial and organizational support as well as their ideological approval was a considerable influence during the 1930s and early 1940s. Indirectly, the influence of the left reached far beyond its own ranks, touching practically all the cultural forces—the Hollywood studios, the Theater Guild, and many federal programs spawned from the New Deal, from the folklore projects of the Works Progress Administration (WPA) to the Federal Theater and the Federal Writers Project. The arguments as to what was folk music and how it was to be harnessed for the political line of the moment was an endlessly shifting sectarian swamp of European-based Marxist doctrine. Between contrapuntal exchanges with the anti-Stalinist left and the trans-political literati, the haggling eventually fell dead. That self-destruction, along with the post–World War II McCarthy savagery and blacklisting, did not entirely destroy the political component of the folk stream, however. Those events simply cleared the road for new political forces that would appear at the end of the 1950s.[62]

How the Small Streams Compare

A few concluding observations about the three smaller streams are appropriate here. The designation "smaller" seems immediately and entirely accurate with respect to jazz, folk, and gospel. The reason is not so much their actual size but rather their inherent self-limiting tendency. The musics of these three streams can be difficult to appreciate, even impenetrable at the core, while at the same time inviting an audience by their charm and by their extra-musical appeals. To appreciate them fully, an audience must make considerable effort. The selective narrowing of the audience that results also reinforces the performers, who cannot make many concessions without compromising their integrity. That quality of unyielding purity is one of the highest and most fragile attributes of these streams. Artistic achievement in the streams rests upon the complete personal commitment of its performers and creators to the transcendent values of their traditions. To sing for money before unbelieving audiences is a betrayal inviting expulsion from the ranks. Yet, not too far below the surface, a desire for an expanded audience surely operates.

Among the three larger streams, there is no such ambivalence. Their personnel will do almost anything musically to enlarge their audience. The pop stream's most insistent dream is a worldwide audience of unlimited size. In short, the three small streams would rather sell one person ten records, while the three larger ones prefer to sell a hundred persons one record. This is not to say that there aren't any strongly held values, beliefs, and attitudes at the center of the three larger streams. There were and are indeed such values; they will be discussed below.

The guardians of jazz, folk, and gospel value their musical integrity, since it is the marker of that state of the spirit which allows them to mediate the presence and the powers of grander forces. They are the agency by which the congregation, in gospel's case, is brought into close contact with the living God. Jazz players attempt to carry their audiences out of themselves and into the realm of artistic ecstasy. Whether the mood be light-hearted or serious, that release is achieved by the artists' intense emotional commitment, surpassing the mere technical skills of performance. It is an experience shared by the listener, an experience that goes beyond the ordinary mode of being. The folk artist, with the same intensity and conviction, is able on occasion to bring his or her audience into a larger sense of communion with the legitimating power of the folk, "the people." All three of these symbolic journeys across the boundary separating everyday life from more elevated (and even dangerous) transcendent moments involve special circumstances and preparation. The normal paraphernalia of show business serve this purpose, even though the look and feel may appear to be only simple entertainment.

Jazz, folk, and gospel are nestled up against the pop, country pop, and black pop streams in ways that allow their powerful commitments to trans-musical values to nudge the moral spines of those commercial streams into a more upright position. By providing a cornucopia of musical and human riches, jazz, folk, and gospel have continued for ninety years to infuse some of those values into the three larger commercial streams.

Each of the smaller streams expresses its values in different ways.

Perhaps the most important and life-enhancing quality of the jazz-folk-gospel triad is its unresolving asymmetry in almost everything musical and otherwise. If gospel and jazz, for example, are at opposite poles in matters of sin and salvation, the folk stream is either indifferent or cynical with respect to that moral struggle. If jazz regards folk as musically incompetent and simple-minded, folk reciprocates by declaring jazz corrupt and decadent, and gospel ignores them both on that issue. Every artistic problem and every related sociological issue appears to be handled differently by the three streams. The three have different ideas and histories as to what is a performance and what are its acceptable times and places; further, they differ on what is a career and what is a calling. They also have taken different routes into the worlds of serious concert music.

Jazz, folk, and gospel recruit and train their performers differently, and reward them differently. They each respond differently to the racial boundaries within the nation. Jazz was, at least in its early days, tied to the encompassing black community (including its role as the devil's tool) and only had a limited connection to the white community through its entertainment vehicles. White gospel and black gospel approached their political and social boundaries with different attitudes, the white side effortlessly connecting to the secular musical world, the black side, only with great resistance. The folk stream, insofar as possible, denied the racial barrier altogether.

Above all, each stream has taken a different stance towards the larger issues relating art to life and life to art; for that is, indeed, their ceaseless mission—to punctuate the rhythm of everyday life with a musical presence strong enough to inform the community with their ethos, to give, in short, the assembled people a helluva show. Attempts by jazz musicians to expand life into art via the studio jam session, for example, or to bring art into life via the rent party were quite different from that of a black gospel performer to "destroy" the congregation in a Sanctified church or a white Sacred Harp convention. Both were different from the folk-sing at a family gathering in the Blue Ridge Mountains or at a hootenanny on Long Island.

Finally, it should be emphasized that none of the six streams lay exactly athwart any social line of cleavage. Neither region, race, religion, class, nor gender or age can claim exclusive dominion over any of them. Significantly, rocknroll, with all its music and its values (which incorporated all six musical reservoirs and the whole set of their extra-musical values), devolved on one social category—the youth. What a powerful set of tools, and what a pre-potent line of stress was to be laid across the age boundary! How this boundary was laid, how the intrinsic contradictions and tensions among those values were handled (or not handled) is visible in rock's stormy maturity. The outcome was determined by the configuration of the six streams with respect to one another and to rockn-roll. The routine work of their personnel and the state of their property rights constituted those configurations. It is to that tangle I now turn as the 1930s and the Depression moved toward the transformative days of World War II.

4. The Pop Stream Leads
It All to 1940 and the War

The 1930s, the second decade of commercial radio, held several fateful turns in the road to rocknroll, as the popular music industry continued to construct its house around the new broadcasting technology. The result was a structure far more complex than its architects had envisioned. The previously simple map of 1900 gave way to a system with new leaders and followers. Although the pop stream contained the same basic elements, that is, the creative artists, distributors, audiences, and critical voices, it had become larger, far more differentiated, and was augmented by other interested parties. It was a densely packed mosaic. This new arrangement would guide the way, after World War II, to a different world for all six streams, preparing the ground for their meeting in rocknroll.

The basic unit of the pop stream had decisively changed. This change included the physical product itself. Sheet music had given way to the phonograph record. But it entailed even more than that. The *song* as written notes, inviting varied interpretations by any performer, was gradually being replaced by a unique recorded *performance* by a single artist (soloist, vocal group, or a band). The performer came to dominate the creative side, overshadowing the songwriter and lyricist. Consequently, it was the record company with its producers, talent scouts, and exploitation machinery that displaced the publisher as impresarial center.

The geography of music was also decisively changed in that process. New York, after reigning as the nation's undisputed musical capital throughout the Depression and war, was dethroned. The regional musics of the South came to the fore, and the large cities all over the country became the sites of the music-making apparatus.

Perhaps least visible but most consequential, the speed of the entire system was substantially increased by shifting the emphasis from old favorites to new songs in an ever-accelerating "hit parade." The resultant need for new material and talent put the pop stream "on the send" for new musical lodes to mine. Black pop and country pop were thus drawn into the pop stream's maw. This whole rearrangement took place behind the scenes, although at least twice during these years the production and distribution of popular music was halted for extended periods in full view of the American public.[1]

Very much in the public eye or, rather, ear and eye, was the Swing Era. During the years of the basic shift from sheet music to the phonograph record, popular song was carried by a new vehicle. This was the swing band, which not only brought the publishers' new songs to a growing audience at home but got that audience out of the house to listen to and dance to those bands. Beginning around 1935 but already on the scene at the beginning of the decade, the swing band swept across the nation's social and geographical landscape, filling the airwaves and the phonograph records with its sounds.

Radio Sustains the Music

The 1920s, a happy time for the young pop stream, ended in the stock market crash of 1929, tipping over the publishers' three-legged money

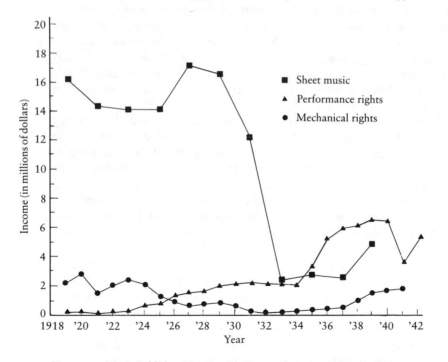

Figure 4-1. Music Publishers' Income (1918–1942). Source: See Notes, Chapter 4, note 2.

stool. Figure 4-1 shows the dramatic changes in the publishers' three sources of income between the two wars.[2] Sheet music sales, which had produced almost 90 percent of their income, plummeted from over $16 million in 1929 to about $2 million in 1933. Sheet music would never return as either the dominant material form of the pop stream or its primary money source. The publishers' glory days were over.

The phonograph industry was almost wiped out by the crash of 1929, further reducing the "mechanicals" share of the publishers' income. Performance rights fees had already surpassed the "mechanicals" fees and by 1935 were the largest slice of a much reduced pie. No wonder the publishers and ASCAP were fighting mad at the radio industry. Not only were the broadcasters resistant to every ASCAP demand, but they were preparing an even greater threat, the creation of a pool of music independent of ASCAP's control. For the rest of the 1930s, radio's golden goose became the target of ASCAP's efforts, generating struggles that affected all of show business.

Throughout the 1930s, radio was growing steadily. The number of American households with a radio increased, on the average, about 10 percent annually during the decade, continuing the strong growth that had begun in 1920.[3] Although the number of AM radio stations did not increase to any appreciable extent during this period, the need for fresh music, live or recorded, was unabating. How that music was to be made and delivered was decided by the outcome of several continuing struggles among the parties involved.

The phonograph and recorded music industries became major actors in those decisions as they recovered from their near demise. The major companies of the 1930s, RCA Victor, Columbia, Decca, and Brunswick, with little history of creatively bringing performers and songs together, soon learned the hit-making game. The first innovation that brought the record industry up from ground zero was Decca's decision in 1934 to record top entertainment names on disks priced at thirty-five cents, a radical reduction from the seventy-five cent record of the other major companies. The Kapp brothers who ran Decca, still unfamiliar with the practices of the publishers' song plugger, relied for sales mainly on newspaper and magazine advertising and the jukebox.

With the repeal of Prohibition in 1933, the automatic coin music machine revived. Jukeboxes instantly appeared in the newly opened bars, taverns, and roadhouses, which needed an inexpensive source of entertainment. From a low of 25,000 operating in 1934, their number had increased to an estimated 500,000 in 1940, having overflowed the bars into ice cream parlors, bowling alleys, skating rinks, and so on.[4]

The jukeboxes purchased a significant number of records; estimates range as high as 60 percent of the total American output in 1938, declining to only 15 percent in the early 1950s.[5] In spite of this impressive share of recorded music, the jukebox did not break new tunes. It made money, not hits, even though the issue was hotly debated in the trade press, especially after the giant and totally unexpected hit, the "Beer Barrel Polka," came out of the jukeboxes in 1939.[6] The reason jukeboxes could not make hits was simple and important. The jukebox was only an instrument of *exposure*; it could not *exploit* a song. The publishers knew that simply exposing a tune once or twice was not enough; they had to implant the song into the ears, mouths, and feet of its several audiences. With the strategic and persistent work of the songpluggers, those audiences would soon find it essential to acquire some of those implanted tunes. Even though it was routine to place a "plug" record in as many jukeboxes as possible and in the most desirable slots on each machine, these efforts would not come close to the effectiveness a song plugger could achieve on radio or from live bands.

The trade press, keeping track of these developments, began to report on the rising importance of the phonograph record in the pop stream. In addition to editorial coverage, *Billboard* gave the new trend full recognition. When a new market is judged large and stable enough, and its transactions are cash and in public, at some point it gets a chart. Since 1931, in the front of the paper, there had been a Music section containing a chart for sheet music sales and another showing the extent of exposure through radio plugs. In January 1936, *Billboard* initiated a listing of each week's "10 Best Records for Week Ending . . .", a list provided by the leading record companies. This chart, however, was placed in the "Amusement Machines (Music)" section at the *back* of the paper, not in the regular music pages.

The existence of two music departments accentuated the chasm between Tin Pan Alley and radio on the one hand and the phonograph record-jukebox complex on the other. No one saw the necessity to connect them, and the publishers could not see any way of converting the massive *exposure* capability of the jukebox into a directed and selective *exploitation* mechanism. It would take the disk jockeys, flourishing after World War II, to unite the two parts of the hit-making process. By then, however, the effort was mainly in the service of the record companies rather than for the publishers.

At each of the strategic assemblage points on the way to the pop stream's current structure, the trade press announced the changes in the relevant markets and technologies and introduced new charts where appropriate.

The Performers Want Their Share

By the mid-1930s, band leaders and rank and file musicians, recognizing the importance of the phonograph record, attempted to gain their share of that growing pile of dollars. Inadvertently, they paved the way for the rise of the singer-songwriter and, ultimately, rocknroll.

There were two main episodes. One began in 1936 when band leader Fred Waring successfully sued the independent Philadelphia radio station WDAS for playing his recordings without permission. His legal claim stated that the performer has a common law property right in the *unique rendition* of a musical composition. The suit arose after Waring was paid $13,500 by a network for an hour's live broadcast. The contract was exclusive; he was to play for no one else. Yet it cost the radio station WDAS only seventy-five cents for a copy of Waring's phonograph record, of which he received a few cents per record sold.[7] Clearly, this extreme cost differential could not be justified by the superior sound quality of live versus recorded music. Waring's suit was simply to protect his exclusive contract with the more lucrative network and its higher advertising rate structure, which was threatened by the low-cost, independent stations' unauthorized use of his music.

There was, though, another consideration for Waring. Perhaps two to three thousand bands during that period were vying for a limited number of dance hall dates, broadcast opportunities, and recording contracts. A band leader's major strategy was to develop a distinctive sound for the band, a unique style. Thus Waring was not just protecting his artistic creativity, he was defending his commercial signature.

With his court victory in hand, Waring founded and led the *National Association of Performing Artists* (NAPA), enlisting band leaders and arrangers, mainly in the East. The members assigned their rights as performers to NAPA, which, in turn, licensed radio stations to play their members' records for an annual fee, much in the same way music publishers assigned ASCAP the right to collect performance rights royalties. NAPA lawyers drafted a new addition to the copyright bill, seeking a way of giving legislative strength to the admittedly weak legal basis for performers' rights.[8] Finally, NAPA sought to extend the outcome of the Pennsylvania case to other states, an enterprise that met only limited success.

NAPA's whole enterprise was wrecked with the suit Paul Whiteman brought against the owners of the independent radio station WNEW on grounds similar to those Waring had used. An appeals court swept aside his victory, and in December 1940, the Supreme Court refused to review the decision. The Whiteman case was dead, and, along with it, the movement for performers' rights—at least for a decade.[9] Performers were simply unable to realize a separate legal hold on their contribution to a song's recorded rendition.

The immediate effect was to remove another barrier to the use of phonograph records on radio. NAPA was not to become another ASCAP. Radio station managers, particularly small, independent ones, were now free to play as many records as they pleased at practically no cost. As a result, the radio stations drew closer to the record companies as they increased their programming of recorded music. These friendships between local record distributors and station personnel formed the skeleton of the system that would later carry the pop stream's hit game out of New York and into cities all across the country.

The long-term consequence of the defeat of performers' rights was the rise of the singer-songwriter. In the pop stream initially but also in all other streams, a song's creator and performer were soon likely to be the same person. If the performer could not find a legal basis for earning anything from his or her unique, interpretive version of a song, the next best thing, the *only* thing, was to become the copyright holder as writer, composer, or publisher, or as all three. The institutional basis for rock-n-roll's strong reliance on the singer-songwriter clearly lay in this earlier failure of performers to secure a property right in their performance.

A second battle waged during the performers' search for their share of the music dollar was the 1938 attack by the American Federation of Musicians (AFM) against *all* mechanically reproduced music. This resistance was a reversal of the union's earlier position. From 1900 until the late 1920s, musicians' employment had expanded as a result of increasing sales of phonograph records for home use. They also benefited from the expansion of the silent motion picture. Thousands of musicians found steady work in movie theater pit bands. When the talking motion picture appeared in 1928, however, the situation changed. The leadership of the musicians' union became convinced that mechanically reproduced music now threatened their livelihood.

The phonograph record industry was too weak and held no treasure for a union lawsuit. The movie industry was too strong to attack. So, the AFM, under the fiery leadership of James Caesar Petrillo, took on the broadcasters.[10] After threatening a strike, the AFM in 1938 negotiated contracts first with the network affiliates, then with the independent stations. Both were to increase spending on staff musicians. Both, however, were allowed unlimited use of electrical transcriptions (a sixteen-inch, acetate phonograph record containing multiple musical selections, used only in broadcasting facilities). This retreat from the union's earlier threat to ban the use of all recorded music turned out to be of no import, because the electrical transcription soon gave way to the individual phonograph record as the technology of choice.

One part of the settlement was to have consequences beyond anyone's imagination. The 162 independent stations that grossed less than $20,000 (in the year 1937) were exempted from the above conditions; thus, fully *half* of all non-network stations, or almost a quarter of the seven hundred AM radio stations, were freed from the necessity of using live music.[11]

They were allowed, even encouraged, to rely entirely on the reviving record industry. The small, independent radio station became thereby, the laboratory that incubated a new strategy of broadcasting and a new way of teaching the radio audience the "hit game." The experiment interspersed extensive programming of popular records with local (rather than national) advertising spots, tying the whole together by the "personality" of the staff announcer. Only after World War II would the full impact of this strategy be realized in the rise of the disk jockey.

That 1938 settlement by Petrillo inspired the National Association of Broadcasters (NAB) to remake itself as a stronger and more representative organization. By that time, it had included almost two-thirds of all stations in the nation, divided into fifteen districts, each represented on the board of directors. It chose its first fulltime president, Neville Miller. The executive committee and the other committees of the NAB, moreover, were representative of the entire range of station types, large and small, network affiliate and independent, all on a nationally dispersed grid.[12]

The Formation of BMI

By 1938, then, the music publishers had endured five years of low sheet music sales, with no sign of an upturn. Recorded music was on the rise but still not yielding very much. Radio's growing profits were the only target. ASCAP top negotiators prepared for battle, and so did the broadcasters. The new directors of the NAB advised their new president "that he consider copyright as his number one task." Miller replied, "The NAB will try to avoid trouble and controversy. We intend, however, to assume an aggressive attitude in the defense and prosecution of our legal rights."[13]

The expiration of the contract between ASCAP and the broadcasters was 31 December 1940, two years away. Each side began to mobilize. The music publishers were not the only ones eyeing the broadcasters. Early in 1938, the trade press reported on the preparations by several other parties. Three of the radio industry's major contracts were to expire in 1940: those with ASCAP, with the American Federation of Musicians, and with the American Federation of Radio Artists (AFRA). These three groups differed in strength and in the nature of their demands. Separately, each was a formidable adversary. The thought of concerted action by all three was a nightmare for the broadcasters. The common date of their contract expirations, though inadvertent, invited joint action, and throughout the two years prior to that moment, there were rumors, flirtations, and, on occasion, serious attempts at joinder.

The radio industry responded to this triple deadline by choosing ASCAP as its primary target. After legislative action in Washington failed to produce any results, the NAB made a fateful decision. It tried, for a third time, to bypass ASCAP altogether by creating its own pool of music for radio. It fell to the young CBS attorney Sidney Kaye to design a system that would provide radio stations with a continuing source of new popular music, independent of and competitive with ASCAP. The system he constructed was based on a previous NAB study and an analysis of its two earlier attempts (both unsuccessful).[14]

The broadcasters' preference was for a per program or even a per piece rate as opposed to a blanket license; they wanted a "measured service," one in which they could immediately and accurately count the amount of music used. That system is just what they got. The keys to success, Kaye concluded, were money and organization. Both of these elements were needed to create a supply of music, to discover and publish new musical talent, to strategically acquire some established publishers with a catalogue familiar to radio audiences, and, finally, to remunerate the writers and publishers lavishly enough to win their continued loyalty.

The 1939 NAB convention unanimously agreed and accepted the creation of Broadcast Music Incorporated. "BMI," as Kaye's new system was soon called, was wholly owned by the broadcasters and funded initially at a level of $1.5 million; $300,000 was given in cash with the rest to be paid by individual stations licensed to use BMI music. In this fashion, the radio industry entered Tin Pan Alley. BMI assembled a large staff to do exactly those jobs a major New York music publisher would do. Sidney Kaye was its operative head as vice president and general counsel.[15]

After pointedly ignoring BMI's birth and early growth, ASCAP presented its terms for contract renewal in March 1940. E. Claude Mills, the shrewd negotiator for the music publishers, proposed a few minor adjustments for most radio stations but dropped a bomb on the networks. Under Mills' terms, most stations were to be charged 3 to 5 percent of their *net* income plus modest sustaining fees, while the regional and national networks were to be charged 7.5 percent of their *gross* income. This last item was the new move. Not only did the proposed fee schedule have the political potential of dividing the recently united broadcasters, but it made good economic sense for the music publishers. As *Billboard* bluntly put it:

ASCAP . . . learned a lot when the Federal government was conducting its network monopoly probe. At that time revenue of the nets was $58,000,000 and that of the indies at $30,000,000. The performing rights Society, is is said, came to the conclusion that it would obtain no more money from the independents.[16]

Up to this point, many broadcasters, even Kaye himself to some extent, had considered BMI a mere bluff, but, with this ASCAP proposal poised like a dagger at the throat, BMI extended and intensified its efforts. It first secured the performing rights to several important catalogues, including M. M. Cole of Chicago (mainly hillbilly and cowboy songs) and Peer International (also largely southern music), then leased the catalogue of the respected New York publisher, E. B. Marks. Kaye then stepped up the pressure on the individual stations to replace ASCAP music with BMI-licensed tunes. He explicitly urged stations not to use ASCAP songs. The networks requested band leaders to program non-ASCAP music. "When this request was practically ignored, one of the networks flatly required as a condition for broadcast, that remote bands must schedule some non-ASCAP music during their show. No compliance, no pickup." [17]

The federal government reentered the scene with a *criminal* case against ASCAP and, to everyone's surprise, a *criminal* action against BMI, along with the two major networks, NBC and CBS. The charges against all the parties included illegal pooling of copyrights to monopolize supply, discrimination against non-member composers, illegal price fixing, and illegal restraint against member composers in their right to bargain for the sale of their own music. In spite of these attempts to get the parties to accept a consent decree on the civil antitrust suit pending against ASCAP and the equivalent one binding BMI, and in spite of last-minute efforts by external mediators, nothing stopped the train.

On the first of January 1941, almost all the broadcasters closed the switch on ASCAP-licensed music. The ban lasted ten months, during which time several crucial events occurred. The first and most important was actually a nonevent; that is, there were no complaints from the public nor from the advertisers about the absence of ASCAP music. It was a case of "out of sight, out of mind" rather than "absence makes the heart grow fonder." [18] The broadcasters had to replace only a small number of songs. In 1938, only 2 percent of all the ASCAP songs were played on the air, and these constituted fully half of all performances aired that year. In other words, just a few songs were repeated many times over. [19]

The second event that occurred during those ten months was that ASCAP and BMI made their peace with the federal criminal cases, both agreeing to conduct their business under a consent decree. In the course of that settlement, ASCAP's much discussed "self-perpetuating" board was shorn of its power to elect its own members. The entire general membership would carry out the vital task of allocating the society's income in the future, based on formulae that were not so heavily weighted in favor of its senior and inactive members. This step was a small but definite one in favor of granting financial reward to new songs rather than to old ones.

ASCAP won the day, however, with its brilliant tactical contract with the Mutual Network, signed on the eve of the NAB's annual convention. The terms of the nine-year agreement granted ASCAP 3 percent of Mutual's gross receipts for the first four years in return for a blanket license and 3.5 percent thereafter, until the termination of the contract in January 1950. By a close and ambiguous vote, Mutual's 170 affiliates approved the network's contract.[20] This agreement drove a wedge into the solid front of the broadcasters, exacerbating an already inflamed cleavage between Mutual on the one side and NBC and CBS on the other. The reason for this rift was the long-awaited congressional antimonopoly *Report on Chain Broadcasting*, which treated the two major networks quite differently (and more harshly) than Mutual (more on that report later).

The tactic worked. Soon after the shattered St. Louis NAB convention, the noise and fight went out of NBC and CBS. They signed nine-year contracts, giving the Society 2.75 percent of their *net* receipts, the same rate to be applied to each of their affiliated stations. Mutual's fees were soon adjusted downward to match the other networks. Peace was announced; everyone had survived.

BMI was now, however, a stronger component of the music business, concentrating on its mission as performance rights collection agency. It did so in a way crucially different from ASCAP's system. ASCAP, it will be recalled, had created over the years a Byzantine formula by which its board divided its earnings ($6.5 million in 1939) overwhelmingly in favor of its older and established members. The lion's share of the Society's rewards were given out for past rather than present achievement. BMI, having no past, had to make a virtue of the present. Its payout was based, therefore, entirely on the number of current performances of every song.

By February 1941, BMI had in place a system that scientifically sampled the music played on all the radio stations in every state of the nation, network and independent, large, medium, and small.[21] BMI's ability to measure the moving contour of the nation's musical life restored peace and profit to radio and had several profound effects that prepared the way for rocknroll. First, BMI's 100 percent payment for current performance, in sharp contrast to ASCAP's rewards to songwriters of the past, tipped the pop stream toward the creation of new songs. Songwriters were spurred on by the unmistakable returns of employment and cash. New songs flooded the markets in great numbers. The speed of the hit game accelerated. The need for more musical material pushed both publishers and record executives to search beyond the usual sources in the pop stream. Among the more exotic places for that search were the two adjacent commercial streams, country pop and black pop.

Second, BMI paid songwriters for a far wider range of performances than did ASCAP. Live *and* recorded performances on radio were treated equally, as were performances on network *and* independent stations. These extensions of performance rights payments gave the entire music industry a longer economic arm into the entertainment business. More importantly, they gave the small, independent radio station a greater chance at making a hit out of a popular song. This ability had been pretty much limited to the network stations, but BMI's placement of the phonograph record on an equal footing with a live performance allowed the small station to plug a record to the point of making it a hit. Recorded popular music of every stream was thereby stimulated. This expansion began to make the phonograph record the major and *common* unit for all the streams, making it easier for a song to move from one stream to another, a fact whose consequences would be far-reaching.

Third, the *national* sampling frame that BMI used to track performances, in contrast to ASCAP's centering on New York, moved the pop stream beyond the Hudson River, and not simply to Hollywood. By extending the reach of the music business into almost every city, BMI opened the pop stream to creative resources beyond what could be found in the New York musical guilds. Black pop, country pop, and the three smaller streams were the beneficiaries. Every local station across the entire country became a potential origin for the making of hits, increasingly defined as a hit *record*.

Advertising and Radio: What Is a Program?

With the costs of radio music stabilized, the question of who was to pay those costs and how the music was to be organized came to the fore. In the late 1930s, the answers were framed by the advertising agencies, who had achieved an augmented role in programming. One of the leading principles of radio had been to maintain as close a connection as possible between the program and its sponsor, in the belief that whatever the audience liked about the program would rub off onto the product.

Full sponsorship of an entire "program" by a single advertiser was the operative schema, requiring three separate program participants. One was the announcer, a station employee, who steered each program through the daily schedule. He introduced the second person, the one who read or sang the commercial messages. This second person was mainly the sponsor's creature, hired by the ad agency, or was a station employee receiving a special "talent fee." The third person was the performer, either the star of a dramatic show, the comedian, the band leader, the solo vocalist, or the news commentator.

Over the decade, the drift was toward skipping the announcer and the commercial reader and simply allowing the performer, the *star*, to deliver the commercials. This schema could take place, obviously, in two ways. One was to persuade an already established star to become the products' spokesman. The other was to elevate the announcer or commercial reader to "star" or at least performer status. There were difficulties with both of these solutions. First, most star news commentators wouldn't sell products on principle and most entertainment stars didn't need the work or demanded too much money. Second, it was difficult to make a star out of the ordinary announcer, especially when there was no program content to which his or her talents could be applied.

New ways to connect program content and commercial messages were tried. One of the most consequential was to move the announcer closer to the program content.

Like hitchhikers and cowcatchers, radio pluggers are gradually being merged into the shows on which they peddle. . . . Today instead of being vocal entities, they are absorbed into shows as actors whose selling job is an integral part of the programs. Advertisers today are laying cash on the line for more than just plain selling before the mike. [T]hey ask for sales spiels created as a production within a production, geared so that while the show delivers the audience, the pitch, in the tempo of the show, delivers sales.[22]

This job description turns out to match that of the disk jockey, the name of precisely that amalgamation of station announcer, commercial salesman, and star personality. His emergence had been prevented by the advertising agency practices, which paradoxically forbade the linkage of program content to commercial message. It had also been blocked by the hierarchies of radio jobs, which held the announcer to technical tasks, and by network practices that took music programming out of the station's hands. Music selection was either turned over to the ad agencies for commercially sponsored shows or to the collaborative publisher's song plugger and band leader for sustaining shows. Beneath all this maneuvering was the still operative belief that the music publisher, not the record company, was the creative source for popular music. Yet, as the record men took over, they formed a natural and easy working relationship with the men who would become the disk jockeys of the postwar era.

The advertising fraternity was also puzzling out the related question, "What is a program?" Since radio's inception, a program was a *block* of uninterrupted time during which the content—news, drama, variety, or music—was presented to an audience. The commercial messages preceding and following were meant to be assimilated into the "credits," that is, into the opening and closing announcements as in a movie's introductory credits or in the theater's playbill. In radio's case, the credits included a reading of the show's producers, performers, and sponsors, and the station's call letters. The midshow commercials on radio were also readily assimilated into the time-honored tradition of the "intermission" (which, in the theater, was actually a "commercial" for the audience, their tailors, dress designers, and hair stylists). These before-, midpoint-, and after-commercial interruptions, still defined as a *break* in the show's main content, were, at worst, tolerated because the sponsor, after all, paid for the show. At best, they could be seen as providing familiar breaks separating a program's subunits, for example, the succession of acts in a play or the sequencing of each performer in a variety show.

As network radio grew to achieve huge, nationwide audiences, the practice of attaching additional brief messages both before and after the main commercial messages in a sponsored program also expanded. Generically, these were called "spot" commercials and received more specific designations, "hitchhiker" and "cowcatcher," depending upon where they were placed in the program. The term "spot" had been used as early as 1929.[23] The networks were eager to sell that air time; the purchaser could "barnacle" his message at lower cost to the program's expensive ship. Not everyone agreed to such practices. The objections were partly financial and partly aesthetic. The "hitchhikers" and "cowcatchers" were clearly not organically connected to a program. If, however, a "program" could be so defined as to include any brief commercial message, then all would be integral components and the program could transfer its magic to all the products. The disk jockey show was to do that job, merging performer with the commercial message, yet at the same time delivering a series of independent sales messages without "sponsoring" a program. Country- and black-oriented stations would follow the pop stream in this use of radio. All six of the streams would draw closer together as the recorded song became the dominant and shared unit under the guidance of the disk jockey.

The Federal Attack on Broadcasting

As radio's internal structure was clarifying, the political debates of the nation reached into broadcasting. The mood was set by the Roosevelt administration, which was turning towards the labor movement as its main ally. That partnership required a renewed assault on the "economic royalists," who were preventing national "recovery" from reaching its targets of full employment and full production. The antitrust guns were reloaded and aimed at selected targets. One of these was the broadcasting industry.

Franklin Roosevelt had an additional reason for this particular target. Most of the nation's newspapers had campaigned editorially against him in the 1936 presidential election. Since a considerable number of these newspapers owned radio stations, he was determined to wound two birds with one stone, to attack the monopolistic nature of radio and to take political revenge on the newspaper owners.

James L. Fly, newly appointed chairman of the Federal Communications Commission (FCC), delivered the final *Report on Chain Broadcasting* in May 1941, a scholarly, statistically bristling 153 pages of smoothly persuasive argument against "chain," that is, network, practices. It brought NBC and CBS executives to their feet in a rage. The Mutual Network smiled and approved.

The report ordered, first, the breakup of NBC's two-network system, claiming that NBC simply used its Red and Blue networks for its own monopolistic purposes. It took NBC two years, but in 1943 its Blue Network was sold to Edward J. Noble, founder and owner of Life Savers.[24] It became the American Broadcasting Company (ABC), headed by Mark Woods, a veteran RCA company man who had risen from junior accountant to NBC vice president. The new ABC network chose the commercial rather than the cultural strand of its NBC heritage. Its philosophy was neatly expressed at the FCC hearings by its new President Woods: "We are in the advertising business, gentlemen, and that business is the business of selling goods to the American people."[25] This attitude was still operative during the 1950s when rocknroll disk jockeys were still on network programs.

The report's second target was CBS, even though its recommendations here applied to all the networks. CBS, in contrast to NBC and Mutual, had maintained the "option" of preempting local programming at any time. CBS claimed that the network concept would collapse without the right of the network to deliver its programs when it deemed fit. The FCC, initially opposed to this egregious example of "chain" control, compromised. It divided the broadcast day into four time periods, within which the network could exercise its option for up to three hours of programming.[26] This arrangement protected the prime evening hours for network programs, which, naturally, the affiliates and the network both wanted. It freed morning and afternoon time periods for local programming. After the war, many network affiliates would find those earlier time slots more lucratively filled with popular phonograph records than with network soap operas.

The report next targeted CBS's and NBC's domination of two adjunct services: the manufacture and distribution of electrical transcriptions and the management of talent agencies. Though it took several years and much creative corporate reweaving, both NBC and CBS shed both these services. NBC's talent agency became the independent National Concerts and Artists Corporation (NCAC). CBS divested itself of its concert bureau, instantly acquired and headed by the ubiquitous Arthur Judson without missing a beat. CBS's artist bureau was sold to MCA (once *Music* Corporation of America, subsequently *Management* Corporation of America). The result of these changes was a more comprehensive national market. MCA, not restricted to a New York broadcasting perspective, used its newly enhanced stable of performers to accelerate the trend toward widely dispersing entertainers to appearances in cities throughout the nation.

One further outcome of the *Report on Chain Broadcasting* was of inestimable importance to rocknroll. Its commissioners expressed the view that the best and most desirable corrective to "bigness was small-ness," recommending that

there is an important function to be served by the smaller local stations. The Commission should continuously strive to improve the technical efficiency of such stations and, within the limits of the Act, afford encouragement to broader economic opportunities for such stations. This should not be attempted by the destruction or impairment of existing services. There is room for both.[27]

This proposal would come to fruition after the war in the FCC's policy on granting new licenses, a policy that would eventuate in the appearance of a new force acting on all six streams of American popular music, that of the small, independent, local radio station.

A final ironic note: There was not a single mention in the *Report on Chain Broadcasting* of newspaper ownership of radio stations. Franklin Roosevelt would have to find his revenge elsewhere. But at least one bird was wounded.

The Rise and Fall of Swing

During the 1930s, as radio created a new set of family audiences and the phonograph record became more important, a dance audience began to revive. Both white and black young people turned to swing for a new set of dances, termed "jitterbug." The story, told many times, of how jazz leaped over its boundaries to infuse the pop stream with an explosive resurgence is sketched here only in its main contours.[28]

Swing included the "hot" bands, which were more serious about their jazz commitments, as well as the "sweet" bands delivering more polite fare in the pop stream traditions of the 1920s. The New York publishers had no difficulty accommodating both types; they were able to make sure every band had at least one vocalist, reflecting the publisher's belief in the power of the lyric in selling songs. The rise to prominence of Bing Crosby, Tony Martin, Dinah Shore, Billie Holiday, and Ella Fitzgerald may have begun in front of a band, but these performers soon became stars in their own right. It was the hot swing band that was the center of attraction, however.

This fourteen- to seventeen-man band (plus vocalists) evolved from two existing models. One was the white popular dance orchestra, of which Paul Whiteman's in the 1920s was the major model. Its descendant and successor from 1929 onwards was the Guy Lombardo Orchestra. This raw and hungry group of musicians was brought to New York in that year by Jules Stein, founder and maximum leader of Music Corporation of America (MCA). Guy Lombardo soon became the leading presence in the pop stream. Stein, erstwhile eye physician and creator of one of the most energetic band-booking agencies in the Midwest, was an imaginative strategist. He had moved the Lombardo band from its origins in Ontario, through Cleveland and on to Chicago, and then, finally, to New York in 1929 with the purpose of breaking that town wide open.

He did just that, first by placing Lombardo in the Roosevelt Grill in the Roosevelt Hotel.[29] He then arranged for three remote broadcasts a week over CBS's flagship station WABC. The Lombardo brothers soon enjoyed a commercially sponsored program, a record contract, and their own publishing firms. From the start, they had the full and unstinting allegiance of New York's batallions of publishers and their song pluggers. By the 1930s, the brothers' opinion was more than a pro forma matter; it was standard procedure for publishers to call upon the Lombardo aggregation with a "black and white" (the simplest form of the sheet music) for a first verdict on the tune's chances. The Lombardos' blessing and plugging never hurt. The band stayed at the Roosevelt for thirty-four years (retiring in 1963), surviving every trend and style in the entertainment business.

The other source for the swing bands were the black jazz bands, a large and diverse group that included Jimmie Lunceford, Chick Webb, Cab Calloway, Lionel Hampton, Andy Kirk, Earl (Fatha) Hines, the durable Jay McShann, classically ambitious Duke Ellington, and Count Basie. Willard Alexander, one of Jules Stein's young talent scouts, was especially interested in bringing jazz into MCA's fold. He was alerted by John Hammond, Columbia Record producer and jazz aficionado, that Basie's band, then working in Kansas City, was both hot and movable. Alexander arranged to bring Basie to New York where, even with changing personnel, it became an instant success, an exemplar of a jazz band with broad popular appeal. Basie played to live audiences at the tiny Fifty-second Street club, The Famous Door (named for its larger counterpart in New Orleans' French Quarter), and recorded studio jam sessions for Columbia and other labels. These extended musical excursions by small combos formed an important link in jazz continuity, connecting the prewar and bop generations.[30]

Between Guy Lombardo and Count Basie, both highly visible success models at each end of the pop stream's dance band spectrum, there arose a large cohort of young, innovative, and highly energetic bands who sought those same successes. The abundance of these bands was due in no small measure to increased phonograph recording.

Even more important, perhaps, was the construction of a national tour network consisting of one-nighters in the major cities from coast to coast and in hundreds of smaller towns as well. These one-night-stand tours were the invention (or reinvention) of Jules Stein, who, along with three or four other major booking agencies, forged an enormously expanded dance hall industry all across the nation. The end of Prohibition in 1933 stimulated this kind of entertainment. Hundreds of young bands were thus creating the new swing form of jazz and educating young audiences for a dance music that spanned the spectrum from "hot" to "sweet."

These audiences for swing were almost entirely racially segregated, North and South, reflecting the pattern of the time. There may have been only one Hollywood and one Tin Pan Alley, but there were two sets of movies, dance halls, dance bands, record stores, and even radio programs, one for whites, another for blacks. The musicians' locals were still segregated by race, and few if any bands were mixed, though gradually the black wing of the jazz stream found a small place in some swing bands. In the main, however, it was the black musical contribution rather than its personnel that crossed to pop.

The swing era burst into full public life in the summer of 1936 with Benny Goodman's sudden and unexpected triumph in Los Angeles. This young, classically trained clarinet player was nurtured musically in the Chicago white jazz tradition. Goodman had played to a Princeton audience in 1929 with a pickup band of Chicago, jazz-oriented sidemen, resolving then to have his own band and to do his own kind of music. Over the next half decade, he paid his dues in every venue possible, recording with all kinds of musicians, white and black, including Bessie Smith in her final sessions.

In 1934, with the encouragement of John Hammond, Goodman organized his first band. His ten-man outfit aimed for and soon achieved a distinctive sound. It was a mixture of the rough Chicago white jazz tradition, the orchestral riches of the big black pop orchestras via the simple and swinging arrangements and originals of Fletcher Henderson (the template for Goodman's subsequent arrangers), and the driving but classically tinged Jewish schmaltz of Goodman's clarinet. After a disastrous start, Goodman won a slot at the Roosevelt Grill where Guy Lombardo, ironically, had recommended the new Goodman band as his first choice for summer replacement in 1934. Neither the dinner crowd to which the band was assigned nor the management was prepared for the pace and the decibel level. The band was fired (with two weeks notice) on opening night for the important NBC network show, "Let's Dance." [31]

MCA, though booking mainly "sweet" bands, immediately took on Benny Goodman as a hedge against the slowly rising tide of white, jazz-flavored sounds. A month's engagement was arranged for the spring of 1936 at Los Angeles' newly opened Palomar Ballroom. The desultory reception the Goodman band received on their one-nighters along the way across country hardly prepared them for the explosion produced on their opening night at the Palomar. Goodman recounts that, after an hour of easy sweet tunes, he called on the strongest Fletcher Henderson arrangements, and the band unleashed its hottest.

To our complete amazement, half the crowd stopped dancing and came surging around the stand. It was the first experience we had with that kind of attention, and it certainly was a kick. That was the moment that decided things for me. After travelling three thousand miles we finally found people who were up on what we were trying to do, prepared to take our music the way we wanted to play it.[32]

It is an important and puzzling fact that the audience at that moment split into those who danced and those who gathered at the stage to listen. This cleavage would remain and ultimately be implicated in the destruction of the swing era. (The same split would reappear with similar effects late in the rock period.) The band was a smashing success and filled the huge Palomar every night of its extended engagement.

The next engagement call came from New York, where full success rained down upon the Goodman band. They had a long engagement at the Pennsylvania Hotel (with a "wire" of course). They were asked to appear in a movie, *The Big Broadcast of 1937*, co-starring with the improbable cast of Leopold Stokowski, Bob Burns, and Martha Raye. They replaced the Casa Loma Orchestra on the prestigious network radio show, "Camel Caravan." They even doubled their assignment with appearances at the Paramount Theater, doing five shows a day to apparently limitless, enthusiastic audiences. They toured, doing one-nighters, and they recorded in the studio.

The floodgates were now open. Swing bands appeared everywhere. George Simon's authoritative book, *The Big Bands*, lists about 450 nationally recognized bands, most of which flourished and died in the short span between 1935 and 1946.[33] The configuration of the dance band quickly standardized itself: four saxophones, three trumpets, two trombones, and rhythm section of piano, guitar, bass, and drums, plus vocalists. This standardization immediately generated the need for some kind of marginal differentiation among the bands. One mark of distinction came from the excellence of the bands' sidemen. Many achieved name recognition and visibility as they moved from band to band. Another difference was in the self-conscious adoption of gimmicks, stylistic trademarks, and distinctive theme songs such as Shep Field's "Rippling Rhythms" and Kay Kyser's "College of Musical Knowledge." The basic distinction remained between "sweet" and "hot" bands, even though a few tried to have it both ways, such as "Swing and Sway with Sammy Kaye."

The swing era infuriated partisans of polite music (and polite society), who railed at the crudeness, the noise, the incomprehensibility, the danger and degeneracy of that "Negroid" trash. To the jazz purists, especially the defenders of the New Orleans traditional style, swing was commercial pap, a collapse of genuine, hot, improvisational creativity.[34] These indictments foreshadow the comparable assaults made on rocknroll. It should be noted that, although swing had a huge following among the young, it was not totally age graded; adults were participants and fans as well.

The hot and sweet dance bands of that era reached their audiences through every entertainment medium. Swing was on network radio via live sustaining and commercially sponsored shows; it was on independent radio via records. Swing was *on* the movie screen (there were dozens of pictures built around name bands); it was *in* the movie houses, often as the feature attraction of the stage show in the big downtown combination houses. It was in the Broadway theater, and it was in the concert halls.[35]

Swing spilled into country pop, appearing as "Western Swing," with Bob Wills and his Texas Playboys as the leading exemplar. The instrumentation of Wills' band evolved from a six-man, all-string group (guitars, banjo, fiddle, string bass) in the early 1930s to a fully horn, reed, and percussion swing band (still with Wills' fiddle) in the 1940s. He was a relentlessly "uptown" musician, repudiating the cowboy and country designation even though incorporating Mexican and local German flavoring: "Our music was never country music. 'Country and Western' is an inappropriate term, in my opinion. I can't think of a country artist we ever listened to. . . . We listened to Benny Goodman, Glenn Miller, Louis Armstrong and Bob Crosby."[36]

Much of country pop, including Nashville's Grand Ole Opry, did, however, resist the pop stream's penetration via the swing dance band until late into the war. Roy Acuff, a major anchor of the Opry, repudiated the Western Swing tradition as vigorously as Wills did the "country" tag. The Nashville establishment fought all and any pop (or black) incursion; "there will be no drums nor horns" on the Grand Ole Opry stage, they told Wills.[37]

If there was a peak moment for swing, having swept to supremacy in the pop stream and having dominated the network radio schedule and recording roster for five years, it occurred during the giant battle of the bands held in New York's Manhattan Center on 18 November 1940. Twenty-eight of the top swing bands, white and black, kept a packed house alive from eight in the evening to four in the morning in an updated version of the great "cutting" contests in the old New Orleans tradition.[38] The audience's favorite that night, Jimmie Lunceford's band, was commanded by the enthusiastic crowd to deliver several encores, even though the band had hardly ever appeared at the top of the polls in *Esquire, Down Beat,* or any other fan or trade publications. The event was a great outpouring of the swing spirit, but it was nearing its end.[39] It may have been past the end, for earlier that year *Variety* had reported under the headline "Swing Knocked Itself Out":

Swing—in the ear-bending style that had been generally associated with the word for the past several years—is nearing extinction. . . . What probably will eventually be evolved . . . will be a white man's style of swing retaining the Negroid bounce but coupling it to more respect for the melody. . . .[40]

It was especially cruel that Goodman's leading audience, the college crowd, voted with their feet. They walked out and wrote the strongest obituary, as reported in the trade press.

The new Artie Shaw and Benny Goodman aggregations have been received with magnificent apathy. Therein may lie some testimony as to the perpetuity of once great heroes. For swing, as they once played it and as evidenced by "Sing, Sing, Sing", the greatest swing record ever cut, is but a memory in wax.

A few still hang on, mulling over sax rides and analyzing Chicago and Dixieland styles. . . . But as far as the general record buying student is concerned swing is as obsolete in bands as the banjo.[41]

The decline of the hot swing bands is a puzzle. Why did the dance-oriented part of the swing audience, always requiring new dance steps, fail to replace the shag (the main, swing-engendered dance step)? With no successors, the vitality in dance for swing froze.[42] The paradox was that even while the swing bands were assisting the record companies in their triumph over the publishers, they themselves were losing their popularity.

The Hit Machine Destroys Itself

During all these events, the music exploitation system itself was headed for dissolution. The transition from the vaudeville and cabaret days to song plugging via radio broadcasting of dance bands had been made with ease. Just as the publishers had subsidized vaudeville, so too had they paid for the wire costs required for remote dance band pickups to the networks. There was nothing new or different about this practice, nor was it any great departure for the band leader to be "cut in" as joint author of a plug tune in return for extensive air play. It was even common procedure for publishers to establish firms and pay ASCAP membership fees for band leaders "to build up a royalty nest-egg that they can look to when their hey-day as bandsmen are over."[43]

It was not these practices per se, but their cumulative impact on the economics of the music industry that made the difference. As long as song plugging was a means to sell sheet music, its cost efficiency could be measured against sheet music sales. But, by the late thirties, it was clear that piano sales were not going to recover and that sheet music income for publishers was on a permanent decline. Phonograph record sales were improving, so "mechanicals" income to publishers were on the rise, as was the performance rights income ASCAP collected from radio. Regardless of the source of income, *exposure* of a song on radio was essential. Song plugging, still carried out mainly via the remote dance band pickup, became the main event.

Soon the tail began to wag the dog. It was easier to get plugs on the radio than it was to sell sheet music. The *Billboard* chart keeping track of these plugs was the main guide for the New York music world. Song pluggers were now paid according to the number of top plugs they secured, not on the basis of sheet music sales. It was this logic that impelled *Variety* to report this example of self-defeating behavior in early 1938:

16 Tunes in 21 Minutes

Publishers who still think that the major function of their business is to sell sheet music are decrying a practice which has made itself particularly evident among the bands picked up by NBC from out of New York. . . . It has become no uncommon thing for an orchestra to do as many as 18 tunes in 15 minutes even though some of them are of the once-over-lightly sort and are tossed in so that some song plugger can help his firm make a showing on the weekly recap of the most played tunes on the networks. . . .

This practice of going after the instrumental chorus only, some of the indie pubs have warned, is what will destroy the sale of sheet music completely within the next five years if not sooner. . . . The plugs pile up in huge number . . . but when an analysis is made of them it is found that the percentage of vocal renditions, which serve as the only stimulant for sheet sales has been negligible.

Meanwhile the constant pounding away at the melody . . . has produced a feeling of surfeit for that particular tune even before the lyrics have had a chance to insinuate themselves with the listeners, with the result that the publisher has no alternative but to drop this song and start working on another.[44]

The older members of ASCAP were alarmed at this situation, warning that the "present method of paying off largely on performances has produced an unhealthy condition not only for the music industry but for the future of the American Society."[45] The established publishers thereupon reduced the dollar value of a radio plug, hoping to diminish the song pluggers' efforts. It only stimulated them. The song pluggers themselves sought relief from the treadmill by getting *Variety* and *Billboard* to stop listing tunes in order of the number of plugs received. That strategy didn't work either. The next attempt to slow song plugging was to differentiate in the listings between plugs on sustaining programs and those on commercial programs, as well as between those with vocals and those with just instrumentals. Another attempt was to include daytime in the reported hours, thus reducing the impact of night band remotes. These measures didn't cure the disease either. Singers complained that they no longer had any control over their material; their instructions were just to deliver the plug and forget the artistry. Band leaders continued their demands for compensation for plugs.

The publishers suffered further blows. Their access to late night sustaining remotes was being closed down as commercial sponsors bought those programs and selected their own music. Then the phonograph record companies refused to cooperate with the publishers' attempts to increase the "mechanicals" statutory fee of two cents per side. Playing one publisher against another, they continued to pay rates fixed early in the 1930s, in spite of the record industry's growing prosperity. This general situation further deteriorated throughout the war years. The tide was turning. By the 1940s, the music publishers and their song pluggers realized that radio exposure, whether on the late night remotes or on prime time commercial shows, was being supplanted by an outlet that could make hits without network exposure, that is, by the local broadcasting of recorded bands.

It was into the hands of the record companies' A&R (Artists and Repertoire) men that the future of popular songs had fallen. The place to be was across the desk from these creative directors in the major record companies, a place hated by the majority of traditionally oriented publishers and feared by the song pluggers. It was now the record company's creative director, the A&R man, rather than the publisher, who initiated the new entries into the pop stream.

Publishers are bound to toy with the notion that maybe their professional staff is too big and unnecessary, so why not concentrate on getting the right kind of records made up by the right artists and pfui with all else. . . . If you can wine and dine the maestri because they control that precious air time . . . then why not use the same tactics on the wax executives for the sake of that equally lovely disk exploitation.[46]

It would take the publishers some time to discover that, in addition to the A&R man, the disk jockey was soon to become the key instrument for exposing the wares of the pop stream to the public.

The trade press, *Variety*, *Billboard*, and *Cash Box*, kept a close watch on these developments, trying to make sense of an industry noted more for foulness of tongue than for quickness of thought. By 1940 it was clear that *Billboard*'s phonograph record treatment had to be expanded, and on 27 July of that year, *Billboard* presented its new "Music Popularity Chart."

The major characteristic of the feature was, in actuality, its two pairs of charts. The first pair compared the listing of records exposed via jukeboxes—"Records Most Popular on Music Machines" (moved from the back of the magazine)—with the outcome of that exposure—"Best Selling Retail Records." The other pair placed the "List of Songs with Most Radio Plugs" (exposure) adjacent to "Sheet Music Best Sellers" (outcome of that exposure).[47] The status of the phonograph record as rival to sheet music was explicitly recognized. *Billboard* treated both with an even hand, now offering equal space to each.[48]

What the War Did

World War II finished the job on the pop stream that show business had already started: It dispersed its hit-making machinery. The four-year ordeal from Pearl Harbor on 7 December 1941 to V-J day on 15 August 1945 touched every aspect of American life, creating for most people an unprecedented break in their lives. All cultural resources were challenged to provide new meanings appropriate to the change, meanings still set within familiar frameworks.

The popular music industry's response rarely reached a very high level of reflection. Soon after the first spastic reaction to Pearl Harbor, which produced a rash of jingoistic songs, heavy patriotic songs became too chancy for live bands. In *Variety*'s formulation, "the bands ducked fighting songs because they found the public generally wanted complete escapology while terping."[49] It was the more personal themes of loss and loneliness, of fidelity and hope, that shared the wartime catalogues with up-tempo dance and novelty tunes. In radio, theater, movies, and jukeboxes during the entire war, no part of show business deserted the highly conscious and public rhetoric of "win the war" and "everything for the boys."

The movement of people was unquestioningly the most pervasive and important fact of the war years. It was the greatest mass migration the country had ever seen. Over fifteen million civilians crossed county lines in pursuit of jobs or family. The crowding, the scarcities, the uncertainty, and, above all, the disruption of the familiar placed a heavy burden on the expressive culture the migrants brought with them or found in strange locales. Even more difficult were the transitions experienced by the ten million men and women in uniform by the summer of 1943, "... piling in at the rate of 100,000 a month. The steady, inexorable transmutation of civilians into soldiers—or sailors or Marines—did more to disrupt the familiar contexts of life on the home front than any other aspect of the war."[50]

As the novels and movies of World War II have shown in endless variation, the enforced, close-quarter mixing of America's youth, while disrupting familiar ties, also created new ones. Country boy met city slicker; college kid met working-class lad; married and single men learned a little from each other. Jewish boys had a hard time with redneck noncoms. Black soldiers (and especially black sailors) had it hard from everyone. Still, the powerful hold of small group solidarity in the squad, the platoon, or the company was able to bridge the differences between most soldiers.

The transformation of the civilian youth into the soldier affected the families at home as well. The emotional focus was on "the boys," "just kids out of school," mysteriously altered by the uniform and by removal from their grownups (except for the even more freighted brief furloughs and leaves). This wrenching carved into American consciousness the cleavage that would widen after the war into the "generation gap." It took several years and some strange excursions to manifest this gap, however. Just as World War I produced in its wake a heightened awareness that separated the young from the adult, so, too, did World War II.[51]

There was also concern over the younger ones left at home. Lurid reports of juvenile delinquency, of "zoot suit" riots and "victory girls" in large cities and around military installations, replaced the usual prewar diagnoses of poverty and parental neglect. New remedies appeared, including the much ballyhooed "teen canteen" program organized and supported by the jukebox industry. Throughout the entire war, *Billboard*'s "Amusement Machine (Music)" pages were filled with stories about the success of this or that city's canteen program, where boys and girls gathered for sanitized fun and danced to their favorite tunes fed by "free" nickels. Whatever the causes or the cures, the term "teenager" entered the American vocabulary as the name of trouble.

Along with that association, though, came the recognition of teenagers as a potential market. One of the most important discoveries in that regard harked back to the 1930s when *Mademoiselle* magazine, specializing in younger women's interests, showed the fashion industry how to subdivide its market by age. The "teen-age" segment was strategically differentiated from the more inclusive "junior" category during the war.[52] By the end of the war, teen radio, magazines, fashion, and other products were rapidly becoming merchandising giants. Kids were independent, tough, and, above all, different from adults. They were building their own culture, including music and dance.

All six streams of popular music experienced comparable dislocations as their boundaries were breached by new audiences, new performance settings, and new demands on their sharply curtailed material and personnel. The military draft took away musicians and their leaders.[53] Musicians and audiences were both under the same severe travel constraints. Even more than usual, entertainment clustered in the population centers, a situation that instantly produced a flood of new clubs and cocktail lounges. Small combos appeared everywhere, staffed largely by musicians and vocalists from disbanded orchestras. This trend toward small musical groups was so vigorous that *Billboard* opened a new section in its pages to highlight and cover its developments.

These small units, working all across the musical spectrum from country to jazz, found larger audiences than their local lounges and honky-tonks could accommodate, mainly through the radio broadcasting of phonograph records and electrical transcriptions. The small combo, typically piano, bass, guitar or clarinet, and vocalist, generally performed without the heavy reliance on arranged scores characteristic of the large swing band. This type of instrumentation and the freer playing style influenced the song repertoire towards more individualized, more intimate vocalized material and more loosely improvised ensemble performance styles, approximating the traditions of the jazz/swing trio or quartet.

Working in a small listening (not a dancing) space, these groups evolved the styles that were to be further developed after the war. These styles ranged from bop and cool jazz, to the small country band such as backed up Elvis on his first records, and to the solo folk performer with guitar.[54] This common thread of small units in different streams educated the industry (record and radio managers particularly) as well as audiences. Both could see and thus learn to accept the overlap and exchanges of personnel and musical languages among the different streams.

The war also had some indirect effects on the entertainment world. Advertising agencies, fearing that wartime curtailments of consumer goods would remove the incentive for advertising (as it had in World War I), successfully fought to sustain the IRS ruling in 1941 that advertising expenditures were a deductible business expense (thereby avoiding the newly enacted wartime excess profits tax). This ruling stimulated American industry to dump a huge fortune into advertising.[55] The shortage of newsprint during the war deflected a major part of the advertising dollar into radio. Radio advertising almost doubled during the war; expenditures for such rose from $195 million in 1942 to $390 million in 1944.[56] This enormous dollar volume naturally enhanced the power ad agencies held over programming. After the war, they put that power to use in ways that encouraged the independent radio stations to include more and more phonograph records in their programming.

The musicians' union was also affected by the war. Not only were its members vulnerable to the draft, but, as AFM President Petrillo endlessly repeated, the expanded use of records on radio and jukeboxes spelled imminent catastrophe for musician employment. The actual AFM membership figures belied his stated fears, however, leading some observers to speculate later that Petrillo's goal was simply to tap recorded music's enormous money reservoir, as ASCAP had done.[57] Nevertheless, the early war years were hard times for dance bands because touring became so difficult. Tires were hard to get, gasoline was rationed, and prices for food and board were ruinous.

The AFM, having no statutory or judicial legitimation for its demands, used its only weapon, raw trade union strength. The tactic Petrillo favored was a ban on all phonographic recording. With full support from the rank and file, the union began a two-year strike in July of 1942.[58] Columbia and Victor feared that if they succumbed to the union's demands, their parent network broadcasting corporations would be the next target. They held out, at great loss, for more than a year after Decca (the third largest record company) signed in September 1943, as did almost one hundred smaller labels.[59]

Petrillo finally triumphed, defying practically every organ of government, judicial, legislative, and executive, including the personal intervention of President Roosevelt himself. A Musicians Unemployment Fund was established, garnering about $4 million a year. The recording ban, described as an economic disaster, was, in fact, not that severe a blow to the major record companies. Most had stockpiled records sufficient to keep the labels' and the performers' presence before the public. Also, the wartime curtailment of shellac for phonograph records (a necessary ingredient largely imported from India) would have cut back production in any case.

There were other consequences more long lasting, however. Because the recording ban was for instrumental music only, vocalists, especially small groups of singers, were allowed to record and did so, stimulating the ascendency of singers during the war years and beyond. Another result was that shoestring operations either took the risk of ignoring the AFM to produce "bootleg" records or quickly signed with the union. This occurrence was especially prevalent in the black pop stream, which was given a boost and thus positioned for a great postwar expansion.

The jukebox also fed and nourished black pop and country pop. *Billboard* reported during the war on the dramatic increase and steady demand for "hillbilly" and "race" records on jukeboxes everywhere in the nation. This demand fed, quite neatly, the needs of the new BMI publishers for new music. The trade press also responded to this new market. On 24 October 1942, *Billboard* expanded its coverage of the black pop stream by introducing "Harlem Hit Parade," a listing of the ten best-selling black pop records in Harlem, as reported by some of the leading record stores. *Billboard*'s announcement of this new chart was accompanied by a notice that the listed records would be aired by a local disk jockey on his regular evening show (fig. 4-2).

A few months earlier, on 28 February 1942, *Billboard* had extended its coverage into the country pop stream by including a column (not a chart) on "American Folk Records." This folk category was a mixed bag, with no clear distinction between country pop (still called hillbilly), the real folk stream, and gospel (called "Spirituals"). Several years earlier, beginning on 5 August 1939, *Billboard* had listed a brief, even simpler, version

TRADE SERVICE FEATURE

The Billboard's
Harlem Hit Parade

Following list of most popular records in Harlem is based on sales reports from Rainbow Music Shop, Harvard Radio Shop, Lehman Music Company, Harlem De Luxe Music Store, Ray's Music Shop and Frank's Melody Music Shop, New York:

1. **Take It and Git**
   Andy Kirk
   Decca 4366

2. **Trav'lin Light**
   Paul Whiteman-Billie Holiday
   Capitol 116

3. **Mr. Five by Five**
   Freddie Slack
   Capitol 115

4. **Stormy Monday Blues**
   Earl Hines
   Bluebird 11567

5. **I'm Gonna Leave You at the Outskirts of Town**
   Louis Jordan
   Decca 8638

6. **When the Lights Go on Again**
   Lucky Millinder
   Decca 18496

7. **Don't Get Around Much**
   Four Ink Spots
   Decca 18503

8. **Let's Be Friends**
   Lil Green
   Bluebird 8895

9. **Every Night About This Time**
   Four Ink Spots
   Decca 18461

10. **Just as Though You Were Here**
    Four Ink Spots
    Decca 18466

Figure 4-2. "*The Billboard*'s Harlem Hit Parade, which makes its debut in this issue as a regular weekly feature, will be aired on Sid Torin's WHOM record program every Thursday night from now on." From *The Billboard*, October 24, 1942, p. 25. © 1942 BPI Communications, Inc. Used with permission from *Billboard*.

1. A new weekly column feature
AMERICAN FOLK RECORDS
COWBOY SONGS
HILLBILLY TUNES
SPIRITUALS, ETC.
News notes, reviews, best nickel-puller recommendations of records of the type of songs which often make money for you. You know how much the Going Strong, Coming Up, Possibilities and Week's Best Releases listings in the RECORD BUYING GUIDE have helped you buy the kind of popular records that make money for you. This new column will help you in the same way with Cowboy, Hillbilly and Country records.

Figure 4-3. *Billboard*'s American Folk Records. *The Billboard*, February 28, 1942, p. 67. © 1942 BPI Communications, Inc. Used with permission from *Billboard*.

of this column: "Hillbilly and Foreign Record Hits of the Month." Given the diversity and still inchoate market structuring of this category, understandably there was no way to rank relative sales strength as there was in the more developed markets (fig. 4-3).

These black pop and incipient country charts were the first steps in bringing those streams into contact with the pop stream. The phonograph record was the technological basis for that convergence, but it was the hit game and the trade press' scorekeeping that knitted the streams together.

As the war unfolded, the outcome of the invisible struggles between the performer and the record company versus the songwriter and the

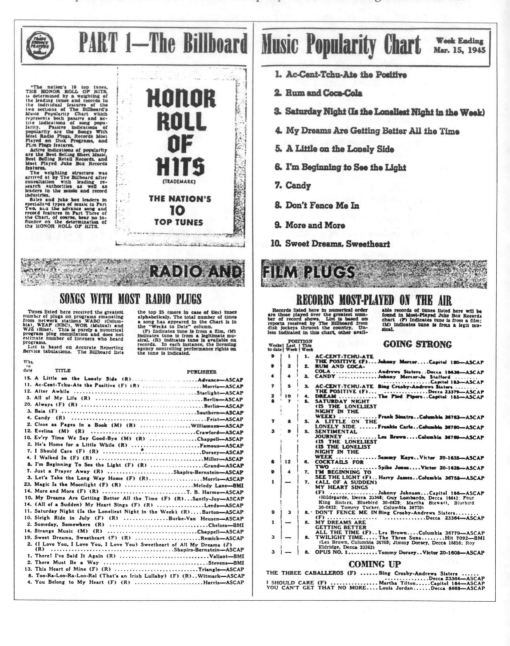

Figure 4-4. *Billboard*'s Pop Charts, March 24, 1945, pp. 16–17. © 1945 BPI Communications, Inc. Used with permission from *Billboard*.

publisher were undecided; tune and record vied for dominion. *Billboard* tracked the battle, serving the industry's need to assess every indicator of the hit game. Its music charts show this unresolved state of affairs quite clearly. On 24 March 1945, a new chart appeared, shrewdly sidestepping a decisive choice between tune and record. It was the new "Honor Roll of Hits" (fig. 4-4).

An authenticated tab of music popularity based upon weekly surveys of every known practical indication of public tune yens . . . so that the "Ten Leading Songs" may be presented each week to the industry and professions to which the music department of *The Billboard* is a vital business guide.[60]

The "honor roll" was an explicit amalgamation of five charts. Two charts assessed exposure: "Songs with Most Radio Plugs" and "Records Most Played on the Air." The latter was a new chart listing records selected by a sampling of disk jockeys throughout the country. It was placed next to the older "Songs with Most Radio Plugs" to emphasize the equivalence of both exposure charts. Two other charts measuring the outcome of that exposure: "Best Selling Sheet Music" and "Best Selling Retail Records." In its first appearance, the latter chart (the lower of the two) contained a nice Freudian slip. Instead of reading "Best Selling Retail Records," it read "Best Selling Sheet Music." The fifth chart was the still useful "Most Played on Juke Boxes" chart. Implicitly, the honor roll was a compromise between the importance of tunes versus that of records. For the reader who needed a consolidated summary of music popularity, the honor roll held the answer. For the moment, *Billboard* was calling the battle between tune and record a draw.

Within a few years, the issue would be resolved with the full victory of the record, carrying the record companies, its producers, technicians, and performers into the next series of transformations. As with most important changes in popular music, the losers still survived. Harmony between antagonists was proclaimed, and the music publishing interests continued their routines. Their interests in the catalogue, with its three sources of income, thrived even as the main action shifted to the phonograph record. Only a few more pieces had to be constructed after World War II for the system to prepare for rocknroll, only a half dozen years away.

PART TWO

ROCKNROLL EMERGES: 1945-1965

5. Redesigning the Machine:
The Disk Jockey Takes Over

In December 1946, within a single month, eight of the nation's top bands broke up—Benny Goodman's, Woody Herman's, Harry James', Tommy Dorsey's, Les Brown's, Jack Teagarden's, Benny Carter's, and Ina Ray Hutton's.[1] Almost a decade later, in January 1956, Tommy and Jimmy Dorsey, the hosts of CBS-TV's "Stage Show," introduced Elvis Presley to a national television audience for the first time. The first of those events, the breakup of the bands, marked the end of swing band era as clearly as the closing of Storyville in 1917 ended the glory days of New Orleans jazz. The second event marked rocknroll's introduction to an adult mass public over the gravestone of one of the thirties' last real bands. Between these two events came ten years of building that new stream from the inside out and the outside in.[2]

This chapter reviews those ten years, concentrating on the disk jockey, the emergent instrument of the pop stream's hit-making machinery.[3] During this period, the presentation of the hit game over AM radio became the major way the pop stream reached its several publics. The success of those efforts invited country pop and black pop radio programming to do the same. The three smaller streams joined the system shortly thereafter with their own disk jockeys.

Collectively, the disk jockeys were the midwives of rocknroll. Some claimed full paternity, most notably Alan Freed, others denied rocknroll's very existence and were forced off the air by their hostility to teenage musical tastes or by underlying racial attitudes. A large proportion of pop stream disk jockeys simply couldn't understand or accept rocknroll because their own musical tastes and sense of artistic integrity were formed during the swing era, with its inescapable linkage to the exalted jazz pantheon.

Postwar Music Developments

At war's end, the entire broadcasting industry—networks, individual stations, hardware manufacturing subsidiaries, and the full array of retail outlets—decided that the moment for the commercial exploitation of FM radio and television had come, but marked for even more immediate delivery were radios and phonographs. As a whole, the nation's entertainment complex was preparing for new markets and new technologies after the war; the public was eager to receive the cultural and material fruits of victory.

In home music, the threefold contest between the radio, phonograph, and piano had been reduced to a two-way contest. Although the piano did not lose its respected place in American cultural life, it never recovered its power in bringing music into the home. Radio was the immediate victor. Ninety-five percent of American households had at least one radio in 1949. By 1954, 70 percent had two or more radios, a third of the homes having three or more. This multiple set ownership reflected the concentrated efforts of the set manufacturers' trade association, which had launched a vigorous campaign to put "A Radio in Every Room."[4]

Further, in their attempts to dampen or obviate altogether the competition between radio and the phonograph, many manufacturers combined the two into one piece, making two versions, one for the adult market, one for the kids.[5] The "classical" musical repertoire on twelve-inch records (either as a single record or more often a set of multiple, twelve-inch records, generically called "packaged" product by the trade) was to be played on expensive turntables mounted in the large, radio-phonograph console. These were not only "the finest musical instruments . . . ever built," according to the advertisements, but were designed to look like a piano or organ. They were even named "Hepplewhite" or "Chippendale" to appeal to the buyers' image of the console as an expensive, "classic" piece of furniture.

The inexpensive small radio and radio-phonograph played popular music on ten-inch, single records. With more or less deliberateness, the broadcasting industry was creating a two-tiered market in the radio and phonograph fields, with a parallel differentiation in recorded music. This marketing decision harked back to the distinction between "teen" and "juniors" fashion. Young people neither wanted nor could afford the high-priced radio-phonograph consoles. The advertisements for inexpensive radio-phonograph combinations therefore emphasized a youthful setting for the product, typically a home dance party.

In 1948, the continuing competition between RCA, with its subsidiaries NBC and Victor Records, and CBS and Columbia Records entered a phase that would deepen the split between adult and youthful musical practices. The competition could be called the "battle of the speeds." The question was over which new system would prevail. Would the winner be Columbia's new vinyl, twelve-inch, 33 1/3 rpm, microgroove long playing (LP) record (introduced in June 1948) or RCA Victor's seven-inch, 45 rpm record (also unbreakable plastic, with its large 1 5/8-inch center hole), presented to the public six months later?

RCA offered the public a range of prices for its new apparatus. At the top end was the redesigned radio-phonograph, retailing from about two hundred to six hundred dollars. At the bottom end was the small, plastic, $12.95 record player that could only play the 45 rpm records. It was this machine that was probably the single most important piece of technology facilitating rocknroll's appearance.

The *Billboard* ad of 4 June 1949, placed by RCA Victor (see figure 5-1), illustrates the wishful thinking of the industry, but also its inadvertant prescience as to the subsequent joinder of the several streams. The little 45 rpm record player is shown, literally, as the way to bind together all the RCA artists into some kind of a whirling, unified program of listening. From the pop stars Perry Como and Tony Martin to country and western singer Hank Snow, from the rhythm and blues performer Jesse Stone to jazzmen Dizzy Gillespie and Illinois Jacquet, all would come together musically via the 45 single and its wonderful player. This blending did happen, but not as advertised. Rocknroll would begin to do it, however, five years later, gradually bringing all these musical streams together, "mixed" by the little machine.

Manufacturers soon were delivering a product line that included all three speeds (78, 45, 33 1/3), either in self-contained phonograph sets or as separate elements for the rapidly growing "components" industry.

But what music could be put on these lengthened aural carpets? At this stage, that is, around 1948, the popular record producers had little idea about what to do with that extended time on the record, except to string together a series of three-minute tunes that would form a plausible program for listeners. Thus the first generation of popular albums contained either songs by a single artist, a collection of specialized ethnic or season songs, dance music (often South American), or even theme songs of the different big bands of the thirties and forties. The surviving dance bands and their singers comprised a major share of the LP repertoire, as did musical scores from the movies and Broadway shows. The clearest illustration that there was little, if any, new popular music being explicitly done to utilize the greater uninterrupted time on an LP record was the heavy marketing of "mood" music, such as Montovani's Strings, Jackie Gleason's "Music for Lovers," and the like.

The album and the singles markets diverged. (A brief attempt to combine the two speeds was made in the EP "Extended Play" record, which

Figure 5-1. RCA Victor Record Ad. *The Billboard*, June 4, 1949. © 1949 BPI Communications, Inc. Used with permission of *Billboard*.

contained three or more songs on each side of what looked like a 45 rpm record. The experiment was effectively dead by 1962.) The split in the market occurred because the two presentational forms were tied into two different exploitation systems. The popular single was initially exposed to the record-buying public through the jukeboxes and over AM radio, almost all now guided by the nation's disk jockeys. The album had no such accepted radio format at that time. Although the entire repertoire of classical music was being poured into the LP format, the public's main exposure to popular music on albums was at the record store via point-of-purchase display and some sparse newspaper and magazine advertising. It was, consequently, a slower, less responsive system, tied to the exigencies of the turbulent retail marketing world and to the corridor politics of the record companies.[6]

The Disk Jockey: His Industrial Base

The new impresario and master tactician of popular music, the disk jockey, came into prominence during the transition years of the 1950s, the very moment when the debris of the swing era was being swept away. The disk jockey's job had been evolving out of the station announcer's position since the 1930s.[7] After the war, with the rise of the record company as the leader of the pop stream, the disk jockey and his three-part job was a crucial figure. First, he was an on-air salesman. Second, he was a radio station performer. Third, he was the musical master of ceremonies. Though the disk jockey's individuality was the key to his personal success, it is the strategic placement of his job that made him so important to the music world.

As air-salesman, the disk jockey's boss was the sponsors, who paid him directly or indirectly to deliver the goods. And the amount of goods moved was large and increasing. The total radio advertising budget rose over 300 percent from $157 million in 1940 to $492 million in 1955.[8] This growth continued even during the time that television was attracting advertising dollars at a much faster and higher rate. Radio's strong performance during these competitive years, while network programming was being virtually abandoned, was due primarily to the growth of local advertising, with some increase in national spot advertising. As network advertising declined from almost half (46 percent) of radio's total advertising in 1940 to less than a tenth (9 percent) in 1956, local radio advertising doubled its share (from 29 to 61 percent). This change in advertising required that someone persuade local merchants to have their products sold over the air. In hundreds of towns and cities across the nation, the disk jockey on the local radio station was that person. In so doing, he was providing a new viable medium for local advertising.[9]

Local advertising rested on the personal touch of the local salesman, since the high-powered production facilities used in national network commercials were neither available nor economic for the local advertiser. The disk jockey as salesman provided that sense of intimacy, not only for the town's used car lot or furniture store but also for the smooth transitions between the highly produced and polished jingles for Coca Cola or General Electric. The local radio air-salesman thus became a distinctive and familiar voice in contrast to the impersonal and polished style of national commercials.

The large number of disk jockeys necessary to handle this greatly expanded volume of local advertising reflected the rapid expansion of local radio stations, which mushroomed immediately after the war. This expansion was not simply a market response to the search for investment opportunities for pent-up capital, though broadcasting was, indeed, a favored target for investment ("a license to coin it," as many observed); rather, the expansion of radio stations was in considerable measure due to deliberate government policy. The promise of the 1939 *Report on Chain Broadcasting* had been fulfilled. Small and independent stations were to have their day. When the FCC ceased licensing new stations in 1940, there were 813 authorized AM stations. In the first few years after the war, the number of stations authorized more than doubled—from 943 in 1945 to 2127 in 1949. Thus, after 1946, the small, independent station, the type empowered and encouraged to program current phonograph records, became the fastest growing entity in radio and, by 1948, was the most numerous kind of station broadcasting to American audiences. A continuing but slower rate of increase brought the number of AM stations to almost 3000 in 1956, as shown in figure 5-2.

AM radio's growth brought local stations to almost every city in the country. Given the economics and politics of broadcasting, it was no surprise that the small, independent station became the postwar meteoric star of the broadcasting industry. They had the most experience with recorded popular music, and, as television became the main evening "family" entertainment, AM radio increasingly filled the *rest* of the day with recorded popular music. Radio and pop records in the years after 1948 became practically synonymous.

Moreover, this growth of local radio changed the competitive situation. In the years before and during the war, each radio station beamed its programs to a market area averaging approximately sixty thousand radio sets. By 1948, the average audience for each station was cut in half. The competitive battle was waged not just against television but also between radio stations. It is not surprising, then, that both station management and the disk jockeys themselves saw radio as a cutthroat business that required strong personalities. As the disk jockeys' second em-

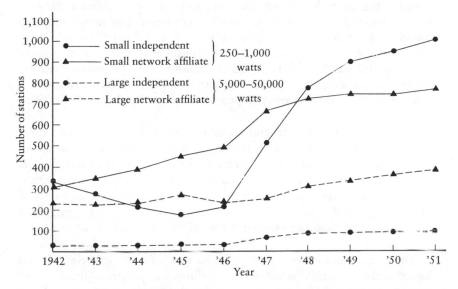

Figure 5-2. Growth in AM Radio Stations (1942–1951). Source: *Radio-Television Yearbook* 1942–1951.

ployer (advertisers being the first), the radio stations were persuaded to give considerable leeway, recognition, and high levels of compensation to their "personality" stars.

The music industry was the disk jockey's third employer, and like the other two, it paid for services rendered. The terms of that exchange were ultimately determined by the sales volume of phonographs and records. There was, in 1945, a sudden spurt in both phonograph and record sales. From 1946 through 1954, however, record sales remained quite stable, although equipment sales experienced a more rapid expansion. Then, between 1954 and 1956, record sales doubled, far outstripping equipment sales. It was during these latter years, I believe, that the disk jockey, standing at the confluence of the advertising, radio broadcasting, and popular music industries, manifested the successful solution to the marketing problems of all three trades.

The Disk Jockey: Working Strategies

For the advertising industry, the disk jockey opened local markets to nationally advertised and marketed products. More importantly, regional and local firms could, through the disk jockey, advertise efficiently in their own area. For radio broadcasting management, the disk jockey was a logical and lucky invention. It allowed a mode of programming that spanned the entire broadcast schedule, gathering and differentiating its diverse subaudiences within its flexible confines. The music industry found in the disk jockey a driver for its new and powerful locomotive. The scope of these interlocking opportunities was summed up breathlessly by *Billboard*: "America's 2,400 stations, with perhaps twice that many disk jockeys, playing a total of 127,000 hours of recorded music a week give the music industry a promotional outlet unique in its long history." [10]

As salesman, personality, and hit-maker, every disk jockey, with varying degrees of awareness and with varying amounts of freedom to do so, constructed an approach that emphasized one of the three parts of his job. The other two parts were still handled, of course, but with less commitment. These strategies were made up of the same basic elements of radio programming that had emerged in 1920 with the first commercial broadcasts and that had evolved for a quarter century of network and independent radio.

The three basic elements were to define a target audience, select certain hours of the broadcast schedule, and delineate appropriate musical and advertising fare. Identifiable groups of people, that is, listened to radio at specific times of the day and night, and they had definite musical preferences. That simple understanding, shared by advertisers, radio managers, and the music industry, had developed into a set of operating rules different for each of the disk jockey strategies.

The sponsor's imperative was to reach a buying audience, the prime members at that time being middle class, married white women between the ages of twenty-five and forty-five. This group controlled the family dollar for the repetitively purchased items: food, drink, tobacco, cosmetics, and home maintenance products. These women were also crucially involved in the purchase of consumer durables, from toasters to automobiles. The man of the family, however, could not be ignored in these big ticket items and thus had to be included in the buying audience. Housewives could be reached after the family left for work and school and before they returned home. Thus the hours from 9 A.M. to 3 P.M. were prime for targeting the sponsor's audience. Of course, the man had to be reached in the morning at home, on the road to and from work in the car, and at home once again before, during, and after dinner. The appropriate music for this predominantly female and adult audience was thought to be the currently popular records. These were to be interspersed with a large number of hits from the past, recalling the real or imagined "good old days" of high school or college, the days before diapers, house cleaning, isolation, and other joys of married life. The ability of the sponsor's disk jockey to thread enough "oldies" into the fabric of current hits to draw an audience with purchasing power, while including enough new records to teach them the hit game, determined his unique appeal, identification, and success.

The disk jockey identifying with the radio station had a different approach. The radio station's definition of its target audience was not defined in status or behavioral terms but in sheer numbers. The broadcasters wanted the *largest* audience it could get. The larger the audience, the higher the station's rate card. It was just that simple. The "personality" of the disk jockey was believed to be the best instrument for building that maximum audience.

The content of that personality was and is, of course, mysterious. It could be wrapped in a smooth, sophisticated manner; it could be "folksy" and comfortable; it could devolve upon a strong and distinctive quality of speech. It need not be a sunny personality; a biting tongue and blunt candor often seemed to win popularity. Examples of the latter include Arthur Godfrey and Henry Morgan, who were both radio disk jockeys in the 1940s before they began their television careers.[11] The majority of disk jockeys who sought to emphasize this part of the job, however, did so in a safe manner, with sunshine, humor, and diversion. They applied, to a fault, the wisdom of honey versus vinegar as flycatcher, avoiding the darker side of everything.

The "personality" disk jockey was likely to use popular music in a different way than did those emphasizing the sponsor. The music was subordinate. It had to fit into radio's lore; the music should get the folks out of bed in the morning, keep them cheerful but not overwhelm them by being too loud or too fast, lift their spirits later in the day, and soothe them at night. It was important to keep things familiar and attractive but not necessarily locked into the context of the hit game. The disk jockey himself and his personal musical tastes were the main attraction. His desired airtime was generally in the morning, preferably from 6 A.M. to 9 A.M., or from late afternoon to early evening, these hours supposedly collecting the largest and most diverse audiences.

Finally, there were the disk jockeys who marked out their career paths in line with the needs of the music industry. They were committed to the systematic exposure and the active exploitation of new releases, the creation and nurturance of a record-buying audience. They organized and mobilized that audience for live, out-of-home dances and performances, presented visiting recording artists, discovered and managed new talent, and even managed and sponsored live pop music shows. In short, they performed the entire impresarial job, a balancing act of considerable risk.

In addition to the normal uncertainty of winning and holding an audience, the hit-making disk jockey put his reputation on the line every time he tried to make a hit out of a new record. It should be recalled that this formative period, from the mid-forties to mid-fifties, witnessed a gradual increase in the sale of popular records. By the early 1950s, the rate of production was up to a rate of two hundred per week. In 1953, *Billboard* estimated, however, that only four out of every hundred records released ever made the charts, not very attractive odds.[12]

The successful hit-making disk jockeys, in the face of these risks, soon devised a set of techniques to minimize the dangers of guessing wrong and to maximize the rewards of being right. The key was to identify the right audience and to select the airtime most likely to reach them. The most identifiable characteristic that distinguished those interested in popular music was age. Young people bought most of the popular records. They knew and cared the most about the music and its performers, and they influenced the rest of the family.

"Young people" were thus the "leading audience," the "opinion leaders" of the pop stream. Although post–high school young working adults and college students were included in the "young" audience, high school students were its most homogeneous and easily reachable part. The logical and most desirable time slots for the hit-making disk jockey, therefore, were primarily after school hours, from about 3 P.M. to the dinner hour on weekdays and to a lesser extent evenings and Saturday morning.

The "young marrieds," the mature adults, and even the older folks were treated as the "following" audience, that is, they were less responsive to advertising appeals and to new records, but, if reassured by friends or family, they acted. Radio broadcasters believed that the separate programs of the full broadcast day had to progress as a seamless whole. The tastes of leading audiences and following audiences, both in music, entertainment, and consumer preferences, were thus presumed to be basically the same; consequently, all those different audiences could be served by a single station that moved through the daily schedule meeting everyone's interests. For the music industry especially, it was believed that "leading" and "following" audiences required each other. Together they made the hit game possible. Even as radio lore began to acknowledge that young people participated in the pop stream more than older people, the music of that stream was the same for young and old alike.

The age differentiation in musical taste is dramatically shown in a table from the radio research of the day (1947).[13] It shows the evening musical programming preferences of adult Americans, stratified by their age and their educational attainment. Out of the twelve types of programs that were reported in the full table, four were musical: popular and dance, semiclassical, classical, and hillbilly and western.

The table states the story simply and clearly. Only the preference for popular and dance music depends on age but not on education. That is, at each of the three levels of education, younger people like popular and

TABLE 5-1

Evening Music Preferences by Age and Education

	College (%)			High school(%)			Grade school (%)		
	21–29	30–49	50 years & over	21–29	30–49	50 years & over	21–29	30–49	50 years & over
Popular and dance music	66	50	29	68	56	32	56	45	29
Semiclassical music	55	48	50	28	36	36	14	20	25
Classical music	53	50	61	21	27	36	15	21	24
Hillbilly & western music	10	8	19	24	22	20	42	39	38

SOURCE: P. F. Lazarsfeld and Patricia Kendall, *Radio Listening in America* (New York: Prentice-Hall, 1948) p. 136, Appendix table 14.

dance music. For the other three types of music, age is essentially irrelevant; schooling is what determines preferences. This data support the belief that classical and hillbilly fans are culturally homogeneous; their musical preferences are resistant to age-grading. The lack of a category for black popular music in the table reflects the minimal presence of that stream on radio at that time. The implications of these findings for radio programming were simple and acted upon. Insofar as the station wanted the *largest* audience, then popular music was the safest course, for it was preferred by a mixture of age and educational categories, maximizing the sheer numbers of people listening. Of equal importance, a popular music policy simplified the ability to program throughout the broadcast day given the succession of age groups.

These, then, were the three main strategies that the disk jockeys evolved. It is difficult to estimate how many disk jockeys carried them out in their pure forms during the decade following World War II, but there were enough, certainly, to influence the rest. Most of the rest, in fact, remained staff announcers, though as many as could do so adopted the new name, disk jockey. The very existence of the disk jockey was important at that time because the founding theory of radio broadcasting had been rendered inoperable. That theory had harkened back to David Sarnoff's basic questions: What is a program? What is a schedule? The answers had been that a program is short, presenting as few units as possible, such as a song or two, a small episode of a continuing story, or a single idea in a short talk. The schedule was a compilation of such brief units, assembled into a day-long mosaic. There was no difference between the morning, midday, and the evening; the schedule could have been played in reverse.

Only gradually was there any differentiation through time, yielding the morning show, the housewives show, and the early evening program. The shows got longer as the commercials got shorter. The guiding idea, though, was that the radio audience was a whole, a unity. There was indeed a rhythm for the day and the week that required modulations of tempo and pace, but essentially the American family at their sets at home, office, factory, and automobile was homogeneous and adult, listening to everything whenever it was presented.

The postwar expansion of radio sets and radio stations rendered that basic theory unusable. Differentiated tastes emerged, and they were sovereign. The three types of disk jockeys became the solution to this diversity. They could handle a differentiated audience at different times of day with different program fares. The new reality could be accommodated if the station management had the courage to go all the way and allow their disk jockeys the autonomy that made each of their strategies so effective. Yet, such autonomy was risky. In the words of one station manager, newly experimenting with the disk jockey style: "If they are good they will take over the station; if they weren't good I don't want them around. I believe in giving them free rein in the program as far as music goes and also as far as their outside activities. All I want is my call letters mentioned every time my boys get some publicity."

Those marching orders, "free rein," were invitations to the three pure types of disk jockeys to do what they did best. Each of the three types had control over the part of his work that was devoted to his main boss. Paradoxically, the very strength of the leading sponsor's disk jockey was his freedom to tear up the sponsor's copy and improvise his own commercials. Similarly, the strength of the "personality" disk jockey enabled him to violate the station's rules of decorum and procedure. So, too, the hit-making disk jockey could ignore the music industry's pressures by virtue of his complete control over the music played on his programs.

As part of this inversion of the normal line of authority, each type of leading disk jockey traded off some significant degree of control over the other parts of the job. The sponsor's disk jockey, for example, could let the station librarian pick out the specific records for his show. The hit-making disk jockey could allow the station's staff to handle all relations with sponsors.

Three Portraits

A closer look at three disk jockeys, Gil Newsome, Bill Anson, and Bill Randle, will demonstrate these three strategies in action.[14] It will become obvious that even these single-minded men deliberately incorporated into their work elements of the other two strategies. The relative emphasis on each was determined by the man's talent and interests and the radio station's history and present needs, both in the context of local and regional musical traditions.

The Air-Salesman Deluxe

Gil Newsome was a nationally recognized, sponsor-oriented disk jockey in his midthirties when he was interviewed in 1952. He had been with a 5000-watt Mutual station in St. Louis for about seven years. There were eight other AM radio and three TV stations on the air in the city at that time. Newsome's station manager sketched the history of the station's policies in this city's sharply competitive atmosphere:

[I]n 1940 we were in the Blue network, part of NBC. We had hit a decline in popularity and needed local programming for revenue. We began to search for something that would fill long stretches of time to compete with the soap operas on the networks. We heard [Martin] Block and [Arthur] Godfrey and noted it was pop music. And we decided to build shows of records around a personality. We gave massive doses of pop music. That was the beginning of the DJ work here. We needed the music and the personality. We were looking for someone of network caliber, who would sell and who knew the bands and pop music.

Newsome filled the bill perfectly. After completing a major in speech at Duke University and working at a small station in Virginia, he got his chance, in true storybook fashion, when he was called to pinch hit for an announcer on the touring Glenn Miller show. He did the job, impressed the band leader, and stayed on until called to the armed forces. He was then offered a job on a St. Louis station. Not enthusiastic, he nevertheless accepted a weekend invitation.

Well, they met me at the airport and took me to the best place in town for lunch. Then after lunch they said that they should go to the steam room for a workout and relaxation. Then in the evening they took me to the Chase Hotel and the next day asked me if I wanted to see a ballgame, they had a box for the season, then to the country club at night. And they told me that if I came out I would need a car, etc., etc. Well they really romanced me and I figured I was making money in New York, but I wasn't living. Out here they made money and they really lived. So I thought I'd try it for one year. . . . At the end of the second year we signed a longer term agreement.

This style of life not only agreed with Newsome—he was soon firmly established in St. Louis's broadcasting life—but he defined his overall situation in these terms:

If I was the station manager I would pay my dj's in five figures, have them get a conspicuous car, a convertible Cadillac or Lincoln. I'd have them belong to the right clubs and keep them clean, no scandal or trouble. The real disk jockey doesn't just spin records. He must be intelligent, have a voice and a knowledge of music. A guy who is a good entertainer is fine, but he must sell. I aim for the upper income group.

In keeping with this approach, Newsome extended his activities into the community to magnify his connections with that upper income audience. He accepted invitations to M.C. major charity events and "big nightclub acts" at the largest hotel in the city. He also hosted local festivals and sports events and was involved in Shrine activities.

In line with this definition of the job, Newsome secured the hours 10 to 11 A.M. and 4:30 to 7:00 P.M. for a rigidly produced and smoothly presented flow of popular music, which he described in these terms:

The basic part of the afternoon show is the five best selling records in town. These are alternated with top selling records of the past. I keep records of what has been the top records in the past. They provoke nostalgia. It's a three-way combination. "These are the records that have sold in the past, the ones you liked in the past, and these are the ones you like now, and these are the ones that I think you're going to like tomorrow, but it's up to you to decide." . . . From 4:30 to 6 I'll take a given year, like 1949, and play the top sellers in that year as the basic ingredient of the show. This is filled with "extras," usually instrumentals and vocals of the band popular in the forties. . . . I lean towards bands and if a record has a name artist or the tune is familiar I'll use it. The artist is the prime concern, you have to see if the record is in the trend of the new sound. And you judge from past experience of a sound if it will become a hit.

The question of who would determine the new records to be played on Newsome's shows, as well as on the entire schedule of the station, had been resolved some years earlier. The station manager reported that, because of the pressure the music industry was exerting on the station's employees, he had taken the programming out of the hands of the disk jockeys and initiated a policy that prevented the extensive plugging of new records. The music director and the librarian were in charge of listing the records to be played, although for his own programs Newsome had established the format and could substitute particular records when he wanted to. It was clear that Newsome was not interested in making hits, nor was he knowledgeable about the newest artists or songs. As part of presenting the most "objective" picture, he kept his distance from the music men universally found in all radio stations at that time, though he maintained polite relations with the industry. His close personal relations were mainly with the sponsors and with their advertising agency representatives. Newsome had no other duties at the station except for his own shows, so his attentions were fully directed towards the sponsors' interests. He had his own airplane, which he used to fly ad agency and musical personnel from city to city in the region for business and for pleasure junkets to lake resorts.

I spend a good deal of time with them, usually go out with our account executives to see the sponsors. They want to feel that you're going to give them a little extra personal touch. The FCC says that the commercials have to be written but I ad lib them and use my own discretion. I used to have a writer who wrote for me but I didn't like his style so I have the station write them and I use my own discretion with them.

Newsome's orientation had not always been directed toward the sponsor. When he first came to St. Louis (1945), he was persuaded to seek out, and to become a leader in, teenage activities. There was a community-wide teenage magazine sold in the high schools that reported community activities of interest to that age group. Although Newsome had previously been lauded for his work with teenagers, he withdrew considerably from the field, finding a more lucrative if not more secure position in the sponsor-based programming. He realized the risky situation the disk jockey was in and the changing state of pop music.

The diversity of pop music has increased. There are new sounds and pseudo new sounds. The thing that makes a pop hit today is a gimmick—either a hillbillish sound or an echo chamber or a multiple taped sound. Then if it's a hit, there is something to build on for the next one. . . . [A] "phenon," an obscure artist can be an overnight hit. It's the disk jockey's responsibility. He is always musically editorializing. You have him looking for, and pushing new talents. . . . But I don't think any dj can make a tune. Gil Newsome is big in St. Louis, but he's nothing in Cleveland. And a network dj is nothing. A disk jockey can start a local hit but can't, shouldn't, make hits for the country.

This self-assessment accurately described his job as it related to the music business; it was to *anchor* the "hit game" at its center. A solid and steady dose of current records was legitimated by a strong connection to the past, leaving a small but definite opening to the future. Newsome's legitimation rested upon his firsthand experience in the big band era and his authority in carrying that aura to his audience.

In consonance with Newsome's place in the implicit division of labor among disk jockeys, others made tomorrow's hits. In Newsome's case, a new disk jockey had recently moved into St. Louis and was giving him the normal kind of trouble. The new man, oriented to the music industry, had airtime that partially overlapped Newsome's. Their competition was part of a direct struggle for the radio audience at a crucial time of the day, the late afternoon. Whichever station controlled the dial from 4 to 6 P.M. had the edge for the evening's main entertainment fare. Newsome's late afternoon show was being nibbled away by the younger man, who had been in St. Louis for only eighteen months. His show, on a 5000-watt, ABC-affiliated station, aired between 3:30 and 6:00 P.M. five days a week.

He thus intersected Newsome's show and competed with him for that particular segment of the audience that could swing the whole family away. Even though the two disk jockeys attempted to capture the *whole* audience at that time, it was only a *partial* audience that would really pay off for each of them, and a different part at that. Newsome wanted the buying audience. The younger disk jockey wanted the music audience and stated his strategy explicitly:

You're important in this business only as long as you have the record buying population, and the industry can knock you off if you don't follow through for them. That's the only way to crack a town. You got to go in and get the teenagers. You got to sell yourself to the kids because you need the audience first.

A comparable crosscutting competition existed between Newsome and some of the early morning men on the other St. Louis stations. These disk jockeys were mainly "personality" types, committed to the station's concern for the maximum audience. It was a daily struggle, move and countermove, to win marginal gains from a fickle public, tracked by a relentless and unreachable scorekeeper, the rating services.

The visible trail of that struggle as well as its chief weapon was the music itself. Of course, there is no better way to understand Newsome's strategy and style than to hear his daily show; its closest approximation is the log of its music. Figure 5-3 shows the log of the 4:30 to 7:00 P.M. show for Thursday, 20 November 1952. His manner, words, and voice, crisp, controlled, friendly, but somewhat distant, can only be imagined. This selection of records for an ordinary late afternoon's show gives a clear snapshot of the pop stream in motion, showing the transition from the dance band era to that of the vocalists.

The first half of Newsome's play list (aimed at housewives and men in cars) consisted of 1949 hits by the remnants of the dance band era. The opening number by Jimmy Dorsey, for example, announces by its position the primacy of the bands and their continuity, since Dorsey was one of the few prominent prewar bands still performing during the fifties. The rest of the records played in that segment were made by surviving or newly created bands. They were keyed around the year 1949, extending the program backwards three years for the young married audience three or more years out of school.

The second feature of the play list is its compromise between two formats, each constituting a particular notion of what is a "program." One was the declining "Bandstand" or "Make Believe Ballroom" format. In radio terms, it was called "block programming," a device that grouped several numbers in uninterrupted sequence, held together by the continuity of the performing groups or by similarity of mood, tempo, lyrical content, or some other thread. This bandstand idea was itself an imitation of the original "wire" remote of a live broadcast from a dance hall or nightclub. The other format was the "Hit Parade" model in which a group of records was played in inverse or scrambled order of popularity. This format was extremely flexible, serving the station programming interests as well as those of the music business.

Both in Newsome's own programming and in the field generally, the

```
                    FIRST FIVE REVUE

            THURSDAY NOVEMBER 20, 1952 (1949)

THEME
OPENER    CHARLEY MY BOY          JIMMY DORSEY          4069
      5.  DREAMERS HOLIDAY        PERRY COMO            2631
EXTRA     BLUE MOON               RAY ANTHONY           8867
                                  (revived by Mel Torme)
EXTRA     CRAZY RHYTHM            HARRY JAMES           2104
      4.  I CAN DREAM CAN'T I     ANDREWS SISTERS &
                                    GORDON JENKINS      8691
EXTRA     WHO'S SORRY NOW         JERRY GREY            6699
EXTRA     DADDY'S LITTLE GIRL     EDDY HOWARD           4236
NEWS ---- ---
EXTRA     DEAR HEARTS AND
            GENTLE PEOPLE         PATTI PAGE            9066
EXTRA     AGAIN                   ART MOONEY            8131
      3.  CANADIAN CAPERS         DORIS DAY             8914
EXTRA     BASIN STREET BLUES      PEE WEE HUNT          8404
EXTRA     DON'T CRY JOE           ROSEMARY CLOONEY      8927
      2.  MULE TRIAN              BING CROSBY           9037
EXTRA     SONG OF INDIA           ENRIC MADRIGUERA      1784
EXTRA     CLANCY LOWERED
            THE BOOM              AMES BROS.            7809
      1.  MULE TRAIN              FRANKIE LAINE         9025



                        FIRST FIVE
            THURSDAY NOVEMBER 20, 1952
THEME
      5.  GLOW WORM               MILLS BROS.           1726
NEW       TWO OTHER PEOPLE        DOLORES GREY          N-201
EXTRA     SKYCOACH                RAY ANTHONY           2541
      4.  MY BABY'S COMIN HOME    LES PAUL &
                                    MARY FORD           7803
EXTRA     BABY IT'S COLD          JOHNNY MERCER &
            OUTSIDE                 MARGARET WHITING    8153
EXTRA     GARDEN IN THE RAIN      PERRY COMO            6743
      3.  I                       DON CORNELL           7793
NEW       NO MOON AT ALL          AMES BROS.            N-216
EXTRA     BRAZILIAN SLEIGH BELLS  PERCY FAITH           2583
      2.  KEEP IT A SECRET        JO STAFFORD           7423
EXTRA     HALLS OF IVY            WALTER SCHUMANN       8905
NEW       FANDANGO                VICTOR MARCHESE       N-221
      1.  WHY DON'T YOU BELIEVE   JONI JAMES            8073

CLOSING   YOURS - VERA LYNN - 9137
          LAZY RIVER - ART MOONEY - 8563
          THE JOKE IS ON ME - FREDDY COLE - N-95
          I SAW MOMMIE KISSIN SANTA CLAUS - SPIKE JONES
          HEART AND SOUL - FOUR ACES -7465
```

Figure 5-3. Newsome's Radio Play List. Source: Archival material for *The Disk Jockey: A Study of the Emergence of a New Occupation and Its Influence on Popular Music in America* by McPhee, et al.

"Hit Parade" format won handily, even though some disk jockeys, especially the personality-oriented ones, preferred block programming. Dick Clark would soon combine the two formats in his "American Bandstand" television show. In the midsixties, the progressive rock FM stations would revive the essence of the block programming format.[15]

The Hit Parade's attractiveness at that time was its efficacy in leading the audience into the hit game by engaging them in its dramatic unfolding, a way of defeating dial switching. The audience was persuaded to hang on to find out which was the number one hit.

The third and final lesson derived from Newsome's play list shows how the pop stream carried its tunes over a long time span during these transitional years. Though most of the records on his list were current hits or new releases, some were written ten to twenty years earlier and presented in a quite self-conscious celebration of the "good old days." This deliberate backpedaling maintained the pop stream as a two-stranded tradition, living both in the past and in the future. That interweaving is what Newsome stood for. Music, while not the primary focus of his strategy as sponsor-oriented disk jockey, was nevertheless its emotional core. Newsome and the rest of the sponsors' disk jockeys threaded the swing era's material into current tunes, thus offering the rocknroll audience, soon to come down the road, a larger pop reservoir.

The "Real" Personality Man

"Personality disk jockey" Bill Anson, a Chicago-born former entertainer, arrived in Los Angeles at the end of a major shootout among that city's leading radio stations. In 1952, there were in Los Angeles County twenty-one radio stations; perhaps as many as forty could be heard in the metropolitan area.[16] The postwar era in Los Angeles, as elsewhere, had stirred radio management into a fever of expansion. The new 5000-watt, independent station KLAC, launching an aggressive disk jockey recruitment plan, began with a raid on KFWB, an established 5000-watt station owned by Warner Brothers.

Two of their most popular disk jockeys were lured to KLAC. One was Peter Potter, a fifteen-year veteran disk jockey and a southerner with strong connections to the substantial and devoted audience for country pop in the Los Angeles area. The other was Al Jarvis, the senior disk jockey presence in the city. Together with four other disk jockeys, KLAC swept the Los Angeles music scene clean. Their highly promoted staff quickly began to dominate the ratings for the entire broadcast schedule. The method was total promotional saturation with their "all–disk jockey staff," each developing his own public personality. An important part of that personality was augmented by visiting movie and recording stars. In addition, tie-in promotions with the record stores and record companies associated with station personnel created the complete machinery for record exposure and exploitation.

KFWB responded by negotiating the return of Martin Block. Billed at that time as America's number one disk jockey, he was a leading member of the group of disk jockeys on New York City's independent WNEW, the eastern seaboard's version of an all–disk jockey station. In the early 1930s, Block had worked briefly for KFWB as a newsman, and he had carried to New York the knowledge of Jarvis' program "gimmick." As legend has it, he invoked Al Jarvis' "Make Believe Ballroom" format as an emergency solution to long gaps of "dead air" during his coverage for WNEW of the trial of Bruno Hauptman for the murder of the Lindbergh child. Whether it was Block's talent as air salesman, his judicious selection of records, or the freshness of the format, he parlayed the initial notoriety surrounding that trial into a large success for himself. The California offer was for Block to take KFWB's strategic 10 A.M. to 1 P.M. segment. The Mutual Network was to carry a major part of the show. In addition, Block was to maintain his WNEW presence in New York by sending his recorded shows there from his California home studio. It didn't work. KFWB and the Mutual Network learned almost instantly that a network disk jockey show could not attract and hold an audience; it had to be entirely a local phenomenon. Block returned to New York after a year.[17]

After the Block fiasco, still seeking a radio personality, KFWB ran a contest to find a replacement. Bill Anson won the job, having no previous experience as a disk jockey. He was not, in his own words,

a dyed in the wool disk jockey. I come here from Vaudeville. I write pop music, and songs recorded by Argot, Herb Jeffries. I also write religious songs and record the sacred songs, happy sacred songs, also a lot of Western and hillbilly songs. I'm a member of ASCAP, and have a contract with Mercury. . . . I was with Paul Whiteman for years, in night clubs and Vaudeville. I write and produce shows.

This story was quite familiar; a substantial number of veterans from the big band days found a place in the disk jockey game in the years after World War II. It was an obvious and readily traversed path, carrying Gil Newsome, Bill Anson, and briefly even Paul Whiteman himself to the microphones.[18]

Anson's skills and connections were those of a broad-ranging entertainment "personality," implicated in many phases of the business. He was not tied to the single-mindedness of hit-making, though he did take pride in the credit he received for discovering the hits "Wheel of Fortune" and "Little Bird" within the Los Angeles area. Though he believed he could spot a hit, he liked to pick out songs from "off-labels." Nor did he have a narrow concern with the buying audience, in spite of the fact

that his main show was scheduled during the critical hours 9 A.M. to
12:30 P.M. This show established the station for the day. Command of
the "hours between the family's departure for school and work and their
return in mid to late afternoon" was vital to all AM radio. The time slot
was highly competitive, with the independent stations bringing out their
strongest guns against each other and against the network battery of
soap operas, game shows, and endless other variations of ladies' daytime
diversions.

Anson was directly pitched against Peter Potter at KLAC and partially
against Ira Cook, at KMPC, two strong disk jockey programs. His
strategy was to emphasize his own public personality as part of the "human side" of the entertainment world:

The chatter is more important than the music, because otherwise they can listen
elsewhere. . . . The show is very loose and free. I'm not a stickler for detail, like
Peter Potter. I do a sloppy show. But I give the listeners the songs they want to
hear. I try not to play the same record every day. I do play the hit parade daily. I
talk about the interesting things I might know about the records and about the
artists' home life. I know 99 per cent of the artists. I predict whether it'll be a hit.
If you don't you're just a staff announcer.

Clearly, this strategy was to expose records to an audience rather than to
exploit them in order to make a hit. Anson's "predictions" were a much
more relaxed matter than those of the hit-maker's. Neither he nor his
show was on the line for the number of hits he made or correctly pre-
dicted. Still, the personnel and the products of popular music were essential to his show. He did not attempt to mold audience taste by the heavy
playing of new releases; he tried instead to simply *reflect* those tastes.
And that reflection required that he participate in activities that gathered
in the largest audience he could muster under the umbrella of his own
personality. Part of those activities were done on the air. In his evening
hour segment, "Strictly for the Girls," which he conducted in a French
accent, Anson offered the comedic side of his personality. In the morning
show, his own talents as entertainer were woven into the succession of
current hits, subordinated to the music but still present. Like practically
all successful disk jockeys in this period, he was led beyond the microphone to participate in the active search for new talent and thus into
managing and guiding the careers of young singers. In Anson's case, however, the call was to TV, where he himself wanted to be the entertainer.
He had by this time established himself as host for a TV program helping needy people ("Have a Heart") and sought to move into fulltime
television.

The larger significance of Anson's type of disk jockey presentation was
in the creation of a loose radio format capable of containing the diversity
of material entering the Los Angeles market. It was the strength of his

"personality" and the flexibility of the programming structure that allowed this eclectic mix of musical styles to hang together. And it was that peculiar unifying totality that allowed him to work successfully with a diverse audience consisting of teenagers as well as mature housewives, of northern and southern Anglos, and of blacks and the Spanish speaking.

The log of his program during the day of the interview reflects in full detail the melange that was the pop stream in 1952. The show was a nicely woven mix of alternating instrumentals and vocals, slow and up-tempo numbers, male and female singers, old dance band numbers and new hits by solo or group singers. It was also interspersed with "hillbilly" tunes, rhythm and blues records, and with records popular in the Spanish community. Each of these minority records on the play list, however, was a safe choice. They were either top hits within their own categories, had been recorded by artists acceptable to the pop stream, or had some local appeal[19] (fig. 5-4).

The few records appealing to minorities were a departure from the programming of Anson's main competition, Peter Potter and Ira Cook, both of whom were strictly sponsors' disk jockeys. They both emphasized the records rather than their personality; they both wanted the adult-buying audience, not the teenagers; they both were heavy on the current hits of the pop stream rather than on those of the adjacent streams. Anson's cautious but consistent use of hillbilly, black pop, jazz, and Spanish records was a recognition of the vigorous musical presence of those audiences in the Los Angeles area. Each record had a musical life that serviced the local community but that also reached into the developing national loops of country pop and black pop and into the emerging Southwest regional Mexican-American musical world.

In fact, at the very moment of the interview in 1952 with Bill Anson in Los Angeles, somewhere across town the song-writing team of Jerry Leiber and Mike Stoller with Johnny Otis were providing Willie Mae (Big Mama) Thornton with one of her big hits, "Hound Dog," on the Peacock label. Four years later, Elvis Presley would continue to mingle the pop, the country, and the black pop streams by bringing his version of that song to the top of all three charts.

The Hit-Making Disk Jockey

Bill Randle was one of the founding members of the small group of hit-makers. At the time of the interview, in late 1952, Randle was twenty-nine years old, a graduate of Western Reserve University. When a youngster he had developed a strong affinity for classical music, jazz, and black music generally. He built his early career around that musical culture, finding in the Detroit jazz disk jockey's job the forum for proselytizing the jazz message. The need for money to complete his education dictated a shift to the pop side.[20]

THEME:
_____

LAMPLIGHT .... RANDY BROOKS ORCH
WHY DO YOU PASS ME BY .... DAVID ROSE ORCH
DANCING ON THE CEILING .... JERI SOUTHERN WITH ORCH DIR
                    NORMAN LEYDEN
TAKE ME IN YOUR ARMS .... FOUR ACES FEAT AL ALBERTS
SIOUX CITY SUE .... JOHNNY MADDOX AND THE RHYTHMASTERS
I DON'T WANT TO SET THE WORLD ON FIRE .... DON CHERRY
A MOTH AND A FLAME .... GEORGIA GIBBS WITH ORCH GLENN OSSER
KEEP IT A SECRET .... JUNE HUTTON AND AXEL STORDAHL WITH THE
                    BOYS NEXT DOOR AND THE STRODAHL ORCHESTRA
A SHOULDER TO WEEP ON .... MILLS BROTHERS AND SY OLIVER ORCH
BECAUSE YOU'RE MINE ... MARIO LANZA WITH RCA VICTOR
DO NOTHING TILL YOU HEAR FROM ME .... AMES BROTHERS AND
                    LES BROWN ORCH
YOU'LL NEVER KNOW .... HARRY JAMES AND ROSEMARY CLOONEY WITH
                    HARRY JAMES ORCHESTRA
WINTER .... SPIKE JONES AND THE CITY SLICKERS
                WITH THE MELLO MEN
WITHERED ROSES .... MARION MORGAN WITH ORCH COND NELSON RIDDLE
ISN'T THIS A NIGHT FOR LOVE .... BOB EBERLY WITH DAVE
                    CAVANAUGH'S MUSIC
JUMP BACK HONEY .... ELLA MAE MORSE WITH ORCH COND JOE LIPMAN
I KEEP TELLING MYSELF .... THE HILLTOPPERS FEAT JIMMY SACCA
WHY DON'T YOU BELIEVE ME .... JONI JAMES WITH ORCH COND
                    LEW DOUGLAS
WITHOUT MY LOVER .... MITCH MILLER ORCH, STAN FREEMAN,
                    HARPSICHORD
ON A LITTLE COUNTRY ROAD IN SWITZERLAND .... DAVID ROSE ORCH
GREYHOUND .... AMOS MILBURN AND HIS ALADDIN CHICKENSHACKERS
CURTAIN TIME .... ACQUAVIVA AND HIS ORCH
IF I HAD A PENNY .... ROSEMARY CLOONEY WITH PERCY FIRTH
                    AND HIS ORCH
PEORIA .... BOB SCOBEY'S FRISCO BAND
TILL I WALTZ AGAIN .... TERESA BREWER WITH ORCH DIR JACK PLEIS
DEEP NIGHT .... HARRY JAMES ORCH AND FRANK SINATRA
SOUTH RAMPART STREET PARADE .... BING CROSBY AND THE
                    ANDREWS SISTERS
YOU DARLIN' .... ART LOWRY, HIS PIANO AND ORCH
CHEROKEE .... THE CONTINENTALS
ROLL ON MISSISSIPPI .... SNOOKY LANSON WITH ORCH
MY FAVORITE SONG .... ELLA FITZGERALD
NOBODY'S SWEETHEART .... JOHNNY LONG ORCH
LITTLE ROCK GETAWAY .... LES PAUL
ROSANNE .... VIC DAMONE WITH ORCH COND NORMAN LEYDEN
AT THE DARK STRUTTERS BALL .,... BENNY GOODMAN ORCH
DON'T TEMPT ME (FOR WHEN I LOVE I LOVE) .... TONY MARTIN WITH
                    HENRY RENE ORCH
I GET A KICK OUT OF YOU .... TOMMY DORSEY ORCH
DANCING GIRL .... VOUGHN MONROE AND THE MOON MAILS WITH
                    VOUGHN MONROE ORCH
OH! WHAT IT SEEMED TO BE .... DICK HAYMES AND HELEN FORREST
THE WORLD IS WAITING FOR THE SUNRISE .... STAN FREBURG WITH
                    BANJOS BY DICK ROBERTS AND RED ROUNTREE
A SUNDAY KIND OF LOVE .... FRANKIE LAINE AND CARL FISCHER'S
                    ORCH
NIGHT OF HEAVEN .... EYDIE GORME
THE UNSEEN RIDER .... DICK BROWN WITH DON COSTA ORCH
BABY WON'T YOU PLEASE COME HOME .... KAY STARR WITH
                    CRYSTALETTE ALL-STARS
POMPTON TURNPIKE .... CHARLIE BARNET ORCH
BACK IN THE GOOD OLD DAYS .... THE PIED PIPERS AND MARK
                    CARTER'S ORCH
INDIAN LOVE CALL .... SLIM WHITMAN
TIRO DE MULAS .... LALO GUERRERO
NOLA .... SIDNEY TORCH ORCH
DRIFTING AND DREAMING .... THE MULCAYS
THE SHEIK OF ARABY .... AMES BROTHERS WITH ORCH
CUBAN LOVE SONG .... DICK LEE WITH DIR FRANK HUNTER
CARIOCA .... LES PAUL
STAIRWAY TO THE STARS .... ELLA FITZGERALD

Detroit, however, was no place to do so, for Ed MacKenzie, "Jack the Bellboy," commanded that city's pop music radio scene. Randle was invited to WERE Cleveland by the owners of this new 5000-watt, independent station a year after it went on the air. That city's radio life was a brawl. The four older stations had been founded either in the earliest days of radio, circa 1920, at the moment of CBS' entry into network radio (1930), or at the divestiture of NBC's Red Network and its acquisition by the newly formed ABC network (1943). After the war, three new independent AM stations, five FM stations, and two TV stations went on the air, significantly crowding the broadcasters' audience potential.

The resulting competition was fought out in the usual ways, including jousting by the disk jockeys for the favor of fickle audiences. Randle's assignment was to win the leadership of the 4 to 6 P.M. time segment, which was then in the fragile hands of an older disk jockey on a new station. Randle said:

He had the audience. But he was tired and careless, an old school guy, just played records. You have to be out, fifteen places at once. He lost his audience. Everyone is shaky. They know some idiot can come into town and knock you off if he's better. But real better; it's not easy to take away an audience.

Randle's success within a brief period was total; his program's airtime stretched from 2 to 7 P.M. six days a week and from 1 to 5 P.M. on Sunday. This uninterrupted span for a single program was unprecedented at that time. The radio schedule of the 1920s, it will be recalled, contained segments ranging from a brief four minutes to a maximum of twenty minutes.

Although Randle did not "invent" the hit-making technique all by himself, he did codify it and apply it with great thoroughness. More importantly, he passed the real test of an innovator; he was able to transmit his understanding of how the system worked. He taught the rest of the disk jockeys on his station and those on other Cleveland stations and in other cities how to make hits. He also taught station management a few things, most of which they didn't like. Randle cut through the conventional wisdom that radio's job was to deliver a pleasant sequence of musical selections reflecting the tastes of the audience and that the disk jockey's job was to sell products.

Unlike many disk jockeys, especially the personality types, and contrary to the honored tradition of radio as culture bearer, the new breed exemplified by Randle did not teach and preach. He was there primarily to *make* the next hit. The passive reflection of the audience's aspirations

Figure 5-4. (opposite) Anson's Radio Play List. Source: Archival material for *The Disk Jockey* by McPhee, et al.

for quality in music was to be bypassed in favor of a single-minded, active commitment to *making* that taste.

The basic premise is that the "public," the record buying public, is the best and *only* determinant of whether or not a song will go. Two problems remain. To identify this public and to get their reactions early—so that they themselves can be resold to themselves.

That public was predominantly the white high school teenager. Black, Spanish, and other minority youths were to be incorporated. No distinction was made between working-class and middle-class kids; it was just *kids* that were to be celebrated.

The high school teenagers were numerous, responsive, and easily shaped into a market, however volatile. Whatever else they were, did, and liked was secondary but still usable in channeling their continuing absorption in the culture of popular music. Randle went along with this narrow perspective to some extent but was careful to touch base with the older audience.

The next question was how to reach that primary audience, how to cross the physical and cultural barriers that separated the radio disk jockey from his public.[21] Randle's solution to the problem set this standard:

One day some kids who came to the station asked me to announce their dance at one of the high schools (or it may have been a teenage organization). So I did and the night of the dance I happened to be out that way and I thought's I'd announce the fact that I'd be coming out to prevent the hysteria. So I started the thing regularly. I had no intention of using the deal this way. This is the way you find out what they want, what is going to go. You ask them, not directly but subtly, what they like, what they think will be a hit.

The second problem, how "to get their reactions early so that they themselves can be resold to themselves," was accomplished both by bringing the teenagers into the station and by meeting them on their own turf. This apparently simple and now obvious strategy was actually a complex social technology, one probably even more consequential for rocknroll than RCA's little $12.95 record player.

Inviting the teenagers to the studios accomplished a number of things for Randle. First, the presence of a live audience gives any show a palpable lift, the crackle of living theater. His studio was sharply divided into audience space and performer's space. (Randle referred to the disk jockey repeatedly as "the performer.") It had the traditional glass-enclosed broadcast booth segregating the on-air performer from the audience. Visitors from the music industry, record distributors, song pluggers, and recording artists with their agents were, on occasion, invited into the booth, visibly demonstrating the disk jockey's links with the music world and his power over its personnel. Randle was clearly on equal terms with everyone, even those who were younger and just starting out.

The audience at the studio rendered an even more important service: It became an emissary to the kids back in the schools. The voluntary nature of this work produced the most motivated ambassadors the disk jockey could hope for. What the devoted students carried to their friends was the confirmation that the disk jockey respected and understood teenagers as a group and, in many cases, individually.

They also carried to the school the message that he would be pleased to set up a dance in their gym: the birth of the sock hop. Again, although the sock hop was probably not Randle's invention, his use of it in the hitmaking game was certainly more systematically developed than what was accomplished by other disk jockeys.

The high school record hop was simply not a dance scene comparable to the swing-era ballrooms—the Avalon, the Trianon, the Roseland. It was a kids' scene, one which raised the difficult issue of how the record industry's increasing concentration on a bewildering diversity of vocalists—solo and groups—could also provide a recognizable and continuing set of danceable rhythms. It did, somehow, even while running a record exposure and exploitation system. Randle, shrewd and thorough, developed the record hop for his own and for the teenagers' enhancement, even to the point of giving the dances a special name. The picture reproduced here of a "Randle Romp," taken by a professional photographer, suggests the nature of this mutual enhancement (fig. 5-5).

The students, generally the high school's "leading crowd," would organize the dance. This role gave them prized autonomy from school authorities and parents, along with the recognition such action incurred. It gave *all* the students an active sense of participation in an important cultural event. The participation was real, for Randle on his side needed not just the support for his "work" as Cleveland's leading champion of teenagers, but he needed their specific reactions to new records. He would bring to the gym his portable sound equipment and a large stack of the current hits and new releases. The kids, respectably and uniformly dressed, listened and danced, commenting freely and immediately to each other and to Randle on which records they liked and disliked.

After learning the potential of new records at the record hops, the studio, or elsewhere, Randle's next step was a concentrated playing and replaying of a selected few. He would play a record he thought had definite hit potential up to five times a day on his own program. Randle had enough influence at his own station to get that same record played frequently by the disk jockeys doing the morning, evening, and late night shows. He would also invoke the mutual obligations that held the infor-

Figure 5-5. Randle's 1950s Record Hop, Cleveland, Ohio. Photo courtesy of William Randle.

mal disk jockey networks together by making phone calls to Pittsburgh, Detroit, Boston, and so on, telling his friends what was happening and inviting them to "lay on the record."

The fragile network of disk jockeys was surrounded and nurtured by several others: the local record distributors and retail record personnel, the song pluggers from the major New York and Los Angeles publishing houses, and the loose network of talent mangers, club owners, performers' agents, and performing artists themselves. All the hit-making disk jockeys were tied into these sources of information and influence to varying degrees, depending upon their career orientation and political savvy.

The record distributors, being local, were relied upon heavily for connecting the disk jockey's programming with his audience's responses. These local distributors often delivered new records to Randle promptly with the "word" on their commercial potential. Then the records that were hot had to be stocked in the stores; the stores had to report what was moving; and to complete the circle, the record distributors had to open the way for the disk jockey to reach the top A&R (Artists and Repertoire) executives of the label.

Randle used all these channels to get the word back to the record's producers that it was or was not "breaking in Cleveland." If the song did not go over well, he dropped it. If it did become a big hit, he immediately ceased playing it once his name was firmly associated with its success.

In each of his programs, those records being given massive exposure were smoothly set within the long sequence of current hits, up-and-coming records, and a large number of brand new ones. There were no oldies. Randle organized the show in his head without the normal preparation of listening, selecting, and typing out a radio broadcast log. Instead of the traditional alternation of instrumentals with vocals and up-tempo with slower numbers, Randle used a different system. During the easy and spontaneous commentary between records, he revealed to his audiences just enough of the music trade reasoning behind his record choices to give the listeners an "insider's" perspective. He had a specific rationale for each record's position on the show and held the entire order in his head, changing it every day. Randle sat in the booth, picking from a large stack of records in an apparently haphazard fashion, handing them to one or another visiting song plugger or record distributor, who in turn carried it to the engineer.[22] What emerged was a living melange. Sometimes two or three records in a row would be by male vocalists; sometimes several instrumentals would be put together. A country tune, a new hit from the rhythm and blues charts, a currently popular choral number would be mixed together, violating the near sacred rules of conventional programming.

Randle's highly conscious progression through the afternoon's records was designed not only to hold each audience segment from the attractions of competing radio shows but also, in his own words, "to research every part of the audience."[23] Randle would play the records on which he was working to every identifiable audience segment—men, housewives, kids, and so on. His public service commitments and activities, which were many and sometimes dramatic, were also shaped to serve these different audiences.

Pretesting records, then heavily exposing them, were two of the major parts of the hit-making disk jockey's machinery. The third part, which Randle did not take for granted, was securing the newest releases from the hottest talent. The strongest card the record company could play in persuading the disk jockey to play its tunes was to offer him an "exclusive." A new record, in the classiest case, would be hand delivered to the disk jockey by the record label's senior distributor in the area, followed by a long-distance phone call from the A&R man. The disk jockey would be informed that he had the record exclusively for a week or ten days; no other disk jockey had it. The rest was up to him. This exchange, record company receiving concentrated exposure in return for the disk jockey's identification as leading hit-maker, was an appealing and legitimate deal. For the hit-making disk jockeys especially, it was a better approach than the paid sponsorship of part of their shows by the record companies or simple cash, both of which deprived the jockey of his most important strength—the freedom to program what he wanted.

The exclusive privilege was a dangerous weapon however. It would and did on occasion outrage the rest of the disk jockeys in town, unless there was an even-handedness in the distribution of such records. For high-prestige disk jockeys like Randle, someone else's exclusive was a difficult situation. It invited competitive "hard ball" countermoves, such as playing the same tune recorded by a different artist, taking over the original record by extremely heavy air play after the exclusive had expired, or simply ignoring it, the latter being the most dangerous course of action. The constant "exclusives" skirmishes among disk jockeys was but one more argument eventually used by station management to end the power of the autonomous disk jockey and to reclaim control over the scheduling of music.

The adventurous hit-making disk jockey sought every chance to move past making hits via exclusives and onto the next step, the discovery and exploitation of new talent (mainly performing rather than song-writing talent).

In the 1930s and 1940s, the New York publisher's office was where new song and performer met. In the early 1950s, it was increasingly the hit-making disk jockey, the outreach instrument of the record companies' A&R men, who brought new performers to the fore. This combination, record company and disk jockey, had replaced the earlier team of publisher and song plugger in this regard.

It was not enough just to bring the newest records to a record hop. As Randle states,

Well, then you have to go beyond that. So you take a performer with you. This of course makes the artist as well as the record. We would take the performers around, not the name people but the unknown. Of course this is what made some of them, like Johnny Ray and the Four Aces. We would put on a show for them and the kids really loved it. They want to show their appreciation for the artist that they know, so they buy the records. When we first made the Four Aces, they saw over sixty thousand people in three days. The station at first was not too happy about it, but then when they saw what it was, they don't say anything. There was opposition from the schools. In Detroit they can't get past the door. The school system is just dead set against it. But here the kids wore them down. So when one school started, the kids in the other school said, why can't we have one, and they would grumble, and the school officials had a near strike situation on their hands. Finally they had to give in and it worked out fine. There was no trouble, the hysteria for some artists was in the assembly hall and was under control. Even the teachers realized that these kids were seeing several thousand dollars worth of talent for free. Things got rough though, the musicians union claimed that this was a theatrical performance and demanded scale. So I had to pay four standby musicians scale, I put out $5500 for these things in a year. It's a captive audience in a way; they have these assemblies that gets a thousand kids.

The way in which Randle selected the few potential hits from the stable of new releases and then rode them to success was the same method used with performers. To find new musical talent he had to catch almost every new act that came through town, listen to every demo record sent or brought to him, and pay attention to the tips that regularly came from industry figures.

Randle was identified with the careers of several artists, some successful, some not. The most prominent, of course, was Elvis Presley. He was also implicated in the brief but significant career of Johnny Ray. The briefest sketch of a new performer illuminates the changing ways in which artists were being connected to the music industry and to their audiences. One of the requirements of the emerging rocknroll performer was youth. Older singers like Bill Haley and Johnny Ray brought something attractive to the teenage record buyer, but that "something" could not carry because the performers were too old. But was youth by itself enough? The following story suggests the obvious answer.

Don Howard, a seventeen-year-old high school student at Cleveland Heights, wrote and recorded in 1952 a song called "Oh Happy Day," accompanying himself on the guitar he could barely strum (not being any kind of a musician). He took the record to WERE disk jockey Phil Maclean, who played it on the air. "The switchboard lit up like a Christmas tree," he said, noting the phenomenal response to the record. Maclean saw a commercial possibility in the doleful rendition of the adolescent lyric. Though regarded as an embarrassment, "absolutely an electronic monstrosity," it was recorded on the Essex label.[24] The disk jockey network was alerted. The song appeared first on *Billboard*'s national "Best Selling Singles" chart on 19 November 1953, remaining fifteen weeks and reaching a high of fourth from the top.[25] Randle commented,

The real thing that started the record was the fact that the kids of the high school that Howard went to really moved. On weekends and during the week some 2000 kids visited every record store in Northern Ohio asking for the record of "Oh Happy Day" by Don Howard. Well these kids' pressure on the stores set in motion the automatic mechanism of the industry. The hype was on. Well it's as dead as a door nail now. . . . I didn't move with it, but if it's a hit you have to. You can't ignore a hit just because you don't like it. You're dead if you do.

Don Howard wasn't the last high school student to attempt a singing career. Within a few years, the significant performers on the pop charts would be under twenty, not far from high school life, and headed for a career path quite different from their elder musical colleagues.

In summary, the autonomous disk jockeys of all three types changed the rules of the game for all the American popular musics. First, they were in the front ranks of those who constructed a new postwar system for the exposure and exploitation of the single phonograph record, the unit for all the popular musics. This structure was built by Randle and perhaps less than a hundred other disk jockeys in ten or twenty cities across the country. They did for the pop stream in the early 1950s what an equivalent number of music publishers did in New York City in the decades before World War II. The hit-making disk jockeys helped create an integrated national grand loop out of the smaller short loops each had constructed in their own cities.

Second, and of ultimately greater significance, the disk jockeys in all the hundreds of smaller cities opened that powerful hit-making machinery to all the other streams. Black pop, country pop, and, just a moment behind, jazz, folk, and gospel would be released from their institutional constraints, even the self-imposed constraints, to find *their* way into the American home on records via the radio, just as did the pop stream. The result would be the breakup of the boundaries separating these six streams and the creation of a seventh.

New artists, new instrumentation, new lyrics, new performance settings, and new audiences were ready. Beneath those shifting musical boundaries, the age cleavage was working in the same direction, thereby creating parallel cultural and social changes that would bring rocknroll into being.

Finally, the autonomous disk jockey was a model for a new impresarial presence, one that would restructure the division of labor within all parts of the entertainment complex. The singer-songwriter was one such new restructuring, and the freelance producer, another; both and still other forms of impresario owed much to the disk jockeys. They embodied and enacted the converging needs of an expanded postwar entertainment world. All its diverse parts would soon congeal into a powerful apparatus, which awaited only a mobilized youth audience to become the seventh stream.

6. The Streams Aligned

I f the "Make Believe Ballroom" was bringing the pop stream to a radio audience, what had happened to the real ballrooms? In spite of the undeniable end of the swing era, in the early fifties the band business was still doing a surprising dollar volume. So, too, were the nation's dance halls. The National Ballroom Operators Association reported that over a thousand ballrooms were packing in three to five thousand paying customers a night for name bands. But the end was approaching. The record hop in the high school gym and the "wilder rock dancing," which deterred the "regular customers" of the ballrooms, reduced the number of ballrooms to about two hundred by the midsixties.[1] Many of those regular customers were now otherwise occupied with house and job and with starting families.

Where, then, were the new sounds of the post-swing era to come from? This question, it should be understood, affected not just the pop stream but the country and black pop streams as well, for each of them had generated its own version of the swing band. The answer is complicated because all three of the larger streams, and the three smaller ones as well, were differently configured. In that inchoate state, each stream had to develop new ways to create, perform, and distribute its songs. Anything was possible; no boundary was sacrosanct.

Not only popular music but all the arts were moving into the "Century of the Common Man" with an ebullience and creativity rarely seen before in America. Not surprisingly, they began to bump into each other, to cross previously unbreachable boundaries. New styles and new art forms were soon to appear as the action at these borders quickened. Rocknroll was one of those innovations, appearing as the structure and metabolism of the pop, country, and black pop streams grew to be more alike and as the speed of their "hit parades" became almost identical, allowing their musics to meet and mix on a regular basis.

This chapter describes the events that brought the three larger streams into alignment. The intersection of their musics happened to be, fatefully, just at the emerging line of cleavage between the young and the adult worlds.

The Pop Stream Retools

In that strategic zone where demographic and cultural changes meet, the disk jockeys, especially the hit-making ones, were reworking the structure of the pop stream. As noted above, they were at the center of a local "scene" consisting of a responsive young audience, of performance sites for music and dance, and of jukeboxes and record stores that provided the latest hits, with the radio stations tying them all together. More importantly, these settings in the cities were the nodes of an emerging *national* fabric connected to each other and to the music centers in New York and Los Angeles via a swarm of highly mobile record men, publishers' song pluggers, and performers with their entourages.

This whole loose structure, even as it was forming, enjoyed unprecedented success. Industry reports revealed new highs in consumer expenditures for radio and phonograph sets, for records and musical instruments.[2] The schools and colleges were the main customers for this burgeoning part of the music business. The future cadres of rocknroll performers were being prepared by the efforts of school music programs, the fruits of which would be the thousands of garage bands and guitar pickers that appeared in every state of the nation. One simple indication of this music education was the resumption of printed guitar and ukelele chords in the sheet music of the day. This practice had been standard decades earlier, and its reappearance was an important indicator of the growing ranks of amateur players of stringed instruments. For many reasons, including the difficulties of technical mastery, horns were out, and guitars were in.[3]

Yet this abundance of novice musicians in the presence of a huge outpouring of records, over one hundred singles released a week, produced a serious incongruity. How could the young players learn their instruments and establish their repertoire except through listening to and imitating phonograph records? Such was how all the American musics had been learned here and abroad since the commercial record appeared in 1920. In the early 1950s, however, the pop stream was producing records that could not easily serve this purpose. The A&R men of the major labels were making records that did not lend themselves to imitation by the young players. In the absence of name swing bands, the studio chiefs were presenting vocalists with all sorts of individualizing markers, backed by complex arrangements played by anonymous studio musicians. Moreover, the new technologies of magnetic tape and electronics invited the A&R men to put their own unique aural stamp on each record. Echo chambers, multiple track overdubbing, and other technological "gimmicks" were used to give each record label's top producers their own personal signature. It would not be easy for future Elvises to go to school on the records of Mitch Miller. They would look elsewhere, finding models in the simpler records coming from black pop and country music. The pop stream, in other words, was not providing a young audience with either a danceable music or one they could learn to play themselves. It was ignoring the youth audience, thereby deepening the generational split and continuing the musical vacuum created by the loss of the big bands.

One reason for this inattention was that the pop stream was busy with television. The FCC freeze on television ended in 1952.[4] Instantly, the number of TV stations nearly tripled. By the end of the fifties, there were 673 stations on the air, an increase of more than 600 percent for that decade.[5] As television became the nation's main entertainment during the prime evening hours, the music publishers channeled into that huge maw the exposure and exploitation energies previously devoted to network radio. For a brief moment, it appeared that television would succeed in turning the clock back to the days when the "sheet" guided the music business. *Billboard* even developed a special chart, "Songs with Most TV Performances."[6]

It was soon apparent that television, especially its top network music and variety shows, could sell a song and make a star. The leading vocalists and even some of their younger protégés found places on such programs, with a repertoire largely comprised of the standards of prewar days. The conservatism of commercial sponsorship, enforced by the advertising agencies, made the older ASCAP catalogues the desirable musical property. This policy paid off; television earnings throughout its first decade were steadily on the increase.[7] By the late 1950s, though, the internal constraints of the nighttime TV rating struggle elbowed popular music programming off the air. There were a few exceptions, spastic attempts to exploit the teenage music boom with cumbersome formats that embarrassed both adults and the young.[8]

During this same time period, the monolithic movie industry's long embrace with the music business was drastically altered. First, the Justice Department, in the famous Alden-Rochelle matter, ended ASCAP's direct collection rights from movie houses. These substantial monies now had to be negotiated centrally with the producers.[9] Then the Justice Department won its major antitrust case against the seven major studios. They were forced to separate the production side from the distribution end of the business. "Block booking" ceased, as did other restrictive practices that had frozen the American movie scene into a highly controlled set of offerings. Independent and foreign films could now more readily enter the market and did so.

The newly unleashed movie distribution system had an even more important result. The number of drive-in movies, an invention of the 1930s that totaled only about one hundred in 1945, grew explosively, reaching 3800 in 1953.[10] The suburbanization of the nation and its attendant baby boom fueled this expansion. Culture in every form followed the people to the suburbs.[11] By 1953, the number of regular movie theaters in the cities had declined by 25 percent, while the drive-in theater commanded 20 percent of the movie theaters, an increase from the less than 1 percent just after the war. Teenagers were believed to be the controlling sector of the drive-in audience, so teenage movies were soon to follow. *Blackboard Jungle* in 1955, *Rock Around the Clock* in 1956, and over 360 others over the next fifteen years flooded out of the Hollywood gates, pairing rocknroll and teenage rebelliousness.[12] Thus the movies, America's most popular commercial, out-of-home entertainment form, were deepening the age-based audience split that the in-home forms (radio, phonograph, television) were also creating. Rocknroll would be linked to movies throughout its development, continuing the entwined fate of music and movies that had begun at the turn of the century.

The dominance of the phonograph record in the pop stream stimulated the jukebox industry, which was feeling its oats with over a half million outlets at its disposal and command of somewhere between a quarter and a third of all record sales. Its pressure on the record labels to generate an ever faster succession of new songs and new performers was considerable. Some jukebox operators wanted even more. As early as 1953, a few, especially those servicing locations that used a lot of black pop and country pop records, were actively creating publishing firms and developing new performers and new record labels. They were using the boxes to pre-test records pressed in their own factories and recorded by artists they controlled—a miniature, vertically integrated operation. More ominously, some jukebox leaders were discussing the creation of their own performance rights licensing organization.[13] They never did organize such, nor were they able to secure any important place in any of the streams' creative departments. They did, though, spread the phonograph record to the wall.

An analogously integrated structure, enhancing the classical end of the pop stream, was forming between the LP record, the high-fidelity phonograph, and FM radio. As the hi-fi craze of the early 1950s ballooned, the proponents of FM radio sought from the FCC in 1945 the right to establish new FM stations, separate and independent of an AM parentage. They were refused. Instead, AM stations were granted complete freedom to broadcast simultaneous programs on an FM band. For these and other complex financial reasons, the number of FM stations actually declined from a peak year of just over one thousand in 1948 to half that number by 1956.[14] Nevertheless, though a minority taste, the classical repertoire on the LP record and the hi-fi home musical system, together with a thin slice of radio programming, kept FM alive. Further down the road, in 1967, it would house the progressive FM rock programming that would appear on the West Coast.

ASCAP and BMI Again: The Schwartz Case

Although the pop stream was growing in this postwar moment, carried along by the successful mix of radio, television, records, jukebox, and movies, it was nonetheless suffering from both diminished adult audiences and the incursion of country pop and black pop. These two musics were largely licensed by BMI, further fueling the hostility of the ASCAP leadership. Some New York music circles, especially those ASCAP members close to the musical theater and movie musicals, had never accepted the creation of BMI or the consent decrees of 1941 or 1950 with the Justice Department. They saw ASCAP's displacement from the creative center of the pop stream as causing not only reduced income but a change in the nation's musical taste. The threat to their status, they believed, came from the alliance of broadcasters, their creature BMI, and the record companies. The threat also applied to the musical culture they had built, a fact made more painful in that radio and records had once played such an important part in creating that culture.

Younger ASCAP members, those prolific in producing current pop hits, also concluded that BMI was responsible for the growth of the pop song on records. To compound all of ASCAP's other difficulties, then, these rebelling young Turks further frustrated the embattled senior members. The main demand in that rebellion was for revision of the Society's distribution system in the direction of greater and more immediate payout for current performances, recorded as well as live. The senior writers' and the publishers' distribution committees of the Society were in no hurry to impoverish themselves, and they distracted everybody with noisy assaults on BMI, the broadcasters, the state of the culture, and so on. It would take years for the near schizophrenic denunciation of BMI and the simultaneous imitation of its methods to subside.

ASCAP's internal dissension was partially deflected by the mobilization of the Songwriters of America. This association was an unofficial ASCAP group, led by Stanley Adams, former ASCAP president, which mobilized money and prominent writers against BMI and others deemed unfair to songwriters.[15] Arthur Schwartz, composer of "Dancing in the Dark" and other standards, was steeped in the Broadway-Hollywood musical tradition. He had practiced law before giving up his amateur status as songwriter to become a highly successful writer, producer, and, later in his career, a performer of his own songs. A highly articulate and litigious spokesman, his views (a deposition of some twelve hundred pages) foreshadowed the dramatic payola hearings of 1958 and 1959 in the U.S. Congress.

It was bad enough, Schwartz argued, that the publishers' earnings were declining both in movies and television. What was worse was that the major record companies, in alliance with the disk jockeys on independent stations, were clearly in the driver's seat in the making of pop hits. The most immediate source of ASCAP's smouldering frustration was BMI's success in scoring so many of those hits.

As early as 1951, some of ASCAP's leading members had prevailed upon the Society to lodge a formal complaint against BMI and the broadcasters. The Justice Department had declined to move. Not deterred, Arthur Schwartz took action in November 1953, leading thirty-two other notables of popular and serious music (including Samuel Barber, Ira Gershwin, Alan Jay Lerner, Gian Carlo Menotti, and Virgil Thomson) in bringing suit in Federal Court against BMI, the major networks, and other individuals. The stakes were far from trivial; the damages asked for were $150 million, valued today at more than four times that amount. The complaint was that the defendants had conspired to deprive ASCAP music of the radio, record, and film exposure necessary for that music to find public acceptance, giving preference instead to the music of BMI's own publishers and writers. That music, the ASCAP accusers were soon the tell the world, was trash, if not dangerous trash. What else but deliberate, collusive exclusion could account for the steady decline of ASCAP's music, the music that had won the hearts of the American people for almost half a century?

The evidence for ASCAP's complaints was embodied in the music popularity charts, where BMI's tunes were increasingly receiving a good showing. The data in Table 6-1 show the percentage of BMI-licensed tunes among *Billboard*'s best-selling pop singles over the years 1942–1951. Nearly identical trends obtained on the other pop charts; sheet music sales, jukebox plays, and disk jockeys plays all showed a decline in ASCAP music.

In its defense, BMI told a different story. ASCAP was doing very well, BMI asserted, in those very broadcasting areas where it *shouldn't* if the networks were successfully leading a conspiracy to keep ASCAP music off the air. On network radio from 1947 through 1951, ASCAP music formed about 75 percent of all musical performances, BMI totaled only 15 percent, and the rest was music in the public domain or licensed by others. In contrast, local radio stations performed ASCAP's music only

60 percent of the time; BMI music, slightly over 23 percent. The same pattern was observed for television; network television, when compared to independent TV stations, gave substantially more performances to ASCAP than to BMI tunes.

The evidence BMI's leaders provided to show that ASCAP was the overwhelming leader both of network radio and network television music could be read a different way, however, and everyone in the music business did so. The significant fact was not the percentage advantage ASCAP enjoyed with the *networks*; it was the rising influence of the local *independent* stations that alarmed the Society. The key figures are those shown in Table 6-2.

The growth in musical performances was clearly at the local level. While in 1947 local stations broadcast three times as much music as did the networks, by 1951 they were producing *five* times as many performances. Thus, it was the local station that was putting the hits on the air. Moreover, BMI's total radio performances increased by almost 100 percent over the years 1947 through 1951, while ASCAP's grew only about 50 percent. These numbers underscored the belief that the future of popular music lay in the hands of the disk jockey on the independent stations.

The Schwartz case would fizzle and sputter for years, floundering in show business' stormy weather, and would finally be snuffed out as new issues in intellectual property rights came to the fore. BMI would survive and flourish. Its two major musical reservoirs, country pop and black

TABLE 6-1

Percentages of BMI and ASCAP Tunes on Billboard's Best-Selling Popular Records Charts (1942–1951)

	1942	1944	1946	1947	1948	1949	1950	1951
% BMI	5	10	7	13	3	14	23	37
% ASCAP	95	90	93	87	97	86	77	63
Number of top records	(20)	(10)	(41)	(30)	(30)	(28)	(30)	(30)

SOURCE: *Annual Tabulations of Music Popularity (1940–1951)*, Bureau of Applied Social Research, Columbia University, 1952.

TABLE 6-2

Musical Performances in Radio, 1947 and 1951

	Network	Local
1947	15.3 million	45.4 million
1951	16.8 million	82.2 million

SOURCE: Affidavit of Carl Haverlin, Civil Action 89–103, United States District Court, Southern District of New York. *In opposition to ASCAP's motion for an order modifying amended final judgment of March 14, 1950*, pp. 21, 21a.

pop, would develop quite on their own into independent streams of great power. Outlined next are the developments that gave both of them their strength and their proximity to the pop stream.

The Country Music Scene

Country music was shaped into a commercially dominated stream quite rapidly during the first postwar decade. As early as 1946 the trade press warned the New York publishing and recording establishment that the hillbillies were beginning to wise up, that the country music market could no longer be harvested in the old way.[16] The days of quick field trips spent collecting songs and performances paid for in small bills were long over. Standard contracts for songwriters, publishers, and performers were being demanded, as was delivery of the royalties. No longer could the New York music scene treat "hillbilly" music as an occasional wild flower to be plucked from the side of the road. It was becoming a steady crop, firmly contained within the business practices that had made the pop stream so lucrative. When country was accurately perceived as a permanent resource of unlimited size, the struggle over its exploitation began.

The first step in that process was geographic. The establishment of Nashville as country music's production center in 1946 began with the joinder of a performance site, the Grand Ole Opry; a radio station, WSM, with its recording studio; and a publishing house, that of Acuff-Rose (a partnership between Roy Acuff, "King of the Hillbillies," and Fred Rose, a former ASCAP-affiliated publisher who switched to BMI after failing to interest ASCAP circles in the potential Nashville gold mine).[17] Almost immediately, the publishers and the major record companies planted offices and studios in Nashville, and its Music Row soon rivaled its sister districts in New York and Los Angeles. The Hollywood-based motion picture industry and the large southern California country music establishment in Bakersfield lost out in the process. The victory went to an eastern alliance of publishers, the major record companies, and the network radio executives that had built the pyramid of country music stations, live performance tours, and barn dance programs for regional network radio. Nashville became the capital of country music.

The next step was the name; *Billboard*, on 25 June 1949, recognizing that "Folk" no longer was appropriate, added the designation "Country and Western" (C&W) to the chart that would gather the diverse strains which made up the country music stream. The various musics were gradually brought together within the rubrics of the broadcasting and recording industries, not an easy task since there were fierce hostilities between those different strains. One of the most resistant was the old mountain music, the "hillbilly" part of country. With a new name, "blue-grass," Bill Monroe in the 1940s domesticated and regularized this passionate and energetic mix of secular dance tunes, sentimental story-songs, and spirituals for the Grand Ole Opry. Its distinctive instrumentation of guitars, fiddle, banjo, and mandolin and a host of performers, including the prolific Lester Flatt and Earl Scruggs, brought that music intact through the fifties. It flourishes today in different venues and with various refreshments from rocknroll and the other streams.

There was generally in the forties a resistance to the new musical technology and its commercial practices, for southern culture was anchored in rural and religious traditions. This integration of diverse country styles took, among other things, the skills of disk jockeys in the South to meld the whole thing together. One example of how unity was achieved is provided by a veteran disk jockey from Memphis, interviewed in 1952:

> I use top hillbilly records and some western. As a whole about 20 per cent of the true mountain type, Bill Monroe. That Kentucky kind is the "countriest" with hymn, semi-religious, and more of folk music. Then about 10 per cent of the Western kind, which is like pop in such people like Pee Wee King—his "Tennessee Waltz," and Spade Cooley—like his "Carman's Boogie." The rest, about 70 per cent is Nashville, the cross between Kentucky and Western. It is more pop-styled guitar—uptown. The pop lyrics are less mature, sound like they're ground out by machine.

It also took the talents, both musical and political, of the major labels' in-house producers to domesticate the independent spirit of country performers. RCA Victor's Chet Atkins was the preeminent example of such an A&R man. His own self-defined position was between pop and country, spiced with as much jazz flavoring as he could get away with. From Hank Snow and Eddy Arnold to Conway Twitty and, ultimately, Elvis himself, Atkins created an elegant, commercial Nashville sound that still sets the standards for performance.[18]

In the course of defining itself, the new country stream created a set of tour routes that reached into the cities and regions responsive to its performance styles and musical content. From Texas to California, the tradition of western swing was strongly entrenched in a vigorous music-for-dancing tradition, which was tied into the gritty efforts of many country performers to translate their musical successes into palpable real estate, commercial ventures, and every other fruit of vertical integration.[19] In the East and Midwest, country artists were mobilized into traveling shows that revitalized a once vigorous network of folk music parks. By 1949, some sixty or more large, outdoor arenas from New England through New York, Pennsylvania, Ohio, and Indiana were hosting weekly shows by top country and western talent. New managers and booking agencies were expanding these successful events into the major cities, for example,

the Jolly Joyce Agency (which booked Bill Haley and the Comets) in Philadelphia, and Colonel Tom Parker (who also represented Elvis Presley after his Sun Records contract) throughout the major cities in Florida.

The audiences for country music, especially for live performances at
this time (the early 1950s), were exclusively white. Once again, the disk
jockey was the one working the intractable boundary between country
and rhythm and blues, trying to find a way those musics might reach
each other and a way for both to cross over into the pop stream. Here is
the lament of a recently transplanted northern disk jockey who was attempting to bring hit-making practices to a large, central Texas city back
in 1952:

There is no teenage activity in this town. I'm now trying with the City Council
to get a regular dance arrangement so that I can bring in shows and conduct
teenage dances. There are only two or three dances a year because of the Baptists
here. The kids like either pop or hillbilly. They're real fanatic, and here the kids,
white, lean to r&b. They call it cat music, so I play some rhythm and blues. I
started it in Cleveland and was surprised that it went so well. I continued it here,
but not the real "low down" stuff.

Within this divided, white record audience, the disk jockeys and the
entire pop stream machinery worked. The aim was to fill the vacuum left
by the swing bands and to extend country music into the as yet untapped
southern regions. One of the main devices in this effort was the "barn
dance" show. These largely musical extravaganzas were at the apex of
the country and western field, conferring great prestige and exposure on
the artists invited to broadcast. Even though the "Grand Ole Opry," the
"National Barn Dance," and the ten or so other major network country
shows were at the top, there were still hundreds of shows on local, independent stations, constituting a large country music pyramid.[20] At the
very base of that pyramid were the hundreds of thousands of jukeboxes
playing country records. Above that base were the thousands of live performers on the more than 650 radio stations using live country musicians.[21] Many of these performers were playing in the thousands of southern roadhouses and dance halls from Norfolk, Virginia, to Los Angeles
(and increasingly, after the war, up into the Northwest and Midwest).

The structure was efficient and crystal clear in its construction. Young
country performers got easy bookings in clubs and roadhouses and also
in the small radio stations that since the 1920s had been hospitable to
live country music. These live music programs were nourished in a mu-
tually sustaining exchange with country disk jockey programming, the
recorded and live performance systems feeding each other. Selection for
an Opry appearance and recruitment into its ranks was the peak achievement for the field. It was also a strong, disciplinary influence that kept

the moral slate clean, if not hypocritically pious. This moral tone existed because the religious component of country music was close to its secular side at the level of national radio shows. A comparable network tradition buttressed the subtle banning or cleansing of the rougher sides of country lyrics. The honky-tonk sound and the lyrics celebrating or mourning the travail of unfaithful married love were so sanitized that the whole tradition could be played just as easily on network radio shows as at Saturday night roadhouse dances.

Closest to the music-making itself were the record companies. Country music was to grow and meet the other streams in the fifties at the hands of a few major record companies, who held an almost complete monopoly over its performers. These companies were, not surprisingly, the majors in the pop stream as well.

The extent of that domination is clear from a summary of best-selling records. From 1946 to 1953, *Billboard's* annual listings of each year's top 20 best-selling country records showed that only seven of those 160 records were from independents, less than 5 percent of the total.[22] Six of those seven records were from labels that had strong rhythm and blues rosters.[23] These labels, as will be discussed later, were located geographically and musically so as to provide an effective outlet for every tendency in country music denied full public view.[24] Country music was a far richer and more sophisticated domain than was at first thought. It was ready to expand beyond its boundaries but prepared to fend off any penetration by "alien" influences, musical or otherwise.

The Black Pop Stream Assembles

A radically different story unfolded in black pop music after World War I. Unlike country music, protected and nurtured within the powerful vehicles of network radio and the major record companies, black popular music began its postwar journey with almost nothing. There was only the wreckage of the "race" record field that had been so vigorous during the 1930s, the disintegrating swing band era, and essentially no black radio. There was, however, a rich treasury of performers, a full reservoir of musical and lyrical material, and a multifarious, if lowly, set of performance sites, sacred and secular.[25]

At this moment, the black parts of jazz, pop, and black pop intermingled their personnel and musical material quite freely, with many attempts being made to create a unitary black popular music combining them all. For example, Billy Eckstine's 1944 band included senior bop founders Dizzy Gillespie and Charlie Parker, as well as Art Blakey, Miles Davis, and Sarah Vaughan. The tunes in that band's book were friendly neither to professional stage tap dancing nor to amateur vernacular dance. Jazz, white pop, and black pop separated. The six streams once again held their boundaries.

What emerged was not a hierarchical pyramid centered in a single capital city as in country music, but rather a new national entity constructed out of a group of cities. Within each of them, built over older institutions that had provided the talent and the performance sites for more than a century, were several new parts: black radio, black-oriented record labels, independent recording studios, and a variety of new performance venues.[26]

Two incidents, trivial in themselves, reveal how the interconnected parts of this new national infrastructure worked. In the mid-1950s, Joe Tex, a rising black rhythm and blues entertainer, met the even younger James Brown just before they were to appear on the same bill at the City Auditorium in Macon, Georgia. Both were touring to promote their current releases on the independent King label. Tex recalls,

I pulled up in front of the theater and he came up and introduced himself, told me who he was, said that he and I was gonna have a battle that night, battle of the blues. I said, "Yeah?" He says "Yeah. Draw the people." And he wanted me to go 'round with him to the local radio station to do an interview. So we got on the air and talked it up and this sort of thing.[27]

The second instance concerns the visit of Art Rupe to New Orleans. Rupe had founded Specialty Records in Hollywood in 1944 and had had surprising successes with Roy Milton, Joe Liggins, and Percy Mayfield (each with chart-topping records). He reports,

I went down to find some talent in New Orleans and I made an announcement on a black radio show called "The Okey Dokey Radio Show" that I was looking for talent. I had no way of getting this talent to come to this recording studio, Cosimo Matassa's. It was one little recording studio in the black section, right off the French Quarter there, where the black people went to.[28]

This emerging, built-by-hand structure that could reach the highest media board rooms as well as the humblest juke joint provided the vehicles to express black aspirations, just at the moment when black political and cultural thought was poised for the coming civil rights struggle. Those vehicles would also revitalize white popular music and provide rebellious white youth with experiences more consequential than anyone expected. Independent black radio stations and record labels, and an increasingly mobile network of performers and producers, would give new power to the black pop stream. Its name, "Rhythm and Blues," was bestowed by *Billboard*'s Paul Ackerman on 25 June 1949.

The spectacular growth of black radio was premised by the wartime experience that black audiences could be profitably reached with appropriate programming. After the war, the dethronement of the radio networks by television and the rapid increase of independent stations occasioned the sidestepping, to a great degree, of radio's established, anti-black broadcasting policies. Even in 1943, *Billboard*, keeping track of this sensitive issue, reported some changes.

For years it has been, and still is, a rule in radio that Negro artists may not be introduced on any *commercial* network show with the appellation of Mr. Mrs. or Miss preceding his or her name. . . . Radio still has a rule that a Negro cannot be represented in any drama except in the role of a servant or as an ignorant or comical person. Also the role of the American Negro in the war effort cannot be mentioned in a *sponsored* program. Despite this, Negroes have made progress on the radio. Golden Gate Quartet had a CBS sustaining for two years and now is on the Amos & Andy *sponsored* show. Teddy Wilson's band was on Duffy's Tavern earlier this year. John Kirby's band had a CBS *sustaining* a couple of years ago—Hazel Scott, the Boogie Boys and other Cafe Society performers have guested on many network and local programs. . . . Negroes have begun to land jobs on radio house bands thanks mostly to John Hammond's persuasions. (my emphasis)[29]

There are three lessons here: (1) commercial sponsors were the main enforcers of anti-black policies; (2) the networks obeyed but were subject to inside, high-level persuasion (such as John Hammond) on the race issue; and (3) only a certain type of black music could get on the air, particularly gospel and sophisticated Broadway or jazz-tinged black pop. This latter lesson was not lost on black performers for more than a decade following the war.

Because of these network practices and the opportunities offered small unaffiliated stations by the FCC, programming to black audiences developed largely on *independent* radio. Still, the attitude was a significant difficulty, expressed precisely in a comment by a southern advertising executive in the early 1950s:

Pillsbury's flour is one of our biggest accounts. If it gets out that we were pushing Negro talent on a Pillsbury program, the next thing you know, it would be branded a "nigger flour" and it would never move.[30]

Neither legal rights nor the artistic merit of black musicians decided the issue, though both were essential. What opened the door to black radio was the demonstration that musical content finely tuned to an advertising message could produce income for the radio station as well as for the advertiser.

All this rethinking culminated in 1949 with the opening of the 250-watt independent WDIA in Memphis, probably the first of many white-owned stations programming almost exclusively to the black community. Memphis, it should be noted, was demographically "the right place at the right time," being a metropolitan city of about half a million people with a third of that population being nonwhite.[31] But it was more than just demographically right for black music. Even prior to W. C. Handy's appropriation of the blues in his Memphis publishing days early in the century, the city was a center for popular black music. It was another inland seaport like Kansas City. This Mississippi riverport, with all its intense nightlife, mixed and melded the musical styles of New Orleans, the Territories (mainly Texas), and the eastern seaboard. Traveling entertainment companies, white and black, from vaudeville to circuses, as well as touring bands paused to refresh themselves and exchange news and music.

Quite naturally, then, WDIA's main programming centered around black popular music, delivered in disk jockey programming and including jazz, gospel, and every style of black pop. In the conventional fashion of the time, the station offered women's shows, religious programs on Sunday, a discussion forum on community issues, a new talent showcase for teenage vocalists, and so on. This programming mosaic is nicely illustrated in the publicity photo issued by WDIA showing both the personnel and the programming (see figure 6-1). That mix of programs worked, and the station flourished. By 1954, WDIA was beaming 50,000 watts to all the mid-South, becoming the most powerful radio voice of the black community in the region if not in the nation. Surveys satisfied the station's belief that it had not lost but augmented its white audiences.

The stature of the station's disk jockeys helped. B. B. King began his career in Memphis as WDIA's combination disk jockey and performer. So, too, did the Reverend Dwight (Gatemouth) Moore, known nationally as a spiritual and blues singer. Sister Rosetta Tharpe, in the midst of her gospel career, was a strong impresarial presence on WDIA.[32] Muddy Waters had also been a disk jockey (at West Memphis' KWEM) and a performer in Memphis, leaving that city for Chicago in 1949, the very year B. B. King arrived in Memphis from Mississippi. The station and its personnel were soon connected to every phase of musical production in Memphis and in its surrounding countryside. Though the segregated dance halls and honky-tonks separated the races, the radio dial allowed both white and black music into everyone's home. Even forbidden stations were listened to by youth of both races. Some of those listeners were likely to have been Elvis Presley and his friends at Memphis' all-white Humes High School.

For the emerging rhythm and blues radio scene to become more than a local phenomenon, it had to find a way to repeat itself in many cities and then connect the cities together. This expansion happened in a rush, primarily in cities with some combination of large black populations, a rich musical tradition, and/or some adventurous entrepreneurial talent, such as in Birmingham, Atlanta, and New Orleans. By 1955, more than

l to r: Joe Hill Louis, Ford Nelson, pno, A.C. 'Moohah' Williams, B.B. King, Maurice 'Hot Rod' Hulbert, Professor Nat. D. Williams (courtesy WDIA)

WDIA

MEMPHIS, TENNESSEE
SPECIALIZING IN THE NEGRO MARKET

JUNE, 1952

Figure 6-1. WDIA Program Log and Station Personnel. Source: *Blues Unlimited* 140, Spring 1981, p. 10. Used with permission of WDIA.

six hundred stations were programming to the black communities large and small in thirty-nine states, with thirty-six stations devoting their entire schedules to black-oriented material.[33] Rhythm and blues vied with black gospel as the two major musics. Each had its own disk jockeys, their numbers increasing steadily over the course of the decade.[34]

The Independents: "Short Loop" and "Long Loop"

The appearance and rapid growth of the independent record labels after 1945 paralleled the growth of black-oriented radio stations. Both were crucial for the development of rhythm and blues. The story of these small record companies has been told many times.[35] They were the inheritors of "race" record production, which was all but abandoned by the majors. The field was thus open territory, with relatively low capital requirements. Hundreds of small firms were created on the approximately $1000 then required to record and press five hundred copies of a record.[36] Anywhere from four to six hundred record labels with some commitment to rhythm and blues appeared in the years immediately following the war. Approximately seventy-five to one hundred had enough activity and stability to be listed in *Cash Box* and *Billboard*'s regular or special coverage of the field.

The ranks soon thinned. After the initial flood, less than ten companies dominated the field by 1949. Of *Billboard*'s fifty best-selling rhythm and blues records between 1949 and 1953, only 8 percent were from the major labels.[37] This distribution is the exact opposite found in country music where, it will be recalled, less than 5 percent of the top records were from independent companies. While practically all recorded country music was in the hands of the six major companies, almost two-thirds of the fifty records on the annual best-selling R&B records were issued by seven independents. These were Alladin, Atlantic, Chess, King, Modern, Savoy, and Specialty. Each of these firms followed the customary policy of using one or more subsidiary labels with different names.

Perhaps the most important accomplishment of these companies, beyond the discovery and grooming of the artists who gave rhythm and blues its vitality and diversity, was the re-defining of black pop's postwar boundaries, both musical and geographic. The black parts of the jazz, folk, and gospel streams were to go their own ways as black pop built its own streambed, wide and deep enough to create and distribute its newly emerging treasure. That stream's structure consisted of "short loops" loosely tied together to form a national "long loop." The short loop was a geographically localized embodiment of the three components of the stream, that is, a flourishing artistic system, a market efficient enough to support it, and a social movement celebrating and expressing the identity of its members. All these were constructed in those major cities that had substantial black populations. The key to each of these city markets was the linkage between the out-of-home performance sites, the jukebox, the emerging black radio, and the new record companies with their distribution and retail outlets. The short loop traced the path from audience demand through exposure points to retail sales; from the discovery of new talent and tunes to their incorporation into marketed phonograph records.

The workings of the rhythm and blues short loop began with and depended on the single record. From 1920 on, the single had been the basic unit, imitating, as closely as possible, the experience of a live, spontaneous performance and carrying it to the black home. Written sheet music was limited to that thin stratum of black musicians who participated in the music publishing world. The recording process was largely that of a studio-captured, "head arrangement."

Records were available in two places, in the jukebox and at the local record store. In the late 1940s and 1950s, before R&B disk jockeys, the jukebox was the main point of exposure. Records moved more slowly and made less of a national impact. Yet the demand for records so far exceeded the supply that almost anyone could enter the market. Enterprising black music men used the jukebox as a radio station:

For this Webb gave them anywhere from $1 to $5 in special quarters painted red, green, and blue so they could play the record he was pushing during peak hours. "I'd tell them to play it when the bar's crowded on Friday or Saturday. When it was baseball night or ladies' night or guild night. They felt important because I brought a record to them. Nobody else was doing that. They usually had to wait for the jukebox operator to come by once a month, but I'd go there personally with a record and say, "You don't have to play it. I'll give you four quarters to play it." It's that personal touch that helps me stay in business.[38]

In this way even the black community's beer drinkers and bartenders subsidized and were part of the short loop.

A surprising number of independent record companies began either in the jukebox industry (e.g., the Bihari brothers, founders of Modern Records) or from the retail record trade. Since most of the R&B outlets were, in the words of Specialty Records' Art Rupe, "little hole-in-the-wall places owned by black proprietors [who] couldn't get credit,"[39] those with the most initiative produced their own records. It was that intimate connection with the marketing of local black records that gave the independent producers their sensitivity to audience taste and the performers their ability to meet it.

Another route to a viable operation came from radio, once black music was programmed. Disk jockeys, both white and black, were magnets that drew thousands of young hopefuls to their studios. The amateur talent show, going back to network radio's "Major Bowes Amateur Hour" in the 1930s, was still a third route for musicians. In the fifties, the reigning exemplification was Arthur Godfrey's Talent Scouts, who were responsible for advancing the careers of hundreds of performers. The Apollo Theater in New York did the same work for black performers. Perhaps a quarter of the recording artists of the fifties began with the help of disk jockeys and/or talent shows.[40] The ports of entry into a singing career were wide open for all, including young black performers.

The manufacturing of records and their distribution were much more troublesome matters. In each of the major cities, the independents found solutions. For manufacturing records they either lured some of the knowledgeable personnel away from the major pressing companies, they started with secondhand parts and built record manufacturing companies from the ground up, or they cajoled the major companies into short-term leasing arrangements. Distribution of rhythm and blues records by the new independents was difficult. It was accomplished piece by piece, using extensions of retail networks or the jukebox distribution routes to which many independents already belonged.[41] The record distribution system itself responded to the rapid growth of small labels by elaborating a new kind of service. By 1952 the "one-stops," as the new firms were called, gave the small labels service to the jukeboxes *and* the retailers. Their financial arrangements were more fragile than those for the major record companies; payment was slow, and discount and full record returns were not as generous.

The "long loop" is the extension of the separate components of the short loop into adjacent and distant cities, bringing all the short loops together into a grand national machinery. It was more or less completed by the early 1950s and included most of the nation's large cities. A few, notably New Orleans, Houston, Memphis, Chicago, Cincinnati, Detroit, Los Angeles, and the San Francisco Bay area, had all the components in place and produced more than their share of the emerging black musical culture that was national in scope. In some cities, there was only a network of small clubs playing to separate white and black audiences. In others, the scene consisted of scattered jukeboxes, social clubs, and other small venues supporting live performances.

In still other cities, the prestigious large theater topped the black community's entertainment calender. In fact, the six great black theaters of the 1940s and 1950s, the Apollo in Harlem, the Lincoln in Los Angeles, the Regal in Chicago, the Paradise in Detroit, the Howard in Washington, and the Royal in Baltimore, were important factors for the whole system. It was in these theaters that many a young performer was discovered, and on these stages the success of others was validated. Each had its own audiences and tastes, producing a mix of styles, yet each could still fit under the capacious "rhythm and blues" designation. Beneath these prime theaters were layers of clubs ranging from "uptown" elegance to the lowest of "downtown" dives. The entire long loop gave black pop a market size and visibility that rivaled the other two large streams. The pop stream was particularly alert to the growing power of the black hit parade.

The connections among the separate short loops in each of the major cities provided the long loop with resources to refresh each of its parts. Their exchanges of local hits and performers injected new material into the stream. This search for new material brings up the issue of satiation again, the perennial need to refresh the stream after its current crop is exhausted. Art Rupe in Los Angeles offers a typical example. He had traveled to New Orleans in 1952, busy with the normal practice of searching out talent in the hinterland. The stimulus to the venture was his impresarial intuition that satiation was imminent. "His LA musicians were getting somewhat glib. 'I didn't feel the spontaneity that I felt originally' he says. 'Either I needed a change or they needed one.'"[42]

Rupe brought back from New Orleans what he went for and more. He reportedly wanted to bring the Fats Domino *sound* back to Los Angeles, not Fats in live performance. The R&B short loop at that time was often based on jukebox venues, so the movement of live talent from city to city was unnecessary to maintain and revitalize the system. The process involved producers moving from city to city, collecting tapes and demos and scouting for performers in local clubs. In this way, Little Richard came to Rupe's *Los Angeles* label. Little Richard had been under contract to Don Robey's Peacock Records in *Houston* for a few years with not much commercial success. Before that he had recorded several songs with RCA Victor as a result of winning a talent contest in *Atlanta*. He sent a demo to Rupe, who took a year to decide that he liked what he heard. He bought Richards' contract from Robey and arranged for a recording session in *New Orleans*. The result was "Tutti Frutti," the first of a long string of hits Little Richard recorded for Specialty.[43] Similar stories were repeated many times in different places. Any city could become the take-off place for an R&B performer in those days. A successful record in one market was tried out in the rest of the cities, sometimes producing a national star performer. Failure in one city was not the end of the road.

The search for fresh material led, of course, to the boundaries of adjacent streams. King Records in Cincinnati is the most dramatic case. Syd Nathan in 1945 formed that company in a city that enjoyed a highly developed country music radio presence. WLW, a 50,000-watt NBC affiliate, and WCKY, a 50,000-watt independent, both programmed country music extensively at that time. Respectable Cincinnati and its sin sister city Covington, Kentucky, across the Ohio River were regularly visited by separate black and white entertainment packages moving along the Midwest tour routes. The racial boundary was, of course, a mile high, but the music and the river flowed under and around it.

Nathan signed a few of the country artists who had eluded the major record companies, including Moon Mullican, Cowboy Copas, and Wayne Raney. They all tended towards a raunchy mixture of country-boogie and honky-tonk style celebrated in Covington and places like it all over the South and Southwest. He also built a stable of black pop performers similar in style to his country acts, notably Bull Moose Jackson and Lucky Millinder. When the 1000-watt, all-black station WCIN opened in 1953, Nathan's operation intensified the pattern it had begun eight years earlier, using the same songs performed by the appropriate artist for the country market or the new black pop audience.[44]

This early crossover of Cincinnati's rhythm and blues short loop into country was perhaps more extreme than that found in other cities, but in Los Angeles, Memphis, Philadelphia, Detroit, and others, country music and black pop flourished side by side. The independent record companies and some of the disk jockeys brought them closer together. Racial segregation, however, obscured the narrowing cultural distance between the three major streams.

The Impresarial Presence

From this story, it is clear that one more element was important in building each short loop and connecting it to the others—the impresario. In the new black pop system, this job was to be filled by as varied and controversial a group of individuals as can be imagined. Hardly any were lovable, but it was this group of mostly white men (including people as diverse as Syd Nathan and Johnny Otis) who did the essential tasks. They found the songs and the talent, shaped the performer and the performance into the confines of the single record, taught the musician the stage presence and the nightclub act to carry it, and organized the tours of performers around the nation. Only a few individuals did all these things, but collectively they put rhythm and blues into operation on a daily basis.

Many impresarios were owners of independent record companies and could do almost everything. Leonard Chess, for example, is reported to have pushed aside the drummer in a band during a recording session and beat out the percussion he knew he wanted.[45] Others came into the full impresarial role circuitously. The career of Irvin Feld illuminates how one could rise with the crest of the tide, bringing rhythm and blues to fruition and then catching the new wave carrying rocknroll. Feld's journey began in Washington, D.C., where in 1939 he owned a drugstore on Seventh Street, one of the main streets serving the black community. The practice of playing current race records from the store into the streets to attract customers was so successful that the drugstore enterprise soon moved almost entirely towards entertainment. When radio offered some black programming in the District, which it did in 1942 with the appearance of station WWDC, the Feld brothers bought airtime, and they continued to use disk jockey programming to the black community as new stations appeared on the scene. By the early 1950s, they had expanded their operation to three large record stores stocking phonographs and appliances, a music and theatrical booking agency, a share of a record company, and a record distribution service to jukeboxes. The events they produced ranged from huge spiritual concerts packing up to 23,000 people into Washington's Griffith Stadium to a summer season of plays, ballets, and popular concerts. All these affairs were closely tied to radio, which promoted the Feld retail establishments, the record stores, the concerts, and the radio disk jockeys.[46]

Feld's next move was to undertake the management of a tour of black rhythm and blues performers. By 1958 his "Biggest Show of Stars" was competing with the several other tours, including one run by Alan Freed. In the course of this activity came the opportunity for personal management. He persuaded Clyde McPhatter to leave the Drifters for a solo career that he would manage, moving McPhatter from Atlantic to MGM and a subsequent departure from the scene.[47] Concurrently, Feld had taken on as client the young (sixteen-years old) and insistent Paul Anka, who had caught the tour's performance in Canada and would not be dissuaded from beginning one of the earliest singer-songwriter careers ever. At some point, Feld's long-standing interest in the circus meshed with his talents as impresario, and he abandoned rocknroll for the Ringling Brothers Barnum and Bailey Circus, which he owns today, an instructive tale of vertical integration helping vertical mobility (poor boy growing up to own the circus is *the* American success story).

There was an important musical dimension to the impresarios' job, especially for those who concentrated on record production. The performance styles in each city took on the qualities of its local recording facilities and its personnel.[48] Most of the R&B records of the fifties bear the marks of their producers, whose specific styles could be attributed to particular cities but were also national in scope. An example that is familiar but illustrative is the Chicago success of the Chess brothers. Their advancement was due to the direct transmission of the Memphis blues tradition to Chicago, including Willie Mabon, Howlin' Wolf, Muddy Waters, Lowell Fulson, and Sonny Boy Williamson, in settings that used any combination of "piano, bass, drums, harp, amplified guitar and horns."[49] Crucial to the whole Chess operation, until 1955 at least, was Willie Dixon. As talent scout, writer, performer, and resident producer, he carried intact from the South its studio recording and performance traditions. "Everything was head arrangements. . . . You have to get a feeling and a mood. You can't work a session like that from something on paper."[50]

In sharp contrast was Jesse Stone at Atlantic Records in New York. The "uptown," sophisticated sound, smooth and controlled, that characterized much of Atlantic's output was the result of Stone's approach, which captured the traditions of an older time and place. Dixon at Chess transplanted the southern recording conditions to a Chicago studio, but Jesse Stone took a different route. On their next southern trip (1951), two of Atlantic's leading executives (Ahmet Ertegun and Herb Abramson)

invited Jesse Stone to come with them: Maybe he'd be able to figure out a way of taking advantage of southern music. He was, and music was never quite the same again. For Jesse Stone managed to find a way of writing down and reconstructing music that had previously been spontaneous and unpremeditated.[51]

The homogeneity of Atlantic's sound was not due, in other words, to the enduring performance style of a group of steady session men (Atlantic had no regular house band); it was due instead to the power of a writing producer-arranger. This rhythm and blues experience of the early 1950s was clearly another triumph of written music over the performance-carried "aural" tradition, thus bringing black pop closer to the pop stream.[52] That this victory took place in New York, capital of written music's main institutional champion—the publishers—is no cause for wonder. The irony was that Atlantic's reliance on this way of domesticating R&B put the company's leadership and its output further away from the creative developments of jazz taking place practically next door. The New York bop style was not the jazz Atlantic preferred.[53]

The whole development among the small independents is summarized in Table 6-3. The lessons summarized in this table are several. One is the close interconnection between black radio and black record production. Where they jointly occurred and interconnected, rhythm and blues developed with particular vigor. Second, the structures of the short loop brought the three major streams together in a way that facilitated the movement of songs originating in one stream to performers in another. Finally, it should be noted that the cities where rhythm and blues were nurtured were not necessarily the places of origin for rocknroll. Although the debt of rocknroll to rhythm and blues is enormous, the two musics were not the same.

The Streams Align in the Charts

As rhythm and blues achieved its national long loop, the three commercial streams came together. Their unit for exposure was now the same; the single phonograph record had become the unit of choice. Disk

TABLE 6-3
Development of the "Short Loop" in Black Popular Music, 1950s

City	Record co. (date of founding)	Founder	Black radio station	Hrs per wk. of black programming
Los Angeles	Specialty, 1944 (Jukebox Rcds.) Exclusive, 1930s (Excelsior) Modern, 1945 (Kent, Crown, RPM, Flair) Alladin, 1945 (Philo) Imperial, 1945	Art Rupe, record man Rene Brothers, songwriters Bhihari Bros., jukebox ops. Messner family, jukeboxes Lewis Chudd, radio exec.	KFVD KGFI KPOL KFOX (Long Beach) KGFR (Long Beach) KALI (Pasadena) KWKW (Pasadena) KOWL (Santa Monica)	21 18 7½ 28 40 23 12 30
Oakland	Big Town, Art-Tone Cavatone, Down Town, Irma, Plaid, Rhythm c. 1945	Bob Geddins, record store owner	KROW KWBR	12 45
Chicago	Chess 1946–47 (Checker, Cadet) Vee Jay 1952–53	Chess Bros., nightclub op. James & Vivian Carter Bracken, Calvin Carter, record store	WAAF WAIT WGES WSBC	16 7 X 20
Houston	Peacock, 1949 (Duke)	Don Robey, talent mgr., club owner	KYOK KCOH KLVL KNUZ	42 98 23 21
Nashville	Excello, 1953 (offshoot of Nasboro, gospel label)	Ernie Young, mail order record sales	WLAC WSOK	5 84
Memphis	Sun, 1953 (Memphis Recording Service, 1950)	Sam Phillips, DJ, engineer	WDIA WCBR WHBQ WMPS KWEM	84 84 17 11 35
New York	National, c. 1942–44 Atlantic 1948 Apollo, c. 1942–44	A. B. Green Ahmet Ertegun, Herb Abramson, Jerry Wexler Ike and Bess Berman, Hy Siegal, Sam Schneider, had a Harlem record store	WEVD WHOM WLIB WMCA WNJR WOV WWRL	1 26 60 7 126 60 46
Newark	Savoy, 1942	Herman G. Lubinsky, record store	WAT WHBI	14 18
Cincinnati	King, 1945	Syd Nathan, record store owner	WCIN WSAI	84 16

SOURCE: *Sponsor*, 20 September 1954.

jockeys served all three in overlapping markets. The travel routes of their performers intersected, gathering audiences for each from the others.

The final act in their alignment was to regulate their metabolic rate so that a record could cross readily from one stream to another. It was as if there were three sets of train tracks, each carrying one of the musical streams. They were now running parallel, and at the moment, the three trains were traveling at about the same speed. It should thus be possible for someone, a single record, for example, to jump safely across the tracks from one train to another.

Of course, the size and even the speed of the three streams were not exactly the same. Pop was clearly the largest of the three in its production, distribution, and exposure of records, followed at a fair distance by country, which was just ahead of rhythm and blues. During the early 1950s, the total number of singles released gradually increased from about three thousand a year in 1950 to over five thousand a year by the midfifties. Their allocation among the three streams for the year 1952 was 62 percent pop, 26 percent country, and 12 percent rhythm and blues.[54] These numbers fluctuated perhaps 5 percentage points in either direction from year to year during this period.

The availability of distribution outlets for those records varied from place to place, of course, with R&B suffering from a less adequate system. *Billboard*'s annual survey of the nation's record distributors for 1953 showed that they were handling pop, country, and rhythm and blues records in roughly the same proportions as were being produced. The percentages were 66 percent pop, 26 percent country and western, 8 percent rhythm and blues. So, in aggregate terms, the distribution part of the complete cycle accurately reflected the amount of production in the three fields.

Such was probably not the case with radio exposure of the music. In a 1948 national survey, *Music Business* reported on the types of musical programs conducted by over eighteen hundred disk jockeys on more than six hundred stations. The distribution of the three main types were as follows: "popular" programs comprised 77 percent, "folk" (i.e., country), 19 percent, and 4 percent were "race" programs.[55] While these data are only suggestive, they indicate that rhythm and blues had far less access to radio exposure than did the other two fields. Pop records were disproportionately played on the air, given the number released and distributed.[56]

By 1953, even if there was some lack of parity among the three major streams in their air play, their music popularity charts were being treated similarly. In *Billboard*, the three streams were given separate sections, but the charts were identical: Best Selling Singles, Most Played in Juke Box, Most Played by Disk Jockeys.[57] From the typography, the organization of the page, and the information contained therein, the markets were made to appear as equal entities, even though the three were of distinctly different sizes. Any song, record, or performer moving among them was instantly recognizable to anyone with any familiarity with pop music. The surface identity of the three major streams by 1955, as seen in their visual presentation in *Billboard*'s pages, is startling compared to their look in 1948 or earlier when "folk" and "race" hardly mattered in the music trade (compare figure 6-2 with figures 4-2, 4-3, and 4-4).

There was one remaining problem: The three streams were not running at the same speed. This problem was soon handled by fine tuning the music popularity charts. Given that the charts were decisive in keeping score of the hit parade, the importance of this adjustment cannot be overemphasized. Transfer of musical or personnel resources from one stream to another required that the material be moving in one market at the same rate as in the others. This matter was not purely a technical issue of how fast a record moved up and down the ranks of the charts; it also involved how many weeks a record in each of the three streams was advertised and written about in the reviews and the news section of the press. The players in all three streams, in other words, must share the same pace and duration of their hit cycles.

The charts, it should be understood, were guides to the *relative* performance of records. Actual record sales figures were proprietary, and performance rights collections by ASCAP and BMI were too slow and isolated to inform the markets. Moreover, the figures on one record or one artist lacked a comparative context. The operative question was on how a specific record stood vis-à-vis the competition. In spite of their weaknesses and limitations, therefore, only the charts in the trade press could tell the industry what was happening.[58] The entire industry relied on the trade press' ability to track the life cycle of each new release. If that tracking was a social fiction too far removed from the reality of the bottom-line figures of sales and performances, then the industry invented its own devices to harmonize the discrepancies.[59] At least the fiction was constant across the major music publications; *Cash Box* and *Billboard*'s popular record charts over the years show a high degree of comparability.[60]

Billboard's best-selling singles chart, the bottom line for the industry, was managed so that the number of records reported each week reflected the action in the markets. As the number of records released in each stream expanded or declined, the number of slots in the charts altered. That is, the size of the "window" looking into each market was adjusted to the size of that market. In so doing, each of the three charts adjusted the speed of the records passing through them in a way that made them comparable.[61] The pop, country, and R&B charts, in other words, were made to appear as if they were all moving at the same speed. This pro-

The Billboard Music Popularity Charts — POPULAR RECORDS

• Best Sellers in Stores

For survey week ending March 16

RECORDS are ranked in order of their current national selling importance at the retail level. Results are based on The Billboard's weekly survey among the nation's top volume pop record dealers representing every important market area. The reverse side of each record is also listed. When a figure is given in parenthesis after the flip title it indicates what position it occupies on the chart.

This Week		Last Week	Weeks on Chart
1.	BALLAD OF DAVY CROCKETT—B. Hayes........... Farewell—Cadence 1256—BMI	3	5
2.	CRAZY OTTO MEDLEY—J. Maddox. Humoresque—Dot 15325	2	8
3.	SINCERELY—McGuire Sisters....... No More—Coral 61323—BMI	1	12
4.	TWEEDLE DEE—G. Gibbs....... You're Wrong, All Wrong—Mercury 70517—BMI	4	9
5.	MELODY OF LOVE—P. Vaughn.... Joy Ride—Dot 15247—ASCAP	5	16
6.	KO KO MO—P. Como.............. You'll Always Be My Lifetime Sweetheart—V 20-5994—BMI	6	8
7.	BALLAD OF DAVY CROCKETT—F. Parker........... I Gave My Love—Col 40449—BMI	11	3
8.	HOW IMPORTANT CAN IT BE?—J. James............... This Is My Confession—M-G-M 11919—ASCAP	9	6
9.	OPEN UP YOUR HEART—Cowboy Church Sunday School.... The Lord Is Counting on You—Dec 29367—BMI	14	13
10.	EARTH ANGEL—Crew Cuts....... Ko Ko Mo—(14)—Mercury 70529—BMI	8	8
11.	HEARTS OF STONE—Fontane Sisters. Bless Your Heart—Dot 15265—BMI	7	16
12.	MELODY OF LOVE—Four Aces..... There's a Tavern in the Town—Dec 29395—ASCAP	15	10
13.	MELODY OF LOVE—D. Carroll.... La Golondrina—Mercury 70516—ASCAP	12	12
14.	KO KO MO—Crew Cuts........... Earth Angel—(10)—Mercury 70529—BMI	16	9
15.	THAT'S ALL I WANT FROM YOU—J. P. Morgan................... Dawn—V 20-5896—BMI	10	18
15.	CHERRY PINK AND APPLE BLOSSOM WHITE—P. Prado...... Marie Elena Rumba—V 20-5965—ASCAP	21	4
17.	BALLAD OF DAVY CROCKETT—Tennessee Ernie Ford........... Farewell—Cap 3058—BMI	19	2
17.	EARTH ANGEL—Penguins....... Hey, Senorita—Dootone 348—BMI	13	14
19.	DARLING JE VOUS AIME BEAUCOUP—Nat (King) Cole..... Sand and the Sea—(32)—Cap 3027—ASCAP	23	4
20.	PLEDGING MY LOVE—J. Ace...... No Money—Duke 136—BMI	17	5
21.	DANCE WITH ME HENRY—G. Gibbs Every Road Must Have a Turning—Mercury 70572—BMI	—	1
22.	ROCK LOVE—Fontane Sisters....... You're Mine—Dot 8570—BMI	22	4
23.	PLANTATION BOOGIE—L. Dee..... Birth of the Blues—Dec 29360—BMI	24	7
24.	TWEEDLE DEE—L. Baker.......... Tomorrow Night—Atlantic 1047—BMI	27	11
25.	MAMBO ROCK—B. Haley.......... Birth of the Boogie—(26)—Dec 29418—ASCAP	18	4
26.	HOW IMPORTANT CAN IT BE?—S. Vaughan.................... Waltzing Down the Aisle—Mercury 70534—ASCAP	26	5
26.	BIRTH OF THE BOOGIE—B. Haley Mambo Rock—(25)—Dec 29418—ASCAP	27	2
28.	IT MAY SOUND SILLY—McGuire Sisters.............. Doesn't Anybody Love Me?—Coral 61369—BMI	—	1
29.	PLAY ME HEARTS AND FLOWERS—J. Desmond.................... I'm So Ashamed—Coral 61379—ASCAP	—	1
30.	DANGER, HEARTBREAK AHEAD—J. P. Morgan.................. Softly, Softly—V 20-6016—ASCAP	—	1

• This Week's Best Buys

UNCHAINED MELODY (Frank, ASCAP) — Al Hibbler— Decca 29441
Initial reaction to this movie tune has been quite strong. Al Hibbler's version already has jumped on the Cleveland and Detroit territorial charts and is a big seller in New York, Pittsburgh and Los Angeles, as well. This disk is also doing nicely in the r. & b. market. Several other versions are sparking considerable action but have not yet gained the acceptance that the Decca record has. Flip is "Daybreak" (Feist, ASCAP).

SILVER MOON (Harms, ASCAP)—Billy Vaughn —Dot 15347
This is another recent release that has taken little time to hit pay dirt. Operators have been particularly enthusiastic about this record. Good sales reports were returned from a wide range of territories that included Philadelphia, Buffalo, Pittsburgh, Cleveland, Chicago, Milwaukee, Nashville, St. Louis, Atlanta and Baltimore. Flip is "Baby O' Mine" (Randy-Smith, ASCAP). A previous Billboard "Spotlight" pick.

According to sales reports in key markets, the following recent releases are recommended for extra profits:

NOBODY (Jerry Vogel, ASCAP)
DOOR OF DREAMS (Roncom, ASCAP)—Perry Como—RCA Victor 6059
While this has been a slow starter for Como, it is beginning to pick up nicely in various parts of the country. This disk is moving at a good rate in Chicago, Milwaukee, St. Louis, Cincinnati, Pittsburgh and Buffalo. Preference as to side is almost evenly split. A previous Billboard "Spotlight" pick.

MAKE YOURSELF COMFORTABLE (Rylan, ASCAP)—Deacon Andy Griffith—Capitol 3057
Southern dealers have been having a field day with this humorous disk. Retailers in the Carolinas, Atlanta, Nashville, Dallas, Baltimore, St. Louis and Kansas City have found a ready response to it. The concentration of strong reports in those territories may put the Griffith record on the national charts in the near future. Flip is "Ko Ko Mo" (Meridian, BMI). A previous Billboard "Spotlight" pick.

• Most Played in Juke Boxes

For survey week ending March 16

RECORDS are ranked in order of the greatest number of plays in juke boxes throughout the country. Results are based on The Billboard's weekly survey among the nation's juke box operators. The reverse side of each record is also listed. When a figure is given in parenthesis after the flip title it indicates what position it occupies on the chart.

This Week		Last Week	Weeks on Chart
1.	SINCERELY—McGuire Sisters....... No More—Coral 61323—BMI	1	10
2.	CRAZY OTTO MEDLEY—J. Maddox. Humoresque—Dot 15325	3	6
3.	HEARTS OF STONE—Fontane Sisters. Bless Your Heart—Dot 15265—BMI	2	15
4.	MELODY OF LOVE—B. Vaughn.... Joy Ride—Dot 15247—ASCAP	5	12
5.	TWEEDLE DEE—G. Gibbs......... You're Wrong, All Wrong—Mercury 70517—BMI	7	7
6.	MELODY OF LOVE—Four Aces..... There's a Tavern in the Town—Dec 29395—ASCAP	4	11
7.	KO KO MO—P. Como.............. You'll Always Be My Lifetime Sweetheart—V 20-5994—BMI	6	7
8.	BALLAD OF DAVY CROCKETT—B. Hayes........... Farewell—Cadence 1256—BMI	13	3
9.	HOW IMPORTANT CAN IT BE?—J. James............... This Is My Confession—M-G-M 11919—ASCAP	10	5
10.	KO KO MO—Crew Cuts........... Earth Angel—Mercury 70529—BMI	11	6
11.	THAT'S ALL I WANT FROM YOU—J. P. Morgan................... Dawn—V 20-5896—BMI	8	14
12.	EARTH ANGEL—Crew Cuts........ Ko Ko Mo—(10)—Mercury 70529—BMI	8	7
13.	EARTH ANGEL—Penguins......... Hey, Senorita—Dootone 348—BMI	12	7
13.	MELODY OF LOVE—D. Carroll.... Golondrina, La—Mercury 70516—ASCAP	14	6
15.	ROCK LOVE—Fontane Sisters....... You're Mine—Dot 8570—BMI	16	4
16.	TWEEDLE DEE—L. Baker......... Tomorrow Night—Atlantic 1047—BMI	17	3
17.	LET ME GO, LOVER—J. Weber..... Marionette—Col 40366—BMI	15	16
17.	DARLING JE VOUS AIME BEAUCOUP—Nat (King) Cole...... Sand and the Sea—Cap 3027—ASCAP	—	1
19.	OPEN UP YOUR HEART—Cowboy Church Sunday School..... Lord Is Counting on You—Dec 29367—BMI	—	1
20.	SINCERELY—Moonglows .... Tempting—Chess 1581—BMI	—	1

• Most Played by Jockeys

For survey week ending March 16

RECORDS are ranked in order of the greatest number of plays on disk jockey radio shows throut the country. Results are based on The Billboard's weekly survey among the nation's disk jockeys. The reverse side of each record is also listed.

This Week		Last Week	Weeks on Chart
1.	SINCERELY—McGuire Sisters....... No More—Coral 61323—BMI	1	11
2.	KO KO MO—P. Como.............. You'll Always Be My Lifetime Sweetheart—V 20-5994—BMI	3	8
3.	HOW IMPORTANT CAN IT BE?—J. James............... This Is My Confession—M-G-M 11919—ASCAP	6	5
4.	TWEEDLE DEE—G. Gibbs......... You're Wrong, All Wrong—Mercury 70517—BMI	4	9
5.	MELODY OF LOVE—B. Vaughn..... Joy Ride—Dot 15247—ASCAP	2	11
6.	EARTH ANGEL—Crew Cuts........ Ko Ko Mo—Mercury 70529—BMI	5	8
7.	CRAZY OTTO MEDLEY—J. Maddox. Humoresque—Dot 15325	8	7
8.	BALLAD OF DAVY CROCKETT—B. Hayes........... Farewell—Cadence 1256—BMI	10	3
9.	HEARTS OF STONE—Fontane Sisters. Bless Your Heart—Dot 15265—BMI	9	16
9.	MELODY OF LOVE—D. Carroll..... Golondrina, La—Mercury 70516—ASCAP	12	10
11.	THAT'S ALL I WANT FROM YOU—J. P. Morgan................... Dawn—V 20-5896—BMI	7	16
12.	HOW IMPORTANT CAN IT BE?—S. Vaughan.................... Waltzing Down the Aisle—Mercury 70534—ASCAP	13	5
13.	MELODY OF LOVE—Four Aces..... There's a Tavern in the Town—Dec 29395—ASCAP	11	10
14.	EARTH ANGEL—Penguins......... Hey, Senorita—Dootone 348—BMI	15	9
15.	DARLING JE VOUS AIME BEAUCOUP—Nat (King) Cole..... Sand and the Sea—Cap 3027—ASCAP	18	4
16.	MAN CHASES A GIRL—E. Fisher..... Wedding Bells—V 20-6015—ASCAP	—	1
17.	PLEDGING MY LOVE—T. Brewer... How Important Can It Be?—Coral 61362—BMI	20	2
18.	DANGER, HEARTBREAK AHEAD—J. P. Morgan.................. Softly, Softly—V 20-6016—ASCAP	17	3
19.	BALLAD OF DAVY CROCKETT—Tennessee Ernie .... Farewell—Cap 3058—BMI	—	1
20.	IT MAY SOUND SILLY—McGuire Sisters.............. Doesn't Anybody Love Me?—Coral 61369—BMI	—	1

Figure 6-2. *Billboard* Popularity Charts for Pop, Country & Western, and Rhythm & Blues.

COUNTRY & WESTERN RECORDS

• Best Sellers in Stores

For survey week ending March 16

RECORDS are ranked in order of their current national selling importance at the retail level. Results are based on The Billboard's weekly survey among dealers throughout the country with a high volume of sales in country and western records. The reverse side of each record is also listed. When a figure is given in parenthesis after the flip title it indicates what position it occupies on the chart.

This Week		Last Week	Weeks on Chart
1.	IN THE JAILHOUSE NOW—W. Pierce................	1	8
	I'm Gonna Fall Out of Love With You—Dec 29391—BMI		
2.	LOOSE TALK—C. Smith..........................	2	21
	More Than Anything Else—Col 21317—BMI		
3.	MAKING BELIEVE—K. Wells.....................	4	3
	Whose Shoulder Will You Cry On?—Dec 29419—BMI		
4.	I'VE BEEN THINKING—E. Arnold.................	4	8
	Don't Forget—(22)—V 20-6000—BMI		
5.	IF YOU AIN'T LOVIN'—F. Young.................	3	18
	If That's the Fashion—Cap 2953—BMI		
6.	ARE YOU MINE?—G. Wright & T. Tall...........	6	8
	I've Got Somebody New—Fabor 117—BMI		
7.	MORE AND MORE—W. Pierce...................	7	25
	You're Not Mine Anymore—Dec 29232—BMI		
8.	KISSES DON'T LIE—C. Smith...................	8	10
	No I Don't Believe I Will—Col 21340—BMI		
9.	THAT'S ALL RIGHT—M. Robbins................	11	6
	Gossip—Col 21351—BMI		
10.	HEARTS OF STONE—R. Foley..................	9	12
	Never—Dec 29375—BMI		
11.	MAKE BELIEVE—R. Foley & K. Wells..........	15	2
	As Long As I Live—Dec 29390—BMI		
12.	MAKING BELIEVE—J. Work...................	12	3
	Just Like Downtown—Dot 1221—BMI		
13.	BALLAD OF DAVY CROCKETT—Tennessee Ernie..	—	1
	Farewell—Cap 3058—BMI		
13.	AS LONG AS I LIVE—K. Wells & R. Foley......	10	4
	Make Believe—Dec 29390—BMI		
15.	ARE YOU MINE?—G. Hill & R. Sovine..........	—	1
	Ko Ko Mo—Dec 29411—BMI		

• Most Played in Juke Boxes

For survey week ending March 16

RECORDS are ranked in order of the greatest number of plays in juke boxes throughout the country. Results are based on The Billboard's weekly survey among operators throughout the country using a high proportion of country and western records.

This Week		Last Week	Weeks on Chart
1.	IN THE JAILHOUSE NOW—W. Pierce............	1	7
	Dec 29391—BMI		
2.	IF YOU AIN'T LOVIN'—F. Young...............	3	15
	Cap 2953—BMI		
3.	LOOSE TALK—C. Smith........................	2	17
	Col 21317—BMI		
4.	ARE YOU MINE?—G. Wright & T. Tall..........	4	6
	Fabor 117—BMI		
5.	MAKING BELIEVE—J. Work.....................	6	5
	Dot 1221—BMI		
6.	HEARTS OF STONE—R. Foley..................	4	8
	Dec 29375—BMI		
7.	I'VE BEEN THINKING—E. Arnold..............	6	5
	V 20-6000—BMI		
8.	ARE YOU MINE?—M. Lorrie & B. DeVal........	10	3
	Abbott 172—BMI		
9.	MORE AND MORE—W. Pierce...................	8	24
	Dec 29252—BMI		
10.	LET ME GO, LOVER—H. Snow.................	9	11
	V 20-5960—BMI		

• Most Played by Jockeys

For survey week ending March 16

SIDES are ranked in order of the greatest number of plays on disk jockey radio shows, according to The Billboard's weekly survey of top disk jockey shows in all key markets.

This Week		Last Week	Weeks on Chart
1.	IN THE JAILHOUSE NOW—W. Pierce...........	1	8
	Dec 29391—BMI		
2.	LOOSE TALK—C. Smith........................	2	21
	Col 21317—BMI		
3.	ARE YOU MINE?—G. Wright & T. Tall..........	3	11
	Fabor 117—BMI		
4.	IF YOU AIN'T LOVIN'—F. Young................	4	19
	Cap 2953—BMI		
5.	HEARTS OF STONE—R. Foley..................	5	11
	Dec 29375—BMI		
6.	I'VE BEEN THINKING—E. Arnold...............	8	9
	V 20-6000—BMI		
7.	MAKING BELIEVE—K. Wells...................	10	3
	Dec 29419—BMI		
7.	THAT'S ALL RIGHT—M. Robbins................	—	6
	Col 21351—BMI		
9.	LET ME GO, LOVER—H. Snow.................	6	14
	V 20-5960—BMI		
10.	AS LONG AS I LIVE—K. Wells & R. Foley......	9	5
	Dec 29390—BMI		
11.	KISSES DON'T LIE—C. Smith...................	13	2
	Col 21340—BMI		
12.	MAKING BELIEVE—J. Work...................	—	1
	Dot 1221—BMI		
12.	DAYDREAMING—J. Newman..................	—	1
	Dot 1327—		
14.	I GOTTA GO GET MY BABY—J. Tubb............	13	6
	Dec 29401—BMI		
14.	ARE YOU MINE?—M. Lorrie & B. DeVal..........	12	12
	Abbott 172—BMI		

RHYTHM & BLUES RECORDS

• Best Sellers in Stores

For survey week ending March 16

RECORDS are ranked in order of their current national selling importance at the retail level. Results are based on The Billboard's weekly survey among dealers throughout the country with a high volume of sales in rhythm and blues records. The reverse side of each record is also listed. When a figure is given in parenthesis after the flip title it indicates what position it occupies on the chart.

This Week		Last Week	Weeks on Chart
1.	PLEDGING MY LOVE—J. Ace....................	1	10
	No Money—Duke 136—BMI		
2.	WALLFLOWER—E. James.......................	3	6
	Hold Me, Squeeze Me—Modern 947—BMI		
3.	I'VE GOT A WOMAN—R. Charles...............	2	9
	Come Back—(9)—Atlantic 1050—BMI		
4.	MY BABE—Little Walter.......................	6	3
	Thunder Bird—Checker 811—BMI		
5.	EARTH ANGEL—Penguins......................	4	15
	Hey, Senorita—Dootone 348—BMI		
6.	TWEEDLE DEE—L. Baker.....................	5	11
	Tomorrow Night—Atlantic 1047—BMI		
7.	CLOSE YOUR EYES—Five Keys..................	12	3
	Doggone It, You Did It—Cap 3032—BMI		
8.	JOHNNY HAS GONE—V. Dillard................	8	5
	So Many Ways—Savoy 1153—BMI		
9.	COME BACK—R. Charles......................	9	6
	I've Got a Woman—(3)—Atlantic 1050—BMI		
10.	FLIP, FLOP AND FLY—J. Turner................	—	1
	Ti-Ri-Lee—Atlantic 1053—BMI		
11.	SINCERELY—Moonglows	7	17
	Tempting—Chess 1581—BMI		
12.	YOU DON'T HAVE TO GO—J. Reed.............	14	4
	Boogie in the Dark—Vee Jay 119—BMI		
13.	DON'T YOU KNOW?—F. Domino...............	13	2
	Helping Hand—Imperial 5340—BMI		
14.	LONELY NIGHTS—Hearts......................	—	1
	Oo-Wee—Baton 208—BMI		
15.	LING, TING, TONG—Charms....................	—	9
	Bazoom (I Need Your Lovin')—DeLuxe 6076—BMI		

• Most Played in Juke Boxes

For survey week ending March 16

RECORDS are ranked in order of the greatest number of plays in juke boxes throughout the country. Results are based on The Billboard's weekly survey among operators throughout the country using a high proportion of rhythm and blues records.

This Week		Last Week	Weeks on Chart
1.	PLEDGING MY LOVE—J. Ace....................	1	8
	Duke 136—BMI		
2.	I'VE GOT A WOMEN—R. Charles................	3	9
	Atlantic 1050—BMI		
3.	MY BABE—Little Walter.......................	4	2
	Checker 811—BMI		
4.	EARTH ANGEL—Penguins......................	7	14
	Dootone 348—BMI		
5.	WALLFLOWER—E. James.......................	5	4
	Modern 947—BMI		
6.	TWEEDLE DEE—L. Baker.....................	6	11
	Atlantic 1047—BMI		
7.	SINCERELY—Moonglows......................	2	20
	Chess 1581—BMI		
8.	FLIP, FLOP AND FLY—J. Turner................	—	1
	Atlantic 1053—BMI		
9.	JOHNNY HAS GONE—V. Dillard................	10	2
	Savoy 1153—BMI		
10.	COME BACK—R. Charles......................	—	1
	Atlantic 1050—BMI		

• Most Played by Jockeys

For survey week ending March 16

SIDES are ranked in order of the greatest number of plays on disk jockey radio shows throughout the country according to The Billboard's weekly survey of top disk jockey shows in all key markets.

This Week		Last Week	Weeks on Chart
1.	PLEDGING MY LOVE—J. Ace....................	1	10
	Duke 136—BMI		
2.	WALLFLOWER—E. James.......................	2	6
	Modern 947—BMI		
3.	EARTH ANGEL—Penguins......................	3	10
	Dootone 348—BMI		
4.	COME BACK—R. Charles......................	6	8
	Atlantic 1050—BMI		
5.	I'VE GOT A WOMAN—R. Charles................	4	10
	Atlantic 1050—BMI		
6.	MY BABE—Little Walter.......................	8	3
	Checker 811—BMI		
7.	CLOSE YOUR EYES—Five Keys..................	13	4
	Cap 3032—BMI		
8.	SINCERELY—Moonglows......................	5	10
	Chess 1581—BMI		
8.	JOHNNY HAS GONE—V. Dillard................	9	4
	Savoy 1153—BMI		
10.	YOU DON'T HAVE TO GO—J. Reed.............	—	2
	Vee Jay 119—BMI		
11.	LING, TING, TONG—Five Keys.................	—	1
	Cap 2945—BMI		
12.	LONELY NIGHTS—Hearts......................	—	1
	Baton 208—BMI		
13.	WHAT'CHA GONNA DO?—Drifters..............	—	1
	Atlantic 1055—BMI		
14.	FLIP, FLOP AND FLY—J. Turner................	11	2
	Atlantic 1053—BMI		
14.	THAT'S ALL I WANT FROM YOU—D. Washington.	—	1
	Mer 70537—BMI		

© 1955 BPI Communications, Inc. Used with permission from *Billboard*.

cedure allowed industry personnel to make recordings, exposure, and exploitation decisions on all *three* markets as if they were one unfolding hit parade.

The following three figures show, step by step, how this was done. First, figure 6-3 shows the number of "slots" in the pop, country, and rhythm and blues best-selling charts over the years 1943–1970. The "race" or "Hot in Harlem" charts, it will be recalled, began in the 1940s with five entries, the same number as the "folk" (i.e., country) chart of that period. As those markets developed, the number of chart entries increased. The sudden spurt in pop chart entries after 1955 reflected the decisive change in all the streams at that time. By 1958, the "hot hundred" concept in the pop stream had replaced the prior chart system.

The unequal, upward meandering of the number of chart slots becomes more understandable when viewed as a response to the gradual but uneven rise in the number of singles flowing through the three markets. Figure 6-4 shows for each year the total number of records appearing on each of the three charts (1943–1970).

The number of records rose suddenly and sharply in the pop field in 1955. *Billboard*'s presentation of the three markets as equals would have been completely unbalanced if it had not increased the size of the pop window, maintaining thereby the same rate of flow compared to the slower growth rate of country and R&B. This strategy is shown nicely in figure 6-5. This figure is a combination of the previous two figures; the number of slots (fig. 6-3) in each market is divided into the number of records moving through that market (fig. 6-4). The result is clear; the rate of flow of records through all three charts was rendered remarkably steady for a period of twenty years (1950–1970), no mean accomplishment for a system undergoing such internal change. Thus, beyond their appearance of equality in size and organization, the charts actually let the hits unfold in the three markets at about the same speed. This method allowed the industry to maximize the cross-market strategy that was so clearly occurring. The three markets were closely aligned and attuned to the pace of their production. The situation was now fully ripe for the era of crossovers.

All the machinery, as described above, was ready. The three streams were now flowing at the same rates. A record in any of them could, after 1950, cross a boundary more readily and speedily than before, and they did so as shown in figure 6-6.[62] There could hardly be more dramatic evidence that the stream boundaries had been breached than this steady drop in the time it took for crossovers to occur. In fact, by the years 1957 and 1958, a maojrity of the records originating with R&B acts appeared first on the pop charts. Whether this peculiarity was a product of *Billboard*'s reporting system (pop retail outlets being quicker to report than

R&B or country and western record stores) or simply a reflection of the greater responsiveness of the white pop teenaged record-buying audience is difficult to assess. This more rapid exchange, in any case, was a mark of the industry's success in teaching the "hit game" to the leading audiences of all three markets.

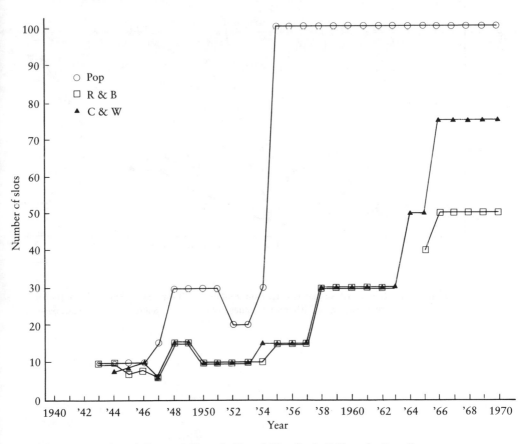

Figure 6-3. Number of Slots in *Billboard*'s "Best-Selling Singles" Chart for Pop, Country & Western, and Rhythm & Blues (1943–1970). For some years (1944–1947 for C & W, 1945–1947 for R & B), the "Most Played on Juke Box" has been substituted for "Best-Selling Singles." Absence of date on R & B charts for the years 1963–1965 is due to *Billboard*'s suspension of the chart during those years. Source: *Billboard* music popularity charts.

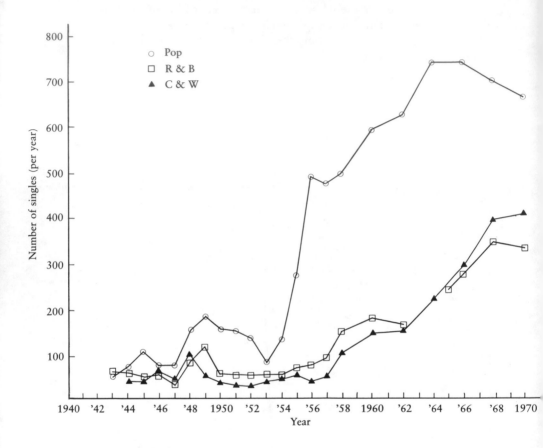

Figure 6-4. Number of Singles per Year on *Billboard*'s "Best-Selling Singles" Charts for Pop, Country & Western, and Rhythm & Blues (1943–1970). Source: *Billboard* music popularity charts.

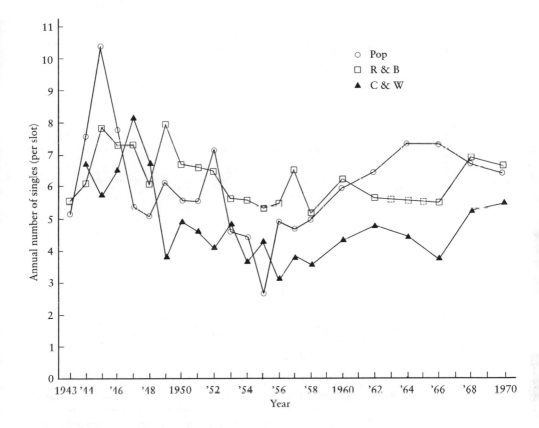

Figure 6-5. Rate of Flow of *Billboard*'s "Best-Selling Singles" Charts for Pop, Country & Western, and Rhythm & Blues (1943–1970): Annual number of singles per slot. Source: *Billboard* music popularity charts.

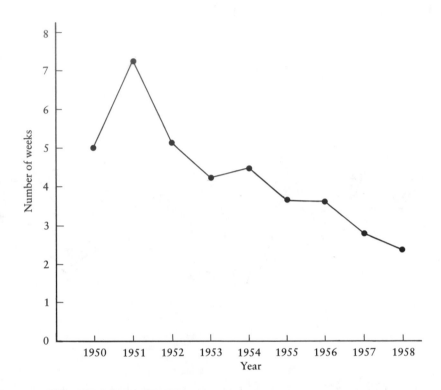

Figure 6-6. Speed of Crossovers between *Billboard*'s Pop, Country & Western, and Rhythm & Blues "Best-Selling Singles" Charts (1950–1958): Number of weeks to cross streams, Pop–R & B and Pop–C & W. Sources: Joel Whitburn, *Joel Whitburn's Top Country Singles 1944–1988* (pub. 1989), *Top Pop Singles 1940–1955* (pub. 1973), *Top Pop Singles 1955–1986* (pub. 1987), and *Top R & B Singles 1942–1988* (pub. 1989), all Menomonee Falls, Wisconsin: Record Research, Inc. compiled from *Billboard*'s Best-Selling Singles charts. © BPI Communications, Inc. Used with permission from *Billboard*.

7. The Early Crossovers

The sixteenth best-selling record on the country music charts for 1953 was Homer and Jethro's novelty, "That Hound Dog in the Window," on the Victor label, words and music by Bob Merrill.[1] Though the record appears to be simply a musical joke about the fact that two songs with a dog theme appeared at the same time, it is more. It contains a useful, if compressed, story about the origin of rocknroll. One of those songs was the much maligned "(How Much Is) That Doggie in the Window," Patti Page's Mercury hit that was 1953's third best-selling pop single. The other song was "Hound Dog," first recorded by Willie Mae "Big Mama" Thornton on Peacock, the number three record on the rhythm and blues chart for 1953.

The significance of the Homer and Jethro record begins with the recognition, shared by the music industry and its audiences, that the three major streams were not only closely aligned but that their boundaries had been breached. The record, though not the first three-way exchange among pop, country, and rhythm and blues, was the earliest self-conscious musical expression of their intersection. It made *only* the country charts, Homer and Jethro being too broadly "country bumpkins" to be accepted by either a pop or a black audience.[2] The country audience, most assuredly, knew of *both* the pop stream's Patti Page and R&B's Big Mama Thornton. Disk jockeys all over the country, but especially in the South and along its borders, had played enough of all three musics to have given their audiences an airing of the two records. Lest there be any doubt, *Billboard*'s review of the Homer and Jethro record spelled it out explicitly for the Country and Western record review readers: "By coincidence or intent, the use of 'hound dog' also recognizes the top r&b record of the moment."

Substantively, Patti Page's "Doggie" instantly became Exhibit A in the case against the pop stream's trivia, its failure to keep a dance pulse, to inspire some kind of passion and excitement, or to carry any artistic merit sufficient to hold the young audiences that were ready to give more than eighty-nine cents a record. Willie Mae Thornton's performance of the Leiber, Stoller, and Otis "Hound Dog," in contrast, was prophetically on target. Its lyrics said something strong, it was danceable, it was a credible member of an accepted black song style, and it was *written*. The authors were part of the growing development in black pop wherein the written song and arrangements were supplanting the older oral tradition and its "head" arrangements.[3]

"Hound Dog" was aimed not only at a black audience; it also stimu-lated answer songs elsewhere, a legitimate way to invoke Rule One (to duplicate last week's hit as closely as possible) while skirting the plagia-rism issue. One tune was by Bill Haley and the Comets, who immediately released "Two Hound Dogs" and moved it fairly well up the pop charts. (Mickey Katz did an answer to the Page "Doggie in the Window" for Capitol entitled "How Much Is That Pickle in the Window.") The logic of the answer song was appealing enough in 1959 to prompt the entitling of Philadelphia teen vocalist Fabian's first movie, *The Hound Dog Man*. Only the title was hooked to rocknroll, however, since the movie was a period piece set in 1912. The really successful answer was Elvis Presley's re-recording of "Hound Dog" in the summer of 1956.[4]

Thus, though light as air, "That Hound Dog in the Window" was a profound diagnosis of the situation and a hint of a solution. The diag-nosis was that the pop stream was fully dessicated; the A&R men in the studios had failed to find a replacement for the swing bands. The easy and immediate solution was to find a rhythm and blues and/or country refreshment. Both in fact would soon pour into the pop stream. The more difficult solution was to search outside the pop stream's usual sources for new material. Songs from the musical theater, the movies, music from England, the Continent, anywhere would be relentlessly tracked.

This chapter reviews the paradoxical process that began at the mo-ment when the three major streams were almost exactly equal in struc-ture but still clearly separate. Everyone thought they would simply unfold on separate, parallel tracks. Their boundaries were shattered, however, by the workings of Rule One and its converse, Rule Two (make this week's hit the *opposite* of last week's). The search for new hit material also forced the pop stream to reach towards those sectors of the three smaller streams ready for a commercial embrace. All six streams were aware of the new young audience; all six sought ways to capture their share of it without surrendering the family jewels. The resultant upwell-ing richness, diversity, and mercurial flux of all the popular musics in the next decade cannot be overemphasized. The immediate beneficiary of that flooding was the nation's youth. When those born just after the end of the war entered high school, they turned that institution into rocknroll's cookery, its hothouse. The records pouring out of all six streams constituted, for the various high school constituencies, the founding reservoir of rocknroll. The seventh stream's ability to contain a multiplicity of styles, its ability to combine with the music of any other stream, its resistance to commercial manipulation, as well as its susceptibility to that very same exploitation, all these attributes were forged in its combustive origins.

Turbulence in the Streams

All the machinery was in place and working; yet there was disturbance in the system. Over and above the hit game's chanciness was the disquieting fact that no one was sure of the streams' boundaries. The three major streams were either bumping into one another or failing to connect where it might prove useful. While the professional songwriters and performers, the masters at disassembling and reconstructing their own music, were learning to do the same for adjacent streams, the record impresarios and venue proprietors were no longer sure about what went with what. In the late 1940s and early 1950s, they tried everything to test the boundary limits. Some bizarre combinations were offered; Ezio Pinza teamed up with the Sons of the Pioneers in a tune called "The Little Ol' State of Texas," for example.[5] Other combinations proved more successful, such as the pop-styled duets by country-folk artist Tennessee Ernie Ford and R&B-tinged Kay Starr. This particular example is not trivial. It pointed out a way to refresh pop with domesticated materials or to stimulate performers with mild mixtures of country and black pop.

Pop also needed what swing-era jazz had given it, vitality in dance, the musical competence and personification of a strongly felt engagement in the song and its story. Now that the pop-jazz moment had ended, country and R&B beckoned. They, in turn, yearned for pop's huge market, for the road to television and the movies, and for access to the highest realms of all the popular arts. The young audiences sought action wherever it was. If *downtown* had the dance pulse, the "party songs," the "real stuff," then that's where the *uptown* traffic went. It moved not only geographically but across stream boundaries, generating strong turbulence throughout the entire system.

Actually, the big swing bands did not just disappear. Some stayed and fought stubbornly. Their official banner, raised and carried by such organs as *Down Beat*, announced that dance would bring back the bands and that the bands would bring back dance, a doomed proposition. The surviving big bands had largely become studio or TV aggregations in the hands of the arranger-leader, whose records were either showcases for vocalists on their way to stardom or were exotic instrumentals engineered by the A&R men looking anywhere for the next hit. These goods were hardly what the hit-making disk jockey wanted to bring to high school teenagers. Yet these bands were energetically toured by packagers who would mix them in with any act that looked like it could draw a crowd. Woody Herman toured with Dinah Washington. George Shearing, Billy Eckstine, and Count Basie were the main acts for Norman Granz' Jazz at the Philharmonic (JATP) concert tour. One of the most revealing of these attempts to rebuild a dance audience was the heavily ballyhooed 1952 Los Angeles concert featuring the unlikely combination of the Harry James band, Big Jay McNeeley, the Four Lads, and Johnny Ray, whose best-selling record "Cry" had attracted an emotional young audience. A reviewer of that event noted with distaste McNeeley's climactic performance, "lying on his back, kicking his feet while honking and snorting hysterically on his tenor into the mike," and then observed that "it was interesting to note the same youngsters who screeched and moaned in real or pseudo excitement for Johnnie [Ray] were the same ones who screeched and moaned for Big Jay's honking and snorting."[6]

This lesson was not lost on record producers and their audiences. A mixture of rhythm and blues and jazz seemed to generate excitement, but what was the boundary between the two? Johnny Otis' story is illustrative of the heavy traffic in that zone. Otis, a Greek-American, decided as a child growing up in a "prematurely" integrated Berkeley neighborhood that he preferred to be among blacks, that he was, in fact, black. Just as the neighborhood went all black, so did he. He was active in black music as a teenager and in 1947 ended his touring with several of the black popular bands of the war period. Was jazz the direction to head now? What else was there since the big band era was over for everyone, white and black?

'Round '47 jobs became extremely scarce for big bands. I remember meeting Billy Eckstine during a date in Washington, D.C. We bemoaned the fact that we were both "too late" with big bands. . . . When I put together a new group I was still thinking of brass section, reed section, so I used two saxes, trumpet and trombone, and piano/bass/drums/guitar. This became like the standard rhythm-and-blues ensemble. . . . Watching the records that were making it—like my friends T-Bone Walker, Roy Milton, Joe Liggins and the Honeydrippers, Charles Brown with Johnny Moore's Blazers—we began to develop something with something. It was a hybrid form that wasn't country blues. It was what was to become known as rhythm and blues, a hybrid form that became an art form in itself. It was the foundation of rocknroll.[7]

Otis went on to become producer, impresario of one of the most successful touring R&B groups, discoverer of important R&B talent (Etta

James, Johnny Ace), hit-making performer, and writer of R&B hits, including "Hound Dog" with Leiber and Stoller.[8]

Essentially the same choice affected most of the black musicians whose talents and previous commitments hadn't foreclosed the option to move into jazz or toward the pop side. Some worked in both without difficulty. The musical grounds for so doing were anchored preeminently in the Kansas City tradition, where, by the end of World War II, jazz and blues styles became so tightly fused that the musicians themselves made no distinction between them. "Jimmy Witherspoon and Al Hibler . . . still see blues and jazz as one entity."[9]

Out of the very same pool of musicians, Dizzy Gillespie, Thelonius Monk, Miles Davis, and Charlie Parker went on to become the pioneers of bebop. Perhaps the closest amalgamation between jazz and pop was the short-lived black band (noted previously) put together by Billy Eckstine in 1944. Other performers, like Sonny Stitt, moved from R&B sideman to bebop soloist with no difficulty. Louis Jordan took a different path and is quoted as saying, "Those guys, except Dizzy, who's the master, the king, really wanted to play mostly for themselves, and I still wanted to play for the people. I just like to sing my blues and swing."[10]

And sing he did, with a small band—the Tympani Five—which was one of several models of the "jump band," the basic instrumentation being almost identical to Johnny Otis'. Louis Jordan steadily entertained both black and white audiences for over a decade (ending in 1951) with about six humorous and danceable singles charted each year. With the exception of Jordan's and Gillespie's unquenchable sense of humor, though, jazz got serious. Stan Kenton was serious. Dave Brubeck and the other young white cool jazzmen were serious. "Seriousness" meant not only difficult music (no dancing allowed), aiming for joinder with classical music (hence the dream of what was called "Third Stream" music), but also a deliberate refusal to enter the commercial hurly-burly.[11]

The jazz stream had, by such a posture, moved away from black pop for the moment. The folk stream also took a share of the older black pop performers, enfolding into its ranks many of the now renamed "Heroes of the Blues." T-Bone Walker was one of these, as was the musical namesake of the "Honey Dripper," Roosevelt Sykes, an early bluesman who recorded some 125 sides between 1929 and 1942.[12] Sykes made the transition from typical "race record" performer to postwar folk stream icon, recording for Folkways, and finally appeared for canonization at festivals such as the Ann Arbor Blues and Jazz Festival of 1973.

Thus, rhythm and blues, with its decks cleared, was ready to go with anything that the independent record companies discovered in the rich talent pools of their cities. It still had to deal, however, with its older and still productive stars near the end of their recording careers. The same was true for country music, where a whole generation of aging performers was still firmly seated at the heights of the country music pyramid and would hang on for some time. Their replacements would be quite an event.

A final point about the jazz stream's contribution to rocknroll at this early stage: In addition to extensive touring at home and abroad and the successful invasion of the college campus, jazz promoters and some record executives were dedicated to the preservation of the jazz performance, both live and in the studio. It soon became clear that the single record, whether 78 or 45 rpm, was not capacious enough for the extended duration of good jazz sessions. Record companies began, as a matter of routine, to contract for longer sessions, producing typically eight sides at a time, an album's worth of material. This procedure soon became standard; by the early fifties, practically all of jazz's history and most contemporary work were in the long playing album format.[13] These technological and marketing decisions were guided as much by the promises of a strong dollar return as by the jazz ethos of celebration and respect for the specific performance and its players. This latter attitude, however, was manifested in the eponymous honor given the players in the meticulously prepared personnel listings on the liner notes and in the critics' jazz commentary. Such respect was implanted into some of rocknroll's founding generation and would find expression in rock's maturity.

Finally, the leadership of the pop stream itself, the publishers especially, tried several tactics to stabilize the turbulence. One was a vigorous campaign that offered the standards of the 1920s and 1930s to performers and A&R men as an antidote to the fad-wracked popular music scene. As will be apparent later, the scheme yielded some successes. Another move was to rekindle older ties with the London and European music scene. This idea too produced some hit records and a few new stars, who briefly flashed onto the charts. Even the insular Syd Nathan, from his King record bastion in Cincinnati, was drawn into the overseas talent search after the likes of Vera Lynn had been imported with great fanfare and impressive record sales.[14] The tours of American packages to England and the Continent also accelerated, with every kind of performer being shipped over in the hopes of launching a career and discovering material for the American hit parade. *Billboard*'s charts reflected these efforts; in 1945 it began a listing of the top 20 tunes in England, and in 1956 it extended its coverage by adding a chart of the top 20 English records. All this effort built part of the bridge that would carry the Beatles to America a decade later, bearing a load of music that had previously been carried the other way over that same bridge.

The Crossovers and the Charts

Rocknroll's formative moments are difficult to retrieve. They lie scattered in the thousands of records by singers and bands who tried to find a fresh path among familiar grooves leading to that young audience everybody knew was ready and waiting. Those moments might be reconstructed through disk jockey logs or the record collections of the high school and college youth at the time. But perhaps the most accessible way for that history to be tracked is through the music popularity charts of the three main streams. These charts were what the players in the music game read then, week by week, in the trade press. The music industry's routine procedures had produced a magical transformation; though the pop stream commanded fully 50 percent of all record sales, country pop, 13 percent, and black pop, 6 percent, the three major streams by 1950 looked exactly alike in their charts and were treated as fully equal to one another.[15]

This triumph, due in considerable measure to *Billboard*'s and *Cash Box*'s presentation of the music charts, allowed easy management of records that had transferred from one market to another. The actual transfer, it should be quite clear, took place in the air via the nation's disk jockeys and on the ground in the nation's record stores and jukeboxes.

All the charts, useful though they may be, obscure the all-important context—a song or record does not live through its relatively brief life cycle alone. It is surrounded by others in various stages of their life span. Most songs are gone in a flash; a few become standards. All live within a large and crowded company, the totality of which gives meaning and placement to each one. The American high school of the 1950s was a four-year container of records, songs, dances, and performers that constituted a slowly moving whole. Through its weightier mass, the momentary hit parade wiggled. Some parts of the parade quickly evaporated; others became the framework of rocknroll's house. Full understanding of a period's music is not to be achieved simply by listing its greatest hits; its junk, its average member, its underground favorites, all must be recognized.

The flow of hit records through the charts, while of key importance, is thus not a complete retelling of rocknroll's origin. Not only those records at the *top* of their own streams but also the records that crossed the *boundaries* between the three major streams have to be considered. The "crossover," a term familiar to us now, was a new and puzzling phenomenon in the early 1950s. A record that crossed over from one chart to another was a mysterious entity, raising questions about what had allowed it to cross that boundary and what that stream boundary really was. Clearly, more than music and lyrics is carried across the boundaries. These questions can be reformulated to ask each record or song: What is your *passport*? that is, What combination of musical and extra-musical schema gives you acceptable passage into this stream? Second, what is in your *carrying case*? This question refers to the full range of the performer's artistry and that of his friends from "over there" that can weather the border crossing and flourish "over here" (once we have determined that we can accept it).

The crossover takes several forms. One is a *record* that carries a unique performance of a song into two or more streams. Bing Crosby's rendition of Irving Berlin's "White Christmas" was such a hit, appearing on all three charts for several years beginning in 1943. What could be more universal than the passport that combined the nation's most representative songwriter with a performer of national repute, who was celebrating a prayerful holiday moment in the midst of war's anxieties; it was clearly a cultural event transcending the insularities of the three streams. Such a crossover was understandably rare, but its carrying case was full of the Christmas records that pleased and annoyed audiences in every market for decades.

Another form of the crossover was the three-chart appearance of a *song*. The gifted Hank Williams, for example, provided a group of them, such as his MGM recording of "Cold Cold Heart." It appeared on the country chart on 17 November 1950, climbed to the number two position, and remained forty-six weeks, a giant hit. Seven months later, Tony Bennett brought his Columbia rendition of that song to the top of the pop charts. Five months after that, Dinah Washington brought the song for Mercury to the number three position on the rhythm and blues chart. The three versions were quite different, each rendered in vocal styling that lay at the center of their streams' canons.

The crossover that almost never occurred was the two-way exchange between country and rhythm and blues. In the first half of the fifties decade, hundreds of two-way crossovers took place between pop and country and between pop and rhythm and blues; but there were only two recorded songs that crossed *just* between country and rhythm and blues.[16] The only way the wall between country and black pop could be surmounted was through the pop stream. The hidden musical reservoir that black and country pop shared was called "country boogie," "cat music," and, finally, "rockabilly," which referred to the meeting of several diverse dance and song forms shared by country and black pop from both contemporary practice and from older traditions. Peculiarly, the pop chart was the shoehorn that allowed a song to fit both a country and a black pop shoe. An early example was the crossover of the song, "Why Don't You Haul Off and Love Me" written by Wayne Raney (with Lonnie

Glosson) and recorded by Raney in 1949 on the King label. It reached the country charts in July of that year and crossed directly over to the pop chart in October. Bull Moose Jackson, also signed to King, then recorded a version of this fast dance tune for the rhythm and blues trade, his version reaching the R&B charts in November. Both performances were similar, yet each was within acceptable stylistic boundaries of their respective streams. Did it take the pop stream's validation to get the song across that racial barrier?

The Crossovers Begin

The year 1950 is exemplary for what was on the charts and for what crossed between them, and it is a convenient point of departure. Figure 7-1 shows the *Billboard* annual summary of the top 30 best-selling singles in pop, country, and rhythm and blues for 1950. The three charts reveal several things. Most apparent is the difference in their performers and song titles; clearly there were three separate worlds with limited overlap. A closer look shows the diversity of musical forms represented in the pop stream as compared to the other two. That variety includes ten records that crossed over to or from other streams, three records from prewar dance bands, three from the movies, some from young solo vocalists, a few from established vocal groups, a mix of instrumentals, ballads, and novelties, the whole thing a thorough gallimaufry. This diversity is to be expected in the largest of the streams, where an implicit invitation welcomes any and all of the nation's varied musical tastes.

The rhythm and blues chart is much more restricted. Most of the black pop records are within a narrow range of performance styles and lyrical content. Only one record on the black pop chart appeared anywhere else (that is, on the pop chart since there was no two-way traffic between country and black pop)—Nat Cole's "Mona Lisa," the Academy Award-winning movie song for 1950.[17] The rest of the records on the R&B chart are by veterans such as Ivory Joe Hunter, Amos Milburn, Johnny Otis, and Louis Jordan. Among the new performers, including Little Esther, Joe Liggins, and Larry Darnell, was Fats Domino. Following his first charted record, "The Fat Man," the young New Orleans piano stylist and singer became one of the most influential crossover R&B artists, thereby generating a major resource for rocknroll's reservoir.

The top country records for 1950 are even more restricted in musical range and in number of performers—thirteen singers as opposed to twenty-one on the pop chart and twenty-two on the R&B chart. Practically all the artists were established male vocalists with long histories of successful record production. (There was not one record featuring a female soloist.) Most of the music was strictly confined to country audi-

THE YEAR'S TOP POPULAR RECORDS
(Specific Recordings)

... according to

RETAIL SALES

RECORD, ARTIST & LABEL	POINTS	POSITION
Goodnight, Irene (Gordon Jenkins-Weavers—Decca)	8488	1
Mona Lisa (King Cole Trio—Capitol)	6445	2
Third Man Theme (Anton Karas—London)	3967	3
Sam's Song (Gary & Bing Crosby—Decca)	3810	4
Simple Melody (Gary & Bing Crosby—Decca)	3801	5
Music, Music, Music (Teresa Brewer—London)	2933	6
Third Man Theme (Guy Lombardo—Decca)	2538	7
Chattanoogie Shoe Shine. Boy (Red Foley—Decca)	2470	8
Harbor Lights (Sammy Kaye—Columbia)	2315	9
It Isn't Fair (Sammy Kaye-Don Cornell—Victor)	2101	10
If I Knew You Were Coming I'd've Baked a Cake (Eileen Barton—Mercury-National)	2076	11
Bonaparte's Retreat (Kay Starr—Capitol)	1968	12
Tzena, Tzena, Tzena (Gordon Jenkins-Weavers—Decca)	1892	13
There's No Tomorrow (Tony Martin—Victor)	1883	14
The Thing (Phil Harris—Victor)	1647	15
Sentimental Me (Ames Brothers—Coral)	1627	16
I Wanna Be Loved (Andrews Sisters-Gordon Jenkins—Decca)	1619	17
Tennessee Waltz (Patti Page—Mercury)	1512	18
I Can Dream Can't I (Andrews Sisters-Gordon Jenkins—Decca)	1485	19
I'll Never Be Free (Tennessee Ernie-Kay Starr—Capitol)	1484	20
All My Love (Patti Page—Mercury)	1470	21
My Foolish Heart (Gordon Jenkins—Decca)	1461	22
Rag Mop (Ames Brothers—Coral)	1407	23
Bewitched (Bill Snyder—Tower)	1380	24
Hoop Dee Doo (Perry Como—Victor)	1158	25
Bewitched (Gordon Jenkins—Decca)	1142	26
Can Anyone Explain? (Ames Brothers—Coral)	1022	27
My Foolish Heart (Billy Eckstine—MGM)	1020	28
Dear Hearts & Gentle People (Bing Crosby—Decca)	1014	29
Cry of the Wild Goose (Frankie Laine—Mercury)	984	30

THE YEAR'S TOP COUNTRY & WESTERN RECORDS

... according to

RETAIL SALES

RECORD, ARTIST & LABEL	POINTS	POSITION
I'm Movin' On (Hank Snow—Victor)	3518	1
Chattanoogie Shoe Shine Boy (Red Foley—Decca)	3196	2
I'll Sail My Ship Alone (Moon Mullican—King)	3043	3
Why Don't You Love Me? (Hank Williams—MGM)	2315	4
Long Gone Lonesome Blues (Hank Williams—MGM)	2114	5
Goodnight, Irene (Red Foley-Ernest Tubb—Decca)	1736	6
Cuddle Buggin' Baby (Eddy Arnold—Victor)	1588	7
(Remember Me) I'm the One Who Loves You (Stuart Hamblen—Columbia)	1348	8
Birmingham Bounce (Red Foley—Decca)	1231	9
Lovebug Itch (Eddy Arnold—Victor)	1202	10
Mississippi (Red Foley—Decca)	1191	11
Throw Your Love My Way (Ernest Tubb—Decca)	1156	12
I Love You Because (Ernest Tubb—Decca)	1071	13
Cincinnati Dancing Pig (Red Foley—Decca)	1033	14
I'll Never Be Free (Tennessee Ernie-Kay Starr—Capitol)	953	15
Let's Go To Church (Next Sunday Morning) (Margaret Whiting-Jimmy Wakely—Capitol)	842	16
Enclosed One Broken Heart (Eddy Arnold—Victor)	835	17
Little Angel With the Dirty Face (Eddy Arnold—Victor)	808	18
Why Should I Cry Over You? (Eddy Arnold—Victor)	797	19
Slipping Around (Margaret Whiting-Jimmy Wakely—Capitol)	739	20
I Love You Because (Leon Payne—Capitol)	675	21
Broken Down Merry-Go-Round (Margaret Whiting-Jimmy Wakely—Capitol)	663	22
Letters Have No Arms (Ernest Tubb—Decca)	631	23
Hillbilly Fever (Little Jimmy Dickens—Columbia)	623	24
Just a Closer Walk With Thee (Red Foley—Decca)	605	25
Tennessee Border #2 (Red Foley-Ernest Tubb—Decca)	561	26
If You've Got the Money I've Got the Time (Lefty Frizzell—Columbia)	561	27
Mona Lisa (Moon Mullican—King)	530	28
Bonaparte's Retreat (Pee Wee King—Victor)	442	29
Moaning the Blues (Hank Williams—MGM)	440	30

THE YEAR'S TOP RHYTHM & BLUES RECORDS

... according to

RETAIL SALES

RECORD, ARTIST & LABEL	POINTS	POSITION
Pink Champagne (Joe Liggins—Specialty)	2717	1
Double Crossing Blues (Johnny Otis, Little Esther, Mel Walker—Savoy)	1891	2
I Need You So (Ivory Joe Hunter—MGM)	1578	3
Hard Luck Blues (Roy Brown—De Luxe)	1534	4
Cupid's Boogie (Little Esther, Johnny Otis, Mel Walker—Savoy)	1476	5
I Almost Lost My Mind (Ivory Joe Hunter—MGM)	1434	6
Well, Oh, Well (Tiny Bradshaw—King)	1429	7
Blue Light Boogie (Louis Jordan—Decca)	1382	8
For You My Love (Larry Darnell—Regal)	1333	9
Mistrustin' Blues (Johnny Otis, Little Esther, Mel Walker—Savoy)	1331	10
Everyday I Have the Blues (Lowell Fulson—Swingtime)	824	11
Blue Shadows (Lowell Fulson—Swingtime)	732	12
Anytime, Anyplace, Anywhere (Joe Morris—Atlantic)	731	13
Why Do Things Happen to Me? (Roy Hawkins—Modern)	687	14
Mona Lisa (King Cole Trio—Capitol)	645	15
I Wanna Be Loved (Dinah Washington—Mercury)	584	16
Please Send Me Someone To Love (Percy Mayfield—Specialty)	536	17
I Love My Baby (Larry Darnell—Regal)	507	18
Saturday Night Fish Fry (Louis Jordan—Decca)	505	19
Cry, Cry, Baby (Ed Wiley—Sittin' In)	440	20
Teardrops From My Eyes (Ruth Brown—Atlantic)	431	21
Love Don't Love Nobody (Roy Brown—DeLuxe)	402	22
The Fat Man (Fats Domino—Imperial)	320	23
My Baby's Gone (Charles Brown—Aladdin)	300	24
Information Blues (Roy Milton—Specialty)	295	25
I'm Yours To Keep (Herb Fisher—Modern)	289	26
It Isn't Fair (Dinah Washington—Mercury)	289	27
I'll Get Along Somehow (Larry Darnell—Regal)	273	28
Bad, Bad Whiskey (Amos Milburn—Aladdin)	270	29
Deceivin' Blues (Johnny Otis, Little Esther, Mel Walker—Savoy)	268	30

ences, but there were five records that reached the pop chart, mostly by performers experienced in threading the two streams. Among the youngest in that group was Hank Williams. His brief career was one of the most fruitful links between pop and country, and even influenced rhythm and blues performers.

Though Hank Williams had experience in radio and in touring with both country and pop acts, it was the alchemy of his own performance and the penetrating insinuation of his songs that provided the passport into the other streams. His carrying case was bulging with material from the music publishers ensconced in their Nashville base. In stories about past musical influences, performers as diverse as Dion (of Dion and the Belmonts), Chuck Berry, and Bob Dylan attest to the power Williams' music had on theirs. Country music was ready to become the major alternative source of new material for the pop stream. Besides Hank Williams, others trafficked heavily the zone between pop and country and the commercial side of the folk stream. Frankie Laine, Tennessee Ernie Ford, and the team of Jimmy Wakely and Margaret Whiting among others, produced records that readily crossed over to the pop market.

One of the most influential was Patti Page's huge success, "The Tennessee Waltz." The song was written in 1948 by Redd Stewart and Pee Wee King, western swing veterans familiar with the pop stream machinery. It was aimed, under the guidance of Rule One, at duplicating Bill Monroe's 1946 country hit, "Kentucky Waltz." The song went nowhere until several years later, when this southern, mournful tale of lost love was revived by Patti Page in a studio-gimmicked recording that presented the singer accompanying herself. It sold two million copies the first year of its release in the pop and country markets and some ten million records by 1960. (In 1965 it was adopted as the official song of the state of Tennessee.) By a fluke, Erskine Hawkins, a veteran R&B band leader with a talent for reaching into the pop stream, brought his version to the black pop charts. Patti Page's bellwether record generated within three years at least eight other songs with "Tennessee" in their title; Rule One gone rampant.

In 1950 there were thirty-one crossover songs.[18] These are listed in Table 7-1. Six of them were three-market crossings. Besides "Tennessee Waltz," the other five illustrate the range of musical materials the three streams could share. The first such song—"Rag Mop"—and its recording history reveal the complex ways the jazz stream, through its historic association with pop and country in the swing and western swing traditions, created passports for musicians working around those borders.

Figure 7-1. (opposite) *Billboard*'s Top Records of 1950: Pop, Country & Western, and Rhythm & Blues. *The Billboard*, January 13, 1951, pp. 18–20. © 1951 BPI Communications, Inc. Used with Permission from *Billboard*.

TABLE 7-1
Crossovers Among the Pop, R & B, C & W Charts: 1950

Chart	Song title	Performer	Record label	Date of first appearance	Peak chart position
Three-market crossovers					
Pop	"Rag Mop"	Ames Brothers	Coral	6 Jan. 1950	1
		Lionel Hampton	Decca	3 Feb. 1950	7
		Ralph Flanagan	RCA Victor	10 Feb. 1950	10
		Johnny Lee Wills	Bullet	17 Feb. 1950	10
R & B		Lionel Hampton	Decca	4 Feb. 1950	12
		Doc Sausage	Regal	4 Feb. 1950	4
		Joe Liggins & His Honeydrippers	Specialty	18 Feb. 1950	4
C & W		Johnny Lee Wills	Bullet	28 Jan. 1950	2
Pop	"Mona Lisa"	Nat King Cole	Capitol	2 June 1950	1
		Victor Young	Decca	23 June 1950	10
		Art Lund	MGM	30 June 1950	14
		Dennis Day	RCA Victor	11 Aug. 1950	25
R & B		Nat King Cole	Capitol	8 July 1950	1
C & W		Moon Mullican	King	26 Aug. 1950	4
		Jimmy Wakely	Capitol	23 Sep. 1950	10
Pop	"Goodnight Irene"	Gordon Jenkins and the Weavers	Decca	30 June 1950	1
		Frank Sinatra	Columbia	28 July 1950	12
		Jo Stafford	Capitol	1 Sep. 1950	26
		Dennis Day	RCA Victor	22 Sep. 1950	22
R & B		Paul Gayten	Regal	2 Sep. 1950	6
C & W		Ernest Tubb, Red Foley	Decca	19 Aug. 1950	1
		Moon Mullican	King	26 Aug. 1950	5
Pop	"I'll Never Be Free"	Kay Starr and Tennessee Ernie Ford	Capitol	18 Aug. 1950	3
R & B		Paul Gayten, Annie Laurie	Regal	29 Apr. 1950	4
		Dinah Washington	Mercury	7 Oct. 1950	3
		Ella Fitzgerald	Decca	4 Nov. 1950	7
C & W		Kay Starr and Tennessee Ernie Ford	Capitol	16 Sep. 1950	2
Pop	"Tennessee Waltz"	Patti Page	Mercury	10 Nov. 1950	1
		Guy Lombardo	Decca	8 Dec. 1950	6
		Les Paul and Mary Ford	Capitol	22 Dec. 1950	8
		Jo Stafford	Columbia	5 Jan. 1951	17
		Fontane Sisters	RCA Victor	12 Jan. 1951	29
		Spike Jones	RCA Victor	12 Jan. 1951	16
		Anita O'Day	London	16 Dec. 1951	24
R & B		Erskine Hawkins	Coral	30 Dec. 1950	6
C & W		Patti Page	Mercury	6 Jan. 1951	2
		Pee Wee King	RCA Victor	17 Feb. 1951	6
Pop	"My Heart Cries for You"	Guy Mitchell	Columbia	1 Dec. 1950	2
		Dinah Shore	RCA Victor	15 Dec. 1950	11
		Vic Damone	Mercury	22 Dec. 1950	12
		Jimmy Wakely	Capitol	22 Dec. 1950	12
		Victor Young	Decca	16 Feb. 1951	29

TABLE 7-1
(continued)

Chart	Song title	Performer	Record label	Date of first appearance	Peak chart position
Three-market crossovers (continued)					
R & B		Dinah Washington	Mercury	3 Mar. 1951	7
C & W		Jimmy Wakely	Capitol	20 Jan. 1951	7
		Red Foley and Evelyn Knight	Decca	17 Feb. 1951	6
Pop ⇄ R & B crossovers					
Pop	"I Almost Lost My	Nat King Cole	Capitol	1 Apr. 1950	26
R & B	Mind"	Nat King Cole	Capitol	22 Apr. 1950	7
		Ivory Joe Hunter	MGM	1 July 1950	1
Pop	"Sitting by the	Billy Eckstine	MGM	27 Jan. 1950	23
R & B	Window"	Billy Eckstine	MGM	4 Mar. 1950	6
Pop	"It Isn't Fair"	Sammy Kaye and Don Cornell	RCA Victor	3 Feb. 1950	3
R & B		Dinah Washington	Mercury	8 Apr. 1950	5
Pop	"My Foolish Heart"	Gordon Jenkins	Decca	3 Mar. 1950	3
		Billy Eckstine	MGM	3 Mar. 1950	6
		Mindy Carson	RCA Victor	28 Apr. 1950	13
R & B		Gene Ammons	Chess	29 July 1950	9
Pop	"I Wanna Be Loved"	Andrews Sisters	Decca	5 May 1950	3
		Billy Eckstine	MGM	9 June 1950	9
		Hugo Winterhalter with the Fontane Sisters	RCA Victor	16 June 1950	24
R & B		Dinah Washington	Mercury	17 June 1950	5
Pop	"Tenderly"	Lynn Hope Quintet	Premium	26 Aug. 1950	19
R & B		Lynn Hope Quintet	Premium	12 Aug. 1950	8
Pop	"Harbor Lights"	Sammy Kaye	Columbia	1 Sep. 1950	1
		Guy Lombardo	Decca	6 Oct. 1950	2
		Ray Anthony	Capitol	20 Oct. 1950	15
		Ken Griffin	Columbia	20 Oct. 1950	27
		Ralph Flanagan	RCA Victor	27 Oct. 1950	27
R & B		Dinah Washington	Mercury	6 Jan. 1951	10
Pop	"Oh Babe"	Louis Prima	Robin Hood	10 Nov. 1950	16
		Kay Starr	Capitol	17 Nov. 1950	12
R & B		Jimmy Preston	Derby	11 Nov. 1950	5
		Larry Darnell	Regal	25 Nov. 1950	5
		Roy Hilton	Specialty	2 Dec. 1950	5
		Wynonie Harris	King	2 Dec. 1950	7
Pop ⇄ C & W crossovers					
Pop	"Chattanoogie Shoe	Red Foley	Decca	21 Jan. 1950	1
	Shine Boy"	Bing Crosby	Decca	27 Jan. 1950	9
		Bill Darnel	Coral	3 Mar. 1950	26
		Frank Sinatra	Columbia	10 Mar. 1950	24
		Phil Harris	RCA Victor	17 Mar. 1950	26
C & W		Red Foley	Decca	21 Jan. 1950	1

TABLE 7-1
(continued)

Chart	Song title	Performer	Record label	Date of first appearance	Peak chart position
Pop ⇄ C & W crossovers (continued)					
Pop	"Bonaparte's Retreat"	Kay Starr	Capitol	9 June 1950	5
		Gene Krupa	RCA Victor	11 Aug. 1950	16
C & W		Pee Wee King	RCA Victor	21 Jan. 1950	10
Pop	"Quicksilver"	Bing Crosby and the Andrews Sisters	Decca	27 Jan. 1950	8
		Doris Day	Columbia	24 Feb. 1950	20
		Elton Britt and Rex Allen	RCA Victor	25 Feb. 1950	3
Pop	"Cry of the Wild Goose"	Frankie Laine	Mercury	3 Feb. 1950	4
		Tennessee Ernie Ford	Capitol	24 Feb. 1950	15
C & W		Tennessee Ernie Ford	Capitol	11 Feb. 1950	2
Pop	"Broken Down Merry-Go-Round"	Margaret Whiting and Jimmy Wakely	Capitol	24 Feb. 1950	12
C & W		Margaret Whiting and Jimmy Wakely	Capitol	11 Feb. 1950	2
Pop	"Sugarfoot Rag"	Red Foley	Decca	(data unavailable)	24
C & W		Red Foley	Decca	18 Feb. 1950	4
Pop	"Peter Cottontail"	Mervin Shiner	Decca	17 Mar. 1950	8
		Gene Autry	Columbia	24 Mar. 1950	5
		Jimmy Wakely	Capitol	8 Apr. 1950	7
C & W		Gene Autry	Columbia	8 Apr. 1950	3
		Mervin Shiner	Decca	1 Apr. 1950	6
		Jimmy Wakely	Capitol	8 Apr. 1950	7
		Johnnie Lee Wills	Bullet	1 Apr. 1950	7
Pop	"Shotgun Boogie"	Tennessee Ernie Ford	Capitol	16 Mar. 1951	14
C & W		Tennessee Ernie Ford	Capitol	16 Dec. 1950	1
Pop	"Let's Go to Church Next Sunday Morning"	Margaret Whiting and Jimmy Wakely	Capitol	7 Apr. 1950	13
C & W		Margaret Whiting and Jimmy Wakely	Capitol	22 Apr. 1950	2
Pop	"Birmingham Bounce"	Red Foley	Decca	(data unavailable)	14
C & W		Red Foley	Decca	13 May 1950	1
Pop	"M-I-S-S-I-S-S-I-P-P-I"	Red Foley	Decca	1 July 1950	22
C & W		Red Foley	Decca	3 June 1950	1
Pop	"I'm Moving On"	Hank Snow	RCA Victor	(data unavailable)	27
C & W		Hank Snow	RCA Victor	1 July 1950	1
Pop	"Cincinatti Dancing Pig"	Red Foley	Decca	25 Aug. 1950	7
C & W		Red Foley	Decca	9 Sep. 1950	2

TABLE 7-1
(continued)

Chart	Song title	Performer	Record label	Date of first appearance	Peak chart position
Pop ⇄ C & W crossovers (continued)					
Pop	"Our Lady of Fatima"	Red Foley	Decca	25 Aug. 1950	16
		Dick Haymes	Mercury	1 Sep. 1950	10
		Phil Spitalny	RCA Victor	20 Oct. 1950	23
C & W		Red Foley	Decca	4 Nov. 1950	8
Pop	"A Bushel and a Peck"	Margaret Whiting and Jimmy Wakely	Capitol	20 Oct. 1950	6
		Perry Como	RCA Victor	27 Oct. 1950	6
		Doris Day	Columbia	5 Jan. 1951	30
C & W		Margaret Whiting and Jimmy Wakely	Capitol	18 Nov. 1950	6
Pop	"Rudolph the Red-Nosed Reindeer"	Gene Autry	Columbia	24 Nov. 1950	3
		Bing Crosby	Decca	8 Dec. 1950	14
		Spike Jones	RCA Victor	15 Dec. 1950	11
C & W		Gene Autry	Columbia	16 Dec. 1950	5
Pop	"Frosty the Snow Man"	Gene Autry	Columbia	1 Dec. 1950	7
C & W		Gene Autry	Columbia	9 Dec. 1950	4

SOURCES: *Billboard* music popularity charts, 1950; *Top Country Singles 1944–1988* (pub. 1989), *Top Pop Singles 1940–1955* (pub. 1973), and *Top R & B Singles 1942–1988* (pub. 1989), all Menomonee Falls, Wisconsin: Record Research, Inc., all compiled from *Billboard*'s Best Selling Singles charts. © 1950 BPI Communications, Inc. Used with permission from *Billboard*.

"Rag Mop" was written for Bob Wills' Texas Playboys by Johnnie Lee Wills and Deacon Anderson, both members of that band. In 1946, Henry "Red" Allen recorded it for Victor in a session that was aimed at getting some records into the "race" market in the style of Louis Jordan's Tympani Five, riding high at the moment. It was then entitled "Get the Mop," a mildly naughty party song done in a jazz-pop style not for radio play.[19] It was a moderate success, and, having crossed from its country origins in Wills' western swing band to a rhythm and blues version, it now appeared to have an unlimited passport. In 1950, Regal Records released for the rhythm and blues market Doc Sausage's version of the song, now cleaned up and retitled "Rag Mop." The publisher, following established practice, sought other recordings and was successful with a black pop version from the young Joe Liggins.

In the pop market, the first attempt was the hit. It was by the Ames Brothers for Coral Records. This group of four actual brothers was one of the younger quartets modeled on the earlier big band-affiliated vocal groups such as the Modernaires and the Pied Pipers. Their rendition made the pop charts even before Doc Sausage's reached the R&B chart.

This rendition was followed immediately by Lionel Hampton's big jazz-pop version, which was a hit in both the pop and R&B markets. Ralph Flannagan's band also released a version that made the pop charts. His was typical of the arranger-led postwar bands, which sought every likely black pop song that might rekindle the prewar dance band days. To finish this saga, one of the original writers of "Rag Mop," Johnnie Lee Wills, now with his own country band, released a version that appeared on both the pop and country charts. The publishers' practice of securing multiple recordings of a single song was nearing its end. The major record companies' tactic of "covering" a hit was a different matter.[20] The story of this record indicates the vitality of jazz, even as it worked itself into musical zones diluting its essence with pop or country or even rhythm and blues flavorings.

The next three-market crossover of 1950 came from the same quarter. "I'll Never Be Free" began with the Regal label's attempt to repeat its "Rag Mop" success. Fred Mendelsohn of Regal found in New Orleans Paul Gayton's small jump band and his powerful vocalist Annie Laurie. Their recording of "I'll Never Be Free" made the R&B charts in April 1950, and four months later, Kay Starr and Tennessee Ernie Ford's duet version on Capitol made the pop chart and then the country and western chart. Both performers of the duet version had careers that straddled all three markets. Kay Starr's long association with black pop music and her tough and torchy renditions of late night love songs gave her enough credibility to cover materials from the R&B field. Tennessee Ernie Ford occupied a comparable position between country and pop, aided in that anomalous zone by an association with the folk stream. His 1949 hits on the country charts, "Smokey Mountain Boogie" and "Anticipation Blues," were early (commercial) versions of the "country boogie" style that was blending R&B material with country performers and string instrumentation. Starr and Ford therefore held passports that allowed easy passage among the three streams.

The fourth of these three-way crossovers came from an entirely different quarter. It marked the beginning of the folk stream's incorporation into pop, a mutual embrace that would provide rocknroll with one of its strongest reservoirs, both musically and politically. The record was Huddie Ledbetter's "Goodnight Irene," done on Decca by Gordon Jenkins' orchestra with the Weavers.[21] The latter were the renamed Almanac Singers led by Pete Seeger. In 1950, Folkways, the pioneering folk stream record company headed by Moses Asch, released "Goodnight Irene" as part of a ten-inch, LP memorial album to Leadbelly, who had died in Bellevue Hospital a year before, poor, sick, and on relief. The Gordon Jenkins/Weavers version quickly garnered at least five cover records, three in the pop market, including ones by Frank Sinatra and Jo Stafford.

The high prestige of these two vocalists indicates the importance the pop stream's record chiefs gave to the folk stream. Improbably, Red Foley and Ernest Tubb did a duet version for Decca that made the country and western charts, as did Moon Mullican's country piano rendition for King.

It should be noted, as shown in figure 7-1, that there were three other best-selling records in 1950 that were folk in styling or origin but that appeared only on the pop charts. These were the Weavers/Gordon Jenkins' "Tzena, Tzena, Tzena," an Israeli folk dance tune; Bing Crosby's "Dear Hearts and Gentle People," a pseudo-folk concoction written by Bob Hilliard and Sammy Fain; and the off-beat, folklike novelty, "Cry of the Wild Goose," sung by Frankie Laine for Mercury. The folk presence was definitely in the air, and the music trade knew what to do about it.

The final three-way crossover of 1950 was an example of the industry's response to that folk presence. It was a creation of Mitch Miller, senior A&R presence for Columbia Records. The song, "My Heart Cries for You," was an adaptation of a French folk song constructed by Carl Sigman and Percy Faith, whose orchestra backed the singer Guy Mitchell. Perhaps in deference to Mitchell's producer Mitch Miller, who not only used his knowledge of classical music with great commercial panache but also was a national TV star, four pop versions of "My Heart Cries for You" soon reached the pop charts. One was by Jimmy Wakely, who put his recording on the country chart as well. Another was by Dinah Washington, workhorse of the pop crossover to R&B, who put Mercury's contribution on the black pop charts some months later.[22]

In addition to these six records that crossed over into all three markets in 1950, there were twenty-five two-market crossovers: seventeen between country and pop, eight between pop and R&B, but none between country and R&B. Among the country-pop crossovers, all but one began in the country field or were originated by country artists. Moreover, practically all were *direct* crossovers, that is, the artist's original country record crossed over into pop. The artists included Gene Autry, whose movies had made him as much a pop personality as a country and western singer and whose seasonal hits like "Rudolph the Red Nosed Reindeer" were cross-market pushovers. Also included was the duo of Jimmy Wakely and Margaret Whiting, a show business team that worked in both pop and country with such innocuous materials as "A Bushel and a Peck" and "Let's Go to Church Next Sunday." Red Foley was another artist whose crossovers harkened back to the success of southern-styled dance band hits of the 1940s. The 1950 hits were "Chattanooga Shoeshine Boy," "Cincinnati Dancing Pig," and the religious "Our Lady of Fatima."[23]

The other performer who crossed the country-pop boundary was Tennessee Ernie Ford with "Shotgun Boogie" and "Cry of the Wild Goose," which had been introduced into the pop field by Frankie Laine, another folk-tinged pop singer. These major artists, in other words, whose careers were anchored in prewar traditions, were responsible for practically all the traffic between country and pop at the level of hit records.

Only three of the eight black pop crossovers were direct. Two of these were by the song stylists Billy Eckstine and Nat King Cole, whose diction, delivery, musical backing were well within the pop limits. The other direct crossover from R&B to pop is one of those inexplicable blips on the radar screen. It was the balladlike pop song "Tenderly," recorded by the Lynn Hope Quintet on the Premium label. The six other crossovers between pop and rhythm and blues were *cover* records, that is, black artists doing their version of a white performer's record. Within a few years, the situation would be reversed; white artists would be "covering" black records.

Rocknroll Assembles Its Canon

As the twig is bent, so grows the tree. The year 1951 produced records that decisively founded the reservoir of rocknroll. Those records, not so much in number but in their location and meaning, were to generate the canon that subsequently offered passage to materials that served the young audience as no other popular music could or did. The total number of crossovers was much the same as for the previous year. The main difference was the increased traffic between rhythm and blues and pop; the number of crossovers between these two streams almost doubled compared to 1950, while the country-pop crossovers declined considerably. Most of the records that moved between rhythm and blues and pop were again those by artists doing songs well within the limits of white pop performance styles (Nat Cole, Billy Eckstine, Tommy Edwards) or by performers carrying versions of a giant pop hit to a black audience (for example, Les Paul and Mary Ford's jazz standard "How High the Moon," or Tab Smith's instrumental version of the 1940 hit "Because of You," revitalized in 1951 by Tony Bennett). Whatever the manner, a black presence was becoming apparent in pop vocal records.

A more important signal came from the direct crossing from the rhythm and blues charts to the white pop charts of four records by black performers, delivering unmistakable black musical styling. These were:

Johnny Hodges, "Castle Rock" (Mercury).
Hodges fronted his own orchestra for this instrumental record after years of exemplary service with Duke Ellington. This group was a black swing band at its most mature. Frank Sinatra immediately put a vocal version on the pop charts as well.

Joe Turner, "Chains of Love" (Atlantic).

This veteran blues shouter from Kansas City's glory days, with a contemporary song written by Van Walls with lyrics by Ahmet Ertegun, bridged the generations (and the races).

John Lee Hooker, "I'm in the Mood" (Modern).
One of the few working older bluesmen whose career spanned the 1930s "race" records era, Hooker put nine singles on the R&B charts from 1949 to 1968.

The Dominoes, "Sixty Minute Man" (Federal).
This tune was a typical party song, a male vanity anthem by a young vocal quartet. It opened a path leading directly to rocknroll.

Before discussing the rocknroll path, which was, in fact, quite circuitous, it is important to note that these four records represented four different stylistic strands of black popular music during the prewar era. Because each was given a strong contemporary framing through disk jockey programming, gymnasium sock hops, and live traveling entertainment packages aimed at young white audiences, these records became the founding black pop and jazz roots of rocknroll.

Now the "Sixty Minute Man" story. The Dominoes' record was their second effort on Federal, one of King Records' subsidiary labels. It made the R&B charts within a few weeks of its release, went immediately to number one, and stayed on the charts for thirty weeks. It sold over a million copies. There was no other recorded version of the tune. Two and a half months later, in August 1951, it appeared on the pop charts. Although "Sixty Minute Man" remained there for just a month and reached only to the number twenty-three position, its very presence there was a landmark. What was there about this rather typical record that stirred so deeply the ranks of black record buyers and, for the first time, penetrated a sector of the white audience as well?

The song was unmistakably framed with gospel harmony and rhythm, including the instrumentation of piano, drums, bass, guitar, and organ. Black gospel would not, however, enter the rocknroll canon directly at this time, or ever. Its personnel and musical resources would be transmitted only indirectly, infusing rocknroll with one of its greatest gifts, the ability to deliver passion at the edge of control. Both sides of the record were set in the vocal styling of the Ink Spots, whose contrasting falsetto and bass voices had earlier and successfully journeyed from a black gospel sound right into the pop stream. "Sixty Minute Man," however, is completely secular, with a bold and driving bass voicing, in the familiar genre of explicit male praise songs of sexual prowess. How these lyrics got through enough white station managers to allow the disk jockeys to play it is still a wonder. Even during the early fifties, when the autonomous disk jockey pretty much called the tunes, station policy on "suggestive" material was still operative and quickly triggered, especially when the offending sounds were black.

Sixty Minute Man *

Sixty Minute Man
Sixty Minute Man
Look here girls I'm telling you now
They call me loving Dan
I rock 'em roll 'em all night long
I'm a sixty minute man
If you don't believe I'm all I say
Come up here and take my hand
When I let you go you'll cry
Oh yes, he's a sixty minute man

There'll be fifteen minutes of kissing
Then you'll holler, please don't stop
There'll be fifteen minutes of teasin'
There'll be fifteen minutes of squeezin'
And fifteen minutes of blowin' my top
Mop! Mop! Mop!

If your old man ain't treatin' you right
Come up and see old Dan
I rock 'em roll 'em all night long
I'm a sixty minute man
Sixty Minute Man
They call me loving Dan
I rock 'em roll 'em all night long
I'm a sixty minute man

These are not teenage lyrics, nor are they like the rough, prewar shouting blues. They are more reminiscent of the "party song" lyrics popularized by Louis Jordan. Just three years later, the Midnighters with Hank Ballard, on the Federal label, kept the R&B charts filled for most of the year with "Work with Me Henry" and the "Annie Had a Baby." Both were number one best sellers whose lyrics barely disguised their sexual celebrations. Such party songs did not cross over to pop directly, but early in 1955 Georgia Gibbs for Mercury drove "Dance with Me Henry" up to the number two position on the pop charts. This rendition was a whitened version of the Hank Ballard tune "Work with Me Henry." The same tune was rewritten by Johnny Otis for Etta James (also given writer credits) who, with a different title, "The Wallflower," took it up to number two on the R&B charts. "Sixty Minute Man" was of intermediate material, strong enough to be easily recognized, rich enough to be musically unfolded in a hundred ways. Unquestionably, "Sixty Minute Man" can

* "Sixty Minute Man," by William Ward and Rose Marks. © 1951 (Renewed) Trio Music Co., Inc. and Fort Knox Music, all rights reserved. Used by permission.

be placed among the first rocknroll records. That placement gets some support in that Billy Ward himself located the record in the naming of rocknroll by Alan Freed (see Chapter 1).

"Sixty Minute Man" was a powerful marker. It reverberated for a considerable time down the rhythm and blues stream and the just-assembling rocknroll path. Its descendants form an extended, if obscure, sequence of answer songs (a major schema used to pursue Rule One). The first was Ruth Brown's "5-10-15 Hours" on Atlantic; clearly this tune is a prayer for a longer experience. It was introduced in April 1952, reaching the number one position on the R&B charts. It remained there thirteen weeks but did not cross over to the pop charts. The next answer song came shortly after, in October of 1952. It was a return to the male vanity song, "Rock Me All Night Long," done by the Ravens on Mercury. This group had been unsuccessfully trying to follow the Mills Brothers and Ink Spots route into the new R&B, and this record was their final attempt to capture a contemporary hook. The record stayed on the R&B charts for eight weeks, reaching the number four position.

Yet the point was made, and it carried into the next promise of even more heroic sexual delivery in "Rock Around the Clock." This song would be picked up by Bill Haley and the Comets in 1955 for Decca, and it went on to both the pop and the R&B charts. It was the number one best-selling record; only eight other records up to that date had stayed on the pop charts longer than did "Rock Around the Clock." Though Haley's rendition was in lineal continuity with "Sixty Minute Man," it was definitely a retreat in the sense that it referred to dance rather than sex. It did, however, clearly serve a youth audience. When the movie *Blackboard Jungle* (1955) used Haley's record to set the tone of the picture, the message was more explicitly stated; rocknroll became a banner of rebellion for the young.

The end of this belabored answer song series was not yet in sight. On 1 August, 1970, Rufus Thomas, the veteran Memphis entertainer, once more hit the R&B charts with a re-release of "Sixty Minute Man" on Stax. The song reached only number forty-three and stayed only a month on the chart, but it was sufficient to stimulate, for the second time, an instant answer.[24] This time the answer song was by the Presidents, imitating Ruth Brown's title. On 26 September 1970, their "5-10-15-20 (25-30 Years of Love)" made the R&B charts, reached the number five position, and remained there for fifteen weeks. This respectable hit crossed over to pop in December of that year, climbing to number eleven and also lasting fifteen weeks.

"Sixty Minute Man" and its long career teaches several lessons. One is that rhythm and blues is not rocknroll, but both can claim the original record as one of their own. The Dominoes, that is, can rightly claim to be in the main line of rhythm and blues through the sequence of records just described, as well as a progenitor of Bill Haley's founding contribution to rocknroll. The chain of answer songs, though a minor matter in itself, formed an important part of the machinery that, piece by piece, made rocknroll the synthesis of all the streams. The answer song linked not only one record to another, but it interconnected the streams as one or more member of the sequence crossed and recrossed boundary lines.

An equally important lesson is that the success of "Sixty Minute Man" as a crossover publicly announced that youngsters, white and black, were taking out-of-school classes in the complexities of love and sexual discovery. The curriculum for that course is printed in the lyrics of "Sixty Minute Man" and Nat King Cole's "Too Young," the number one best-selling pop record of 1951 and twenty-second best seller in the R&B market.

*Too Young** *

They tried to tell us we're too young
Too young to really be in love
They say that love's a word
A word we've only heard
And can't begin to know the meaning of

And yet we're not too young to know
This love will last though years may go
And then someday they may recall
We were not too young at all

"Too Young" was introduced by Johnny Desmond, one of several young vocalists competing for the places vacated with the demise of the big band singers. It was one of the first attempts by pop record executives to conjoin a young musical persona to lyrics that would appeal to a young audience. The smooth and fastidious styling of Nat Cole's version was too appealing, however, and it took the play away from the Desmond record. Young audiences, readily appropriating both "Sixty Minute Man" and "Too Young," invited themselves into that highly sensitive exploration of young love and sexual adventure. The forbidding presence of parental authority was clearly the unspoken enemy. These two records, and others that would soon follow, sounded the beginnings of youth's assertiveness in matters of personal life.

Nat Cole, however attractive he may have been, was an adult performer. His "look" as well as his career were simply out of touch with the teenagers of that day. The question was, Could the young audiences being assembled by the nation's disk jockeys find their hero in an adult performer? The Al Martinos and Johnny Desmonds, however, were not

* "Too Young," words by Sylvia Dee, music by Sid Lippman, copyright 1951, renewed 1979 Worldwide by Aria Music Co. (ASCAP).

doing the job, and the pop stream repeatedly tried to find performers who could embody the dreams of the young.

The next attempt was the sudden and unexpected *direct* crossover of Johnnie Ray's "Cry." It appeared on the pop charts in November of 1951 and on the black charts a month later, climbing to the top of both. Designated by the general press as well as by the trade press as some kind of phenomenon, Ray's sudden popularity in both pop and R&B markets raised the question then being formulated in the industry: Could they find a white boy who could sing black?

Born in 1925 in Dallas, Oregon, Ray had an early familiarity with black gospel and black pop. After World War II, he drifted through the Midwest nightclub scene. While performing in Detroit's Flame Show Bar, that city's headquarters for rhythm and blues, he attracted the attention of the disk jockey–record distributor network connected to Bill Randle, who tipped off Mitch Miller to Ray's remarkable performing presence. Miller recorded Ray's "Cry" and "The Little White Cloud That Cried." The record sold over two million copies in 1951–1952, both sides making the R&B as well as the pop charts. Ray had the direct emotionalism and a black voicing that was newly appealing to the young audience. Yet, in spite of a few more recordings and some exciting appearances in the big combination houses, his career faded. He was deserted by a significant group of disk jockeys, including Randle. Ray's personal history, including brushes with the law, left him too off-beat and off-base. He was not a guitar player and had no linguistic or musical passport to deliver country music, which was still the favored alternative to the pop stream. Above all, he was too old and looked like an adult performer. If he had been young in actual age or in the social connections of youth, he might have anchored rocknroll; but, having no ties to school (as did the Four Freshmen and Lettermen) or to the family-church setting (as did Pat Boone), and lacking the prettiness that was so startling in Elvis' face, there was little chance of a big success, even though he was white.

Another crossover in 1951 of considerable significance was the Clovers' "Fool Fool Fool" (writing credits to Ahmet Ertegun), a catchy and inoffensive tune produced in the arresting but controlled Atlantic manner. Its vocal style was halfway between the extreme falsetto to bass range of the Dominoes' gospel style and the pop silkiness of the Ink Spots. A strong hit, reaching the top of the R&B chart and remaining twenty-two weeks, "Fool Fool Fool" was covered soon after by Capitol's Kay Starr. Her version of the song in August 1952 was a moderate hit and reopened the door to the practice of pop performers covering R&B hits. This record can also claim to be a rocknroll first in that it was the earliest instance of the new R&B vocal groups popping up in every city and triggering an important "cover" record by a leading pop artist. The trend was thus begun of channelling pop practices, musical and nonmusical, into an emerging core of rocknroll values. In the case of "Sixty Minute Man," R&B values were what was brought into the rocknroll reservoir, because the song was a *direct* crossover to pop. With "Fool Fool Fool," it was the *cover* crossover that merged pop conventions into the canon of rocknroll.[25] The cover records that followed, of which there were a flood and a half, were like training wheels for the emerging rocknroll—useful in the beginning but soon to be discarded in favor of freewheeling.

Rocknroll Is Named and Launched

During the next few years, up to 1955, the separate elements of rocknroll slowly, almost invisibly, unfolded. Those elements included the appearance of performers emblematic of the young audience, fresh dance music and dances that anyone could learn, and meaningful lyrics. All these were developing more or less independently of one another and would increasingly depart from adult musical fare in all three major streams. While the major record companies used their established artists to pump out records shadowing yesterday's hits, a scattered group of young and/or amateur producers offered new sounds and new singers to the disk jockeys eager to win the loyalty of their young followers. The conservative stasis continued though; the number of crossovers among the streams actually declined somewhat in 1952 and 1953. The vigor of R&B did occasionally cross over to pop via a few sides by Fats Domino and Joe Turner, both of whom put records on the R&B and pop charts, along with a few young vocal groups. And from country music, Hank Williams scored hit after hit, with several crossing over to pop either directly or covered by pop vocalists.

Along with these small but necessary steps along the way was one record in 1953 of lasting significance for rocknroll. It was "Crying in the Chapel." Originally it was a country "sacred" song written by the father of a young country artist, Darrell Glen, who moved it onto both the pop and the country charts via the Valley label. It was covered quickly by Rex Allen for Decca, who also achieved a moderate success on both the country and pop charts. June Valli was assigned to do a cover version for RCA, which took the play away from the other records. But it fell to the Orioles, a young but experienced vocal group from Baltimore, to do the definitive R&B version. It was the number one record for the fall of 1953 in that market and crossed over *directly* to the pop chart, where it reached the number eleven spot and stayed on the chart for two months.

This record was important mainly because it showed that "Sixty Minute Man" could be repeated, that is, an explicitly black-styled, young vocal group could bring a song appealing to teen-aged audiences directly to the pop market. "Crying in the Chapel" also displayed to its young audiences four different versions of the same tune, one each from the pop and R&B traditions and two country stylings. (In 1965, Elvis would restate them all in his own version.) These records enhanced the readiness of all three commercial streams to accept "sacred" or gospel subject matter as stimulating a teenaged amalgam of passions at once religious and romantic. The exploitation of that murky set of feelings involving death, cars, and unrequited love continued for a decade.[26] The gospel roots of country and R&B helped fuel those suffused emotional fires in teenaged hearts.

Not the least of the important aspects of the "Crying in the Chapel" series is that it built not just an abstract acceptance of diversity, but offered specific test cases by which to judge the quality of the variegated musical materials filling the rocknroll reservoir. Youngsters were to learn more about the difference between the genuine article and a slavish imitation as the cover records by white pop artists attempted to dominate the crossovers from rhythm and blues.

Given the exhaustion in the pop stream, it is entirely understandable that "Crying in the Chapel," or something like it, was to be the signal for flooding the crossover market. The wave swelled in 1954, which produced a 50 percent increase in the total number of crossovers. Of the total, almost twice as many records moved from R&B to pop than from country to pop—the exact reverse of the previous year. The largest group of these crossovers was direct R&B hits that went from the black to the pop charts. They introduced to young white audiences black artists, whose appeal could extend into country audiences if a white country performer could be persuaded to do a song identified with a black artist.

And, given the fading strength of many country singers, this was readily achieved. An important example is "Hearts of Stone," initiated by the Charms on Atlantic, covered by the Fontane Sisters for Dot in the pop field, and recorded by Red Foley for the country stream. Another three-way crossover was "Goodnight Sweetheart Goodnight" by the Spaniels on the Vee Jay label, covered for the pop market by the McGuire Sisters for Coral and by the young but traditional group Johnny and Jack for the country market. Again, white pop validation preceded the R&B to C&W crossing.

Also in 1954, the Chords' "Sh-Boom," recorded on Atlantic's subsidiary Cat label, informed the New York industry leaders in unmistakable terms of the power of the new R&B material. That hit, in addition, illuminated the safest way for the ever-nervous broadcasting industry to accommodate such material, that is, to produce a cover record by a white performer, in this case the Crew Cuts for Mercury. Both versions were overnight successes, with the cover version becoming one of the pop stream's most provocative developments in years. The New York music world took a special interest in this pair of records because it involved such a dramatic meeting of tradition and innovation. Ralph Shaw (Mr. Tradition) was general professional manager for Hill and Range. He was offered and bought from Jerry Wexler (Mr. Innovation) of Atlantic Records a half interest in the copyright of "Sh-Boom" on the basis of the Chords release. With the help of Bill Randle (another Mr. Innovation), the Crew Cuts entered the picture and brought both recordings to the top of their charts. This episode was another founding incident of rocknroll, the beginning of many episodes in which fresh, young, amateur energy met wily old industry practice.[27]

Events moved further down the same road in 1955 with Alan Freed's move to WINS in New York City. Here the drama involved rocknroll's raucous and uncouth name giver, who was invading the citadel of music's staid publishing and recording capital. The message being delivered, but not fully understood by anyone, was that rhythm and blues was turning into something else. It would take more than a decade and considerable hindsight to identify that something as one wing of rocknroll. Neither the message nor the messenger was warmly received. The old line ASCAP publishers trotted out the familiar blasts against Freed for playing smutty records. They found allies in some black circles, who accused Freed of putting black deejays out of work by stimulating the trend towards white disk jockeys programming black popular music.[28] His denials of playing suggestive materials were as unavailing as his protests to the very same black spokesmen who had a year before praised his showcasing black talent to a wider audience.

Freed's programming not only increased WINS's ratings but forced the other largely white pop music stations into a scramble for a black pop presence. He also alarmed the pop stream's music establishment by the success of his New York concerts and dances, which flushed hundreds of young black performers off the street corners and into recording studios. As mentioned earlier, Freed had put together in 1952 a melange of rhythm and blues acts, including some white pop performers, for his first Moondog Coronation Ball held in the Cleveland Arena.[29] The outcome of that event was explosive and prophetic. The ten thousand seats were oversold by estimates ranging from eight thousand to twenty thousand; there was a near riot; Freed was arrested but later released.[30] The tag of disreputability in the history of rocknroll was fixed at that concert. It was repeated a few years later in Boston with full national press orchestration at a similar fracas before one of Freed's concerts.

The years 1954 and 1955 witnessed a brief moment of abundance and tranquility in the nation. The Korean War had ended, the Cold War, though chilly, was quiet, and the ferocities of the McCarthy witch hunts had ceased. The factories and the schools were packed and humming; the Eisenhower presidency was in command of a thriving "suburban-industrial complex."[31] But changes in American life were just about to take off. They had already arrived for some; others would experience them tomorrow. The people involved in the creation of rocknroll and those in the on-going struggle of black Americans certainly knew something was happening, but it was news to the general public.

The two social dangers of youth's rocknroll and organized black-led protest against segregation were seemingly independent of each other. Both, though, were steaming in the American high schools all through the South and in the border states. Rocknroll and school desegregation played out their origins in the same place at the same time. The Supreme Court decision *Brown* v. *Board of Education*, though barely a headline in many newspapers, was the main event setting off the new active phase of the civil rights movement of the fifties.

With more noise and perhaps less consequence, rocknroll got its name at around the same time. Though the designation "rocknroll" (in a variety of spellings) had been in use since 1951, there had been essentially no mention of rocknroll in the popular American press until 1956 when the *Encyclopedia Britannica's Book of the Year* reported that

the most popular music was almost all either a resurrection of old materials or a flagrant imitation of folk songs, the latter reaching its lowest ebb in the so-called "rock 'n roll" style of rhymetic chant [which] concentrated on a minimum of melody line and a maximum of rhythmic noise, deliberately competing with the artistic ideals of the jungle itself.[32]

By the spring of that year, the weekly news magazines had begun to translate for the entire nation what *Billboard*'s Paul Ackerman had been trying to tell the music industry for more than a year:

The shouting and the tumult had died, but rhythm and blues, or as the teenagers call it, rock and roll, has not departed.

Rather, it may be stated that it has achieved respectability. . . . On the Roxy Theater's stage, for instance, "The Rock 'n' Roll Ice Revue" opens February 1, billed as "the hottest production ever staged on ice." . . . Another indication of this acceptance at high levels is the upcoming CBS radio program featuring so called rock and roll, with Alan Freed as the deejay.[33]

Ackerman's article continued for several columns to chronicle the number of R&B acts that had appeared on radio and TV, including the prestigious Ed Sullivan show. At that time, neither he nor the industry was too finicky about the distinction between rhythm and blues and rocknroll. Whatever it was, it was unmistakably there, a billboard-sized notice to adults.

To return to the charts and the crossovers, the year 1955 saw the boundaries of the pop stream explode; yet a study of the best-selling singles on the three charts—pop, R&B, and country and western—for that year almost totally obscures that fact (fig. 7-2).

In the pop stream, the number one record was Perez Prado's "Cherry Pink and Apple Blossom White." According to Roberts, this song was one of Prado's finest balancings of Spanish authenticity within an accommodation to white pop's constraints.[34] It was also the Latin dance's swan song on the national scene for a while, though in the several Spanish-speaking enclaves (New York, Los Angeles, Florida), the dance halls and social clubs never ceased their successive re-invention and abandonment of South American and Afro-Caribbean dance forms.

The number two pop record in 1955 was Bill Haley's "Rock Around the Clock." This title was the strongest direct statement the assembling rocknroll audience could make at that time. It stood alone, so much so, it requires a word about Haley's achievements and failures, since he was one of the most original experiments in the search for a pop artist who could deliver that special something to a teenage audience.

Bill Haley brought to rocknroll the black performance styles of Louis Jordan and other similar bands, but he was white and born and raised in the North. His work in small AM radio stations familiarized him with all the popular musics and directed his musical interests and commercial instincts to where pop, black pop, and country pop met. His first band reflected this interest, as its name states—the Four Aces of Western Swing. The Four Aces were a Philadelphia-based, pop vocal group that achieved their first notoriety in 1951, the same moment Haley was developing his performance style.

That same attraction to a mix of country, pop, and black pop led him next to respond to the number one rhythm and blues hit of 1951, "Rocket 88" by Jackie Brenston on the Chess label.[35] That sound influenced Haley so much that, even though that particular record did not go anywhere in the pop field, he changed the name of his group to "Bill Haley and the Comets" (a variation of the answer song tactic). After that time, his successful records were increasingly derivative material that sought for a passport into pop, such as "Mambo Rock" and "Birth of Boogie," which made the pop charts in 1955 just before the release of "Rock Around the Clock."

Bill Haley kept trying to find that musical combination of the three streams that would open all their markets. He put twenty-four records on the pop charts, only three of which reached the R&B charts. None made the country charts. It was simply not enough to call himself a country artist, nor enough to get on the country music circuit, though Haley did both. The fact remained that his musical weight was on the "swing"

1955'S TOP RECORDS

POPULAR

according to RETAIL SALES

Pos.	Record, Artist & Label	Points
1.	CHERRY PINK AND APPLE BLOSSOM WHITE (P. Prado, Victor)	14575
2.	ROCK AROUND THE CLOCK (Bill Haley, Decca)	13514
3.	YELLOW ROSE OF TEXAS (Mitch Miller, Columbia)	10026
4.	AUTUMN LEAVES (Roger Williams, Kapp)	9528
5.	UNCHAINED MELODY (L. Baxter, Capitol)	9519
6.	BALLAD OF DAVY CROCKETT (Bill Hayes, Cadence)	9010
7.	LOVE IS A MANY-SPLENDORED THING (Four Aces, Decca)	8951
8.	SINCERELY (McGuire Sisters, Coral)	8484
9.	AIN'T THAT A SHAME (P. Boone, Dot)	7628
10.	DANCE WITH ME, HENRY (G. Gibbs, Mercury)	7036
11.	CRAZY OTTO MEDLEY (Crazy Otto, Decca)	6992
12.	MELODY OF LOVE (Billy Vaughn, Dot)	6440
13.	SIXTEEN TONS (Tennessee Ernie, Capitol)	6242
14.	LEARNIN' THE BLUES (Frank Sinatra, Capitol)	6163
15.	HEARTS OF STONE (Fontane Sisters, Dot)	5873
16.	TWEEDLE DEE (G. Gibbs, Mercury)	5814
17.	MOMENTS TO REMEMBER (Four Lads, Columbia)	5653
18.	MR. SANDMAN (Chordettes, Cadence)	5393
19.	LET ME GO, LOVER (Joan Weber, Columbia)	5380
20.	BLOSSOM FELL, A (Nat "King" Cole, Capitol)	5385
21.	UNCHAINED MELODY (A. Hibbler, Decca)	4998
22.	BALLAD OF DAVY CROCKETT (Fess Parker, Columbia)	4431
23.	HONEY BABE (A. Mooney, MGM)	3685
24.	BALLAD OF DAVY CROCKETT (Tennessee Ernie, Capitol)	3628
25.	KO KO MO (Perry Como, Victor)	3615
26.	NAUGHTY LADY OF SHADY LANE (Ames Brothers, Victor)	3410
27.	HARD TO GET (G. MacKenzie, X)	3403
28.	THAT'S ALL I WANT FROM YOU (Jaye P. Morgan, Victor)	3357
29.	ONLY YOU (Platters, Mercury)	3214
30.	IT'S A SIN TO TELL A LIE (Somethin' Smith & the Redheads, Epic)	3163

C&W

according to RETAIL SALES

Pos.	Record, Artist & Label	Points
1.	IN THE JAILHOUSE NOW (Webb Pierce, Decca)	7378
2.	MAKING BELIEVE (Kitty Wells, Decca)	3990
3.	I DON'T CARE (Webb Pierce, Decca)	3956
4.	LOOSE TALK (Carl Smith, Columbia)	3353
5.	SATISFIED MIND (P. Wagoner, Victor)	3357
6.	CATTLE CALL (Eddy Arnold & Hugo Winterhalter, Victor)	2560
7.	LIVE FAST, LOVE HARD AND DIE YOUNG (Faron Young, Capitol)	2219
8.	IF YOU AINT LOVIN' (Faron Young, Capitol)	2193
9.	YELLOW ROSE (Hank Snow, Victor)	2100
10.	I'VE BEEN THINKING (Eddy Arnold, Victor)	2100
11.	MORE AND MORE (Webb Pierce, Decca)	1883
12.	LOVE, LOVE, LOVE (Webb Pierce, Decca)	1778
13.	SATISFIED MIND (Red & Betty Foley, Decca)	1778
14.	BALLAD OF DAVY CROCKETT (Tennessee Ernie, Capitol)	1694
15.	JUST CALL ME LONESOME (Eddy Arnold, Victor)	1564
16.	THERE SHE GOES (Carl Smith, Columbia)	1563
17.	ARE YOU MINE? (Ginny Wright & Tom Tall, Fabor)	1446
18.	SATISFIED MIND (J. Shepard, Capitol)	1375
19.	LET ME GO, LOVER (Hank Snow, Victor)	1307
20.	ALL RIGHT (Faron Young, Capitol)	1078
21.	SIXTEEN TONS (Tennessee Ernie, Capitol)	997
22.	KISSES DON'T LIE (Carl Smith, Columbia)	884
23.	HEARTS OF STONE (Red Foley, Decca)	877
24.	THAT OLD HOUSE (Stuart Hamblen, Victor)	871
25.	CATTLEMAN SONG (Eddy Arnold, Victor)	835

R&B

according to RETAIL SALES

Pos.	Record, Artist & Label	Points
1.	PLEDGING MY LOVE (Johnny Ace, Duke)	6617
2.	AIN'T THAT A SHAME (Fats Domino, Imperial)	4997
3.	MAYBELLENE (Chuck Berry, Chess)	4653
4.	EARTH ANGEL (Penguins, Dootone)	4676
5.	I'VE GOT A WOMAN (Ray Charles, Atlantic)	4171
6.	WALLFLOWER (Etta James, Modern)	3600
7.	ONLY YOU (Platters, Mercury)	3465
8.	MY BABE (Little Walter, Chess)	3341
9.	SINCERELY (Moonglows, Chess)	2775
10.	UNCHAINED MELODY (Roy Hamilton, Epic)	2688
11.	HEARTS OF STONE (Charms, Deluxe)	2591
12.	TWEEDLE DEE (L. Baker, Atlantic)	2490
13.	EVERYDAY (Count Basie, Clef)	2346
14.	IT'S LOVE, BABY (L. Brooks, Excello)	2171
15.	FLIP, FLOP AND FLY (J. Turner, Atlantic)	2167
16.	DON'T BE ANGRY (N. Brown, Savoy)	2060
17.	BO DIDDLEY (Bo Diddley, Checker)	2006
18.	WHATCHA GONNA DO? (Drifters, Atlantic)	1982
19.	UNCHAINED MELODY (Al Hibbler, Decca)	1936
20.	STORY UNTOLD (Nutmegs, Herald)	1866
21.	SOLDIER BOY (Four Fellows, Glory)	1842
22.	I HEAR YOU KNOCKIN' (Smiley Lewis, Imperial)	1666
23.	FOOL FOR YOU (Ray Charles, Atlantic)	1667
24.	AT MY FRONT DOOR (El Dorados, Vee Jay)	1657
25.	ALL BY MYSELF (Fats Domino, Imperial)	1420

Figure 7-2. Billboard's Top Records of 1955: Pop, Country & Western, and Rhythm & Blues. The Billboard, January 7, 1956. © 1956 BPI Communications, Inc. Used with permission from Billboard.

side rather than on the "western" side of western swing. Not only was this strain an exhausted musical base, but Haley himself was simply too old and too square. His visual appearance with his band would hardly frighten the parents, much less inflame the kids.

Haley's considerable contribution to the young rocknroll was, however, twofold. First, he emblazoned its new banner with the musical expression of teenage assertiveness. Secondly, he gave that musical expression a specific embodiment. In spite of the incongruity of Haley's chubby adult persona, the live performance of his small group of musicians thrashing their instruments and leaping about emblazoned rocknroll with a visual vocabulary. This movement, mainly from black theatricality, was essential and laid the basis for the subsequent rock superstars and their settings—the huge festival and arena concert. Haley was gone from the top 40 ranks of the pop charts by 1956, though he continued to record, placing his final charted single in 1974 (a remake of "Rock Around the Clock").

The number three record in 1955 was Mitch Miller's boisterous "Yellow Rose of Texas," a choral interpretation of an anonymous Civil War song. This arrangement was part of the pop field's continuing excursion into a country-folk mix, which also produced the chart entries "The Ballad of Davey Crockett" (three versions) and "Sixteen Tons" by Tennessee Ernie Ford. Both the latter records originated on television shows, as did Joan Weber's "Let Me Go Lover" (the number nineteen record) and Gisele MacKenzie's "Hard to Get" (number twenty-seven). Television was a major performance site for the embattled pop publishers and record men. So were the movies, which generated three of the records on the chart: "Unchained Melody," "Love Is a Many Splendored Thing," and "Honey-Babe," the marching song from the movie *Battle Cry*. The whole list was the usual pop melange.

In 1955, there was not one Brill Building song in the first ten best-selling singles that had arrived there by way of the conventional route, that is, via live performances and radio exposure. Only seven such records were on the entire chart, less than a third of the total.[36] The old days of the radio remote–dance band–publisher nexus were over. The disk jockeys, especially the hit-making ones, were in charge. They were the ones to find the talent and to showcase it before an audience that could make the hits. That talent, needless to say, was coming from those places supplying country music and black pop with its resources.

This source pool is seen dramatically in the sharp rise of crossovers in that year (see table 7-2). The strong action was in R&B. While there were only three three-market crossovers, they were indicative of the trend, all coming from black artists who strongly shaped the rocknroll canon. The first was the classic case. "Most of All," written by Harvey Fuqua (lead

TABLE 7-2
Crossovers Among the Pop, R & B, C & W Charts: 1955

Chart	Song title	Performer	Record label	Date of first appearance	Peak chart position
Three-market crossovers					
Pop	"Most of All"	Don Cornell	Coral	14 May 1955	14
R & B		Moonglows	Chess	9 Apr. 1955	5
C & W		Hank Thompson	Capitol	20 Aug. 1955	6
Pop	"Maybellene"	Chuck Berry	Chess	20 Aug. 1955	5
R & B		Chuck Berry	Chess	6 Aug. 1955	1
		Jim Lowe	Dot	24 Sep. 1955	13
C & W		Marty Robbins	Columbia	1 Oct. 1955	9
Pop	"Love, Love, Love"	Diamonds	Mercury	23 June 1956	30
		Clovers	Atlantic	28 July 1956	30
R & B		Clovers	Atlantic	23 June 1956	4
		Diamonds	Mercury	7 July 1956	14
C & W		Webb Pierce	Decca	24 Sep. 1955	1
Pop ⇄ R & B crossovers					
Pop	"Tweedle Dee"	LaVern Baker	Atlantic	15 Jan. 1955	14
		Georgia Gibbs	Mercury	29 Jan. 1955	2
R & B		LaVern Baker	Atlantic	15 Jan. 1955	4
Pop	"Dim, Dim the Lights"	Bill Haley	Decca	20 Nov. 1954	11
R & B		Bill Haley	Decca	22 Jan. 1955	10
Pop	"Earth Angel"	Penguins	Dootone	21 Dec. 1954	8
		Crew Cuts	Mercury	29 Jan. 1955	3
		Gloria Mann	Sound	12 Feb. 1955	18
R & B		Penguins	Dootone	8 Dec. 1954	1
Pop	"Ko Ko Mo"	Crew Cuts	Mercury	29 Jan. 1955	3
		Perry Como	RCA Victor	5 Feb. 1955	2
R & B		Gene & Eunice	Combo, Atlantic	29 Jan. 1955	6
Pop	"That's All I Want	Jaye P. Morgan	RCA Victor	27 Nov. 1954	3
R & B	From You"	Dinah Washington	Mercury	19 Feb. 1955	8
Pop	"Pledging My Love"	Johnny Ace	Duke	19 Feb. 1955	17
		Teresa Brewer	Coral	19 Mar. 1955	17
R & B		Johnny Ace	Duke	22 Jan. 1955	1
Pop	"The Wallflower"	Georgia Gibbs	Mercury	26 Mar. 1955	1
R & B	("Dance With Me Henry")	Etta James	Modern	19 Feb. 1955	1
Pop	"Two Hearts"	Pat Boone	Dot	2 Apr. 1955	16
R & B		Charms	DeLuxe	5 Mar. 1955	8
Pop	"It May Sound Silly"	McGuire Sisters	Coral	16 Mar. 1955	23
R & B		Ivory Joe Hunter	Atlantic	30 Apr. 1955	14
Pop	"My Babe"	Little Walter	Checker	(data unavailable)	106
R & B		Little Walter	Checker	12 Mar. 1955	1

TABLE 7-2
(continued)

Chart	Song title	Performer	Record label	Date of first appearance	Peak chart position
Pop ⇄ R & B crossovers (continued)					
Pop	"Unchained Melody"	Al Hibbler	Decca	9 Apr. 1955	3
		Les Baxter	Capitol	9 Apr. 1955	1
		Roy Hamilton	Epic	23 Apr. 1955	6
		June Valli	RCA Victor	14 May 1955	29
R & B		Al Hibbler	Decca	23 Apr. 1955	1
		Roy Hamilton	Epic	30 Apr. 1955	13
Pop	"Don't Be Angry"	Nappy Brown	Savoy	30 Apr. 1955	25
		Crew Cuts	Mercury	30 Apr. 1955	14
R & B		Nappy Brown	Savoy	16 Apr. 1955	23
Pop	"Chop, Chop, Boom"	Crew Cuts	Mercury	30 Apr. 1955	14
R & B		Danderliers	States	23 Apr. 1955	10
Pop	"Ain't That a Shame"	Pat Boone	Dot	9 July 1955	1
		Fats Domino	Imperial	16 July 1955	10
R & B		Fats Domino	Imperial	14 May 1955	1
		Pat Boone	Dot	24 Sep. 1955	14
Pop	"Rock Around the	Bill Haley	Decca	14 May 1955	1
R & B	Clock"	Bill Haley	Decca	11 June 1955	3
Pop	"The Door Is Still Open to My Heart"	Don Cornell	Coral	(data unavailable)	14
R & B		Cardinals	Atlantic	23 Apr. 1955	4
Pop	"Rollin' Stone"	Fontane Sisters	Dot	4 June 1955	13
R & B		Marigolds	Excello	4 June 1955	8
Pop	"Story Untold"	Crew Cuts	Mercury	25 June 1955	16
R & B		Nutmegs	Herald	4 June 1955	2
Pop	"Seventeen"	Boyd Bennett & His Rockets	King	9 July 1955	5
		Rusty Draper	Mercury	20 Aug. 1955	18
		Fontane Sisters	Dot	20 Aug. 1955	3
R & B		Boyd Bennett & His Rockets	King	13 Aug. 1955	4
Pop	"Forgive This Fool"	Roy Hamilton	Epic	23 July 1955	45
R & B		Roy Hamilton	Epic	30 July 1955	10
Pop	"Only You (And You Alone)"	Platters	Mercury	11 Oct. 1955	5
		Hilltoppers	Dot	12 Nov. 1955	8
R & B		Platters	Mercury	30 July 1955	1
Pop	"Why Don't You Write (To) Me?"	Snooky Lanson	Dot	20 Aug. 1955	45
		Jacks	RPM	12 Nov. 1955	82
R & B		Jacks	RPM	6 Aug. 1955	3
Pop	"I Hear You	Gale Storm	Dot	22 Oct. 1955	2
R & B	Knocking"	Smiley Lewis	Imperial	3 Sep. 1955	2
		Gale Storm	Dot	19 Nov. 1955	15
Pop	"At My Front Door"	El Dorados	Vee-Jay	15 Oct. 1955	17
		Pat Boone	Dot	29 Oct. 1955	7

TABLE 7-2
(continued)

Chart	Song title	Performer	Record label	Date of first appearance	Peak chart position
Pop ⇄ R & B crossovers (continued)					
R & B		El Dorados	Vee-Jay	28 Sep. 1955	1
		Pat Boone	Dot	29 Nov. 1955	12
Pop	"My Boy—Flat Top"	Boyd Bennett & His Rockets	King	12 Nov. 1955	31
		Dorothy Collins	Coral	3 Dec. 1955	16
R & B		Boyd Bennett	King	8 Oct. 1955	13
Pop	"He"	Al Hibbler	Decca	15 Oct. 1955	4
		McGuire Sisters	Coral	29 Oct. 1955	10
R & B		Al Hibbler	Decca	22 Oct. 1955	13
Pop	"Come Home"	Bubber Johnson	King	12 Nov. 1955	92
R & B		Bubber Johnson	King	22 Oct. 1955	9
Pop	"Adorable"	Fontane Sisters	Dot	19 Nov. 1955	71
R & B		Colts	Vita	29 Oct. 1955	11
		Drifters	Atlantic	5 Nov. 1955	1
Pop	"Burn That Candle"	Cues	Capitol	19 Nov. 1955	86
		Bill Haley and His Comets	Decca	19 Nov. 1955	9
R & B		Bill Haley and His Comets	Decca	19 Nov. 1955	9
Pop	"Tutti-Frutti"	Little Richard	Specialty	28 Jan. 1956	17
		Pat Boone	Dot	4 Feb. 1956	12
R & B		Little Richard	Specialty	26 Nov. 1955	2
Pop	"When You Dance"	Turbans	Herald	12 Nov. 1955	33
R & B		Turbans	Herald	26 Nov. 1955	3
Pop	"Smoky Joe's Cafe"	Robins	Atco	10 Dec. 1955	79
R & B		Robins	Atco	3 Dec. 1955	10
Pop	"Are You Satisfied?"	Sheb Wooley	MGM	17 Dec. 1955	95
		Rusty Draper	Mercury	31 Dec. 1955	11
		Tony Arden	RCA Victor	4 Feb. 1956	78
R & B		Ann Cole	Baton	28 Jan. 1956	10
Pop	"The Great Pretender"	Platters	Mercury	24 Dec. 1955	1
R & B		Platters	Mercury	17 Dec. 1955	1
Pop	"Gee Whittakers!"	Pat Boone	Dot	17 Dec. 1955	19
R & B		Five Keys	Capitol	25 Feb. 1956	14
Pop	"White Christmas" *	Bing Crosby	Decca	24 Dec. 1955	7
		Drifters	Atlantic	31 Dec. 1955	80
R & B		Drifters	Atlantic	18 Dec. 1954	2
Pop ⇄ C & W crossovers					
Pop	"The Cattle Call"	Eddy Arnold and Hugo Winterhalter	RCA Victor	16 July 1955	42
C & W		Slim Whitman	Imperial	15 Jan. 1955	11
		Eddy Arnold and Hugo Winterhalter	RCA Victor	25 Jan. 1955	1

TABLE 7-2
(continued)

Chart	Song title	Performer	Record label	Date of first appearance	Peak chart position
Pop ⇄ C & W crossovers (continued)					
Pop	"I Gotta Go Get My	Teresa Brewer	Coral	26 Feb. 1955	59
C & W	Baby"	Justin Tubb	Decca	19 Feb. 1955	8
Pop	"Ballad of Davy	Bill Hayes	Cadence	26 Feb. 1955	1
	Crockett"	Fess Parker	Columbia	12 Mar. 1955	5
		Tennessee Ernie Ford	Capitol	19 Mar. 1955	5
		Walter Schumann	RCA Victor	9 Apr. 1955	14
C & W		Tennessee Ernie Ford	Capitol	26 Mar. 1955	4
		Mac Wiseman	Dot	28 Apr. 1955	10
Pop	"I'm In Love With	Pat Boone	Dot	9 June 1956	57
C & W	You"	Kitty Wells	Decca	24 Sep. 1955	12
Pop	"The Kentuckian	Hilltoppers	Dot	30 July 1955	20
C & W	Song"	Eddy Arnold	RCA Victor	9 July 1955	8
Pop	"Yellow Rose of	Mitch Miller	Columbia	6 Aug. 1955	1
	Texas"	Johnny Desmond	Coral	13 Aug. 1955	3
		Stan Freberg	Capitol	22 Nov. 1955	16
C & W		Ernest Tubb	Decca	17 Sep. 1955	7
Pop	"The Richest Man (In	Eddy Arnold	RCA Victor	12 Nov. 1955	99
C & W	the World)"	Eddy Arnold	RCA Victor	10 Dec. 1955	10
Pop	"Searching"	The Hilltoppers	Dot	12 Nov. 1955	81
C & W		Kitty Wells	Decca	7 July 1956	3
Pop	"Sixteen Tons"	Tennessee Ernie Ford	Capitol	12 Nov. 1955	1
		Johnny Desmond	Coral	3 Dec. 1955	17
C & W		Tennessee Ernie Ford	Capitol	11 Dec. 1955	1
R & B ⇄ C & W crossovers					
R & B	"Baby Let's Play	Arthur Gunther	Excello	29 Jan. 1955	12
C & W	House"	Elvis Presley	Sun	16 July 1955	5
R & B	"Thirty Days (To	Chuck Berry	Chess	29 Oct. 1955	2
C & W	Come Back Home)"	Ernest Tubb	Decca	17 Dec. 1955	7

SOURCES: *Billboard* music popularity charts, 1955; Joel Whitburn, *Joel Whitburn's Top Country Singles 1944–1988* (pub. 1989), *Top Pop Singles 1940–1955* (pub. 1973), *Top Pop Singles 1955–1986* (pub. 1987), and *Top R & B Singles 1942–1988* (pub. 1989), all Menomonee Falls, Wisconsin: Record Research, Inc., all compiled from *Billboard*'s Best Selling Singles charts. © 1955 BPI Communications, Inc. Used with permission from *Billboard*.

* First charted by Bing Crosby in 1942 and every year for the following twenty years; the Drifters charted it in the pop charts in 1955, 1960, 1962; and in the R & B chart in 1955 and 1956.

singer of the Moonglows) and Alan Freed (who sponsored the group), was an augmentation of their Ink Spots' styling with a more contemporary R & B sound for Chess. Coral Records, Decca's R & B subsidiary, covered the record with its young "belter" Don Cornell, exactly as it had before with the McGuire Sisters covering the Moonglows' first hit, "Sincerely." The crossover to country was by Hank Thompson, one of the last Western Swing performers looking for any way into that contemporary sound. The second three-way crossover was the Clovers' "Love Love Love," which made the R&B charts, crossed over directly to the pop charts, and was covered on the country charts by Webb Pierce, one of the leading honky-tonk-styled Nashville performers.

The other three-way crossover was Chuck Berry's "Maybellene," his first record for Chess. This driving number, recounting the competitive and romantic life of fast cars in high school, went to number one on the R&B charts, then crossed over directly to pop and climbed to the number five position. It was covered by Jim Lowe (of subsequent "Green Door" fame) for Dot, also making the R&B charts. "Maybellene" was additionally covered by the young country singer, Marty Robbins, who moved the record up to number nine on the country charts. Berry's appeal to country audiences was not an accident. He was a skilled performer of current "hillbilly" hits, amusing his mixed white and black audiences in the St Louis area with interpretations of Hank Williams' songs. Idolizing the styling of both Nat Cole and his friend and mentor Muddy Waters, and influenced by the guitar of such jazz masters as Charlie Christian, Berry synthesized all these musics in the service of the high school experience. His compositions, drawing on his own school days, were instantly understood as the authentic statement of that life.[37] That acknowledgment didn't stop the teenagers from buying in that same year a record of far less achievement, Boyd Bennett's "Seventeen," which reached the top ranks on both the pop and R&B charts. In subsequent years, even worse trash pitched to teenagers would flood the record stores; the gates were opening wide to any and everything that had the teen label on it.

The two-way crossovers revealed the same story. The exchanges between country and pop remained at ten records, that is, no change from 1954, and almost all of them were songs by established country artists covering adult-oriented pop tunes or pop artists covering country songs. The forty-nine crossovers between R&B and pop, more than double the number compared to the previous year, were divided between those that crossed directly from the R&B market to pop and those that were covers, close imitations by pop artists. They brought to the fore artists who would join such durable performers as Fats Domino, Little Richard, the Platters, the Drifters, the eponymous Bo Diddley, and some performers who were but momentary flashes, such as the Penguins ("Earth Angel"), the Nutmegs ("Story Untold"), and Johnny Ace ("Pledging My Love"). Among those white artists who covered the R&B hits, including the vocal groups such as the Crew Cuts, the McGuire Sisters, the Fontane Sisters, and Georgia Gibbs, were a few, notably Pat Boone, who continued to be strong presences in rocknroll. Also in that year, Ray Charles' "I've Got a Woman," though by no means his first chart appearance, was the first record successfully integrating the gospel and R&B styling that characterized a career that would span all the black popular styles for more than two decades. It would take several more years, however, for Charles' records to cross over to the pop stream.

The contrast between black pop and country pop could not be more sharply drawn than in their 1955 best-selling singles charts. Country music was locked into its hierarchy of established performers, resisting both young performers and the styles that would get beyond the Nashville establishment. Even the newcomers Faron Young and Carl Smith were well within the limits of Nashville's country sounds, although the former's "Drive Fast, Love Hard and Die Young" approached the teenage romantic and murky affection for that song's subject matter. Tennessee Ernie Ford held sway in country pop's meeting with the folk stream, which, in fact, closely overlapped the pop field. The whole list, almost all coming from major labels, was holding, white-knuckled, a position established just after World War II.

In summary, the picture at the end of 1955 was that of a new and energetic rhythm and blues stream, with a roster made up almost entirely of young performers with new sounds and with the whole enterprise still dominated by the independent labels. The pop stream, always ready to accept a winner, opened the crossover route, allowing both black and white cover performers the glare of celebrity. Country music resisted everything. Having seen one pillar of its southern white mansion fall to the pop stream's invasion, it was waiting, so it seemed, for the other shoe to fall. That shoe was, of course, one of its own, made in the South of genuine southern materials even to the distinctively regional flavor of its name—Elvis.

8. The King and His Court

The liner notes of an elaborately designed Extended Play (EP) album entitled *A Session with Chet Atkins* opened with these words: "Chet Atkins has built a bridge. With six steel guitar strings for material and the songs in this album for blueprints, he has done much to span the gulf between country and popular music and the followers of each."[1] The eight numbers on this "New Orthophonic High Fidelity Recording," including "South," "Frankie and Johnnie," and "The Birth of the Blues," were typical of the jazz-, pop-, and black pop-influenced music that was the mark of this celebrated musician who was, as noted above, RCA Victor's main Nashville record producer. The writer of the notes was Nelson King, a leading country music disk jockey from Cincinnati. The year was 1955. The expensive promotional effort in this record was a prayer whose urgency was understandable.

Record sales in the United States had been growing explosively. The Recording Industry Association of America (RIAA) reported that total record sales in 1956 increased by $100 million to a figure of $331 million. This was an increase of 43 percent over the previous year, a huge jump in a growth rate that had averaged, over the previous decade, just over 4 percent per year.[2] Though the LP record and the hi-fi craze were surely somewhat accountable for the stimulation in sales (which explains the prominent hi-fi advertisement on the Atkins album), the industry believed it was the youth market responding to the rhythm and blues efforts of the independent labels that was largely responsible. So RCA Victor turned loose Chet Atkins, "The Country Gentleman," in hopes of capturing a part of that new market. Perhaps he did influence some of the young guitar pickers whose ranks were still relatively small, but the main bridge from country to pop with a whiff of black pop was to come from a different place.

That place was the deep South, the city of Memphis, where the eighteen-year-old Elvis Presley would be found by Sam Phillips. Their oft-told story, leading to the crowning of the "King of Rocknroll," still contains substantial questions that this chapter seeks to examine. The idea that rocknroll has a king at all is certainly not out of the ordinary, being one version of the individualism so dominant in the culture.

Another version of this individualism is the star system in the arts and entertainment worlds. From at least the 1830s onward, show business hoopla celebrating a leading figure in the theater or concert hall circuits organized the routines of the entertainment world. The celebrated methods of P. T. Barnum brought him fame and fortune as he promoted the talents of "The Swedish Nightingale," Jenny Lind, and the endless curiosities ranging from the Feejee Mermaid (a fabrication of half fish and half monkey) to the redoubtable midget Tom Thumb. The evolving star system paid off handsomely.[3] At the other pole, the respectable, genius end, David Sarnoff carried forward the same logic a century later in his creation of the NBC Symphony Orchestra for the star presence of Arturo Toscanini. It was a masterful merger of the NBC dedication to public service with the publicists' bubble of star-centered promotion.[4] The next extension was the rock "superstar," the vertical integration of a performer's talents into every possible money source that could be generated.

The emphasis on the individual is so deep and distorting that it is almost impossible for Americans to recognize a social movement until it surfaces a leading figure. This "cult of personality" also feeds the American infatuation with royalty. Half serious, half self-mocking, the elevation to kingship, at one time received by virtue of bloodline, is now given to a person who has *earned* highest honors, regardless of parentage. Achievement triumphing over ascription is nevertheless adorned with the latter's emblems; an irony worthy of American mores.

There is more to this matter, however. In the jazz world, the title "King," once awarded to the winners of New Orleans "carving contests," as in King Oliver, and carrying on to Benny Goodman's crowning as the "King of Swing," descended to the ranks of "Count" as in Basie and "Duke" as in Ellington. Though used in a respectful yet jocular fashion, these titles point to the problematic relationship between a single reigning presence and a surrounding group of gifted but lesser figures. This chapter thus seeks to examine the nature of such ranking, since it runs counter to rocknroll's strong if implicit egalitarian stance towards its diversity of musical styles and performers. The matter is the same one, touched on previously, that Charles Rosen and the folk stream's theorists met head on.

Finally, I note that in New Orleans, Louis Armstrong was crowned

"King of the Zulus" for the 1949 Mardi Gras. This custom is as close as the American Protestant ethos got to allowing the Catholic-Latin carnival's "King of Misrule" to reign over the ceremonies of release on American soil. The same disdain, which adds racism to the venom, is applied to rocknroll generally and to Elvis specifically when he is designated the "King." The considerable ambivalence white adults felt towards rocknroll is coiled within this title. Not surprisingly, the negative side of that ambivalence is almost always directed at the part that comes from rhythm and blues, from the culture of black Americans. The emergence of rocknroll as unquestionably "a white boy's" music therefore raises the question, Where did the black part of rocknroll go?

Elvis in Memphis

The familiar story about Elvis is that this poor country boy with a heart full of music and mother love came out of the South to bring together country music, rhythm and blues, and pop and to form a new thing. Rocknroll, the story continues, was its name, and it carried off the nation's teenagers in exactly the same way and for the same reasons the Pied Piper took away the children of Hameln; that is, the greed and violence of the adults was so ferocious that the children sought out each other and Elvis to conquer their fears (of the bomb), to repair their abandonment (by the family), and to escape their oppression (by the school). This origin story is true in the sense that all myths eschew the particularities of historical fact in order to state unchallengeably an intolerable contradictory situation that exists on the ground, and then to solve those contradictions in the air.

The facts are interesting, though, and perhaps more sustaining than the myth. Other cities were very much like Memphis, and each would have its own rocknroll moment within a short span of years; but it was in Memphis that youth rebellion found its musical voicing in the merging of black, country, and pop. That city's unique constellation of contemporary musical resources and its history made it a predisposed point of confluence for the pop, country, and rhythm and blues streams.

Memphis is a major river port connecting the agricultural delta of the Mississippi River states to the industrial urban cultures of the deep South and to the mountains of Appalachia. Its cultural life, reflecting the diversity of the great Mississippi River port cities, was concentrated in its colorful, if shabby, downtown sprawl. Radiating out of Beale Street was every show business technology and organization that could nurture the city's entertainment richness. Its theaters, saloons, and nightclubs presented a full and continuing parade of local and national black entertainment.[5] The city was also part of the more egalitarian but invisible "League of Rhythm and Blues Cities," with the new station WDIA (1948) bringing in black popular music in all its varieties.

Memphis had an equally rich country music tradition, which was carried to the smallest rural community via the radio stations. The country disk jockeys carried on the entrepreneurial traditions of organizing local shows and contributing to the major tours headed by the top stars. Country music had expanded its presence dramatically in the city after the war and in the expansion days following World War II. The four radio stations founded in the 1920s were augmented by five more, along with two TV stations. Memphis had a huge, multistate radio audience, but only a small number of country disk jockeys. It was a relatively small stop far from the peak of the pyramidal hierarchy of country music.

Popular music was also thoroughly covered by both the network stations and the independents. The three major music markets were therefore all present and thoroughly interconnected in the city, though none of the three dominated the others. Its disk jockeys were similar to those in all the other urban centers but with far less emphasis on the high-pressure, hit-making procedures. The city was located, in short, at just the right place to bring together the reservoirs of all three musics. It had a rich, unharvested pool of artists and responsive audiences in a low-pressure atmosphere. The scene invited experiments across those boundary zones protecting each of the musics from the overbearing presence of the others.

Memphis is also a southern city. From 1909, the first elected mayor, E. H. Crump, virtually ruled the city via his control of the Democratic machine of Shelby County. He was a strict segregationist, yet the black voters supported him at the polls in spite of the principled opposition of local black elites. "Boss" Crump finally fell in 1954, the year the Supreme Court struck down school segregation, though the Memphis schools did not begin to integrate until 1961.

Sam C. Phillips, Alabama born, was sidetracked from an anticipated legal career by the death of his father and the coming of World War II in the year of his graduation from high school.[6] He began his radio career as a disk jockey at WLAY, Muscle Shoals, Alabama, in 1942. He then moved to WHSL, Decatur, Georgia, then to WLAC, Nashville, and reached WREC, Memphis, in 1946, where he remained as record spinner and talent agent. By 1950 he had opened the Memphis Recording Service and secured enough capital to begin Sun Records on the model of hundreds of other small enterprises living at the edges of the rapidly growing music scene in the South.

In spite of a lack of local expertise and enterprise in recording, Phillips saw that he had a good purchase on a growing market. In the radio environment of that time, the race issue was at maximum alert. The struggles over how the hit-making disk jockey used his crucial exposure and exploitation machinery often had a racial dimension that sometimes reached the surface. A self-imposed censorship was a common device. In the words of a disk jockey in Louisville, Kentucky (about four hundred miles northeast of Memphis but not a mile beyond its thinking), who was replying to a question about why he didn't play rhythm and blues records,

> Not because the person is colored, but it's the rhythm and tone of the things. It's not melodic. Our audience doesn't like this sort of thing. They would be ashamed if they thought that their friends knew they were listening to it. The quality of the music is poor, it really is. It brings out the . . . well . . . the savage in people.[7]

Phillips did not hold to such racial views. In fact, he was looking for exactly that kind of music. He became involved with one of the more successful incubations of a music that could be acceptably simple and savage. He got his appetite whetted by recording Jackie Brenston's "Rocket 88," sending it to Chess in Chicago. He saw it top the R&B charts, not realizing that he had participated in making what some have called the first rocknroll record. He continued recording sides by local black and white artists, including B. B. King and Rufus Thomas, which he sold or leased to independents in the North. In 1954, *Billboard* reviewed his recording of Harmonica Frank's "Rockin Chair Daddy" as "an unusual mixture of r&b and country music. The singer is a country artist, instrumentation is the type used for down-home blues wax."[8] This success intensified Phillips' search of the clubs and radio stations in the Memphis region for white performers working the small roadhouses and cocktail lounges. There was a surprisingly diverse range of styles in the regional "country boogie," basically soloists and small combos playing a danceable blues rhythm out of a stripped-down country instrumentation.

It was in this dense atmosphere that Presley appeared at Phillips' studio to cut a birthday record for his mother, two songs of his own choosing.[9] Some eight months later, in the summer of 1954, Phillips thought Elvis might be right for a ballad he had acquired. Although the recording session was unsuccessful, Phillips later thought that mixing minimal instrumentation behind Presley on vocals might be the right combination for merging the country and the rhythm and blues sounds for the pop market. After some six months rehearsal with Elvis and two local musicians familiar with the studio and the local club scene—Scotty Moore on guitar and Bill Black on bass—Phillips thought he had found his man.

Presley was the singer he had talked about so often. Mississippi born, poor, religiously soaked, strictly raised, Beale Streete smart, musically and theatrically adept though a complete amateur, young, and strikingly handsome in the face, Elvis was indeed the answer.

The selection of the tunes for the first record, dictated certainly by Phillips, was as obvious as it was effective: one-half black, one-half country, both pop.[10] Memphis-based blues singer Arthur "Big Boy" Crudup's "That's All Right Mama" was the "A" side. The tune had been recorded by its writer for Victor's Bluebird label in 1946 and had achieved only local jukebox play. The "B" side was Bill Monroe's 1947 "Blue Moon of Kentucky."

The two sides are both remarkable. The clean and austere instrumentation of Scotty Moore's electric guitar and Bill Black's string bass was unquestionably a country sound. Elvis' vocal style—tentative, self-consciously experimenting, but exuberant—was, however, the main part of the appeal. The manner on "That's All Right" was softer and more balladlike compared to the more exaggerated blues roughness of the "Blue Moon of Kentucky" side. The deliberate stylistic reversal—the black, up-tempo song done in an almost dreamy country feeling and the slow country anthem unceremoniously given a brusque treatment—is somehow acceptable because of the youthful, honest, but playful voice. It was in that reversal that Phillips saw the road to pop, and he said so at that first session. All the garbled versions of the tape contain Phillips' line, "That's different. That's a pop song now." It should be clear that these first two sides as well as the rest of the records Elvis made for Sun were in the current reservoir of R&B and country and western. They were *not* part of the folk stream. It would be some years before Bill Monroe and Arthur Crudup would be lionized by the museum wing of the folk stream and the major record companies would reissue their old records, RCA labeling Crudup the "Father of Rock and Roll."[11]

Presley's first record is clearly another candidate for the first rocknroll record. Arguably, it was the first *regional hit* to launch a national star on the basis of his performance. The "It's All Right" side brought an R&B sound in a country voicing to pop, enlarging rocknroll's young reservoir with a white as well as a black component. The "Blue Moon of Kentucky" side was a shrewd choice to record at that time. Nashville was still assembling, not at all the "capital" of country music it would become, and Bill Monroe's place as an established easterner and hillbilly stalwart was an important component for the Phillips strategy. Elvis, as a deep southerner, did the song with such surprising boldness that his reach into white mountain music carried. Presley's country music credentials, which he passed on to his descendants a full decade later, were validated in that record.

The question was where to expose these two sides. Sam Phillips went to disk jockey Dewey Phillips (no relation) who aired them to an immediate deluge. The telephone board lit up; the radio audience wanted to hear the record again and again, and they wanted to know where they could buy it. They also wanted to know something about the singer. Dewey Phillips, in the radio interview that evening, quickly and diplomatically identified Presley as white by answering a question about what high school he had attended. "Humes High" was more than a sufficient answer. L. C. Humes High School was one of the all-white schools in the city. The telephone callers may have even recognized Elvis as the acne-ridden, shy kid who wore the outrageous clothes seen in Beale Street shop windows. He was certainly not part of the school's leading crowd.

The first record sold well in the Memphis area. *Billboard* put its "Review Spotlight" on Presley as "a potent new chanter who can sock over a tune for either the country or the r & b markets."[12] This success was not enough. It was a blind alley, in fact, for Elvis to ignite the mixed white and black teenage radio audience with only the rhythm and blues side. He had to reach the country audience. This meant live appearances on the country circuit. Sam Phillips got Elvis onto Webb Pierce's tour, in the local clubs, and on the Opry itself within a few months. The reception was mixed. The name "Elvis Presley" was off-beat; so was the act. The conservative Opry audience was cool; Elvis was crushed. Phillips did not give up, nor did Elvis' first manager, Bob Neal, one of Memphis' senior country and western disk jockeys.

Neal proceeded to book him both locally and in the "high minors" of the country circuit. The pop thrust was accentuated by naming Elvis' act (now formally including Scotty Moore and Bill Black) the Blue Moon Boys.[13] Following the traditional practice of placing an ad when a record is reviewed, the review and display ad reprinted here appeared on the same page in *Billboard*. Note the now-common designation of the emerging style as "folk blues." This label served the obvious tactic of tying together Elvis' first record, "Blue Moon of Kentucky," to the authentic and unassailable country artist Bill Monroe. Elvis was on his way. The country

Figure 8-1. Early Elvis Ad. *The Billboard*, January 29, 1955.
© 1955 BPI Communications, Inc.
Used with permission from *Billboard*.

Figure 8-2. Early Elvis Record Review. *The Billboard*, January 29, 1955. © BPI Communications, Inc. Used with permission from *Billboard*.

> **ELVIS PRESLEY**
> **Milkcow Blues Boogie** 80
> SUN 215 — Presley continues to impress with each release as one of the slickest talents to come up in the country field in a long, long time. Item here is based on some of the best folk blues. The guy sells all the way. Ops will particularly like it. **(Leeds, ASCAP)**
>
> **You're a Heartbreaker....76**
> Here Presley tackles the rhythmic material for a slick country-style reading. What with the good backing this one should get action, too. **(Hi Lo, BMI)**

music establishment designated Elvis as the "Most Promising Country Music Singer" of 1955. The trade press announced that the revival of country music was at hand, that a new day had arrived. Elvis' releases on Sun were highlighted in "Pick of the Week" reviews (figs. 8-1, 8-2).

At the same time, an articulate minority of the country music establishment was in opposition. It was clear to some that Sam Phillips was trying to use Elvis' country music style as a passport to the pop stream, while carrying a full case of rhythm and blues. They blew the whistle. The clearest statement appeared in, of all places, a front-page *Down Beat* article by a well-known country disk jockey. Elvis, the major culprit, though unnamed, is not the only problem mentioned. Rhythm and blues was leaking into country, breaching the deepest line of cleavage in all the American popular musics. This voice did not come just from one petulant country disk jockey. The situation was recognized by the entire industry. Everyone saw the generational failure of country music to produce new talent, but the experts were divided on how their ranks were to be replenished (fig. 8-3).

Presley stayed with Sam Phillips for about a year. When his contract expired, the mysterious Colonel Tom Parker took over. The sale of this poor Mississippi boy was about to commence. The Colonel saw in the nineteen-year-old not only what Sam Phillips and Bob Neal had seen, but he could also read the charts. By late spring of 1955, Elvis' latest Sun side, "Baby Let's Play House" (a cover of Arthur Gunter's R&B hit), was, for the first time, climbing the national country charts (but never making the pop charts). By fall, his "Mystery Train," a cover of Junior Parker's R&B hit of 1953 for Sun Records, and its flip side, "I Forgot to Remember to Forget," had topped the country charts.

Colonel Parker's vision was far grander than that of either Phillips or Bob Neal; he had been closer to the pinnacle of the country music structure as Eddy Arnold's former manager and, by 1954, head of the Hank Snow Jamboree Attractions. The exact route that took Presley from Sun

(Trademark Registered U.S. Patent Office)   Printed by John Maher Printing Co., Chicago

Vol. 22—No. 2   **Chicago, January 26, 1955**

Part One of Two Parts

Disc Jockey Urges Return To Spinning Only Country Music

By RANDY BLAKE
Disc Jockey, WJJD, Chicago

Chicago—Suppose you are building a house. You have the finest carpenters in the country. The finest electricians, the finest plumbers and stone masons. Each an expert in his field. But suppose the stone masons started installing the electrical wiring, the electricians started doing the masonry work, and the plumbers turned to carpentering.

Wouldn't you say somebody should have his head examined? *You*, particularly, if you didn't stop these goings-on?

Yet, this is just the way the music business is attempting to rebuild its house.

*   *   *

Country music is country music, period. Rhythm and blues is a field unto itself. Pop, likewise. So is grand opera. Each has enjoyed the fullest extent of its own prosperity by, and only by, catering to its own established audience. Things were all right in these fields —until somebody yelled panic.

One day everything was normal. The next day it wasn't. Overnight, somebody had said rhythm and blues was on the upbeat.

*   *   *

The news spread. The panic—call it trend if you like—was on.

And country music disc jockeys the nation over had become the unwitting, or otherwise, appointees for spreading the panic.

*   *   *

Suddenly we were deluged with records by country music artists that were not country music—gosh-awful, brazen attempts at something these artists can't do and never will be able to do.

*   *   *

Placing the blame really doesn't matter.

The thing that does matter is that there is one person who can halt the whole thing—quick. That person is the country music disc jockey.

Isn't it time we started realizing that an r&b song isn't a country tune, even though it be recorded by a heretofore top-rated country singer and bears a major label?

We know country music. We know our audience.

*   *   *

So why should we — knowing these things — be swayed by the turncoats of an otherwise honest business? Let such persons destroy themselves if they will. But why should we permit them to drag down our integrity?

*   *   *

Mackinaws are ready sellers in Alaska. Bikini bathing suits are hot items in Florida. But you couldn't sell a combination Mackinaw-Bikini anywhere. So let's play nothing but country music!

Figure 8-3. Commentary on Country Disk Jockeys in *Down Beat*. DOWN BEAT, January 26, 1955. Reprinted with permission from *DOWN BEAT* magazine.

Records to Victor for $25,000 and the publishing rights from Hi Lo Music (Sun's publishing arm) to Hill and Range for $15,000 is well known, involving such familiar characters as Arnold Shaw and Bill Randle. Shaw, after hearing Elvis' records, met with Colonel Parker and then with Sam Phillips. On the basis of what the Colonel told him, that "Presley had not really made his mark on wax, that he was *dynamite* in personal appearances, affecting Southern girls, white and black—as Sinatra once had", he called Bill Randle. Randle, whose audience response was immediate and positive, arranged to have Elvis booked onto the Dorsey Brothers' "Stage Show." [14]

The personal appearances on television, particularly on the Ed Sullivan show, handed Elvis the nation. In spite of the blast of parental disapproval, more likely because of it, Elvis could do no wrong. He began the long march of some 150 records on the pop charts, and then it was off to the movies. Ever since a quarter of Tin Pan Alley had moved to California when the talkies appeared in 1928, there was an unflagging appetite for singers and bands in motion pictures. That appetite was fully fed by the ambitions of singers who wanted nothing more than the worldwide glamour accorded a movie star.

The Court Assembles

While Elvis was beginning his reign as the King of Rocknroll, that young stream was filling its ranks with performers as appealing as they were diverse, coming from every other stream in great number. The lucky break for rocknroll was the eclectic taste of its audience. Any music that was danceable, exciting, or funny; any lyrics that were passionate or spoke their condition would receive a hearing by teenagers who, with characteristic directness, would act on their immediate preferences. "I like the beat; I give it an 86," was the quick and merciless system of evaluation moving records through the system. As with every other art form, 90 percent of rocknroll's output was junk, but out of the huge pot that held this melange emerged a smaller number of strong and enduring performers. They formed the court that accompanied Elvis.

The scope of rocknroll's pantheon can be seen most clearly in the charts and the crossovers, which show the extent to which the boundaries between the three major streams were collapsing. The array of records in 1956 was remarkably different from that of just a year previously, not to speak of 1950. The old guard in country and black pop were barely in evidence. Younger performers such as Marty Robbins and Little Richard swamped the lists; half the pop best sellers were rocknroll records that were also spread across the other charts. Elvis simply crowded the scene; among the top 30 best-selling singles, he had six on the country chart, five on the pop chart, and three on the R&B chart. Young white country performers appeared on the R&B chart. At least one black performer made the country chart (Fats Domino doing the pop standard "Blueberry Hill"). Clearly, the grid had been taken out of the ice cube tray.

The extent to which records flowed across their stream boundaries during the entire fifties decade is directly demonstrated in the number of crossovers between and among the three major markets. Figures 8-4 and 8-5 present the number of two-way crossovers from pop and country and from pop and R&B during the years 1950–1960. There were, as noted above, no two-way crossovers between R&B and country. Each illustration shows the number of direct crossovers and cover crossovers, although the direction of the flow is not shown. For both country and R&B in the beginning of the decade, records flowed both ways. Later, the two smaller streams initiated the move into pop.

Though the number of country crossovers was significant in the mid-fifties, it was nothing compared to the direct release of rhythm and blues records into the pop stream, in surprising numbers and at an explosive rate after 1956. It startled the whole music world. Any young black sound, it was thought, had an automatic invitation into the pop stream. The search was on, accordingly, for every aspiring street corner group of kids and every gospel soloist or quartet.

Elvis Presley, it was also believed, opened the country door to black pop with his crossing into that forbidden territory. His records and those of some other country performers did cross over to the black pop charts, but, as noted above, only after they had been validated by an appearance on the pop charts. The break-out of the country boogie performers into both pop and black pop is visible in the rise of the three-way crossover.

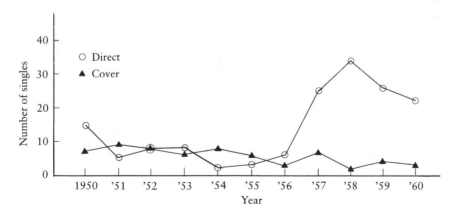

Figure 8-4. Crossovers: Pop and Country & Western (1950–1960). Source: *Billboard* music popularity charts.

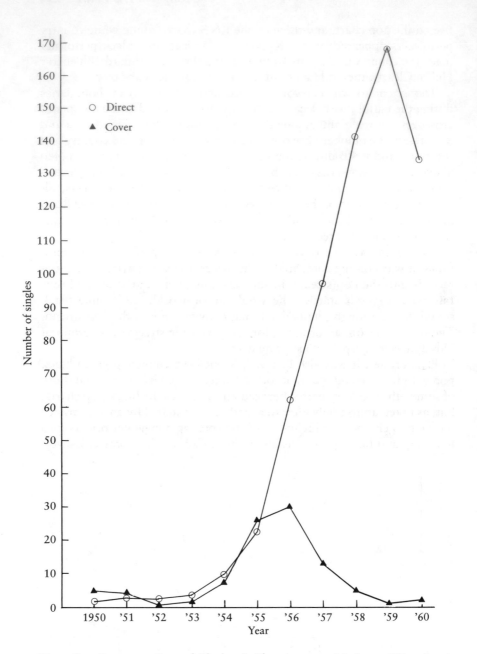

Figure 8-5. Crossovers: Pop and Rhythm & Blues (1950–1960). Source: *Billboard* music popularity charts.

Elvis dominates the records in 1956 that reached all three charts—on nine of the twelve three-way crossovers. This saturation by one performer simply had no precedent in any of the popular musics. It would trigger not only the imitative reflex, with every record company on the send for its own Elvis look-alike, but it would change show business thinking as to what a "star" was. The word "superstar" would now enter the vocabulary. But the phenomenon was not caused by Elvis alone. A whole system of separate musical markets was collapsing, the full extent of which is best grasped from the data in table 8-1. This table shows the proportion of records from each stream that crossed over to another area during the 1950s. It should be noted that this extensive breakdown was not the result of an increase in the number of records flowing through the three markets, nor was it an artifact created by enlarging the number of records reported on the charts.

It occurred, once more, because of the relatively steady interchange between country and pop and the dramatic flooding of pop by R&B. The fact that, in less than a decade after World War II when "race" records were almost extinct, black pop could move over 90 percent of its records to pop, attests to the vigor of that crop and the assiduousness of its harvesting.

This huge transfer of records, mixing diverse musics of all three streams throughout the 1950s, was poured into the great teenage vat. That kettle of resources was the memory bank, the reservoir of rocknroll. As it was boiled down, it produced the canon of songs and performance styles and the artists who would accompany Elvis into the great hall of rocknroll to be crowned king. Who were these others, and why were they different from Elvis? A litany of names of those who first appeared can

TABLE 8-1

Volume of Crossover, 1950–1958

(Percentage of all records on the pop, country & western, and rhythm & blues charts that crossed boundaries)

	Pop		C & W		R & B	
	Percentage	Base no. of records	Percentage	Base no. of records	Percentage	Base no. of records
1950	16	(168)	43	(49)	15	(67)
1951	11	(167)	20	(46)	17	(66)
1952	8	(144)	24	(41)	3	(65)
1953	17	(94)	23	(48)	11	(57)
1954	15	(136)	21	(56)	25	(57)
1955	9	(276)	3	(65)	29	(80)
1956	14	(499)	33	(46)	76	(82)
1957	23	(483)	64	(59)	87	(99)
1958	35	(500)	53	(107)	94	(155)

SOURCE: *Billboard* music popularity charts, Best-Selling Singles. The numbers listed alongside the percentages are the total number of records on the chart for that year.

be cited: Chuck Berry, Fats Domino, Little Richard, the Coasters, the Platters, the Drifters from the R&B side. Then from country came Carl Perkins, Jerry Lee Lewis, Johnny Cash, Roy Orbison, Gene Vincent, Eddie Cochran, the Everly Brothers, Ricky Nelson. The pop stream provided fewer performers at the beginning, but Pat Boone, Connie Francis, and Tommy Sands were among the early stars on the charts.[15]

For every name cited, there were hundreds of performers whose records in all three streams filled the bins of the local record stores. Somehow, rocknroll's initial vast and untidy cornucopia was winnowed to reveal the King and his court. It took several different kinds of procedures to do that sifting. One of the most important was the closing of the boundary crossings. The warning the country music disk jockey gave to Elvis was backed by more persuasive measures that ended promising crossover careers. Marty Robbins, for example, briefly explored rocknroll territory, especially with the success of "A White Sport Coat (And a Pink Carnation)" in 1957 and a few more teenage-oriented sides, but he ended up returning to a long and steady career in the country stream. Other performers felt the same pressure, some being driven out of town precipitously, as with the Burnette Brothers who left Memphis to back up Ricky Nelson in Los Angeles with an authentic country sound that made this thoroughly pop personality a credible and enduring rocknroll performer.

Just the opposite response came from the black pop stream. Every independent label, the talent managers, the freelance producers, writers, and would-be scenemakers put forward their own versions of what would cross over to pop as well as sell records in their own market. There were more than the "five styles of rocknroll" Gillett reported on in his pioneering study of early rocknroll.[16] One discography identifies more than sixty subspecies of early rocknroll.[17] Black pop would find a powerful and continuing place in rocknroll with a succession of performers from Motown gathered by Berry Gordy, Jr., along with the New York independents who provided a parade of doo wop vocal groups, "the girl groups," and solo performers like Sam Cooke and Jackie Wilson. Durable performers such as Ray Charles, the Impressions, and the Temptations had recording careers that put records on the black pop charts and on the pop charts for years.

The pop stream was of two minds about rocknroll. While some of the senior leadership of the old line publishing houses hated it and all it stood for, others jumped right in. The creation of the "teen idols" was one such tack; another was the cadre of young writers and composers working for Don Kirshner's Aldon Music in New York's Brill Building (which I will discuss further later).

The country field sported Bill Justis, performer of "Raunchy" on the

Phillips label, a strong crossover hit from country to pop in 1957. Justis was the leader of Sam Phillips' house band, and like his boss, he was determined to understand what this rocknroll was all about. He did just what his friends had probably often done when scouting out a new patch of music they hadn't heard before:

One night, upon reading a newspaper article about an arranger in New York named Buck Ram, who had to do with the success of the vocal group scene, I found out how much money he had made out of rock 'n' roll. So I said, "That's for me" and I immediately set out to a record shop in Memphis and bought about 80 dollars worth of the all-time rock 'n' roll hits, the ones that set the styles. I studied the stuff, found it was real simple compared to the jazz I had been into, yet it was so basic and savage that it was difficult in a way. This was 1956.[18]

That eighty-dollars worth of records, among the earliest of the Golden Oldies collections, never yielded its hidden treasure to either Phillips or Justis, but it is clear that it contained the secret of rocknroll—that simple and savage communication of a danceable version of sexual celebration.

All the streams except gospel and jazz attempted to find that secret and apply their streams' musical schema toward harvesting it. Gospel, white and black, was deeply immersed in its own expansion of recordings, disk jockeys, and tours of its star performers, even while training some of its young adepts for a secular career. Jazz similarly was self-absorbed, dealing with a succession of arcane styles following bebop. It was building its network of festivals, both national and international. The summers in Newport beginning in 1954 and in Monterey in 1958 constructed the infrastructure and the consumer habit of a summer music celebration, a tradition mature rock would inherit directly in those very venues. Jazz's main connection to young people was on the college campuses where cool jazz, à la Dave Brubeck, Chet Baker, Gerry Mulligan, and others, laid down a set of attitudes and cultural resources that would also serve the rock culture, in part through its connection to the San Francisco–based Beat poets and writers.

What Did Elvis Have That the Others Didn't?

The question remains, What made Elvis greater than any other performer on either side of a decade? Elvis' record production, first of all, underscores his distinctiveness. A fair comparison, given the similarity in physical appearance and the nature of their appeal, could be made between Elvis and the teen idols, from Frankie Avalon to Bobby Rydell. These youngsters from the pop stream's factories put an average of five singles a year on the pop charts during their brief heyday, which lasted from the late fifties to the early sixties. They put only a scattering of records on the R&B charts, and none on the country charts. The other useful comparison is to Pat Boone, about whom I have more to say later. He was also a rising young star in 1955, and over five years or so, he put almost as many single records on the pop charts as did Elvis. Like the other white boys singing black he did not reach the country charts at all and placed just a few on the R&B charts. He, too, faded rapidly after 1960.

Elvis in those same early years put an average of nine records per year on the pop charts and five per year each on the R&B and the country charts. He was thus only a little more productive than the teen idols but had a definite reach into all three markets. The real impact of this attainment is that, after 1960 when the teen idols had totally vanished from the charts, Elvis went on to put 105 singles of his total 149 on the pop charts, 54 of his 84 singles on the country charts, but only 6 of his 35 records on the R&B charts. Elvis' achievements, which included more singles than anyone else, twice as many records in the top 40 than anyone else, about fifty albums placed on the charts, and the making of thirty-three movies, make him unquestionably rocknroll's most productive performer, its first superstar. Both the suddenness and the durability of his musical career raise important questions about the nature of rocknroll.

Was that productivity the creative fountain of the "man as artist" or the factory assemblage of RCA Victor/Paramount's "man as machine"? The output was awesome in any case. How did Elvis' rise happen? Within three years of graduation in 1953, Elvis went from an ugly duckling high school student to a gorgeous swan appearing on national television and selling records to millions. It took twenty years more to complete the portrait as Dorian Gray.

Elvis was trouble from the start, embodying the contradictions in the American family concerning parental authority, youth independence, and sexuality.[19] His rebellion was masked in southern manners bordering on obsequiousness. Even the restraint religion imposed went awry in Elvis's case. His church training and gospel music experience did not prevent the incipient excesses of sexuality from living beside (being, in fact, augmented by) the religiosity that fired the most explosive emotional yearnings in southern Protestant life, white and black. Those themes of rebellion, religiosity, and ungovernable sexuality were emblazoned in all his performances and in his public presence.

Every biographer has noted that Elvis lived for performing, that he had been rewarded beyond any other experience by performance. They also repeat the stories of how he sang "Old Shep" in the fifth grade to the applause of his teachers and fellow students, how he won the five-dollar second prize for singing the same song at the Mississippi-Alabama Fair when he was ten, and how in high school he triumphed at the annual variety concert where for the third time he opened a medley of songs with

"Old Shep." He knew then that the stage was where he could both lose himself and control an audience; he was born to performance.

A deeper experience was also at work in Elvis' life that has, to my knowledge, not been discussed before: his peculiar relationship to the trauma of World War II and the Korean War. No American soldier would face a major enemy for a dozen years. Rocknroll was born and flourished, it should not be forgotten, in an era of relative freedom from actual warfare.[20] Neither Elvis nor his father ever served in the armed forces in wartime. The distance from those life-threatening but honor-giving statuses set them apart. That distance, I suggest, allowed him to formulate his own situation freed from the adults who guided the nation through the great war.

Although most families who lost fathers and sons in the "big" war found the personal and cultural resources necessary to rebuild their lives, the younger children affected, those from six to thirteen years, suffered. They had experienced the terrors of abandonment by absent fathers and older brothers. There were no reassurances sufficient to their condition. Shepherded by women, they moved through strange cities and new schools, with only their own teenage scenes in which to make sense of the world and work things out. Elvis was a lightning rod for all that dislocation and urgent need for identification. In 1956, the year Elvis first reached a national audience, there was another group of youngsters from fourteen- to seventeen-years old whose older brothers had either been in the Korean War or who were eligible but didn't serve for one reason or another. They were natural allies of the slightly older kids who had felt abandoned during World War II.

It is not too extreme an assertion to say that Elvis delegitimated the adults' command over these kids by making any authority conferred by World War II irrelevant. Ten years later, that deauthorization was still operative. The following reminiscences are those of a Berkeley professor on the heirs of Elvis:

I saw that the students represented the first generation that hadn't experienced World War II directly. . . . For their elders the war was culturally non-negotiable. It was a good thing; Hitler was wrong; America was right. But the war did not settle the problems of the world, and the young expressed a certain impiety toward it.[21]

There was one other component in Elvis' life that made his contribution to rocknroll a distinctive one. It was what could be called, tabloid style, Elvis' "missing twin" phenomenon. Practically without exception, the biographies of Elvis announce early and portentiously that Elvis Aron Presley arrived on 8 January 1935, the first of twins. His brother, Jesse Garon Presley, was stillborn and was buried the next day in an unmarked grave.[22] Just as Elvis' real twin brother disappeared from view, so, too, did his second "twin"; that is, nobody today thinks of Pat Boone as the "good" twin to Elvis' "bad" twin, but this precise notion was in circulation for a few important years. The parallels in their lives as "cultural" twins tell an important part of the rocknroll story.

Both performers were southerners, Charles Eugene Boone being born in Jacksonville, Florida, on 1 June 1934 (making him six months older than Elvis). The Boones, descendants of Daniel Boone, were a religiously observant middle-class family that regularly attended church (twice on Sundays). The father had been deferred from active service during World War II, so Pat, like Elvis, as part of that minority of families without father or sons in the military during the war. Pat, an obedient son, found in high school the easy success that totally eluded Elvis. Pat was the model member of the "leading crowd." After graduation in 1953, he married his high school sweetheart, the daughter of Red Foley, one of country music's senior stars. It was in part family connections and in part the availability of a microphone provided by the Ted Mack "Amateur Hour" that launched Pat's singing career in 1954.

Pat's career took off with his association with Randy Wood, founder of Dot Records. Wood's recording strategy was similar to Sam Phillips'. They both knew that the three pop streams were coming together and that the trick was to find a young white performer who could carry R&B to pop. Pat Boone was Wood's answer. In April they found and covered the Charms' hit on Deluxe, "Two Hearts," that made the R&B charts in February 1955. Pat's first effort was thus a moderate chart hit. Real success followed with the same tactic, a cover version of Fats Domino's "Ain't It A Shame." Pat, with slightly "corrected" lyrics and a pop styling, took the sales action away from the Domino recording, making for Boone his first number one record. From that point on, it was a horse race for leadership of white rocknroll, with Elvis from the country side and Pat from pop, both carrying the R&B repertoire.

The Mr. Bad and Mr. Good images were apparent from the start, and their early successes closely rivaled one another's. The photographic images of the two in performance shots, in publicity stills, and in candid poses can be instantly and accurately decoded in those terms. The photographs reveal Pat's squeaky-clean image, which carried to the Kingston Trio and the Beach Boys, while the Beale Street sharpie shines right out of Elvis (figs. 8-6, 8-7, 8-8, 8-9).

Rocknroll and American Youth Culture

In the second quarter of the twentieth century, two cultural inventions came together. One was adolescence; the other was the high school. As a distinctive period in the life course, adolescents were thought to suffer the peculiar deformities of transition that lay in the years between child and adult. The high school was the triumph of a social movement and a bureaucratic practice. It would continue the age segregation that had proceeded steadily in the twentieth century. After 1945, it was to be the vehicle that would carry the war's first great peace dividend, its teenagers, to the land of peace and plenty. By the 1950s, the high school was as nearly a separate world as could be tolerated by a society that still held onto the family as its basic unit of morality and economy and to the local community as the site of a family-based power.[23]

Within this "adolescent society," American teenagers from every class, race, and religion grabbed onto the whole set of solutions that Elvis and rocknroll offered to their problems. They drew strength, affirmation, and a load of savvy from that culture, which made it okay to love your mother and God and, at the same time, hunger for the wild promises of love and sex. These were on youth's agenda, as always. Their operative distinctions were not coded in explicit sexual terms but in social groupings that ordered the entire high school scene.

The leading crowd, as pictured in the Randle Romp scene (see Figure 5-3), was the pinnacle in every high school in America. That crowd reigned successfully by way of a public acceptance of adult values and a manipulative ability to explore their violation. Every high school also had its rough crowd, its "fast" crowd, ranging from just a few youngsters, nearly always in some kind of trouble, to perhaps as many as 10 to 20 percent of the students. The middle majority yearned to have it both ways, to earn the rewards of obedience as well as to enjoy the pleasures of the disreputable.[24] They followed the "leading crowd" in some things, the "fast crowd" in others.

Besides the middle majority and the malleable leading crowd, there were in the schools several deviant minorities. These, as noted in Chapter 1, were named by David Matza in 1961 as the "subterranean traditions of youth"—Delinquency, Radicalism, and Bohemianism.[25] These categories may appear to be simple-minded by today's standards, but they encompass much of what was going on then and now. The rebellious direction, a favorite of sociologists that has been tagged "juvenile delinquency" since the 1920s, placed physical prowess and dangerous action as the number one requirement for making and maintaining individual reputations. The "hoodlum element" in every high school after World War II found its dominant form in the motorcycle gang. If the "Dead End Kids" were the embodiment of that stance in the thirties and forties, the Hell's Angels were its successor in the fifties and sixties. The black leather jacket, the greasy hair, the menacing look with equipment to match, and, above all, the deliberate affront to middle-class values represented attitudes that found a home in rocknroll and, in fact, provided its symbol-

Figure 8-6. Pat "Good Twin" Boone Studying. From *'Twixt Twelve and Twenty*, written by Pat Boone, published by Prentice-Hall, Inc.

Figure 8-7. Elvis "Bad Twin" Presley Also Studying. Copyright © Alfred Wertheimer 1979.

Figure 8-8. Elvis
Performing. Copyright
© Alfred Wertheimer 1979.

Figure 8-9. Pat Per-
forming. From *'Twixt
Twelve and Twenty*, writ-
ten by Pat Boone, pub-
lished by Prentice-Hall, Inc.

ism. An early and innocent Elvis had shifted from the country boy with his guitar to the city leather boy.[26]

The Bohemian direction of high school deviance moved past the Greenwich Village artists and gypsies of the thirties and forties to the Beat and the Bopster. From their defanged versions on television, Dobie Gillis and his "beatnik friend" Maynard Krebs, to the serious literary figures—Kerouac, Ginsberg, and the other Beat poets—the Bohemian repudiation of the straight life was storing up its resources for reappearance as the "hippie."

The radical wing of teenage life in the 1950s was smaller and weaker than the others. Its main elements, as Matza describes them, were apocalyptic, populist, evangelical. All three of these tendencies had, it is interesting to note, a strong religious base or a scientific urgency. Part of that underlying foundation included the compression of time into a millenial collapse: Salvation now. The unwillingness and/or inability to sustain a more extended temporal conception of the social process was also part of the delinquent and Bohemian cultures. Something *now*.[27]

Teen industries, which included fashion, movies, and music, courted all groups but wooed especially the rough kids and the other subterranean minorities in the hope of controlling the middle majority. This strategy worked not only because of the irrelevance of adult culture in the schools but because of the leading crowd's infinite capacity to give in to the rough crowd and the rough crowd's infinite capacity for excess. It was this social dynamic that led the high school population into rocknroll.

Those students, collectively, had great influence over that music. Their feedback to the disk jockeys was definitely consequential. Their preferences were individualistic and quite varied, reflecting the charts and the crossovers. Unlike the record producers, the teenagers were not particularly eager to boil down rocknroll into its essence. Their preferences were catholic; a typical record collection would contain everything from Elvis and Perry Como to Little Richard and the McGuire Sisters.

Table 8-2, which charts the preferred music of teenagers, comes from one of the most systematic studies of teenage life during the early days of rocknroll.[28] The categories are those of the researcher, based on pretest interviews with high school students.[29] The data are unmistakable. The single most frequent category of preferred music is rocknroll, accounting for half the total. No other single category is even close. It carries the day for both boys and girls. The presence of definite minority tastes for country music, jazz, and folk is an important confirmation of their presence not just in the music world but in the living assertions of their audiences. The assembling rocknroll canon would heed those assertions.

The second part of the table indicates both the fleeting and the fixed

TABLE 8-2
High School Student Music Preferences: 1957

	Percentage*	
	Boys	Girls
Favorite Types of Music		
Rocknroll	55	53
Pop	19	31
Country & Western	7	4
Folk (Calypso)	8	6
Jazz	11	6
	100	100
Total =	(3722)	(3724)
Favorite Singers		
Pat Boone	44	45
Elvis Presley	22	18
Tommy Sands	8	11
Perry Como	11	10
Frank Sinatra	5	7
Harry Belafonte	10	9
	100	100
Total =	(3960)	(4113)

SOURCE: From *The Adolescent Society*, by James S. Coleman. Copyright © 1961 by The Free Press, a division of Macmillan, Inc.; copyright renewed 1989 by James S. Coleman. Adapted with the permission of the publisher.
* Figures rounded to whole number; "No answer" removed.

qualities of teenage taste. Pat Boone is the nearly two-to-one favorite over Elvis Presley among boys and preferred almost three-to-one by girls. Pat represented to the middle majority their safe dreams; Elvis, their more dangerous fantasies.

Pat Boone and Elvis served as competitive anchoring points for the industry's response to the basic competition between the two "fantasies" for dominion over the teenage market. The prize was the loyalty of the vast majority of kids in the middle. Both performers gave the deauthorization of adult authority strength and legitimation. Hollywood and the pop stream swallowed them both, offering their domesticated good/bad personae as alternatives that moved no one to alarm. On one side was Pat's *'Twixt Twelve and Twenty*, a friendly, earnest advice book for teenagers on the Christian road to the future, an instant best seller when published in 1958. Four hundred thousand copies had been sold by the early seventies, and it was in its twenty-second printing.

On the other side was Elvis himself. But perhaps it was what stood beyond Elvis that upset the adults who were worried that the "catch up" game the schools' leading crowd had to play would bring the whole school to ruin. There is no doubt who and what the "rough" crowd liked, including the incipient radicals and hippies. Coleman summarizes his findings about the minority of kids who formed cliques crosscutting almost every status and school grade and who

... constitute the "rough crowd." Their black "rock and roll" jackets are a symbol in this school of orientation to a good time, cars, music, the skating rink, and unconcern with school. Almost all smoke or drink or both. Their favorite singer is Elvis Presley, while that of most of adolescent culture is Pat Boone, who dispenses rock and roll without the implicit deviance and rebellion in Presley's image. In short, these girls are extremely hedonistic, antischool, and rebellious. . . . They are not "part of the background." . . . They count in the system, but they are so oriented to out-of-school activities that even in this culture, where adult values have little currency, they do not have status among the adolescents as a whole.[30]

These cliques of girls can be compared to the cliques of boys who were deeply committed to religion; they both have members from every grade in school.

That these two interests, religion and rock and roll are at opposite poles of a continuum of hedonism is not so important as that they set off a boy or girl from his fellows and lead him to look beyond the confines of his own grade for fellow-devotees. "Fans" and "fanatics" have an interest that pervades their behavior, including their selection of friends.[31]

This environment would produce the social movements of the sixties. The "continuum of hedonism," including sex, music, drugs, religion, politics, would soon expand beyond the high school boundaries. The social skills of the leading crowd would move with the times to provide the leadership for college student movements. Their vulnerability to the excesses of the rough crowd would grow as well. The high school dynamics would thus work on the nation's college campuses. The straights, hippies, radicals, and bikers would fight it out many times.

The Legacy of the Pantheon

Perhaps it is an error of enthusiasm to freight Elvis Presley with too heavy a historical load; yet, he clearly outshines the other performers in rocknroll's first pantheon. He, more than the others, has become a national icon. The legacy of rocknroll's founding years, therefore, is largely Elvis', even though it was a collective accomplishment. That legacy can be defined as follows:

1. Early rocknroll brought together the three commercial streams of American popular music into a unified reservoir and a public presence that was economically viable and musically creative.

2. The main performers, Elvis most notably, coalesced into a loose but discernable code the attitudes of American youth, a code that would serve

them as a personal and political guide in their dealings with adult authority for decades to come.

3. Elvis alone, but inviting imitation, provided a template for the American entertainment industry's solution to the problem they had themselves created. The "superstar" model fit the scope of the artistic and economic arrangements they had generated.

Each part of this legacy calls for some further elaboration. First, early rocknroll allowed every performer to draw on the full musical resources of pop, country, and rhythm and blues. Their songs, lyrics, instrumentation, and performance styles, everything from Broadway's grand songwriting tradition to the lowest downtown hootchie-cootchie act, became grist for rocknroll's mills. All these materials were offered and evaluated in commercial terms. If the record sold, it was a good record—the simplest evaluative ax.

As the most dramatic focus of the three-stream convergence, Elvis was the founding figure of "blue-eyed soul." In this and other respects, his utilization of black music and black dance were artistic achievements of "mythic" dimensions. That is, a myth tells of a complex and consequential matter, coiling it into a simplifying form, which displays its tensions and contradictions even as it resolves them within an isolated structure, be it story, song, or other form.[32] Elvis stated a real contradiction on the ground—in this case, the incongruence of white doing black—and then solved the contradiction in the air—he did black being white. Equally important for the reality of rocknroll, Chuck Berry, the Coasters, Smokey Robinson, Frankie Lymon, and others were also "mythic" in that they were black doing white. Rocknroll became a racially integrated stream even before the appearance of, for example, the Del-Vikings in 1957, one of the first integrated rocknroll groups.

The locus of that transformative symbolic process was the ability of these performers to invoke the pop stream's greatest gift: its capacity to transcend race, religion, gender, or region in the name of music. The presence of racism and sexism among the pop stream's personnel and policies often prevented this symbolic transformation from working; yet no petulant dismissal of Elvis' work or of rocknroll's founding performers can erase the fact that the pop stream, and therefore rocknroll as well, can transcend racial and other prejudices, no matter how justified may be the cries of theft, imitation, or exploitation.

The meeting of the three streams mixed the instrumentation; in rocknroll, then, there are many acceptable musical forms. Elvis, though beginning with a three-man country band, soon went to the Nashville studio band and then to the Hollywood and Las Vegas monster orchestras. It was Buddy Holly who substituted drums for the guitar, thereby turn-

ing the country group into a little rhythm and blues jump band. And
Jerry Lee Lewis was a virtuoso piano player as well as compelling vocalist. There were a cappella doo wop groups, solo singers, and almost every
other possible configuration. A rock star could play anything.

Rocknroll's second legacy was essentially nonmusical. It was a set of
attitudes about how a young person confronts the world. These attitudes
were, in the very words of Elvis' early song titles, both tender and cruel.
"Don't Be Cruel" and "Love Me Tender" were his back-to-back, number
one hits in September and November of 1956 for RCA Victor. He was
assertive, sullen, and determined. He was also sensual and yearning. With
his guitar grasped almost as a weapon, singing out his feelings directly
and strongly in a fully adult musical idiom, Elvis' performance armed
millions of young Americans. Regardless of Elvis' apolitical stance, any
set of words, any rejection of adult authority, any declaration of an alternative future was protected by Elvis' compelling model. Moreover, in the
early 1950s, rocknroll put the personal questions of love and sex into the
hands of fifteen-year olds, who never relinquished them and probably
never will.

The third part of rocknroll's legacy, with Elvis as its central figure, is
the "superstar" phenomenon. Elvis was one of the first superstars in
American entertainment, larger in the popular imagination than Frank
Sinatra ever was and setting the model for the Beatles and others. One
part of that complex exaggeration of the entertainer is in the transmission
of the message that any kid can learn the guitar and cut a record. The
highly publicized story of Elvis doing just that announced to teenagers
that it could be enacted again anywhere in the country. It would take
several more years before great numbers of American young people, boys
and girls, would themselves pick up the guitar, but, in the meantime, the
local disk jockeys served as the ubiquitous and friendly avenue to show
business. Presley not only opened great reservoirs of music to rocknroll,
he showed young people how to use them.

Another component of the superstar was its place in an increasingly
corporate entertainment complex. From the very start, the direction rocknroll took was towards its own consolidation into larger corporate formations. There was no other direction for it to go, having begun with
maximum dispersion in the short loops scattered throughout the nation's
cities. The small independent record companies, the independent radio
stations as bases for the autonomous disk jockeys, the performers moving
through the network of little clubs and coffee houses, the teenage audiences in their individual high schools—all these elements were spread
from coast to coast with only the slightest thread connecting each into a
loose, national "long loop." The grand loop of rock was assembled over
an extended time period. Each part relentlessly pursued the logic of ver-

tical integration; each part raised the "ante" as it progressed—just add the zeros. Colonel Parker quickly moved from selling publicity stills and programs of Elvis' concerts for ten cents to the creation of a multimillion-dollar Elvis products division.

The saddest outcome was that the investment in Elvis as a teen rock superstar was so great and so inscribed in corporate stone that his career development was stifled. The pop stream had made it easy for its performers to grow old. It accepted its audience's aging as a part of its own renewal. It even found a way for that gerontological process to give its own rewards; Las Vegas, Tahoe, the entire state of Nevada, with its polite refusal of American morality's legal codes, wrote its own.

It is a mistake, I believe, to say that Elvis was locked into being permanently young, even though youth was the central definition of the rock stream. He did age, but he did so in a strange way. He became something like Sleeping Beauty. He was intact, as attractive and magical as ever in each appearance. He would disappear after each movie or infrequent live show to indulge his private youthful excesses, then reappear more resplendent, maturing but still younger than the audiences who were indulging, for the moment, in their own past. Although this subtle contrivance might have preserved Elvis' shelf life, it cost him dearly and scarred the unfolding rock canon in a particular way. It made Elvis the symbol of an aging rock establishment, another target for youth assertiveness. This time the arrow pointed at the head of the pantheon. Rocknroll has been able to save itself from the dead-end position that the country stream found itself in during the late 1950s by the invention of its own museum wing. It is still a young person's music, but, myth-like, it has found a place for its old folks as well.

There is a triple irony in the end. First, Elvis as the angry young man with the guitar made it okay to sing out your rage, but he himself had nothing to say. Second, he gave everything he had to give most vividly and fully in live performance, yet his career mentors prevented his participation in the building of rocknroll's own live performance traditions. Finally, he brought the song reservoirs of three full streams of American music to rocknroll, yet he was only a singer of other people's songs. Rock's own singer-songwriters would have to wait just a little while longer. Nevertheless, he was and is the one and only, the King of Rocknroll. The pantheon surrounds him.

PART THREE

ROCK MATURES:

1965-1970

9. The Industry Refuses, Then Accommodates

To the pop stream, rocknroll was *the* enemy, the "fad" that would neither go away nor soften its assault. It was the spawn of BMI, proving that the broadcasters could not be entrusted with the riches of American popular song. At the center of the New York music world in the late 1950s was a relatively small group of individuals whose strategic position and personal strength gave them considerable influence. These senior professional managers of the music publishing houses, their established writers, some top talent managers, the broadcasting and record executives, and the usual ripened show business lawyers, wise men, and publicists were prepared to use all their resources to destroy rocknroll.

This chapter reviews the attempts of these forces to do so. It also traces their accommodation to the resilient and ever-growing rock stream. The attacks were made in the public press, in the halls of Congress, and wherever the deals that characterize the music business were made. The target was the hit-making disk jockeys and, behind them, BMI. The echoes of these struggles in broadcasting and the recording industry are also sketched as the technology and the audiences changed and as each of the other streams sought to adjust to rocknroll's presence.

The Legislative Assault

The ASCAP publishers, for they were the core, first invoked all their old political connections in Congress. In the 1959–1960 hearings before the friendly Senate Subcommittee on Communications, their sharpest legal wits were aimed at constructing a legislative device that would destroy BMI's alleged power over popular music. The Smathers Bill, S2834, was "to provide that a license for a radio or television broadcasting station shall not be granted to, or held by, any person or corporation engaged directly or indirectly in the business of publishing music or of manufacturing or selling musical recordings."[1] Its hearings attracted the testimony of the entire music industry on one side or the other. There was no quarter given as the notables in all the arts were invited to write or telegraph the committee.

Arthur Schwartz was back on the stand, arguing for immediate passage of the bill. His assertion was that the public airwaves, lent to the broadcasters via the FCC licensing process, were being abused. CBS and NBC, as the senior broadcasting networks, were unfairly securing exposure for records produced by their subsidiary companies Columbia Records and RCA Victor Records (and their smaller labels). BMI, being wholly owned by the broadcasters, was implicated in this conspiracy of selective exposure. More than two thousand publishing firms were lavishly subsidized by the networks. These funds, it was stated, were used to enhance air exposure for BMI-licensed records via payments to the nation's disk jockeys. The entire weight of the music industry, from writer to publisher, from record company's A&R man to performer down to the radio station's disk jockey, the whole apparatus led by the giant broadcasting networks was a threat to genuine American music by manufacturing rocknroll and shoving it into the nation's ears.

It was the Distinguished Professor Arlan Coolidge, Chairman of the Department of Music, Brown University, who set the tone of the hearings:

Not long ago I took an extended trip in my own car which led into many States. . . . I kept the car radio on for long intervals. . . .

I was shocked by the perpetual blanket of banality encountered hour after hour. The almost complete absence of the fine tunes by Berlin, Jerome Kern, Cole Porter, and many other gifted composers in the area of musical comedy was regrettable because it is a natural step from music of this kind to much concert music of high quality. . . .

Every advertiser knows that constant repetition of an idea gradually sinks into public consciousness. . . . The teenagers . . . haven't a chance even to hear Hammerstein's music very much, they have heard the rock and roll and the cheaper music and that to them is music.[2]

Out of the more than 1100 pages of testimony emerged the position that rocknroll posed a threat to the entire graded series of the arts, lower to higher. To reach the heights, the ladder must be available to all. Other leading authorities lent the weight of their names and organizations to this belief. Clarence Derwent, theatrical producer and chairman of the National Council on the Arts and Government, signaled the committee as follows:

The National Council on the Arts and Government which represents all seven major arts and is composed of such prominent Americans as Henry Seidel Canby of Columbia University, Rene D'Haroncourt of the Museum of Modern Art, Norman Dello Joio, world famous composer, Lillian Gish and Howard Lindsay of the Broadway stage, wants to express a strong hope that your committee will give favorable consideration to the Smathers bill. The growth and freedom from monopolistic control for every creative artist in our land is synonymous with the growth and culture of America.[3]

Statements agreeing with this position by musical personalities such as Dean Martin, Georgie Jessel, Aaron Copland, Morton Gould, and others occupied almost ninety pages of the hearing's printed testimony. The full outrage of the American art leadership was vented. Within a decade, however, almost all those prestigious art leaders would be replaced by a new set of faces and voices, who were only too happy to meet the rock stars of the day. Some of the new painters, dancers, musicians, and theater artists would share not only celebrity but creative exchanges with the rock stream.

The full array of medical-theological-educational experts was also mobilized for the hearings. The following statement was typical:

As physicians and psychologists who come into daily contact with people of all ages and walks of life, we urge you to give serious heed to the Smathers bill. If the broadcasting interests are allowed to continue their dominance and manipulation of America's musical taste, they will shortly strangle all true creative effort, and consequently jeopardize the future development of our culture. To jeopardize our culture is to weaken an intrinsic ingredient of our leadership in the world. (Walter Hyden, Ph.D., President, The Association for the Scientific Study of Psychotherapy)[4]

This was the line, then: a highly dramatic identification of rocknroll with juvenile delinquency, with youth rebelliousness, with unbridled sexuality, with racial "mixing," with musical trash.

The Smathers bill failed. Though the pain within the music industry was somewhat assuaged by the rising tide of record sales, the continuing dominance of the disk jockey still upset the older publishers, so they turned their efforts towards that target. The very next year, 1960, saw the phalanx of respectable culture once more mobilized for another set of payola hearings. They produced fifteen hundred pages of testimony and exhibits before Oren Harris' (Democrat, Arkansas) Special Committee on Legislative Oversight. The charges of "payola" in the music business were not new, of course, and Paul Ackerman's professorial lecture to the committee on payola's prevalence since vaudeville days did nothing to soften or swerve the congressmen from their cleansing fury.

This particular committee had been reaping headlines from their investigation of the quiz show scandals, and some ASCAP leaders were credited with persuading the chairman to extend their "media" hearings into an examination of payola among radio disk jockeys. ASCAP felt that the animosity of the press toward media corruption on the one hand and toward rocknroll on the other would spill over to affect radio's main impresarios, the disk jockeys. If their wide-ranging entrepreneurial activities in all the major cities outside of New York City could be shut down, the "legitimate" publishers believed they could rebuild a more adult audience from their New York base. Then, high-quality music, which was being driven out of American culture by the greedy exploitation of susceptible teenagers, could return.

The major record companies were the reluctant allies of the ASCAP publishers in this attack on the disk jockeys. They were reluctant because they could not find young performing talent without the help of local disk jockeys, nor could they compete effectively against the thousands of singles produced by small labels for local markets without disk jockey help. The major record companies had tried to compete with the independent labels for disk jockey favor and had been made the laughing stock of the industry. The specific occasions were the 1958 and 1959 disk jockey conventions, held in Kansas City and in Miami Beach. There the major record labels had, in an undisguised and gross attempt, tried to stuff "Booze, Bribes and Broads" into the mouths, pockets, and beds of the twenty-five hundred pop disk jockeys who had accepted the hospitality of the convention.[5] It was clear that the major record companies wanted it both ways. They wanted the good will of disk jockeys, who so completely influenced teenage audiences, but they also wanted to deliver to those audiences the music of the older artists of the pop stream they had under contract. They pretty much wound up with neither.

The two most highly visible disk jockeys in the nation then were Alan Freed and Dick Clark. They both fell. Freed was caught up in the Manhattan grand jury probe into payola. He had moved his operation from Cleveland to New York in 1954, built a sizable radio audience with his WINS show, and, after the Boston "riot" that erupted during his "Rock 'n Roll Party," had resigned to join ABC-TV's channel 5 with an hour-long TV rocknroll show. The accelerating demand for a solution to the payola problem naturally focused on Freed. ABC sought to diffuse the attack by having him sign an affadavit denying he had ever taken payola. He declined on principle, was fired, and the road down was greased by a combination of industry indifference and Freed's self-destructiveness.

This result was in the sharpest contrast to the outcome of Dick Clark's travails. This ever-young-looking disk jockey had become the focus of a highly productive local music scene in Philadelphia. His nationally televised teenage dance party was a huge and surprising success, even though violating the industry's first premise—that disk jockey shows had to be local. ABC tailored a special affadavit for Clark to sign, which he did. The multiple and complex business arrangements Clark and his friends had developed became the centerpiece of Oren Harris' hearings. The committee staff had produced extensive evidence that Clark was the cen-

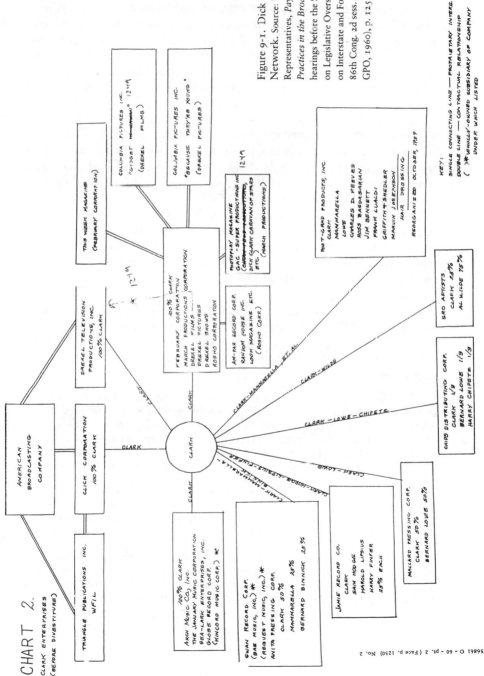

Figure 9-1. Dick Clark's Financial Network. Source: U.S. House of Representatives, *Payola and Other Deceptive Practices in the Broadcasting Field*, hearings before the Select Subcommittee on Legislative Oversight of the Committee on Interstate and Foreign Commerce, 86th Cong. 2d sess. (Washington, D.C.: GPO, 1960), p. 125f.

ter of a huge and convoluted impresarial network, reaping unconscionable profits from every breathing pore of the huge musical apparatus he had allegedly constructed. Large Rube Goldberg charts showing its structure were offered to the committee and the press[6] (fig. 9-1).

This apparatus, the committee alleged, produced a series of "wholly owned," no-talent teenage performers whose endless prefabricated records received undue exposure on Clark's show, propelling them, thereby, into hundreds of thousands of undeserved sales and their singers into an undeserved stardom. The committee huffed and puffed its moral outrage for all it was worth in the press, but even Clark realized what the game was all about. In his frank retelling of those events, Clark says that, during a lunchtime recess between sessions, the committee's chief counsel, Robert W. Lishman, brought his teenaged son to meet Clark: "I gave the kid his autograph. It was at that point that the light suddenly came in on my head. I realized the whole thing was a shuck. This man had been saying terrible things to me in public, really gunning for me, and then he turned up with his kid for an autograph!"[7]

By his own assessment, Clark was both burned and rescued. He had to divest himself of those holdings, no matter how garbled they were on the big wall charts. "When the Government put me out of the music business I estimate I lost more than $8 million. The hearings taught me a lot about politics and business. I learned not just to make money, but to protect my ass at all times."[8]

The radio broadcasting industry also learned a lot, partly from *Billboard*'s learned Paul Ackerman. He taught the committee, and the attentively listening station managers, an important lesson: a way to control the autonomous hit-making disk jockey in fact and in the eyes of the public.

A significant question, then, is whether a system can be installed which can guard against the weakness of any individual employee who might fall prey to venality. . . . It is our belief that only the group or committee system of responsibility can provide an adequate safeguard. . . . It has been many years since we installed the group or committee at the Billboard, a procedure which has made us secure in the knowledge that even if any individual were so foolish as to have dishonest intentions, our editorial columns, record reviews, and popularity charts could not be influenced to a point where our readers could be misled. . . .[9]

To make sure the point could not be missed, Ackerman explicitly laid out the avenue that was already available:

We have been interested to note that many radio broadcasters now seem to be switching over to the group system, to avoid placing the tremendous responsibility of record selection in the hands of a single individual who must, as a result, be subject to pressures which some simply cannot withstand.[10]

The hearings concluded with a paltry piece of legislation proscribing payola. Its real impact, an apparent victory for ASCAP, was in the publicity, which effectively ended the era of the autonomous, hit-making disk jockey. A new configuration of marketing popular music was in the making.

Radio and Records Respond

The committee system of selecting records was but one suggestion to station managers, who were facing a sharpened competitive struggle for audiences. By the early 1960s, the entire entertainment complex was restructuring itself. The movie industry had recovered its balance after a decade of fearful or blustering attacks against the television screen. The entire music market was expanding. The upscale hi-fi sector was stimulating the production of albums rather than singles. The record companies, accordingly, were scouring the neighborhood for album-length material. To make matters more competitive, the FCC was allowing the number of television and FM and AM radio licenses to increase almost freely.

The result was that radio audiences, if not diminishing in absolute size, were at least being segregated into smaller and more differentiated tastes. In 1950, the heyday of the autonomous disk jockey, there were about two thousand AM stations, seven hundred FM ones, and about one hundred TV stations. A decade later, the AM stations had increased 70 percent to thirty-four hundred, the number of FM stations had actually declined in number, but television stations had increased to about six hundred.[11]

How was a radio station to win a reliable if smaller part of the audience? One answer that fit a substantial number of AM stations was the "top 40" format. The earliest appearance of this procrustean arrangement seems to have been early in 1950 on the NBC affiliate WDSO. Several years later, in 1952, a young disk jockey named Bob Howard inherited the on-air name "Bob Hamilton," along with a two-hour, late afternoon show, "The Top 20 at 1280." The show was a standard pop stream segment aimed at the broadest audience possible. Howard picked his own records with the help of the station's informal survey of local record stores, jukebox operators, and the local record distributors. He played the safe top hits, with few new records. Several years later, Robert "Todd" Storz simply extended the format to the top 40, applied it to a stable of stations that were forming a "regional" network, and expanded it to cover a full broadcasting schedule. Soon other stations and mini-networks followed suit.

This committee choice favoring the top hits soon turned into an elaborate shell game of rating wars and audience demographic studies. The rhetoric of the industry basically came down to giving a name to the range of tastes of a group of listeners, for example, Easy Listening or Middle of the Road (MOR). It was a shell game without a pea, because there was little if any credible evidence showing the necessary, three-way correlation among the audience's demographic characteristics, their product choices, and their music preferences. The lack of such evidence almost didn't seem to matter. As the stations increased in number, each one sought a single, identifiable trademark and style. Unless a station was going to deliberately cater to extreme tastes—audiences that were too old, too ethnic, or too anything outside the white, middle-class range—the "Top 40" was the generic answer for scheduling a narrow and uncontroversial music policy.

Once the idea of a single identifying characteristic for a station began, the normal imitation and differentiation among stations produced an endless set of minor format labels. Each sought to carve out of the pop stream a distinctive name and musical range that made it different from the others yet somehow reached the desired broad audience. This task was obviously impossible, that is, the reliance on marginal differences among stations which insisted on their uniqueness. Middle of the Road, Easy Listening, and other such formats, however, were interpreted by the music industry as a return to sanity, a resumption of the plugging system that approximated the old days. It meant dealing with a centralized station management on the basis of musical plugs, exchanged in the traditional "friendship" manner. It would take only a few years for the weakness of the committee system to appear, opening the door to a rash of consultants and newsletter services. Radio station play lists were compiled from the best-selling records, spiced with a few new sides chosen as if by oracle. These witch doctors promised to pick the hits from the flood of new releases that were continuing to increase. The abuses of this system would take years to reach the headlines once reserved for Alan Freed and Dick Clark.

At that moment, though, the result was the closing down to a great extent of teenage music on AM radio. This move drastically reduced the programming of newly released, 45 rpm singles and de-emphasized the hit game in popular music. It did not mean the end of the disk jockey as a whole or even the demise of those disk jockeys committed to rocknroll. There were, in fact, several that emerged as new heroes for young music, "Murray the K," "Wolfman Jack," Kal Rudman, and others just as colorful. Their strategy, somewhere between that of a personality and a hit-making disk jockey, was to identify themselves as closely as possible with the careers of one or more performer.

The result was a severe loss to the singles-oriented music publisher and the small record company, exactly the intent of the major record companies and the older publishers. They saw in the dominance of the long playing album the new basic unit that would solve most of their problems; an era of "good" popular music could resume. What the ASCAP forces couldn't do in the marketplace, they accomplished politically. Some AM stations, unnerved by the coverage of the payola hearings, were already changing their programming. *Cash Box* offered an astringent seminar on the fate of those stations that were too hasty in their retreat from danceable singles in favor of album cuts of standards and instrumentals.

A number of stations who made that transition during the past three months have run smack into a cement wall engraved with the words, "YOUR RATINGS ARE LAYING AN EGG." As a result, many of these stations (enough to indicate that this could be a trend) are returning to the records their audiences want. Almost immediately their ratings are recovering.[12]

Things did not return to normal though. The effect was to further segregate the markets by age. Adults were to be served an expanded menu of LP albums containing Broadway musicals, movie themes, and a flood of popular orchestras serving up mood music. But the Mantovani's, the Peter Nero's, and the Burt Kaempfert's couldn't carry the pop stream for long. It would soon have to look elsewhere for a new musical lode to mine. The young audience was given a special fare designed for it; the moment of teen idols and the first "death of rocknroll" approached.

For the moment, the years 1958–1962, the strategy of age stratification appeared to work. Home phonograph equipment sales increased sharply as the hi-fi craze spread beyond its initial hi-brow audience and into the mass public. The little RCA 45-rpm record player, retailing at $12.95 in the early 1950s, or its updated version, was upstairs in the kids' room playing rocknroll, while in the living room was an expensive hi-fi costing hundreds of dollars that played wallpaper for the grown-ups. The inauguration of LP record clubs and the introduction of stereophonic sound in the late 1950s separated still further the adult and youth constituencies.

In one of their surveys of radio personnel, *Billboard* revealed unequivocally that the album was surpassing the single as the dominant recorded form. The results showed that, in the decade from 1953 to 1963, the stations had radically reduced their plugging of the single record and that, by 1963, cuts from albums received the dominant exposure and exploitation efforts.[13] This outcome was certainly the victory sought by the New York musical establishment. A soggy "top 40" system provided the industry a more politically controllable, if slower, hit-making system than did the faster and more accurate way the hit-making disk jockeys were servicing the teen market.

But what was the "album"? At the beginning of its use in the pop stream, it served several purposes. One was to differentiate artists. For the new performer with one or more hot singles, the album was a way to mark him or her as a classy act. It was also a way to move the goods. As Otis Williams of the Temptations put it "Basically, selling an album was like reselling one, two, or three hit singles plus some throwaway filler tracks that nobody really gave a damn about."[14] It would take more time and the triumph of rock superstars to explore the creative possibilities of the album form.

Rocknroll's New Structure

While the payola hearings reflected the popular music industry's refusal to accept a young people's music, that very same industry was organizing the machinery that would, nevertheless, accommodate a rocknroll presence. The recognition that rocknroll was a performers' medium generated a set of structures that significantly changed the players and the power relations in the pop stream, as well as in black and country pop. The young performer, solo or group, was the crop to be harvested. Every young performer aspiring to the superstar status that Elvis had so suddenly achieved with such apparent effortlessness would be looking for someone to guide his or her career, someone who could offer both regular live performances and a record contract.

Since there was an extraordinary number of such youngsters around, it is no surprise that a whole flock of new specialists appeared on the scene. They included talent agencies, personal managers, and others who facilitated the movement of performers to live performance sites and to radio and record studios. Premier Talent, Creative Management Associates (CMA), and dozens of regional and local talent and concert agencies built new connections between the record companies and the performance venues. It was this brokerage position between record labels and the concert system that would make Premier Talent President Frank Barsalona "the most powerful man in the music business, bar none," in the words of Ahmet Ertegun at that time.[15]

Another change involved a vital part of the assembling rocknroll infrastructure, generated by the mostly backstage friction between two of the new actors in the picture. The heat developed over who was in charge of making the record, the performer (rapidly becoming superstar) or the producer (master of the studio technology). Their quarrels not only raised questions regarding the source of musical excellence and the nature of the music itself but also what constituted artistic growth and where to direct career lines. The answers to these questions would occupy rocknroll audiences and critics for some time as they fought through the various ways of evaluating the music.

The performance sites were also changing. The places where kids could dance and listen to their favorite performers were expending beyond the high school gym to downtown theaters, concert halls, and ballrooms, as well as to smaller bars and coffee houses. Every city's music community fashioned these new venues, the radio stations, recording studios, and their audiences into more or less coherent entities that were increasingly interconnected to become a national rocknroll constituency.

The trade press, especially *Billboard*, ever responsive to industry trends, sought to track these events. In March of 1959, in recognition of the emerging rack jobber (a new type of distributor who provided a full current array of records from all labels to retail outlets), *Billboard* introduced "On the Racks." This feature reflected the separate audiences in supermarket locations, the regular LP market, bargain albums, the Extended Play record, and the kiddie disk. *Billboard* also sought to accommodate the age segregation in record sales and radio preferences. In July 1961, in addition to its "Hot 100 Best Selling Singles," *Billboard* introduced into its programming guide a listing of the top twenty "Easy Listening" singles and the top twenty "Teen Beat" records, an attempt to contain the teen's range of tastes. The difficulty of segregating the adult from the teen components of the white pop stream was too much, however. It was too subjective and became too tangled as all three major streams ebbed and flowed around and into each other. *Billboard* retreated from the attempt, withdrawing the Teen Beat chart four months later. Over the course of the next decade, the charts shifted fitfully in response to the industry's ever-changing market boundaries and its technological packing-merchandising practices. But never again was any popularity chart based on teenaged tastes. Rock never got its own chart in *Billboard*; the industry accepted the inescapable fact that rocknroll was to be housed, if barely tolerated, within the vehicles of the pop stream, charts and all.

The industry also accepted the equally recalcitrant fact that, while the 45 single served several markets and had a crucial exposure function on radio, the LP album was becoming the profit maker and star builder for the industry. So, in addition to the Hot 100's list for the 45 single, *Billboard* expanded its coverage of album sales. From a listing of "25 Best-Selling LP's" in 1957 and 1958, the charts proliferated and differentiated into separate listings of mono and stereo basic inventory, "action," and best-selling records, and were finally consolidated into a "150 Top LP's" chart in 1963 (which was expanded to a 200 listing by 1967). These charts reflected quite accurately the programming practices of AM radio, as well as the whole record configuration.

The Spread into the Cities

All these processes were not taking place in a vacuum; rocknroll was constantly growing and changing. It experienced moments of consolidation and collapse, meandering and sudden spurts forward. The period 1958–1963, for example, has been widely designated as having failed to achieve rocknroll's explosive promise, a "treacle time," the "death of rocknroll," a precursor of at least one other major pause point. It was clearly a moment of loss. Rocknroll's founding pantheon had been scattered. Peter Guralnick repeated a "familiar litany. . . . Elvis in the Army, Buddy Holly dead, Little Richard in the ministry, Jerry Lee Lewis in disgrace, and Chuck Berry in jail." [16]

It was also a period when the pop stream mobilized towards winning a piece of the youth market by constructing its own versions of what teenage music and teenage life were all about. The period also saw vigorous exploration and growth in black popular music. As Ray Charles, the strongest exemplar, worked toward bringing a secular black gospel presence to an adult black audience, others continued down the road toward the young white audience. Finally, and most invisibly, this period incubated the widest and deepest penetration of musical literacy and participation among young people the nation had ever seen.

All this action was carried out in the cities. New York, to begin with, was regaining influence and was the scene of what might be called "the battle of the producers," a contest that had a consequential geographical element. On one side was Mitch Miller; Phil Spector was on the other. Spector was a "bicoastal"—born in the East, in Los Angeles during his formative teen years, then back and forth between New York and Los Angeles to produce highly innovative records. He later spent time in London, invigorating the New York–London circuit. The rocknroll life was thus an international alternation of journey and pause. All the cities may have been different, but they were all interconnected.

Mitch Miller, however, reigned in New York. Beginning in 1956 when his first "Sing Along with Mitch" reached the number one spot on the pop album charts, he produced a long series of albums in this genre (bolstered by his own television show) that was primarily aimed at a family audience. Miller also had designs on the teenage market in a way that was different from rocknroll. He showed his instincts in this direction by securing for "The Yellow Rose of Texas" the lead position for the record

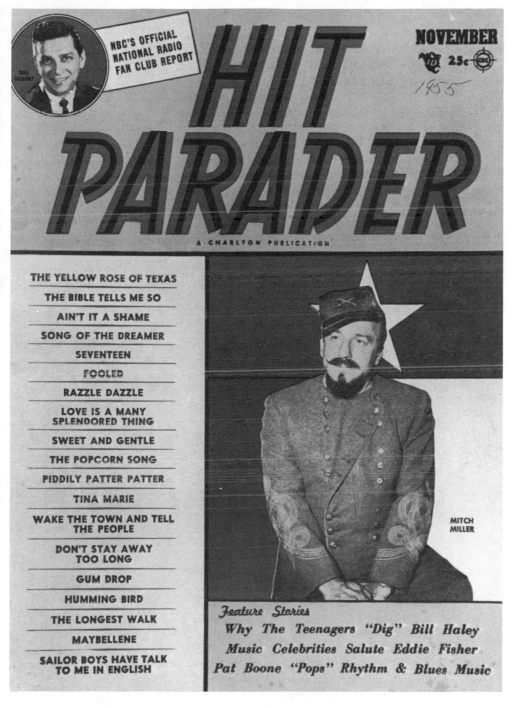

Figure 9-2. *HIT PARADER* Cover with Mitch Miller. Reprinted courtesy of *HIT PARADER* magazine.

and a cover picture of himself in *Hit Parader*, the foremost magazine since 1943 in providing popular song lyrics to teenagers (fig. 9-2).

Mitch was on the wrong side of rocknroll, as his presence and testimony at the congressional hearings of the late 1950s indicate. While his regal pronunciamentos blasted rocknroll up front, his backroom mechanics were transforming the twenty-eight-year-old, Detroit-born Al Cernik into Guy Mitchell (Miller's first name). Mitch coaxed five singles that made the charts (from 1956–1959), two of which crossed over to the R&B charts, out of this overaged fabrication of a rocknroll singer. Miller's strategy was as obvious as it was shrewd: Get a country sound, and give it a black beat and a clean, white, and hopefully young styling. Both of Guy Mitchell's number one pop records, "Singing the Blues" in 1956 and "Heartaches by the Number" in 1959, were simply covers of country and western chart toppers by Marty Robbins and Ray Price, respectively. The other records, "Rock-A-Billy" and "Knee Deep in the Blues," didn't go very far, even with the appropriate teen-appealing titles. Some time later, Columbia Records abandoned the southern strategy, "The Yellow Rose of Texas," the singalong, and Mitch himself.

Phil Spector was only about five years younger than his mentors, Leiber and Stoller, with whom he worked under Atlantic's umbrella. He had quickly moved from performer (the Teddy Bears) to producer, asserting, "my dream was to invent the word 'producer.'" [17] He thereby obliterated any debts to all previous producers—Mitch Miller, Sam Phillips, the steady hands at Atlantic, and all others. Spector, like Miller, participated in the transition from sheet music to the phonograph record, making the producer the steersman of all the popular musics. [18] Spector, though, became a genuine "maestro" of rocknroll, creating the Teddy Bears, Bob B. Soxx, the Crystals, the Ronettes, and the Righteous Brothers. On his own label he provided them with a string of hit records, fashioning a distinctive sound with his own hands on the studio controls. Later he produced hits for established rock stars, made and flashily spent a fortune. He was the model rock impresario before he was twenty-five years of age.

Spector achieved something more though. He produced that rare melding of superior technical craft with genuine emotional expression. His records and the techniques that generated them were benchmarks for the rock stream in later years, all the more surprising since its materials were the commercial sounds of AM radio. He was a perfect magpie, absorbing whatever he heard and saw from the full reservoirs that rocknroll had brought together since the early 1950s. If he took from Buddy Holly, from Chuck Berry, from the Monotones, and from the most obscure R&B singles, he transformed them into a unique sound signature that supported his performers in a seamless musical event. [19] The "wall of sound" made by repeatedly overdubbing the instruments of the studio band, thus transforming the tracks into "little symphonies for kids," was a serious innovation that did more than enhance the creative significance of the producer. Spector's records, in fact, built a wider and deeper rocknroll connection between R&B and pop, sufficient to transform the issue of "blue-eyed soul." Up to that point, being white and doing black had come from the country side, the main route passing from Elvis to Buddy Holly. Spector did it by providing a new sound and performers who mysteriously transcended a primary racial identification. Of Spector's main performing groups, at least half put their pop chart singles on the black pop charts as well; the Crystals put *all* of their records on both charts.

A final observation illustrating Spector's impresarial gift is pertinent here. Just as he opposed the introduction of stereophonic sound, Spector was not particularly fond of the album in any form. His reliance on the 45 rpm single presented him with a dilemma, however, which erupted from his characteristic urge to control everything. The single record had two sides. If he put two of his strong creations on a single, the *disk jockeys* would have the choice of playing either side. This would not only put control in other hands but would dissipate exposure and exploitation efforts. Since Spector apparently refused the usual practice of giving the "B" side to friends, using a "trunk" song, or aiming at another market (as Sam Phillips did on Elvis' releases), what was he to do? His solution was to let the studio musicians jam away as freely they wished, take the most appealing two minutes, put it on the B side, and give it an outrageous title. A disk jockey receiving a copy of a Phillies record with "Be My Baby" on one side and "Tedesco and Pittman" on the other would have little difficulty deciding which to play. Yet those B sides, "Bebe and Susu," "In Dr. Kaplan's Office," and so on, have their own integrity. At some point, some rock curatorial enterprise will collect all those B sides into a CD and embroider them with learned textual critique.

There was no victor in the contest between Mitch Miller and Phil Spector. They both spread out the carpet for subsequent producers, generating an estimable body of work and, in the normal course of things, burying themselves in the process.

New York offered other roads to rocknroll. One was the young group of writers, composers, and publishers who reinhabited the Brill Building (the music publishers' historic Broadway bastion). Midtown Manhattan was reconnecting its ties to record production. The most prominent group was the stable around Don Kirshner and Al Nevins of Aldon Music. This publishing house fed to major and independent record companies the work of a gifted group of young writers, including the young Canadian Paul Anka, Jeff Barry, Bert Berns, Neil Diamond, Harold

Greenfield, Ellie Greenwich, Gerry Goffin, Carole King, Jerome "Doc" Pomus, Neil Sedaka, Mort Shuman, and Cynthia Weil. Their songs worked the teenage market with every mixture of schlock and honest song. Those who also had performing talent were to become one branch of the singer-songwriter combination that was to dominate the sixties.[20]

The other significant New York contribution during these years was the folk scene in Greenwich Village, which was gathering a pool of talent and performance styles, and an audience that would soon attract the money men of the pop stream. That whole scene developed a set of attitudes that would expand the rocknroll ethos far beyond its teenage preoccupations.

In Philadelphia, another effort to catch the young audience appeared—the single-minded search for commercial gold in the young performer. Though the "Teen Idols" were a national phenomenon, it was the accidental density of black pop and pop-oriented radio stations and its well-trained audiences that gave Philadelphia a jump-start to the careers of Frankie Avalon, Fabian, Bobby Rydell, Leslie Gore, and perhaps ten to twenty others. Here were also the entrepreneurs operating new and small labels, such as Cameo and Chancellor Records, who provided innocuous teenage lyrics with a domesticated rocknroll sound to the unsinkable Dick Clark. His televised "American Bandstand" opened the eyes and ears of an even broader section of American young to a parade of young performers, including Buddy Holly, Sam Cooke, Jackie Wilson, and other young R&B acts. In addition, Clark hosted Bobby Vee, Connie Francis, Annette (of Mouseketeer origin), and others who were in and out of the teen-oriented movies of the moment, notably the beach and surf films. Anywhere from a quarter to half of the records put on the pop chart by the teen idols crossed over to the R&B charts (some moved over to country), but they were off all the charts by the early 1960s. Of more lasting importance (but who could tell at the time) were the more mature pop artists such as Bobby Darin, Eddie Fisher, Eydie Gorme, and Steve Lawrence.

The Detroit contribution to rocknroll at this stage came, of course, largely from the Motown label, whose founder, Berry Gordy, Jr., worked long and hard in the rhythm and blues vineyards to generate one of the first and strongest black music empires in the nation. That oft-recounted saga tells of the resoluteness of Motown's struggle to win a place in its own market and to storm the pop stream as well.[21] The success of their main performers, Smokey Robinson and the Miracles, the Supremes, Martha and the Vandellas, the Temptations, Marvin Gaye, the Four Tops, and others, owed much to the total preparation their productions entailed. This fine tuning relied on dance instruction from the longtime veteran Cholly Atkins, the creative writing-producing work of the Hollands and Lamont Dozier, and the gritty steadfastness devoted to securing performance opportunities for the performers. Although Motown's acts were all black-oriented, the tours and the venues in which they played stimulated rocknroll audiences' easy acceptance of black pop as part of their music.

Los Angeles made a significant mark during the late fifties and early sixties. With few exceptions, the large cities that had generated rocknroll under the tutelage of the hit-making disk jockeys fell silent. In Los Angeles, the most unpredictable combination of talents would suddenly come together to capture the entire nation's attention, or someone else's creative first step would be repeated to exhaustion. The movie industry's half-century tenure, and more recently television production, have augmented a large, diverse, and intricately interconnected music scene. From classical to jazz, a rich mix of composers, performers, technical support personnel, and above all a lively layer of entrepreneurial talent keeps the pot simmering. By 1957 Elvis' presence in the movies was a beacon. The two hundred or more rocknroll-tinged movies made from the early fifties onward extended the new stream's dance and performance vitality and the accessibility of its vocabulary.[22]

The more than twenty radio stations, old and new, large and small, in metropolitan Los Angeles served a mosaic of specialized audiences with a diverse musical menu to match. In this rich soup, it was not surprising to find, in the late fifties, a record industry that contained outposts of the major companies and a spurt of new small labels, along with the still-active independents so vital to rocknroll's birth. The loose network of performers, scenemakers, and producers in Los Angeles at that time is illuminated best, perhaps, from the circles flowing around Lou Adler. The future senior organizer of the Monterey Festival of 1967 was in 1958 "already circulating in the L.A. scene, . . . organizing dances at roller rinks."[23]

His friends and sometime partners included Herb Alpert, Lester Sill, Lee Hazelwood, and Phil Spector, all searching for new talent. In that atmosphere, it is not surprising that Adler was involved in the founding of a movement that would equip American youth with the tools of their own music making. He found two teenagers who, like thousands of others, had formed their own high school band. "Jan and Dean," as they came to be known, had recorded a tune of their own composition in Jan's parents' garage on a couple of home recorders. They sold it to a local record label (Arwin); it was picked up by a local disk jockey and, to everyone's surprise, made the national charts. In 1963 after a shift to the Liberty label, Jan and Dean's "Surf City" appeared on the pop charts, going to the top. Both these first two Jan and Dean records, it should be noted, also reached the rhythm and blues charts. This fact clearly suggests that the emerging southern California surfing culture contained in its music something sympathetic to black youngsters, few of whom would ever "hang ten." The sound is not hard to trace. Brian Wilson of the Beach Boys collaborated with Jan in the writing of "Surf City." The Beach Boys, almost ordinary teenagers (their father was a songwriter), were also new to the music game, having at that time (1963) only their second single on the national charts. Their strong musical influences had been Spade Cooley, the Four Freshmen, and Chuck Berry, another triangulation into rocknroll via the Wollensack tape recorder in the garage.

Brian Wilson, the creative omni-talent for the Beach Boys, had a self-taught writing and producing energy unmatched to that date. Like many less successful performers, he moved from amateur to professional status through on-the-job training. The Beach Boys' route was different from that taken by apprentices of a Phil Spector, who worked from the bottom up and from the inside of the industry. They were both, however, the heirs of Mitch Miller, Sam Phillips, and all the other A&R men in the independent record companies, who knew that the unit was no longer the song but the record.

Lou Adler was a friend of Brian Wilson's, part of the circle that bridged the gap between the professionals and the teenagers themselves. While Adler was handling the new Brill Building sound in Hollywood for Don Kirshner's Aldon Music, he was at the same time tracking the shifting Los Angeles youth scene. Later, with the Mamas and the Papas on his own record label (Dunhill) and with a close connection to the emerging rock and folk scene, Adler would be a key figure in rock's maturity.

Lee Hazelwood, though only briefly in the public eye, was a strategic member of the freelance producers of the late fifties. He crafted a string of about a dozen hit singles for Duane Eddy on the Philadelphia-based Jamie label from 1958 to 1962. Eddy's first hit, "Rebel Rouser," was a three-market crossover, appearing on the pop, R&B, and country charts in July 1958. It was his last record to make the country charts, but over the next five years he placed five more crossover singles on the rhythm and blues charts. His impact on the pop market was considerable, delivering twenty-six more singles and ten albums to respectable chart positions. Whitburn states that he was the "all time No. 1 rock and roll instrumental artist—worldwide." [24]

Duane Eddy, a guitar-toting son of Elvis, inspired hundreds of groups into a comparable instrumental style. Even the lusher guitar sound of Roy Orbison enhanced the instrumental side, although his vocal work anchors his reputation. The Pacific Northwest, in particular, spawned bands that had important national impact, the Ventures being the most prominent in the early sixties. Further down the West Coast, the surf scene grew stronger, riding the wave of guitar-based music. This rapid epidemic of simple guitar groups was a part and portent of the pop stream's other accomplishment in that otherwise fallow period: putting the guitar and the inexpensive tape recorder into the hands of more young people than had ever before participated in music.

The boy with his guitar became a national phenomenon. The models of rockabilly—rebellious, troubled, but still fun-loving music makers—found a broad range of expression. These bands were almost entirely white and reached mainly a white audience. Dance, romance, youth independence, and a blast or two at the adult world were their main concerns. Soon thereafter would come the girl with her guitar. The high school band playing tough rocknroll, the use of local, inexpensive, do-it-yourself recording studios, local radio exposure of 45 rpm singles, accessible dance floors and clubs with a supportive attitude towards not-too-polished performers, a strong reliance on "other people's music," all built a huge and musically literate audience base. The capital required for making a recording ranged from a few hundred to slightly more than a thousand dollars.[25] Access to an independent record company was easy. Local disk jockeys were still in daily contact with the record distributors, and the major record companies were clearly opening the doors to "deals" with independent producers. A local hit could make regional or even the national charts, as Don Howard's "Oh Happy Day" had in 1952. The garage bands learned to make their own "new ones out of old ones" without effort and to distribute them on the rash of new independent labels that sprang up steadily during the sixties.

The extent of amateur performers in the nation and their increasing participation in its musical life is shown in figure 9-3. The data trace the unit sales of fretted instruments (mainly guitars) compared to the piano and all other instruments combined from 1950 to 1971. The story is somewhat complex. Compared to the nongrowth of the piano market from 1950 to 1970 and the steady but slow market expansion of other instruments, guitar sales showed a more pulsed increase. A slow growth occurred at rocknroll's beginnings around 1950, but sales eventually doubled and held at a plateau from 1959–1962. Then, in 1963, even *before* the Beatles arrived on the scene, it should be noted, there began a huge growth. From 1963 to 1965, guitar sales doubled. After another plateau during rock's maturing, 1965–1969, came an even more explosive expansion. The total number of guitars strummed by American fingers grew by a third during the period 1969–1971 to yield a total of almost sixteen million pickers in the nation.

This deep reservoir of guitar players and, more significantly, of ex-guitar players, formed the critical mass of a knowing and paying audience for a guitar-driven youth music. The real guitar fans would bring to stardom the guitar virtuosos, who could do on record and on stage what the fans had wanted to do themselves. These stars came from every stream

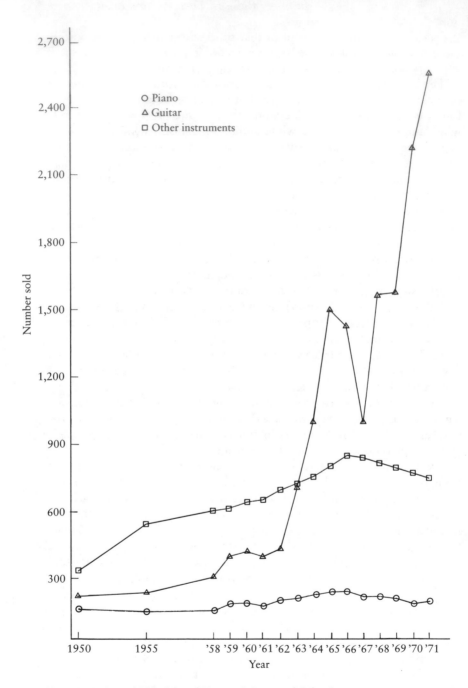

Figure 9-3. Annual Unit Sales of Pianos, Guitars, and Other Instruments, 1955–1971 (in thousands, rounded to the nearest thousand). Source: *Music USA: Review of the Music Industry and Amateur Music Participation, 1973* (Chicago: American Music Conference).

and from every part of the United States, and a particularly heavy crop came from the United Kingdom.

In the hands of the young, teenagers and college youth, this shared instrumental preference created a strong bond between rocknroll and the accelerating folk revival. Both were guitar-based musics, as was country music. Competence with the guitar, especially with some knowledge of its traditions, would be a passport into rock for a long time to come, just as competence with horns had served the swing era during the 1930s. In fact, the adulation given virtuoso guitar players whose repertoire was blues based was part of the reason black musicians held that rock of this style was old hat and not worthy of their attention.[26]

It is unfortunate that the available data do not show the popularity of electric versus acoustic guitars. In general, the electric guitar rarely reached beyond a quarter of all guitar sales, gradually increasing from the early 1960s to a peak in 1967 and declining gradually after that point.[27] Record executives would ignore those guitar players and that instrument only at their peril. Record sales during this entire period were also steadily on the rise, it will be recalled, indicating that listening and performing were not antithetical.

The Larger Context

As the Eisenhower years of relative calm and domestic steadiness ended, several other developments limited the attempts of the pop stream's upper echelons to scotch rocknroll. Their efforts to supersede the single record with the album, using the Caribbean and American folk idiom as material, would not stop the "fad." Performers such as Harry Belafonte and the Kingston Trio would become the inadvertent agents for the subsequent mingling of the folk stream and rocknroll. Rocknroll was on its way. It was able to survive the attacks of its enemies and was freed from the embrace of its friends. Country music was retreating into its geographical and cultural bastion, and black pop was heading towards the pop stream directly rather than through rocknroll. So the pop stream, like it or not, was where rocknroll would have to stay, using its charts and its exposure and exploitation machinery. Facing dilution rather than extinction, the supporters of rocknroll were prepared to nestle into a corner of pop, close to the boundaries of the other streams, ready to use all musics.

Central to the main story are three other events that took place in the beginning of the sixties. From hindsight's vantage, it is now clear that these events represented a new breath being drawn, a great journey begun. Actually, they involved several journeys, perhaps resumed more than started anew. They were not closely interrelated at that time, for they involved entirely different social and cultural spheres.

One of these events was the civil rights movement. There had been no quiescence after the 1954 Supreme Court decision on school segregation. The Montgomery, Alabama, bus boycott of 1955, in fact, began a steady acceleration in organization and resolution challenging every facet of racial discrimination in the nation. Young people of both races were drawn into those struggles, sometimes as allies, sometime as enemies. Their efforts to find justice were always accompanied by the sounds of popular music and its dances. Public commitment and private release lived side by side.

The second event was actually a process, the spread of American popular music into world markets. The oldest and most traveled tract was the London–New York short loop. From the early 1700s on, a steady two-way traffic had exchanged the literary, theatrical, and musical offerings of American and British culture. (The term "British" refers to the United Kingdom, the term is but a shorthand compression of the separate streams that brought Irish, Scottish, Welsh, and English song and story.) In addition, London, as metropole to a vast but shrinking imperial tradition, attracted considerable talent from its world outposts. As colonials made their marks in political, literary, and artistic London circles, their products and notoriety were carried to the equivalent sister circles in New York. The reciprocal contribution of the Caribbean to American music and politics, to mention an important case, was mediated largely from a London base.

In 1960 came a flash of recognition of this worldwide audience for popular music. The usual myopia of the music moguls and their troops required correction. One straightforward voice educating the parochial leaders of the vending industry came from George Albert, *eminance grise* of *Cash Box* (see figure 9-4). His message about the one world market may have seemed premature. There were, however, already indications that the specific pop stream traffic between London and New York was quickening. This loop was especially real for jazz, which had by the year 1960 laid down the bases for resuming its world routes that dated from World War I. As John Wilson recounts in his succinct coverage of the important jazz years 1950–1960, American jazz in all its phases of development created or revitalized viable local music scenes in every major European and Asian capital. Jazz clubs, record stores, periodicals, and concerts and tours by American or expatriate American performers were the vehicles and events that kept jazz alive during those years.[28] They also laid the groundwork for extending the world market referred to by *Cash Box*. The assemblage and subdivision of that world market into a series of "tours" and stopping points that accommodated the seven American streams was a growing reality by 1960.

The third event of that period was entirely different in scope and direc-

The Cash Box

FOUNDED BY BILL GERSH   Vol. XXI—Number 17   January 9, 1960

The Cash Box

(Publication Office)
1721 Broadway
New York 19, N. Y.
(Phone: JUdson 6-2640)
CABLE ADDRESS: CASHBOX, N. Y.

JOE ORLECK, President and Publisher
NORMAN ORLECK, VP and Managing Director
GEORGE ALBERT, Treasurer

EDITORIAL—Music
MARTY OSTROW, Editor-in-Chief
IRA HOWARD, Editor
IRV LICHTMAN, Associate Editor
ALLEN BURZOFSKY, Editorial Assistant
TED WILLIAMS, Statistical Editor
MIKE MARTUCCI, Statistical Assistant
POPSIE, Staff Photographer

ADVERTISING—Music
BOB AUSTIN, Director, New York
MARVIN SCHLACHTER, New York
BRUNO DUTKOWSKI, Art Director

MANAGERS
MARTY TOOHEY, Coin Machine Dept.
A. MARINO, Business Manager
T. TORTOSA, Circulation

———●———

CHICAGO
LEE BROOKS
Larry Karel
29 E. Madison St., Chicago 2, Ill.
(All Phones: Financial 6-7272)

———●———

HOLLYWOOD
JACK DEVANEY
Erv Malec
6272 Sunset Blvd., Hollywood 28, Cal.
(Phone: HOllywood 5-2129)

———●———

ENGLAND	BENELUX
NEVILLE MARTEN	SKIP VOOGD
9a New Bond Street	P.O. Box 1141
LONDON, W. 1,	THE HAGUE,
ENGLAND	HOLLAND
Tel: Hyde Park 2868	Tel: 070

GERMANY	
EVA MORELL	AUSTRALIA
Freiherr Vom Stein	RON TUDOR
Strasse 15	8 Francis St.
FRANKFURT,	HEATHMONT,
GERMANY	VICTORIA
Tel: 778381	

ITALY	SCANDINAVIA
VITTORIO	EVY FORSBERG
de MICHELI	Kaggeholmsvagen 48
Via P. Lomazzo 27	Tel: 59-46-85
MILANO, ITALY	STOCKHOLM-ENSKEDE
Tel: 341189	SWEDEN

———●———

SUBSCRIPTION RATES $15 per year anywhere in the U. S. A. Published weekly. Second class mailing privileges authorized at New York, N. Y.
ADVERTISING RATES on request. All advertising closes Friday at 12 Noon preceding week of issue. Advertisements subject to approval of publishers.
THE CASH BOX covers the entire music industry, ranging from retail record and music stores to disk jockeys, music publishers, recording artists, record manufacturers, music composers and arrangers, radio and TV stations, and all others allied to the music industry throughout the world.
THE CASH BOX covers the entire coin machine industry all over the world. Operators, jobbers, distributors, manufacturers and suppliers of automatic music vending, service and amusement machines are covered.
Copyright under the International Copyright Convention. All rights reserved by the Pan American Copyright Convention. Copyright 1960 by The Cash Box Publishing Co., Inc.

World Market— 1960

Recognition of the foreign market as a major area for record sales has made tremendous strides during the past year. However, the advances made in 1959 should be dwarfed by the tremendous growth we can expect in the next twelve months.

The record industry is today where the motion picture industry was half-dozen or so years ago. At that time, films were made strictly for the United States market and whatever additional grosses came in from Europe and the other continents, were considered gravy. Today, film producers are very much aware of the fact that a film often can gross more throughout the world than it can in our own country. And today top level thinking, when a new film is being produced, takes into consideration the appeal of potential members of the cast in other countries.

Although record manufacturers have not yet reached this stage, the past year has brought a noticed awakening of the extra profits that can be earned from a record that meets with broad acceptance in foreign lands.

During the past half year, we have heard some truly startling reports about singles, big hit singles in the U. S., which have sold more records abroad than here. Considering that some of these singles topped the 600,000 mark here, this should be sufficient evidence that the foreign market is one with which to be reckoned.

Another phenomenon which has been making its impression on record company brass of late is the artist who has been clicking with his waxings abroad even though he has not "made it" big here in the States. Such an artist is a valuable asset to any company since the cost of his sessions can, at least, be covered by the foreign sale and the artist can continue to be recorded without a loss. Should the artist "catch on" in the States, then, ironically, the U. S. sale will be the gravy. And from what we've been hearing in recent months, there are a number of recording artists in this category.

Almost every company today recognizes, in varied degrees, the importance of such markets as England, the European continent, Australia, etc. But in 1960 we can expect to see strides made in many other foreign lands.

Film companies are already well aware of a "World Market". It's just a matter of time before record companies recognize the world as one market.

Figure 9-4. *Cash Box* editorial, "World Market 1960." *Cash Box* 9 Jan 1960.

tion. This effort was indifferent if not hostile to the music of the young; rather, it was directed towards the "music of the spheres." On 25 May 1961, the young John F. Kennedy in the first spring of his New Frontier presidency announced to the Congress that Americans were going to the moon. The Russians had begun the manned space era a month before, 12 April 1961, with the successful orbital flight of cosmonaut Yuri Gagarin.[29] Three weeks later, Alan Shepard, one of the original group of American astronauts, completed a suborbital launch and safe return to earth. The space age invited the human species "to sail on this new sea," as Kennedy described it, but in a context of competition with the Soviet Union. Negotiations for a joint exploration of space had failed at that time. President Kennedy therefore announced that Americans would go to the moon, land a man there, and return him safely to earth. The competitive tone was unmistakable; we were going to the moon to beat the Russians.

The success of that decade-long effort would produce in 1970 the first major branching away from rock as the cultural banner of youth.

But in the early sixties, rocknroll had its music, its audiences, and the machinery to connect them. The work that young people had before them blended the music with the politics.

10. The Youth Movements

Never send a boy to do a man's job; send a girl"—that is, the difficult truth is that sometimes it is better to send the young to do a difficult job. If they fail in the task, what a cackle, what a fullness of venom will decry the effort. And the shrillness escalates if the boy—with the girl—go off and do something on their own. The re-writing of the history of the sixties reeks with this attitude.[1] Out of the silliness, the embarrassing utopian nonsense, the downright insulting and sometimes dangerous behavior of the young came results, nevertheless, that are undeniable. They are denied, however, just as the crimes and stupidities of the adults-in-charge are denied. A small example: the "all natural" breakfast foods so relentlessly advertised on television are the direct consequence of youthful experimentation with diets that were nutritious, not gambits for market share, chemically poisoned, or threats to the environment. A large example: the end of the Vietnam War.

The grown-ups of post–World War II America provided the youth with dreams of peace, freedom, and plenty, along with the tools to achieve them. When these well-intentioned instruments—the schools, the jobs, the nation's highest culture—were applied like a "boot," it was difficult to tell the screams of pain from the shrieks of joy. Those sounds, ever so much like rocknroll, had interchangeable lyrics. Jesse Belvin's "Earth Angel" (which the Penguins enlivened beyond the imitation by the Crew Cuts) was the first verse of more extended words provided by Herbert Marcuse, Paul Goodman, Norman O. Brown, Allen Ginsberg, Timothy Leary, Peter Marin, John Cage, Ken Kesey, Gary Snyder, Frank Zappa, and R. Crumb, among others.

The works of these social critics constituted replies to the command of the State that its artists and teachers prepare the young for citizenship. These learned guides finessed the official order by posing, each in his own way, the more important question: What is commitment, and what is release? It was that question that spun the dreams of the young, uniting them at one point; its answers divided them some time later. The matter was complicated because those adults, some quite young themselves, who would not obey the State could not agree among themselves. Their recipes for social change were all differing mixtures of art and politics; commerce was definitely in the background. Some threw out the arts altogether; others did the same with politics. Some took the view that art was not school, that artists had nothing to teach; artists just lived, and so should everyone else.[2] Others asserted that school had become the equivalent of a factory and the students had to act like (revolutionary) workers.[3] The students themselves were even more divided.

This chapter explores the movements that they made. Rock music can be understood, I believe, only in terms of its young audiences, who shared one important understanding from high school to college—that adult authority was suspect. There was a sure sense that adult institutions sought to harvest youth for purposes not their own and in ways not to their liking. There was an equally sure belief that there were alternative roads to life besides those announced by parents, teachers, and so on, even if those paths were only dimly seen.

The Structural Base for Alternative Youth Perspectives

The history of youth movements in the western world is many stranded. Sometimes the focus rests on the *teachers* of a generation strategically placed among the warring factions of adult power; Socrates and his spokesman Plato were in actuality the targets of a curriculum battle. Sometimes youth movements derive from the students themselves, rebelling against something specific to their interests or participating in more general uprisings. From plain bread riots of the seventeenth century to the nationalistic movements that swept Europe in the nineteenth century, youth and students were in the thick of it. Their participation moved, in the twentieth century, to traditional societies in the process of freeing themselves from colonial rule. Beneath the specifics of geography or social structure, all generational conflict, it is held, is generic, endemic, but rarely fatal.[4]

In the United States, however, there has been no extended record of youth rebellion. Somehow, the dethroning of cruel adult authority or repudiation of faithless or failed fathers never incited the sons and daughters to more than passing rebellious episodes.[5] Thus it was a thin soil that nurtured the youth movements of the 1950s and 1960s. Young people could not look to the history of their colleagues of the past; they thus looked all around their on-going world for answers. The generational transmission of culture became entangled with the generational succession of power, producing a thoroughly perturbed period.

Rocknroll during the 1950s was one of the main banners under which the search for alternatives was conducted in the high school. During the sixties, the search moved to the college campus and beyond. The music moved as well, and as it matured into rock, teenaged and college-aged youngsters merged into a seamless category—"youth." This chapter traces that process, which was only partially a musical story. The process was actually sociological and gives specificity to Kenneth Kenniston's insight that, in addition to the familiar stage of "adolescence" announced at the turn of the century, there was in the 1960s a definite period of the life-cycle called "youth."[6] The youth category included adolescents in high school but also college students, working young people, those in the armed services, and those between schools or jobs or adrift. And there was a lot of drift.

"Youth" posed anew questions as to personal identity and the meanings and boundaries of family, neighborhood, even nation. These questions were the issues on the agenda, as was the serious underlying question of what was work and what was play. The answers most definitely became political because national and world events brutally reached into young lives across increasingly distant age-graded boundaries. Youth responded appropriately by seizing the age category and using it as a weapon against the adults. The groundwork had been laid earlier. Age-grading, appearing in selected institutions beyond the family after World War I, was spread further into American society during the 1930s and 1940s by the consumer industries reawakening from the Depression. The women's garment trade in particular showed the way, it will be recalled, by marginally differentiating its product lines by age. The schools then reinforced age segregation from kindergarten onwards. Whether by design or not, some legal matters became actively challenged youth policies. The draft was the main one, the laws governing liquor service following close behind, with voting age also a consequential matter in 1968.

The founding structural element of the story is demographic. One part, discussed earlier, was that a significant sector of the earliest rocknroll generation came from families in which no one had served in the armed forces in either World War II or in the Korean War (like Elvis himself). These youngsters were, as a consequence, immunized from the blood-sanctioned authority of the adults who had been in those wars. These young people found in rocknroll a legitimating and guilt-free commitment to alternative values.

The second and familiar demographic element was the baby boom, which began after the war. The birth rate in the year 1946 and 1947 showed a greater increase over all the previous years since 1929. In just one year, 1946, the annual birth rate increased by 20 percent for whites; in 1947 it rose by 12 percent over 1946. The birth rate then declined for four straight years, after which it continued at a high level until the late 1950s. For non-whites (about 95 percent blacks) the birth rates had been substantially higher than for whites since World War I, but they increased much more slowly, albeit more steadily, after 1945.[7] In absolute terms, the number of children under five years of age increased by over 5.5 million between 1940 and 1950, most of the increase coming in the last half of the period. This growth represented an increase of 53 percent.[8] This massive growth of the young was not, however, distributed equally in the population. Surprisingly, the greatest increases in the birth rate were "more pronounced among those with more schooling (and status)."[9] Whatever middle-class life had to offer the nation, the nation was going to get a lot more of it.

The entire educational apparatus, from kindergarten through high school, to the colleges and universities, was soon pressed to expand its facilities. There is no better way to appreciate this thrust than to note the following figures: In 1945, at war's end, there were almost 20 million Americans between the ages fourteen and twenty-four. Only 730,000, less than 4 percent, were in college. Over 7 million, 37 percent, were in school below the college level, and the largest proportion, almost 60 percent, were not in school at all. In just five years, by 1950, the number of young people in college had doubled. By 1960, a decisive moment for both rocknroll and the youth movements, the institutions of education had enfolded half the young population—almost 3 million in college, more than 10 million in junior and high schools. By 1970, at the peak of rock's maturity, the height of countercultural activity, and the greatest strength of youth's political wing, there were 6 million college students and over 15 million in junior and high schools. Together, those in school constituted about 65 percent of young people fourteen to twenty-four years of age.[10] The proportion of young people packed into schools and in the military had, since the end of World War II, swollen from about 15 percent to almost a quarter of the entire population.[11] A tremendous human reservoir was ready to burst its seams.

The launching of the Russian Sputnik in 1957 increased the influence the educational system could exert in young lives and offered youth an entirely new perspective. The American space program that was instantly called for included the National Defense Education Act. It pumped millions of dollars into teacher training, the provision of laboratory equipment, and the organization of science and math programs in schools at every level all over the country. Inadvertently, this huge effort stopped, to some extent, the draining of educational resources from the inner cities, and the suburban expansion now had a high-priority competitor that brought science and space exploration to everyone. The space program was thus provided with a wide base for future recruitment and support. The new job title "astronaut" was soon to have a visually compelling embodiment in Alan Shepard, the first American in space. The long-running TV series from Cape Canaveral, culminating in the triumphal moon landing of 1969, was an enormous educational advertisement. It provided another alternative for youth, even though its devotees, the "nerds," "grinds," and "squares," would be the butt of disdainful jokes.

It is no mystery how youth had become such a potent force in the nation, given this explosive increase in their numbers, their containment within common institutional frameworks, and, most importantly, a mobilized self-consciousness about their life situation. The psychological aspects are more problematic. How could the passive conformity of the fifties turn into the active movements of the sixties? One common answer is that the permissiveness engendered by popular child-rearing practices prepared the young only for self-indulgence and petulant outbursts when the going got rough. Dr. Benjamin Spock is still taking it on the chin for the entire decade. It is more likely that more specific things were happening to different groups of youngsters. Some turned rebel because of poor academic performance and anticipated downward mobility.[12] This faction included, it should be noted, the growing number of "drop-outs"—poor and mainly black kids who were in fact pushed out of the schools. Others, raised in a family pattern that emphasized humanistic values beyond achievement in the marketplace, repudiated the increasingly institutional pseudo-rationality that treated students as products to be batch-processed.[13] Whatever the individual motivation, American youngsters were being gripped by social policies that tightened too closely about them.

Alternative Paths

Although teenagers created their own culture within the locked framework of their high schools, they never found during the 1950s either an organizational form or a belief system that could bring them together into a coherent social movement. They were a dispersed or at best a locally aggregated mass that was activated by strong but elusive forces, the greatest of which was youth itself (for them a gift easy to squander). But never before had that mass been so neatly and visibly packed together for the harvest. After World War II, some literary artists sensed the coming struggle youth would engender. Colin MacInnes, writing in England, was one who sensed it.

... Youth has power, a kind of divine power straight from mother nature. All the old tax-payers know of this because, of course, for one thing, the poor old sordids recollect their own glorious teen-age days, but yet they're so jealous of us, they hide this fact, and whisper it among themselves. As for the boys and girls, the dear young absolute beginners, I sometimes feel that if they only *knew* this fact, this very simple fact, namely how powerful they really are, then they could rise up overnight and enslave the old tax-payers, the whole damn lot of them—toupets and falsies and rejuvenators and all. . . .[14]

The adults, half realizing that power, half realizing their own loss, could do nothing but press their institutional containers more fiercely upon youth. Adult authority proclaimed crises of teenage criminality and irresponsibility while confronting a maddening recalcitrance: "Slaves, slum dwellers, teen-agers, and enlisted men do, indeed, often display a defensive stupidity and irresponsibility, which quickly abates in situations which they feel to be free of officious interference, with which they can deal, by means of their own institutions, in their own way."[15]

The social life around rocknroll was, from this viewpoint, a pitifully thin and cynically manipulated framework for that magical immanence of youth to celebrate itself. Nevertheless, it was a world of youth's own making, even if only a partial shield against adult incursions. The high school was not a "total" institution in the same sense a prison was, even though the buildings looked a lot alike. Within the high school grew a student-managed social structure and a cultural dynamic that reached to the walls and beyond. That social structure was, as described earlier, the three-fold division of the leading crowd, the great majority of ordinary kids, and the rough, radical, and Bohemian minority cliques.

A dynamic process allowed any of these smaller groups to achieve practically anything they wanted in the school, except, of course, a working relationship with the teachers and the principal. The reason was the "catch up" game; the leading crowd had to accede to or bless the preferences, musical or political, of the "hoodlums," "beatniks," and on occasion even the radicals, if it was to maintain its leadership. Not all matters were acceded to, of course, mostly those things in the realm of release rather than those of commitment. So Jerry Lee Lewis and Little Richard were included along with Elvis, at the dangerous pole of rocknroll, with Pat Boone and the subsequent teen idols at the other, safer end. Rocknroll was the major cultural outlet offering teenagers conventionalized and more acceptable versions of the more fully committed outlaw, radical, and Bohemian responses to the times. The music and the dancing may have been weapons, but they were also a safety valve, substituting symbolic action for more dangerous behavior in the streets.

The despised alternatives would sometimes come together, sometimes diverge, as the separate strands underwent their specific trajectories of surge and decline. They were gradually shaped into a homogenized melange. An American youth culture was forming. Not only distinctive dress styles, including preeminently hair, but a wide variety of visual and ideological guides were being fabricated in high schools and colleges to mark the boundaries of the spreading alternative culture. Many voices were articulating weighty rationales why each of the alternative visions should be enacted.

Some of these voices were simply announcing the headlines. In 1954, Dien Bien Phu in distant Vietnam fell to Ho Chi Minh's troops. Four years later, the first Americans would fall in that country, beginning an agony that was not to end for another decade and a half. Also in 1954, the Supreme Court decided *Brown* v. *Board of Education* in favor of ending legal segregation. Just one year later, prestigious black political forces in Montgomery, Alabama selected Rosa Parks to challenge the segregation practices in that city and invited Martin Luther King, Jr., to join the struggle. Both accepted, and thus began the work that also took fifteen years to climax. The peace and civil rights movements, with common dates of activation in separate places, would later meet and join forces for several consequential moments.

Within the realm of ideas there were also stirrings in the fifties that would subsequently arm the youth movement, either directly or by trickling down the age ladder. Even the very young were targeted, for the publishing industry had caught the drift of age segregation. By 1957, fully a third of the publishers surveyed by *Publishers' Weekly* were carrying specifically teen-oriented books in their juvenile lists.[16] Hardly any of these would come up to J. D. Salinger's *Catcher in the Rye*, published in 1951, in quality or appeal, but books addressed to the young heightened their awareness of the distinct position named for them in society. New publications appeared to challenge the general complacency. In politics arose the *Village Voice*, *Dissent*, *Ramparts*, and *Liberation*. SANE and a flurry of nonviolent civil rights organizational voices chimed in.

In popular sociological books, David Riesman's *The Lonely Crowd*, Vance Packard's *The Status Seekers*, Sloan Wilson's *The Man in the Gray Flannel Suit*, and William Whyte's *The Organization Man* pointed to the penetration of a corporate-driven society. In a more literary voice, Gore Vidal offered a spleeny view of the inside of society, while Allen Ginsberg's *Howl*, Jack Kerouac's *On the Road*, and Norman Mailer's *The White Negro* pointed outward with road signs announcing Hip versus Square.

Further afield, some previously unvoiced constituencies spoke on gender and sexual matters, forces that would later coalesce into fighting phalanxes. Simone de Beauvoir's *The Second Sex* and Betty Friedan's *The Feminine Mystique* reopened the women's struggle. The appearance of *Playboy*, with an ideology as up-front as its pictures, was not simply an affront to conventional prudery. Hugh Hefner laid a time bomb alongside American hypocrisy, exploding some years later in the so-called sexual revolution. The widespread use of "the pill" (first introduced in 1960) gave women not only a technological basis for greater sexual freedom but provided an actualizing experience for their autonomy in other realms as well. The Mattachine Society published *ONE*, announcing a gay presence in the political arena.

In addition to these ideological materials, some of the assembling youth culture would soon augment their thinking with ideas from Albert Camus, Frantz Fanon, Alan Watts, and William Burroughs. Then, one of their own, Jerry Farber, made any implicit understanding quite clear with his *Student as Nigger*. Some teachers were less academic, such as the belatedly canonized Lenny Bruce, and some used more modulated voices, such as Mort Sahl and Dick Gregory. For the young explicitly, there was *Mad* magazine, an irreverent and undogmatic forum for a wide range of social commentary. *Mad* also facilitated the underground press in that Paul Krassner, the founder of *The Realist*, said, "I found *The Realist* as a *Mad* for adults."[17] This paper, though one of a kind, spread as if by spontaneous contagion. At its peak in the late sixties, there were an esti-mated three thousand underground papers alone in the high schools all across the United States, and more than three hundred serving larger publics.[18]

The comics revival included creative figures such as Robert Crumb, whose *Zap Comics* and its off-shoots were an especially important teach-ing tool for the creation and dissemination of youth ideological currents. Largely based in loose high school networks, thousands of young car-toonists laid out the dilemmas of the times and probed for answers, as shown in the reproduced 1969 cartoon by a thirteen-year-old. This visual inventory mirrors quite accurately the alternatives to adult life talked about in most high schools and colleges in the sixties. Each would have its own following and its moment in the sun (fig. 10-1).

There were other alternatives to be sure, and a bewildering array of more specific pathways among the main ones mentioned. Within them all was a set of choices reflecting much older and much deeper issues. How much should one live for the moment; how much should one think ahead to the future? Where are one's energies to be placed—in the world of work or in free celebration of love, art, drugs, and all other paths to ecstatic release? What makes the moral community, and where is it? Is the right course engagement with or retreat from the forces of the adult world?[19]

The young people who grappled with these questions did not, could not, abandon their cultural inheritance. Those traditions gave the over-whelming majority of them some kind of a religious grounding; their biology gave them some kind of sexual interest.[20] Rocknroll probed di-rectly those religious-sexual minglings. The youth movements of the six-ties would explore every kind of sexual notion and its religious shadow—

Figure 10-1. Cartoon: "Life in the Counter Culture." With permission of Michael M. Ennis.

Figure 10-2. Students at Jesus Rally. From *Life* magazine, June 30, 1972, p. 42, Photo: Jack and Betty Cheetham.

Figure 10-3. The Chicago Plaster Casters. Photo: Baron Wolman.

androgyny, multiple relationships, Satanism, the occult. Every excessive personal cult with a pan-emotional fervor would get a hearing. For example, the white plaster casts of a closed hand with one upraised finger carried by young celebrants of the 1972 Great Jesus Rally in Dallas, Texas, symbolized the religious direction of such passions manifested by the seventy thousand kids from all over the nation who came to celebrate with Billy Graham, Johnny Cash, Rita Coolidge, and Kris Kristofferson during this religious festival. One cannot view those upraised fingers without a sliver of recognition of a similar plaster cast from the previous decade. Whether or not the "four high school students [who] made plaster-of-Paris versions of the 'one way' symbol and carried them to all the meetings"[21] knew about the Chicago Plaster Casters is not important.

The erect plaster digit could thus be adapted to serve either God or sex. The same symbolism had a collective manifestation. *Life* magazine ends its story of the Dallas Jesus Rally with a two-page photograph of the final night when seventy thousand candles were held in upraised hands—two pages of gleaming dots of light. Anyone who has attended a rock concert knows of the strong feeling evoked when thousands of flaming cigarette lighters are held aloft at the end of the concert.

The artistic representations of the tensions inherent in sexual and religious zeal back in 1968 by no means resolved the issue. Less than a decade later, and again in Dallas, the general manager of gospel radio station KWJS announced he would lead teenage participants from twenty-four area churches in a rock record-smashing rally. It was being held to call the music industry's attention to the fact that popular music had fallen into a

... deep void of bestiality, sexual debasement and violence. ... A devilish but obvious question facing the evangelical promotor ... is what kind of music to play. It sounds like a silly question, but he wanted music that would attract the kids yet not the kind of music they were asking be destroyed. ... The planners settled on a contemporary gospel sound and a group that used the instruments and rhythms of a rock band.[22]

Elvis and rocknroll can't be blamed for all the ways religion and sex accommodate their entanglements. The young in the sixties must be given some credit, though, for the boldness and the resoluteness with which they put them together.

Such explorations, testing the alternatives to the adult scripts, were carried by the high school graduates of the fifties into college in the sixties. To a considerable extent, the same structure and dynamic was rebuilt to fit the college campus. As historians of the sixties have noted, the leading elements of the Students for a Democratic Society (SDS) and related student activists came from a secure background of middle- and upper middle-class professional and well-educated parents.[23] In their high schools, they were the sunny, competent, take-charge kids who also be-lieved, when they got there, that college was their oyster. If it worked in the high school for individual interests, it would work on the college campus for larger social matters. One of the SDS leaders made this state-ment about that experience after he had learned a thing or two.

My high school . . . was a finishing school for men and it was meant to teach the sons of the rich how to rule the empire. . . . I ran most of the extra-curricular activities—debating, newspaper, press club, drama workshop—and hustled my way out of classes and required athletics. Only later did I see that it was I who had been hustled. I learned the hustling game. I am afraid that when my ideas shifted allegiance from nuclear physics to the Blacks and the Vietnamese that at first I shifted en masse all my ways of operating. I organized my corner of the movement the way I had organized the newspaper, top down, . . . with structures that looked democratic, but let hustlers with my traits, chiefly other men, rise to the top. . . .[24]

The leading crowd, it is clear, was to be a major player in the maturing youth movement. So would the radical and Bohemian minorities as they developed their more mature forms. The rough crowd, the criminal alter-native, was largely sustained by J. Edgar Hoover's publicity machine, by the movies, and by the sociologists fueling the "juvenile delinquency" fires. They were a definite reality and would find expression in the sixties in the too often romanticized Hell's Angels motorcycle life. The Diggers in San Francisco, at that same moment, were also rooted in the experi-ence of the high school criminal element, if Emmett Grogan's life story is to be believed. This New York urchin went from child prodigy in theft to leader of the Diggers' similar game, this time in the service of providing free food and shelter to the flower children.[25]

The remnants of the adult social movements of the 1930s had but a shadowy influence on the youth movements of the sixties. In their heyday, those left-wing movements had represented the adult working man and his family. Even such youth formations as the American Youth Congress as well as the regular youth outcroppings of the left were "auxiliaries," firmly under the discipline of their adult leadership. After World War II, this situation would change. In spite of the reflex attempts of the Old Left to control the returning veterans and the postwar college youth, most eluded its organizational and ideological grasp. Between Senator Joseph McCarthy's anticommunist crusade and its own frozen and bankrupt thinking, the Old Left was politically destroyed and its liberal friends silenced.[26]

The New Left offered a different diagnosis and remedy, premised on the observation that American youth had become a social formation of considerable economic weight. Some people estimated its consumer value in 1970 to be $40 billion.[27] Youth supported an educational establish-ment valued at ten times that amount.[28] With the growth of that educational Gargantua, American youth interests were gradually separated from any and all other social groups. Within the schools and college campuses, students invented their own organizational forms, belief systems, and culture, set within specific territorial enclaves. That whole youth entity was readily assimilated into a classical Marxist definition of a modern social class. As the young, especially college students, felt more and more boxed in, they behaved more and more like a class and, by the late sixties, were driven by their own spokesmen and teachers into believing they were not only a class but a revolutionary class, one whose mission was to deliver the nation from the oppressive, corrupt, and doomracing adult establishment.

Not many young people believed in the revolutionary class business, and the cultural side of the youth movement was not shy in telling the "politicos" to stuff it. In turn, the "freaks" and "hippies" took a lot of heat from the political activists. They were regarded as unreliable, having no stomach for the confrontation with the police and the "class enemy." This quarrel was the main fault line that would later divide the youth movement. Yet, the overwhelming majority of kids were somewhere in the middle, just trying to understand, trying to get on with their lives, but not afraid to jump right into the pudding. All students and other young people were united in their response to bureaucratic adult authority. "Do Not Fold, Spindle, or Bend" was more than a button worn by the students at Berkeley; it was youth's diagnosis of the entire social structure's smothering hand on their lives.

The Movements Pick Up Speed

The college youth movements after World War II started almost from scratch.[79] Their freshness and broad outlook came from the war veterans pouring into American colleges and universities on the wave of the GI bill. These new students had a surprisingly global perspective, which they translated almost immediately into organizational form with the founding of the many college chapters of the American Veterans Committee and, more importantly, the establishment of the National Students Association (NSA) at the University of Wisconsin at Madison in 1947.[30]

The NSA founding convention attracted almost a thousand delegates and observers from 350 colleges and universities. The enthusiasm for a national student organization easily overrode all the differences in experience and perspective among the students. Not even the political maneuvering of the radical Left and Catholic leadership against each other (they were a small minority of the delegates) could dampen the sense that a great democratic, national network of students was being formed in a shared cultural moment of surprising intensity.

A significant aspect of those Madison meetings was the ubiquitous presence of folk music. Folk performers, some of whom were students, some in that limbo between amateur and professional status, charmed the delegates, imprinting them with the entwined heritage of world folk music and world political concerns. Both the political role of the NSA and its student services would suffer fatal damage in March of 1967 with the revelation by *Ramparts* of its crippling and ignominious subversion by the intelligence agencies of the Federal government.[31]

Towards the end of the 1950s, and out of the wreckage of the Old Left, there began to appear in the colleges and universities local nodes of student activism, which took several forms. One was the organization of student journals. They appeared in considerable number; Feuer lists twenty-seven that appeared after the war.[32] They spanned the range of commitments to art, scholarship, professionalism, and politics in a variety of mixtures. *New University Thought*, begun in 1960, was an early and leading example. Its editors, almost all graduate students in Chicago, went on to productive careers in academe and politics. Their seriousness of purpose in developing a principled politics blended with a commitment to professional careers is shown in the following excerpts from the editorial in their first issue (Spring 1960) and in its table of contents (fig. 10-4). Its purpose was clearly stated.

In a world facing enormous problems, including threatened nuclear death, American intellectuals, students and professionals have withdrawn from participation in public life. Valuable knowledge and training, which could be directed toward solving social and intellectual problems, become increasingly overspecialized; professions and disciplines are isolated from one another and from society. Our generation has been accused of being "silent" because it has not produced any ideological and political movements.

New University Thought is a political magazine. It is also a scholarly journal. And it is a journal of opinion. These functions appear to be disparate only because they have been so long dissociated from one another in our overspecialized thought.

The editors of *New University Thought* are students, young faculty members and professionals. We are from the natural and social sciences, as well as the humanities. Our readers, like the editors, span three different groups within the "young" generation—veterans of World War II whose careers, though established, are still new; the student generation of the Korean War, many of whom are still in graduate schools; and the undergraduate students in colleges and universities. You who read this magazine will also participate in it. More than merely reading *New University Thought*, the readers must themselves identify problems, analyze them, write articles, suggest solutions and, with the aid of others involved in the magazine, carry these solutions into action. . . .

The common characteristic of the articles in *New University Thought*, however diverse their subjects, will be their *radical* mode of analysis, radical in the original sense of "going to the root." . . . We look forward to academic and professional careers. We would like to live in a community of intellectuals, a community which does not suffer from internal fragmentation or alienation from the

new university thought

spring, 1960

volume 1, number 1

Published and
copyright 1960,
by New University Thought
Publishing Company

mailing address
909 East 55th Street
Chicago 37, Illinois

New York representative
Robert Stein
615 West 113th Street
New York City

subscription rates
one year $1.50
outside of U.S. $2.00
two years $2.75
outside of U.S. $3.25

editors
Nicolette Carey
Mady Chalk
Otto Feinstein
Martin Goldsmith
Lawrence Landry
Ralph Nicholas
Leo Stodolsky
Donald Villarejo
Carl Werthman

managing editor
Nicolette Carey

designer
Hap Smith

associate editors
Claire Arguelles
Arlene Hirsch
Robert Jacobs
Paul Levy
David Margolies
Richard Merbaum
Cynthia Smith

legal advisor
Albert Sciaky

corresponding editors
Donald Anderson
Carlie Anderson
James Flynn
Keith Guy
Robert Perlman
Linda Rosenberg
Joel Rosenthal
Robert Stein

contents

Figure 10-4. Table of Contents, *New University Thought* (1960).

larger society. . . . We want to begin creating this community, and we think it can be done at least in part through the medium of *New University Thought*.[33]

The neighborhood around the University of Chicago had, since war's end, nurtured its nonmatriculated "University of the Street," which included rabbit-warren apartment houses and a variety of coffee houses, local bars, community theater, and the like. Every university town in America had such a "scene." Along the tree-shaded streets of Hyde Park in the 1950s there walked (probably headed for Jimmy's) not only the young men and women who wrote that editorial but also an overlapping bunch who founded the Compass Players (subsequently Second City), one of the nation's first and most influential, postwar improvisational theaters.[34]

In 1955, the very year rocknroll became the banner in the high school the Compass Players moved to the South Side (55th near Greenwood). The group was composed of a highly charged and diverse set of talents in search of an audience.[35] The audience that did assemble to see Paul Sills, Severn Darden, Mike Nichols, Elaine May, Andrew Duncan, Barbara Harris, Eugene Troobnick, Paul Sand, Mina Kolb, Anthony Holland, Shelley Berman, and others was largely made up of students and ex-students. The range of material was broad, held together by an explicit commitment to contemporary American life.

It was a church we were running in Hyde Park. I have met girls and boys who were ten years younger than I who said they first woke up in Playwrights Theater Club or the Compass because it was their first contact with situational morality. And also it was a very heavy attack on their parents going on all the time at the Compass.[36]

They acted out teenaged life in exactly the same way the Shirelles sang "Will You Still Love Me Tomorrow?" (1961), at almost the exact same time. Nichols recalls that time:

I said "Let's do two teen-agers in the back of the car" and we did and it was a terrific scene and then it kept changing and growing and we kept adding to it. . . . It's just two kids screwing around in the back seat and getting their arms tangled up, talking about what they talk about and it had the line in it where she says "If we went any further, I know you wouldn't respect me" and I say "Oh. I'd respect you like *crazy*! You have no *idea* how I'd respect you".[37]

What Elvis and rocknroll had done for teenagers nationally, the Compass was doing for the college-aged audience in the evolving Chicago "scene."

The mixture of culture and politics may have been adventitious, but gradually it all hung together. It was not difficult for the basic theatrical attitude of the Compass, exemplified by their earlier productions of Brecht's *Caucasian Chalk Circle* and Berg's *Wozzeck*, to mix with folk music evenings. This "Tonight at 8:30" series briefly included Omar Shapli and Mike Nichols, both of whom worked at WFMT, one of the nation's first FM radio stations. Under a "liberal" management, the station broadened its classical music fare to invite the Chicago literary scene into the city's living rooms. Studs Terkel, Chicago's indestructible, unbuttoned boulevardier, hosted a series of essentially freeform interviews, musical potpourris, and soliloquies. On Saturday night, WFMT's "Midnight Special" was an eclectic show of the current folk recordings and occasional interviews with touring performers.

The station was an important element of a short loop connecting radio to the several folk nightclubs then operating. It created a record-buying and listening home audience for the increasing number of folk *albums*, making a small national market in a few metropolitan areas. The clubs had an out-of-home audience mainly in the Near North Side. This area, just above the Loop's businessmen's night spots and restaurants, had begun in the 1950s to develop a nightlife and a shopping area with chic art galleries that catered to the young married professionals, working middle-class singles, the graduate student crowds from Northwestern in Evanston, and the University of Chicago on the South Side.

The Gate of Horn was the leading folk club in town. Paul Sills had been house manager there briefly in the 1950s, followed after a time by Albert Grossman, a Chicago boy who quickly learned the scene. As manager of the Gate of Horn, Grossman participated in the revival of old black performers, especially Big Bill Broonzy, and young folk performers such as Odetta, whom he managed and took to New York in 1958. Soon afterward he began a career as a personal manager, serving clients such as Bob Dylan, Peter, Paul, and Mary, Paul Butterfield, Janis Joplin, and others. The college cultural and political scene, in short, quickly spread into the rest of Chicago's nightlife. As the Second City succeeded the Compass Players, it continued its critical opposition to the straight adult life, diffusing its stance and its personnel into the places youth would gather. The Compass/Second City structure became a training ship and a placement agency for the talent that tumbled forth on the wave of its success.[38]

The University of Chicago continued to be an important place where the student movement put its music together. Within a few brief years, three important concerts were held at the university's Mandel Hall. In 1962, Joan Baez stopped there during her first national tour, a fresh young folk singer whose shy manner did not obscure the strength and clarity of purpose in her program. The repertoire was a balance of the old "singer of songs" and the new political awareness, both carried in a personal voicing. She swept away a full house, packed even to the stage, that was filled with chairs, leaving Baez almost entirely surrounded by the audience. The program and the setting were emblematic of the beginning of an important journey.[39] In that same year, Muddy Waters did the same in another concert at Mandel Hall, as did Paul Butterfield and his Blues Band. These concerts indelibly linked the folk, black pop, and rock streams together. Thus, the new politically engaged folk stream, the new white electric rocknroll based on old black pop and jazz, and the black carrier of that tradition pointed the way to an authentic synthesis of the movement's cultural base.

In New York, Los Angeles, Ann Arbor, and in perhaps a dozen cities in which there was a major university, college-aged youth were assembling into loose agglomerations that were part audience, part social set, part social movement. Rocknroll's creative pulse also shifted to the college campus, helped by the music industry's turn to the *album* instead of the single and by the pop stream's enfolding of the folk stream. The college student culture held the spotlight as it formed a new and barely definable synthesis.

Politics and Culture Conjoin

The political part of that synthesis was the result of *New University Thought* and other similar journals releasing a logic that instantly burst into organizational form.[40] Political groups were founded in two different places in characteristically different ways. One was the Students for a Democratic Society (SDS) in 1960, based initially at the University of Michigan, Ann Arbor.[41] Within months there were up to thirty chapters of SDS on paper, some being little more than that. Paper or not, the SDS cadres enabled students on hundreds of campuses to organize and express themselves loudly and effectively for the next decade.

The other place of organizational importance was Greensboro, North Carolina, where, on 1 February, 1960, four black students sat down at the Woolworth's lunch counter ordinarily reserved for whites only. Their arrest flashed through North and South the message that direct, nonviolent action to end segregated public facilities was the tactic most likely to advance the cause. Within a few months there had been at least sixty sit-in activities all through the mid-South and the border states. By April the Student Non-Violent Co-ordinating Committee (SNCC) was formed under the guidance of Ella Baker at a conference sponsored by the Southern Christian Leadership Conference (SCLC).[42]

Both white and black youth movements, on the campus and off, accomplished several remarkable tasks. Those successes led, after a series of delicate dealings among all the active players and chilling confrontations with southern segregationist forces, to the culminating triumph of that period, the August 1963 March on Washington. This event was the first and almost the last peaceful, positive, political outpouring of the decade. The bombings, assassinations, and murders of civil rights workers were the gruesome cost to be paid. These events were brought into the living rooms of the American people with the evening news—a television college of the airwaves—as was the murder of President John F. Kennedy in Dallas in November of 1963, indicating that a different and more sinister set of forces was loose. Whatever they were, they were operating under conditions that made the sure identity of friend and foe problematical.

Some elements of the youth movements, white and black, concluded that the alternative to nonviolence was a possibility that now had to be considered. That perspective was also a means of asserting their own autonomy vis-à-vis the adult leadership of the movement. The brand new SNCC and SDS had, in fact, met with each other in May of 1960, when SDS's first conference on the theme "Human Rights in the North" brought together some of the leading adult civil rights activists and theorists—Bayard Rustin, James Farmer, Herbert Hill, Michael Harrington, and some of the leadership from SNCC. The normal difficulties in maintaining a steady alliance between white and black was made even more complicated by virtue of several hidden fault lines.

The different stance each would take toward adults was a serious one. Young black leaders had to orchestrate their double opposition to white authority and to black authority. They had to find ways that didn't weaken the thrust against the former but also didn't succumb to the latter, a difficult road that more than once resulted in public excess and distortions, along with a permanent undertone of resentment. Young white leaders blundered into comparable over- and underestimations of the power and reasonableness of both white and black forces, and nurtured comparable rages. Within a few years, and in different ways, those attitudes surfaced over the issue of nonviolence as a political constraint. Increasingly, the authority of the gun beckoned. Both SDS and SNCC would be superceded by groups that heeded that call. The Black Panther Party and the Weathermen were gathering just around the corner.

There were two other issues that were to drive the young black and the young white political activists in different directions. Attitudes and practices towards women was one of them. The important context that shaped both the black and white youth movements was the different kinds of relations between the sexes that obtained in the black and the white adult communities. The other issue was the extent to which college youth would and could separate themselves from their home community, from the urban community as a whole. With the exception of a few urban, middle-class members and some West Indians, most black activists were poor, and many were southern. Their ties to the black communities maintained a strong mixture of personal history and ideological commitment. On the other hand, the predominantly middle-class backgrounds of most of the white college student leadership sent them in a different direction in the search for community.

As a result of both these issues, there was a permanent tension and constraint in the dealings between white and black activists. The recognition of the vulnerabilities of black women and black men to white contact, plus fears on the part of whites, generated a strange mixture of reserve and excess that soon led to a separation of the races. The situation so closely merged individual and group identity that this plaintive refrain was not uncommon. One black civil rights worker stated, "I hate myself for hating Albin, because he's a friend; and I hate Albin for liking me, because he's White." [43]

Even at the political level the distrust that blacks held for whites in the early 1960s southern civil rights days was nearly fatal to cooperation. SDS's brilliant tactical "participatory democracy," so effective on northern college campuses, backfired:

The emphasis on "freedom organizations" is an example. The theory behind them is that to the extent the local people are influenced by the organizer, they are also being manipulated. It has been described by whites as "participatory democracy" but the phrase intellectualizes the process, and thus defeats one of its objectives since intellectualizing is considered one of the unfair advantages of white organizers. [44]

The belief, perhaps a rationalization, was that the strengths of whites and blacks were resources best husbanded in separate settings. The outcome was obvious; whites and blacks kept their organizational distance, freeing personal relationships from the pressure. By 1965 the separatist tendencies of black politics were clearly ascendant. Neither the political desires of the white radicals nor the cultural reliance of the rock stream on black music would bring any substantial black presence into the movement and only a small presence into the counterculture.

Black politics and culture were devising new militant and separatist recipes. "Huey Newton, minister of defense for the Oakland, California, based Black Panther Party; Ron Karenga, the cultural nationalistic leader of the Los Angeles based "US" organization; and Charles Kenyatta, the head of the New York City's Mau Mau's all commanded significant respect among young blacks in various local areas where these organizations had set up offices. [45] The problem of white women in the black movement thus lost any significance "after 1965," when the black power slogan came onto the agenda, because whites of both sexes were entirely forced out of youth and almost all adult civil rights formations. The "beloved community" days were over; the sacred value and personal worth of every individual were to be submerged in disciplined obedience to organizations defending single status politics.[46]

The emerging feminist movement strengthened the resolve for equality of all women in civil rights or in student activism. To that degree, some men, feeling threatened or ignored, could and did invoke the defensive cultural resources at hand, male bravado being the preferred response. That style proved, for blacks, even more attractive as the struggle for civil rights was transformed into a demand for black power, with all its attendant bluster. As a *cultural* style, moreover, a strong male presence on the dance floor was the traditional and preferred model, just as its inversion had a place in black culture, for example, Flip Wilson's Geraldine. Black popular music served a sophisticated dance audience, and male and female were expected to exhibit a graceful and knowledgeable command over a literate and changing dance vocabulary.

This music was not strictly, or at all, in the service of a male vanity culture. There was a long-standing tradition of using popular music in the service of the celebration of black identity. Rhythm and blues was a party music, and a dance party was just as much a place to state a person's black pride as in church and, increasingly, in the streets. After the black teenagers and college youth had given all the help they could to assist the bus boycott during the days in Montgomery, they listened to and danced to the current top R&B hits on the weekend. Thus a thriving, good-time music lived all through the sixties, come revolution, black power, or whatever.[47] In addition, the black gospel canon was invoked and expanded into the category of "Freedom Songs," raising the fighting spirit of the civil rights participants, young and old, white and black.[48]

A different configuration of male-female relationships gave the white student movement its own internal tensions. Women's demand for equality was acceded to in principle much more readily in the white student movement than among blacks (recall Stokely Carmichael's assertion that the only position for women in SNCC is prone) but was probably given no more reality in practice; until, that is, women took it. They did so as the level of political commitment deepened. The conscious eradication of "monogamy" proceeded most completely for the minority of SDS members who transformed themselves first into the Weathermen, then, logically, into Weatherpeople:

We do not view ourselves as sex objects but as part of the revolution. Sex isn't something to happen isolated from daily work. Destroying the one man one woman relationship was perhaps the most liberating thing that happened to us. We could speak at meetings without being uptight or being on an ego trip and most important we were upfront at demonstrations along with men.[49]

This radicalization took place over the five-year period 1965–1970, during which the youth movement expanded most rapidly and consolidated its ranks. Two events particularly strengthened its ties. One was the Free Speech Movement at Berkeley that commenced on 14 September 1964. The other was President Johnson's escalation of the Vietnam War. In February 1965, Johnson ordered the bombing of North Vietnam and an increased draft call. Students in greater numbers than ever before began to see themselves as directly threatened by the "university" and the "government." They began, also as never before, to define themselves as their own constituency, one that included their younger brothers and sisters. Students were receiving threats to free thought, speech, and action, so they focused their attention on those two institutions that most students had heretofore held aside from condemnation. Slum lords, racist sheriffs, and greedy corporations were the familiar enemies in their vocabulary. The conclusion that the university and the government were hand-in-glove partners oppressing the youth (and everybody else) was the road to a far more radical stance.

It was the road that led to a serious and extended national discussion. Was American youth actually a part of a revolutionary new class? Or were young people only a volatile and unstable element that could merely spark imminent political events? Didn't the real work of revolution lie in the hands of the working class? But, on the other hand, wasn't the working class hopelessly compromised by its cheap pay-off for silence and complicity in the war machine's economy? Didn't the real revolutionary burden fall on the American blacks and their third world allies? Didn't Che Guevara's "Two, three, many Vietnams" point the way?[50]

The answers were not easy, in good measure because the input was so fragmented. American society during those years living through an unparalleled, five-screen video show, revealing five separate realities. The first screen showed the adult and family fare that dominated both daytime and evening programming, soap opera, game shows, sports, variety entertainment, and the like. A second screen stoked the music industry fires for its youthful customers (from Dick Clark's "American Bandstand" to "Hullabaloo"). A third screen showed those customers being whacked over the head for protesting what was on a fourth screen, Vietnam and the burning of Newark and Watts. A fifth screen was putting on the space travel show "from lift off to splash down." Of course, all was a seamless whole, all five screens.

The cultural scene, luxuriant and diverse, did nothing to make political choice easier. From vegetarian diets to the meditative wisdoms of the East, from long hair and Salvation Army clothes to arcane or just plain filthy language, all became personal and idiosyncratic expressive decoration, the statement of almost any political leaning. Within a remarkably brief time period, however, the styles of hair and dress were conventionalized into a clear continuum indicating the degree of a student's activist commitment. Figure 10-5 provides some persuasive pictorial evidence. In a questionnaire, including photographs, administered to a random sample of about four hundred Berkeley students in the spring of 1967, political activism and dress style were perceived to be closely correlated, as was dress style and drug use.[51] The line drawings picture the four main dress styles on a continuum from least to most active in the counterculture. Their predictive power was quite high: Two of the most important of those results are shown in the figure. The study illustrated here shows that the more unconventional the dress a student adopts, the more likely the student is to be involved in left-wing politics, and the more likely the student uses marijuana. The association is strong and unequivocal. The study also reveals that the dress code works because the perceived association of dress and attitude by the external observer parallels the actual association intended by the wearer. In short, culture and politics among the male college student of the sixties were closely aligned and publicly understood.[52]

High school kids developed a comparable series of hair and dress styles (both boys and girls) to express their own growing political leanings. The very statement that high school kids *had* political interests clear enough to join college-aged young people is to announce that politics in the sixties had definitely changed. Those politics may have been only the attitudes lying inchoate within the musical syntheses that Elvis created. When joined to the rocknroll-folk-jazz synthesis of 1965–1970, the resultant mature rock stream was a tightly woven part of the fabric connecting political and cultural movements. The assertive independence from parents that Elvis had called for was now thrust at the other adults, the ones carrying out educational and military policy. Music and attitude from both age groups and from both races gave the movement and the musics of the young an enviable unity.

Achievement and Dissolution

The situation in the late sixties was difficult to assess; it was neither a "nation on its feet" nor a "silent majority" enduring a noisy but tiny claque, but something in between. The numbers of young people involved in rock concerts and political demonstrations during the 1960s was without precedent. The very existence of a huge counterculture and a huge movement appearing simultaneously and surviving indistinguishably for a decade clearly announced that politics and culture in the United States had indeed changed. But the string did run out.

In spite of its initial and shrewd posture of being the catalyst and fa-

Conventional (9%) Clean Cut, well
groomed with conventional off-campus
wear: jacket and tie, white shirt,
wool slacks.

Collegiate (61%) Clean cut, well groomed
but casual-in California, the campus
norm: no jacket or tie, conventional,
long-sleeved shirt with rolled-up sleeves,
cotton slacks.

Perceived and actual activity in left-wing politics

	Convent.	Colleg.	Shaggy	Earthy	N
Perceived as active	14%	16%	58%	71%	(410)
Actually active	13%	20%	77%	74%	(266)

cilitator for all campus and nonstudent activism, SDS was gradually drawn into a dreary factionalism. The sources of that friction are too complex to track here; yet the very power of the youth movement, its labile, almost directionless energies, must have driven the SDS leadership wild with anticipation and frustration as they tried to harness that power, tried to ride the tiger. The issues were maddening in that cultural and political developments were proceeding at a pace far faster than the leaders could handle. This pace kept up for both black and white sectors as the 1960s unfolded. On the cultural side, the music, the dress and hair styles, the language, the drugs were all coming together to make the word "hippie" a disturbing reality to parents, a joke far beyond the TV humor of Maynard Krebs. On the political side, the escalation of the civil rights movement into its black power manifestation had become a deadly reality to the authorities, a matter far beyond the irritation of lunch counter sit-ins.

Shaggy (23%) Definitely not clean cut, only casually groomed but not outrageously unconventional: dark, slightly scruffy shirt, corduroy pants, hair definitely on the long side.

Earthy (7%) Distinctly (if not aggressively) long-haired and unkept, deliberately unconventional: scruffy work shirt and jeans; work boots; long, dissheveled hair.

Perceived and actual use of marijuana

	Convent.	Colleg.	Shaggy	Earthy	N
Perceived use	18%	31%	56%	78%	(410)
Actual use	4%	26%	80%	90%	(266)

Figure 10-5. Correlation of Dress Styles with Political Activity and Marijuana Use. Source: Paper presented to the annual meeting of the American Sociological Association, 1971, by Jonathan Kelley and Shirley A. Starr.

By 1967, Martin Luther King, Jr., and the SCLC had joined the anti-war National Mobilization, and SNCC had formally opposed the war. Yet a gulf deeper than the differences in attitude about the proper relations between men and women divided the white and the black movements. They each searched in different places for community and the sense of personal worth and identity that membership in that community would give. Probably these differences were best concretized in the famous cartoon circulating in black student circles. It showed a burning schoolhouse labeled "Integration." "Are you sure you want to enter that place?" was the caption. The reference was not to the danger of the struggle for desegregation, but to its purpose. Black liberation, black pride, "black is beautiful," the very name "black" instead of "Negro" were signs of change. Black identity and black community were not simply matters of age or of class. The intellectual search for what they were occupied the black movement with nationalisms, political and cultural, for some time.[53]

Its nonviolent commitment weakened by the legal and armed resistance it encountered, the civil rights movement was shattered by the assassination of Martin Luther King, Jr., in 1968. The young leaders of black power and black liberation groups shared with the white radical leadership a recognition that they were slipping further and further from their mainstream bases and, of course, further from any real cooperation among themselves. Even geography worked to divide black and white leaders, and to isolate both from their main constituencies. The black community was worlds away from the college campus, even if the black ghetto was right next door to the school as it was at the University of Chicago, Columbia, and UC Berkeley. Thus, while the main body of the white youth movement held fast to the campus bastion as the most secure base from which to mobilize against the war, the search for "the community" led some black students and their allies out of the colleges under the black power banner. In another direction went the left SDS splinter groups to mobilize the white working-class youth and to blitz the high schools.

The romance between the movement's political wing and its cultural side cooled and heated alternately, but they ultimately frayed apart. One reason for the split was that some of the student radical theorists paying attention to the relevant events were assimilating them into an inappropriate theory. The grip of a Marxist class analysis apparently was unbreakable, perhaps because it seemed better than the other alternatives. One such alternative was a nationalistic one, coming mainly from black theoreticians and based on the observation that the black population in the United States was neither a separate caste (because full legal equality was theirs if they struggled for it) nor a class (because its members occupied almost every economic position, even though mainly concentrated as workers in manufacturing and agriculture). Moreover, class consciousness among blacks never triumphed over a mix of racial pride and trade union and other associational loyalties. What remained was a nationalistic vision mixing Third World identifications with a not entirely foolish dream of a geographical-political League of Black Cities,[54] or simply with the free-floating slogans of Black Power for Black People. None of these solutions attracted more than a minority of believers. The black populace was making its own political philosophy manifest in the streets, while protecting itself at home.

Another alternative for members of the movement was to get out. The great North American continent was wide and rich. Many young people believed its present owners were too mean, too strong, too stupid, the situation too dangerous. They believed it was hopeless to fight, moreover, since the struggle would transform the youth into their enemies. Peace and love could be achieved only by creating new lives in new communities. The explosive growth of intentional communities during the sixties attests to the popularity of that notion. Most experiments at community building failed, some publicly and painfully.[55]

A third alternative route away from the idea of "youth as revolutionary class" was the notion that their culture would show the way.[56] Music, drugs, the new consciousness, these would bring power to the assembled people, giving themselves, along the way, incidentally, a helluva show. It was an easy laugh, if a sad one, to see the trust and the naivete of the young being so easily exploited by the gurus and hustlers selling the dope and the new consciousness. It is equally easy, with no laugh at all, to identify the leading characters who led that parade. Timothy Leary had the goods and the message. He led the chemical wing of the escapist alternative, offering LSD as the main vehicle. Speed, marijuana, cocaine, and other substances filled out a menu despised and feared both by the adult world and by the more politically single-minded youth.

Less a player than a prophetic sideline commentator, Charles A. Reich put into the conventional form of a best-selling book the same naivete as the flower children. His *The Greening of America* had digested all the required reading of his youth clientele, from Marx and Marcuse to Ken Kesey. How can these sentiments about the new consciousness be faulted? "There is a revolution coming. . . . It will originate with the individual and with culture, and it will change the political structure only as its final act. It will not require violence to succeed. . . . This is the revolution of the new generation."[57]

These prophets married the logic of individualism to the belief in the effectiveness of symbol over action and came up with their own cultural road to freedom. If work can be made erotic in the same way that art is an erotic form of work, then all is whole again through the hidden magic that art carries—the "gift of life." Release transcends commitment through the power of consciousness.

Sadly, history cancelled the checks. Programs based only on the institutions of release can not do the job of reclaiming the institutions of commitment. Consciousness of a situation by itself does not bring about change. However, the consciousness industry was flourishing in the sixties; pieces of the whole world's culture, especially the wisdom of the East, filled many holes in American life. From the Hare Krishna cult to the spread of a home-grown Zen Buddhist practice, even to the Tantric esoterics, new ways of living were finding a home.

The simpler political alternatives for the Movement were also clear:

Either cut your hair and go "Clean with Gene" into electoral politics, or go down to the working class, black or white, with Marx, Marcuse, and Mao. On the other side was the smiling assertion that long hairs don't fight; they sing and dance. The youth were, in fact, doing both in a way that bothered everyone. The individuals leaning toward the cultural side of the student movements matured rocknroll. Those interested in the electoral/political side found their road, improbably enough, by following the coalition led by more adult forces but that included the vital Yippie! fabrications of Abbie Hoffman and Jerry Rubin. After 1965, event after event drilled into the young the unrelenting and ferocious nature of the struggle. The Moratoriums, the Mobilizations, the 1968 Democratic Convention in Chicago, all brought the resistance face to face with the steely face of the Johnson administration and its increasingly direct use of violence. The more radical political activists were thus driven beyond the students to a chimerical revolutionary constituency. That movement led only to political defeat and personal erasure.[58]

It was almost over. The excesses that characterized the counterculture and some of its political sweepings were producing a horror show for the American public. The kidnapping of Patty Hearst, the Los Angeles SWAT team's destruction of the crazed Symbionese Liberation Army in a blazing inferno, the Sharon Tate murders by the Manson "family," all signaled a Götterdämmerung, Disney style. In the same mode, this time in the style of the Keystone Kops, the last act of joint solidarity between the political and cultural wings of the movement was achieved in Timothy Leary's escape from a California prison (held on a marijuana possession conviction), assisted by the Weatherpeople. The preparations for a long and lonelier fight by those SDS members who were determined upon a course of armed struggle were made in the black neighborhood of the working-class city of Flint, Michigan, in the winter of 1969.

The war council was a frenzy, a frenzy in anticipation of the armed struggle they were calling for. Most Weatherpeople slept an hour a day; the rest was heavy, heavy rapping, heavy listening, heavy exercising, heavy fucking, heavy laughing, a constant frenzy-strain that went through the whole four days, all the time no flab, no looseness, no ease in anything that was done.[59]

The distance from the early days of the Movement and from rocknroll is clear. As they prepared to go underground, they gave voice to their feelings, as soldiers are wont to do, in song. The music was old pop and rocknroll; the words were in the Weatherman songbook. For example, to the tune of "White Christmas," these words were sung:

> I'm dreaming of a white riot
> Just like the one October 8,
> When the pigs take a beating

And things started leading
To armed war against the state.
We're heading now toward armed struggle,
With ev'ry cadre line we write.
May you learn to struggle and fight
Or the world will off you 'cause you're white.

To the tune of the Beatles' "Nowhere Man" was sung:

He's a real Weatherman,
Ripping up the mother land,
Making all his Weatherplans
For everyone;
Knows just what he's fighting for,
Victory for people's war,
Trashes, bombs, kills pigs and more,
The Weatherman.[60]

These completely wooden words attached to the tunes that Bing Crosby and the Beatles had made part of their lives suggest the distance these young people had traveled from their culture of origin. How could these Weatherpeople, with such an attitude, relate to young people committed to Janis Joplin, the Airplane, Zappa, and Crosby, Stills, and Nash, and how could those young people relate to the Weatherpeople?[61]

To sum up, whatever their failures, weaknesses, and excesses, the positive accomplishments of the young during the sixties are considerable. They played a major part in the immediate decisions that ended the Vietnam War. They changed the ways whites and blacks behaved towards one another. They expanded the constituencies of the arts and their interrelations. Entire new art forms emerged along with rocknroll to enliven and confuse the Parade of the Muses. They redefined the age-graded arrangements within every American institution. Though neither Head Start nor retirement communities can be regarded as achievements of the young, they both began in age-linked encounters.

The young launched alternatives to the ordinary ways Americans handled everyday life and experienced extraordinary events. The marches, demonstrations, festivals, and concerts were the morphological triumphs of the youth movement. To paraphrase Parker Tyler, who was speaking of Hollywood studio movies of the 1930s and 1940s, there was no irrelevant rock festival in the 1960s. They were all embodiments of the counterculture, that loose structure par excellence of the sixties. The creation of alternative forms of political discourse equaled the ingenuity of youthful innovations in market exchanges and modes of personal living. The adults may have sniggered at the hippies in their "tribes," "communes," "crash pads," and so on in the sixties, but they inherited those social forms when they became conventionalized into the new family forms and living arrangements of the seventies and eighties.

Finally, youth carried all these things to young people all over the world through rocknroll and its cultural entities. The Movement and the counterculture did this with such force and penetration that each of those outcomes lives on today, in the 1990s.

11. Rock

I f the youth *movements* of the 1960s attacked the adult establishment like a spear thrust at the body politic, the youth *cultures* of the time enveloped that establishment like a fog, unsettling every social institution. Those cultures, what has come to be called "the sixties," were not a mysterious Zeitgeist, a disembodied emanation descending from the heavens. They had specific historical roots, geographic nodes, and discernable structural components. They were still aimed at adult authority, even while carrying out their own youth-centered interests. The core of those youth cultures was the maturing rocknroll. This chapter traces that stream's coming of age.

What Is a Stream's "Maturity"?

In 1965, at the culmination of the widespread experimentation with the guitar, there was a crystallization of rocknroll's resources. Rocknroll was maturing into rock.[1] Such an efflorescence in any artistic system requires that all four of its elements be functioning at a high level. In the case of rock, its separate audiences were blended into a single one, and musical materials and performers from the separate streams were combined to form a new and different musical idiom with its own artists and its own music. There was also the creation, from previous performance and distribution vehicles, of a new and distinctive rock infrastructure. Finally, a critical apparatus was emerging, a self-conscious, self-proclaiming voice of rock.

Rocknroll reached a minimal level of maturity when it stretched beyond its teenage concerns and constituency, past the trauma of puppy love and the problems of parental authority. *Hit Parader*, the established teen fan magazine, spelled out the process in this way in 1962:

Let's face it, we of this generation have our own hits, our own idols, who sing and play our own particular mood and beat. The other singers recognize this. They understand it, having been through the same thing themselves. They stick to the "mature" sound they have developed over the years, just as many of the better Rock and Roll singers of today will gradually "mature" and develop into the polished professionals of tomorrow. No doubt, the time will come when we teen-agers will smooth and polish our own tastes to a more mature sound.

But, for now, while we're young let's live young and sing young, with Rydell and Elvis and Darin—and all the others who give us the beat and the sound that we want to hear.

Sure we dig the Comos and Fishers and all the other big names, but we dig our own stars the most, the kids who will become the Comos, Dean Martins, and Eddie Fishers of tomorrow.[2]

Hit Parader's editors were hearing rocknroll's age-graded music with old, nonage-graded ears. Between those ears lay the belief that young performers would simply mature along with their audiences. It never happened. There was no way that Frankie Avalon or Elvis, for that matter, could grow into mature *rocknroll* performers. Unless they went into movies or to Las Vegas, they were to come as close to being permanent teenagers as their audiences would permit. That was their fate, caught in rocknroll's perpetual sandbox with a brief shelf life.

What did, in fact, happen was that, as the youngsters grew up and changed, their music changed as well, reaching down to and enfolding the succeeding generations of teenagers. It did so by virtue of the incorporation of folk and jazz elements into its canon and by the expansion of the "youth" category to include kids from a wide range of ages.

A set of "music memoirs" written by college students in the early 1970s offers a look at the simultaneous maturation of rocknroll and its first-generation audience. The typical story of an individual's musical interests shows a haphazard and idiosyncratic progression through the years. The journey often began with lullabies and party songs, the "Mickey Mouse Club" seen on television at age eight, or the little phonograph with records such as "Tubby the Tuba." For some, musical education continued with violin, piano, or trumpet lessons. Many mentioned the shock or distaste of their parents as they all watched Elvis on the "Ed Sullivan Show," and at least one delighted in watching the kid on the school bus imitating Elvis' "Blue Suede Shoes." Many wrote about their first record purchase of Del Shannon's "Runaway" at age twelve, or maybe it was a record by David Seville and the Chipmunks. They tell of being terrified at seeing the Rolling Stones on television's "Hollywood Palace," and then as college freshmen listening to Simon and Garfunkel. By their junior year, they were getting into Crosby, Stills and Nash and The Band. Each cohort, year by year, dropped off some of their earlier favorites, moving on to what was closer to the more sophisticated preferences of their immediate circle of friends. The embedding of musical taste in peer groups was widespread.

The music industry, either hostile or indifferent to such progressions of taste, bullheadedly insisted on a strategy of further differentiation of the market by age. They were assisted in this direction by a narrower range of age-group bonding that yielded clumps of younger teenagers susceptible to a music which came to be called bubblegum.

In the fashion area, which was vital in defining the youth culture, the screws were being tightened to the extent that retailers were "urgently" advised to offer "four entirely different departments for girls 5 to 18" years of age.[3] The purpose was explicitly to encourage young people to choose styles along familiar and predictable lines as they matured. The resistance was nationwide. Young people were going to make their own fashion statement, as Andy Warhol observed in New York in 1963.

It was the summer of the Liz-Taylor-in-Cleopatra look, long, straight dark shining hair with bangs and Egyptian-looking eye makeup. . . . [The scene] was divided mostly between the collegiate-looking kids and the "hitters." . . . [T]he folk singer look was in—the young girls with the bangs were wearing shifts and sandals and burlapy things; but looking back, I can see that maybe by way of the Cleopatra look, folk evolved into something slick and fashionable that would eventually become the geometric look. But this summer, at least, *folk and hip were blending.* (my emphasis)[4]

"Folk and hip" as dress styles were not only specific unifying elements among young people, from the youngest teenager to twenty-year olds, but the terms were also concrete symbolic markers indicating that the folk and jazz streams, with all their richness and sophistication, were keeping company with rocknroll. Warhol further noted that "in England the kids eighteen and nineteen were having a ball. Or starting to, anyway—it was a new age classification."[5] That "new age classification," was, of course, the young. In the United States, blue denim jeans, old clothes from the Salvation Army, and the "earthy" look described above, outrageous at the time, would become the fashion standard for white youth. Black youth fashion, also headed for the outrageous, was nevertheless quite distinct from its white counterpart, but youth as a cultural entity was maturing together, producing a single rock audience.

The maturing of the music itself involves two quite different notions. The first is that an art form has the ability to reproduce itself. A mature art is one that makes its *own* "new ones out of old ones"; that is, its canon at a certain stage of development contains not only siblings but progeny. This reproduction requires initially that somebody love the stuff to the point of imitation. Given that dedicated affection, an art form large enough in productivity and extended enough in time can grow its own artists, audiences, distribution systems, and critical apparatus. Such a mature stream can also produce mixed progeny with adjacent streams. One of the most important of these offspring would come from a mix with jazz, the most artistically and technically demanding stream. "Fusion," as this meeting has been called, was exemplified early on in the short-lived Electric Flag of Michael Bloomfield, the more durable Mahavishnu Orchestra led by John McLaughlin, and the even more complex Earth Wind and Fire.

An art form's maturity is also evidenced by its deepening expression of the human experience. If rocknroll couldn't get past "I love you madly, they're tearing you away from me, I'm gonna die, and I'm only nine years old," there was not much hope for its maturation. There is something to be said for the ancient wisdom that insists on suffering as a precondition for the achievement of a high art. The journey past the surface of life into a greater appreciation of its mystery and absurdity, its struggles and simple joy, creates a mature art form when expressed through a greater technical mastery and when subtlety is achieved in both hiding and revealing its messages. There is, in other words, a strong but paradoxical correlation between the profundity of an art form's wisdom and the technical level of its musical accomplishment. On occasion, that is, just the opposite is true; crudity of expression can dwell with a great passion, with a depth of understanding.

The curve of maturation, moreover, does not necessarily move from youthful, high-spirited vulgarity to a ripe adult mastery. Neither does it merely shift from simplicity to complexity, nor does maturity imply any particular direction for its content, for example, the movement from private emotion to public declamation or vice versa. It does move, however, through a course of exploration, elaboration, then exhaustion of an art form's resources. That satiation is not just an audience response; the artists themselves at some point have nothing more to say along a particular line.[6]

The Influence of Folk and Jazz

The meeting of rocknroll with the folk and jazz streams was the main event that formed mature rock around 1965. Folk delivered to rocknroll its music, its performance sites, and a set of beliefs about "the people." Rock was built over jazz's unique distribution network and used its presentational forms, as well as absorbing its ethos rather than its musical techniques and repertoire. Behind both folk and jazz was the gospel reservoir, which nurtured both, and through them gave rock some of its spiritual energy. The story of rocknroll's mingling with folk and jazz is full of genealogical influences, a musical "begat" of artists, at the extremes a gossip column of who met whom. Those meetings were at specific places, at performance sites and hangouts, on tour, in the recording studios, wherever the streams' personnel gathered to work and to listen. The charts were less important in tracking the changes, though the dollar volume was still the bottom line.

After the blows dealt to the autonomous, hit-making disk jockeys by the 1960s payola hearings and the surge of the pop stream into rocknroll (the Philadelphia Teen Idol scene and the new Brill Building producers), there wasn't much of a place for raw rocknroll on top 40 AM radio. The thousands of dispersed garage bands played in the high school gym and in small clubs and dance halls, but success was chancy. A few bands opened for prominent acts in large performance venues and recorded a few singles that were played over local radio stations. All were praying for a scene-maker who could make them stars.

The reviving folk stream entered the picture in the unpromising atmosphere of the coffee house in large cities and around colleges and universities. The academic, ethnographic, and folkloristic sides of the folk stream flourished. The new tape recording technology, the long playing record, and high-fidelity component systems were also creating a broader audience for high-quality, authentic folk music. The pop stream was beginning to regard folk music as part of its market. Conversely, the "folk" guitar players appropriated some songs from the current pop stream into their repertoires.

The folk collectors and entrepreneurs, both wary of and attracted to the pop stream, were on guard for the twin dangers of topicality and commercialism. Their scholarly mission of preserving and understanding all the world's great anonymous song and music traditions was being eroded, they believed, by activist politics and by commercial looting. Yet their own needs for an audience put them in the dilemma of trying to encompass both fully documented folk music and living performance— the musty museum and the lively show.

The Old Left rallied its shattered voices around a number of organizations and publications, especially *Sing Out*. The rediscovery of the hootenanny inspired a set of audience participation forms, networks of coffee houses, folk nightclubs, and college and community-church groups.[7] The weekly "hoots" at the Village Gate, New York's main folk club, and the publication *Broadside* were given a sense of urgency by a growing exchange of personnel with southern civil rights militants. The "Sing for Freedom" meetings, begun in 1960 under the auspices of the Highlander Folk School, held a particularly memorable meeting in Atlanta in May of 1964, jointly sponsored by the school and SCLC and SNCC.[8] The more commercial part of the folk stream flowed through the same venues but was more closely connected to the record companies. The Weavers with Gordon Jenkins, the Tarriers, the Brothers Four, and the Kingston Trio proved that both the political and commercial wings would follow any path that led to a full house.

With New York's resurgence as a significant city in rocknroll, one of those paths to success reappeared. It was the bridge that had been established in 1938 with the founding of Cafe Society Downtown, the legendary Village nightclub that gave Billie Holiday, Josh White,[9] and other pop-folk-jazz performers a local, then national showcase. In 1938, while organizing the first Carnegie Hall musical parade of contemporary black popular music entitled "From Spirituals to Swing," John Hammond was introduced to Barney Josephson, founder and owner of Cafe Society Downtown. They hit it off, agreeing on the need for a racially integrated night spot in New York, and Hammond agreed to supervise the club's music policy. He was able to bring his black artist friends to a larger audience, being a producer for Columbia Records.[10] The two simultaneous events, Hammond's Carnegie Hall concert and the opening of Cafe Society Downtown, crystallized an arrangement that for years would nurture an urban audience's taste for folk and jazz in "respectable" settings.

That specific three-way meeting of the small club, the large concert, and the record company was the template that would contain the emerging folk and jazz streams as they connected to rocknroll twenty years later. That three-way combination of presentational forms was a symbiotic arrangement that enhanced each part. The jazz concert, predecessor to the rock festival, was where true believers met in a setting large enough to confer the strength of numbers to both audience and artists. Together, the assembled people were getting a helluva show. The small club or coffee house, at the other extreme, provided a different kind of encounter. Structurally, it was the place for audience and performer to form strong bonds, ties that would hold as the distance between them increased in large concerts and even further with the phonograph record. The small club was also the most economical presentational form for showcasing the flood of new jazz, folk, and rock talent that was spilling out of the nation's high schools and colleges. Those clubs trained the performers in the rigors of the road, on inattentive audiences, noisy drunks, sleazy owners, and cheating managers. They also trained audiences to use their own critical eyes and ears.

A new self-reinforcing and self-maintaining molecule of cultural action was thus forming to meet the evolving political movement. These new short loops in the small folk and/or jazz clubs in New York's Village, Los Angeles's Sunset Strip, San Francisco's North Beach, or in Chicago's Near North Side of the 1960s were the white and more affluent cousins of the 1950s small black clubs in every major city that showcased new rhythm and blues talent.

John Hammond's continuing presence in New York's music world reasserted itself dramatically when he was asked to organize the music for a summer jazz festival in Newport. The sedate Rhode Island summer compound for the old eastern robber barons became the setting in 1954 for a modest two-day event, predictable and by all accounts delightful. Stan Kenton was master of ceremonies; Eddie Condon, the Oscar Peterson trio, and Ella Fitzgerald exemplified the vintage and style of the performers.[11] That success assured continuity, and in 1956 the third Newport Festival invited Mahalia Jackson and a large black and white audience. The large concert-festival form was continuing to carry its political message of desegregation. It was also maintaining its record connection; Vanguard Records released a version of the next year's festival.

The rock festival that grew out of this vehicle gave the maturing rock stream its own "City," a device that would link the separate rock scenes scattered across the nation. The form was built on the experience of all the other festivals, including the traditions of Newport.

The first real festival, one that claims San Francisco as its home, was the Fantasy Faire and Magic Mountain Music Festival in June of 1967, held across the Golden Gate Bridge in the amphitheater carved into the sides of Mt. Tamalpais.[12] It was the move out of the city (The Human Be In, the predecessor gathering, took place in Golden Gate Park six months earlier) that made it a special journey. Eleven bands played for two days; the acts ranged from the local Jefferson Airplane and Country Joe and the Fish to the Byrds, Dionne Warwick, and Smokey Robinson. It was a beginning that proved rock's claim that it could reach and contain all the other popular music streams.

The festival that launched rocknroll into rock most dramatically was in Monterey, held a week later, 16–18 June 1967. It was organized by Lou Adler and John Phillips, with Derek Taylor (formerly of the Beatles organization) as head of publicity. All of these men were emblematic figures of the era. Phillips was the organizer of the Mamas and the Papas, the quintessential pop-folk group of the moment. Clean harmonies, a laid-back attitude, their ability to cruise with the inner circles of the folk-rock hierarchy, and their chart-topping "California Dreaming" and "Monday, Monday" made them serious business and opened the way to Monterey.

That small Pacific coastal town connecting (or separating) Los Angeles and San Francisco held fifty thousand people for three days and nights while twenty-seven of the top acts in rocknroll, folk, and black pop gave the listeners more than their money's worth (tickets cost three to five dollars). From all reports, it was a dream festival with relatively little of the hassling, money grubbing, and panic that would haunt succeeding festivals. There were some outstanding performances that launched careers, as in the case of Janis Joplin. Her intensity not only stunned the audience but impressed Clive Davis, the new head of Columbia Records Artists and Repertoire who was in attendance. He signed her on the spot, so to speak, and the record industry thus learned that the tour and the festival were crucial in discovering talent and exploiting it.[13] Otis Redding's set was also a smash, one of the few black acts to appear. His San Francisco anthem "(Sittin' on) The Dock of the Bay" went to number one on both the pop the R&B singles charts. The extremes of rock's musical and emotional ranges were displayed. At one end was Jimi Hendrix, whose repertoire respectfully included Dylan's "Like a Rolling Stone" and disrespectfully exploded into a frenzy of first copulating with then burning his guitar right on stage. Barely controlled excess combined with musical mastery of a high order. At the other end was Ravi Shankar, who played with comparable intensity to a rapt audience.

This festival launched rock artistically. It also raised the money issue; while some of the bands were playing to the paying audience at Monterey, the Grateful Dead and the Jefferson Airplane were giving a free concert across town. The question of who paid what to whom would continue the stormy romance between art and money.

The small club part of the developing rock system appeared in every major city. It linked several kinds of clubs together, including the blues clubs. It was in these black pop venues that the Paul Butterfield Blues Band of Chicago, one of rock's premier acts, fashioned an idiom of their own out of the South Side bar blues on which they were raised. Though there was a lively mix of other white blues players in Chicago at that time—1965—[14] Butterfield was the strongest. After Butterfield's impressive visit to the Bay area, the late Bill Graham, impresarial leader of the Fillmore, declared Butterfield "the king of San Francisco." It should be noted, though, that the crown on Butterfield's head and the ones that adorned the Blues Project were only the gold of critical acclaim. They were not made of greenback dollars. Neither the Butterfield Blues Band nor the Blues Project ever put a single or an album on any chart. This brief "blues revival" by white artists in the late sixties was not a passing fad, but a restatement and continuation of rock's origins.

The maturing rock audience was also finding its own independent, small record labels, even though the majors were by this time ready to sign new rock acts. Several of these new companies were assisting the album's victory over the single as the main presentational form for rock and its folk heritage. Folkways, Electra, Vanguard, Caedmon, and Verve were the main folk-oriented labels, another example of a powerful loop connecting intimate clubs, large concerts, and record labels. What John Hammond and Barney Josephson had done in 1938 and again in the midfifties, these record companies were doing in the sixties. At this time, however, the scope of the loop was not only national but worldwide. Its basis was the international rock tour. Rocknroll had matured into rock not only by synthesizing the *music* of the six streams but by selectively appropriating their live performance networks. The hit-making disk jockey on AM radio was noticeable by his absence in this system, having been superceded by the conductors of the tour. The main world stops were New York, Los Angeles, Chicago, San Francisco, London, five or six cities on the Continent, Japan, and Australia. These and other foreign venues had first been tied together in the postwar jazz expansion described earlier.[15] The rhythm and blues tours of the fifties, which hit most of the same cities, added to rock tours its facilities and audiences (or the part of them that could make the transition from jazz, to R&B, to rock).

In the major cities, the small club, concert-festival, and recording loops for rock continued to expand. The performers and their audiences were discussing the perennial issues of artistic growth and commercial interests, which were inescapably connected to the tensions between racial politics and artistic expression. Kenneth Rexroth, literate friend of jazz, put the problem before *Metronome*'s readers in 1961. His question touched the sensitive race issue in the context of jazz musicians' relationships to their new and huge audiences:

[That] audience is not a normal musical audience, setting out there beyond the stand primarily to listen to music. . . . It doesn't do any good to be "cool" and pretend there is nobody out there. . . . It doesn't do anybody any good to get up there with a horn and pretend you are Elijah Muhammad and the Vassar girls at the front table are the Georgia mob that lynched your grandfather. You aren't and they aren't.[16]

The jazz clubs, Rexroth reminded his readers, as descendents of the speakeasy, were best at delivering hot dance tunes; they were not designed for orchestral-scaled music. These intensely fought issues could not but help influence the growing rock stream. Until the midsixties, the dominant position had been in favor of racial integration. Club managers and tour promoters were punctilious in "balancing" their programs with both white and black acts. After 1965, when separatist racial views dominated youth politics, the situation became more difficult.

The issue was authenticity. Who spoke in the truest, deepest way for the people? Was a song and its performance genuine? How had the performer paid his or her dues? These questions became important as an evaluative criterion when the folk stream began to move from the pop stream to rocknroll. Even the Kingston Trio's first big hit in 1958, "Tom Dooley," selling 2.5 million singles, produced a spate of articles from the popular press explaining how Tom Dula was a real person, how he was hanged, and so on. On the musical side, many people in the industry thought that record simply could not stand by itself, because it had none of the pop sweetening that would acceptably enfold the folk base. They were wrong; the freshness of the folk instrumentation was fully "commercial." Harry Belafonte's hits at the same time and in the same folk vein never needed such musical rationalization, even though they had too many strings to sound genuinely Calypso. He was, like John Jacob Niles and Richard Dyer-Bennett, working under the mantle of the "stylist," the "singer of songs." His specifically black musical presentation was confined within that New York-international, folk-supper club circle, just as Josh White's had been a decade earlier.

As the stakes in rocknroll were socially escalated to include "the assembled people," deeper resources were needed. That is, as the student movement became a close companion to the emerging rock stream, the music required a commitment beyond adolescent romance. Since those ideals were most immediately manifest in the black civil rights movement, a key test was the "blues," including both the musical form and its embodiment in old prewar "race" performers. White folk stream producers and audiences wanted to canonize them. Black pop music producers, especially Motown, wanted to move past them or at least modernize them.[17] In any case, white performers tended to sound as black as they could manage without making complete fools of themselves. A southern accent had long been a show business mannerism signaling affiliation with jazz, late night blues-torch songs, or some populist affinity. In the 1960s, that voicing became a more consequential testing ground. The generosity of the culture provided, thankfully, enough acceptable modulations along the road from white to black to allow every artist a place. While these arguments continued, the first step was accomplished: Folk moved from folk club to folk festival and then to record successes that matched the Four Aces and other mainstream acts still dominating the pop charts.

Folk Rock

In 1959, George Wein, in conjunction with Albert Grossman, produced the first Newport Folk Festival, the high point of which was Joan Baez's stunning success. Within two years, Baez had put two albums on the charts, her picture on the cover of national magazines, and by 1963 had accomplished the incredible feat of getting her rendition of the civil rights anthem "We Shall Overcome" onto the pop singles chart. There would be many other young women who walked through the door she opened, propelled by their own talents. Some, including Judy Collins and Joni Mitchell, would join the ranks of rock's mature performers.

Joan Baez was a committed folk singer whose pure voice could carry the English and French ballads of her repertoire with the same conviction as the topical songs of Bob Dylan. At the Newport Festival of 1963, she sang with Dylan, "With God on Our Side." The showcase the festival gave to Baez and Dylan was important in connecting the limited folk apparatus to the widening audience for the pop-folk idiom.

The sour folk purists, especially the English folk revivalists, would have none of it. The politics of the British folk movement were entirely different from its counterpart in the States. The Oxbridge "scenes" were characterized by a strong antiestablishment strain, as were American college circles, but British snobbery mixed with a mooncalf yearning for the working class completely missed the direction of the American sons and daughters of Woody Guthrie. Ewan MacColl, a Scot and one of the leading types in this regard, commented on the American folk revival at a notable New York "symposium" held in 1965. After chiding the audience for failing to base its work on traditional music and its special disciplines, MacColl delivered himself on Dylan:

I have watched with fascination the meteoric rise of the American Idol and I am still unable to see in him anything other than a youth of mediocre talent. Only a completely non critical audience, nourished on the watery pap of pop music could have fallen for such tenth-rate drivel. "But the poetry?" What poetry? The cultivated illiteracy of his topical songs or the embarrassing fourth-grade school boy attempts at free verse? [18]

MacColl's understanding of the relationship between what he calls American "pop" and the folk movement is just as congealed as his understanding of the antiwar movement and its relationship to rocknroll and folk.

Phil Ochs was also at that symposium. He tried to remind MacColl and everybody else about what they already knew but were wont to forget.

There are two major revolutions going on in music today: one is the revolution in song writing, adding perceptive protest and valid poetry; the other is the solidifying of the pop revolution of the fifties started by Hank Williams, Elvis Presley, Buddy Holly and Chuck Berry and now being carried on by the Beatles, the Rolling Stones, the Righteous Brothers and the Lovin' Spoonful; that is, the firm entrenchment of rhythm-and-blues slightly flavored by country-and-western that led to the sudden and final destruction of the big band sound. [19]

Phil Ochs never lost that connection between the beginnings of rocknroll and its implicit political imperative, even after a large part of the rock audience had forgotten it or repudiated it.

Most of the folk performers centered around Gerde's Folk City, the Wha?, and the dozen other Village clubs had pretty much the same history as Ochs, including Dylan. The songs of Tim Buckley, Dave Van Ronk, Tom Paxton, Tim Hardin, and so on constituted the political voice of folk; Dylan was its more personal, poetic side. [20] The artists were dealing with the mixed emotions and motivations that made the economic,

artistic, and political meeting of rocknroll and folk difficult. As for all
American young people, the Beatles were an important catalyst for
Dylan. He had apparently heard several things in the Beatles that showed
him the way and gave him the desire to bring folk and rock together:

They were doing things nobody was doing. Their chords were outrageous, just
outrageous, and their harmonies made it all valid. You could only do that with
other musicians. And it started me thinking about other people. . . . Everybody
else thought they were just for teeny boppers, that they were gonna pass right
away. But it was obvious to me they had staying power. I knew they were pointing
the direction of where music had to go. I was not about to put up with other
musicians but in my head the Beatles were *it*.[21]

For Dylan, the incompatible elements of art, commerce, and politics in
the folk-rock antagonism were resolved almost instantly in 1964. He
couldn't get over the fact that the Beatles had eight of the top ten songs.
The following views, reported by Anthony Scaduto, state both Phil Ochs'
and Bob Dylan's stance at this crucial moment.

[Ochs:]   I thought then that there was no end to what he [Dylan] could do now.
I thought that he could become Elvis Presley on that level. Essentially he could
physically represent rural America, all of America and put out fifteen gold records
in a row. . . . My feeling at that time was that he *did* want that. . . . What
happened then was the Beatles got in the way. Dylan wrote the lyrics, and the
Beatles captured the mass music.
[Dylan to Ochs:]   The stuff you're writing is bullshit, because politics is bullshit.
It's all unreal. The only thing that's real is inside you. Your feelings. Just look at
the world you're writing about and you'll see you're wasting your time. The
world is, well . . . it's just absurd.[22]

The bitchy tone of these words is probably not characterological. The
interpersonal style of that Village club scene, set by the manners of the
various scene-makers, ranged from southern-spiced barbs and New York
brusqueness, through the normal show business character assassination,
to black confrontational rhetoric. Whatever the motivation, Dylan and
Ochs were responding to severe pressures. The folk stream was being
devoured by the pop stream. Everyone in both camps was highly nervous
about choosing the terms of the meal. Few could maintain a completely
graceful composure under the stress, when hundreds of thousands of dollars were at stake in every record and a real shot at the big time was in
the offing. The battleground was mainly over the integrity of the performer, his choice of songs, his inclusion of profanity, and issues of dress
and manners. The rules of the game played by the pop stream were not
the same as in the folk stream. Art, commerce, and politics had different
meanings, were given different priorities. Dylan was clear, again according to Scaduto, on where he wanted to be. It was with the kids, and they
were wise to the futility of student protest.

The kids today, by the time they're twenty-one they realize it's all bullshit. I know it's all bullshit. Kids realize it's really a drag to plan for tomorrow their whole life, realizing in really hard terms that tomorrow never comes. You always wake up and it's today. There is no yesterday: tomorrow never seems to come, so what's left is today. Or nothing. There's no reason for anybody not knowing what's real, if they'd only open their heads.[23]

This motto is what is written on every artist's flag: "Time stoppeth here." Dylan, in picking up art's banner, put himself in a strategic place in the unresolving quarrel between politics and commerce. He also allied himself with Albert Grossman at approximately the same time he was signed by Hammond for Columbia. Hammond's impresarial stamp had considerable weight, giving Dylan a more powerful entree into musical and political circles than he might have received from a younger and less well connected record producer. In turn, with the legitimation he had won from Hammond, reinforced by his own presence in the South at dangerous times, Dylan commanded the vehicles that could cross the pop-folk bridge to rock; he was, indeed, fulfilling the promise of his first idols, Hank Williams and Little Richard, a promise to bring it all together for the young people.[24] His first album had even made a respectable showing on the pop album charts in September 1963.[25]

When Clive Davis took over supervision of A&R at Columbia in 1965 and continued to shepherd Dylan's career, the merging of folk and rocknroll had an even better chance. Davis did not harbor Mitch Miller's anti-rock bias that had prevented Columbia and the other major record companies from harvesting the crop they themselves had planted. That change at the top of the recording industry echoed down the ranks and changed the ways in which musical performance was judged. The absence of mastery in instrument or voice was irrelevant in the presence of the authenticity and personal power of the performer.

The year 1965, a year of success for Dylan, was for folk rock the year of its most dramatic appearance and its first public acceptance. The Byrds' first chart single, "Mr. Tambourine Man," went to number one on the pop chart in June of 1965, remaining thirteen weeks. Dylan is reported to have had the same reaction to the Byrds' version of his "Mr. Tambourine Man" as he did to the Animals' version of "The House of the Rising Sun," which Dylan had put on his first album. When the Animals' recording of the traditional song hit the top of the American pop chart in 1964, he allegedly said, "Rock worked." The Byrds later that year had another number one hit, Pete Seeger's biblical statement, "Turn, Turn, Turn." The Los Angeles-based Turtles instantly followed with another Dylan song, "It Ain't Me Babe," and Sonny and Cher put still another Dylan song, "I've Got You Babe," into the number one position on the pop charts. Folk rock's moment had arrived.

The Byrds were probably not much different from hundreds of bands with lead and bass guitars, drums, and a headful of songs. Their success with the Dylan material spurred them into making a full genealogical statement. The placement of their musical coat of arms in *Hit Parader* clearly shows that their target was the mass rocknroll audience (fig. 11-1). Their statement is one of the first, if not the first, formal genealogical statements that attempted to define the mature rock stream at the moment of its birth. It might be a publicist's tongue-in-cheek puffery, but, nevertheless, it is on target. The Byrds' origin story is illustrated as the meeting of the six streams, forming a seventh. Beyond that, the identification of Bach as their great grandfather underscores their "serious" musical heritage and interest, as does the claim to their jazz origin via John Coltrane's influence. The reference to the folk stream is a double one, Pete Seeger for political purity and Odetta for the shading of politics into entertainment. The debt to Ravi Shankar as part of the world music scene is a recognition of the remarkable respect with which that specific artist, his instrument the sitar, the raga form, and the ideology behind it was held by the emerging rock movement on the West Coast.[26] The acknowledgment of the Beach Boys appears as a left-handed recognition of their dominance in the American white rocknroll tradition, substituting for Elvis who is understandably missing (being very much in the movies and gaining weight). Their respect for Chuck Berry is in the context of a testament to the Beatles as the synthesizers of rocknroll, who took it from the founders to a place where "serious musicians could go to."[27] The Byrds formed and reformed with changing personnel, eventually putting out eight chart-making albums before 1973 as well as seven singles before 1967.

To return to the drama that was beginning in the summer of 1965, Dylan appeared at the Newport Folk Festival's major Sunday night program in hot English mod clothes, with a solid body electric guitar and backed by Paul Butterfield's Blues Band. Accounts of the events that followed vary considerably. Whether it was an imbalance in the sound system that blotted out Dylan's voice, or the shock of seeing the full electric rock presence overwhelm the acoustic folk-hero, there was considerable audience upset.[28]

That encounter signaled stormy seas. East Coast folk fans held no love for the rock-tinged electric blues that was growing into their own folk club scene; yet the pressure for a fully instrumental, strongly rhythmic, and loud sound came from the rocknroll concerts and clubs that were keeping the kids dancing. The Young Rascals, for example, were a highly

Figure 11-1. (opposite) Geneology of The Byrds' music in *HIT PARADER* July 1965, p. 8.
Reprinted courtesy of *HIT PARADER* magazine.

ALL MUSIC IS FOR THE BYRDS

BACH

Johann Sebastian Bach was the greatest master of Counterpoint. Counterpoint is a related but independent melody played simultaneously along with the basic melody. The most simple example of this is when you sing "Row row row your boat gently down the stream" and someone else sings "Merrily merrily merrily merrily, life is but a dream" at the same time. See! You've been singing counterpoint for years.

THE BEATLES

The Beatles made the largest jump in the whole development pattern. They were aware of Bach and Chuck Berry at the same time. The Beatles were the primary catalyst of the synthesis. They brought rock and roll to a place serious musicians could go to.

RAVI SHANKAR

In India, pop music, classical and jazz are all the same thing. The man who has given this music a worldwide audience is Ravi Shankar, India's master musician.
After years of rigorous training in the technique of the sitar and music in general, he started anew as a classical soloist and soon established himself in the front rank of young musicians. Richer with the foundation of classical values, he started experiments in orchestrating Indian music on a hitherto unattempted scale, and successfully founded, composed for, and conducted the National Orchestra at All India Radio.

THE BEACH BOYS

The Beach Boys are associated with the West Coast sound and the Byrds use a little of it when Dave sings the high lines. "I think I got just as much church music as the Beach Boys," is the way Dave puts it.

THE SITAR

The sitar is the most popular stringed instrument of India. It has existed there in its present form for approximately seven hundred years. Fashioned from seasoned gourds and teakwood, it has a track of twenty metal frets and 6 or 7 main playing strings above them, and thirteen sympathetic resonating strings. The strings are also strummed upon occasion with the little finger of the right hand inserted in the main strings. The instrument is tuned to the Raga being played and the main strings are plucked by a wire plectrum worn on the index finger of the right hand.
Sitar-like sounds can be produced on a 12-string guitar, as recently demonstrated by The Byrds, by tuning the E string to the key of D to produce a modal chord. The bottom three strings provide the drone sound and the upper strings are bent to play the "melody."
The last time we saw the Byrds they told us that an instrument manufacturer is making a sitar that can be played through an amplifier. They haven't gotten their hands on one yet, but when they do — watch out!

JOHN COLTRANE

Jazz critic Martin Williams said of tenor saxophonist John Coltrane, "There was a time when Coltrane was placing the notes in his rapid tenor runs so as to imply that he wanted the eighth-note rhythms further subdivided into sixteenths." Don Heckman, writing in Down Beat said, "The use of harmonics, both as an extension of the instrument's range and as a method of producing two or more notes simultaneously; the running together of massive streams of notes into tonally indistinct blurs of sound; the gradual inclusion of such noise elements as squawks and honks - all this became a part of Coltrane's instrumental vocabulary." Byrd leader Jim McGuinn digs it because of "the note cluster concept and random improvisation. They're going against the establishment."

BOB DYLAN

Dylan added words. He caused a wave of awareness-cresting-and it spread out like ripples. The Byrds happened to be close to the center. They were the first to put Dylan's songs in the pop field.

PETE SEEGER & ODETTA

Pete Seeger and Odetta were early influences on Jim McGuinn before the Hootenanny explosion. Jim used to hang around at the Gate of Horn and the Old Town School in Chicago and watch. He learned a lot. "It was really beautiful then," says Jim.

favored New York band that drew some of the same crowds seen at the folk clubs. The group had been rebuilt in that year (1965) from the remnants of Joey Dee's Starlighters, who had had a number one hit with "Peppermint Twist" back in 1962. They now turned to rock.

The mingling of folk with rocknroll was unstoppable. Even the Blues Project was to spin off some of its personnel in that direction. That group, whose very name implied its noncommercial purity, was right in the middle of the Village's political wing of the folk revival. Yet, from its ranks it extruded Al Kooper. Brooklyn born in 1944, Kooper at the age of fourteen joined the Royal Teens (of "Short Shorts" fame) as guitarist and was soon a familiar figure at the New Brill Building, writing and arranging for commercial rocknroll groups. In 1965 he played organ on the Columbia session that recorded Dylan's "Like a Rolling Stone" for the "Highway 61 Revisited" album, and he was on hand for Dylan's appearance at the 1965 Newport festival. After leaving the Blues Project, he formed Blood Sweat and Tears in 1967, producing their first album and then leaving before that first rock band to introduce horns had found its commercial niche.

The commercial success and the consolidation of two full streams— rocknroll and folk—made the Byrds the equivalent of Elvis. With that rock-folk passport, their carrying case brought a whole brigade of performers into a new perspective. Both young musicians and record executives could now accept the synthesis of folk with rocknroll. Disheartened folk singers from the Village and from Los Angeles had a chance at that point to regroup under the rock banner. It was large enough to enfold even the seasoned Los Angeles professionals Sonny and Cher, surf music refugees, the Turtles, and the Mamas and the Papas. Others with more folk and/or country roots soon put together combinations that worked, and the melange of music in the San Francisco Bay area would do its share. Mature rock in the United States was a homemade bread, but the yeast came from the other side of the Atlantic.

The British Caravan

The British invasion, as it has been called, was actually more like a revival of the old London–New York short loop. From the earliest days, British standards set American preferences. In return, American vigor and exoticism flavored the bland British palate and cultural insularity.[29] The snob value of British upper-class elegance in language and manners, if not in clothes and decor, was a never-ending source of pleasure and reassurance for American audiences, especially when that elegance carried anti-establishment ideas. The differences between London and New

York were large enough to guarantee interest in any cultural product moving from one to the other but minimal enough to fit into the marketing and evaluative categories of both. Marginal variation within familiar frames was once more the formula for stoking the fires of the two cities' cultures.

Aside from the flood of British actors who poured onto the new sound stages of Hollywood after 1928, the main traffic from the United Kingdom to the United States was in exchanges of fashion and music. From London came considerable help to America's youth, bypassing the categories proffered by the consumer industries. On the music side, there was an increased pace in the R&B tours to the United Kingdom, including Big Bill Broonzy, Sonny Terry and Brownie McGhee, and Muddy Waters, implanting there a crop of young bands enamoured with the purity of the blues and its modern offshoots. The visiting rocknroll acts, especially Gene Vincent and the Blue Caps along with Buddy Holly and the Crickets, provided a powerful model for British bands, the latter influencing the choice of name for both the Hollies and the Beatles.

One of the lesser-known attractions was jazz; and one of the most consequential, if invisible, British visitors to American shores, with respect to rocknroll, was Ken Colyer. The context of his story is this. The British popular music scene after the war was in flux. It was burying its music halls, as the United States had done for vaudeville in the 1930s. The British pop record companies were attempting to domesticate their variegated club scene, the major exposure point for records since radio was not a commercial exploitation medium. After World War II, the pirate ships broadcasting from the English Channel and from Radio Luxembourg gave British kids an earful of American music from every stream. Jazz styles in Britain ranged from purist to commercial, with each position fiercely defended by its partisans. Pop was less tidy, larger, and more volatile. Chris Barber and Humphrey Lyttleton had been the best-known figures in the traditional and revivalist jazz styles after World War II, but both were outflanked by the unexpected surge of the traditionalists led by Ken Colyer.[30]

A working-class youth, Ken Colyer had organized the Crane River Jazz Band in 1950 before he left in 1952 for the States to listen to and play with George Lewis' band, then playing in New Orleans.[31] Lewis was the living link to Buddy Bolden, to Louis Armstrong, and to the original and pure American black jazz, and when he invited Colyer to play with the band, it was a high honor. Colyer returned to London where, sadly, the interest in traditional jazz had sunk like a stone.[32] The irony was that it was Lonnie Donegan, one of Colyer's own sidemen, who used the skiffle form to launch his own career and help short-circuit the "trad" boom.

Donegan's "Rock Island Line," a copy of Huddie Ledbetter's then current recording of the same tune, quickly found a top chart position in both the United States and Britain. The Beatles went to school on that sound, completing, for the hundredth time, the loop that exchanged the musics of the United States with that of the United Kingdom.

Tommy Steele, the first English teenaged star, was a lucky find by the older music industry forces, who were trying to connect the American sound to English tradition. They were "to use him [Steele] to attract audiences into the failing music halls," which had a "surprisingly strong influence on British pop."[33] When the Beatles appeared with their echo of British music hall performer George Formsby, the New York–London music publisher network was on the road to a resurgence.[34] Their explosive popularity was undeniable, so it is not surprising that the Beatles were picked up by the London music apparatus scanning all the young groups for another Tommy Steele with a valid passport to America. In February 1964, the Beatles' records reached the States. In that month, "I Want to Hold Your Hand" reached the number one position on the singles pop chart and their first album, *Meet the Beatles,* went to the top of the best-selling albums chart.

John, Paul, George, and Ringo followed their records to America shortly thereafter. Their impact was immediate and surpassed, by far, what either Frank Sinatra or Elvis Presley had generated among young people. The Beatlemania that had burst in England the previous October (1963) repeated itself in America. The Beatles were like the cork in the bottle. Once pulled, everything in the United Kingdom came pouring out. The music was packaged into singles and albums and shipped to the States. The live performers followed immediately. These early groups are now forgotten or, more accurately, are safely enshrined in the museum. Mickie Most, one of the British producers quickest off the mark in the early 1960s, helped bring over several plane loads of "beat groups"— Herman's Hermits, the Cherokees, the Symbols, the Moquettes, and so on. Most's most successful group, the Animals, reworked Dylan's songs and some older black blues materials and were one of the first British groups to reach the number one position on the album charts. The Rolling Stones put four singles on the pop charts in 1964 and launched their first U.S. tour in June of that year. The London–New York pump was primed.

The London end was, as George Melly sketched it, a hustle requiring the assemblage and rapid circulation of this or that musical, lyrical, and visual part of the Anglo-American rag bag of pop resources. Impresarial talent, as in the U.S., was essential:

Secunda [a pop manager] can stand as the most perfect of all those ex-public school layabouts who'd been sitting on their asses up and down the King's Road for almost a decade wondering what to do with the only talent most of them had—an instinct for style.

Some had become criminals, some hustled in the fringes of the art world, some went into advertising, some married heiresses. For those who'd hung on, pop was the answer; a simple world without precedents or an established hierarchy, prepared to accept any fantasy as a potential and profitable reality.[35]

The game continues to this day.

Stylish bands pasted over with trendy colors were not the only products sent over the ocean. In the sixties, any passport containing the "blues" was a welcome product. From John Mayall's Blues Breakers on through the permutations that brought together Eric Clapton, Ginger Baker, Jack Bruce, and others, the substantial British guitar import has mixed creatively with the American counterparts. All too many, however, were pale imitations of older sounds. The main act to follow the Beatles was the Rolling Stones, led by the indestructible Mick Jagger. If these two British bands did not mirror the good twin-bad twin image that Elvis Presley and Pat Boone projected, it was only because they looked and sounded too much alike to American kids at first. Moreover, their music was different; the Stones worked American rhythm and blues to near exhaustion, and the Beatles explored everything in the world. The Stones never achieved the Beatles' breadth, although their move to Atlantic via Ahmet Ertegun was a full step forward in their maturation. Following right behind were the blues bands, notably Mayall's, Clapton's, and a variety of jazz-blues-rock bands including Cream, Blind Faith, the Yardbirds, and the Moody Blues, exchanging personnel as they moved towards the British contribution to hard rock via Led Zeppelin. The strong anti-pop, anti-commercial attitudes that characterized these groups were partially expressed in the passion expended on the guitar.

As a whole, the British contribution to mature rock has been threefold. First, the Beatles and others, in opening wide the London–New York short loop, accelerated the entire world involvement with popular music, which was increasingly a youth music. In the States, that opening meant a British validation of the emerging youth culture. What had been a despised and frightening cultural compacture of adolescent sex and race-mixing was rendered almost acceptable by the "moppets." The contemporary world rock tour owes much of its vitality to the special nature of the London–New York, two-city short loop. London drew in all the colonial cultures that sought closeness to the metropole.

The Caribbean, especially, provided the music scene with a melodic richness, an instrumental color, and a political sense that refreshed Britain's almost exhausted rehashing of old American rocknroll, pop, and R&B. It is paradoxical that Jamaican dance forms themselves (from Ska, to Rock Steady, to Reggae) were influenced by American black pop dance music. The same process occurred with Soca, the synthesis of American soul and Trinidadian Calypso musics.[36] New York, at the other end of the loop, was attempting a comeback as the center for all American culture, competing with the West Coast for dominion. It could still deliver, once in a while, the huge American public.

The second contribution of the British to rock's maturity was a result of the immense popularity of the Beatles first, and the rest of the groups shortly afterward. This popularity froze the rock band's schema, its formal characteristics. It now had four, possibly five, players, drum kit, bass guitar, lead and supporting guitar (all potentially electrified) plus vocals delivered by one and all. It is essential to understand, though, that the Beatles, Stones, and so on did not create the mature small rock band. The mold had been made in the U.S.; from 1946 onward, the three commercial streams had been evolving the smaller band. By the mid- to late sixties, anything was possible—a solo act such as Judy Collins or Neil Young, the duos like Simon and Garfunkel, or larger aggregations such as Crosby, Stills and Nash. The Beatles, nevertheless, provided a powerful and constraining model that thousands of young American garage bands found exactly to their liking. The Beatles were not only British; they were white. They formalized in 1964 the live performance rock band led by writer/performer.

By 1966, the Beatles had finished touring but continued their development in the studio, from which *Sgt. Pepper's Lonely Hearts Club Band* emerged. It may not have been the first concept album (Zappa's *Freak Out* may earn that honor), but it dramatically stretched past the three-minute single. Its immense popularity, critically and financially, beyond the normal bounds of the rock audience firmly established the album as the basic artistic unit for rock performers. It must be said that the Beatles were chameleons and magpies partaking of every musical and cultural trend in the 1960s. This statement may be an ungenerous way of describing their own maturing, but that's what the youth culture was all about, continual exploration and improvisation around some steady if general ideals.

Third and finally, the British rock groups, and here I refer primarily to the Beatles, taught the American music industry that the young singer-songwriter, already a factor in the person of Paul Anka or Bob Dylan, and the young producer-writers, such as Leiber-Stoller, could even further vertically integrate the music business. With their own record company (Apple) and with full control of a series of worldwide tours and movie projects, the Beatles just about completed the maturation process. Rock grew up as it learned the three lessons that built the superstar machinery essential to the record industry.

Bay Area Synthesis

San Francisco is a small city. In the sixties, it sustained a series of interconnected scenes. Some of the people browsing on a Saturday afternoon in City Lights Bookstore in North Beach might see each other later that night as they moved from the Matrix to the other clubs there, then bump into each other at the Russian bakeries along Clement Street on Sunday morning. From Minnie's "Can Do" on Fillmore in San Francisco to the line of Telegraph Avenue luncheon spots on the way to Oakland from Berkeley, there was enough overlap to provide a diverse but unified audience for the densely packed musical scene.

The Haight-Ashbury area, one of the main wings of the Bay area's youth scene, was, in 1965, the focal point. Ralph Gleason, respected jazz critic for the *San Francisco Chronicle*, described how the area's reputation began with the visit of the Family Dog, a young group who wanted to put on dances in the Haight. They had sought his help, for he had been publicly identified as a champion of rocknroll. Luria Castell, a member of the Family Dog, had recently returned from Los Angeles where she had visited the Trips, one of the few nightclubs that permitted kids to dance: "Dancing is the thing. . . . they've got to give people a place to dance. That's what's wrong with those Cow Palace shows. THE KIDS CAN'T DANCE THERE. There'll be no trouble when they can dance."[37]

This complaint unmistakably echoed the situation that had produced rocknroll in the first place back in the early 1950s, when the dance pulse had gone out of the pop stream. Now, since rocknroll had been drained of its original R&B sources and Elvis' rockabilly heritage had been smoothed out, the challenge was to put a dance beat into a music that was, at the same time, trying to merge folk with rocknroll. The bands of San Francisco were able to do just that, and the effort produced not only mature rock but its incandescent cultural atmosphere.

Radio was important for this effort, just as it had been earlier, and here again San Francisco pioneered the way. Tom Donahue, veteran disk jockey of the late fifties, found for a failing FM station, KMPX, the frame for a new kind of programming.[38] Within a short time, Donahue had assembled a staff and a style that was to be called "progressive" FM programming. The air play for album cuts and the interviews with the artists tightened the new short loop that was appearing. The hippie community took over the place as one of their own. On air and off, the station was the conduit for Bay area music. Commercials were aired at a minimum, albums were played in part or in full, and the radio lore of forty years was given the heave-ho. Even after a strike at the station and a move to KSAN, progressive FM was there to stay.[39] It quickly traveled down the coast and across the country to the major cities where rock was also incubating.

There was another element that was to make San Francisco the reputed capital of the counterculture. On 21 February 1965, Augustus Owsley Stanley III was arrested and charged with operating a methedrine laboratory (a speed factory). He beat the charge, left town, and returned with enough materials and know-how to make 1.5 million doses of LSD. He supplied the city's youth with an important new tool for their already well-packed stash of drugs—marijuana being the staple, with speed, cocaine, and heroin also available. Drug use and its commerce became part of the alternative lifestyle in the Bay area, down the coast, and everywhere else, giving the term "acid rock" a local designation.

Finally, San Francisco maintained a tradition of public display. This practice was derived not only from its Italian and Latino festivals, parades, and street fairs, but also from the murals that brought Diego Rivera to the city for a public celebration in 1930, when he fulfilled his commissions to paint the walls of the San Francisco Stock Exchange Luncheon Club and the School of Fine Arts. He received a warmer welcome than he did in New York City.

The acceptance of public artistic life sheltered for the next few years a variety of adventures, which ranged from Ken Kesey's Trips Festival, the Vietnam Day March over the Oakland bridge, the appearances of Allen Ginsberg at Berkeley's Poetry Conference, Bob Dylan's opening in December with his electric band, the Human Be In of 1967, and other more or less regular happenings. Music was everywhere. Gleason listed 387 bands, with whimsical and improbable names, that had appeared in San Francisco following the first Family Dog dances in October 1965.[40]

Only two of these groups have survived to the present (though individual performers from other groups are still at work)—the Grateful Dead and the Jefferson Airplane (after 1970, the Jefferson Starship, now simply Starship). Building upon the synthesis within the Bay area during 1965, these two bands created two of mature rock's strongest styles. Internally, their members' histories are as diverse as any of the youngsters who wandered into San Francisco in the early sixties. Jerry Garcia nicely states the process of growth for the Dead in the idiom of the sixties:

See, it's all very strange because we all came from such far-out backgrounds into the rock'n'roll scene. . . . I think it might be like Phil Lesh was saying the other day. He mentioned that when he had sort of like run out of his musical bag, . . . and things were looking pretty down, . . . and then all of a sudden here was the Beatles movies. . . . It was very high and very up, you know. And high and up looked better than down and out, really. . . . So that like for me, my musical bag had run out as well, there was no, like, people who were really interested in bluegrass music and nobody to play with. . . . It was like a bankrupt scene. . . . You never got a chance to play or anything. And playing the music is a real immediate, satisfying thing. It's like if it's going good, everybody knows it's going good, everybody in the band and everybody in the audience. . . . You know, it's a faster thing. You don't have to worry about the form or anything. It's really cleansing somehow.[41]

It is the fact that the members of the Dead came from diverse backgrounds, each member having lived through some part of most of the musical streams, that is important. They were prepared for the new thing by the exhaustion of their musical pasts. And they found enough intrinsic musical satisfaction and personal compatability to stave off the disruptions of ego-clash and money-burn. They, like so many other bands in the Haight, lived more or less communally, part of the "tribes." They were one of the first rock bands to be signed by a major record label. After years of debt-peonage to Warner Brothers, they set up their own label in 1973 but have lived and thrived in the midst of probably one of the largest bootleg tape operations in history (Deadheads pride themselves on their freely traded tape collections of Dead concerts). Their musical reliance was on a jazz-improvisation type of performance. The seventeen- or twenty-five-minute versions of "Dark Star" are mature rock, a cousin to a long jazz jam but certainly no close relative to a pop, R&B, or country piece. Their readiness to spin off solo and other configurations of recording groups also comes from the jazz tradition.

The most important strategic accomplishment of the Dead, however, has been their success in permanently bonding to their audience. This remarkable and self-renewing attachment of fans to the Dead is not entirely a result of escapist, retreatist, or drug-filled nostalgia. The existence of the Deadheads and their tribal-like practices might make it appear so, but the live concerts from 1970 to the present almost always completely sold out, have extended their audience's age range from the veterans of 1967 to the teenagers of the 1990s.

The Airplane, now the Starship, though a stormier and more volatile band, is of that same historic significance. They looked America straight in the eye as they celebrated their own youth-drug scene, challenging the adults to look in the mirror. Their 1970 *Blows Against the Empire* album was an important response to changed conditions. Perhaps the successful landing on the moon by American astronauts in July 1969 changed youth's basic perspective. The band's concern with space travel may have been a metaphoric way of recognizing that the eyes of some segments of the youth movement were lifted to the skies rather than focused on Vietnam.

Which city first achieved the synthesis that matured rock will be argued about for some time. The case for San Francisco rests upon that city's claims that it all came together there in its most complete and colorful form. San Francisco even had a theme song, Scott McKenzie's 1967 pop single "San Francisco (Be Sure to Wear Flowers in your Hair)," which signaled the dangerous extent to which young sincerity would become marketable. The year 1965 witnessed a confluence of all the forces in the political movement and in music. Though this process was happening everywhere in the nation, "San Francisco had turned on the world to the adult rock sound. Rock 'n' roll came of age in San Francisco and its birth pangs were flamboyant to say the least."[42] This judgment came from jazz critic Ralph Gleason, participant observer and chronicler of the scene.

The Bay area was producing other musicians who would illuminate rock's diversity as it matured. Janis Joplin, Sly and the Family Stone, Country Joe and the Fish, and Carlos Santana were among those who wrested enough control over their music and their extra-musical life to carve different niches in the rock life. San Francisco will always be in their music. During these maturing years, every permutation of rock's founding streams found embodiment in some band or group. The development of what became "hard rock" moved forward, for example, with Blue Cheer. This band, formed in 1966, asserted a genealogy different from the folk-rock line in its 1968 hit record, "Summertime Blues." This song was a remake of Eddie Cochran's 1958 original, but it was done in a manner that earned them the name "power trio." Blue Cheer was also linked to the psychedelic, their name being the same as one of Owsley's LSD variations. They were like the Detroit white band, Mitch Ryder and the Detroit Wheels, and would transmit that rough manner to the Who, a second-wave British band who also scored a hit with their even louder and more exaggerated version of Eddie Cochran's hit. The biker connection Blue Cheer had (its manager was a former Hell's Angel) was but one way to reach out to that important component of the rock audience.

Another example of San Francisco's rock diversity was the Pacific Gas and Electric Company. This band put three singles on the charts just at the end of San Francisco's moment in the sun and was one of several integrated bands trying to blend rock with "soul." San Francisco had a band for every taste.

The city's youth culture also had that quality of self-consciousness, generosity, and panache that suggests a brief life span. The youth called their shots quite cleanly, announcing that the city was a Human Be In at the start of the fireworks and declaring the show over when it was over, that is, with the "Death of Hippie" ceremonies in October 1967.

The Los Angeles Swarm

Los Angeles is another matter. Too large, too diverse and complex to be exemplified in a single image, L.A. is the basis for the futuristic city in the movie *Blade Runner*. It is also a major entrepot for world music, world film, and world television markets. The music of all seven streams is mixed in every combination possible by the highly energetic hurly-burly of creative writers and performers, strong studio producers, and equally creative session musicians. Swimming among these are the deal-makers who keep the whole system moving. Their talent is to bring the right somebodies together at the right time. Los Angeles in the midsixties was the equivalent of Memphis in the early 1950s and more, since all seven streams had their own short loops in that area.

The sprawling Los Angeles produced unique rock forms, for example, the GUAMBO (Great Underground Arts Masked Ball and Orgy) spon-sored by the Los Angeles *Free Press* in July of 1966. Even though the exact location of that event (which promised music, lights, film, dancing, and so on) was changed two days before, word of mouth brought thou-sands of people out in their cars, young and old, straight and gay, all flashing together for the experience, while the police, the union musi-cians, and the rest of the onlookers gaped helplessly. No organization, no leaders, just the whirling but definitely assembled people. The closest thing to it, some say, was the phenomenon described in Nathanael West's *Day of the Locust*.

The musical scene was not always peaceful, though. A gradual politi-cization of entertainment zones from San Diego up to Seattle-Vancouver had developed. Los Angeles, with its history of cultural violence dating back to the 1943 Pachuco riots, exploded in 1966 with a series of com-parable commotions on Sunset Strip. These highly publicized nights were the first serious encounters of a nonsouthern police force with white youth. (Actually, the 1963 police sweeps through Manhattan's Washing-ton Square, clearing out the menace of folk singers, was probably the first such event.) The police during these years were regularly screening out underaged youngsters at beer and liquor-serving establishments. It is dif-ficult to say who learned what from those encounters, but the question about whether "youth" were to be treated as children to be protected or as hoodlums to be corralled was unequivocally answered. Here was an-other instance when all young people, regardless of age, were treated as a single category.

Los Angeles also produced in the midsixties hundreds of rock bands, ranging from the Beach Boys to the Buffalo Springfield. The latter was a strategic band formed in the spring of 1966. Stephen Stills had worked himself all around the country to the New York folk scene, where he met Richie Furay then with the Au Go Go Singers (the East Coast version of California's New Christy Minstrels and Serendipity Singers, both pop-folk groups). Like others struck by the Beatles movie *A Hard Day's Night*, they decided their next move was to form a rocknroll band. So, off to California and the legendary meeting on Sunset Boulevard with Neil Young in his hearse with Bruce Palmer. The Buffalo Springfield never made a charted album, and their five singles are but bare indicators of the weight these individuals and their various groups were to carry in rock's mature flowering.

Crosby, Stills, and Nash emerged from the wreckage of Buffalo Springfield. Their elegantly produced albums yielded some of the most enduring works in the rock canon. "Suite: Judy Blue Eyes" and "Marrakesh Express" extended the range of the concept album, and celebrated the rock culture and its heroes (in the former case Judy Collins, in the latter the drug culture).

Graham Nash, a founder of the Hollies (the British rocknroll band formed in the wake of Buddy Holly's visit to the United Kingdom), brought the country music side of the group to the fore and led genealogically to country's durable place in rock via Creedence Clearwater Revival, Poco, and subsequent bands.[43] Followers included Gram Parsons, who had also paid his Greenwich Village dues and played briefly with the Byrds. His personal magnetism and strong commitment brought a strong country sound to the influential Flying Burrito Brothers, which he formed with Chris Hillman of the Byrds. Neil Young, another of mature rock's restless actors, after leaving Buffalo Springfield joined Crosby, Stills, and Nash for a time, but carried his acoustic instrumentation and personal vision all through the sixties and for two more full decades mostly by himself.

The compatibility of the several diverse strands that made up mature rock can be demonstrated by the meeting that brought together Al Kooper, graduate of the New York Brill Building, now producer for Columbia records, Stephen Stills of the California rock scene, and Mike Bloomfield of the Paul Butterfield Blues Band in a one-time album, *Super Session*. Like most of rock's finest achievements, it was unduplicable.[44]

Los Angeles' contribution also includes the Doors, who were but one of many bands that came from the region's college and university campuses. That academic hothouse atmosphere nurtured Jim Morrison's infatuation with the literature and practice of extremes, the artistic attempt to reach beyond everyday experience into any kind of transformed state. One of the most important of these exemplars was the "Living Theater" of Julian Beck and Judith Malina. Their confrontational, orgiastic company so impressed Morrison with its quasi-religious purification theatrics, including mass disrobing on stage, that he was subsequently led into lugubrious indecent exposure misadventures in Miami.

The Los Angeles scene also contained Frank Zappa. With and without the Mothers of Invention, Zappa has been able to create one of the longest and strongest catalogues in rock history. He was another self-taught, classically enamored writer-performer. Zappa brings together all the streams. As a "kid I used to save up for a month so I could get an R & B album and, the same day the complete works of Anton Webern."[45] Zappa has successfully managed a vertical integration to the point of owning his record company, and, more recently, a video cassette production company; he is the Wagner of Rock. He is at the same time the social commentator par excellence, wearing the mantle of Lenny Bruce and R. Crumb in the self-appointed role of "Central Scrutinizer." From *Freak Out*'s tribute to Elvis, "Help, I'm a Rock," to "Trouble Every Day," a distanced recapitulation and warning about the Watts riot, to "Drafted Again" on the *You Are What You Is* album, Frank (as with Elvis, his fans are on an easy, first-name basis) is responsive to the larger political issues relevant to the young. His suited appearance in 1988 before the Senate hearings on rating rock records was memorable, yielding the hippest defense of the First Amendment heard in a long time. Frank reigns in the rock pantheon.

Los Angeles also sheltered the commercial side of the music. Just as true rock bands were coming together in the midsixties, Don Kirshner of Screen Gems, formerly of the Brill Building, was assembling the Monkees, a fabricated rock group designed to capture the teen audience for television. The success of the Monkees surprised everyone. Despite the fact that the actors were not even musicians, the Monkees were a hot property in movies, television, and records during the succeeding five years. They opened the West Coast road to bubblegum. The Archies, the Cowsills, and the Partridge Family would follow and lay the basis for the heavy metal bands to come after 1970; that is, if you have been raised on Mickey Mouse, King Kong will scare the pants off you. Television had the ability to deliver the sound of rocknroll but not its fury.

Finally, rock in movies continued the romance between music and the motion pictures. Just as fad-ridden as the music business in America, movies experienced a trajectory of maturity remarkably akin to that of rocknroll. Jonas Mekas, senior New York–based movie critic, said that "in the years 1960 to 1965 the 'cinema' had come to maturity."[46] The intersection of rock and the cinema still awaits full analysis and appreciation.

The New York Order

New York maintained a more structured tradition in its musical components, and its geography was determined by an uptown-downtown distinction that was perhaps more stylistic than physical. Going uptown to Harlem in the 1920s and 1930s was more like going downtown to the Village in the 1950s and 1960s. The Village produced the Blues Project, the Lovin' Spoonful, and the wilder Fugs, bands that would assist in the rock-folk amalgam and in the coalition between cultural and political rebels. But there were several other scenes in the City. One was Broadway. The musical theater, always on the lookout for hot properties, had sneered at rocknroll during all the years that the senior ASCAP mentality had held sway. With *Hair* in 1968, *Jesus Christ Superstar*, and *Tommy*, rock was taken more seriously—but still not very.

Another, most peculiar scene helped blur if not destroy the comfortable distinction between uptown and downtown, and in the process, it added another vital component to maturing rock. The band was the Velvet Underground, and the band's sometime impresario Andy Warhol held a place in the Pop Art ambiance of the moment large enough to shelter the Velvets. The classical musical training of Lou Reed and John Cale, their founding members, was masked by the brutal blast of their short songs. Nevertheless, the band had the basic New York passport— mastery of their instruments, commitment to serious music, and a creative songwriting capacity. Their sophisticated, knife-edged decadence was exactly in line with Warhol's strategy of erasing the lines between art and commercialism, between fashion and music. They managed a committed fury while maintaining the fatigued distance requisite to breaching the city's boundaries separating uptown from downtown sensibilities. This breach into forbidden areas so aroused the *New York Times'* irate scorekeeper, Bosley Crowther, that he delivered himself of this in 1966:

It has come time to wag a warning finger at Andy Warhol and his underground friends and tell them, politely but firmly, that they are pushing a reckless thing too far. It was all right as long as they stayed in Greenwich Village or on the south side of 42nd Street. . . . But now that their underground has surfaced on West 57th Street and taken over a theater with carpets, . . . it is time for permissive adults to stop winking at their too-precocious pranks.[47]

It was not only New York that was offended. When the Velvet Underground toured the West Coast with the Warhol entourage, they met the San Francisco music scene with contempt and distaste, which was equally returned. The New Yorkers' political cynicism and cool attitudes towards drugs and sex were almost totally opposite. The response of the Velvets to their counterpart in San Francisco, the Grateful Dead,[48] and to the city itself, is best summed up in Paul Morrisey's remark of 1967, quoted by Warhol:

Oh God, the music in this city is so incredibly bad. Just think: San Francisco has not managed to produce even one individual of any musical distinction whatsoever. Not a Dylan, not a Lennon, not a Brian Wilson, not a Mick Jagger— nobody. Not even a Phil Spector. Just some nothing groups and some nothing music. They delude themselves that music is a *group* thing—the way they think everything is. . . .[49]

The Velvet Underground didn't record much, got hardly any air play, and disbanded after their last album in 1969. Freed of the Warhol influence, and after a period of limbo, Lou Reed and John Cale resurfaced in the 1970s. Their work constituted an important anchor in rock music during those vital early years, representing both meticulous musicianship and rough energy and bringing hard drugs and androgynous sexuality into the rock world.

Rock Criticism

The final element of the maturing rock stream was its critical apparatus. The rock critics' job was to persuade the relevant publics that they as critics were in charge of elaborating the standards of evaluation for this new stream. They first had to find a platform from which to apply those standards to the new records and performances as they appeared. The underground alternative papers and the rocknroll fanzines coming out in the midsixties provided that platform. But what were the standards for rock? Charles Rosen's radical assertion about the pantheon's dominion in any stream of music framed the issue. This view, hardly available to rock's young critics, was nevertheless at work, leading to a clearing of the decks, a new start.

But an entirely new start was not possible, for rocknroll was the synthesis of all the other streams and had also inherited their critical vocabulary. In part, that vocabulary was built from the two-line reviews of new releases in *Billboard, Cash Box,* and the other trade press organs. The shrewd reviewers of those papers were masters at identifying for each record its musical style, its ancestors and influences, the merit of its performance, and the likelihood of its commercial success. This was basic criticism, but it was directed to jukebox owners and record distributors. The disk jockeys of the 1950s were also critics. Their selection of records, the making of hits, the management of talent, their championing of the teenagers, however, was more than a critic's disinterested evaluation. They were partisans and participants, serving themselves and the industry; they were not autonomous critics.

A major barrier to formal rock criticism was the fact that, until the midsixties, teenagers were the audience for rocknroll. Young people had neither the resources nor the reason to express to themselves or to their disk jockey champions more than simple preference—the familiar, "I give it an 86; I like the beat." Besides, who would bother to elaborate a critical language for a kid's three-minute rocknroll record?

The only literary sources aimed exclusively at those teenaged audiences were organs such as *Hit Parader.* These publications mainly reprinted the lyrics of currently popular songs and filled their pages with the usual fluff of Hollywood-type fan magazines. In December 1963, *Hit Parader* began the long march from teenaged gossip to a more serious level of music criticism. "Teen" was dropped from the magazine's cover page, and a new editorial staff and policy were installed. Jim Delahant became its editor and guiding presence (a decade later, he moved to a senior position in Atlantic Records) at about that same time the folk and jazz streams were being brought into rocknroll.

Crawdaddy: The Magazine of Rock emerged in 1964 with an air of musical knowledge and commitment that clearly indicated that rock had found a mature critical voice. This pioneer "fanzine," founded by Paul Williams, was one of hundreds of such small, generally mimeographed magazines that ranged from simple adulation to a polemical-analytical stance by and for the developing rock audience. These were the literary equivalent of the garage band and were spread across the entire nation.[50] *Crawdaddy*'s sense of its role as the learned and dedicated critical guide for a brand new art form was evident:

"Rock and roll has given us a whole new playground" Paul Williams said in an interview in the fall of 1967. "If it weren't for rocknroll we'd have to play in some one else's playground. I mean its hard to groove on Plato because other people have done it for so long that you have to learn the rules. But we're creating standards for criticism, a whole new aesthetic.[51]

In November 1967, *Rolling Stone* appeared in San Francisco under the editorship of Jann Wenner and the guidance of Ralph Gleason, considered to be the closest mentor Wenner ever had.[52] It was from the start a brilliant mixture of the new dedicated rock journalism and the alternative youth culture flourishing in the Bay area. At the same time, it was a financially oriented operation aimed not only at the national youth audience but also at the major industries that served that market. In this anomalous position, straddling the boundary between youth and the Establishment, it was a major incubation point for the new and developing language of rock criticism.

Part of that language came from the styles of *Sing Out* and *Broadside* and soon moved towards the academic-literary style largely supplied by students from the American Studies programs building up in many universities at that time. Part of the language, perhaps the most extensive part, came from jazz. Rock had been assisted by a few jazz critics who welcomed the seventh stream. In addition to Gleason, Nat Hentoff and Michael Zwerin, to name just two others, forged a friendly and literate link between jazz and rock. The early *Rolling Stone* even looked like the early *Down Beat*, with its tabloid-sized pages folded in half to make a smaller magazine.

Rock criticism soon developed the analytical style that characterized much jazz writing. An example from a critical appraisal of Phil Spector's first record, the Teddy Bears' "To Know Him Is to Love Him," illustrates that style.

"To Know Him" demonstrated in its structure that Spector had already mastered the kind of harmonic devices which then ruled pop. Most of the New York vocal group records, like the Five Satins' "In the Still of the Night," or the Penguins' "Earth Angel," were based on a cyclic progression: E-C sharp minor -B-A. It had an inevitability about it which let the listener know what was coming next and made him feel comfortable. Spector made one switch in the progression without losing any of the harmonic certainty, and wrote an eight-bar bridge whose declamatory appeal contrasted beautifully with the body of the song. Annette's confident little "oh-oh" at the end of the bridge after the words "that he was meant for me," is pure New York in content, just the kind of small improvisation which an East coast singer would consider second nature, but the style is softer and whiter. In retrospect this record can be seen as the beginning of a Los Angeles style which later culminated in the Mamas and the Papas, whose records were really little more than an updated Teddy Bears sound based on youthful, clean-cut, heavily arranged harmonies.[53]

The tone and vocabulary of that paragraph comes from the international jazz critical tradition. It almost sounds like the critical voice Alec Wilder used to dissect the pop stream's canon. Jazz criticism in its early days faced exactly the same hostile atmosphere that rocknroll criticism experienced in the 1960s. But, gradually, jazz writing was accepted by even the most classically dedicated stuffed shirts.[54]

Rock criticism sought to establish that same musical legitimacy once the music had the complexity to match (which it did, along with its fair share of junk). Rock's critical establishment flourished, expanding its mission beyond sorting out the junk and telling the news to laying down the history of the stream and interpreting its artistic canon in the light of larger cultural and political events.

In sum, the period 1965–1970 was the classic age of mature rock. It had all its own vehicles in place, vigorously and exuberantly giving forth a music distinct from all the other popular musics in America. It had worked through the most complex problems of its artistic life, finding its own way. Yet it had lively and respectful relations with each of the other six streams, having assimilated their riches. Rock was large and untidy enough to gather underneath its banner every sector of its audiences— teenagers, college kids, working youth, of every political tendency. From surfers to Maoists, from dope smokers to straight arrows, all found a place in rock's capacious halls and in its darkest cellars. The seventh stream was also a world music of youth, and still had much to give.

12. The Pause Point

In the year 1970, the mature seventh stream reached a point not so much of change but of pause. Rock soon resumed and continued to generate new music, new performers, new ideas; yet that moment contained the seeds of a deep branching in rock's future. Separate paths for both the youth movement and for rocknroll began at that juncture. It was not one specific event that produced this brief cessation. A whole set of things did it, some small, some large, within rock itself, in the other six streams, and in the society at large. It was a shudder, youth's sense of the fragility of the world they were trying to remake, a recognition that forces darker and stronger than previously known had suddenly come down on them. This chapter describes that pause.

From the Inside

The music was doing well. Rock's merger with folk and jazz had firmly set. Enough of these streams' musical reservoirs, their performance traditions, and their general ethos had been absorbed into rock to give it greater range and depth. Rock now had a purchase into all the other six streams of American popular music. In the course of that transfer, the industry had shifted its resources and practices to make the LP album the dominant unit for all the streams' musical "product." This shift was not a simple matter, and the trade press, especially *Billboard*, was obsessed with the relative strength of single versus album sales in every part of the world as well as in every market in the United States. AM radio was still an important exposure medium; its play list makers paid attention only to the singles market or to an album only after a single from it had broken out. Record executives performed the delicate balancing act of putting out a single that could command attention without ruffling the feathers of their artists, who were intent on making a fully extended statement in an album.[1]

The major victory for rock was in its share of the total LP market. Over the decade of the sixties, the dollar sales volume of all records had increased by 67 percent to top the billion dollar mark, with albums gradually yielding more than ten dollars to every one earned from singles.[2] Figure 12-1 shows for the sixties (1959 through 1970) how the three major streams and rock divided the expanding album pie. The three smaller streams fluctuated in their percentage share from 5 to 16 percent during the decade. Since the total pie had grown so much, however, jazz, folk, and gospel had actually increased in absolute terms and in the number of performers reaching the public.[3]

The story in this table is the steady, relative decline of the pop stream and the rise of rock. These two streams had completely reversed themselves, with rock holding half the entire market by 1970. Without question, rock had found a commanding place within the pop stream's major distribution apparatus, including its popularity charts. The long playing record had, in fact, brought all seven streams into the same stores all over the country and allowed each of their wares to mingle. Both country

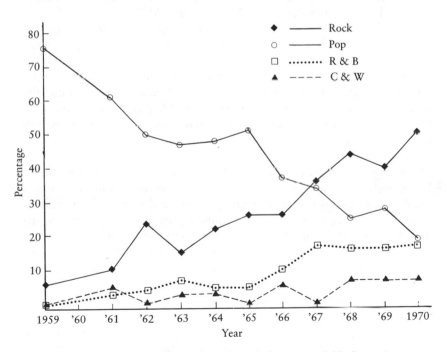

Figure 12-1. Shares of the LP Market (1959–1970). Data unavailable for 1960. Source: *Billboard* music popularity charts.

music and R&B, as previously noted, lagged behind rock in adopting the album as its main carrier, but by the late sixties both had gotten the hang of it. Black pop steadily increased its share of the market over the decade, sharply rising above country music in the late sixties, the very time during which the Beatles had allegedly driven black pop out of rocknroll. The early sixties' folk explosion had conjoined rock to folk successfully enough that folk was headed for a small but steady place on the charts, about as big as jazz.

Behind these overall statistics was a familiar economic pattern. Within the American entertainment complex, which was by the early sixties thoroughly implicated in world capital markets, the wave of mergers continued to gobble up the independent record companies. The creative layer of record producers and talent scouts that had nurtured the first generation of mature rock bands were either shackled or dismissed. Elektra Records, for example, was sold in August of 1960 to Kinney International Service, a giant conglomerate that had already swallowed Atlantic, Atco, Warner Brothers, Reprise, and Cotillion.[4] The "bottom line" men, the "suits," were the masters in the conversion of rock authenticity, with all its excesses, into a more commercially reliable product. By 1970, "five major manufacturers controlled half the market—Columbia, Warner/ Seven Arts, RCA Victor, Capitol-EMI, and MGM."[5]

Within each of the streams, events unfolded that influenced rock in different ways. A double crisis occurred in country music. First, Nashville's major stars were aging. Roy Acuff was long gone. Ernest Tubb was near the end of his quarter-century career of steady chart-making singles. The senior members of the bluegrass wing of country music were also falling silent. Eddy Arnold, Hank Snow, Webb Pierce, and Kitty Wells could still put singles on the country charts, but their audiences were fading. The other difficulty was that many of country's new stars were minimally country artists. Anne Murray, Olivia Newton-John (from Canada and Australia, respectively), John Denver, Glen Campbell, Jimmy Dean, and others like them had clearly diluted the traditional country vocal quality, its instrumental distinctiveness, and its lyrical content—so much so that the blurring of the boundary between pop and country music threatened to divide country into a museum wing at the Ryman Auditorium in Nashville and a pop wing anchored somewhere between the executive offices of the major record companies and their television studios.

As if in response, there appeared in Texas, especially, but also in Georgia and in Bakersfield, California, a new rock-country music. The sound was definitely not Nashville. In Austin, a rambunctious local music scene had been merging the country, rock, and folk streams since the mid-1960s. Its culmination was the 1970 opening of Armadillo World Headquarters, a large and comfortable performance site run by a sympathetic group of serious young impresarios led by Mike Tolleson.[6] The Austin scene soon reached past the local performers (Michael Murphy, exemplar) to attract rock and rock-country acts ranging from John McLaughlin and the Mahavishnu Orchestra to John Prine, thus placing the city visibly on the national rock map.[7] Willie Nelson's departure from Nashville and his setting up shop in Austin reinforced not only the position of that city but also rock-country music as a new and important component of the seventh stream. The "outlaw" group, Nelson, Waylon Jennings, Merle Haggard, later Kris Kristofferson, and some others, plus the strong emergence in 1970 of the Allman Brothers from Macon, Georgia, gave the rock world something to chew over. It would take some time to assimilate this addition, which would soon be enriched by other bands such as the Charlie Daniels and the Marshall Tucker bands. Even closer to the core was the country-folk-rock direction taken by Gram Parsons, mentioned before. This southern-born and Harvard-educated musician joined the Byrds in 1967, left after six months, formed the Flying Burrito Brothers in 1968, and died in the desert east of Los Angeles in 1973. His commitment to threading together country music and rocknroll bore considerable fruit, beyond his own albums. He definitely arched rock's reach back to its country origins and influenced the Byrds' *Sweetheart of the Rodeo* album and the music of Commander Cody and the Lost Planet Airmen, Asleep at the Wheel, and the Eagles. He left a strong imprint on the early music of Emmylou Harris, who, after Parsons' death, negotiated her way back across the folk rock border to mainstream country. She still radiates from that platform the spirit of rock's deeper mysteries, dredged from country's "mountain" wing, exemplified by the music of the Louvin Brothers.

The black pop stream was experiencing, besides its definite growth, a consolidation and restructuring. The market for "soul" singles and albums was expanding, but the change of name of the stream signified the unresolved place black pop occupied. On 23 August 1969, *Billboard* announced that "Rhythm and Blues" would be replaced by "Soul" because that term "more properly embraces the broad range of song and instrumental material which derives from the musical genius of the black American."[8] Black pop had exhausted part of its resources. Motown, which had dominated the black pop charts since the early sixties, was suffering its own crisis of success and the breakup of some of its established performing units. The Supremes, like the Beatles, had dissolved, with Diana Ross poised for a brilliant solo career. Rock audiences had been enthusiastic about some black pop acts, the Temptations, particularly, but also the Supremes who in 1967 headlined a show with the Buffalo Springfield, the Fifth Dimension, and Johnny Rivers. But the long-range dream of black pop surpassing country music in dominating the vehicles of the pop stream went only so far. Ed Ochs, a wise observer of the nation's black music scene, repeatedly called attention to the situation for *Billboard* readers:

Top 10, pop, the dream destination of soul disks too heavy to hold down on the soul charts, has become harder to reach these days as the stagnancy of soul music coupled with the rapid changeability of pop has left soul by the wayside.

On the eve of a new year, the rock'n'roll revival is threatening to throw soul back to the yesteryears of hard-earned radio play and defunked pop-soul.[9]

James Brown and Aretha Franklin, indeed the royal couple of "soul," were giving black pop a different direction. The shift of recording influence to the South, to the Memphis Stax-Volt scene and to the Muscle Shoals, Alabama, studios, underscores the important shift of mood. Black pop's concern with racial pride, with self-respect, and with the black community's response to the catastrophic events surrounding it had shifted the balance subtly away from joyous party music and the ever-necessary telling of love's waywardness.[10]

This change was but a reflection of the political reality in 1970. Repeatedly during that year, black civil rights leaders and their white allies charged the Nixon administration with willful neglect in enforcing the hard-won legislative protection of black civil rights. The Temptations' single, "Ball of Confusion (That's What the World Is Today)," carried comments on the antiwar movement and unemployment in the ghetto in a musical form that moved past their previous Smokey Robinson stylings. Many black pop acts were influenced by the Last Poets, whose first album was making waves in white as well as black circles and had surprisingly risen to the twenty-ninth position on the album charts.

Nina Simone was not as fortunate. Her decision to leave the States in late 1969 symbolized the impasse of black pop. She earned the name "the High Priestess of Soul" the hard way, taking the condition of her people seriously enough to reject the ordinary settings in which black artists could speak and sing. She went beyond the boundaries of commercial R&B, could not enter gospel, was not invited into jazz very warmly, and, of course, never came anywhere near rock. She neither chose nor could find an organized political platform from which to concertize her ideas.[11] Simone drove herself musically out of mainstream black cultural and political circles and ended up in a burning rage that took her out of America and into the shelter of Europe. Like almost all those who fought too far out past their audiences' musical tastes and political understanding, she fell harder than those who went easier.[12] Some of rock's warriors would sadly soon follow this path.

Jazz, in its perpetual hard times, was finding its way beyond the achievements of the free jazz of the sixties that Ornette Coleman, John

Impulse in Commercial Swing

LOS ANGELES — Impulse and BluesWay product will take on a more commercial sound as a result of a&r director Ed Michel's aim.

Impulse's roster of hard avant-garde artists is now experimenting with forms out of this spectrum, which is helping move the jazz line into new avenues.

Tenor saxophonist Archie Shepp is recording an LP of songs four or five minutes in duration and with a vocal group.

The vocal group provides a stronger melodic framework for the audience to hang onto, explains Michel, who replaced Bob Thiele in the position.

Ornette Coleman, the "father" of the avant-garde movement, has just recorded a single, "Man on the Moon," combining rock rhythm with electronic music plus his own eclectic style of saxophone playing.

Another avant-garde player, working with-in new framework, is Pharaoh Sanders, whose new

LP, "Karma," features a vocalist for the first time.

"A lot of jazz records are made that are very good but they're not focused. Jazz can go between 15,000 to 30,000 copies. Most get made and don't sell 5,000 copies because I don't think record companies treat jazz like something special.

Figure 12-2. Commentary on Jazz's Commercialism. *Billboard*, August 23, 1969, p. 8. © 1969 BPI Communications, Inc. Used with permission from *Billboard*.

Coltrane, and Cecil Taylor had pioneered. Not only were players such as Sonny Rollins circling back to older R&B masters such as Louis Jordan and Junior Walker, but jazz's avant garde was coming back into the warmth of a more commercial stance, as the *Billboard* article reproduced here indicates (fig. 12-2).

Paradoxically, gospel flourished in this drought. *Billboard*, actually Paul Ackerman, opened a Gospel Music Section in that trade organ on 6 December 1969, gave Edward M. Smith a full column, allocated a page for gospel news, and added gospel charts later. The Gospel Music Association, organized in 1964, was a strong centralizing force, and the Black Gospel Association, headed by James Cleveland, could boast of five thousand members.[13]

Finally, there was the pop stream, still the largest in terms of its overall reach and control of all the popular musics. Its older performers were also losing their hold on the current record charts. The young stars, such as Neil Diamond and Barbra Streisand, were closer to the rock scene and were replacing pop's older audiences, who had carried Frank Sinatra and Tony Bennett into the museum. In short, with the exception of gospel, the other streams were all experiencing an encroachment by rock's expansion. Rock music at the height of its maturation was finding itself, peculiarly, closer to the music of the other streams than it had ever been before. It was different from them and, at the same time, of their cloth. The entire popular music picture in America was being held in a freeze-frame.

The Festival Coda

Within rock, the unique innovation that had brought all its separate city scenes and scattered audiences together was rising to a peak. The rock festival, beyond anyone's expectations, had become the dominant performance site for mature rock. Over three hundred festivals were held in the sixties in every part of the nation, involving perhaps an audience of 15 million young people.[14] The high visibility of the youth culture, with its music, hair, (un)dress, and drug use, was so strong a statement of independence that the adult world, including the music industry, had to recognize it. The anti-war movement with its demonstrations and marches had developed the performance styles of the rock performers; there was a genuine symbiosis between movement and music. As Country Joe McDonald said, "The Fish and the other San Francisco bands that went over well playing rock festivals owed much of their success to the years prior to the big-rock festival days when everyone learned the ins and outs of outdoor concerts at political rallies and free appearances in Golden Gate Park." [15]

From the 1958 and 1965 Newport festivals in the East, to the Monterey Pop Festival of 1967, to Woodstock in August of 1969, there was a continual upward expansion in numbers of people attending and in the internal development of rock. Its mechanics were perfected, its star performers recognized, its command over its repertoire made secure, its creativity and energy maintained at a high plateau.

Woodstock, perhaps overvalued as the founding of a youth's nation, nevertheless was a startling and energizing affirmation of rock culture. The music had its high points as well as its flops, and the record companies went to work again to harvest that particular crop. The movies, albums, and other products flooded out, as did the printed reports of the event. The inside story of the Woodstock adventure has been written up with all its chicanery, greed, and double-dealing villians as well as its idealism, good guys, and victims.[16] However, it was the sense of community and the coiled meanings within that scene that are of more import, I believe. Greil Marcus for *Rolling Stone* noted that the young people, forming the "third largest city in New York state, . . . were able to do things that would ordinarily be considered rebellious . . . but can now take the stars as benchmarks and move out . . . to build their own instant communities on their own terms with no thought of rebellion." [17] Andrew Kopkind, reporting in the same issue, was equally impressed but took a more political stance, stating that a new oppositional force of great strength had emerged. "It's not a 'youth thing' now but a generational event; chronological age is only the current phase. . . . When the dope freaks and nude swimmers and loveniks and ecological cultists and music groovers find out they have to fight for love, all fucking hell will break loose." [18]

The question as to whether it was a "youth thing" or a "generational" one is still open. There is no doubt, on the other hand, about whether the Woodstock nation fought for love and unleashed "all fucking hell." They didn't; what broke instead was the once solid youth ranks. The branching of young people into a cultural and a political wing was a step toward a general unraveling of the coalition. Indeed, the sheer size of the festivals had now brought to the fore the tensions that had been managed and contained until then. Not only was there an exhaustion of the festival form itself, evidenced by the reports that at least two highly advertised festivals had fizzled, but the sharks and incompetents had also entered the scene.[19]

The alternative culture was finding its meeting with the straight music industry and local officialdom so problematical that a conference of some of its leading members was held in October 1969. The "Sympowowsium," held in New Mexico, was attended by some sixty music and movement figures including Kesey, John Sebastian, Rock Scully from the Grateful Dead, Paul Krassner, and other senior rock leaders. The question was, What happens after Woodstock? The key problem was "the architecture of mass gatherings." A tentative organization was formed that pledged to support the evolving lifestyle: "We've got to prove an alternative life style works. We've got to come up with something besides communes and dealing," one of the leaders was quoted as saying.[20]

Then, in December 1969, Altamont. After considerable initial confusion as to place and price (it was finally a free concert), some 300,000 Bay area young people gathered at the Altamont Speedway some fifteen miles east of Berkeley to hear Santana, Crosby, Stills and Nash, the Jefferson Airplane, the Grateful Dead, and other local performers, and to see Mick Jagger lead the Rolling Stones into a triumphal climax to their hugely successful third American tour. The Stones had hired the Hell's Angels to provide stage security in return for five hundred dollars worth of beer. According to most accounts, the Angels' presence was from the start surly and aggressive, giving the entire event an uneasy and fearful mood. In one fight that broke out, one Angel knocked the Airplane's Marty Balin unconscious with a pool cue. Then, during Jagger's performance of "Sympathy for the Devil," one of the Angels patrolling the stage leaped off and stabbed to death an eighteen-year-old black youth. The concert somehow continued. There were three more deaths (two people fatally injured by automobiles, one drowned in a puddle) and about one hundred wounded.[21]

Whatever Woodstock was, Altamont wasn't; it was the proverbial watershed. Jann Wenner, founder of *Rolling Stone*, would "never after Altamont . . . proclaim that 'rock and roll can set you free.'"[22] The disaster, many commentators repeatedly asserted, was not just the Stones' fault. The scene was a repetition of the continued failure to hold a secure alliance between the Hell's Angels and the rock community. The first occasion had been a moment of promise five years before when the slim possibility that radical, hippie, and "criminal" youth minorities could come together and lead the more conventional mass of young people. That moment was prayerfully nurtured, only to be dramatically shattered in the paradigmatic October 1965 confrontation at the Oakland-Berkeley border where 14,000 marchers and 400 police paused at a moment of truth in the very place and at the precise moment that rocknroll was becoming rock. Ken Kesey, one of the leading figures in the Bay area's alternative culture, had developed some kind of a working, if fragile, relationship with Sonny Barger, leader of the Oakland Hell's Angels. The Berkeley radical mix was out in force, seeking that political synthesis that would parallel the musical one taking place. Kesey was on good terms with all the elements, the San Francisco Bohemian community, the Berkeley students, and the Hell's Angels. Hunter Thompson reports on the lost opportunity:

The Angels blew it in 1965 at the Oakland-Berkeley line, when they acted on Barger's hard hat, con boss instincts and attacked the front ranks of an anti-war march. This proved to be an historic schism in the then Rising Tide of the Youth Movement of the Sixties. It was the first open break between the Greasers and the Longhairs, and the importance of that break can be read in the history of SDS which eventually destroyed itself in the doomed effort to reconcile the interests of the lower/working class biker/dropout types and the upper/middle, Berkeley student activists.[23]

However prophetic that 1965 event was, the reality of 1970 provided a heavy and continuing dose of bad news. Part of the news was economic. Even though Altamont chilled, and almost finished, the festival movement, the escalation in fees for rock acts continued. A consequence was that small clubs could not afford to bring in name performers and were thereby endangered. Bill Graham and other club owners complained in 1970, with more than mere self-interest, that without the small clubs new talent could not be showcased, thus stifling the industry and the rock stream.[24]

The Political Toll

The main bad news was political; the climate had become much meaner. The assassinations of Robert Kennedy and Martin Luther King, Jr. set the tone in the States for the escalating and unstoppable murderous war in Asia. The governor of California, Ronald Reagan, stated with respect to campus militants, "If it takes a bloodbath, let's get it over with. No more appeasement."[25] From the White House came similar verbal abuse and threats. The public polls showed a nation of adults adamantly and furiously against the student opposition to the war. Not that the public was behind the Nixon administration, the situation, in fact, was an impacted collective ambivalence of millions of Americans not liking the war yet hating the students more. The radical theorists were nervously asking, Would the soldiers shoot the students? The answer in 1970 was, yes, repeatedly. After the invasion of Cambodia, a wave of spontaneous actions by students occurred all over the country. The authorities, civil and military, acted and overreacted. On the fourth of May, the National Guard was called out, and four white students were shot dead and eight injured at Kent State University in Ohio. On the fourteenth of May, the National Guard and police fired one thousand rounds in seven seconds into a student dorm, killing two black students at Jackson State in Mississippi.

The chilling effect of those shootings was incalculable. Though the Weather Underground reported for duty and suffered their own casualties, as in the explosion of the bomb factory in Greenwich Village that took three lives and destroyed a townhouse that had nurtured a generation of honest left activists, most ordinary students were outraged to the extent of shutting down their education. By the middle of May, some "268 colleges were reported closed or effectively boycotted."[26] Those who showed up for the demonstrations were likely to have become much tougher than those who fled after the defeats of Chicago in 1968. The aftermath of that event ground on with Judge Hoffman gagging (literally and figuratively) the "Chicago Seven" activists being tried for crimes of political protest.

The efforts to enlarge the youth constituency increased even as the mood darkened. Jerry Rubin and Abbie Hoffman published a flood of books, one of which was entitled, *Do It* (1970). That book was aimed at maintaining the fraying alliance between "the hippies and the New Left" via the fictive Youth International Party (Yippie!). Rubin sought to hold the teenagers and the college-age youth together with an important history lesson. His teachings included the plausible and absurdist assertion that rocknroll was the ultimate source of the youth movement fighting against the Vietnam War, that Elvis was the common point of origin for both hippie and radical:

The New Left sprang, a predestined pissed off child, from Elvis' gyrating pelvis. . . . Elvis Presley ripped off Ike Eisenhower by turning our uptight young awakening bodies around. Hard animal rock energy beat/surged hot through us, the driving rhythm arousing repressed passions. Music to free the spirit. Music to bring us *together*.[27]

It was too late for that line however. The rock situation in 1970 was such a mixture of puzzling change and despair that such lessons just couldn't reach the youth.

The Personal Losses

The litany of casualties was indeed depressing. The excesses of the rock life were beginning to kill. Brian Jones (age twenty-seven), the Rolling Stones' most starkly and idealistically committed musician, was found dead in his swimming pool in July of 1969. The Beatles finally disbanded in early 1970. The Paul Butterfield Blues Band was at the end of its creative life. The same was the case for Simon and Garfunkel and for the Doors (Jim Morrison was dead the following year, at age twenty-seven). Then, in September, Jimi Hendrix died at age twenty-seven, and in October Janis Joplin succumbed, also at age twenty-seven. Many tears, much print, and an overall numbness.[28] By 1969, even the Haight was dead:

There was no such thing as a San Francisco sound anymore. The ballrooms had closed; most of the bands had broken up or moved away. The Haight had become a ghost town. Berkeley was now peopled by razor-cut over-achievers bustling from class to class, visions of good careers dancing in their heads.[29]

Emblematic of this moment of dissolution and the courage of some parts of the rock life to fight it, and fight in the same terms that had spawned rocknroll in the first place, was the action of Phil Ochs, one of the veteran folk singers of the early 1960s New York Village scene. He had been a stalwart and cheerfully unyielding singer-songwriter at the political end of the rock stream, a friendly antagonist of Dylan, but committed to the fusion of music and politics. After nearly two years of recovering from the defeats of 1968 at the Chicago National Democratic Convention, he returned to Carnegie Hall for a solo concert. John S. Wilson, senior jazz critic of the *New York Times*, reviewed the event. Its reprinting here in full is merited, I think, not only because of the drama of the evening but because it illuminates rock's pause period more fully than any other (fig. 12-3).

Ochs' personal musical development, from Elvis to the Kingston Trio and then to politics, was probably the route taken by millions. His plea to acknowledge and continue the journey may have succeeded that magical evening in Carnegie Hall. The gold lamé suit (see figure 12-4), also worn by Elvis, certainly was a shocker. It didn't work anywhere else, though, and it worked for him only partially and painfully. After several years of touring and a benefit concert in 1974 for victims of the Chilean junta with Dylan, he committed suicide in 1976.

While 1970 was the pause point for Phil Ochs and tens of thousands of average youngsters who simply couldn't take the unyielding brutality of the government and its police, some of rock's strongest performers resisted. They shut their eyes and held on, ignoring both the political steam rising around them and the increased commercial pressure for

Phil Ochs Fans Are Won Over by Rock

By JOHN S. WILSON

Enough time had passed since his two tumultuous concerts at Carnegie Hall last Friday night to give Phil Ochs a chance to reflect on the experience. The concerts, which threatened to be the most disastrous of his nine-year career, have turned into a major breakthrough for the politically oriented folk singer.

Instead of presenting only his customary protest songs, he offered also rock songs of the 1950's associated with Elvis Presley, Conway Twitty and Buddy Holly. Mr. Ochs appeared in a glittering golden suit, patterned on one worn by Mr. Presley. His audience's reaction to this was a rising barrage of boos and hisses.

"I expected something like this to happen," Mr. Ochs said the other day. "I've been a political singer for nine years and New York has been my strongest base. I knew that going from total rebel to total rock stylist would be a supershocker."

Program Cut Short

The shock was compounded by the fact that the first concert was presented without an intermission and was cut short after an hour and a half because Carnegie Hall had received a bomb threat. The puzzled and disgruntled audience that left the first concert was not aware of this.

"After the first show," Mr. Ochs said, "I went next door to the Carnegie Tavern with Jerry Rubin and my mother and some other friends. I was furious because I'd had to cut the show short.

"And I was furious at the sound people because they were three hours late getting to the hall and there wasn't time for a sound check. Then about 20 or 25 angry kids walked in and said: 'How can you charge money to put on a show like that?'

"I told them to give me their names and I'd get them into the second show. I took the list and left it at the box office. About 10 minutes later the kids were back and they said the list was torn up. I blew up.

"I went back to the box office and I was pounding on it and I was pounding on a door and I smashed my hand through the glass, right in front of all the people in the lobby. They cheered this as a revolutionary thing."

After a bandage was put on Mr. Ochs's thumb, which had a tendon cut by glass, he returned for the second concert. It began shortly after midnight and continued for more than three hours.

Change of Heart

"This time I talked a mile a minute explaining what I was doing," Mr. Ochs said. "But still they'd boo a Conway Twitty song and cheer a protest song. But during the second half, the audience completely turned around to an extent that never happened to me before.

"By the end, when I was doing my Elvis Presley medley, they were jumping on the stage and shaking my hand. It was like an old time 50's rock concert — total ecstasy.

"When I began doing encores the Carnegie Hall man-

agement got uptight, what with the unions and overtime and everything, and they cut off the power. Me being crazy, I shout, 'Give me the power!' And 2,000 people shout, 'We want power!'

"It was a fantastic theatrical moment. The management had no choice. They turned on the power and I did Chuck Berry's 'Schooldays.' It became a total magic moment."

The magic of the moment continued into the next day when David Frost called and asked Mr. Ochs to be on his television show.

Trying to Get on TV

"You know, for nine years I haven't been able to get on television," Mr. Ochs said. "Except at a straight news level where I'm singing in the background. I taped the show Monday—a 20-minute segment of what I did at Carnegie Hall without the booing."

Mr. Ochs said that change from protest to rock had been in the back of his mind for years.

"At 15, my idol was Elvis Presley," he said. "Then, in college, it was the Kingston Trio and I became infatuated with folk music. I've been a folk singer and a political singer ever since.

"But even in 1958 people were saying there would be something like folk-rock. Bob Dylan did it but by then I'd become so totally political that I didn't do it.

"Eventually I found myself in a stale position I could go on and be a sort of Pete Seeger. But after Chicago I was so depressed, so

full of despair that I just went crazy and didn't care anymore. I decided to do just what I wanted to do.

"I thought, 'Wouldn't it be funny to come out in a gold suit like Elvis Presley?' It was a leap into fantasy, into a musical area that I really like. Suppose it was Elvis who became the Vietcong to America. Elvis Presley is America and that music is the music of America. Imagine—the man in the gold suit who sang 'I ain't marchin' anymore!'"

Mr. Ochs plans to continue doing the show he gave at Carnegie Hall, and possibly take it to Europe. And after that?

"Maybe I'll go back to being a regular guy," he said. "Or maybe I'll just get crazier."

Figure 12-3. Phil Ochs Concert Review. *The New York Times*, April 3, 1970, pp. 44.
Copyright © 1970 by the New York Times Company. Reprinted by permission.

quick hits and packed concerts. There was thus an unmistakeable elegiac quality in "Layla," Eric Clapton's near-farewell session with Duane Allman and the alumni from Delaney and Bonnie and Friends. As the levels of anger and frustration rose with every Rolling Stones tour due to the drugs, groupies, and the generally unhinged entourage accompanying Jagger and company, the cynicism rose to the point of repudiating the whole rocknroll venture. It is said that their 1972 *Exiles on Main Street* does just that. Dylan finally accepted the end of the period in 1975 with his *Blood on the Tracks*.

The clearest evidence that 1970 was the year that things cracked is seen in the self-announced shift between Jonathan Eisen's 1969 *The Age*

Figure 12-4. Phil Ochs in gold lamé suit. Photo courtesy Michael Ochs Archives / Venice, CA

of Rock to its successor volume issued a year later. The first edition was filled with history, scholarship, and a straightforward curiosity and celebration of rocknroll. The second exudes a pained awareness that the beautiful part is over, that the music hype has reached the precincts of a mature rock music, that too many of the Gods have forked tongues and feet of clay. West Coast innocence is ridiculed, and the Boston sound is excoriated as the publicity game that it was. Unquestionably, the level of cynicism among the rock writers had increased to the point that some reassessment of the value of the whole rocknroll world was called for.

During the brief period of rock's maturity, art, commerce, and politics suspended their usual warefare to give everyone an opportunity for the fullest achievement possible. Some promises were fullfilled; but each performer came to a recognition sooner or later that the moment had passed. It was not the geographical place but the passing that counted. Even

"Kent State" evoked a picture not of a particular campus but of the meaner, more dangerous era that had begun.

The unity of teens and college-age youth was breaking up. Record executives were aiming more towards the teenybopper side as the old strategy of submarket differentiation singled out a younger section of the audience. The Archies, Monkees, and so on were the merchandising acid dissolving the "youth" adhesive that had been holding the full youth alliance together.

At the same time, the rock entrepreneurs themselves were fashioning a more regularized mode of "mass gatherings." The music industry was also searching for something beyond "communes and dealing." The answer was found in the specific types of performance sites that were to dominate the seventies. These included, first of all, "arena rock." This innovation was an attempt, ultimately successful, to regularize the chaotic and unpredictable festival schedules. Another change was to stabilize the club scene. The coffee houses gave way to small clubs with liquor licenses. The younger teens were excluded, both as audiences and as musicians, since Governor Reagan had vetoed a bill passed by both houses of the California legislature that would have allowed players under twenty-one to play in clubs that served alcoholic beverages.[30] Youngsters were being corralled into a set of consumer arenas designed for their age group and playing appropriate bubblegum music.

The Final Frontier

A pair of events occurred at this time that could not be more unrelated yet were conjoined, as figures 12-5 and 12-6 indicate. What appears to be another smart publicist's hook for catching the reader's eye is, in fact, a serious statement. Space exploration was commanding the attention not just of the general public but of a strategic sector of the young, record-buying audience. The launching of astronauts and their return had been a steady and compelling television show for the dozen years that rocknroll grew into rock. The education on space travel had been augmented during that period by the seminal motion picture about space, Stanley Kubrick's 1968 *2001, A Space Odyssey*, based on Arthur C. Clarke's novel, and by the weekly television show "Star Trek" (Trekkies have become a continuing cult movement)

On 21 July 1969, the grand finale of the first phase and the opening act of the next were seen all over the world. It seems quite likely that, with the moon landing, a certain proportion of the young in the United States (and in all other countries as well) were permanently imprinted with a space age commitment. Their eyes and thoughts turned towards the heavens. Was it just a coincidence that the regional hit "In the Year

Figure 12-5. "Men Walk on Moon," *The New York Times*, July 21, 1969. Copyright © by the New York Times Company. Reprinted by permission.

Figure 12-6. Sun Records Ad, "Jerry Lee Lewis Hits on Sun," *Billboard.* © 1969 BPI Communications, Inc. Used with permission from *Billboard.*

2525 (Exordium and Terminus)" by Zager and Evans reached the number one position on the Best-Selling Singles Charts at that moment—July of 1969—and remained there for thirteen weeks? The lyrics of that record, without any dance beat whatsoever, clearly reflected a popular understanding of the mutual interpenetration of time and space inherent in the realm of space travel.[31]

It is probably not an hyperbole to assert that the Age of Aquarius ended when men walked on the moon. Not only was the countercultural infatuation with astrology given a strong, television-validated antidote of applied astronomy, but millions of kids who had not signed up for either belief system were totally convinced. A significant proportion became part of a new generational pulse, moving toward the imperatives of the space age rather than toward the politics of the rock era.

Within minutes of the lunar landing, the rest of the United States, especially the supersensitive marketing organs in the economy, said "me, too." The advertisement for Sun Records' revival of Jerry Lee Lewis exemplifies rock in 1970. The industry seized upon the moon landing as the peg for the copy, but the real response was to the sudden revival movement in rock that had been reported in *Billboard* and *Rolling Stone* and was given a powerful reality by the Madison Square Garden shows produced by Richard Nader. Nader twice filled the hall with thousands who came to hear and cheer Chuck Berry, Bill Haley, Bo Diddley, Jackie Wilson, the Five Satins, Penguins, Capris, Belmonts, and others. Nader then proceeded to organize a road tour headlining Little Richard and Bill Haley and featuring the Coasters, the Shirelles, Chuck Berry, and Jackie Wilson. The package went to Hartford, Boston, Pittsburgh, Houston, Chicago, and other cities, and a European tour was planned.[32] The Golden Oldie movement was a commercial bonanza, a refresher course for serious rock fans and performers, and a recycling kindergarten for the next generation.[33]

The pause of 1970 was a strange moment. It was marked by the absence of creative movement in rock's central core and the upsetting mixtures taking place at the boundaries with pop, country, and soul. It was equally due to the dangerous political climate that shattered the youth movement's unity and thus drove rock away from its natural base. The breakup of bands, the deaths, the personal crises, the restless movement of performers, the record companies' insistent attempts to pull out solo acts from ensemble bands so that they could be turned into superstars, all these led to a reconsideration of what constituted the stable unit for rock. The revival of old rocknroll further slowed the stream, reflecting the publishers' grab for the museum dollar rather than a genuine search for roots.[34]

Nevertheless, the music continued, and the world rock tour was in motion; but in Middletown, Connecticut, rock's pause was palpable. Even though the Grateful Dead had appeared at Wesleyan University in May of 1970 for a free concert in support of the student strike ("Free Bobby Seale and All Political Prisoners"), and even though Abbie Hoffman had resolutely announced that "we won't let them separate our culture from our politics" in rebuke to Yale's Kingman Brewster's remark that the New Haven May Day Rally "would not be another Woodstock."[35] Even so, the Powder Ridge Festival in Connecticut was to be a different story.

The local establishment was not pleased that the Zemel Brothers, long identified with the left and operators of the area's only commercial ski slope, were to be the hosts for the proposed festival. The normal excitement over such a quiet place being the scene of a rock festival became even more of a tense hurly burly. There was a shrill series of police announcements, warnings, and insistent pressure to shut the event down. The listed program was typically broad, including Sly and the Family Stone, Eric Burdon and War, Van Morrison, the Allman Brothers, Little Richard, Ten Wheel Drive, Joe Cocker, Chuck Berry, Janis Joplin, Ten Years After, Richie Havens, Melanie, and others. Only Melanie actually performed.

The following hastily typed note was left on a kitchen counter in the course of preparations by a group of local kids ready for the Powder Ridge concert.

28 July 70
10:30 PM
Calls going all the time, here is the story. The Powder Ridge festival. Is it on or off. News—Injunction. Producers say they'll pay the fine and its [a big] one, about 40,000 there now. If you don't have a ticket don't go, Roads are all sealed off. Going to a festival is like going to Las Vegas. It could be a Woodstock or it could be an Altamont. It is a risk. That's what the summer is all about, that's what 1970 is all about.[36]

That was it; an existential consciousness of choice manifest in the conversation of fifteen-year olds. Mature rock meant "live the moment"; it stood for the brief ecstatic release in opposition to the ordinary with its incessant Achtung. Rock fought everything ordinary, from oppression and war to parents and the school, all the visible encroachments on youth's release. And here in Middletown that release was calmly being evaluated as to its risks. The dangers were real; the "high" was chancy. But the kids were ready to go. They had yet to settle for the sure wisdom that ecstasy is the short trip, everyday life, the long trip.

Continuum

More than twenty years have passed since that
moment in 1970 when rocknroll paused at its full maturity. The seventh
stream soon resumed its life, but it had changed. The intimate connections between the youth political movements, the youth cultures, and the
music were broken. All three gradually went their own ways, subsequently to recombine into new configurations. The music was largely returned to its commercial owners. The political youth grimly fought on
through 1975 to the final withdrawal of American forces from Vietnam,
after which almost everyone retired from politics. The flower children,
the hippies, the communes, the rock festivals, the whole youth culture,
hair, clothes, and all, straightened up and dispersed.

The Sixties' Shadow in the Present

Although there was no victory and no victory celebrations at the end,
the true ceremonial closure for that time is the recognition that American
youth during the sixties punched a huge hole in American institutions.
As is generally the case, such recognitions become embodied in sacred
places. Graceland in Memphis and the Vietnam War Memorial in Washington are the two that have appeared, both being among the most
heavily visited shrines in the United States. They attest to the living presence of those times to this day.

During the seventies and eighties, the effects of the age-based rebellion
were quite visible, and they are still working their way from the cradle to
the grave. With their demands for alternative learning environments, for
instance, young people decisively shook the public high schools. The entire public school system, in fact, became a marginally exhausted institution, thus opening it in the 1980s to the predatory attacks of its real
enemies.

In many other fields—health, nutrition, leisure, and family life—a comparable evolution of alternative experimentation moved into conventional practice. The entire New Age culture is the contemporary coagulation of ideas spawned in those times or now gathered under its noumenon. Comparable notions in community design, architecture, and domestic regimens, those of parsimony and simplicity, smallness of scale, and modesty in scope, are also carryovers from the earlier days of experimentation with alternative designs for living.[1] The self-help movement got a definite boost from young people, who had learned to grow their own and heal their own. Among the institutions of the spirit, the continuing vitality of eastern religions and philosophies, albeit domesticated into American organizational forms and purged of their more extreme hysterical edges and authoritarian practices, also harks back to the sixties. Strong social nodules all over the country carry on the quest for enlightenment that began during the sixties.

In world politics, the years after 1970 are more difficult to narrate. The relatively quiescent period following the final withdrawal of American forces from Vietnam was punctuated by the local ferocities of third world wars, the brutalities of state-supported terrorism, and the rise of narco-militarism (our own as well as others). All this turmoil climaxed in 1989 with the destruction of the Berlin Wall. The attendant collapse of the Soviet-established regimes in East Europe and the dissolution of the Soviet Union itself has brought an end to the Cold War and a new set of international cleavages. The poisonous Mideast conflict is now the focus of a widening circle of alignments—Palestinian versus Israeli, Arabs versus the West, Muslims and their third world allies against the industrialized powers, a new chapter of the Crusades.

The reflection of this still fluid situation in American political movements is disarray and confusion. Yesterday's allies are today's enemies. The penetration of corporate culture into every phase of American life continues apace as the federal government retreats from active melioration and regulation. A wired executive class allied to a rampant military caste orchestrates a bubble economy, while the cities choke. A drugged and leaderless underclass (what a hateful term) is held as a threat over a sweated working class and a nervous and overextended middle class. The intelligentsia looks the other way while the Bill of Rights erodes under the attacks of a resurgent radical right and the Supreme Court itself. Some individual writers and artists, and some broader forces, especially church based, speak out. Too many have signed up as frontline word soldiers for the corporate phalanx or do their scholarly chores in silence.

The retreat into private life spreads as the bipartisan alliance for stagnation at home and adventure abroad drives more than half the eligible voters out of the political arena altogether. Cocaine and money dealing generate a contempt for an economy that spends fortunes on credit card promotions accompanied by an army of credit card "collectors" who harass those who can't or won't pay the bills for goods they have been persuaded to buy from an intrusive and relentless marketing armada. There is consequently an underground economy of considerable strength and an alternative political consciousness that, as yet, has only displayed negativity, and even that potentially explosive stance is dissipated by the everyday hustle and hassle.

Yet, American politics, always volatile, is capable of mass ignition, even though nothing comparable to the civil rights and peace movements of the sixties has yet emerged. The attempts to replay some of the scenarios of that time have met with audiences hungry for some political direction; but in the context of the joint lecture tour of G. Gordon Liddy and Timothy Leary, who can take such things seriously. And when some old stalwarts of the sixties hawk the old call for grassroots organization in local communities as the basis of a New Society, there is sadness and cynicism.

Gathering at one pole of the political spectrum is every kind of political-military pirate, survivalist, terrorist, and racist adventurer, along with the usual crop of millenarian and messianic cults. At the other end are the organized movements centered upon status protection—the elderly, the ethnic minorities, the disabled, the gay and lesbian communities, animal rights activists, environmentalists, everyone except youth and labor who are still absent. The women's movement, perhaps the largest single group, seems to be recovering from its own divisiveness and advancing into the entangled legal thicket of reproductive rights, free speech boundary lines, population policy, and the environment.

These problems are unfolding amidst unprecedented threats: the AIDS epidemic, hunger abroad and at home, the poisoning of the land, the sea, the air, our bodies. The scenarios predicting how all these problems will play out, given national rivalries and global economic conflict, range from an apocalyptic near-fatal wounding of the planet to a full flowering of a new garden of Eden, most often located in the Pacific Rim nations.

Rocknroll Comes Up to the Present

The arts are still on a rising trajectory begun at the end of World War II, although the current recession has slowed their markets. The towering geniuses produced may be few, but there is an undeniable democratizing sweep of artistic activity in the nation. The National Endowment for the Arts reported an 81 percent increase in the number of artists in the United States from 1970 to 1980.[2] From the New York and London auction houses with their startling prices, to the suburban shopping malls, to the weekend arts-crafts fairs in the country, the arts are ubiquitous.

As painting, dance, music, and literature took off in the 1950s, bursting their own boundaries, they created a whole set of new art forms and styles. Along with "happenings" and other puzzling presentational forms of the sixties, there is now "performance art," the melding of many extant art forms breaking their boundaries. Video art, a large movement of considerable technological virtuosity nurtured by the video music network MTV, exudes an untamed political bravado. The whole Parade of the Muses is sloshing around as if someone had taken the grid out of the ice-cube tray. Such formerly despised arts as the cartoon, the comic book, graffiti, the circus, and commercial advertising, not to speak of rock, have refreshed and enlivened the other arts. It has been a long trek from 1959 when ASCAP's highbrow composers told the Congress that rocknroll had to be fumigated from the ranks of American music. We have even seen Frank Zappa play with Zubin Mehta, Twyla Tharp celebrate in dance the music of Chuck Berry and Frank Sinatra, and the New Music composer-impresario Philip Glass proclaim that he is more at home with rock-pop-jazz musicians than with the uptown conservatory music crowd.

Rocknroll, now forty years old, is still a youth music but now also contains aging performers and audiences who are much alive. Though not many members of rock's museum wing appear on *Billboard*'s Hot 100 Singles Chart, some are still making music. The Grateful Dead, Frank Zappa, Paul Simon, Joni Mitchell, the Rolling Stones, and Neil Young are on tour or on records, each with an audience of considerable age range. These and other performers from rock's maturity continue to shape the music, either as revitalized groups or as individual players or producers.[3]

Rock as a whole has spread wider rather than climb higher. It now reaches further into the boundary zones of the other streams that gave it birth. The restructured disco movement at the edge of black pop and Latin pop, for instance, has brought a durable format to dance music. At its core, rock in the seventies and the eighties took shape as arena rock and punk, two quite different styles on the surface but closely related in underlying attitude. The folk-rock performers either moved off stage into the singer-songwriter category or left town. Yet in the late 1980s, there appeared a whole new crop of singer-songwriters too diverse to form a single sensibility yet all personal in their perspectives.

The festivals of the sixties, lasting several days, with their full mix of diverse folk and rock acts, gave way to the high production values of arena rock shows, featuring one headlining band or solo performer. These national or international tours, generally paid for by the record label, would be organized around the release of the performer's latest album. Up to three or four local or regional opening acts would serve to link the headliner to the local scene or to accommodate the record companies' politics. By 1976, such large-scale concerts had become such a regularized and massive feature of rock that *Billboard* initiated (on 20 March 1976) a "Top Box Office" chart that tracked the gross receipts of the major arenas and auditoria across the country.

The unity of teenagers and college-age youth had unraveled. "Youth" was no longer the single powerful entity in either a political or a cultural sense. The entire music industry, at every level, quickening to this fragmentation, proceeded as always towards differentiation of audiences and specialization of marketing strategies. The arena concert audiences were younger, the musicians more conventional, the performances more outrageous—the heavy metal rave up, guitar smashing, bizarre costuming, high-tech light shows, exploding sets, all the paraphernalia of "a helluva show" without the "assembled people." The music became flashier with louder and more familiar guitar riffs, augmented with elaborate keyboards and exotic percussion. The lyrics carried some residual menace and passion, spiced with satanic or occult overtones, as in bands from Led Zeppelin to Black Sabbath, giving some plausibility to the costuming.

Punk appeared in several places around the midseventies in the New York–New Jersey late nightclub. It is the inheritor of rocknroll's dark side. Punk may ultimately stem from the Elvis figure and blasting guitar, but it is amplified and distorted in the direction that Jimi Hendrix took his instrument individually and where the heavy metal bands took theirs collectively. Punk is also a retreat from the extended piece, the long cut on a conceptually unified album, the form that mature rock pioneered and exemplified. The seismic, two-minute blast on a single record is punk's desired unit.

Most importantly, punk concentrates all the passion once carried by mature rock into an explicit repudiation of adult life. In its lyrics and implied in its whole ethos—language, clothes, hair, postural stance, excessive sound levels, and grungy venues—punk and its contemporary version, hardcore, have only this to say: "Fuck you; get off my back." Yet, as Greil Marcus observes, British punk spoke not just for the ordinary rebellious youngster but for the already failed, "fat, anorexic, pockmarked, acned, stuttering, crippled, scarred, and damaged" kids, allowing them to "appear in public as human beings."[4] This redemptive act in no way diminished the punk rejection of the mature rock era, the contemporary rock establishment, and likewise any punk-rocker who sold out by producing a commercially successful record. The specific content of punk's politics ranges from right-wing primitivism, often with Nazi and racist paraphernalia, to a left-wing, sometimes explicitly socialist, program.

The exemplar of this type is the Clash. This London-based band was formed on the model of the Sex Pistols, opened for them on occasion, and carried on some of their irreverences. They differed in their political stance—a sharp left-wing critique tied closely to the headlines. They had a quick musical ear and the gift of lyrical invention, picking up black American riffs and West Indian reggae. Rejecting the self-destructive elements in punk, the Clash survived and were commercially viable. In spite of any steadiness on the job, there is a definite negativistic strain in the punk movement. This nihilism on occasion triggers an apocalyptic spasm that simply declares the end and pulls down the curtain on the world, the Sex Pistols being the exemplary clinical case.

Though there seems to be a deliberate amnesia in punk historiography, its roots are all-American, discernible in the hundreds of garage-type bands of the sixties, typified by Paul Revere and the Raiders. One discography lists forty-two bands from 1963–1968 that put out short, hot, guitar-based singles and then disappeared soon thereafter: the Trashmen, Sonics, Nightcaps, Sam the Sham and the Pharaohs, ? and the Mysterions, Mouse and the Traps, Castaways, and so on.[5] In a related line, the Detroit-based MC-5, house band of John Sinclair's White Panther party, provided the same kind of politically angry, simple, loud, and short songs. Also out of Detroit, Iggy Pop and the Stooges, led by leader James Osterberg, imprinted a sector of young rocknrollers with an anxiety-provoking, spastic, and gross performance style and today is a senior presence on the scene. Excess and primitiveness were the basic elements of punk, but it also received, from an unlikely source, another inspiration. This came from Lou Reed, originally of the Velvet Underground. Reed's influence may have come from the decadence, the drugs, the cynicism, the New York mini-max hip, but it probably also had a lot to do with the fact that Reed was a professional and unceasingly creative performer. He rode each crinkle in rock's hothouse production of the next new thing. In any case, he was a model and guide for New York's downtown scene, which crystallized around another updated version of the small club–record company short loop.

This time it was CBGB, named for country, bluegrass, blues, but showcasing mainly punk bands. After the New York Dolls had opened the way in 1973, the poet-musician Patti Smith turned this barely renovated Bowery bar into punk rock headquarters. The Ramones, Television, Blondie, the Talking Heads—altogether 110 bands and solo acts passed through or performed there on a more or less regular basis beginning in 1974.[6] Not surprisingly, some of the punk groups toured the United Kingdom. The Ramones particularly found more than a sympathetic response. The Sex Pistols then traveled to the States for its twelve-day triumph and unmourned debacle.[7]

The punk or hardcore movement, with little or no radio exposure, makes hundreds, perhaps thousands, of inexpensively produced singles and albums that are carried to its substantial audiences through a vigorous fanzine press. One of the most durable and articulate of these, *Maximumrocknroll* (issued from Berkeley, California), fills its pages with columns, letters, comics, and reviews of movies, books, and records. It reflects the interests of a young audience sophisticated and cynical enough to appreciate the underground tradition of the sixties without falling into reverence. From the East Coast, Mike Gunderloy's *Factsheet Five* is of the same party and does a service by tracking the other fanzines, reviewing their work, and listing their addresses. In sum, the punk movement stubbornly seeks an alternative way of music and life in a nation indifferent or hostile to its aspirations, inchoate as they may be.

The main train of rock was carried for a while on new radio formats. The Middle of the Road (MOR) chart of 1961 evolved into the "Easy Listening" listings of 1965, which then branched into the Album Oriented Rock (AOR) and Urban Contemporary charts of the 1970s. There is now "Lite" and "Soft" rock programming, which offers blandness old and new. *Billboard*, as always, attempted to guide the industry through the confused seventies with new charts and editorial features. Rock, carrying half the album sales in the country, finally in 1980 after twenty years, was rewarded with its own chart via the "Best Selling Rock Albums and Tapes." Until then, rock records had of course been tracked, but only on the charts of the other streams, primarily pop and to some extent on the country and R&B listings.

The Grammy awards, the National Academy of Recording Arts and Sciences' annual ceremonial accolade to the different parts of the music world, didn't help rocknroll either. In the twenty-six years of its presentations (beginning in 1958), the Grammys only fitfully and idiosyncratically recognized rock's existence. Chubby Checker's "Let's Twist Again" was the first-named acknowledgment in 1961 under the category "Best Rock and Roll Recording." After five years of an expanding recognition of "R&R" artists and recordings (up to three categories in 1966), there was a total blackout of rock for twelve years in the Grammy awards. In 1979 rock was once more given four categories out of the fifty-eight different Grammy awards, and they have continued since to include the seventh stream with the typical subcategories of best vocal performance female and male, best vocal duo or group, and best instrumental performance. It was a long time in coming.

Black Pop and Country Pop at Rock's Border

The black component within mature rock has been steady but limited in scope. The nearly two-year struggle to get any black act onto MTV, the new exposure medium of the 1980s, ended with cuts from Michael

Jackson's spectacular *Thriller* album being given airtime. The MTV executives' mealy-mouthed assertions that black performers were not doing rock but rhythm and blues (and therefore should go elsewhere) had given way to a combination of pressure from Columbia Records and the market success of the Jackson album. The fight was not over, but the success of rap has opened the MTV screen to a considerable black presence, including mixed black and white groups.

Not that mixed race groups are an anomaly. From the start rocknroll has produced them, beginning with the Del Vikings in 1957, then Memphis' Booker T. and the MG's in the early 1960s. The Jimi Hendrix Experience and Sly and the Family Stone were the preeminent mixed groups of mature rock in the late sixties. Richie Havens was and is a folk-based stalwart of the sixties, with many more strings to his bow than was thought for some time. Bruce Springsteen's E Street Band, with Clarence Clemons on saxophone, continues the tradition, as does Prince, which exemplifies top black bands with a few white sidemen and back-up (generally female) vocalists. Fully black acts, such as the Temptations, Aretha Franklin, and James Brown, have also become a close part of the rock canon, although still a step apart.

Disco appeared in the midseventies as a meeting of rock and black pop, doing an end run around both the pop and the "soul" radio, record, and club scenes.[8] Its high-decibel delivery of a simple, insistent beat once more brought a black rescue to a white music that had lost its dance way. What Donna Summer gave to disco's largely black audience by the midseventies, the movie "Saturday Night Fever" and the Bee Gees gave to a larger rock-pop audience in 1978. Disco became a more or less permanent part of the crossover pathways between the pop, rock, and black pop streams. "Hot Dance Music," as disco is now called, has its own chart in *Billboard*, its own twelve-inch single recorded form, and a vigorous club life.

This particular zone of exchange between rock and disco has been one of the reasons for adding a new chapter to the continuing attempt to define the name, content, and direction of the black pop stream. A *Billboard* story on 25 February 1989 focused on Reverend Jesse Jackson's well-publicized campaign to introduce the term "African-American" as the name of black people in the United States. The issue of appropriate names immediately echoed into music circles, where some executives of black-oriented record companies expressed dissatisfaction with the term "urban" as being too euphemistic and R&B as being too dated. Black was considered a useful umbrella term, but no term described the crossover phenomenon that characterized the pop, rock, and black charts.

Another incident that triggered controversy over this issue occurred when the expected winner of the 1989 "Soul/R&B Performer of the

Year" award at the 16th Annual American Music Awards—either Michael Jackson or Bobby Brown—was by-passed. Instead, George Michael was chosen. He also took the award for "Best Soul/R&B Album" of the year. In the words of Greg Peck of Island Records: "I don't have a problem with George Michael's album being the album of the year, but I do have a problem with him being the black artist of the year. When you make him black artist of the year, you know . . . he's not *black*."⁹ Indeed, this very white, young, handsome, and British lad also won the "Pop/Rock Album of the Year" award. The confusion will not subside as long as there are categories that, more or less deliberately, slip between a racial designation and a musical one. And such categories are necessary for pouring the industry's product into containers that can be carried across the airwaves to the record counters in every neighborhood's retail outlets.

Rap, the current explosive black pop form, is derived from hip hop sensibilities and the poetic-social commentator tradition heard in the sixties from such artists as Gil Scott-Heron's "The Last Poets." These ways of combining social and political commentary with a danceable beat come from much older black and Afro-Caribbean traditions. Rap in the early 1990s carries not only a more articulate message but a sense of deliberate menace. Thus, rap and white hardcore share a respect for each other and on occasion make direct musical exchanges. In 1986, rap's first top ten single was Run-D.M.C.'s cover of Aerosmith's "Walk This Way." Since that time, the Beastie Boys and Vanilla Ice have pointed the way for white groups trying on the rap style. The tour joining the white heavy metal band Anthrax with the black rap group Public Enemy underscores the point. Their separate audiences had no trouble celebrating together the music and the messages.

Jazz, thoroughly involved with its own evolution, and always concerned with its music and its public from a principled point of view, has been a steppingstone for some black musicians in crossing to rock and beyond.¹⁰ Retreating from the extremes of the New Thing and its Third World musical explorations in the late 1970s, jazz sought to double back to the pop stream. Since it was impossible to do so in the old swing and big band manner, rocknroll provided the route. This view was expressed in a jazz symposium some time ago but is applicable today:

People who have grown up listening to rock have rudiments of jazz in rock'n'-roll. . . . White kids took the music of the black musician and black blues singer and sophisticated it. They made it palatable to their audiences from dancing and listening standpoints. Now the young fine black jazz players have taken the rock beats from the white kids and incorporated them; they've stolen them back to where their records sell like white rock bands.¹¹

Miles Davis was one of the main explorers of this whole venture. His 1970 *Bitches Brew* marked the way opened by such jazz groups as the

Charles Lloyd Quartet, which reached rock audiences as early as 1964. Traffic, John McLaughlin's Mahavishnu Orchestra, Santana, Blood Sweat and Tears, and War moved the jazz-rock synthesis even closer to the jazz side in the late 1960s. In 1970 Weather Report was formed—the closest genealogical link of contemporary jazz to rock, to Brazilian and other world pop rhythms, and to the new musical technologies. The jazz stream has connected to the rock-pop boundary zone, utilizing the latest musical technologies while maintaining its black traditions of drive, swing, and hip stance.

The deeper struggle in all the American popular musics is that between country music and black music for dominion over the vehicles of the pop stream (that is, radio, television, movie outlets, and the large venues for live performance, especially Las Vegas and Atlantic City). The pop stream tolerates that struggle with no difficulty, thrives on it in fact, and is able to mediate the deep if buried hostilities between country and black music.

Even though Ray Charles could record highly successful albums of country tunes (his 1962 album *Modern Sounds in Country and Western Music* was a number one best seller, remaining an incredible 101 weeks on the charts), it didn't mean country and black pop would mix. Charlie Pride has been a successful black country artist for twenty years, with many best-selling singles and albums, but he is still just about the only one. And although Gary Burton and his quartet, a white jazz group to the core, could use Nashville musicians to make an important jazz-country album in 1967, *Tennessee Firebird*, it had no offspring and failed to breach the walls between country, jazz, and black pop. These boundaries penetrate too far into American culture and geography. On occasion, the emotions involved in maintaining them erupt into blunt public utterance, as in Stan Kenton's alleged statement to the *Nashville Banner* in 1975: "I hate country and western music. It is ignorant music and perverted music. As a professional musician—a jazz musician—I abhor it." He went on to say: "Country music is a lot of whining and crying and I cannot understand why the American public is buying it."[12] This statement is *too* blunt, failing thereby to convey the complexity of this almost unbridgeable gap.

Yet nothing seems to stop the country stream from trying to get into pop's tributaries. The Nashville Network, closely associated with the Grand Ole Opry, is cut from the cloth of old radio and early television, featuring talk shows, game shows, and all the other current types of television programs, as well as, of course, country music new and old. As Nashville's music industry, now the main southern branch of the Brill Building tradition, expands into high-tech music, including long-form videos, compact disk programming, and so on, it fulfills the dour warnings of Chet Atkins (veteran RCA-Victor A&R man in Nashville), who said in the midseventies, "I hate to see country going uptown. We're about to lose our identity and get all mixed up with other music. We were always a little half-assed anyway, but a music dies when it becomes a parody of itself. . . ." [13]

There is no danger of that happening though. Country music is heard on radio programs all over the nation; new performers appear whose records make them stars in the full sense of the word. Randy Travis, the Judds, Reba McEntire, and Rosanne Cash, to name a few, work closely enough to the traditional country voicing and material to allow a widening cohort to follow them, some grazing close to rock and to pop stylings.

Inside and Outside Rock's Boundaries

The core of rock is still developing, and one of its directions is toward modifying its "white boy" image. The simple presence of women as performers does not exhaust their significance in that stream, although it might be the most visible vantage point for the assessment of change. And change there has been. Women in rocknroll bands and as solo performers have not been carbon copies of the leading women performers of the sixties, for example, Janis Joplin or Grace Slick. Nor are they cut from the folk mold of Joan Baez, Joni Mitchell, or Judy Collins. They are, instead, more closely related to their male generational cohorts, tough, direct, musically literate, and multitalented. To a great extent, they are leaders of their own bands, suffering or celebrating the same industry-inflicted distortions that pull superstars out of genuinely collaborative aggregations. And there is much diversity of musical style and socio-political orientation. From Patti Smith, Debbie Harry, Pat Benatar, Joan Jett, Bonnie Raitt, the Go-Go's, Heart, the Bangles, and a host of others that are straight-out rockers with varying degrees of feminist wit and bite, to the more media-hyped pop acts such as Madonna and Cher, the women's presence in rock is strong, and their place is assured. The work behind the scenes is another story; women's careers in the rock-corporate life are marked with the same difficulties as in any other industry.

Also coming from the center of rock is its growing implication in the other adult arts, especially in outcroppings from classical, conservatory, or serious music. As new instruments have come from the technological sphere, precipitating a rethinking of the aural implications of the very performance spaces that the avant garde is now exploring, rock is part of their thinking. "I saw a bridge between [Jimi] Hendrix and Stockhausen. The challenge was to understand noise in an emotional manner." [14] This not atypical response is from one of the members of Rhythm and Noise, a Bay area ensemble formed in 1980 after the usual drenching in San Francisco's light and rock shows of the sixties. There are too many currents in the Bay area to chart here; it is still creatively a strong counterpresence to New York. Even deeper into conservatory music circles, the Kronos Quartet has breached the exclusive precincts of chamber music to seek new and younger audiences with a repertoire that includes some of the classics of rock. There is hardly a musical stream that rock has not creatively encountered. The ultimate indicator of mass acceptance is rock's narcoleptic presence in the shopping mall, the supermarket, the high-rise elevator, and the dentist's office.

Perhaps the largest part of the sixties folk rock heritage continues via its participation in the world music system. Among several contradictory tendencies working themselves out during the 1970s and 1980s, the most important was the two-way traffic, the flooding of the world's pop-rock into the United States and the massive export of American music. The estimates are that at present two-thirds of all "American" record sales go to overseas markets. The term "American" is in quotation marks because those same estimates assert that a substantial share of the record companies are held by foreign corporations.[15] America has become the key stop on the world's criss-crossing rock tour. Most of the young rock stars in almost every country seek a chance to crack the American market, and many do. By 1983 *Billboard* reported that a third of its hot hundred singles were foreign-born acts, not only from Britain and Australia, but from thirteen different countries.[16]

Some of the diverse musical traditions of the world have been received in the United States with immediate understanding and affection. Most Latin dance music fits in without difficulty, even though it has a limited audience. African pop, on the other hand, required some explication from the critics. It was necessary to tell the American public that the strangely named and exotically instrumented bands carried nevertheless familiar schema. Here, for instance, is the New York *Times*' critic Jon Pareles instructing his readers on the constituent geographical-musical elements of the makassi music of Cameroon, being presented probably for the first time to a New York audience:

The basic rhythm . . . is eight beats, in a syncopation that continually bounds forward. It is a dance music with a trans-Atlantic heritage—guitar arpeggios like those of Zairian music, horn riffs akin to calypso, and a percussion arsenal including American trap drums, Caribbean congas and timbales, and African log drums.[17]

There was a larger base for Worldbeat (one of many names for the rock-pop-folk music of the world's nations and peoples). It grew out of academic programs devoted to world music on many American college and university campuses. During the sixties, there had been generous

funding for visiting and resident artists from all over the world and for
the founding of several Indonesian gamelan orchestras, South Indian music aggregations, and other enclaves of distant musical traditions. Perhaps
the most important outcome of those seedings was the growth of an educated world music audience. Its core was the graduate student proletariat
and their friends, augmented in the seventies and eighties by the growth
of college radio programming of significant amounts of world music.

Some nations who were nurturing their own homegrown mixture of
traditional folk music, their local, postcolonial commercial entertainment, and their new, youth-based rock did not export. The three-year,
groundbreaking study of the music industries in twelve small countries
on four continents, conducted by a Swedish research team headed by
Roger Wallis and Krister Malm, is essential in understanding this world
traffic and its blockages.[18] The difficulties of copyright law, technical radio standards, corporate organization, governmental practice, music industry rivalries, the mix of high and low technologies, all make a situation of rapid change and paradoxical impasse. Old ethnic musical
traditions are grist for a commercial mill that grinds faster than can be
controlled by the interests of indigenous musicians and their local supporters. The recent General Agreement on Tariff and Trade (GATT)
meetings on intellectual property have been called an attempt by the
United States to impose its own copyright laws and practices on the
world. In the name of preventing the piracy of records and tapes, there is
a definite attempt to squeeze out from third world countries an added
slice of profit.[19]

From this worldwide network of rock and pop systems, questions arise
about the various short loops in each country and the ways in which they
are connected to the vast international exchanges of musical culture.
What are the equivalents of the early fifties hit-making disk jockeys and
the record exposure and exploitation systems? How do these commercial
activities meet the indigenous folk music traditions? Then, most importantly, what is the relationship between the music scenes and the various
youth movements that are on the march? The American question of
1970, "Would the soldiers shoot the students?" is now being asked of the
Chinese, of the Korean, and of the Middle Eastern nations.

Not only is there a lively rock presence in Western Europe and the
East bloc countries, but it can also be found in mainland China, India,
Turkey, Bali. Indonesia boasts a particularly strong example of this
musical-cultural-political syncretism in the deeply religious and nation-
alist rock star Rhoma Irama. His records, movies, and live appearances
are based on the urban popular music "dung dut" and are nationally
celebrated as an anthem to Islam, his country, and rock music.[20] In the
Caribbean, the influence of American soul, rock, and jazz continues. The

unfolding of Jamaican dance music has paused for the moment as new American audiences are given refresher courses in its evolution from Ska, Rock Steady, Reggae, and so on. A similar cessation in its formal evolution appears to be occurring for the other great musical style of the Caribbean—the Calypso of Trinidad and Tobago. Its creative meeting with American black pop to form "Soca" in the late sixties momentarily diverted the satirical-social commentary tongue in Calypso in favor of a super hot dance form. But in recent days, there has been both a renewed political thrust among the Calypsonians as well as academic defense and celebration of its history and contribution to all the Caribbean cultures.[21] The flow of Caribbean musics into American popular music continues to run mainly through the jazz and black pop streams, but it is also carried by rock via black Caribbean musicians in the United Kingdom who give white or mixed bands the music to bring back to the States.

At the same time, there has emerged a self-consciously assertive "American" idiom within rocknroll. This "nationalistic" strain, opposing the world music flow into the United States, is in part a nativistic reassertion of its rockabilly roots. The strain is typified by the Stray Cats, a relentless, oldtime rockabilly group whose initial appearance in the eighties was a predictably short blast, until they called in one of their nine lives to issue another album in 1989. The music of this mode is partly a topical political commentary, originally closely allied with country performers who were articulating the unemployment and economic dislocation of the early eighties. It continues into the present with the "Farm Aid" concerts associated with relief programs, organized by Willie Nelson and others. That direction is also, and perhaps most deeply, a search to reclaim the sense of relevance rock had in the heady days of the late 1960s. John Cougar Mellencamp's "Jack and Diane" aims glancingly at the power and fragility of the teen-age moment;[22] Billy Joel evokes the eastern seaboard's postindustrial, nostalgia-ridden anxieties; and Grand Funk's attempted self-revival petulantly proclaims, "Rock and Roll American Style." But it is Bruce Springsteen who has inherited rock's crown and who wears it lightly as "The Boss."

Certainly, Springsteen's credentials are blue-ribbon rock. He was discovered and signed by John Hammond and managed in his early days by Mike Appel. (He is managed now by pioneer rock critic Jon Landau, formerly of *Rolling Stone*.) Undoubtedly, Springsteen has paid his dues in the record business, surviving lean days and creating in the E Street Band a distinctive sound and a stage presence that earns for him the respect of a critical and engaged audience. As writer-performer, moreover, his works from "Born in the USA" to "My Hometown" evince the authenticity manifest in rock performers of the days just before the pause point in 1970. His physical presence on surprise occasions, with free performances at a benefit for striking workers in an Asbury, New Jersey, bar, gives that authenticity a stamp of modesty and commitment all too rare at the moment.[23] Not that there isn't a strong and responsive sense of social activism among the young rock audience. The response to the Live Aid and Band Aid concerts as measured by the sales of "Do They Know It's Christmas" and "We Are the World" is clear testimony. So, too, is the response to the more politicized issue behind the record "Sun City"—a campaign to discourage entertainers from appearing at the resort complex in Bophuthatswana, South Africa.

Though it has certainly lost its integrated connection to the present movements of social protest, rocknroll has kept alive its tradition of sharp social commentary. The subject matter includes predictable contemporary concerns. Nuclear destruction, social alienation, loss of individuality, the corrosive intrusion of bureaucratic control are themes that vie with satirical jabs at contemporary politics, mores, and culture. Their musical tone ranges from punk sharpness and excess to Bruce Springsteen's somber and elegiac reading of the American landscape typified in the album *Nebraska*.

Technology and the Corporation

Rock's drenching in corporate culture is certainly undeniable when you consider that, by the midseventies, six major record companies (ABC, CBS, EMI, Polygram, RCA, and Warners) held slightly over 80 percent of the record market, with the four large independents (A&M, Motown, 20th Century, and United Artists) getting practically all the rest. The pie they were dividing was estimated to be worth almost 2.5 billion dollars.[24] By 1984 it was estimated that the entire record business had reached a new dollar worth of about 4.5 billion, and it was increasingly concentrated into the hands of a few.[25] The industry is approaching the point where two or three media empires, that of Time-Warner Communications, and the super vertically integrated Sony-Columbia Pictures/ CBS Records, will rule in such a ducal manner as to make the medieval period look like small potatoes.

The significance of corporate domination is that money considerations outweigh the musical ones in almost all decisions. The infrastructure required to sustain those giant bureaucratic enterprises involves a complex set of international relations; the legal, technical, diplomatic, and commercial staffs are bigger than the governments of most members of the United Nations.

During this consolidation, the quarrel between ASCAP and BMI that indirectly launched rocknroll in the first place has been long settled. The Congress and its Revised Copyright Act of 1978 is but one small body in a proliferating group of international bodies that regulate the bundle of rights that have to be respected and monies that have to be exchanged to sustain the musical traffic around the world. In the United States and the other developed nations, though leaking downward to the poorest of the nation states, the plugging of records is now entangled in the exploitation of consumer products. The soft drink companies, to take the noisiest of examples, are now easily more important in music than Proctor and Gamble ever was in soap opera, although the latter was the largest single theatrical producer in New York. Is it too much for Pepsi-Cola to foot the 5 million-dollar bill for Madonna's "Like a Prayer" video, only to turn it down as a television commercial?

Here are a few other indications of the way things are:

Item: Arlo Guthrie's hit folkish single, "City of New Orleans", was utilized as the background music for television commercials for Olds mobile's Cutlass. The original version of Phil Spector's "Be My Baby" with the Ronettes was the musical backing for the television commercial for Mercury's Topaz. The MTA School of Truck Driving in East Hart-ford, Connecticut, used Willie Nelson's "On the Road Again" for its tele-vision commercials.

Item: Pepsi-Cola sponsored Michael Jackson's Victory Tour of 1984–1985. Michael Jackson starred in "Pepsi generation" commercials. This move, of course, triggered the introduction of the new (and sweeter) Coke. Pepsi retaliated by unleashing Lionel Richie into the trenches of the cola wars. Coca-Cola brought back the old, now "Classic," Coke and lucked out by signing the Grammy winner Whitney Houston for its commercials.

Item: Michael Jackson bought the Beatles catalogue for 40 million dollars. Paul McCartney couldn't afford it, but "Ebony and Ivory" found a way. In 1991, Sony and Jackson concluded a contract for a billion dollars.

The problem here is not simply the captured songbird. The question is who owns the musical heritage of a nation and its various peoples. Does the implacable logic of corporate accountability and control make grant-ing artistic freedom to its employee artists somewhat problematical? If, as I have suggested at the beginning of this study, the publisher's catalogue was the key instrument in retrieving, organizing, and shaping the many musical reservoirs of rocknroll and the other streams as well, then those who control those catalogues can determine tomorrow's music. And in-sofar as those catalogues become expensive enough to become attractive chips in corporate crap games (as radio and television licenses have be-come), then artists' and audience participation in the unfolding of musi-cal streams becomes if not trivial, then simply a factor to be manipulated. The economic-political side of rocknroll will not go away just because the sixties are long gone. That side of rock's life has yet to be fought for. There is some evidence that world music is an abiding adversary of the gray corporate lock step, even if the examples are meager. From the appearance of Bob Marley and his band at the Independence Day ceremonies of Zimbabwe, to the concerts against famine organized by Bob Geldorf, to the simple durability of the guitar-backed voicings in the night by youth all over the world, they testify to that strange and durable power of music.

Technological Advance; Musical Retreat

It was a shock when Jimi Hendrix played "The Star Spangled Banner" at Woodstock; he pushed the distortions, blastings, and screechings of electric music into an artistic statement. That performance was more, though; implicitly it was youth's unmistakable assertion of opposition to the war in Vietnam. What meanings can be attributed to that same song being lip-synched by Whitney Houston at the televised opening of the 1991 Super Bowl, a performance dedicated to the troops in the Persian Gulf and punctuated with televised flybys of a formation of fighter planes? This was not the first time either. Huge rock concerts are regularly treated in this way; a canned tape replaces the true voice of the gyrating lead singer on the platform. When Milli Vanilli does the same and gets caught, the matter is all too quickly shrugged off. But the issue about what is a performance and who is in charge is a real one. This issue is especially pertinent if the musical decisions are being made in the corporate offices. When album sales, concert box office receipts, the sale of T-shirts, the parking, and the beer concessions are more important than the aspirations of the band, the question arises, why bother? Once again, it is *not* the technology per se; it is the mindset of the owners of that technology that threatens.

It is a long way back to the little $12.95 RCA record player that played 45's. The recordings that were listened to by the teenagers of the 1950s are now appearing on compact disks. What, then, is the real unit in rock? Also in question is the advance in instrumentation. If the drum machine is essential in supporting Def Leppard's one-armed drummer, what else can the electronic synthesizer and its descendants do?

The unlikely mixture of the ultramodern and traditional music from diverse cultures, accepted by audiences quite readily as the next new thing, illuminates another technological innovation of the seventies—the instantaneous, worldwide exchange of words, music, and pictures. The first real communications satellite in space was the American Telstar, launched in July 1962.[26] Now, several thousand objects in the heavens send and receive signals, auditory and pictorial, to every part of this globe. As the world has become so intensively interconnected, it has changed not only its internal boundaries but also its thinking about what constitutes a national boundary.

Then there is MTV, whose music has been, until recently, almost entirely from the rock stream. A few pop performers were able to join in, and after considerable political and market pressure, black pop performers at the boundary of rocknroll also found a place. "Videos," first popularized in Great Britain in the late 1970s, set the pattern for the MTV channel. Phil Spector's "little symphonies for kids" have now grown beyond even little operas or little movies for kids. Videos are a new art form in their own right. Indeed, they are a slave form—dedicated to the song—but a free-standing one nevertheless.[27] The ghost of Richard Wagner, evil magician of the total art experience, beckons such video makers as Madonna, David Byrne, Peter Gabriel, and others down a road too narrow to sustain their ambitious visions.

Television technology has assisted in breaking up the once unified youth audience so that now the college component is a special target. Every one of rock's tendencies, stylistic and political and especially the internationalization of the music, finds intensive exposure on the nation's campuses. The new video technology operating through specialized music-video services now brings to over six hundred college campuses all across the nation weekly shows of new videos, mainly rock but some from the country, black, and other streams.[28]

Does all this technology inevitably remove youth from its music? Is this observation made in the early 1980s by Paul Rappaport of Columbia Records typical of the present scene? "What we have now is like the 50s. Music was part of my life, but it was an also-ran. I wasn't *waiting* for the next Bobby Darin album, but when the 60's came, I *waited* for the next Rolling Stones album, I *had* to have it! Today it's just songs again."[29]

One More Frontier

Finally, there is the realm of space exploration, an item already on youth's agenda and a subject in their curriculum for almost as long as rocknroll has existed. The future of space exploration at this moment is bleak. Both the American and the Soviet efforts are stalled; there is no public appetite for the adventure. Even the military use of space, so threatening a few years ago, has retreated from its more extreme Star Wars scenarios.

Peaceful uses of space are quietly advancing, its important work being the LANDSAT photography of the planet, the augmentation to weather prediction and weather science, and world communications via satellites. These palpable achievements, even the promise of vast harvestable resources in space, are not, however, the real story of space exploration.

The real story, in the words of Michael Collins of the Apollo Eleven crew, is "about leaving, it's about leaving the planet." Consider this stunning sequence: Our oldest ancestors are between 2 and 3 million years old. *Homo sapiens*, the contemporary human, has been on this planet for somewhere between 100,000 to 200,000 years.[30] Then, after 30,000 recorded years of swarming all over the planet by ship and caravan, humans achieved powered flight. Only sixty-three years after Wilbur Wright barely flew over his brother Orville's head in 1903 at Kitty Hawk, North Carolina, less than the span of one lifetime, the human species had left the planet, had landed on the moon and returned safely. *That* is acceleration. Since then, men and women from almost a dozen nations (whose populations constitute more than 80 percent of all humans) have repeatedly visited or scrutinized in manned and unmanned space vehicles not only our moon and sun but most of the nine planets in our solar system. This spectacular acceleration in the ability of the human species to go wherever it chooses is the single most important beacon to the future. We are a swarming species, and we are headed for the stars.[31]

The rocknroll generations are the first space age generations. The pause point in rocknroll was also a rekindling of an ancient aspiration. It is now possible for some humans to travel to distant stars in search of habitable planets. What remains are the political questions: Who has the will and the vision to establish the passenger list? The humans who walk onto those starships will not be the people who walk off. What will be transported to distant planets will be the double essence of the human species—the inextricable mixture of genes and culture. The "passenger list" is more than a metaphor for future dreams. It is the invisible core of current politics.

The immediate issues are the military versus peaceful uses of space, the precedence of manned or unmanned exploration, the relative priorities of a space station, the merits of colonizing the moon, and the exploration of Mars. The long-range and more difficult questions are: what is a human being, how is it made and nurtured, who is in charge of it? These matters are now being decided with every court decision, congressional act, and corporate investment. They will come to a sharp focus when the decision is made about whose genes will walk onto the starships and what cultures will be taken aboard.

How will the institutions of commitment and release be arranged on those long voyages through space? Will rocknroll, youth's cultural banner, be in the ranks of those fighting the gene police and military domination of space?[32] Will rocknroll be just a dockside band playing farewell at lift-off, or will this music be among the passengers and crew? And will one of the starfleet's ships be named *Elvis Forever*?

Notes

Introduction (pp. 1–14)

1. This spelling of an essentially one word utterance is not meant to hide its linguistic history, some parts of which are told below. "Rocknroll" is cleaner than the various apostrophe-littered spellings, and it is nice to have such a neat word of origin counterposed to the equally imposing word of its maturity, "rock." Rocknroll grew into rock, generating the quarrel between those who want to celebrate the beginning and those who want to move on. The one-word spelling will be used throughout this work, unless a quoted passage spells it otherwise.

2. See Philip Rieff, *The Triumph of the Therapeutic: Uses of Faith after Freud* (New York: Harper & Row, 1966), pp. 232, 233.

> Every culture has two main functions: (1) to organize the moral demands men make upon themselves into a set of symbols that make men intelligible and trustworthy to each other, thus rendering also the world intelligible and trustworthy; (2) to organize the expressive remissions by which men release themselves in some degree, from the strain of conforming to the controlling symbolic, internalized variant readings of culture that constitute individual character.

What Rieff emphasizes as an individual process I prefer to see as the job of the culture. The releases from conformity, that is, are built into every society's leisure and cultural resources. This material is available for every person to select and shape in his or her individual manner.

3. See Philip H. Ennis, "The Definition and Measurement of Leisure," in *Indicators of Social Change: Concepts and Measurement*, Eleanor B. Sheldon and Wilbert E. Moore, eds. (New York: Russell Sage Foundation, 1968), pp. 525–572.

4. See Marghanita Laski, *Ecstasy, A Study of Some Religious and Secular Experiences* (Bloomington, Indiana: Indiana University Press, 1961).

5. Philip H. Ennis, "Ecstasy and Everyday Life," in *Journal for the Scientific Study of Religion* 6, no. 1 (Spring 1967): 47.

6. Bernard A. Grossman, "Cycles in Copyright," in *The Complete Guide to the New Copyright Law*, New York Law School Law Review, eds. (New York: New York Law School, 1977), pp. 373–377.

7. Civil Action no. 89–103, United States District Court, Southern District of New York.

8. William N. McPhee, Philip H. Ennis, and Rolf Meyersohn, *The Disk Jockey: A Study of the Emergence of a New Occupation and Its Influence on Popular Music on America*, Bureau of Applied Social Research, Columbia University, July 1953.

9. Paul L. Berkman and Sydney S. Spivak, *The "Rhythm and Blues" Fad: An Exploratory Study of a Popular Music Trend*, Bureau of Applied Social Research, Columbia University, October 1955, p. 69.

10. *Variety*, 30 June 1971.

11. The Zeigarnik effect is that incompleted tasks tend to be recalled better than completed tasks. The study by B. Zeigarnik was part of Gestalt psychology's efforts to show how perceptual closure, or wholeness, was an organizing principle in behavior. Failure to achieve such closure sets up a tension that activates the memory. (See "Über des Behalten von erledigten und unerledigten Handlungen," *Psychol. Forsch.* 9 (1927):1–86.)

12. See Philip H. Ennis, "The Simulation of an Artistic System," in *Gaming-Simulation: Rationale, Design, and Applications*, Cathy S. Greenblat and Richard D. Duke, eds. (Newbury Park, California: Sage Publications, 1975), pp. 410–417. See also Ennis, "Perspectives on Assessing Actors' Employment and Unemployment: Some Short and Long Term Problems on Research into the Arts," in *Research in the Arts: Proceedings of the Conference on Policy Related Studies of the National Endowment for the Arts* (Baltimore, 1977), pp. 76–79; and Ennis, "Sociological Theory and the Arts," in *Contribution to the Sociology of the Arts*, reports from the 10th World Congress of Sociology, Mexico City, 1982, ISA Research Committee no. 37, pp. 48–53.

13. The youth movements were enacting the main theoretical thrust of B. F. Skinner's work on operant conditioning. Punishment shuts down the whole organism. Selective positive reinforcement shapes behavior. If you want people to learn, therefore, don't punish them; just reward the behaviors you want. The young understood and adopted that lesson. Home, the schools, factory, and office had too much invested in making and using rules to have any interest in such nonsense. See B. F. Skinner, *Walden Two* (New York: Macmillan, 1948), on whose model the intentional community, Twin Oaks, was founded in 1967.

14. See Diana Crane, *The Transformation of the Avant-Garde: The New York Art World, 1940–1985* (Chicago: University of Chicago Press, 1987); and Irving Sandler, *The Triumph of American Painting: A History of Abstract Expressionism* (New York: Icon Editions, Harper & Row, 1970).

15. See Sally Banes, *Terpsichore in Sneakers: Post-Modern Dance* (Boston: Houghton Mifflin, 1980).

16. See Stephen Bayley, Philippe Garner, and Deyan Sudjic, *Twentieth-Century Style and Design* (New York: Van Norstrand Reinhold, 1986).

17. See *The New Yorker*'s profile of Ahmet Ertegun, 29 May 1978.

18. See Ken Colyer's memoir, *New Orleans and Back*, produced by Arthur Brooks and Ron Pratt, (England: Delph, Yorks, nd). See also Tom Bethell, *George Lewis: A Jazzman from New Orleans* (Berkeley: University of California Press, 1977), pp. 1, 214, 229, 234, 246–247.

19. This recording was on the *Good Time Jazz* label, owned by Neshui Ertegun. It was recorded in San Francisco in 1944.

20. See Howard S. Becker, *Art Worlds* (Berkeley: University of California Press, 1982).

21. Personal communication, Robert Farris Thompson, 1958.

1. *The Organization of Popular Musics (pp. 17–41)*

1. See Introduction, note 1.

2. Richard Robinson, ed., *Rock Revolution* (New York: Curtis Books, 1973), p. 9.

3. The date and source of this interview are lost. All that remains is a single xeroxed page with enough internal evidence to suggest that it was conducted in late 1957 for an entertainment magazine.

4. The "Century of the Common Man" was a phrase popularized by Henry Wallace, then vice president of the United States, in a 1942 speech supporting Roosevelt's and Churchill's Atlantic Charter. It was explicitly designed to dispel the notion of the "American Century," an earlier grandiose vision of America's imperial aspirations.

5. The occasional equivalence between a named creative person and an equally creative, anonymous mass of creators is noted by Levi-Strauss in his description of the artistic riches among the Pacific Northwest Coast Indians:

> This unceasing renewal, this inventive assuredness that guarantees success wherever it is applied, this scorn for the beaten track, bring about ever new improvizations which infallibly lead to dazzling results—to get any idea of them, our times had to await the exceptional destiny of a Picasso. With this difference, however: that the daring feats of a single man, which have been taking our breath away for the past thirty years, were already known and practiced by a whole indigenous culture for one hundred and fifty years or even longer.

(Claude Levi-Strauss, *The Ways of the Mask*, Sylvia Modelski, trans. [Seattle: Washington University Press, 1988], p. 4.)

6. In this scattered literature, see Philip H. Ennis, "The Social Structure of Communications Systems: A Theoretical Proposal," *Studies in Public Communication* 3 (Summer 1961): 120–44; Charles Kaduchin, *The American Intellectual Elite* (Boston: Little, Brown, 1974); Mark Granovetter, "The Strength of Weak Ties," *American Journal of Sociology* 78 (1973): 1360–80; Paul Hirsch, "Processing Fads and Fashions: An Organization-Set Analysis of Cultural Industry Systems," *American Journal of Sociology* 77, no. 4 (1972): 639–59; Thomas Smith, "Conventionalization and Control: An Examination of Adolescent Crowds," *American Journal of Sociology* (Sept. 1968): 172–83; and Orrin Klapp, *Opening and Closing: Strategies of Information Adaptation in Society* (Boston: Little, Brown, 1974).

7. Charles Rosen, *The Classical Style: Haydn, Mozart, Beethoven* (New York: Viking, 1971), p. 21.

8. Russell Sanjek, *American Popular Music and Its Business: The First Four Hundred Years*, vols. 1 and 2 (New York: Oxford, 1988).

9. Alec Wilder, *American Popular Song: The Great Innovators 1900–1950*, edited and with an introduction by James T. Maher (New York: Oxford, 1972), p. xxiv.

10. Russell Sanjek, *American Popular Music and Its Business: The First Four Hundred Years*, vol. 3 (New York: Oxford, 1988), p. 23.

11. Charles R. Townsend, *San Antonio Rose: The Life and Music of Bob Wills* (Urbana, Illinois: University of Illinois Press, 1976), p. 102.

12. Paul Oliver, *The Meaning of the Blues* (New York: Collier, 1964), p. 7.

13. See Oliver, *Meaning of the Blues*, pp. 8 and 24–28. See also Marshall Stearns, *The Story of Jazz* (New York: New American Library, 1958), pp. 77–80.

14. Robert M. W. Dixon and John Godrich, *Recording the Blues* (New York: Stein and Day, 1970), p. 6.

15. Oliver, *Meaning of the Blues*, p. 22.

16. Black jazz and black pop were then, as now, closely related, as evidenced by the participation of Charlie Parker in Jay McShann's Kansas City band of the 1940s.

17. E. B. Marks observed that by 1900 there were over a hundred published songs about the telephone. Edward B. Marks, *They All Sang: From Tony Pastor to Rudy Vallee* (New York: Viking, 1935).

18. Personal communications with George Marlo and Russell Sanjek.

19. See *The Hartford Courant*, 26 August 1990, for the story of copyright problems involving rap record sampling of previous hits.

20. Immanuel Kant's definition of "schema" appears in the Oxford English Dictionary: "Any one of certain forms or rules of the 'productive' imagination through which the understanding is able to apply its 'categories' to the manifold of sense perception in the process of realizing knowledge or experience."

21. See Myron Matlaw, ed., *American Popular Entertainment: Papers and Proceedings of the Conference on the History of American Popular Entertainment* (Westport, Connecticut: Greenwood Press, 1977); Don B. Wilmeth, *Variety Entertainment and Outdoor Amusements: A Reference Guide* (Westport, Connecticut: Greenwood Press, 1982); and Abel Green and Joe Laurie, Jr., *Show Biz: From Vaude to Video* (New York: Henry Holt, 1951), p. 183.

22. See Rhys Isaac, *The Transformation of Virginia, 1740–1790* (Chapel Hill: University of North Carolina Press, 1982), p. 131. "The defining characteristic of gentility are elusive. . . . Appropriate demeanor, dress, manners, and conversational style were essential. . . . The status of gentleman could be confirmed only if one unmistakenly possessed the means of personal independence. In this slave holding colony customary English valuation of manly independence was carried to very great heights."

23. In 1849, for example, thirty-one people were shot to death by the police and 150 were injured in New York City during a riot at the Astor Place Opera House. The provocation was the support given the British actor William Macready by his upper-class audiences. The "man in the street," celebrated and empowered by the Jacksonian democracy, championed the American actor Edwin Forrest, who had for a decade or more brought the issues of an American identity to dramatic focus in plays about the American Indian and Roman slave revolts. Robert C. Toll, *On with the Show* (New York: Oxford, 1976), pp. 20, 21.

24. The Spanish contribution to that civilization cannot be ignored. The geography of Mexico and the Caribbean Basin, and the movements of their peoples in and out of the United States, have made the "Latin tinge" more than a coloration. If there is a candidate for the eighth stream in American music, it is clearly the Hispanic in all its multifarious accents and styles. Its current importance is reflected in *Billboard*'s "Hot Latin Tracks" and "Top Latin Albums" charts, whose origins are in the rotating regional chart, "Hot Latin LP's," begun on 9 December 1972. As that stream grows in specific regions and cities, it will be carried by the vehicles of the other streams and will bring, in its fullness, more of the world's popular music to the American scene.

25. See Paula S. Fass, *The Damned and the Beautiful: American Youth in the 1920's* (New York: Oxford, 1977).

26. See David Matza, "Subterranean Traditions of Youth," *The Annals of the American Academy of Political and Social Science* 338 (November 1961).

27. See Ennis, "Ecstasy and Everyday Life," in *Journal for the Scientific Study of Religion*; and Rieff, *The Triumph of the Therapeutic*.

28. Marks, *They All Sang*, p. 3.

29. In lyrics and in industry practices, sex was acknowledged by each secular music stream at its own pace. The traditions of late nineteenth-century womanhood, the delicate female on a pedestal, whether wronged, abandoned, or luminously virtuous, lingered long in most American popular musics:

Yes, the songs of the late seventies and eighties, which rose from the flamboyant rough-and-tumble of the Bowery, were particularly innocent. They were intended for the home piano. Only ladies played the piano, and ladies never admitted that they were not innocent. Today songs are aimed at the radio audience, and unless they are hot, sister will turn the dial to another program. (Marks, *They All Sang*, p. 38.) In country music, female soloists achieved recognition much later than in pop and black pop.

30. Quoted in Green and Laurie, *Vaude to Video*, p. 183.

31. Wilder, *American Popular Song*, pp. xxxvi–xxxvii.

2. *The Basic Struggle: Publisher against Broadcaster (pp. 42–70)*

1. This discussion draws upon Sanjek, *American Popular Music*, vol. 3.

2. *Census of Manufactures*, 1900, vol. 7, table 4, group 6, p. 366.

3. Sources are U.S. Bureau of the Census, *Historical Statistics of the United States: Colonial Times to 1957* (Washington, D.C.: 1960), series P187–232, p. 417.

4. Green and Laurie, *Vaude to Video*, pp. 84–86; and Foster Rhea Dulles, *A History of Recreation: America Learns to Play* (New York: Peter Smith, 1952), p. 219. See Robert C. Toll, *On with the Show: The First Century of Show Business in America* (New York: Oxford, 1976), chap. 10, pp. 265–294.

5. For a discussion of the origins of the word and an extensive description of the history of such practices in the United States, see William Randle, Jr., "Payola," *American Speech* 36, no. 2 (May 1961): 104–116.

6. Gerald Bordman, *Jerome Kern: His Life and Music* (New York: Oxford, 1980), p. 260.

7. The jukebox industry, with its coin-operated music machines, was exempted from the "mechanicals" fee provision, a fact that gave that industry a tremendous advantage in subsequent developments during the 1930s and 1940s.

8. Special Report, *Census of Manufactures*, 1905, Part IV, p. 240, table 3; p. 248, table 13; p. 243, tables 6 and 7. *Abstract of the Census of 1919*, table 178, p. 259.

9. Roland Gelatt, *The Fabulous Phonograph: From Edison to Stereo* (New York: Appleton-Century, 1965), p. 49.

10. I am indebted to Lewis Allen Erenberg's *Steppin' Out: New York Nightlife and the Transformation of American Culture, 1890–1930* (Chicago: University of Chicago Press, 1984), for this discussion of the origins of the cabaret.

11. Lucia S. Schultz, "Performing Right Societies in the United States," *Notes* 35, no. 3 (March 1979): 513.

12. *Herbert v. Shanley Co.*, 242 U.S. 591 (1917).

13. *Variety*, 7 January 1914, p. 17.

14. R. Leiter, *The Musicians and Petrillo* (New York: Bookman Associates, 1953), p. 56.

15. *Minutes of a Conference Held at Fifty-Six West Forty-Fifth Street in Of-

fices of the American Society of Composers, Authors and Publishers, 20 September 1922, New York City, p. 32.

16. One of the first such attempts was in 1914 with D. W. Griffith's *Birth of a Nation.* The movie's producers commissioned opera composer Joseph C. Breil to write an orchestral score for the epic film. The sequel to that movie, *The Fall of a Nation* (1918), also had original music composed, ironically, by Victor Herbert, turning his talents for a moment to the medium that threatened the very existence of the New York musicians' organization he had helped form. David Ewen, *All the Years of American Popular Music* (Englewood Cliffs: Prentice Hall, 1977), p. 275.

17. *Minutes,* ASCAP, 1922, p. 18.

18. Marshall Stearns and Jean Stearns, *Jazz Dance: The Story of American Vernacular Dance* (New York: Macmillan, 1968), p. 22.

19. Ibid., p. 98.

20. Ibid., p. 13.

21. Marks, *They All Sang,* p. 166.

22. Ibid., pp. 169, 170.

23. Schultz, "Performing-Right Societies," p. 51.

24. Simon Kuznets, *Commodity Flow and Capital Formation,* vol. 1 (Washington, D.C.: National Bureau of Economic Research, 1938), p. 81.

25. Erik Barnouw, *A Tower in Babel; A History of Broadcasting in the United States Volume 1—to 1933* (New York: Oxford, 1966), p. 53.

26. See Gleason Archer's *History of Radio to 1926* (New York: American Historical Society, 1938), pp. 151–155, 163, which makes the strongest possible case on circumstantial evidence that it was President Woodrow Wilson himself who signaled the navy, the Congress, and industry leaders that he did not want the British to gain possession of the fruits of American technology.

27. Admiral William H. G. Bullard, quoted in Archer, *History of Radio,* p. 165.

28. The rules of incorporation specified, happily, that only U.S. citizens could serve as officers or board members and that no more than 20 percent of the stock could be held by aliens. (Barnouw, *Tower in Babel,* p. 59.)

29. These, according to Archer in *Big Business and Radio* (New York: American Historical Society, 1939), p. 7, were the firms linked together in cross-licensing covenants, the so called Radio Group: Radio Corporation of America, General Electric, Westinghouse, United Fruit, Tropical Radio Telegraph, Wireless Specialty Apparatus, and, from the telephone group, American Telephone and Telegraph and its equipment manufacturing subsidiary, Western Electric.

30. See Oliver Read and Walter L. Welch, *From Tin Foil to Stereo: Evolution of the Phonograph* (Indianapolis: H. W. Sams, 1976), pp. 287–288, for additional examples of the Rockefeller-Morgan contest.

31. The furor over the murals by Mexican painter Diego Rivera, planned for the main entrance of the RCA Building, was emblematic of the full range of ideas and sympathies uneasily contained within the Rockefeller outlook. In this instance, the stern Baptist temperament, allied to a near-religious affirmation of American capitalism, triumphed over the Rockefellers' more tolerant attitude that came from their cosmopolitan international artistic, political, and intellectual connections.

The result was a cruel censorship. Rivera had designed the murals around the theme provided by the Rockefellers, "Man at the Crossroads Looking with Hope and High Vision to the Choosing of a New and Better Future." His wholehearted embrace of that theme, however, was carried in strong color, to which the architects objected, and in an explicitly revolutionary socialist interpretation, including a prominent portrait of Lenin. The young Nelson Rockefeller demanded that Rivera substitute, "the face of some unknown man" for Lenin's. When Rivera refused, he was ordered to cease work on it. In spite of nationwide protests by public figures in the arts, letters, and politics, and in spite of assurances to the contrary, the mural was "removed from the wall by the process of smashing it to powder" on Nelson Rockefeller's explicit order. Bertram D. Wolfe, *Diego Rivera: His Life and Times* (New York: Knopf, 1939), p. 369.

32. Archer, *History of Radio*, p. 112.

33. Archer, *Big Business and Radio*, p. 29.

34. Until cable and satellite transmission changed the situation, FM and television were capable only of a limited broadcasting distance, limits set by the characteristics of their wave lengths and the topography of their setting. The fact that FM sound was ultimately married to the TV picture by Federal decision in 1941 is thus not surprising. The two technologies shared the line-of-sight limitation.

35. *Sears Roebuck Catalogue*, 1928, information cited in Read and Welch, *Tin Foil to Stereo*, p. 214.

36. See Archer, *Big Business and Radio*, p. 32.

37. Archer, *History of Radio*, p. 199.

38. The usual wars over who was first to broadcast commercially involve Detroit's station WWJ owned by the *Detroit News* and others. See Barnouw, *Tower in Babel*, pp. 61–63; and William Peck Banning, *Commercial Broadcasting Pioneer: The WEAF Experiment 1922–1926*, (Cambridge: Harvard University Press, 1946), p. 50.

39. Banning, *Commercial Broadcasting Pioneer*, p. 90.

40. Ibid., pp. 85, 86.

41. Bill C. Malone, *Country Music USA* (Austin: American Folklore Society, 1968), pp. 35–36.

42. See William Randle, Jr., "History of Radio Broadcasting and Its Social and Economic Effect on the Entertainment Industry 1920–1930,"vol. 1, Ph.D. diss., Western Reserve University, 1966, chap. 10, for a discussion of those exceptions, which include records of some eight hundred radio programs by black artists from 1921 to 1930. The low ownership of radios among black families in the South did nothing to dissuade radio managers from the policy of excluding black performers. See Paul Oliver, *Songsters and Saints: Vocal Traditions on Race Records* (New York: Cambridge University Press, 1984), p. 273.

43. Malone, *Country Music USA*, chapter 1.

44. Archer, *Big Business and Radio*, p. 68.

45. Ibid., pp. 66–67.

46. These call letters underwent a series of changes, reflecting the outcomes of corporate and governmental decisions.

47. The engineering bases for these changes were developed, ironically, by Bell Laboratories and offered to Victor Records.

48. Stanley Lebergott, *The American Economy: Income, Wealth, and Want* (Princeton: Princeton University Press, 1976), p. 287.

49. *Minutes*, ASCAP, 1922.

50. Randle, *History of Radio Broadcasting*, p. 369.

51. This account is taken from David R. MacKay, "The National Association of Broadcasters: Its First Twenty Years," Northwestern University, unpublished, 1956, pp. 10–12.

52. E. Claude Mills had tentatively accepted the offer to leave ASCAP and

lead the NAB if broadcasting's major industrial powers would join. When attempts to induce RCA, GE, Westinghouse, and AT&T to join the NAB failed, the young organization lost Mills' services (MacKay, *NAB*, p. 17).

53. *Buck* v. *Jewell-LaSalle Realty Co.*, in which the Supreme Court held that each unlicensed performance of a song was subject to infringement penalties. Every station in a network had to have an ASCAP license.

54. ASCAP had threatened to get into broadcasting, and NBC had tried to create its own music licensing agency. Randle, *History of Radio Broadcasting*, p. 370.

55. John G. Peatman, "Radio and Popular Music," in *Radio Research 1942– 1943*, Paul F. Lazarsfeld and Frank Stanton, eds. (New York: Duell, Sloane and Pearce, 1944), p. 336.

56. George T. Simon, *The Big Bands* (New York: Macmillan, 1967), p. 4.

57. MacDougald in 1941 regarded the *Enquirer* as the most important version of the sheet because it marked the results at the end of the week. *Variety* and *Billboard* came out on Wednesday, and the industry, especially the song pluggers, wanted as early a reading as they could get. More importantly, the *Enquirer* commented on the activities of the song pluggers, using their actual names; for example, "'All the Things You Are' took first place with 11 lengths to spare, guided by Eddie Wolpin and staff, who also spotted 'I Didn't Know What Time It Was' in a third-place tie with Henry Spitzer at Chappell's. Clever work boys." Duncan MacDougald, "The Popular Music Industry," in *Radio Research 1941*, Paul F. Lazarsfeld and Frank Stanton, eds., (New York: Duell, Sloan and Pearce, 1942), pp. 99–100.

58. MacDougald noted in 1941 that:

as publishers seize every possible opportunity to spread favorable propaganda for their songs, it would be logical to assume that they would concentrate on getting announcers to introduce songs in this pseudo-enthusiastic manner. However, as far as could be ascertained from interviews with the announcing staffs of the two major networks, announcers are rarely approached by publishers requesting favorable introductions of this nature. Such "build-ups" are prohibited at NBC by a regulation which requires announcers to present *sustaining programs* [my emphasis] of dance music as simply as possible without any unnecessary plugs concerning the popularity or "outstanding" character of any song.

CBS has no specific ruling against announcements which might serve to influence listeners favorably toward a particular song, but according to information obtained, the network would be quick to act against any excessive plugging on the part of its announcers.

(MacDougald, "The Popular Music Industry," pp. 101, 102.)

59. Peatman, "Radio and Popular Music," p. 352.

60. MacDougald, "The Popular Music Industry," p. 101, quoted from *Variety*, 24 January 1940.

61. Peatman, "Radio and Popular Music," p. 57.

62. Arnold Passman, *The Deejays* (New York: Macmillan, 1971), p. 47.

3. Gospel, Jazz, Folk: Their Paths in Development (pp. 71–99)

1. See Bill C. Malone, *Southern Music: American Music* (Lexington: University Press of Kentucky, 1979); Robert Palmer, *Deep Blues* (New York: Viking, 1981), pp. 255–277; and Richard A. Peterson and Paul Di Maggio, "From Re-

gion to Class, the Changing Locus of Country Music: A Test of the Massification Hypothesis," *Social Forces* 53 (March 1975): 497–506.

2. C. P. Jackson, *White Spirituals in the Southern Uplands* (Chapel Hill: University of North Carolina Press, 1933), p. 214.

3. D. K. Wilgus, *Anglo-American Folksong Scholarship Since 1898* (New Brunswick, New Jersey: Rutgers University Press, 1959), pp. 357–358.

4. John Lovell, Jr., *Black Song: The Forge and the Flame* (New York: Macmillan, 1972), p. 14. The following discussion of the spiritual draws from this work.

5. Kip Lornell, *Happy in the Service of the Lord: Afro-American Gospel Quartets in Memphis* (Urbana, Illinois: University of Illinois Press, 1988).

6. Burleigh was one of the few black students of Antonin Dvorak, who, as director of the National Conservatory in New York City in the 1890s, stimulated the incorporation of indigenous materials into classical music settings. This nationalistic-oriented music also guided several white composers into the use of black spirituals in a variety of concert forms.

7. Black concert circuits parallel to the black pop tours kept alive the steady if thin flow of black opera and "art" music. See Eileen Southern, *The Music of Black Americans: A History*, 1st ed. (New York: Norton, 1971), pp. 278–309.

8. Ibid., pp. 500–501.

9. LeRoi Jones, *Black Music* (New York: Morrow, 1967), pp. 181–182.

10. There were a few exceptions. Aimee Semple McPherson, a California evangelist, preached or, more accurately, performed to integrated audiences, as did a few white churches that occasionally invited black gospel groups to sing.

11. Anthony Heilbut, *The Gospel Sound: Good News and Bad Times*, rev. ed. (New York: Limelight Editions, 1985), p. xxix.

12. Lornell, *Service of the Lord*, pp. 500–501.

13. See Heilbut, *Gospel Sound*, chapter 2, for a full description of Dorsey's contributions and his life. See also Dorsey's reminiscences in Dominique-Rene De Lerma's *Reflections on Afro-American Music* (Kent, Ohio: Kent State University Press, 1973), pp. 189–195.

14. Heilbut, *Gospel Sound*, p. 25.

15. John Godrich and Robert M. W. Dixon, comp., *Blues and Gospel Records, 1902–1942*, rev. ed. (Essex: Storyville Publishing, 1969).

16. Estimates made from Godrich and Dixon, comp. *Blues and Gospel Records*; and from *Billboard* estimates of the new releases issued per week.

17. See James H. Cone, *The Spirituals and the Blues: An Interpretation* (New York: Seabury Press, 1972); and E. Simms Campbell "Blues," in *Jazzmen*, Frederick Ramsey, Jr., and Charles E. Smith, eds. (New York: Harcourt Brace, 1939).

18. Jackson, *White Spirituals*, pp. 216–217.

19. Stanley H. Brobston, "A Brief History of White Southern Gospel Music and a Study of Selected Amateur Family Gospel Music Singing Groups in Rural Georgia" Ph.D. diss., New York University, 1977.

20. Ibid., p. 212.

21. Ibid., p. 213.

22. Malone, *Country Music USA*, p. 204.

23. Ibid., p. 22.

24. Nor did the gospel stream develop any specialized publications devoted to its music, as did the jazz stream. In both jazz and gospel the result was, paradoxically, the same—the relative isolation of the two streams from their commercial neighbors.

25. Ross Russell, *Jazz Style in Kansas City and the Southwest* (Berkeley: Uni-

versity of California Press, 1983), pp. 31, 32, who asserts that the New Orleans jazz was a melding of "the French quadrille, the French opera, French brass band music, the German march, the Spanish tango, the Caribbean meringue, the African bamboula, and the tribal chant, not to mention country folk song and the popular music-hall tunes of Europe and America."

26. *Jazz New Orleans 1885–1963: An Index to the Negro Musicians of New Orleans* (New York: Oak Publications, 1963), pp. 2, 4.

27. Stearns, *Story of Jazz*, pp. 52, 53.

28. Rudi Blesh, *Shining Trumpets: A History of Jazz*, 2d ed. (New York: Knopf, 1958), p. 205.

29. Stearns, *Story of Jazz*, p. 58. Stearns also notes that black and Creole bands had moved out of New Orleans even earlier, such as Freddie Keppard, who reportedly left New Orleans to tour nationally "in 1912, turned up in Los Angeles in 1914 and played Coney Island in 1915" (p. 117).

30. Ibid., p. 47. The relation between these extensive secret societies as a type of social organization and the pervasiveness of deliberately hidden meaning in black song is too complex to be discussed here. See Robert Farris Thompson, *The Flash of the Spirit: African and Afro-American Art and Philosophy* (New York: Random House, 1983), for the broader cultural meanings in Afro-American symbolic systems.

31. See Marshall Stearns and Jean Stearns, *Jazz Dance* (New York: Macmillan, 1968), pp. 36–42; and T. O. Ranger, *Dance and Society in East Africa 1890–1970: The Beni Ngoma* (Berkeley: University of California Press, 1975).

32. Ramsey and Smith, ed., *Jazzmen*, p. 78.

33. She played in 1915 with bands on the Mississippi excursion steamers and later with King Oliver's band, when she met and married Louis Armstrong (Blesh, *Shining Trumpets*, pp. 218, 233).

34. Ibid., pp. 233–234.

35. See Charles R. Townsend's full biography, *San Antonio Rose: The Life and Music of Bob Wills* (Urbana: University of Illinois Press, 1976).

36. This description of the Southwest and Kansas City jazz owes much to Ross Russell's splendid *Jazz Style in Kansas City*, and to Gunther Schuller's *Early Jazz: Its Roots and Musical Development* (New York: Oxford, 1968).

37. Russell, *Jazz Style in Kansas City*, pp. 4, 5.

38. Ibid., p. 45, lists sixteen other such prolific pianists.

39. Not only learned piano players were called "professor." Pioneer photographers or daguerrotypers were also given that title, being "but a step from the anvil or the sawmill to the camera." Richard Rudisill, *Mirror Image: The Influence of the Daguerrotype on American Society* (Albuquerque, New Mexico: University of New Mexico Press, 1971), p. 121.

40. Russell, *Jazz Style in Kansas City*, p. 49.

41. See Simon, *Big Bands*, p. 12, for the quasi-official template of a swing band's instrumentation. Stearns counts thirteen as standard—five brass, four reeds, four rhythm, in *Story of Jazz*, p. 141. The number varied, of course, and during the swing era there were many recordings and performances by smaller groupings of large bands and independent trios, quartets, quintets, and sextets.

42. Soon after Whiteman had hired Bix Biederbecke, Ben Pollack, another established band (infused with the white Dixieland spirit) hired some of the best of the young Chicago players. The hiring of a few jazz performers who could give a few hot solos has a current counterpart in the club date sector of contemporary pop music. In the New York area, at least, (and probably in all other major cities)

almost all of the huge number of anonymous bands who play wedding parties, bar mitzvahs, and lodge functions, find it necessary to hire at least one "rock and roller" to satisfy their audiences' taste for something "hot" and current. See Bruce MacLeod, "Music for All Occasions: The Club Date Business of Metropolitan New York City," Ph.D. diss., Wesleyan University, 1979.

43. Glenn Miller studied briefly with Joseph Schillinger, preeminent guru of jazz arrangement and composition during the 1930s.

44. Blesh, *Shining Trumpets*, p. 237.

45. The opposite tendency, that of separation, even hostility, between artist and audience, is expressed at the extreme by the performer turning his back to the audience, thus stating, as Miles Davis is alleged to have said, "I'm only playing for myself." For an early statement of this problem see Howard S. Becker, "The Professional Dance Musician and his Audience," *American Journal of Sociology* 57 (1952).

46. See Charles Seeger, "Professionalism and Amateurism in the Study of Folk Music," *Journal of American Folklore* 62 (1949): 107.

47. Wilgus, *Anglo-American Folksong*, p. 4.

48. Quoted in Wilgus, *Anglo-American Folksong*, p. 8.

49. The fruition of this period, Wilgus asserts, came after World War II with the publication of many indexes and summary volumes assessing and classifying the known collections of folk song (American and British mainly). The folk canon was then closed. Peculiarly, the initial premise of communal authorship resurfaced in one of the leading examples of these summarizing volumes, *A Guide to English Folk Song Collections: 1882–1952* (1954), compiled by Margaret Dean-Smith. The *Guide* indexed folk song texts from previously published collections, omitting those that "only after examination of all collections with music disclosed no associated tune, or where, sofar as judgment could decide, by the standards of the Folk-Song Society the item must be deemed '*composed*' [my emphasis]." Cited in Wilgus, *Anglo-American Folksong*, p. 246.

50. The American Anthropological Association was founded in 1902, the Modern Language Association in 1883, its more specialized offshoot, the Linguistic Society of America in 1924, and the American Musicological Society later in 1934. See Manfred Bukofzer's *The Place of Musicology in American Institutions of Higher Learning* (Indianapolis: Bobbs, Merrill, 1957).

51. See Lovell, *Black Song*, pp. 89–100, for a critique of the major white folkloric work, which claimed the black spiritual and other music as well was a late "burnt-cork" imitation of white music.

52. See Charles Seeger's warning about this state of affairs after World War II in "Professionalism and Amateurism."

53. From the Introduction to *Checklist of Folksongs*, Library of Congress, Archive of American Folksong, 1942.

54. Missouri (1906), Texas (1909), North Carolina (1912), Kentucky (1912), Virginia (1913), Nebraska (1913), West Virginia (1915), and Oklahoma (1915). Cited in Wilgus, *Anglo-American Folksong*, p. 79.

55. See Wilgus, *Anglo-American Folksong*, p. 212.

56. Malone, *Country Music USA*, p. 62.

57. Ibid., pp. 56, 57.

58. Over the decades, *Porgy and Bess* has become a near-sacred cultural icon, offering black performers a prestigious capstone to their careers. The show is not without its critics. Rudi Blesh, one of the few who combine a high level of jazz performance with an equally virtuoso jazz scholarship, excoriates *Porgy and Bess*

as "Negroesque," a work that creates a new cultural stereotype for black artists who must sing not their own popular music but a "music that the white public finds to be just like *its own* [Blesh's emphasis]." This harsh judgment is not made gratuitously but in the context of defending early New Orleans Dixieland jazz as an authentic and respectful white response to the black jazz of the time in that city (Blesh, *Shining Trumpets*, pp. 204, 205).

59. This was an old issue. As early as 1909, for example, Henry Belden had shown, on the basis of his collections, that the ballad was a living and changing form. New music was still, as always, coming out of old music.

60. See John Greenway's *American Folk Songs of Protest* (Philadelphia: University of Pennsylvania Press, 1953); and the work of George G. Korson during the 1920s, who recorded the songs of the anthracite coal miners through the states of the mid-South and Midwest, with financial and appreciative support from the United Mine Workers.

62. From Richard Brazier's memoirs, reprinted from *Labor History* (Winter 1968) in *The Sounds of Social Change*, R. Serge Denisoff and Richard A. Peterson, eds. (Chicago: Rand McNally, 1972), pp. 60–71. The *Little Red Songbook* was a collection of songs created by many talented writers who put new words to old tunes, words with wit, righteous outrage, and political direction. The first printing of the *Little Red Songbook* was a run of ten thousand copies, with standing orders for ten thousand more. It is still available. In counter-punch to the Salvation (called the "starvation") Army, the Wobblies formed their own marching bands. Musics old and new, folkish and otherwise, were indiscriminately enlisted.

62. See R. Serge Denisoff, *Great Day Coming: Folk Music and the American Left* (Urbana, Illinois: University of Illinois Press, 1971).

4. The Pop Stream Leads It All to 1940 and the War (pp. 99–128)

1. These were (1) the fourteen months' hiatus in the broadcasting of ASCAP's music in 1941 due to the breakdown in negotiations between the music publishers led by ASCAP's top negotiators on the one side, and the broadcasters (both network and independent stations) and BMI itself on the other; (2) the AFM national ban on the recording of instrumental music during the war years, 1942–1944.

2. Time series data for the music publishers' three income sources have never, to my knowledge, been consolidated into a single compilation. The material for this figure has been drawn from the following:

Bernie L. DeWhitt, "The American Society of Composers, Authors and Publishers (1914–1938)," Ph.D. diss., Emory University, Department of History, 1977, Table 1, p. 416.
Business Week, 11 January 1936
Variety, 22 December 1937
Variety, 16 February 1938
National Association of Broadcasters, *Let's Stick to the Record* (Washington, D.C., n.d.), p. 9
Schultz, "Performing Rights Societies"
Billboard, 29 December 1934, p. 35
Randle, "History of Radio Broadcasting," pp. 317, 318
ASCAP, *Nothing Can Replace Music: Newspaper Editorials and Comments on Music and Radio* (New York, 1933), p. 7

Variety, 27 December 1939
Recording Industry Association of America, Inc., press release, 1981
Kuznets, *Commodity Flow and Capital Formation*, vol. 1, p. 81
Biennial Census of Manufactures, 1935, C3.24/4, p. 563
Census of Manufactures, 1939, vol. 2, part 1, p. 683

3. *Historical Statistics*, Table R 90–98, p. 491.

4. Read and Welch, *Tin Foil to Stereo*, pp. 293, 297.

5. Sanjek, *American Popular Music*, vol. 3, pp. 136, 305.

6. The vending industry, of which automatic music machines are part, has been tied to circuses, carnivals, and fairs. Individual jukebox operators repeatedly tried to make hits and stars in the pop music stream. The alleged connections of some of these operators to organized crime was no predictor of either success or failure in those efforts, all of which are generally regarded as minor.

7. Sanjek, *American Popular Music*, vol. 3, pp. 121–122.

8. *Billboard*, 22 February 1939.

9. Stan Kenton, still another band leader with a strong commitment to a written, jazz-based performance style, resumed the battle after the war to no avail. And in the 1960s there were further but futile efforts to secure performers' rights in the extended copyright hearings before Congress. More recently, Bette Midler raised the issue in a successful suit defending her own performance style as an infringed property (*New York Times*, 12 November 1989). The last word on performers' rights has definitely not yet been uttered.

10. The struggle against the record industry was postponed until the middle of World War II, and the comparable fight against the movie industry was resolved only in 1944. In 1938, the AFM won the prohibition of using a sound track for one movie in another. This was a Pyrrhic victory, because the movie producers immediately reduced the number of musicians employed by the studios (Leiter, *Musicians*, p. 82).

11. Ibid.

12. MacKay, "The National Association of Broadcasters," chapter 12.

13. Ibid., p. 591.

14. Ibid., chapters 10, 11.

15. Ibid., chapter 13.

16. *Billboard*, 23 March 1940.

17. MacKay, "The National Association of Broadcasters," pp. 633, 638. Years later, this strongarm tactic would haunt the BMI and broadcasting leadership, for it came back at them wrapped in an antitrust suit, the famous Schwartz case.

18. There was precedent for this reaction. In 1936, when the popular songs controlled by the Warner Brothers' movie empire were withdrawn from radio for six months, there were also no complaints, hardly any notice taken. The music in those catalogues constituted somewhere between 10 and 40 percent of the entire ASCAP reservoir and included the work of such notables as Victor Herbert, Cole Porter, and Jerome Kern. There was, however, a powerful and immediate effect in the reduction of sheet music sales. In that six-month period, sheet music sales dropped to $299,000 compared with $718,000 for the comparable period a year previously ("Let's Stick to the Record," NAB pamphlet, n.d.).

19. *Advertising Age*, 28 October 1940; and Russell Sanjek, "Informal History of BMI," unpub. ms., p. 5.

20. MacKay, "The National Association of Broadcasters," pp. 658, 659.

21. Stanley Rothenberg, *Copyright and Public Performance of Music* (The Hague: Martinus Nijhoff, 1954), p. 51.

22. *Billboard*, 20 November 1943.

23. Passman, *Deejays*, p. 42.

24. The Blue Network included three wholly owned and operated stations, WJZ, New York, renamed WABC (at which point CBS changed the call letters of its flagship station to WCBS), WENR, Chicago, and KCEO, San Francisco.

25. Quoted in Barnouw, *The Golden Web: A History of Broadcasting in the United States, Vol. II—1933 to 1953* (New York: Oxford, 1968), p. 189.

26. Ibid., p. 171.

27. *Report on Chain Broadcasting*, p. 138.

28. See Shapiro and Hentoff, *Hear Me Talkin' to Ya* (New York: Rinehart, 1955); Arthur Taylor, *Notes and Tones: Musician to Musician Interviews* (published by author, 1977); and Frederic Ramsey, Jr., and Charles Edward Smith, eds., *Jazzmen* (New York: Harcourt Brace Jovanovich, 1939).

29. Lombardo notes: "We dismissed the St. Regis, . . . an uptown favorite spot for the social register crowd, . . . because we felt the social clientele might be too restrictive in their musical demands. And we thought the New Yorker . . . in the garment district . . . would not attract the collegiate crowd, which was among our biggest boosters." Guy Lombardo, with Jack Altshul, *Auld Acquaintance* (New York: Doubleday, 1975), p. 91.

30. One of its best representations is the Buck Clayton Jam Session of 16 December 1953, produced by George Avakian and John Hammond for Columbia (CL 548). Not only is this a highly creative and swinging pair of numbers, but the album is notable for several other reasons. First, it is one of the few early extended sessions allowing the musicians full and free time to unfold their ideas. Second, and in apparent contradiction, the original "takes" were cut and spliced according to the producers' sense of what made the best final outcome, even to changing the order in which the improvised choruses actually proceeded. Third, the album tells the listener all this in an extended set of liner notes. This presentational form of jazz criticism reached its peak soon afterward, then giving way to the marketing directives that dictated pictures on both sides of the album covers—no words.

31. Simon, *Big Bands*, p. 206.

32. Benny Goodman, with Irving Kolodin, *The Kingdom of Swing* (New York: Ungar, 1939), p. 198, 199.

33. Lombardo, in *Auld Acquaintance*, estimates that by 1940 there were "800 bands in an industry doing a reported billion-dollar-a-year business" (p. 182).

34. Blesh, in *Shining Trumpets*, opens his polemical anchorage of jazz primarily in the musical traditions of West Africa, with a six-page chart contrasting those African survivals with their deformations. The "hot" concept is the first he develops. Swing, he asserts, is one of the main deformations jazz has suffered.

35. Perhaps the pinnacle was Sol Hurok's presentation of Benny Goodman's band at Carnegie Hall for an evening entitled "Benny Goodman and his Swing Orchestra." The program was warmly received; the dancing in the aisles and boxes was not booed; but the classical music world was by and large intractable. When Benny Goodman was invited to perform with the Philadelphia Orchestra in 1941, its conductor Jose Iturbi withdrew. His reason, "Beneath my dignity" (quoted in Green and Laurie, *Vaude to Video*, p. 517).

36. Leon McAuliffe, Bob Wills' closest collaborator, quoted in Charles R. Townsend, *San Antonio Rose: The Life and Music of Bob Wills* (Urbana, Illinois: University of Illinois Press, 1976), p. 285.

37. Quoted in Townsend, *San Antonio Rose*, p. 102. Bob Wills was allowed

his full instrumentation (including drums and horns) at his 1945 Opry appearance after telling his boys to "pack up, we're going home." Ten years later, the same story is repeated: The rockabilly style failed to impress such institutions as the Grand Ole Opry, where drums were not allowed on stage and where Presley "died" on his first appearance in 1955.

38. Simon, *Big Bands*, p. 328.

39. An ironic note was that Martin Block, one of the first disk jockeys to become part of the pop stream, was the MC that evening. One game ends; another begins.

40. *Variety*, 24 January 1940.

41. *Variety*, 31 December 1941, "College Rhythm" report on UCLA, one of a series of invited commentaries on the college scene by a member of the student body.

42. ". . . since the shag, which gave much impetus to the swing era and which has long since knocked itself out, no jitterbug hop requiring speedy tempo has come to favor." *Variety*, 24 January 1940.

43. *Billboard*, 2 March 1938.

44. *Variety*, 16 March 1938.

45. Ibid.

46. *Billboard*, 3 November 1945.

47. Actual sheet music sales were carefully guarded secrets. When "Best Selling Sheet Music" tunes were charted, only rankings were used, based on reports from publishers, hardly an objective estimate.

48. It even introduced a regional breakdown of record sales, parallel to the regional sheet music sales chart introduced earlier that year. Geographic dispersion and geographic variation was a reality for both sheet music and records.

49. Green and Laurie, *Vaude to Video*, p. 512.

50. Cabell Phillips, *The 1940's: Decade of Triumph and Trouble* (New York: Macmillan, 1976), p. 193.

51. It is probably not entirely mistaken to view the Great Depression (1929–1932) and the slow recovery (1932–1940) as a suppressant to the developing generation gap, which thus began only after World War II. See Fass, *The Damned and the Beautiful*, chapter 3.

52. *Business Week*, 8 June 1946.

53. Some reappeared in khaki soon after, though, for the armed forces were expanding their entertainment apparatus, for example, Glenn Miller.

54. The small "chamber" jazz group goes back beyond the Benny Goodman trio and quartet of the midthirties to the duos and trios of the mid- to late twenties; the Louis Armstrong, Earl Hines trumpet and piano records of 1928 are exemplary of this style. That line of small jazz groups continued more or less independently, finding vigorous expression on Manhattan's West Fifty-second Street during and after the war and subsequently in Birdland—the jazz cellar in midtown Manhattan.

55. Barnouw, *Golden Web*, pp. 165–167.

56. Geoffrey Perrett, *Days of Sadness, Years of Triumph: The American People 1939–1945* (New York: Coward, McGann & Geoghegan, 1973), p. 390.

57. The membership in the AFM had grown from about 84,000 in 1917 to a peak of 146,000 in 1929. During the depression years, membership had declined to slightly over 100,000 but in 1939 it had risen to 131,000 and by 1944 it was about 147,000 (Leiter, *Musicians*, p. 80).

58. The AFM's annual conventions of 1941 and 1942 authorized Petrillo to

try to end the production of records and transcriptions. Members supported the action as much by loyalty as by fear, since Petrillo had exacted from the union a rule expelling any member who recorded with any company not under AFM contract. Without the AFM card, employment for musicians was nigh impossible.

59. Leiter, *Musicians*, p. 140.
60. *Billboard*, 24 March 1945.

5. Redesigning the Machine: The Disk Jockey Takes Over (pp. 131–160)

1. Simon, *Big Bands*, p. 32.
2. Large bands continued to play after 1945, of course. They were in the television, radio, and movie studios, with their personnel interchangeably assembled for recording studio work. Some bands continued touring, including Stan Kenton, Buddy Rich, Sauter-Finnegan, Ray Anthony, Les Elgart, and Buddy Morrow. The college prom circuit kept other more traditional bands busy until the mid-fifties. Ellington, Basie, and other black big bands went on, oblivious to all the changes. It took two more decades for a recognizable "museum" resurgence of the "big bands" to appear, for example, public television's "Wolf Trap" concerts in the late 1970s and early 1980s.
3. Passman, *Deejays*, pp. 10, 11, finds deeper linguistic-historical anchorage for the term "jockey." Disk jockey as performer is somewhere between the realms of impresarial agent, mimic, clown, and holy fool. Take your choice.
4. *Sponsor's 11th Annual TV/Radio Basics*, July 1957, p. 181 ("Radio in Every Room" campaign).
5. The tactic of piggybacking one product onto another is a perennial American practice: In the late 1880s, some models of the newly invented sewing machine were equipped with a parlor melodeon (a reed organ); see Patsy and Myron Orlofsky, *The History of Quilts* (New York: McGraw Hill, 1974), p. 59. Some elegant models of the early jukebox dispensed a candy bar at the close of a coin-induced musical selection (Read and Welch, *Tin Foil to Stereo*, p. 304).
6. The release of postwar buying power burst the boundaries of prewar retail store definitions. What constituted a line of goods was up for grabs. "Music" stores were diversifying their stock in every direction. A large number moved from a record and radio-phono mix into a product line emphasizing the full catalogue of electrical products—kitchen ranges, refrigerators, toasters, blenders, irons, and so on (see *Radio and Television Retailing*, June 1946, pp. 56, 57).
7. It will be recalled that the evasion of anonymity began early in the history of radio. Announcers in the 1920s successfully adapted an old convention from the days of wireless wherein each operator or announcer identified himself with a three-letter signature indicating his job (A for announcer, O for Operator), the initial of his last name, and an initial for the city originating the broadcast. Station management, ever wary of depending upon celebrity names but every greedy for larger audiences, soon joined what they couldn't lick. As long as the station's call letters were associated with their named disk jockeys, they went along. see Barnouw, *Tower In Babel*, pp. 163, 164.
8. *Broadcasting Yearbook 1969*, p. 28.
9. *Statistical Abstracts*, 1971, table 1215, p. 745; and *Broadcasting Yearbook 1969*, p. 28.
10. *Billboard*, February 1953, p. 16. As early as 1947, *Billboard* began its annual disk jockey surveys, expending tens of pages every year describing the

programming practices and musical preferences of hundreds of the nation's disk jockeys who responded to the extensive questionnaire sent by *Billboard*. In every issue, in addition, Billboard's column "Vox Jox" described the minutae of disk jockey culture as it unfolded, perhaps the best teacher after all. *Sponsor, Broadcasting, Cash Box,* and *Variety* to a lesser extent also tracked disk jockey activities.

11. Television provided a larger stage for the "personality" than did radio. Along with Godfrey came Robert Q. Lewis, Dave Garroway, Steve Allen, Ernie Kovacs, Jack Paar, and others; all were radio disk jockeys before they came to TV. Even contentiousness brought notoriety to some "personalities." Barry Gray, Jack Eigen, Mike Wallace, Les Crain, and others made their careers as disk jockeys in this way, where music played a negligible part in the programming. The late night talk show was one outgrowth of this exaggeration of the disk jockey's personality.

12. *Billboard*, 26 December 1953.

13. P. F. Lazarsfeld and Patricia Kendall, *Radio Listening in America* (New York: Prentice-Hall, 1948), p. 136, Appendix table 14.

14. The following discussion is drawn from a study carried out by Columbia University's Bureau of Applied Social Research in 1952 for BMI (see Introduction), in anticipation of the suit entered by Arthur Schwartz. The project as a whole was directed by Robert O. Carlson. William McPhee headed the disk jockey study, with Rolf Meyersohn and Philip H. Ennis as associates. The latter two carried out the interviews for the national sample of disk jockeys. The final report issued by the BASR in July 1953 was entitled *The Disk Jockey: A Study of the Emergence of a New Occupation and Its Influence on Popular Music in America* by William N. McPhee, Philip H. Ennis, and Rolf Meyersohn.

The material described here is based on the visits and discussions with the total of forty-two pop stream disk jockeys located in twenty-four cities in all parts of the country, carried out in the winter of 1952–1953. In addition to the leading nationally recognized disk jockeys, an interview with a less important disk jockey in each city was arranged.

Disk jockeys identified by name have given their permission for such citation. Those who were unavailable or who refused direct attribution are described in ways designed to protect their anonymity as promised forty years ago.

15. They did so under the double imperatives of the album (rather than the three-minute single) as the musical unit and the repudiation of the Hit Parade pressures to force the hit game on an audience who took rock music as part of their culture, not as a "product."

16. *1954 Broadcasting-Telecasting Yearbook*, pp. 80–93.

17. Passman, *Deejays*, p. 187.

18. In 1947, the ABC network hired Whiteman in a $2.3 million disk jockey package billing him as "the King of Jazz" (See ibid., p. 118).

19. "Jump Back Honey" was an R&B tune written and recorded by Hadda Brooks, a Los Angeles-based singer. The version used here was the record by Ella Mae Morse, a black, jazz-tinged big band singer. "Greyhound" was a hit on the R&B charts, here offered by the original artist, Amos Milburn, instead of the cover record by Vic Damone. "Peoria" by Bob Scobey and "South Rampart Street Parade" by Bing Crosby and the Andrews Sisters were traditional jazz numbers that had reached the pop audience. "Indian Love Call," the 1924 Harbach-Hammerstein II song from the Friml musical of that year, revived by Jeanette McDonald and Nelson Eddy in the 1930s movie of the same name, appeared once more and hit the top of the Country and Western charts in this Slim Whit-

man rendition. The Spanish tune "Tiro de Mulas" by Lalo Guerrero was a local hit by a West Coast Mexican-American singer.

20. Randle did go on with his education, leaving radio at the peak of his disk jockey's career to resume his academic interests. He completed his doctorate in 1966 at Western Reserve University with a rich thesis on early radio's impact on the entertainment industries (See Randle, *History of Radio Broadcasting*).

21. This boundary crossing has been described as "para-social" interaction (Donald Horton and R. Richard Wohl, "Mass Communication and Para-Social Interaction," in *Psychiatry* 19, no. 3 (Aug. 1956). It is still a useful notion showing the importance of contact between performer and audience.

22. In the two afternoon sessions I observed, the visitors, experienced and highly sophisticated veterans of the song plugging game, said not a word other than the usual show business banter. They were in the presence of a pro; they wisely saved their "hype" for the younger, more naive disk jockeys. I had just come from visits with a few of them in other cities, and the difference in treatment and demeanor was unmistakable.

23. In a particular time period, for example, he might run a baking recipe contest against a disk jockey with a strong housewife appeal or place especially popular musical selections to hold potential dial turners at news breaks or other interruptions as a competing show was about to begin.

24. *Down Beat*, 14 January 1953, p. 3.

25. The Four Knights, a short-lived white quartet from Charlotte, North Carolina, whose career was launched via a local radio station, also recorded the song. It reached the eleventh position and remained six weeks on the charts. For reasons too deep to fathom, Lawrence Welk also recorded "Oh Happy Day." If ever there was a case of divine justice, this was it, for the Lord had said, "If I give you rocknroll then I gotta give you Lawrence Welk." Also mysterious is the fact that in 1970 Glen Campbell, then early in his career, also recorded this tune and drove it to number twenty-five on the country charts.

6. The Streams Aligned (pp. 161–192)

1. National Ballroom Operators Association, personal communication, Otto Weber, Managing Director, 20 August 1969.

2. *Billboard*, 24 July 1954.

3. *Billboard*, 1 October 1949.

4. The FCC had stopped issuing licenses for TV stations in 1948 due to a technical logjam. NBC's relatively simple and inexpensive black and white picture was being challenged by CBS's more complex, more expensive, and not yet perfected color system. It would take several years to resolve this issue, during which only one hundred existing stations served a TV audience that was expanding rapidly from 1 million sets in 1948 to 27 million in 1953. Richard E. Chapin, *Mass Communications: A Statistical Analysis* (East Lansing, Michigan: Michigan State University Press, 1957), p. 90.

5. *Broadcasting Yearbook 1969*, p. 131.

6. It began on 17 March 1951 and ended 24 November 1951.

7. ASCAP and BMI's settlement with the television broadcasting industry, however, took over five years to regularize, during which there was a year-by-year extension of the 1950 contracts with both the licensing agencies.

8. There were a few fitful attempts to bring youth-oriented music and dance shows back, such as "Hullabaloo." *Billboard*, 28 April 1956.

9. *Billboard*, 19 January 1952.

10. Chapin, *Mass Communications*, p. 132.

11. Not included were those forms that were locked into metropolitan centers or at least thought to be at that time. The leadership of New York's opera, dance, orchestral music, and theater in the early 1950s began a series of discussions and studies aimed at assessing the results of the suburban development for the performing arts. (See P. H. Ennis and S. Spaulding, *The Suburban Migration: The Implications for the Future of the Performing Arts in the New York Area*, Bureau of Applied Social Research, Columbia University, 1956.) The Rockefeller interests primed the pump for dance particularly and for the arts generally in New York State. The New York Arts Council subsequently became the model for the National Endowment for the Arts' efforts in spreading the Federal dollar for the arts across the American landscape through its block grants to all fifty states. The tension continues between urban concentration of artistic resources and their dispersion in smaller centers.

12. Philip Jenkinson and Alan Warner, *Celluloid Rock: Twenty Years of Movie Rock* (New York: Warner, 1974), see filmography, pp. 127–132.

13. *Billboard*, 3 October 1953, p. 16.

14. Chapin, *Mass Communications*, p. 82.

15. Sanjek, *American Popular Music*, vol. 3, p. 308.

16. *Billboard*, 16 February 1946, p. 20.

17. Malone, *Country Music USA*, p. 252; Sanjek, *American Popular Music*, vol. 3, pp. 288, 289.

18. Chet Atkins, with Bill Neely, *Country Gentleman* (Chicago: H. Regnery, 1974).

19. Spade Cooley, for instance, owned and performed at a ballroom at Santa Monica, "which drew between five thousand and six thousand customers every Saturday night." Bob Wills did the same. Cited in Malone, *Country Music USA*, p. 211.

20. See Linnell Gentry, *A History and Encyclopedia of Country, Western and Gospel Music* (St. Clair Shores, Michigan: Scholarly Press, 1972), pp. 168–175, for a listing of these radio barn dances.

21. Malone, *Country Music USA*, p. 210.

22. The newly formed MGM Records is included among the majors. This is important not just because of its ties to a major motion picture firm, but because it had signed perhaps the most important artist who reached beyond the country and western stream, Hank Williams.

23. Four of these were on King: Wayne Raney's "Why Don't You Haul Off and Love Me," covered immediately by Bull Moose Jackson, Moon Mullican's "I'll Sail My Ship Alone," the Delmore Brothers' "Blues Stay Away from Me" (written by the Delmore Brothers, Wayne Raney and Henry Glover), and Jack Cardwell's "The Death of Hank Williams." Imperial produced Slim Whitman's "Indian Love Call." On National, Bing Crosby took Dick Thomas' 1945 hit "Sioux City Sue" to the top of the pop charts. Finally, there was "Mexican Joe" by Jim Reeves on Abbott Records.

24. The earthy sexual lyrics, celebrations of drugs and drink, and blatant racial assaults are chronicled in Nick Tosches, *The Biggest Music in America* (New York: Stein and Day, 1977), pp. 167–228.

25. See Katrina Hazzard-Gordon, *Jookin': The Rise of Social Dance Formations in African-American Culture* (Philadelphia: Temple University Press, 1990).

26. In Birmingham, Alabama, to take an exemplary case, the control over

licensing jukeboxes in both white and black places of entertainment was fully in the hands of "Bull" Connor, commissioner of public safety. He exercised that power to keep a tight rein on black nightlife.

27. Peter Guralnick, *Sweet Soul Music: Rhythm and Blues and the Southern Dream of Freedom* (New York: Harper & Row, 1986), p. 228.

28. John Broven, *Rhythm and Blues in New Orleans*, (Gretna, Louisiana: Pelican, 1974), p. 37.

29. *Billboard*, 2 January 1943, p. 28.

30. Estelle Edmerson, "A Descriptive Study of the American Negro in United States Professional Radio 1922–1953," University of California, Los Angeles, PhD. diss. 1954, p. 354.

31. *Statistical Abstracts, 1967*, table 17.

32. *Sponsor*, emphasizing the commercial possibilities in black radio, credits her show "Songs of the South" for selling 456 General Electric washing machines in ten weeks (*Sponsor*, 14 August 1950, p. 28).

33. Ibid., 19 September 1955, pp. 110–113.

34. Ibid., 10 October 1949, p. 55; Passman, *Deejays*, p. 184; and David Dachs, *Anything Goes: The World of Popular Music* (Indianapolis: Bobbs-Merrill, 1964), p. 113.

35. See John Broven, *Rhythm and Blues in New Orleans*, (Gretna, Louisiana: Pelican, 1974); Nelson George, *The Death of Rhythm and Blues* (New York: Pantheon, 1988); Charlie Gillett, *The Sound of the City: The Rise of Rock and Roll* (New York: Pantheon, 1983); Peter Guralnick, *Feel Like Goin' Home: Portraits in Blues and Rock'n'Roll* (New York: Outerbridge and Diestfrey, 1971); Charles Keil, *Urban Blues* (Chicago: University of Chicago Press, 1966); and Arnold Shaw, *Honkers and Shouters: The Golden Years of Rhythm and Blues* (New York: Macmillan, 1978).

36. Steve Chapple and Reebee Garafalo, *Rock'n'Roll Is Here to Pay: The History and Politics of the Music Industry* (Chicago: Nelson Hall, 1977), p. 173.

37. The four records from the majors came from two record companies, Decca (Louis Jordan's "Saturday Night Fish Fry" and "Blue Light Boogie") and MGM (Ivory Joe Hunter's "I Need You So" and "I Almost Lost My Mind"). *Billboard*, 24 April 1954, p. 16.

38. George, *Death of Rhythm and Blues*, pp. 76–77.

39. Shaw, *Honkers and Shouters*, p. 183.

40. For one compilation of data on career lines, see Norm N. Nite, *Rock On: The Illustrated Encyclopedia of Rock N' Roll* (New York: Crowell, 1974; reprint, Popular Library, 1977). The fact that Nite himself is a disk jockey should be kept in mind.

41. Shaw, *Honkers and Shouters*, pp. 154, 185, 195, 197, 198.

42. Ibid., p. 187.

43. Ibid., pp. 189, 190.

44. Nathan's ability to match the performance of black and country artists was based in part on his resident producer/writer Henry Glover, who had played with the popular traveling black dance bands in the 1930s (Shaw, *Honkers and Shouters*, pp. 278–279).

45. Palmer, *Deep Blues*, pp. 164–165.

46. *Sponsor*, 24 January 1955, pp. 50, 82.

47. Charlie Gillett, *Making Tracks: The Story of Atlantic Records* (London: Panther, 1975), p. 5.

48. The New Orleans studio of Cosimo Matassa was legendary for its sound

and for the parade of artists whose records there established or continued their national reputation. See Broven, *Rhythm and Blues in New Orleans*, pp. 13–17.

49. Shaw, *Honkers and Shouters*, p. 290.

50. Ibid., p. 292. Dixon was discussing the evolution of a tune in the studio session, which began as "Little Black Angel" and became, as Shaw wryly notes, "in the atmosphere of the time," "Little Angel."

51. Gillett, *Making Tracks*, p. 50.

52. This contrast between Chess' and Atlantic's production styles is a restatement of the situation experienced by the jazz bands of the 1930s. Then, it will be recalled, the problem was securing a reliable ensemble performance from players who could not read music. The solution came from Kansas City with the appearance of the arranger, usually the piano-playing leader, Basie's band being the exemplar.

53. The *Billboard* headline on 22 April 1955, "Atlantic Records will enter the jazz pop album field," signaled quite early the significance of the LP *album* for jazz (and later for rock), as well as the Erteguns' abiding interest in jazz. Atlantic's commitment to jazz was embodied to a great degree in the work of King Curtis, Atlantic's contract sideman and solo performer for years. Curtis represented the branch of the Kansas City tree that grew over the fence into rhythm and blues. The progenitor, Lester Young, was a strong influence on the young Curtis. Atlantic's jazz interests also included young New York jazz performers in a more sophisticated mode, such as the elegant styling of Tommy Talbert and the innovative vocals of Patty McGovern. But this was not the direction of Atlantic's close neighbors. Bop was heading elsewhere.

54. *Billboard*, 27 December 1952.

55. *Music Business*, May 1948. This nonscientific sampling did generate replies from 32 percent of all AM stations on the air.

56. This composite table is suggestive of the relative prevalence of these three streams in recorded music during the early 1950s. Note the progressive diminution of R&B records in their journey from studio to audience.

Types of Records Released, Distributed, Programmed, 1948–53

	Released	Distributed	Programmed on radio
Pop	62%	66%	77%
Country	26	26	19
R&B	12	8	4
	100%	100%	100%

SOURCES: Released, *Billboard*, 27 December 1952; distributed, *Billboard*, 26 December 1953; programmed, *Music Business*, May 1948.

57. The "Most Played by Disk Jockeys" chart for the R&B field came on board last. It was added on 22 January 1955.

58. *Billboard*'s charts were rich enough to satisfy every level of sophistication in the music trades. Busy, lazy, or conservative record dealers and jukebox operators could stock their inventories by simply following the best-selling singles charts and the "Best Buys" by *Billboard*'s staff reviewers, a shrewd and knowledgeable staff. The more adventuresome in the trade could and did use the reviews and the performers' track records to handicap their selections much as did veteran horseplayers.

59. *Billboard* itself offered a service to its readers that went beyond the pre-

sumptions of the regular charts. The service began in 1951 (February), was called the "Billboard Disk Jockey Monitoring Service (not published in the Billboard)", and provided its subscribers with a "factual, comprehensive and confidential weekly report on actual disk jockey performance."

60. Technically, this means that the charts should be considered on an ordinal not an interval scale. That is, the difference between the number one best-selling single and the no. 2 is not necessarily the same distance (in number of records sold) as between the number two and the number three, and so on. Any statistical manipulations of the charts on the assumption they are interval data is an exercise in mythology; useful perhaps, but still mythological.

Further, the primary report on which side of a two-sided single sold the record was guided by local conventions that need to be studied for the nature and degree of distortion introduced at that level. Walter Rassbach, unpublished comparative study, Wesleyan University, 1971.

61. The "real" speed of the three markets is difficult to ascertain. The actual number of new releases, the sales, extent, and duration of radio and jukebox exposure are the relevant measures but are generally beyond full collection for any stream over any extended period. There was considerable but fragmentary street knowledge about the relationships between chart position and sales in the three markets. Shaw (*Honkers*, p. 311) cites a typical example of the early 1950s. The Moonglows' 1955 hit "Sincerely" reached the number nine position in *Billboard*'s year. It sold about 250,000 copies. The McGuire Sisters' cover version reached number eight on the pop charts and sold over a million copies. Chart position and actual sales had only a "more than–less than" relationship.

62. These include all crossovers, direct and cover records moving between all three markets.

7. *The Early Crossovers (pp. 193–228)*

1. *Billboard*, 19 December 1953, p. 29. It first appeared on 16 May 1953 and remained nine weeks, reaching the number two position. The other side of the record contained a parody of Hank Williams' 1952 hit "Kaw-Liga," entitled "Pore Ol' Koo-Liger."

2. There was, however, a ready audience for spoofs of the hillbilly life, if the performers showed sufficient distance; for example, "Cigarettes, Whusky, and Wild Wild Women" by the sophisticated Sons of the Pioneers, and pop balladeer Jo Stafford's "Timtayshun," both strong hits in 1947.

3. The Atlantic Records' strategy developed by Jesse Stone, described previously, was to triumph over Willie Dixon's style at Chess. Leiber and Stoller, still teenagers when they wrote the song, worked for Atlantic briefly on their way to becoming one of the first freelance producing teams as well as among the first writer-producer-label owners of the new rocknroll era. *Billboard*, 25 April 1953, p. 54.

4. This precipitated a flap about who wrote the song. Johnny Otis was apparently cut into a third of the writer's credits in the beginning but was given sole credit on the Big Mama Thornton record. With Elvis' success, the lawyers went to work, and ultimately Leiber and Stoller got their credit and probably some of the money. See Gillett, *Making Tracks*, pp. 150–152.

5. Green and Laurie, *Vaude to Video*, p. 547. There was a spate of duets by various father-son, mother-daughter teams, as well as pairings from different musical genres including the improbable but winning duets of Helen Traubel and Jimmy Durante.

6. *Down Beat,* 31 December 1952, p. 21.
7. Shaw, *Honkers and Shouters,* pp. 160, 161.
8. Ibid., pp. 158–168; and Johnny Otis, *Listen to the Lambs* (New York: Norton, 1968).
9. Keil, *Urban Blues,* p. 62.
10. Ibid., p. 64.
11. Eddie "Lockjaw" Davis, a veteran jazzman, nicely sums up the situation, looking back from the late 1960s.
> There was a different atmosphere about jazz years ago. . . . There was a margin of humor in playing, there was a happier atmosphere. Today the jazz musician comes to the bandstand with a grim outlook, he's too serious. . . . The people who come to the club are afraid to talk loud, afraid to laugh among themselves because the musicians are looking grim. So the whole joint looks like a graveyard. . . . Jazz was never meant to be that way. To me, jazz has always meant an outlet, a form of expression, a relief, a relaxation and a listening pleasure. (Taylor, *Notes and Tones,* pp. 92, 93.)
12. R. Crumb, *Heroes of the Blues* (New York: Yazoo Records, 1980).
13. The beginnings of multimedia production of musical recording began at this time with such pioneering efforts as Norman Granz's "The Fred Astaire Story," a set of LP's containing thirty-four tunes sung by the dancer or made famous by him in movies. The musicians were an all-star group of jazzmen; a series of photographs by Gjon Mill and a biographical text accompanied the fifty dollar limited edition. *Down Beat,* 31 December 1952.
14. *Down Beat,* 31 December 1952.
15. See Sanjek, *American Popular Music,* vol. 3, p. 245. Classical records comprised 20 percent and the new field of children's records reached fully 10 percent of the total record sales. Jazz and folk comprised about 1 percent each, and gospel less than 1 percent.
16. These were Arthur Gunter's recording of "Baby Let's Play House" on the Excello label, which reached the R&B chart at the end of January in 1955. Then, in the middle of July of that year, Elvis Presley's first chart record for Sun Records was that very same song. The second record to cross from R&B to country was Chuck Berry's "Thirty Days (To Come Back Home)" for Chess, which appeared on the R&B charts in October of 1955, followed two months later by Ernest Tubb's Decca recording. This recording was, perhaps, somewhat of a comedown for the great country star, reduced to covering a rhythm and blues upstart.
Actually, there were two earlier such crossover records, if the time period between the appearances on the two charts is extended beyond the six month period used to define a crossover in this study. One was "Country Boy" recorded by Little Jimmy Dickens, which appeared on the country charts in June of 1949. Eight months later, in February 1950, Dave Bartholemew put his version on the R&B charts. The other was "Bloodshot Eyes" sung by Hank Perry, which appeared on the country chart in February of 1950. A year and a half later in August of 1951, Wynonie Harris put his version on the R&B charts.
17. Nat Cole's version for Capitol sold 3 million copies and was the second best-selling record on the pop chart. The record's success generated three cover records in white pop by prewar performers (Victor Young's orchestra, Art Lund, and Dennis Day). Jimmy Wakely did a country version for Capitol, as did Moon Mullican for King Records, both of which were moderate chart successes. There would be many other detachable movie songs that were successful in the three markets during the fifties.
18. A crossover in this study is defined by the movement of records across the

Billboard music popularity charts. The specific titles of songs, their performers, and their record labels are taken from those charts, as is the duration on a particular chart and the top position achieved.

In this study, the crossovers are the pop, country, and R&B records that have appeared on their own best-selling singles charts (including the hot 100 in the pop stream) and/or are the most played on jukeboxes, and/or are those receiving the most disk jockey exposure. To be considered a crossover, a title has to have made its first appearance on any of the charts of two or more streams within a six month period.

The sources for these listings are the weekly *Billboard* charts themselves or the Whitburn compilations: Joel Whitburn, *Joel Whitburn's Top Country Singles 1944–1988* (Menomonee Falls, Wisconsin: Record Research Inc., 1989); *Joel Whitburn's Top Pop Singles 1955–1986* (New York: Billboard Publications, 1987); and *Joel Whitburn's Top R & B Singles 1942–1988* (Record Research, Inc., 1988).

The Whitburn volumes blur the distinction between the best-selling, most played on jukeboxes, and most played by disk jockeys. A test analysis of the rate of crossovers over time among the three streams, comparing the best-selling singles chart taken directly from the weekly *Billboard* with the Whitburn volumes, yields the same story. They are essentially equivalent for the analyses presented here.

There are occasional discrepancies in the date of first appearance of a record listed in the weekly *Billboard* and in Whitburn. Moreover, in the late 1950s, an R&B artist would often have an R&B record appearing on the pop chart before it appeared on its own chart.

Whether this is due to the quicker response of the pop market during those years or is an artifact of *Billboard*'s reporting is not clear.

19. Such naughty party records were a small but regular part of the pop stream's output. The performers, such as Dwight Fiske and Nan Blakstone, both appearing on the Gala Records label, were mainly supper club performers.

20. An ironic note to this song's career and to the new era it heralded was that Elvis Presley attempted a version of "Rag Mop" in 1954. At Sam Phillips' suggestion and supervision, Elvis was called in to the Sun Records studio to do a demo version of the song that a black singer had sent Phillips from Nashville. Phillips knew the action was at the confluence of pop, country, and R&B, but this recording didn't work (from liner notes on *Elvis the Sun Sessions*, a 1976 album of uncertain origin, even though bearing an RCA logo).

21. Gordon Jenkins himself, a veteran of the Woody Herman band, was one of the few pop band leaders with aspirations beyond the pop song. His "Manhattan Towers," an impressionistic, orchestral-like suite written as a background for a television show, was one such example. Another was his encounter with the folk stream, testing the receptivity of pop to that as yet unexplored zone, discussed earlier.

22. It is puzzling that far more critical respect is given to Billie Holiday's treatment of pop tunes than has been accorded Dinah Washington's. It is difficult to say whether Washington resisted a full commitment to the material she was given or whether it was simply inferior to the songs Billie gave life to. It may have been the result of the generally low esteem of commercial rhythm and blues where Dinah lived compared to the doubly elevating prestige Billie received by being in the top ranks of both the jazz and pop streams. The two pop hits Dinah covered

in 1950 were both high-class tunes from 1933. One was from the nightclub revue "Casino de Paris," titled "I Wanna Be Loved" (words by Billy Rose and Edward Heyman, music by John Green), redone by the Andrews Sisters for Decca. The other was a Richard Himber song revived by Don Cornell for Coral.

23. This crossover pattern was part of Foley's personal version of an established country music bringing in white gospel as a parallel to secular songs. His "Just A Closer Walk with Thee," "Steal Away," and "Peace in the Valley" had been hits along his way.

24. Thomas, it might be recalled, was a lively figure in Memphis entertainment in the 1950s—a disk jockey on WDIA and a recording artist for Sam Phillips' Sun Records. "Bear Cat" was his 1953 best-selling answer song to "Hound Dog."

25. Not entirely though, for the *song* carried black cultural material, specifically the term "fool," into white speech. This black linguistic piquancy caught on in the songwriting field in both pop and rhythm and blues, binding them closer together; so much so, in fact, that *Billboard*'s musical sleuths commented on the rash of song titles using this new concept in a variety of manifestations:

Since the first of the year, at least 13 different songs hyping or discounting the "fool" have appeared on the scene and snatched at least 20 different recordings. . . . To date only "A Fool Such As I" has attained what might be loosely described as hit proportions. This made it first in the hillbilly field and more recently has opened up in the pop category. (*Billboard*, 7 March 1953, p. 17.)

26. Included are such mawkish records as the 1958 "Endless Sleep" by Jody Reynolds, "Tell Laura I Love Her" by Ray Peterson, "Teen Angel" by Mark Dinning, "Running Bear" by Johnny Preston, and "Patches" by Dickey Lee in 1962, released again in 1970 by Clarence Carter. They also include the western narrative epic "El Paso" by Marty Robbins, "Moody River" in 1961 by Pat Boone, and in 1965 "Laurie," again by Dickey Lee, and the 1967 "Ode to Billy Joe" by Bobby Gentry.

27. See Shaw, *Honkers*, p. 421, for a slightly different version of this story.

28. *Billboard*, 9 October 1954, p. 16.

29. Freed's adoption of the name "Moondog" certainly had more to do with his identification with the recording he used as his theme song, the popular R&B record "Blues for Moondog" by Todd Rhodes on the King label, than with Moondog himself. Moondog's real name was Louis Hardin, and he had been influenced by American Indian and Oriental sources. He came to New York in 1943 where, bearded and wrapped in a blanket, he was a familiar figure in midtown Manhattan streets. In 1952, Tony Schwartz produced a 45 rpm EP (Mars MREP-A2) of eight of Moondog's street performances, including his wife as singer and accompanist. When Freed came to New York, Moondog successfully sued to prevent him from using the name Moondog, hence moving to center stage the name rocknroll as the designation of his shows.

30. Passman, *Deejays*, p. 177, estimates that eighteen thousand tickets were sold. Gillett, *The Sound of the City*, 1st. ed. (1970), p. 16, states that it was thirty thousand.

31. Godfrey Hodgson, *America in Our Time* (Garden City: Doubleday, 1976), p. 51.

32. *Encyclopedia Britannica Book of the Year 1956* (Chicago: Encyclopedia Britannica, Inc.), pp. 468, 469.

33. *Billboard*, 4 February 1956. This review of press coverage of rocknroll's surfacing draws upon the 1970 student paper by Peggy Kobacher, Wesleyan University.

34. John Storm Roberts, *The Latin Tinge: The Impact of Latin American Music on the United States* (New York: Oxford, 1979).

35. Chess had purchased the master from Sam Phillips, who was still recording black performers, including Jackie Brenston, a member of Ike Turner's band at the time.

36. "Melody of Love," "Learning the Blues," "Moments to Remember," "Mr. Sandman," "A Blossom Fell," "Naughty Lady of Shady Lane," "That's All I Want from You."

37. Chuck Berry, *Chuck Berry: The Autobiography* (New York: Harmony, 1987).

8. The King and His Court (pp. 229–258)

1. Nelson King, liner notes for *A Session with Chet Atkins*, 45 EP album # EPB 1090, 547–0535, RCA Victor, 1955.

2. Record Industry Association of America, *U.S. Record Sales 1921–1963*.

3. See Neil Harris, *Humbug: The Art of P. T. Barnum* (Boston: Little Brown, 1973).

4. See Joseph Horowitz, *Understanding Toscanini* (New York: Knopf, 1987).

5. This discussion draws upon Margaret McKee and Fred Chisenhall's *Beale Black and Blue: Life and Music on Black America's Main Street* (Baton Rouge: Louisiana State University Press, 1981).

6. See Colin Escott and Martin Hawkins, *Catalyst: The Sun Records Story* (London: Aquarius Books, 1975).

7. McPhee, Ennis, Meyersohn et al., *The Disk Jockey*.

8. *Billboard*, 17 July 1954.

9. One was "My Happiness," a 1933 tune that had reached the pop and the country charts in 1948 in versions by Ella Fitzgerald, the Pied Pipers, Slim Whitman, and Jan and Sondra Steele. The other was an equally mawkish ballad "That's When Your Heartaches Begin," a 1940 tune released in 1952 but never making the national charts.

10. Robert Palmer, *A Tale of Two Cities: Memphis Rock and New Orleans Roll* (Brooklyn: Brooklyn College of the City University of New York, 1979), p. 25.

11. *Rolling Stone*, 9 December 1971, p. 10.

12. *Billboard*, 7 August 1954, p. 39.

13. *Billboard*, 29 January 1955, p. 51.

14. Shaw, *Honkers and Shouters*, pp. 496–500; *Billboard*, 3 December 1955, p. 1.

15. The brevity of the early rocknroll stardom and the intensity yet fickleness of its young audience is shown in the case of Tommy Sands. At the peak of his eleven-record career, which began in 1957 with the hit "Teen Age Crush" (reaching number two on the pop chart and number ten on the R&B chart), Tommy Sands was the favorite of 8 percent of high school students in a reputable study, exceeded only by Pat Boone (45 percent) and Elvis (20 percent). See James S. Coleman, with the assistance of John W. C. Johnstone and Kurt Jonasson, *The Adolescent Society: The Social Life of the Teenager and Its Impact on Education* (New York: Free Press of Glencoe, 1961). In spite of major record company sup-

port (Capitol), starring roles in four movies, and a marriage to Frank Sinatra's daughter, Sands was gone by 1960.

16. Gillett, *Sound of the City*, 1st ed., 1970, Chapter 2.

17. Mirek Kocandrle, *The History of Rock and Roll* (Boston: G. K. Hall, 1988).

18. Escott and Hawkins, *Catalyst*, p. 102.

19. As experts in that field attest, the mother-son relationship is crucial, and Elvis, though outwardly a devoted and loving son, pushed the role past the point of parody. It was his mother who bought him his first guitar at age eleven. It was for her birthday that he walked into Sam Phillips' Recording Studio to sing a song. It was in her name that his publishing firm, Gladys Music, reaped the rewards of his devotion. Yet his petulant demeanor was instantly recognized as a refusal to accept parental or other adult authority.

20. The TV series "Happy Days," by its very title, carries the understanding that no external enemy can take young lives on conventional battlefields. The anxiety over nuclear war was a different order of concern, with the innocent victims in their own homes in such number and so out of the control of ordinary politics that a deeper level of frustration and terror was experienced. It was due to the threat of the bomb that adults blamed Elvis and rocknroll for exploiting the fears of youth—too much projection of their own intertwined feelings of powerlessness and terror, perhaps.

21. Larzer Ziff, The Johns Hopkins University alumni newsletter (1981), affirmed by personal correspondence.

22. Dee Presley, Billy, Rick and David Stanley, as told to Martin Torgoff, *Elvis We Love You Tender*, (New York: Delacorte Press, 1979), p. 6.

23. See *Youth Transition to Adulthood: Report of the Panel on Youth of the President's Science Advisory Committee* (Washington, D.C.: GPO, 1973; reprint, Chicago: University of Chicago Press, 1974), pp. 27, 28.

24. A. B. Hollingshead, in *Elmtown's Youth: The Impact of Social Classes on Adolescents* (New York: J. Wiley, 1949), p. 221, concluded that there were three groups, the "elite" (the leaders in school and community activities), the "good kids" (those self-described as "never this or never that"), and the "grubbies" (those with unfortunate family position or the troublemakers). In the late 1950s, I asked the California-raised teenage daughter of a friend about her high school. She got my drift and said that there were three groups. At the top were the "sharp crowd"; next was the majority, kids like herself—just ordinary. At the bottom was the "sharp and cheap" crowd. In reply to my query about the difference between the top and bottom groups, she replied, "Oh, there's not much difference, the 'sharp and cheap' ones are just nymphomaniacs." Fifteen years old.

25. Matza, "Subterranean Traditions of Youth," in *Annals*, pp. 102–118.

26. This was one of the few ways Elvis was allowed to develop. The other was the late and brief flirtation with political relevance, as in "In the Ghetto." The main direction, however, was the exaggeration of the "total entertainer" image, Las Vegas style—huge collar, neckline cut to the waist, glitter.

27. This urgent telescoping of time into the omnivorous present, the only locus of meaning, was diagnosed by the social scientists as a failure of socialization. The pattern was designated as an inability to sustain "deferred gratification." As a cultural alternative to a social structure that excluded the young as significant actors, the "now" became a banner carried into the control centers of the school, the corporate office, and the government bureau, with well-known effects.

28. See Coleman et al., *Adolescent Society*.

29. The use of "Calypso" (which I have assimilated to folk) probably reflects the chart prominence of Harry Belafonte at that moment. The absence of rhythm and blues as a category is most likely due to its relative invisibility to the students.

30. Coleman et. al., pp. 205, 206.

31. Ibid., p. 206.

32. See Michael Cherniavsky, *Tzar and People: Studies in Russian Myth* (New Haven: Yale University Press, 1961), pp. 45f. In the analysis of Russian-painted domestic icons, Cherniavsky traces the images in which the contradictions of the Russian Tzar as simultaneously saintly prince and princely saint were stated and resolved.

9. The Industry Refuses, Then Accommodates (pp. 259–282)

1. U.S. Senate, [The Smathers Bill], *Amendment to Communications Act of 1934 (Prohibiting Radio and Television Stations from Engaging in Music Publishing or Recording Business)*, hearings before the Subcommittee on Communications of the Committee on Interstate and Foreign Commerce, 85th Cong., 2d sess., S. 2834 (Washington, D.C.: GPO, 1958), p. 1.

2. [The Smathers Bill] *Amendment to Communications Act of 1934*, pp. 25, 26.

3. Ibid., p. 953, 954.

4. Ibid., p. 954.

5. U.S. House of Representatives, [The Payola Hearings], *Payola and Other Deceptive Practices in the Broadcasting Field*, hearings before the Select Subcommittee on Legislative Oversight of the Committee on Interstate and Foreign Commerce, 86th Cong., 2d sess. (Washington, D.C.: GPO, 1960), p. 225.

6. Clark in his memoir says, "There, facing me, were diagrams with dozens of names and corporations interconnected with solid and broken lines. It was mad; everybody I ever met was on the charts at one place or another. There were people listed on the charts who had the same names as people I knew but were the wrong people. There were companies that I'd owned and other companies that I'd never heard of." Dick Clark and Richard Robinson, *Rock, Roll, and Remember* (New York: Thomas Y. Crowell, 1976), p. 215.

7. Ibid., p. 216.

8. Ibid., p. 225.

9. *Payola and Other Deceptive Practices in the Broadcasting Field*, pp. 906, 908.

10. Ibid., p. 908.

11. *Broadcasting Yearbook 1969*, p. A–131.

12. *Cash Box*, 26 March 1960.

13. *Billboard*, 6 April 1963, p. 36.

14. Otis Williams, with Patricia Romanewski, *Temptations* (New York: G. P. Putnam's Sons, 1988), p. 75.

15. Quoted in Chapple and Garofalo, *Rock 'n' Roll*, p. 126.

16. Guralnick, *Feel Like Goin' Home*, p. 4. See also Chapple and Garafalo, *Rock 'n' Roll*, p. 49; Ed Ward, Geoffrey Stokes, and Ken Tucker, *Rock of Ages: The Rolling Stone History of Rock and Roll* (New York: Rolling Stone, 1986), Chap. 12 and 13; and Greg Shaw, who adds Eddie Cochran (dead) and Gene Vincent (out of the country) to the list in *The Rolling Stone Illustrated History of Rock and Roll*, Jim Miller, ed. (New York: Random House, 1976), p. 96. One might well add Ritchie Valens (dead) given his recent and belated recognition via Los Lobos in the movie *La Bamba*.

17. Richard Williams, *Out of His Head: The Sound of Phil Spector* (New York: Outerbridge and Lazard, 1972), p. 14.

18. The actual division of labor within the studio varied considerably. Sometimes the "engineer" at the session was simply technician, sometimes unacknowledged creator, sometimes the total producer. As studio work became more complex, the engineer-mixer-producer elaborated into many gradations. The credits on current rock albums generally identify the producer unequivocally and prominently. The variety of engineering and mixing assistance is less definitely identifiable. The development of the "mixer" as the key figure in the maturing of rock is more fully described by Edward R. Kealy, *The Real Rock Revolution* (Amherst: University of Massachusetts Press, 1980).

19. In Joseph C. Smith's roman à clef *The Day the Music Died* (New York: Grove Press, 1981), an ill-disguised Phil Spector is portrayed as achieving his successes by looting, bar by bar, collections of old R&B 78s.

20. For a fuller discussion, see Gillett's chapter 9, *The Sound of the City,* rev and expanded ed. (New York: Pantheon, 1983). Also see Greg Shaw, "Brill Building Pop," and Greil Marcus, "The Girl Groups," in *Rolling Stone Illustrated History.*

21. See Nelson George, *Where Did Our Love Go? The Rise and Fall of the Motown Sound* (New York: St. Martin's, 1958).

22. See Jenkinson and Warner, *Celluloid Rock.* In "Mister Rock'n Roll," to take a typical case of Hollywood's loony understanding in 1957, Alan Freed, Lionel Hampton, Frankie Lymon, LaVern Baker, Little Richard, Brook Benton, Clyde McPhatter, and Ferlin Husky collaborate in a story about rocknroll's virtue in the face of adult duplicity—a musical mix defying all history.

23. Williams, *Out of His Head*, p. 27.

24. Joel Whitburn, *Top Pop Artists and Singles 1955–78* (Menomonee Falls, Wisconsin: Record Research, 1978).

25. Robert Karshner, *The Music Machine* (Los Angeles: Nash, 1971), p. 76.

26. See Nelson George, *Death of Rhythm and Blues*, p. 109.

27. American Music Conference, *Annual Reports 1963–71.*

28. John Wilson, *Jazz, the Transition Years 1940–1960* (New York: Appleton-Century-Crofts, 1966), chap. 7.

29. They had also initiated the age of space exploration itself in 1957 with the launching of Sputnik, the first of the thousands of manmade satellites now traveling around the earth.

10. *The Youth Movements (pp. 283–312)*

1. That re-writing of the sixties began barely after the decade had ended. See Clifford Adelman, *Generations: A Collage on Youthcult* (New York: Praeger, 1972).

2. See Judith Adler, *Artists in Offices: An Ethnography of an Academic Art Scene* (New Brunswick, New Jersey: Transaction Books, 1979), pp. 44, 45, for a statement that exactly mirrors this view and unfolds the story of what happened to those who believed yet violated this dictum.

3. See John and Margaret Rowntree, "The Political Economy of Youth," *Our Generation* 6, no. 1–2 (May/July 1968); and Richard Flacks, "Revolt of the Young Intelligentsia: Revolutionary Class-Consciousness in Post-Scarcity America," in *The New American Revolution*, Roderick Aya and Norman Miller, eds. (New York: Free Press, 1971), pp. 223–263.

4. Karl Mannheim's "The Problem of Generations, in his *Essays on the Soci-*

ology of Knowledge (New York: Oxford, 1952), is still a useful point of departure. One of the difficulties in the succession of generations is that two things are simultaneously involved. One is the transfer of power in the state and its several institutions; the other is the transmission of culture—that of the whole society and each of its parts. During the sixties, even though both politics and culture were thoroughly entangled, there was no serious run at state power by any youth formation. The construction of alternatives was the main thrust, in addition to ending the war.

5. See Lewis S. Feuer, *The Conflict of Generations: The Character and Significance of Student Movements* (New York: Basic Books, 1969).

6. Kenneth Kenniston, "Youth, a (New) Stage of Life," *American Scholar* 39, no. 4 (Autumn 1970) 631.

7. Clyde Kiser, Wilson Grabill, and Arthur Campbell, *Trends and Variations in Fertility in the United States* (Cambridge: Harvard University Press, 1968), table 4.1, p. 58.

8. *Historical Statistics*, table A–71–85, p. 10.

9. Peter H. Lindert, *Fertility and Scarcity in America* (Princeton: Princeton University Press, 1978), p. 23.

10. *Characteristics of American Youth* (Current Population Reports, series p. 23, no. 30, 1970), table 1, p. 5.

11. Rowntree and Rowntree, "Political Economy," p. 163.

12. See Arthur Stinchcombe, *Rebellion in a High School* (Chicago: Quadrangle, 1964).

13. See Richard Flacks, "The Liberated Generation: An Exploration of the Roots of Student Protest," *Journal of Social Issues* 23, no. 3 (July 1967): 60, 61.

14. Colin MacInnes, *Absolute Beginners*, from the London novels of Colin MacInnes (New York: Farrar, Straus and Giroux, 1969), p. 260.

15. Edgar Z. Friedenberg, "The Generation Gap," in *The Annals of the American Academy of Arts and Sciences*, vol. 382 *Protest in the Sixties*, Joseph Boskin, Robert A. Rosenstone, eds. (March 1969), p. 35.

16. *Publishers' Weekly* 172, no. 5 (29 July 1957): 101–141.

17. See Abe Peck, *Uncovering the Sixties: The Life and Times of the Underground Press* (New York: Pantheon, 1985), p. 11.

18. Robert J. Glessing, *The Underground Press in America* (Bloomington: Indiana University Press, 1970), p. 178–190.

19. Bennett M. Berger, "Hippie Morality—More Old then New," in *The Anti-American Generation*, Edgar Friedenberg, ed. (Chicago: Transaction Books, 1971), pp. 81–95. For the most general statement of these fundamental value alternatives, see Florence Kluckhohn, "Dominant and Variant Value Orientations," in *Personality in Nature, Society, and Culture*, 2d ed., Clyde Kluckhohn and Henry Murray, eds. (New York: Knopf, 1953), pp. 342–357.

20. The tension between these two concerns is proverbial. Elvis both expressed that tension and, again in "mythic" terms, resolved it. He could love God and Woman at the same time. What an example for the young. "Parents weren't afraid of his so called bump and grind, they were afraid of his power" (Alfred Wertheimer, *Elvis '56: In the Beginning* [New York: Macmillan, 1979], p. 37). The violation of ordinary rules separating religion from sex would carry all through the life of rocknroll, a recent example being the flap over Madonna's 1989 music video (and rejected Pepsi commercial) "Like a Prayer."

21. *Life*, 30 June 1972.

22. *The Daily Texan*, 9 October 1981, p. 23.

23. See Flacks, "The Liberated Generation"; and Kirkpatrick Sale, *SDS* (New York: Random House, 1973).

24. Quoted in Sale, *SDS*, p. 356.

25. In his book *Ringolevio: A Life Played for Keeps* (New York: Avon, 1973), Grogan cynically denies any moral worth, or even honesty, to some of the familiar celebrities of the youth movement (Abbie Hoffman especially); a depressing comment on the alienating and corrosive effects of the isolation that goes with the criminal enterprise.

26. See Victor Navasky, *Naming Names* (New York: Viking, 1980).

27. Sale, *SDS*, p. 20.

28. See Rowntree and Rowntree, "Political Economy."

29. World War II wiped out the leaders and organizations of prewar political formations typified by the American Youth Congress. Almost all had been compromised by the political flip-flops of the left as the Popular Front tactics of the 1930s gave way to a false and opportunistic isolationism triggered by the Nazi-Soviet pact of 1939.

30. The beginnings of that convocation were laid at the First World Youth Congress held in November 1945 in London, where over six hundred delegates from fifty countries established the Communist-led World Federation of Democratic Youth and an International Preparatory Committee. The mission of the latter was to convene the World Student Congress in August 1946 at Prague, Czechoslovakia. Students from an even larger number of countries representing every shade of political opinion gathered that year in a series of preparatory meetings, culminating in the congress. The International Union of Students (IUS), the several dozen other national student unions, the looser federations of Christian and Catholic student organizations, all celebrated the Allied victory and called upon the great power of youth to join its idealism with the struggles of the poor and underprivileged peoples all over the world.

The American delegation to the IUS, a mixed bag of left, independent, and Catholic student forces, returned to gather at the University of Chicago at the end of 1946 with 475 delegates and 175 observers representing 295 colleges and 19 national student organizations. (*Operation University: A Report and Analysis*, compiled by the Joint Committee for Student Action of the National Catholic Youth Council, 1947. This pamphlet was the guide to the order of battle for the Catholic forces at the founding convention of the NSA.) Their deliberations called forth the Madison, Wisconsin, convention.

31. W. C. McWilliams, *Commonweal*, 3 March 1967, vol. 85, pp. 611–14.

32. Cited in Feuer, *The Conflict of Generations*, p. 384 (from Robert Martinson, "State of the Campus," *The Nation* 194, no. 20 [19 May 1962]".

33. *New University Thought* 1, no. 1 (Spring 1960): 2.

34. There was at least one such specifically named person who was in both circles. Leo Stodolsky, one of the editors and contributors to the first issue of *New University Thought*, also was in the cast of two scenario plays produced by David Shepherd for the "Tonight at 8:30 Series" at the University Theater. Jeffrey Sweet, *Something Wonderful Right Away* (New York: Avon Books, 1978), p. xxiii. The following discussion relies considerably upon this work and my own recollections of those times and places and people. See also Janet Coleman, *The Compass* (New York: Knopf, 1990).

35. Compass had transformed itself from an experimental theatrical company, the Playwrights Theater Club, begun under the leadership of David Shepherd, into an improvisational topical theater style derived from the techniques of

Viola Spolin's Game Theater, which her son Paul Sills had brought to the company (Sweet, *Something Wonderful*, p. 5).

36. Ibid., pp. 5, 6.

37. Ibid., p. 78.

38. Mike Nichols and Elaine May left in 1958 to do a New York nightclub act. Their success on Broadway led May to a writing-directing stint in the New York theater and Nichols to Hollywood, where he directed two of the landmark youth films of the period, *The Graduate* in 1967 and Joseph Heller's *Catch-22* in 1970, involving Paul Simon and Art Garfunkel. Nichols' and May's successful comedy recordings were an early signal to the record industry. The record companies soon invited a flood of stand-up comics. Comedy had found a new audience, a new stance, and a new set of performance sites. Sweet (*Something Wonderful*, pp. 377–380) lists over two hundred names as having done a turn or two at the several Second City companies that moved around and touched down in many major cities in the nation.

39. At least twice during the ensuing years I have met people who were at that concert and will not forget when Baez asked the audience if anyone had a capo to "mute" her guitar for the next number. Embarrassedly, a tall young man seated on the stage was seen to put his hand in his pocket and slowly draw out the desired object. He even more slowly rose, and as everyone realized the problem was solved, they warmly applauded. A trivial incident but typical of the intensity that burned in the folk stream.

40. The following discussion draws upon Sale's *SDS*; Harry Edwards' *Black Students* (New York: Free Press, 1970); and Todd Gitlin's *The Whole World Is Watching* (Berkeley: University of California Press, 1980).

41. Its parentage was the mixed marriage of the Student League for Industrial Democracy (itself the offspring of the prewar remnant of liberal, social-democratic, and Trotskyist splinters held together by a barely bankable anti-Communism) and independent white and black students drawn into the rising civil rights movement.

42. Martin Luther King, Jr., *Why We Can't Wait* (New York: Signet Books, 1968), pp. 54, 55.

43. Charles J. Levy, *Voluntary Servitude: Whites in the Negro Movement* (New York: Appleton-Century-Crofts, 1968), p. 173.

44. Ibid., p. 115.

45. Edwards, *Black Students*, p. 43.

46. This discussion draws upon Sara Evans, *Personal Politics* (New York: Knopf, 1978), chap. 4.

47. Perhaps only the smallest minority of black movement members repudiated all black popular music with a contempt and totality akin to the way Islamic or African names were used to repudiate an American identity. The jazz that moved in that same direction, that of Pharoah Saunders, Sun Ra, or Archie Shepp, for example, was still connected to the full body of Afro-American music. For the overwhelming mass of black youth there was no difficulty in accepting the Dells, Temptations, James Brown, Marvin Gaye, *and* Nina Simone.

48. See Bernice Johnson Reagon, "Songs of the Civil Rights Movement 1955–1965: A Study in Culture History," Ph.D. diss., Howard University, 1975.

49. Sale, *SDS*, p. 585.

50. In France, these questions were posed in the streets, raising substantial fears that the youth and the left-led organized French working class would jointly mount a genuine revolution. All sectors of French society were mobilized, includ-

ing the arts. See *Art and Confrontation: The Arts in an Age of Change* (Greenwich, Connecticut: New York Graphic Society, 1968).

51. See Jonathan Kelley, "Dress As Non-Verbal Communication," paper presented to American Sociological Society, August 1971.

52. In a panel study over the important period September 1965 to May 1967, William Eaton, Jr. ("Reference Groups and Educational Values"), traced a dramatic shift in student philosophy towards a nonconformist stance from less than 10 percent to almost a quarter of the students, thereby creating a sizable political force. The distribution of student philosophy found at Wesleyan University in Connecticut was almost exactly that at Berkeley, if the dress styles are matched as follows:

Wesleyan May 1967		Berkeley Spring 1967	
vocational	11%	conventional	9%
collegiate	40	collegiate	61
academic	21	shaggy	23
nonconformist	23	earthy	7
	95%		100%

53. See the *Black Scholar*, first published in November 1969, for a fair sampling of that discourse, particularly in its earliest issues.

54. This fanciful dream was floating in political and academic circles in the late 1960s. It had some basis in reality in that there was a strong black presence in the major cities in the South, in the border states, and in some cities in the North and the West. In 1968 the election of Richard Gordon Hatcher as mayor of Gary, Indiana, and Carl B. Stokes as mayor of Cleveland were encouraging signs. Sharing and exchanging culture, plus the flow of families to schools and jobs, had established a network of travel routes and pause points in the major cities of such strength as to invite their transformation into political terms.

55. One such was Morningstar, the commune built by Lou Gottlieb of the Limelighters on northern California's Russian River. It began in the spirit of its name and ended as a dangerous slum of heroin, theft, and despair. Others may still be going, Stephen Gaskin's Farm being one, the subject of friendly ridicule in the Grateful Dead's "St. Stephen."

56. See J. Milton Yinger, *Countercultures: The Promise and Peril of a World Turned Upside Down* (New York: Free Press, 1982).

57. Charles A. Reich, *The Greening of America* (New York: Random House, 1970), p. 4.

58. See Jane Alpert, *Growing Up Underground* (New York: Morrow, 1981).

59. Sale, *SDS*, p. 627.

60. Ibid.

61. Yet it is puzzling that their musical practices in hiding was, if the memoirs are any indication, like that of the PL and SDC cadres still fighting it out in public. Motown, Marvin Gaye, the Temptations, early Dylan, and later Bruce Springsteen were accepted as parts of the woodwork.

11. Rock (pp. 313–343)

1. Even observers generally unsympathetic to rocknroll have acknowledged this fact. See George, *Death of Rhythm and Blues*, p. 106: "'Rock and Roll,' that

straightforward, unambitious consumer product, was now evolving into something more experimental, less categorizable, roughly dubbed 'rock.'"

2. *Hit Parader*, July 1962.

3. Eugene Gilbert, *Advertising and Marketing to Young People* (Pleasantville, New York: Printers' Ink Books, 1957), p. 311.

4. Andy Warhol and Pat Hackett, *POPism: The Warhol 60's* (New York: Harcourt Brace Jovanovich, 1980), pp. 28, 29.

5. Ibid., p. 28.

6. In fact, artists burn out the symbolic materials faster than the audience due to their greater immersion in and knowledge of its units. This differential rate of satisfaction gives artistic systems just one of their several sources of internal instability. See Theodore L. Shaw, *Don't Get Taught Art This Way!* (Boston: Stuart Publications, 1967), chap. 9.

7. See Josh Dunson, *Freedom in the Air: Song Movements of the Sixties* (New York: International Publishers, 1965).

8. The senior members of the northern folk movement were there—Theodore Bikel, Phil Ochs, Tom Paxton, Len Chandler—along with their musical and political southern counterparts—Mrs. Fannie Lou Hammer, Bernice and Cordell Reagon, Betty Mae Fikes, and the influential Guy Carawan. Not only the ancient slave music but the modern gospel movement was being retooled for the quickening civil rights struggle. The Summer Mississippi Voter Registration Project got a boost at that meeting. Its musical echoes reached the Village and all the folk musicians there, including Dylan as well as the Blues Project. See Dunson, *Freedom*, chap. 9.

9. Josh White was heir to Blind Lemon Jefferson, Blind Willie Johnson, Blind Joe Taggert, and many others—all great men in the making of the modern urban black guitar styles. His first album, with liner notes by Alan Lomax, clearly represents a transitional moment in folk. The record had a double quality. It was a stylist's performance in a commercial setting and, at the same time, a politically mobilizing event. The high point of the record was the uncompromisingly stark "Strange Fruit."

The folk stream would soon be aggravated by the gradually increasing tension between those two modes. Only the joinder with rock would bring them together. White's fastidious guitar and controlled emotional intensity carried over into the rock stream to influence many young performers who fought out the authenticity crisis of the midsixties. But because of White's New York sophistication, his breadth of repertoire, and, unfortunately, his political guilt by association, his influence was restricted to that small club circle of players and fans pioneered by Cafe Society Downtown.

10. John Hammond, with Irving Townsend, *John Hammond on Record: An Autobiography* (New York: Ridge Press, 1977), pp. 206–210.

11. George Wein, young Boston jazz club owner and promoter, Marshall Stearns, aficionado, collector, and jazz scholar, the critic Leonard Feather, and Hammond himself became part of the governing group that, until the 1970s, produced a widening range of music festivals.

12. See Robert Santelli, *Aquarius Rising: The Rock Festival Years* (New York: Dell, 1980), for a fuller account of this and subsequent festivals.

13. Clive Davis recounts how, in 1968, at the high point of his reign at Columbia, he invited Richard Rodgers to listen to the tapes of the newly signed Janis Joplin. After listening to several selections, Rodgers signaled that he didn't want to hear any more.

He said that he just didn't understand it. He'd take my word that the record would be meaningful to young people—but he didn't understand what the music's appeal was, what the *basis* for the appeal, why anybody would think this particular piece of music was good, or for that matter why anyone would consider *Janis* a good singer. He became upset. He shrugged his shoulders and his left arm flailed as he talked. "If this means I have to change my writing," he said, "or that the only way to write a Broadway musical is to write rock songs, *then my career is over* [emphasis, Clive Davis]. In no way could I possibly do this." Clive Davis, *Clive: Inside the Record Business*, p. 42.

14. These included the Barry Goldberg Blues Band and, for a moment, Steve Miller and others such as Nick Gravenites and Charles Musselwhite.

15. Wilson, *Jazz: The Transition Years*, pp. 108–138.

16. *Metronome*, May 1961, p. 21.

17. See George, *Death of Rhythm and Blues*, p. 108: "The black audience's consumerism and restlessness burns out and abandons musical styles, whereas white Americans, in the European tradition of supporting forms and styles for the sake of tradition, seem to hold styles dear long after they have ceased to evolve."

18. David DeTurk and A. Poulen, Jr., eds., *The American Folk Scene: Dimensions of the Folk Song Revival* (New York: Dell, 1967), p. 157.

19. Ibid., p. 153.

20. The folk stream throughout the sixties was almost entirely white. Odetta, Richie Havens, and a few others were exceptions. Harry Belafonte, one of the originals of the pop-folk meeting in 1956, was at a definite remove from the rest of the downtown folk crowd. Nevertheless, the black presence, musical and attitudinal, was definitely voiced.

21. Anthony Scaduto, *Bob Dylan: An Intimate Biography* (New York: Grosset & Dunlap, 1971), p. 175.

22. Ibid., pp. 223, 176.

23. Ibid., p. 177.

24. Ibid., pp. 6, 7.

25. At the same time, Grossman's other top folk act, Peter, Paul and Mary, pushed Dylan's "Blowin' in the Wind" to the number two position on the singles chart, staying for fifteen weeks. This was the trio's third top chart single in a row. Their first was Lee Hays and Pete Seeger's "If I Had a Hammer," introduced in 1958 by the Weavers. There was still a clear association with the left's folk establishment.

26. One of the early articles in *Crawdaddy* (no. 7, 19 January 1967) by Sandy Pearlman was a long and technical explanation of the raga form and its vital place in rock.

27. *Hit Parader* (as shown in Figure 11-1), July 1965, p. 8.

28. See Scaduto, *Dylan*, pp. 212–215, for a full statement of the event. Al Kooper's version is completely benign; see Al Kooper, with Ben Edmonds, *Backstage Passes: Rock 'n' Roll Life in the 60s* (New York: Stein & Day, 1977), p. 60. Ellen Sanders' *Trips; Rock Life in the Sixties* (New York: Charles Scribner's Sons, 1973), p. 62, probably best catches the mood and historic significance of the moment.

29. This influence was especially clear with respect to black culture and music, at least as far back as the turn of the century. In 1902 the musical "In Dahomey," the first black play in a major New York hall, was received coolly, lasting only for fifty-three performances. It ran to acclaim for 251 performances in London (Bordman, *Kern*, p. 31).

30. For a full and moving description of the whole experience, see Colyer, *New Orleans and Back*, pp. 24, 25.

31. See Tom Bethell, *George Lewis: A Jazzman from New Orleans* (Berkeley: University of California Press, 1977).

32. The sad conclusion to Colyer's story is the following note in *Down Beat*, 13 August 1964:

Britain Buys Big Beatled Beat

There is a drastic change of wind blowing through Britain's club scene, for at the moment the country is in the stranglehold of a gigantic big-beat revival, spear-headed by the Beatles.

With the demand for danceable—beat—music a large number of so-called rhythm-and-blues groups have emerged as popular club attractions. In their ea-gerness to cater for the new trend and boost business, most clubs have changed their policy to introduce r&b and "blue beat" bands.

"Jazzshows" jazz club, which until recently featured an all trad program, now presents various r&b combos three nights a week. This also applies to Ken Colyer's trad stronghold, which now devotes four evenings to the big beat.

33. George Melly, *Revolt into Style: The Pop Arts* (New York: Doubleday, 1971), p. 50.

34. Formsby had visited the States briefly in 1947 but left no strong impression.

35. Melly, *Revolt into Style*, p. 117. For a full guide through this period, see also Melly's first, largely autobiographical recapitulation, *Owning Up* (New York: Penguin, 1970).

36. See Billy Bergman, with Andy Schwartz, Isabelle Leymarie, Tony Sabour-nin, and Rob Baker, *Hot Sauces: Latin and Caribbean Pop* (New York: Quill, 1985).

37. Quoted in Ralph Gleason, *The Jefferson Airplane and the San Francisco Sound* (New York: Ballantine, 1969), p. 1.

38. In 1965, the FCC had ordered the separation of AM/FM stations that were merely sending out the same signal on both channels. FM stations had to have their own material.

39. See Susan Kreiger, *Hip Capitalism* (Beverly Hills: Sage Publications, 1979).

40. Gleason, *Jefferson Airplane*, p. 330–340.

41. Ibid., p. 323.

42. Ibid., p. 25.

43. See Pete Frame, *The Complete Rock Family Trees, Books 1 and 2 in One Volume* (London: Omnibus Press, 1980), pp. 8, 17.

44. The critical and monetary success of this album led Kooper to produce another, then to continue as a playing and producing presence for such groups as the Tubes (originally a San Francisco band), Lynyrd Skynyrd, and Nils Lofgren. Kooper is particularly candid about having learned on the job, with all the terror and spontaneous joy that went along with the life-in-the-moment atmosphere of the sixties (see Kooper, *Backstage Passes*).

45. Quoted in *The Movement for a New America: The Beginnings of a Long Revolution*, assembled by Mitchell Goodman (Philadelphia: Pilgrim Press, 1970), p. 378.

46. Warhol and Hackett, *POPism*, p. 139.

47. Ibid., p. 185.

48. A neat irony is that *both* the Velvet Underground and the Grateful Dead had called themselves the "Warlocks" in earlier versions of their bands.

49. Warhol and Hackett, *POPism*, p. 235.

50. See R. Serge Denisoff's, *Solid Gold: The Popular Record Industry* (New Brunswick: Transaction Books, 1975), chap. 6, for a fuller discussion of the rock press and its origins; Glessing, *Underground Press*, pp. 178–190; and Peck, *Uncovering the Sixties*.

51. See *Rolling Stone*, 19 April 1969 (Michael Lydon's review of *Outlaw Blues* by Paul Williams), p. 24.

52. Robert Sam Anson, *Gone Crazy and Back: The Rise and Fall of the Rolling Stone Generation* (New York: Doubleday, 1981), p. 301.

53. Williams, *Out of His Head*, p. 27.

54. They would not regard the following words as out of place. They are the words of B. H. Haggin, for years the magisterial proprietor of classical music for *The Nation*:

> When we listen to an early Armstrong cornet solo we hear something similar to what is so exciting in Haydn and Berlioz, the moment-to-moment working of a mind which we observe this time in the very process of creation, operating with an inventive exuberance that is controlled by a sense for coherent developing form. (B. H. Haggin, *The New Listener's Companion and Record Guide*, 3d ed. (New York: Horizon Press, 1971), p. 186.

12. The Pause Point (pp. 344–361)

1. Clive Davis recounts that on one occasion he carefully re-mixed Janis Joplin's "Piece of My Heart" from her *Cheap Thrills* album to make it commercially viable as a single. On another, he warned the members of Blood Sweat and Tears that they were in danger of compromising their anti-establishment credentials with their FM audience because they were too successful with singles (Davis, *Clive*, pp. 95–97, 108, 109).

2. Recording Industry Association of America press release, 31 March 1981.

3. These are the percentages:

	1959	1960	1961	1962	1963	1964	1965	1966	1967	1968	1969	1970
Jazz	3	*	4	2	5	5	8	7	2	1	2	2
Folk	3	*	8	5	12	11	7	5	4	6	6	3
Gospel	2	*	1	0	0	0	0	0	0	0	1	0

SOURCE: Annual compilations of LP sales, *Billboard*.
*Data unavailable.

4. *Rolling Stone*, 3 September 1970.

5. Sanjek, *American Popular Music*, vol. 3, p. 508.

6. See his "The Music Business: Who Pays the Piper" (14 April 1978) in the independent, near-alternative, Austin-based bi-weekly, magazine *The Texas Observer*. At that time, the editor was Jim Hightower, who subsequently made a colorful career in the populist wing of the Texas Democratic Party.

7. See Jan Reid, *The Improbable Rise of Redneck Rock* (New York: Plenum, 1974), for a full discussion of the Texas country-rock story.

8. *Billboard*, 23 August 1969, p. 3.

9. *Billboard*, 22 November 1969.

10. See Reebee Garafalo, "The Impact of the Civil Rights Movement on Popular Music," *Radical America* 21, no. 6 (Nov.–Dec. 1987).

11. Elaine Richards, as deputy minister of information to the Black Panther

party in southern California, released an album on Vault Records in August 1969, the profits of which were donated to the Panther efforts and whose lyrics were simply a political pamphlet.

12. She was touring once again in the States in the spring of 1983. *Avatar*, 25 May 1983.

13. *Billboard*, 6 December 1969, p. 67.

14. See Santelli, *Aquarius Rising*.

15. Ibid., p. 42.

16. See particularly, Robert Stephen Spitz, *Barefoot in Babylon: The Creation of the Woodstock Music Festival, 1969* (New York: Viking, 1979).

17. *Rolling Stone*, 20 September 1969.

18. Ibid.

19. The festival at Shea Stadium in New York, held to memorialize the atom bombing of Hiroshima, drew only twenty thousand and barely broke even. The other, in Philadelphia, also dedicated to a peace memorial, was bureaucratically hassled to death by the courts (*Rolling Stone*, 17 September 1970, p. 10). In Florida, three separate festivals were reported by *Rolling Stone* (2 April 1970) as likely to have been some kind of hustle.

20. *Rolling Stone*, 27 December 1969, p. 18.

21. For a close, descriptive account of these events, see Ralph Gleason, "Aquarius Wept: After Woodstock and Love Came Altamont and Disaster," in *Esquire* 74 (August 1970): 84–92.

22. Anson, *Crazy and Back*, p. 158.

23. Hunter S. Thompson, *Fear and Loathing in Las Vegas: A Savage Journey to the Heart of the American Dream* (New York: Random House, 1971), p. 179.

24. *Rolling Stone*, 3 September 1970.

25. *Rolling Stone*, 11 June 1970, p. 9.

26. Ibid.

27. Jerry Rubin, *Do It: Scenarios of the Revolution* (New York: Simon and Schuster, 1970), p. 18.

28. See, among the flood of materials, Robert Somma, ed., *No One Waved Goodbye: A Casualty Report on Rock and Roll* (New York: Outerbridge & Dienstfrey, 1971).

29. Anson, *Crazy and Back*, p. 313.

30. *Rolling Stone*, 17 September 1970.

31. That same responsiveness to space as the new frontier had appeared once before. In December 1962, the Tornadoes put their instrumental single "Telstar" in the number one position, which stayed on the charts sixteen weeks. This song culminated the year that saw the first American, John Glenn, orbit the planet in February and the launching of the Telstar satellite in July.

32. *Billboard*, 15 November 1969, p. 6.

33. *Rolling Stone*, 21 February 1970, pp. 48–50, reviewed and organized many of the re-releases, defining, thereby, a genealogy of rocknroll.

34. Frank Zappa in this climate even called for a ". . . . 'rock pool.' In a *Rolling Stone* interview, he broached the idea of musicians getting together one show at a time. There would be no rehearsals (no touring! no managers!!), just spontaneous, one-time-only, buy-your-tickets-now jamming" (Ward, Stokes, and Tucker, *Rock of Ages*, p. 420).

35. Stu Werbin, "Troubadours and Politicians: Counter Culture Backlash," *The Middletown Press* (Connecticut), 30 July 1970.

36. These were not the only kids to have this experience. In a pensive 1970

article entitled "The Politics of Rock: Movement vs. Groovement," in *The Age of Rock* 2, Jonathan Eisen, ed. (New York: Vintage, 1970), pp. 83–91, Tom Smucker recounts how he had that same existential acceptance, sitting there on his blanket at Woodstock where

> at some point that becomes a drag. If you aren't a personal friend of Jimi Hendrix and aren't at the performers' party eating strawberries and cream, but in a blanket sharing a Coca-Cola it took an hour to get. Well it was a limited game, and someone should have run down the limits to people. But it had to be someone who understood the game, and related to it, and knew why people were playing it, and what the payoff was or might be.

Continuum (pp. 362–380)

1. This is not to deny, on the other hand, the occasional large vision of the new community. The most grandiose was, and is, Paolo Solari's Arcosanti, at Scottsdale, Arizona, a whole sub-cosmos that began, paradoxically, at the pause point 1970.

2. NEA Research Division Note 3, 27 April 1983.

3. For a thorough review of these trends in post-seventies rock, see Ward, Stokes, and Tucker, *Rock of Ages*, especially the section "The Seventies and Beyond."

4. See Greil Marcus, *Lipstick Traces: A Secret History of the 20th Century* (Cambridge: Harvard University Press, 1989).

5. A full list has been compiled by Benjamin Lyons from his personal collection, augmented by the discography of Robert A. Hull, "That's Cool, That's Trash, Part II," *Creem* 11, no. 2 (July 1979).

6. Listed in Roman Kozak, *This Ain't No Disco: The Story of CBGB* (Boston: Faber & Faber, 1988), pp. 135–143. The success of the Ramones was due almost entirely to the surviving remnants of the alternative press. "The Ramones' commercial potential was not really tried at that point, but their press was so incredible that no one could fault anyone for signing them. Even in those early days the *Voice, Soho News*, and *Aquarian* were there, and the Ramones were the darlings of the press" (Kozak, p. 68).

7. They fell into murder, drugs, and other squalor. Their founding Rasputin, Malcolm McLaren, continues his participation in British-spawned trendlets past the new wave, hardcore, techno-pop, and other mini-moments in rock.

8. *Billboard* instituted on 26 October 1974 a one-column report, "Disco Action," that tracked record sales and spins in New York clubs. Two years later, on 18 September 1976, *Billboard* expanded its coverage to a full page, covering the top disco records in the top sixteen national markets.

9. *Billboard*, 25 February 1989, p. 82.

10. The first weekly jazz album popularity chart had debuted in *Billboard* on 4 January 1969.

11. *Billboard*, 28 June 1974, p. 26. This discussion draws upon the special articles by Eliot Tiegel, Jean Williams, and Jim Fishel in that issue.

12. *Chicago Sun-Times*, 29 June 1975.

13. Chet Atkins, 1976, quoted by Doug Green and William Ivey in *Illustrated History of Country Music*, Patrick Carr, ed. (New York: Doubleday, 1980), p. 246.

14. *Ear: Magazine of New Music* 13, no. 10 (February 1989): 23.

15. Adam Smith, TV report on popular music, May 1989.

16. *Billboard*, 26 March 1983, p. 6.

17. Jon Pareles, "Pop: Sam Fan Thomas at Ritz," in *The New York Times*, 27 January 1986.

18. Roger Wallis and Krister Malm, *Big Sounds from Small Peoples: The Music Industry in Small Countries* (London: Constable, 1984).

19. See *The Nation*, 17 December 1991, p. 770. This same point was made by Jeremy Marre and Hannah Charlton, reporting in book form their adventures in preparing for the television series, "Beats of the Heart." Jeremy Marre and Hannah Charlton, *Beats of the Heart: Popular Music of the World* (New York: Pantheon, 1985).

20. His film *Perjuangan dan Dua* is regarded as a major and first Islamic-rock musical film, a synthesis of local and world musics akin to the process that produced American rock thirty-six years ago.

21. See *Caribbean Contact*, February 1986, p. 12, and January 1986, p. 12.

22. His lyrics about holding onto age sixteen are another example of that existential acceptance of the short trip and the long trip as found in the 1970 kids' thinking about going to the Powder Ridge Rock Festival.

23. *New Haven Register*, 20 January 1986.

24. Sanjek, *American Popular Music*, vol. 3, p. 594.

25. Ibid., p. 653.

26. The American pop single record-buying public of 1963, by no means a cross-section of the nation (being younger, more urban, and whiter than the total population), sprang to the launching of the first American satellite by boosting the Tornadoes' single "Telstar" right to the top of the charts within months. That musical group also put its first and only album of the same name, *Telstar*, on the charts but was never heard from again. This surely indicates that it was the space event rather than the musicians that was holding the public's attention.

27. See *Billboard*, 19 November 1983, for extended discussions of these ventures, along with the commercial firms offering them.

28. Rock World Video Marketing of Albany, New York, is one of the largest of these firms. They provide free videos and sometimes financial assistance in procuring the equipment to play them to about five hundred colleges and universities in forty-nine states. Commercial spots from national advertisers at rates competitive with local TV shows are the basis of the firm's economic operation (personal telephone interview, 4 February 1986).

29. *Musician*, November 1982, p. 80. Emphasis in the original.

30. See Alexander Marshack, *The Roots of Civilization: The Cognitive Beginnings of Man's First Art, Symbol and Notation* (New York: McGraw-Hill, 1972), for an analysis of carved stone and bone artifacts some thirty thousand years old showing lunar and solar observations.

31. In 1977, two *Voyager* spacecraft aimed at the exploration of Jupiter and Uranus were launched by the United States. Affixed to their sides was a gold-coated copper phonograph record containing 118 photographs of our planet and its inhabitants, along with greetings in almost sixty human languages and ninety minutes of the world's music, including Chuck Berry's "Johnny B. Goode." See Carl Sagan's *Murmurs of Earth* (New York: Random House, 1978).

A study of how these particular languages and musical selections were chosen would repay the effort involved, for the biases of the distinguished group of scientists who did so are riveting. Sagan confesses in the book that they "reached a consensus that we shouldn't present war, disease, crime, and poverty . . . [or] any picture that was specifically religious" (pp. 75, 76). It rests with such rocknroll stalwarts as Neil Young with his "Misfits," Nilsson's "Spaceman," Elton John's "Rocket Man," David Bowie's "Space Oddity" (and the movie *The Man Who Fell to Earth*), Elvis Costello's "Satellite," XTC's "This World Over," and the Grateful Dead's "Dark Star" to carry on the discourse with the heavens.

32. The gene police will probably be addressed as "Doctor," being either a physician or some kind of Ph.D. See *The Middletown Press* (Connecticut), 29 December 1991, for a report of a recent mobilization of concern over the power that will reside in scientific knowledge of human genetics. In the shadow of the 3 billion-dollar, fifteen-year Human Genome Project, designed to map the 100,000 human genes, the National Institutes of Health has awarded a $300,000 contract to the Center for Theology and the Natural Sciences at the University of California, Berkeley, to study genetic engineering. The task of this ethical research is to begin to answer the questions: How far should the gene technicians go in playing God by restructuring the human being, and who decides?

Bibliography

Abrahams, Roger D. *Deep Down in the Jungle: Negro Narrative Folklore from the Streets of Philadelphia.* Hatboro, Pennsylvania: Folklore Associates, 1964.

Alpert, Jane. *Growing Up Underground.* New York: Morrow, 1981.

Art and Confrontation: The Arts in an Age of Change. Greenwich, Connecticut: New York Graphic Society, 1968.

Barlow, William. *Looking Up at Down: The Emergence of Blues Culture.* Philadelphia: Temple University Press, 1989.

Barnouw, Eric. *The Golden Web: A History of Broadcasting in the United States from 1933 to 1953.* New York: Oxford University Press, 1968.

———. *A Tower in Babel: A History of Broadcasting in the United States to 1933.* New York: Oxford University Press, 1966.

Berry, Peter E. *". . . And The Hits Just Keep On Comin'."* Syracuse, New York: Syracuse University Press, 1977.

Broven, Robert. *Rhythm and Blues in New Orleans.* Gretna, Louisiana: Pelican, 1974.

Carr, Patrick, ed. *The Illustrated History of Country Music.* New York: Doubleday, 1980.

Chapple, Steve, and Reebe Garofalo. *Rock 'n' Roll Is Here to Pay: The History and Politics of the Music Industry.* Chicago: Nelson-Hall, 1977.

Charlton, Katherine. *Rock Music Styles: A History.* Dubuque, Iowa: William C. Brown, 1990.

Cohn, Nik. *Rock: From the Beginning.* New York: Stein and Day, 1969.

Coleman, James S., with the assistance of John W. C. Johnstone and Kurt Jonassohn, *The Adolescent Society: The Social Life of the Teenager and Its Impact on Education.* New York: Macmillan, The Free Press of Glencoe, 1961.

Coleman, James S., and others. *Youth—Transition to Adulthood: Report of the Panel on Youth of the President's Science Advisory Committee.* Chicago: University of Chicago Press, 1974.

Denisoff, R. Serge. *Great Day Coming: Folk Music and the American Left.* Urbana, Illinois: University of Illinois Press, 1971.

Denisoff, R. Serge, and Richard A. Peterson, eds. *The Sounds of Social Change: Studies in Popular Culture.* Chicago: Rand McNally, 1972.

DeTurk, David A., and A. Poulin, Jr., eds. *The American Folk Scene: Dimensions of the Folksong Revival.* New York: Dell, 1967.

Dunson, Josh. *Freedom in the Air: Song Movements of the 60's.* New York: International Publishers, 1965.

Edwards, Harry. *Black Students.* New York: Macmillan, Free Press, 1970.

Eisen, Jonathan, ed. *The Age of Rock: The Sounds of the American Cultural Revolution.* New York: Random House, Vintage, 1969.

———. *The Age of Rock 2: Sights and Sounds of the American Cultural Revolution.* New York: Random House, Vintage, 1970.

Eisenstadt, S. N. *From Generation to Generation; Age Groups and Social Structure.* Glencoe, Illinois: The Free Press, 1956.

Farber, Jerry. *The Student as Nigger.* New York: Contact Books, 1969.

Frith, Simon. *Sound Effects: Youth, Leisure and the Politics of Rock 'n' Roll.* New York: Pantheon, 1981.

Gelatt, Roland. *The Fabulous Phonograph: From Edison to Stereo* (rev. ed.). New York: Appleton-Century, 1965.

George, Nelson. *The Death of Rhythm and Blues.* New York: Pantheon, 1988.

Gillett, Charlie. *The Sound of the City: The Rise of Rock and Roll.* New York: Outerbridge & Dienstfrey, 1970. Rev. and exp. ed., New York: Pantheon, 1983.

Gleason, Ralph L. *The Jefferson Airplane and the San Francisco Sound.* New York: Ballantine, 1969.

Gottlieb, David, Jon Reeves, and Warren D. TenHouten. *The Emergence of Youth Societies: A Cross-Cultural Approach.* New York: The Free Press, 1966.

Green, Abel, and Joe Laurie, Jr. *Show Biz from Vaude to Video.* New York: Henry Holt, 1951.

Guralnick, Peter. *Feel Like Going Home: Portraits in Blues and Rock 'n' Roll.* New York: Outerbridge & Dienstfrey, 1971.

Heilbut, Anthony. *The Gospel Sound: Good News and Bad Times.* New York: Simon & Schuster, 1971. Updated and revised, New York: Limelight Editions, 1985.

Hentoff, Nat. *The Jazz Life.* New York: Dial, 1961.

Hoffman, Frank. *The Literature of Rock, 1954–1978.* Metuchen, New Jersey, and London: Scarecrow Press, 1981.

Jones, LeRoi. *Blues People: Negro Music in White America.* New York: William Morrow, 1963.

Keil, Charles. *Urban Blues.* Chicago: University of Chicago Press, 1966.

Kocandrle, Mirek. *The History of Rock and Roll: A Selective Discography.* Boston: G. K. Hall, 1988.

Krauthammer, Richard. *Three Christian Capitals: Topography and Politics.* Berkeley and Los Angeles: University of California, 1983.

Lazarsfeld, Paul F., and Frank N. Stanton, eds. *Communications Research 1948–1949.* New York: Harper & Brothers, 1949.

———. *Radio Research 1942–1943.* New York: Duell, Sloan and Pearce, 1944.

Leiter, Robert David. *The Musicians and Petrillo.* New York: Bookman Associates, 1953.

Levy, Charles J. *Voluntary Servitude: Whites in the Negro Movement.* New York: Appleton-Century-Crofts, 1968.

Logan, Nick, and Bob Woffinden. *The Illustrated Encyclopedia of Rock*, rev. ed. New York: Crown, 1977.

London, Herbert I. *Closing the Circle: A Cultural History of the Rock Revolution.* Chicago: Nelson-Hall, 1984.

Malone, Bill C. *Country Music U.S.A.*, Austin: University of Texas Press, 1968.

Marcus, Greil. *Lipstick Traces: A Secret History of the 20th Century*. Cambridge: Harvard University Press, 1989.

———. *Mystery Train: Images of America in Rock'n'Roll Music*. New York: Dutton, 1976.

Marcus, Greil, ed. *Rock and Roll Will Stand*. Boston: Beacon Press, 1969.

Martindale, Colin. *The Clockwork Music: The Predictability of Artistic Change*. New York HarperCollins, Basic Books, 1990.

Matlaw, Myron, ed. *American Popular Entertainment: Papers and Proceedings of the Conference on the History of American Popular Entertainment*. Westport, Connecticut: Greenwood Press, 1979.

Melly, George. *Revolt into Style: The Pop Arts*. Garden City, New York: Doubleday, 1971.

Meyer, Leonard B. *Music, the Arts, and Ideas: Patterns and Predictions in Twentieth-Century Culture*. Chicago: University of Chicago Press, 1967.

Mezzrow, Mezz, and Bernard Wolfe. *Really the Blues*. New York: Random House, 1946.

Nite, Norm. *Rock On: The Illustrated Encyclopedia of Rock N' Roll*. New York: Crowell, 1974.

Ochs, Michael. *Rock Archives: A Photographic Journey Through the First Two Decades of Rock and Roll*. Garden City, New York: Doubleday, 1984.

Oliver, Paul. *The Meaning of the Blues*. New York: Macmillan, 1963. Original title *Blues Fell This Morning*, London: Cassell, 1960.

———. *Songsters and Saints: Vocal Traditions on Race Records*. New York: Cambridge University Press, 1984.

Oliver, Paul, Max Harrison, and William Bolcom. *The New Grove Gospel, Blues and Jazz*. New York: Norton, 1980.

Palmer, Robert. *Deep Blues*. New York: Viking, 1981.

———. *A Tale of Two Cities: Memphis Rock and New Orleans Roll*. Brooklyn, New York: Brooklyn College of the City University of New York, 1979.

Pareles, Jon, and Patricia Romanowski, eds. *The Rolling Stone Encyclopedia of Rock and Roll*. New York: Rolling Stone Press, 1983.

Passman, Arnold. *The Deejays*. New York: Macmillan, 1971.

Peck, Abe. *Uncovering the Sixties: The Life and Times of the Underground Press*. New York: Pantheon, 1985.

Peckham, Morse. *Man's Rage for Chaos: Biology, Behavior and the Arts*. New York: Schocken Books, 1967.

Pichaske, David. *A Generation in Motion: Popular Music and Culture in the Sixties*. New York: Macmillan, Schirmer Books, 1979.

Propes, Steve. *Golden Goodies*. Radnor, Pennsylvania: Chilton Books, 1975.

Ramsey, Frederic, Jr., and Charles Edward Smith, eds. *Jazzmen*. New York: Harcourt, Brace, 1930.

Randle, William. "History of Radio Broadcasting and Its Social and Economic Effect on the Entertainment Industry." 3 vols. Diss. Western Reserve University, Cleveland, Ohio, 1961.

Riley, Tim. *Tell Me Why*. New York: Knopf, 1988.

Robinson, Richard, and the editors of *Creem* Magazine. *Rock Revolution*. New York: Curtis Books, 1973.

Rolling Stone. *The Rolling Stone Record Review*. New York, Simon & Schuster, Pocket Books, 1971.

Rosen, Charles. *The Classical Style: Haydn, Mozart, Beethoven*. New York: Viking, 1971.

Roszak, Theodore. *The Making of a Counter Culture* New York: Doubleday, 1968.

Roxon, Lillian. *Rock Encyclopedia*. New York: Grosset & Dunlap, 1969.

Sachs, Curt. *The Commonwealth of Art*. New York: Norton, 1946.

———. *The Wellsprings of Music*. Ed. Jaap Kunst. The Hague: Martinus Nijhoff, 1961.

Sanjek, Russell. *American Popular Music and Its Business: The First Four Hundred Years*. Vol. 3, *From 1900 to 1984*. New York: Oxford University Press, 1988.

Schuller, Gunther. *Early Jazz: Its Roots and Musical Development*. New York: Oxford, 1968.

Shapiro, Nat, ed. *Popular Music: An Annotated Index of American Popular Songs, 1920–1969*. 6 vols. New York: Adrian Press, 1973.

Shapiro, Nat, and Nat Hentoff, *Hear Me Talkin' to Ya*. New York: Rinehart, 1955; Dover, 1966.

Shaw, Arnold. *Honkers and Shouters: The Golden Years of Rhythm and Blues*. New York: Macmillan, 1978.

Simon, George T. *The Big Bands*. New York: Macmillan, 1967.

Southern, Eileen. *The Music of Black Americans: A History*. New York: Norton, 1971.

Stearns, Marshall. *The Story of Jazz*. New York: Oxford University Press, 1956. Reprint. New York: New American Library, 1958.

Stearns, Marshall, and Jean Stearns, *Jazz Dance: The Story of American Vernacular Dance*. New York: Macmillan, 1968.

Sweet, Jeffrey. *Something Wonderful Right Away*. New York: Avon, 1978.

Toll, Robert C. *On with the Show!: The First Century of Show Business in America*. New York: Oxford University Press, 1976.

Townsend, Charles R. *San Antonio Rose: The Life and Music of Bob Wills*. Urbana, Illinois: University of Illinois Press, 1976.

Wallis, Roger, and Krister Malm. *Big Sounds from Small Peoples: The Music Industry in Small Countries*. London: Constable, 1984.

Walton, Ortiz. *Music: Black, White and Blue*. New York: William Morrow, 1972.

Ward, Ed, Geoffrey Stokes, and Ken Tucker. *Rock of Ages: The Rolling Stone History of Rock and Roll*. New York: Simon & Schuster, Rolling Stone Press, 1986.

Whitburn, Joel. *The Billboard Book of Top 40 Albums*. New York: Billboard Publications, 1987.

———. *The Billboard Book of Top 40 Hits*, 3d ed. New York: Billboard Publications, 1987.

———. *Joel Whitburn's Top Country Singles 1944–1988*. Menomonee Falls, Wisconsin: Record Research, Inc., 1989.

———. *Joel Whitburn's Top Pop Singles 1955–1986*. Menomonee Falls, Wisconsin: Record Research, Inc., 1987.

———. *Joel Whitburn's Top R & B Singles 1942–1988*. Menomonee Falls, Wisconsin: Record Research, Inc., 1988.

Wilder, Alec. *American Popular Song: The Great Innovators 1900–1950*. New York: Oxford University Press, 1972.

Williams, Paul. *The Map: Rediscovering Rock and Roll (a Journey)*. South Bend, Indiana: And Books, 1988.

———. *Outlaw Blues: A Book of Rock Music*. New York: Dutton, 1969.

Williams, Richard. *Out of His Head: The Sound of Phil Spector*. New York: Outerbridge & Lazard, 1972.

Wilmeth, Don B. *Variety Entertainment and Outdoor Amusements: A Reference Guide*. Westport, Connecticut: Greenwood Press, 1982.

Wilson, John S. *Jazz: The Transition Years, 1940–1960*. New York: Appleton-Century-Crofts, 1966.

Yablonsky, Lewis. *The Hippie Trip*. New York: Pegasus, 1968.

Index

Italicized entries indicate the title of a record album, publication, book, film, or theatrical work. Quotation marks around an entry indicate a song title, radio or television program. Footnote references are indicated after a page number by the letter "n" and the note number. Figures are indicated by the letter "f"; tables by the letter "t."

metal, 366; punk, 365–68). *See also*
regional development
"Rock Around the Clock," 164, 213, 220, 221
Rock criticism, 341–43
"Rock Island Line," 330
"Rock Me All Night Long," 213
Rock steady, 331–32, 375
Rockabilly, 200
Rockefeller Center, 51
Rockefeller financial interests, 51, 52, 386n.31
Rockefeller, Nelson, 387n.31
"Rocket 88," 220, 233
"Rockin Chair Daddy," 233
Rocknroll: and aging performers, 255, 314; instrumentation, 253–54, 279; geographic distinctions, 37–41; and movie industry, 164, 275, 409n.22; naming, 18–19, 219; origins, 1–3, 17–20, 29–37; (conspiracy theories, 29–32; in crossovers, 199–201; demographic base, 19, 34–37; in music industry, 30, 32–34, 108; property rights struggles, 3, 104; role of Bill Haley, 222; role of Elvis Presley, 231, 253–54; as seventh stream, 17–23); "pantheon," 241; regional development, late fifties/early sixties, 270–79; styles, 242; (blue-eyed soul, 253, 273; "country boogie," 200, 233, 239; "doo-wop," 242, 252; "girl groups," 242; rockabilly, 200; skiffle, 329–30; surf, 275–76); teen music preferences, 250–52; terminology, 380n.1
Rock 'n Roll Hall of Fame, 40
Rodgers, Jimmie, 92
Rodgers, Richard, 7, 24, 93, 414–15n.13
Rolling Stone, 342
Rolling Stones, 323, 330, 331, 351, 354, 355, 365, 379
Rollins, Sonny, 349
Ronettes, 272, 377
Roosevelt, Franklin, 111, 113, 124
Roosevelt Grill, 11, 114
Rosen, Charles, 23, 89, 230, 341
Ross, Diana, 347
Royal Teens, 328
Rubin, Jerry, 310, 353
Rudman, Kal, 266
"Rule One/Rule Two," 33, 194, 203
Run-D.M.C., 370
Rupe, Art, 172, 177, 179
Russell, Bill, 12
Rustin, Bayard, 301
Rydell, Bobby, 243, 274
Ryder, Mitch, and the Detroit Wheels, 336

Sahl, Mort, 290
Salinger, J. D., 289
Sam the Sham and the Pharaohs, 367
"San Antonio Rose," 10
"San Francisco (Be Sure to Wear Flowers in Your Hair)," 336
San Francisco, 333–36, 354
Sand, Paul, 298
Sands, Tommy, 242, 251t, 406–407n.15
Sandburg, Carl, 91
SANE, 289
Santana, Carlos, 336, 351, 371
Sarnoff, David, 52, 53, 54, 60, 230
"Saturday Night Fever," 369
Saunders, Pharoah, 412n.47
Sausage, Doc, 204t, 207
Savoy (Records), 176
Schillinger, Joseph, 391n.43
School desegregation, 219, 232, 298, 307
Schwartz, Arthur, 5, 130, 165–66, 260
Schwartz v. BMI, 5–6, 30, 31, 166–67
Scott, Hazel, 173
Scott-Heron, Gil, 370
Scruggs, Earl, 169
Scully, Rock, 351
Sebastian, John, 351
Second City, 299
The Second Sex, 289
Sedaka, Neil, 274
Seeger, Charles, 94
Seeger, Pete, 11, 95, 208, 325, 326, 327f, 415n.25
"Seventeen," 227
Sex Pistols, 366, 367, 419n.7
Sexual revolution, 289–90
Sgt. Pepper's Lonely Hearts Club Band, 322
Shankar, Ravi, 320, 326, 327f
Shapiro-Bernstein, 42
Shapli, Omar, 299
Shaw, Arnold, 238
Shaw, Artie, 118
Shaw, Ralph, 218
"Sh-Boom," 217–18
Shearing, George, 196
Sheet music, 34, 42–43, 66, 395nn.47, 48; displaced by record, 34, 99–101, 126–28
Shepp, Archie, 412n.47
Shirelles, 298, 360
Shore, Dinah, 113, 204t
"Shotgun Boogie," 209
Shuman, Mort, 274
Sill, Lester, 275
Sills, Paul, 298, 299
Simon and Garfunkel, 332, 354, 412n.38
Simon, Paul, 365, 412n.38.